HOW TO DO more of just about everything

eHow and other contributors

Contents

How to Do More of *(Just About)* Everything

How to do more of just about every-thing

HarperCollins Publishers
Westerhill Road, Glasgow, G64 2QT
www.collins.co.uk

UK Edition

Developed for HarperCollins by **The Package**
an imprint of White-Thomson Publishing Ltd and Balley Design Ltd.

Director: Stephen White-Thomson
Art Director: Simon Balley
Project Editor: Sonya Newland
Designers: John Fowler and Andrew Li

Printed by Bercker, Germany

A catalogue record for this book is available from the British Library.

ISBN 978 0 00 731513 0

15 14 13 12 11 10 09

10 9 8 7 6 5 4 3 2 1

A Note to Readers

Risky activities: Certain activities described in this book are inherently dangerous or risky. Before attempting any new activity, make sure you are aware of your own limitations and consider all applicable risks (whether listed or not).

Professional advice: The information in this book is not intended as a substitute for professional advice. You should consult a professional whenever appropriate, or if you have questions regarding medical, legal or financial advice.

Physical or health-related activities: Be sure to consult your GP before attempting a health- or diet-related activity, or any activity involving physical exertion, particularly if you have any condition that could impair or limit your ability.

Adult supervision: The activities described in this book are intended for adults only, and they should not be performed by children without responsible adult supervision.

Breaking the law: The information provided in this book should not be used to break any applicable law or regulation.

All the information contained in this book is obtained from sources we believe are accurate and reliable. However, we make no warranty, expressed or implied, that the information is sufficient or appropriate for every individual, situation or purpose. Further, the information may become out of date over time. You assume the risk and full responsibility for all your actions, and eHow Inc. and the publishers will not be liable for any loss or damage of any sort, whether consequential, incidental, special or otherwise, that may result from the information presented. The descriptions of third-party products and services in this book are for information only and are not intended as an endorsement by eHow, Inc. of any particular product or service.

How to Do More of *(Just About)* **Everything**

1 | Oil Paint

Oil painting is not a hobby for the impatient or impulsive, and the vibrant colours and precise, nuanced control offered by this medium are only a reward if you have the patience to master it.

⊙ Steps

Getting Supplies

1   Consider buying a ready-made paint kit that contains a good selection of paints and brushes, canvases, medium, paint thinner, a palette and a wooden case that doubles as a portable easel.

2   Purchase high-quality primary-colour oil paints. Paint is very expensive, so it is better to buy a few relatively high-quality oil paints than a big assortment of lower-quality ones. Be sure to get a primary red, green, blue and white, and perhaps black as well (although you can mix other colours to create black).

3   Purchase a wide selection of brushes. Many art shops stock beginner assortments of oil brushes that will get you started. Then, as you figure out what you like, you can get more.

4   Purchase oil and paint thinner. Refined or cold-pressed linseed and artist-grade turpentine are pretty standard for oil painting.

5   Purchase oil-painting canvases and a painter's knife. The canvases should be pre-primed. Get small ones to start with, as they will be cheaper and easier to work with.

6   Purchase an easel. You should be able to paint comfortably while standing at it without hunching over.

Painting

1   Open the windows or set up some fans. Good ventilation is essential to oil painting.

2   Put down a tarp under your canvas, just in case you spill some paint. You may also want to wear old clothes.

3   Place a canvas on the easel. Make sure that the easel is at a comfortable height for you.

4   Prepare a jar of medium and a jar of turpentine. The jar of medium should follow a turpentine-to-oil ratio of about 2:1.

5   Prepare your paints. Squeeze out the colours you desire on to your palette. Mix them to get the shades you want. Start with just a little: you can always go back and add more.

6   Add medium to the paint. The amount is up to you. More will make for a thinner paint, which is good for delicate washes.

7   Paint the first layer. Try to get out a rough sketch. Don't worry about details yet, and keep the layer very thin.

8   When you have finished the first layer, wait for it to dry. Depending on the amount of oil and turpentine you are using, it can take anywhere from a few days to a week for the first layer to be dry enough to work on.

✳ Tips

Follow the rule of fat over thin: each successive layer should have more linseed oil and a longer drying time, otherwise, the painting can crack.

Oil paint can be changed, or even removed, for a while after you apply it. If you aren't happy with your painting in its initial stages, you can scrub it clean with turpentine and a rag and start again.

9 Once your work has dried, come back to it and paint broad plains of colour. In general, you want to get the basic shapes the first time, the colours the second time and the details the third time. Every artist has a different technique; you might be able to paint it all in one pass, or it might take you four or more tries.

Cleaning Up

1 Dip the paintbrush in the turpentine to clean it. Do this every time you have to change colours.

2 If you have paint on your palette that is still usable, wrap up the whole thing in plastic wrap to keep it fresh.

3 If you have no usable paint left, clean the palette with turpentine and an old rag.

4 Thoroughly clean your brushes with turpentine. Dry paint can easily ruin brushes, so be thorough.

5 Put the painting somewhere where it will not be disturbed or jostled. If you can, keep dust away from it.

| Draw Faces | 2 |

Artists use particular techniques when drawing made-up faces and faces from models. With an understanding of some basic principles – and much practice – drawing faces will become much easier.

⊙ **Steps**

1 Establish the basic shape of the head. Most heads are either oval-shaped or inverted-egg-shaped. Pay careful attention to the shape of the top of the head and the face shape. The face of a heavy person or a child will have a more rounded shape.

2 Sketch in the features lightly – proportions are very important. It is a common mistake to put the eyes near the top of the oval, when in fact the eyes are usually about half way between the top of the head and the chin. The bottom of the nose will be about half way between the eyes and the chin. The mouth will be roughly half way between the bottom of the nose and the chin.

3 Contour the eyes, paying close attention to their shape and the thickness of the eyelid. How much the eye is open will help determine what expression the face has. The top eyelid usually covers a portion of the iris of the eye. Don't forget the eyebrows, which vary greatly in size, shape and thickness.

4 Detail the width, length, line shape and nostril size of the nose. Much of its shape will be determined by shading, but begin by placing the nostrils and making them a careful distance from the eyes and mouth. Draw the line of the underside of the nose. When the basic shape of the bottom of the nose is ready, continue from one side of the nose to the eye with a light line.

✳ **Tip**

Practise observing the details of a person's face and note diversities before you begin drawing.

5   The mouth also has much to do with the facial expression. Consider the thickness of the lips: the upper lip is usually more curved, thinner and darker due to shading. The lower lip is usually lighter in tone and fuller.

6   Add detail to the ears. Ears are very complicated so it is best to keep them simple, using a few lines and some shading. If the face is front view, then the ears will hardly matter at all.

7   Shade the picture to add depth, dimension and life to the face. Shade hits everyone's face uniquely but should be found consistently in some general areas. Shade around the eyes, in the hollows of the cheeks, around the nose, on the sides of the nose and on the chin. Shade around the edges of the face and the chin.

3   Paint in the Impressionist Style

Impressionism was an artistic movement that began in the late nineteenth century. It focuses on the sensationalism of a scene and works to represent rather than faithfully recreate its subjects.

◉ Steps

1   Set up your supplies outside. Not all Impressionists' paintings were done outside, but most were, and the artists made a point of freeing themselves from the studio setting.

2   Look for unusual weather and interesting skies. Impressionists loved to paint the way different types of natural light affected objects in their paintings.

3   Study the way natural light hits objects, especially when the effect is fleeting. For example, watch how light bounces along the edges of waves in the water or flickers when moving objects block direct sunlight.

4   Consider how movement should look in a painting. In a photograph, a running child will be caught in a stationary pose, but in a painting, effects can be utilised to give the viewer the impression of movement over time.

5   Choose ordinary subject matter – find something natural and unplanned. Impressionists liked painting scenes of everyday life.

6   Paint quickly. Contrary to the slow step-by-step process of studio painting, Impressionists liked to finish their paintings in one sitting.

7   Do not blend colours. Advances in photography at the time taught the Impressionists that light is made up of a variety of colours. Instead of blending blue and yellow, they would put blue paint next to yellow paint to create the illusion of green.

8   Use short, quick brushstrokes. Impressionist paintings often dried raised up from the canvas, in the *impasto* style. Detail was not as important as the initial impression of a scene.

9   Do not use strong lines. Dark colours are placed next to light colours to create the illusion of an edge. Wet paint is placed next to wet paint to encourage colour mixing and soft edges.

10 Avoid black paint. True Impressionist pieces had very little black paint. When dark paint is required, mix grey with a strong colour to give the impression of black.

✳ Tip

No two Impressionists painted in the same style – the paintings of Cezanne and Van Gogh were quite different, but both incorporated the ideas of Impressionism into their work. Feel free to develop your own style.

Things You'll Need

❑ Oil paint

❑ Canvas

Draw Disney Cartoons 　4

Disney cartoon characters are drawn using a series of rounded shapes, with details filled in along the way. Following a few basic principles, it is easy to draw your favourite character in just a few minutes.

⊙ **Steps**

1　Find a picture of the Disney cartoon character that you want to draw.

2　Begin by drawing ovals that are the size and basic shape of the head, body and limbs. Depending on what you want the character to be doing, position the ovals according to where you want each part of the character to be. It is best to start with the head.

3　Create an outline of the facial features in their correct proportions. All Disney characters have oval- or almond-shaped eyes. Draw the basic features like the eyes, nose and mouth, but do not add too much detail.

4　Draw the body with rounded lines. For females, draw the hips and upper chest as larger and rounder than the waist. For males, draw the shoulders as the largest part.

5　Draw the arms and legs by making oval shapes for both the upper and lower parts. Draw a circle between the ovals on the legs for the knee, and connect the simple shapes with rounded lines.

6　Draw the hands by making a rounded square with three ovals on top, and two connected ovals on the side for the thumb. For the feet, you can draw a basic shoe shape or be creative if you want your character to be barefooted.

7　Connect all ovals and smooth out the outline with rounded lines. Erase un-needed parts of the ovals in the drawing.

8　Using crayons, markers or coloured pencils, colour in your drawing using the picture as a reference. Change the colours of the clothing if you want, but make sure the character is recognisable.

Things You'll Need

❑ Picture of a Disney character
❑ Paper
❑ Pencil
❑ Eraser
❑ Marker/crayon/coloured-pencil set

Appreciate Van Gogh 　5

Vincent Van Gogh is one of history's most celebrated artists, but his work can be mysterious. Learning more about his talent can help you appreciate his work on a new level.

⊙ **Steps**

1　Observe the details of Van Gogh's actual paintings, rather than looking at poster replicas. Visit a museum to view a Van Gogh painting in person. Observe the work from a distance for the overall effect, and then get close to study the individual brushstrokes. Van Gogh is known for his mastery of the pointillist technique.

2　Feel and experience the art. Merely looking at the subject matter of a painting doesn't always capture the work's spirit. When you view a painting in a museum, note how it makes you feel. Connect to the art on an emotional level.

✳ Tips

Study the manner in which Van Gogh lived, as well as his works.

Note the thick brushstrokes, texture and his celebration of light evident in his paintings.

3　Investigate Van Gogh's popular works, such as "Starry Night" or "Sunflowers", but also seek out his lesser-known paintings. Van Gogh was a prolific painter and he completed numerous works that don't conform to his popular image.

4　Travel to Amsterdam – home of the Van Gogh Museum. Learn about the man behind the art. His training, personal history and the vast collection of his work can introduce you to the multiple aspects of Van Gogh's work. Visit some of the locations around Holland and France where Van Gogh completed his masterpieces.

5　Talk to people who work at a museum and find out why they are so devoted to this artist. Experience what inspired him to create things that remain inspirational today.

6　Become an Art Model

Modelling for artists sounds like a glamorous job, in which one sits about doing nothing and is immortalised in a beautiful painting. The reality is that it's a physically demanding activity that requires practice.

⦿ Steps

1　Examine figure drawings and paintings that you find beautiful or interesting. To be a good art model, you need to have an appreciation of art. Note the poses that you think are interesting and draw inspiration from them for your own modelling.

2　Invent visually interesting poses. As the model, you add much to the art. Use your inspiration and your body to find poses that an artist might enjoy drawing or painting.

3　Become comfortable with nudity. Undraped, or nude, art models are in the highest demand.

4　Practise sitting still. A still model is as important as an inspired model. You will generally have to hold a pose for 25 minutes at a time, after which you will get a short break.

5　Locate a figure-drawing class or open session. They are offered at art centres, private art schools, colleges and universities. Check the phone book and search online for art classes offered in your area.

6　Contact the college or organisation that offers the class and explain that you would like to be an art model but don't yet have experience. They will probably be able to find an opening for you.

7　Bring a dressing gown when you model to wear during your breaks. It is not acceptable to lounge nude before the class or during breaks!

8　Bring all your inspiration and practice to the model stand and try to offer poses that are good for everyone in the room.

✳ Tips

Keep rotating as you pose. If you faced right on the first pose, face forward on the next. When you rotate, the artists will get a variety of angles.

If an artist appreciates your work, he or she may ask you to do private work. Charge at least as much for private work as you earn in group work.

⚠ Warnings

Don't continue posing if you feel faint. Let the instructor or monitor know immediately and break the pose.

Don't accept a private modelling job unless you know the artist or can get references from them.

Build a Wood Sculpture

Artists use many mediums to create their work, but wood may be one of the earliest and most versatile materials for sculpting.

◉ Steps

Choose the Appropriate Wood

1 Select a log or stick that has moderate moisture. If the wood is too wet, your work will be difficult. If it is too dry, it may crack when carving.

2 Purchase wood that has been cut into boards and kiln-dried. These boards can be glued together if you need a large board. Unlike wood from logs, they can also be used to form unusual shapes.

3 Soft wood, like basswood or butternut, is easy to carve and is safer to use for hand-held projects. However, this kind of wood is difficult to stain, so items made from soft wood are usually painted.

4 Choose butternut, cherry, mahogany or walnut if you want wood with a natural finish. There is little finishing work to be done with these woods because of their attractive colours and grain patterns.

Purchase Your Carving Tools

1 Buy your hand-carving tools. For manual carving, you will need a chip carving knife, carpenter's chisels, U gouges, V gouges, bent gouges, spoon gouges, skewed chisels and mallets. These tools, except the mallets, can also be purchased in smaller sizes as palm tools.

2 Speed your work with hand-held power-carving tools. One such item is the flexible shaft tool, which is small enough to reach into tight spaces, cuts down on the time used to carve and sand wood, and can be used for any type of wood regardless of grain.

3 Purchase woodworking machinery. These include a band saw, belt sander, chain saw, drill press, and a planer and joiner.

Carve the Wood

1 Use the dark lines on the wood to determine the direction of the grain. You will need to follow the grain as you build your sculpture to avoid tearing the wood.

2 Carve downwards into the wood grain, diagonally across the grain, or parallel to the grain. Avoid carving up against the grain to prevent the wood from tearing.

3 Use a knife when carving a small sculpture. Hold the wood in one hand and the knife in the other. When making a cut, place the thumb of the hand holding the wood against the back of the blade to control the cut.

4 Begin to build a big sculpture by removing as much unneeded wood as possible. You will need to use a chain saw or a band saw for this.

5 Carve in the details after defining the shape of your sculpture. The U gouges and V gouges help to create small lines and shapes.

6 Sand and finish your sculpture using progressively fine sandpaper, from coarse to extra fine, to smooth the surface. You may finish your sculpture in several ways, including applying a stain, polish or paint.

✳ Tip

When you build wood sculptures, protect yourself with a pair of safety glasses and a dust mask.

Things You'll Need

- ❏ Wood
- ❏ Chip carving knife
- ❏ Carpenter's chisels
- ❏ U gouges
- ❏ V gouges
- ❏ Bent gouges
- ❏ Spoon gouges
- ❏ Skewed chisels
- ❏ Mallets
- ❏ Flexible shaft tool
- ❏ Band saw
- ❏ Belt sander
- ❏ Chain saw
- ❏ Drill press
- ❏ Planer and joiner

8 Enjoy the Works of William Shakespeare

Shakespeare might seem intimidating, but the language of his plays and sonnets can be beautiful, tear-jerking or high comedy. You just need to know how to appreciate it.

⊙ Steps

1 Let go of your fear. These are just words on a page – they won't hurt you (unless the *Complete Works* is hurled at you).

2 Buy a version with both the original text and a modern translation.

3 Read the play out loud. The first few pages might sound a bit rough, but your speaking voice will settle into the natural rhythms of the text quite quickly.

4 Forget everything your English teacher told you about reading Shakespeare. Do not waste your time looking for symbolism or interpreting the dialogue. Enjoy the story.

5 Rent a DVD. Shakespeare wrote plays to watched, not read, and there are many film versions. Start with the film versions of *A Midsummer Night's Dream* and *Much Ado About Nothing*.

6 Don't try and learn iambic pentameter – you use it all the time. It's just the way we speak.

7 Do not read line by line. Instead, read from sentence to sentence. Line by line is like listening to a bad poetry reading.

8 Realise that in his day Shakespeare was just a prolific author. He wrote slapstick. He wrote horror. He wrote romance. He wrote drama. He wasn't writing to write the greatest literature of all time. He was writing to entertain you.

⚠ Warning

Shakespeare is addictive. Once you get the hang of it you'll find yourself spending more and more time in the Bard's company.

9 Perform Shakespeare

Performing in a Shakespeare play is like performing no other work of literature. The Shakespearean actor must take into account the public's expectations, the true meaning of the words, the character, the dialogue and the rhythm of the play.

⊙ Steps

1 Speak loudly and clearly – the language can be confusing to a modern audience. Taping yourself and playing it back can help you master the task and hear improvement in your own voice.

2 Translate your own dialogue into contemporary language so you are sure you understand the meaning. Never rephrase Shakespeare on the stage, but use the tone, emotions and attitude with each line that you would if it were a modern sentence.

3 Break down the rhythm into iambic pentameter, one bit of dialogue at a time, to discover meaning and infuse it into your delivery.

✸ Tip

Stop studying the lines at least a couple of days before performance and focus on the truth of the character for each scene.

⚠ Warning

Don't jump right into performing Shakespeare as if it's simply a play by another playwright. Take the time to truly study both the play and the writer in order to give the best performance.

4   Use wide gestures that engage your whole body. Shakespeare was written for actors to perform in a very active way. Do this in rehearsal, explaining your reasoning with the director. Remember, the director is ultimately in charge, but a great director of Shakespeare will be thrilled that you've done the legwork, too.

5   Rehearse with the director as often as possible. While the actor rarely controls this, you can engage the director in conversation during rehearsal. When he sees your knowledge and general interest, he will probably be more than happy to work with you until you feel you've mastered this play.

6   Read more than one of Shakespeare's plays. Although it may be tempting to simply read the one you are performing, you will gain insight into Shakespeare – and perhaps understand more about your own play – by reading his other works.

Perform Stand-Up Comedy   `10`

People say you're funny, but do you have what it takes to perform stand-up comedy? There's a lot more to it than just telling some jokes…

⊙ Steps

1   Study the acts of professional stand-up comedians. Record their shows, and watch them over and over. Get a feel for their techniques and how they deliver their material.

2   Listen to yourself. Use an audio or video tape to play back your routine. Take notes. Develop your comic timing. Pay attention to body movement and language.

3   Perform at open mics. Call local comedy clubs to see when open-mic nights are held. Coffee shops, bars and nightclubs may also offer open-mic nights at which you can practise.

4   Invite family members and friends to open-mic nights. They may be more critical than a normal audience, but this will get you used to performing in front of a large group of people.

5   Develop your own onstage persona. This may take years to do, but keep at it. Perseverance pays off.

6   Follow the news. Many comics have built successful careers as satirists who take their material from daily events.

7   Consider your autobiography. No, not as a book: look at every aspect of your life, particularly your relationships with family, friends and significant others. You'll find a lot of material in your daily interactions and some of it won't even need a comic twist to be funny. Keep a journal detailing interesting incidents.

✳ Tips

Never steal material from other comedians.

Prepare to face criticism and heckling while on stage. Ignore these interruptions and keep performing.

11 | Get Over Stage Fright

At some point in your life, the chances are you will be on stage or need to speak in front of a group of people. Here's how to make this as painless as possible.

⊙ Steps

1 Practise, practise, practise. Know everything you are going to do and say backwards and forwards so that there is no question in your mind that you know what you're doing once you get on stage.

2 If you are in front of an audience, look at their chairs or to the back of the room. If you are in front of judges, look at the middle of their forehead. It will look to them like you are looking them in the eyes without setting the butterflies loose in your stomach.

3 Pretend the people in the audience are all your closest friends. Tell yourself that they think you're funny and clever and talented, and they will like you no matter what.

4 Stand up straight, take a deep breath and smile!

✱ Tip

Good preparation is vital. If you know your routine, speech or song back to front, it helps your confidence immeasurably. Practice makes perfect.

12 | Mime

Mime showcases the grace of the body in motion and pays close attention to the mechanics of expression, or how the body shows emotion, moods and thought.

⊙ Steps

1 Understand that a mime is conveying a message without speaking. Don't talk!

2 Choose an action to start your routine. For example, opening a door.

3 Ask yourself what objects you would interact with and how you would interact with them. For example, if you were opening a door, you would reach out for the knob, grasp it in your hand and turn. After that, you would push the door open.

4 Try out your chosen action for real. Open a door a few times. Pay attention to every detail of your body as you reach for the knob and turn, then move over the threshold.

5 Recreate the position and motion of your body but without using the door. Practise this until you are comfortable.

6 Give your action a context with a strong emotional component – for example, opening a door to discover your lover with someone else.

7 Examine the emotions inspired by the context. Watch what your face and body does to show emotion.

8 Reproduce the emotional "tell" of your body.

9 Combine the action and emotional response to create your first short pantomime performance.

✱ Tips

Make short performance pieces at first, then link them together to make more complex stories.

Your hands and face are the most expressive parts of your body, but do not ignore the messages that posture can send.

⚠ Warning

Some people suffer from an incapacitating fear of clowns and mimes (coulrophobia), which you may trigger with your performance.

Walk a Tightrope   `13`

Have you ever seen tightrope-walkers at the circus and won-
dered how they managed to learn? While tightrope walking is
difficult and takes lots of practice, anyone can learn how.

⊙ Steps

1   Become reasonably fit. Practise walking on peg stilts first to develop
    your balance.

2   Start with slack rope, which is a little looser than the tightrope. You will
    have to experiment to find out which tension works for you.

3   Set up your rope not more than 30 cm (12 in) from the ground at first.
    You can always raise it as you become more accomplished.

4   Start in the middle. Look forwards and not at your feet. Work on keeping
    your balance from your hips.

5   Keep your arms out straight and move them to keep your balance when
    you place your other foot on the rope.

6   Hold something in your hands to help you balance. Some slack rope
    walkers recommend juggling clubs.

7   Find your footing first when walking on the rope. Keep your weight on
    your back leg when you stand on two legs.

8   Work on standing on one leg. You will actually find it simpler than standing
    on two legs, as you can use one leg to help you balance.

9   Learn to turn on the rope by having your right foot facing ahead on the
    rope, then place the left foot at right angles with the toes facing out.
    Shift your weight to your left foot, and swivel on the ball of your right
    foot. Put the weight on the right foot, and face the other direction. Do
    not look down at your feet.

10 Tighten and raise the rope gradually.

⚠ Warning

Tightrope-walking can be very
dangerous. If you fall, you could
suffer life-threatening injuries.

Put on a Puppet Show   `14`

Kids love puppets, and puppet shows are a great way to
entertain, teach and inspire. Here's how to put on your own
puppet show and spark your kids' imaginations.

⊙ Steps

1   Write a script for your puppet show. Make sure it has a beginning,
    middle and end. Remember that you can't have a good script if it
    doesn't have conflict – there must be a problem to solve. Alternatively.
    find a ready-made script in a library book.

2   Create puppets. You can use simple socks for the bodies of the puppets.
    Sew on buttons for the eyes and nose. Some people might prefer making
    stick puppets – an even simpler choice. Cut some pictures of people or
    animals from magazines and glue them to craft sticks.

✳ Tip

You can also find inexpensive
puppets in toy shops if you don't
want to make your own.

3   Build a puppet theatre for your puppet show. Take a large cardboard box and cut out the bottom of it. Turn it on its side so that you can look through the opening you cut out. This will be the stage of the puppet theatre. Paint the cardboard box. If you don't want to build a puppet theatre, just take a tablecloth and drape it over a table. You can crouch behind the table and hold the puppets above the surface.

4   Practise your puppet show until you feel comfortable with the hand movements and dialogue. Experiment with different voices so you can make each puppet sound unique. Attempt to make the puppets move as naturally as possible.

5   Gather an audience and perform your puppet show for them. Make sure you keep your voice animated so you can keep your audience's attention.

---

15 | Put on Stage Makeup

If you are performing in a play or musical, or are participating as part of the stage crew, stage makeup is an important factor. On stage, both men and women will require makeup.

⊙ Steps

1   Apply foundation to the entire face, jaw and neck. The colour of the foundation should closely match the performer's skin tone. If the performer has very light skin, use a foundation that is slightly darker than his skin. Make sure the foundation covers the skin completely and is blended well, with no noticeable edges.

2   Use brushes to apply shading around features such as eyes, cheek-bones, nose and jaw. By using the right colouring and the correct brush size, you can make features appear larger or smaller. Dark shading along the cheekbone or jaw will make the face look thinner and more defined, while shading around the eye socket will make eyes appear larger. Blend the shading well, except along the cheekbones or eye socket. These features should remain clearly defined.

3   Powder the face well, and then apply highlighting and eye shadow. Bright colours of eye shadow work best. Apply highlighting to the browbone and upper cheeks.

4   Line the eyes along the top and bottom lids, leaving a noticeable space at each corner. By leaving the lines disconnected, the eyes will appear more open. Apply mascara or false eyelashes if desired. Darken the eyebrows with the eyebrow pencil.

5   Use a strong, matte lip-liner and lipstick. If the performer should not look overly made up, use a natural-coloured lip-liner and lipstick. Apply rouge to the apples of the cheeks and blend it back into the cheekbones

✳ Tip

Make sure the skin is very clean and dry before applying makeup. Wiping skin with an astringent will help remove oil.

Tell a Good Joke 16

Do you start off conversations with "Did you hear the one about the...?" Even if you don't, here's how to tell a good joke, from set-up to punchline.

Steps

1 Mentally prepare yourself. Know the joke like the back of your hand. There is nothing more embarrassing for a joke teller than to fill in the joke with ums and errs while scrambling to remember exactly how it goes.

2 Practise in the mirror. Doing so will help you to see how you deliver the joke, what facial expressions work to enhance the humour in it, and what pace to say certain lines. You are your first audience.

3 Practise the joke for the family dog. This second audience will allow you to focus your attention on them, not yourself since you have perfected your art form in the mirror already.

4 Third time lucky? Wait for the right moment to tell the joke. Once you decide to do it, go for it! Don't hesitate; it could stop your momentum in its tracks. Delivery is key. Beginning is key to the key.

5 Give it your all. Once you're telling the joke, keep it up – don't stop mid-sentence (unless, of course, that's part of the joke).

6 Finish the joke with an amused look on your face. Even if no one laughed, at least someone has found it funny!

✳ Tips

Have confidence. Even if it's a bad joke, you had the guts to put it out there.

Have a good sense of humour. Even if it didn't go well, there will always be another opportunity to tell the same joke.

⚠ Warning

Be conscious of your audience. Some people are offended quite easily, others not so much.

Perform the Key Card Trick 17

This is one of the simplest yet most effective card tricks you can perform. The key card makes it work.

Steps

1 Note the card at the bottom of a deck of cards and memorise it. This is the key card.

2 Ask a volunteer to pick a card at random from the deck.

3 Ask the volunteer to memorise the card and show it to the audience. The volunteer should not show it to you or tell you what it is.

4 Have the volunteer place the card on top of the deck once he or she has memorised it.

5 Allow the volunteer to cut the cards as many times as he or she wishes.

6 Look through the deck, starting with the top card, until you find the key card. The one after it is the volunteer's card.

⚠ Warning

One of the most important rules of magic is to never reveal how a trick is performed. If you do, your audience will be disappointed and everyone you know will start doing your trick.

18 | Perform the "9th Card" Trick

This classic card trick will have your audience baffled.

⊙ **Steps**

1 Shuffle the cards and spread them out, being sure to memorise the ninth card from the bottom.

2 Turn the deck face down so that your memorised card is now ninth from the top.

3 Ask a spectator to pick a number between 10 and 19.

4 Deal down the number of cards he or she says. If your volunteer has said 15, for example, deal 15 cards face down.

5 Ask your volunteer to add the two digits of their number. If they picked 15, 1 + 5 = 6. Have them deal – from the previously dealt pile of 15 – six cards.

6 From the new pile of six, ask them to memorise the top card. If they know how to do simple maths, it will be the card you memorised at the start of the trick.

7 After they memorise that card, put the entire deck together, shuffle and spread the cards out across the table. Put your finger over them and then "figure out" which card they memorised.

8 This trick works because adding together the two digits of any number between 10 and 19, and then subtracting that from the original number, always results in the answer 9.

⚠ **Warning**

Not everyone is great at maths, so make sure you go over the calculations very clearly.

19 | Perform "Dream of Aces"

The "Dream of Aces" card trick has become one of the most famous of all time.

⊙ **Steps**

1 Set up the deck as follows: trick Ace of Hearts, trick Ace of Diamonds, trick Ace of Clubs, real Ace of Spades, real Ace of Hearts, real Ace of Diamonds, real Ace of Clubs, then the rest of the deck.

2 Place the trick aces in a row. Place the real Ace of Spades in front of that row.

3 Take the next three cards in the deck (real aces) and place them, face down, on top of the Ace of Spades. Leave a little bit of the Ace of Spades showing so the audience knows it is still there.

4 Remove the next three cards from the deck (random cards) and place them underneath the Ace of Hearts, face down. Repeat this process for the Ace of Diamonds and Ace of Clubs.

5 In each of the three piles, place the ace underneath the cards. Then place the new top card underneath everything. When finished, you should see three columns of face-down cards, and in front of it, the Ace of Spades with three face-down cards on top.

 Things You'll Need

❏ Three "trick" aces (double-backed aces, with an ace on the front and a random card on the back)

6   Going over the three piles, make some sort of a magic motion and turn the piles over. Slowly show each card. The ace in each pile will have disappeared and turned into a different card. The reason, of course, is because by turning the pile over you are now looking at the back of the trick ace. After this, the aces in the top three columns should appear to be missing to the spectator.

7   Go to the pile with the Ace of Spades, which has had three face-down cards on top of it all the time. Turn those three cards over – the aces!

Levitate Small Objects   20

You do not have to be an experienced magician to levitate small objects. Using some simple materials, it is possible to levitate something to amaze, amuse or even scare other people.

⊙Steps

1   Gather your materials. Find a small, light object that you want to levitate and a waxy or clear adhesive; a clear tape can work. The wire should be thin, clear and not easily seen in normal lighting or in the light where the levitation will take place.

2   Place the clear adhesive material on one end of the wire and attach it to one of your fingers. With more adhesive, stick the other end of the string to the other hand.

3   Stick the adhesive on to the object and then attach it to the middle of the string.

4   Test your levitation trick. Experiment by moving your hand around and see how the object moves. It should appear to float in mid-air, between your hands, when you move your hands apart.

5   Try tricking people by telling stories or directing their attention to other things. This way it is less likely they will see the wire. Ask people to give you small things to levitate. As long as the objects stick to the adhesive, you can levitate them.

Things You'll Need

❑ Clear adhesive, such as wax or clear tape

❑ Clear string or fishing wire

Mambo   21

The basic dance steps for this Jazz-influenced Cuban dance take very little time to learn.

⊙Steps

1   Stand with your feet together facing your partner.

2   Place your right hand on your partner's waist.

3   Extend your left hand, palm up, to your side with your arm bent.

4   Grasp your partner's hand in a loose grip.

5   Wait for the music to start.

6   Listen for the first beat.

⚠Warning

This dance is really addictive!

7　On the second beat, step back with your right foot.

8　On the third beat, shift your weight to your left foot.

9　On the fourth beat, step forward with your right to bring your feet together again. Shift your weight back to your right foot.

10　Pause for the fifth beat.

11　On the sixth beat, shift your weight to your left foot and forwards.

12　On the seventh beat, shift your weight back to your right foot.

13　On the eighth and final beat, shift your weight back to your left and back, bringing your feet together again.

14　Repeat.

15　The follower should listen for the first beat and on the second, move forwards with the left foot, then continue the directions in reverse.

---

22 | Pole Dance

Pole dancing was once reserved for gentlemen's clubs, but today it is a fitness craze offering an alternative to normal step and aerobic classes.

◎ Steps

1　Face the dance pole and allow your strongest hand to glide up and down the pole's surface before grasping it. Centre yourself mentally then take hold of the pole, extending your arm, your hand grasping the pole at head level. Place your inner foot securely at the base of the pole.

2　Allow the music to consume you. Let your body move into its own shape, your hips swaying, moving side to side.

3　Let your body arch, your weight leaning back, with your hand still in a secure grip on the pole. Move your body in an S shape and let it sway sensuously to the music's tempo.

4　Bring your body back to a straightened position. Move around the pole slowly. Keep your outer leg straight and in a smooth motion let it swing out to the side, pivoting on your inside foot, allowing your knee to bend slightly as you make your turn.

5　Return to your starting position then bring your dominant leg up and hook the pole. Slowly run your leg along the pole's surface. Lower your leg once more, then place your outer foot down just behind the other foot. Your body should now be shifting its weight to the back foot.

6　Bring the inside leg back up, hooking it around the front of the pole. Make sure your leg has a good grip right behind the knee. Allow your body to use its own weight to swing around the pole as your leg stays grasped about its surface.

✱ Tip

Always check with your doctor to make sure your body is healthy enough to begin this type of physically demanding exercise. Though the movements are slow, each of them will be enduring on all the muscle groups, as well as being a cardiovascular activity.

⚠ Warning

Never use lotions or oils on your body when pole dancing – they will make the pole slippery and dangerous.

Learn Basic Tap Dance Steps   23

Although tap dancing looks complicated, it starts with a series of basic steps linked together. Add timing, fluidity and creativity, and it looks masterful.

⊙ Steps

1 Put on your tap shoes and some cool music.

2 Start by tapping your toe to the beat. Do this faster and faster to gradually build strength.

3 Brush the ball of one foot forwards and then back to shuffle.

4 Step back on the ball of your right foot and step on your left (or vice versa) to do the ball change.

5 Brush forward with the ball of your foot and step on the ball of it for the flap.

6 Do a cramproll by jumping up and landing with your feet. Do this in the following order: land first on the ball of your right foot, then the ball of your left foot, followed by your right heel and, finally, your left heel.

7 Step with your right foot and touch your left toe behind it for the step toe.

8 Learn the stomp – hit your foot on the ground to stomp and then lift it off (placing no weight on the foot when you stomp).

9 Perform the shuffle hop. Do the basic shuffle with your right foot and, leaving your right foot in the air, jump up.

✳ Tip

Tap dance in front of a wall-mounted mirror to check your body posture.

Overcome Writer's Block   24

It's frustrating to be stuck when there are deadlines looming. Here are some tips to get your writing back on track.

⊙ Steps

1 Understand what is causing the writer's block in the first place. It could be a distraction from a household chore or a simple lack of interest in the subject matter. Writing requires concentration and involvement. When you're preoccupied, it's hard to snap back to focus on writing.

2 Distract yourself for a few minutes. Drop the pen and focus on anything else, such as reading a book or watching TV. Make yourself a hot cup of masala chai and wonder about Mesopotamian civilisation.

3 Kick-start your imagination by reading topics of interest. Motivate yourself by reading your favourite author and revel in his or her style.

4 Try not to criticise your work straight away. Even though we reserve the editing job for later, the left side of the brain runs a constant check to perfect the imagination, which affects the natural flow of thoughts.

5 Stop thinking about writing for a few minutes. Get into a meditative state or ankle-crunching pose. Even if you do not succeed in reaching a meditative state, you should have new ideas raking your brain.

✳ Tip

Start your day with some free writing to warm up the grey cells. Write whatever comes to mind to trigger the imagination, even if it is a narration of a dream or a shopping list.

25 | Enter a Writing Contest

Some writing contests offer money, and many others offer vouchers or other prizes. If you love to write, this might be for you.

⊙ Steps

1 Choose your writing genre, such as sci-fi or fantasy, and then search the Internet for relevant competitions. They may offer prizes such as money or gift tokens.

2 Read the rules and guidelines for the contest carefully. Fill out the required admission form. For some you'll have to pay to enter, others will be free.

3 Write your story with all guidelines in mind. Submit it to the contest.

4 Enter another contest if you enjoy writing. Entering writing contests is a good way to improve your writing skills.

✱ Tips

Make sure that you have no misspelled words and that all the punctuation is correct.

Always make sure that the story you submit is in the required genre for that contest.

⚠ Warning

If you have to pay a fee to enter a competition, make sure the prize is worth the entry fee.

26 | Sell Your Novel

Conventional wisdom holds that you have only a couple of minutes to convince an editor that your novel is worth buying, so every second is critical in presenting your work in the best light.

⊙ Steps

1 Pay a professional editor to review your book and polish it. Editors can be a big help when it comes to identifying flaws in the plot or smoothing out stilted dialogue.

2 Make sure your manuscript is clean, free of mistakes and neatly bound. Although non-fiction books are generally bought based on a sample chapter, outline and proposal, fiction is only purchased after reading the entire manuscript.

3 Get an agent. Most publishing houses won't even look at a manuscript unless it comes via an agent.

4 Choose publishing houses that sell the genre of book you've written. If you think you're the next Danielle Steel, don't pitch your romance novel to a house that deals exclusively in history.

5 Write a solid covering letter to accompany your manuscript. Start the letter with a "hook" – something unique or provocative about the book. Also include why you chose this particular editor to show you've done your homework.

6 Include any information about prior publishing experience you have. If you have none, however, don't let on that you're a beginner.

7 Give a brief summary of the novel – no longer than three paragraphs – with an estimated word count and a description of who you think your novel will appeal to.

✱ Tips

Get a copy of *The Writers and Artists Yearbook*, which lists all publishers and useful contacts.

Get a personal introduction to publishers. This will help you to stand out from the hordes of author wannabes.

Include a stamped, self-addressed envelope in the package so that an editor can send back your manuscript.

8 Post the manuscript to as many publishers as you think are potential buyers, but tell the publisher if you are submitting to other publishers or if they are the only one.

9 Wait. Depending on the size of the publishing house, it can take several months before you hear anything. Hold off emailing or phoning to ask about the status of the book.

10 Turn over any offers to your agent. He or she is more objective and will work to get you higher advance payments, which in turn means higher percentages for the agent.

Start a Book Club   27

When you start a book club, you get to make up the book list and format the type of discussion. The goal is to generate lively discussions about thought-provoking books.

⊙ Steps

1 Have a plan. How many people do you want at your club? Do you fancy intellectual or light discussions? Do you want to read contemporary bestsellers or classic novels?

2 Organise the details. Will you meet in your home, take turns in members' homes, or locate a welcoming bookshop, hall or classroom?

3 Create a reading list before you find members if you want to control the types of tomes you'll read. But keep in mind that working folks have little leisure time, so they may want to have a say about how they spend it.

4 Advertise your book club through email to friends or by leaving leaflets in bookshops and on library notice boards. Get into literary chatrooms on the Internet, visit online book clubs or put an ad in the local classified section if necessary.

5 Network where you work, go to school, exercise or shop to see if anyone is interested in joining.

6 Create an outline listing the first book, the meeting place, what you expect from each other and a mission. For example, "This is an irreverent group whose aim is to dish characters, gossip about authors and muckrake bad plots." Or, "We will dissect this book in its original Latin to pinpoint cultural, political and social contexts."

7 Serve refreshments at the book-club gatherings. If the meetings are at members' homes, rotate the location.

8 Read great books.

✽ Tip

Aim to have around eight to 12 people in your book group. Too few and there may not be enough to generate lively debate. Too many and not everyone will get their opinion heard.

28 Find Rare Books

Whether you want a rare book as an investment, to add to your personal collection or just to read, here's how to find it.

◎ Steps

1   Know exactly what you're looking for before you begin your search. Having the complete title, author's name, edition number and publication year will help you locate the book.

2   Lurk at car-boot sales, antique shops, estate sales and bookshop sales, and scan book-dealer catalogues.

3   Check out eBay's and Amazon's auctions as well as some of the larger used book sites. Some webites have a search option that checks many small shops across the world.

4   Decide what condition is acceptable for your collection. If you're a collector, you'll generally want first editions and well-cared-for volumes.

5   Look for books printed on early presses or with wooden type. Woodblock pictures indicate a good investment, as do hand-coloured illustrations and first editions that have been signed by the author.

6   Focus on books concerning art, diaries and atlases if you're looking for items that will appreciate in value. Bibles and other religious books generally do not.

✳ Tips

Compare prices at several places. The same book may sell for substantially less at a place that has more than one copy on the shelf.

Remember that the book's condition, binding type and edition number, and the presence of an autograph will affect its price. The book's age usually matters, but not in all cases.

⚠ Warning

Make sure that any seller you deal with will guarantee the quality of the book before you buy it.

29 Read Horror Stories

Reading horror stories can bring you fear, sleepless nights, entertainment, and a respect for the genre that drives you to buy the next one.

◎ Steps

1   Turn off the lights and grab a book light. Especially if you are alone and want a good scare, read horror stories in the dark. This will help you set the right environment to breed the heebie-jeebies.

2   Plan ahead in case of nightmares. Not every horror story will induce nightmares, but the really good ones will. If you know you are going to read horror stories, plan to take the next day off or go into work late. And if you have trouble sleeping, you may need to turn on a light to ensure there are no creepy-crawlies around.

3   Include your friends. The best way to have fun and get the frightened giggles is to read horror stories to your friends. Read them out loud with everyone in a circle, and practise the stories beforehand so that you can give the right emphasis to the really scary parts.

4   Know first where your limit is. If you are choosing books for your child, make sure you read over them first to ensure they aren't too graphic or terrifying. The same goes yourself. If you want to read horror stories, but know there are certain things that are too gruesome for your tastes, look over books and read reviews before you buy them.

⚠ Warning

Don't underestimate the power of a well-written horror story – the fear can linger for days!

Write a Haiku

Haiku is a form of Japanese poetry that combines three different lines and a noticeable grammatical break. The break, or *kireji*, is often replaced with commas or hyphens in English haiku.

⊙ Steps

1. Think about a theme for your haiku and write down some of the words that come to mind on that theme. Haiku usually includes nature and everyday objects and situations, so don't think too hard about what to use as a topic.

2. Organise your thoughts roughly on to three lines. First, set the scene, then expand on that by expressing a feeling, making an observation or recording an action. Keep it simple.

3. Polish your haiku into three lines, the first with five syllables, the second line with seven syllables and the third line with five syllables. It may take some time and substitution of words to make it fit.

✳ Tips

Express a single mood or emotion in your haiku. Think about a common experience or sight in a new and different way.

Some writers incorporate a pause into the poem, indicated by the use of a colon, semicolon, hyphen or ellipses. This helps to focus attention on the insight your poem presents.

Buy Your First Guitar

Buying your first guitar is one of the most important steps for beginner musicians. Here's what to look for and what to watch out for when making such an investment.

⊙ Steps

1. Decide on whether you want an acoustic, classical or electric guitar. Classical guitars use nylon strings and are made for fingerstyle music. Acoustic guitars are abundant and are versatile: from rock, to pop, to the blues. Electric guitars are extremely versatile but require the extra investment of an amplifier. Electric guitars, by nature, are easier to learn on because of the action (low string height), the smaller body styles and ease of the fretboard.

2. Set a budget on how much you are willing to spend. If you are serious about learning the guitar as a profession, side gig or hobby, consider this for what it is – an investment opportunity. In general, the motto "you get what you pay for" holds true with musical instruments.

3. If you chose an electric, the next step is to decide what kind of guitar body you would like: solid, semi-hollow or hollow. Solid-body guitars are good for general rock and blues music; semi-hollow and hollow for jazz.

4. Do some research. Look online at suppliers and read reviews on guitars that interest you right from the start. Even though you should never buy your first guitar online, this process helps clarify exactly what you are looking for in a guitar, as well as what you're not.

5. Find a local guitar shop and try out guitars. The most important part of the buying process for any guitar player is to find the guitar that fits you like a glove and looks, sounds and feels right in your hands. Try and direct your attention at finding models you were interested in, but keep your mind open to anything.

✳ Tips

Never buy a guitar online if you are a first-time guitar player. It is even more important for beginners to get their hands on lots of guitars to find out what they like best and what body style suits them.

Guitar playing is ultimately an investment – of your time, your patience and more noticeably your wallet. The more you are willing to put into a guitar, the more you will get from it. Pay more upfront to reap more down the road.

6   If purchasing an electric guitar, remember that the guitar itself is only half the equation. At least 50 per cent of your tone quality comes from the amp and how it interprets the vibrations of your guitar. Because of this, don't plan on spending any less than £300–400 for a practice amp.

7   Once you have found the right guitar for you – one that fits your price range and style – figure out what accessories you will need. You should consider a guitar case for your instrument, some picks, an electronic guitar tuner and a strap.

32 | String a Guitar

This stringing technique applies to the standard folk guitar, which is the most commonly used acoustic guitar. However, the principles of good stringing are the same for any guitar.

⊙ Steps

1   Secure the string to the bridge of the guitar.

2   Put the string through the posthole mounted on the head of the guitar.

3   Bend the string sharply to the right.

4   Slightly turn the tuning key anticlockwise and lock the string to the right from where you started.

5   Turn the tuning key anticlockwise to wrap the string around the post: three turns on the wrapped (low E, A and D) strings; twice as many turns on the unwrapped (G, B and high E) strings.

6   Stretch the string to increase stability.

7   Tighten the string with the tuning key and tune it up to approximate the pitch.

8   Repeat this procedure for all six strings of the guitar.

✳ Tip

You may start stringing your guitar with any of the six strings it takes (E-A-D-G-B-E). Just ensure you can match all your strings to their corresponding pitches when you have finished.

⚠ Warning

Sloppy stringing will get your guitar untuned quickly and repeatedly, which can be quite annoying, so take the time to string your guitar properly.

33 | Play the Drums

Drumming might look easy, but it's not. Here are some basic steps to get you started on the road to rock 'n' roll stardom.

⊙ Steps

1   Listen to a song of your choice and count along to the beat.

2   Count the beat in fours: 1-2-3-4. In this example, we'll use the Beatles' "Lucy in the Sky With Diamonds".

3   Put your right foot on the bass drum pedal and your left foot on the high-hat pedal.

4   Keep the high-hat pedal pressed down while you play.

5   Begin with the music playing, and use only your right stick on the high hat.

✳ Tips

Hold the drumsticks in the middle, loosely between your thumb and second and third fingers.

Keep your arms and shoulders very relaxed.

6   Hit the high hat once for every syllable in the chorus: "Lu-cy-in-the-sky..." Keep this steady rhythm throughout the song.

7   Add your bass-drum pedal on beats 1 and 3 when you can keep a steady beat on the high hat. For our example, the bass drum would sound on "Lu-", "Sky" and "Dia-".

8   Add the snare drum to complete the beat.

9   Use your left stick on beats 2 and 4, which is when you might naturally clap to a song. In our chorus, it would be played on "in" and then just after the word "sky" and on "-monds".

10 Try playing your rhythm throughout an entire song without a missed beat.

11 Try new songs with different tempos.

⚠ **Warning**

Most new drummers put a death grip on the sticks, which can cause fatigue and/or injury. Relax your grip, and your arms and shoulders, as much as possible.

Write a Song   `34`

Here's how to form the basic structure of a song and how to put your thoughts into that structure in order to create a song.

◉ **Steps**

1   Grab a pencil, paper and eraser and find a quiet place to work.

2   A song has a chorus and three verses. The first step is to create a catchy chorus – a pleasant-sounding couple of sentences that capture a point of view about any universal idea. The best choruses are those that root themselves in clichés, i.e.: "Big Girls Don't Cry", "Party Like a Rockstar".

3   You don't need music to write to, but it helps. There are many websites where you can purchase pre-made instrumental music. Search for instrumental music in the genre of your choice, and the selections are endless. With or without music, the lyrics should come easily and fluidly. The important thing to remember is to be candid and basic about one central idea.

4   The chorus is the foundation. You can repeat the same chorus twice, or make the second a variation of the first. To create the verses, just delve deeper into the idea of the chorus in chronological order. For example, the first verse is an introduction to the idea, exploring it and variations of it. The second verse is the body of the song. The third verse is a combination of punchline, final points and sometimes a reflection or reference to ideas in the first verse.

5   If writing without music, practise your song to different basic melodies. This is not necessary, though – once the structure is written you can always find a musical composition that feels right for your story. Experiment with different tempos and moods: you may discover new, more interesting aspects of your song.

⚠ **Warning**

Don't overexpose yourself to popular music. Otherwise you'll probably end up just regurgitating what's already on the radio. Make sure you take time to isolate yourself and search for your own creative voice

35 | Start a Rock 'n' Roll Band

Being in a band can be a whole lot of fun. Here are some tips to help you rock – even if you've never been in a band before.

☉ Steps

1   Find a drummer. Everyone plays guitar, but once you locate a good drummer, the band will fall into place. More important, find a drummer with a drum kit and a place to play it – an area that tolerates a drum set will usually be a suitable rehearsal space.

2   Find a bassist. Bassists are almost as hard to find as drummers, but once you get a rhythm section into place, things start looking up.

3   Invest in a microphone and keyboard amplifier. When a band first forms, a common problem is that everyone shows up with a guitar and an amplifier, but overlooks the importance of hearing the singer. Purchasing a PA system is a daunting task and very expensive, so a keyboard amplifier is a cheaper way to make the singer's voice heard.

4   Start with a song that everyone in the band knows and wants to play. It might be helpful to go over the song at a low volume to make sure everyone knows all the parts and chord and time changes. Pick a relatively easy song in an easy key, such as G major or D major. Start with no more than three different chords in each song.

5   Practise the song with little or no amplification at the beginning. Concentrate on making the chord changes at the same time.

6   Practise it more. Learn to listen to one another. Keep the same tempo. Stay together.

7   Practise it until the band is playing something that people would want to hear.

8   Showcase your hit to family and friends. Pay attention to their responses.

9   If you get positive feedback, keep on playing together. If you do not get positive feedback, keep on playing together anyway. It takes time to become a great band.

10 Learn some more songs. This is a very gradual process. One well-rehearsed song is better than 10 sketchy songs.

✳ Tips

Using foam earplugs is an effective but annoying way to reduce hearing damage. Musicians' earplugs are the way to go since they do not muffle sound as foam earplugs do.

If you are not having fun or enjoying the company of the other band members, there is no point in doing it. Be positive and patient with yourself and the others.

36 | Build a Home Recording Studio

Although the cost of setting up a home recording studio can be high, it can also be rewarding and you can rent out studio time to help cover the costs.

☉ Steps

1   Decide on the components you want included in your home recording studio. This will include the space you are going to use, the equipment and how everything will be arranged. The equipment should include the microphones, computer and software you plan to use.

✳ Tip

You can download professionally produced midi files free from the Internet of just about any imaginable genre, performer or specific song.

2 Choose good-quality microphones. The microphones are the most important part of the set-up. Without quality sound in the first place, it will be harder to edit and sync your recording for optimal quality. You need to have a variety of microphones, including dynamic, condenser and ribbon microphones.

3 Find a computer fast enough and with enough memory to support the software you plan to use. Recording software has many components to it and requires a large amount of space on the hard drive. It's a good idea to just have a separate computer for this, rather than trying to use your personal computer to do multiple jobs. Also, invest in some quality computer speakers. If you can't hear where the problems are in the recording, you'll have difficulty fixing them.

4 Invest in quality and well-known home recording software. Pro Tools software is one of the best-known and widely used software for home recording studios. It has all the applications of a professional recording studio and with a little reading and practice can be easy to use.

5 Purchase a MIDI board. This is the switchboard-like device that allows you to play with the sounds, add depth, add instruments and many other aspects of recording music. It will have its own software to load as well, so take this into consideration when choosing a computer.

Attend an Indie Rock Concert   37

Has a friend invited you to hear a new band but you're afraid to go because you'll look out of place and awkward? Nobody wants that. These quick tips make it easier for one to slip into the music scene and leave behind that out-of-place feeling.

⊙ Steps

1 Be knowledgeable about the band playing. Almost every band has a Myspace page; check out their profile before the show. Listen to the songs posted, and try to remember your favourite one. When (or if) they play it, you can turn to your friend/date/whomever and say "this is my favourite song!" They'll be so impressed, they'll think you've been doing this for years. Fun facts about the band never hurt either. For instance, while the band is setting up, you can make casual conversation by saying, "Did you know the lead singer has been vegan for seven years?"

2 Take your wardrobe into consideration. If you don't want to feel out of place, skip the khakis and polo. Skinny legs and V-necks are musts at most shows. Bold colours work best (the more neon, the better). Hair is usually dramatically swept to one side and dishevelled. Accessories don't hurt – scarves, chunky bracelets, facial piercings and sleeve tattoos are commonplace.

3 Be organised and observant. Most concert-goers will have an "I don't care" feel to them, but this is a lie and a strategically practised attitude. Have tickets (or money) ready well before the show, and secure the location of the club or venue (it's always a good idea to call ahead and confirm when the band takes the stage). Walk around the venue. Be sure

✳ Tips

Remember: comfortable, closed-toed shoes! Crammed crowds are the best places to get smashed toes.

You will sweat, so heavy deodorant is recommended.

Be early! You may just catch the band walking around.

⚠ Warnings

Music will be loud.

You will want a cold drink and a hot shower afterwards.

to locate the toilets, bar and band entrance. Avoid carrying a large bag in with you, as you may not leave with it. Store all mobile phones, cameras and cash in your pockets, and check them frequently.

4   Show an appropriate amount of enthusiasm. As you will notice along the course of your indie rock-concert adventure, the die-hards will push into front row and may form a mosh-pit. It is strongly advised to stay away from this area. The sides of the stage usually remain mellow, or the back of the venue may prove easier for conversation. Singing and dancing are encouraged to an extent, but rember that this is not an NSync concert and behave appropriately. Nod along and clap after songs; lighters and mobile phones usually come out during slower numbers and this is perfectly acceptable.

5   Hang around after the show. The band will more than likely talk to fans afterwards. Walk around the venue outside; normally, word gets out where a band is greeting fans and a small dedicated group will already be gathered. This is your moment to observe and learn more about the scene, or even make new friends. Conversations with strangers prove easier when everyone is still on a post-concert high and anticipating meeting the band. If the band does come out, strike up an interesting conversation ("there's this great vegan restaurant in town"). Some bands will hang out afterwards at bars, clubs or even house parties. Keep your ears and eyes open and you may find yourself partying with the band that night. At that point: congratulations, you have successfully assimilated into the music scene.

38 | Get Backstage

Many people dream of meeting their favourite star at a concert or event, but going backstage requires a backstage pass. With the right approach and some persistence, you may be able to get a pass and enjoy the experience of a lifetime.

⚠ **Warning**

Never fabricate a story to get backstage as such methods are unlawful and can get you in trouble.

⊙ Steps

1   Narrow down the concerts or plays that you want to see. Ask friends and relatives if they know anyone who is involved in the upcoming event. Having a connection is the biggest key to making your way backstage. Once you locate a connection, ask for the favour and offer your services in return.

2   Keep an eye out for any promotional contests that are giving out backstage passes to the winners. Work hard to win the prize!

3   Working for a print or Internet magazine can also help you get backstage because the stars often seek publicity. Try to get assigned to cover your dream event.

4   Contact the venue to see if it needs event volunteers. Offer to help with security, equipment handling, handing out fliers or any off-stage duties. This is a sure way to get backstage and meet your favourite stars.

Sing the Blues

Blues music expresses the frustration, loneliness and bad luck of folk in trouble. If you want to sing the blues, feeling is more important than a trained voice – sing from the heart.

☉ Steps

1   Wipe that smile off your face. Blues songs are about pain, death, losing your boyfriend or girlfriend, cheating or being cheated on. Sound hurt, but don't whine. Blues songs are about feeling too deeply, not self-pity.

2   Work your lower register. Most blues songs are meant to be sung in a low or medium pitch. Higher-pitched voices are too spry and chirpy for songs like Leadbelly's "Where Did You Sleep Last Night?"

3   Learn to sing with a slide guitar or harmonica in the background. Blues instrumentation is slow and sensuous, often with a shuffle rhythm.

4   Shed your inhibitions. You'll sing about shooting your lover in a barroom, sneaking off with a married lover, being broke and drinking cheap wine. You have to sing the blues like you mean it. There's no faking it while singing "Little Red Rooster" or any other Willie Dixon song.

5   Adapt a blues moniker before your first performance. No one will buy the blues from a Tiffany or Jason. Try names like Wille Jo or Big Sadie.

✳ Tip

Seeing blues performers live will give you a good idea of how to properly sing the blues.

Listen to and Appreciate Jazz Music

Listening and appreciating jazz music will enrich your life, your musical tastes and your sense of musical history.

☉ Steps

1   Learn a little jazz history. In the 1910s and 1920s, New Orleans Dixieland and ragtime led to the big band and swing styles of the 1930s and 1940s. Bebop began its reign in the 1940s with the likes of John Coltrane and Miles Davis. The 1950s and 1960s brought about the Latin-jazz fusion genres such as Afro-Cuban and Brazilian jazz. The 1970s brought about the jazz-rock fusion, which developed into the acid and smooth-jazz genres from the 1980s to today.

2   Do a little research. Look up artists whose names you have heard and read about. Most people have heard of Duke Ellington, Miles Davis, John Coltrane, Kenny G, Grover Washington Jr. and David Sanborn. Look up the songs and artists you have heard or that interest you. This will give you a general sense of the kinds of music you are interested in.

3   Find and purchase albums by a few of the artists you have looked up or have heard on the radio. Consider purchasing a few jazz compilations to get a broader view of the genre. Consider purchasing a few albums across a span of a genre, a time period or from a specific or collective group of artists.

✳ Tips

Go to jazz concerts and festivals to experience the music live.

Talk to jazz musicians and other jazz-music fans. Ask them who their favourite artists are. Ask the artists about their music and their instruments.

Talk to jazz historians and music-shop owners who are aware of the history of jazz. Ask them any questions you may have or about artists you are interested in.

4   Listen to the music that you have purchased. Start small so that you can really focus on the music and learn it. From this, explore the sounds you seem to enjoy most. Read up on the artists you have chosen to begin your exploration. This reading will help you delve deeper into the music and to get a true feel for it.

5   Continue your exploration of jazz music. Explore more artists in the same sub-genre or other sub-genres. Read and learn the history of the specific sub-genre that you are listening to. Learn about and listen to how each distinct sub-genre began and developed over the years. Your musical taste and experience will expand and you may discover some new favourite artists to add to your list.

6   Get out and experience live jazz music. There is nothing better than the sound of live music. It will enhance your senses and add further to your feel for the music. You will hear and see the sounds that you enjoy first-hand. Watching live musicians creates an interaction between you and the music, therefore creating a live connection.

⚠ **Warning**

Do not go out and purchase too many albums all at once. You'll be overwhelmed and won't have the time to really appreciate the music you have purchased. Try buying only a few at a time, no more than three or four.

41   Tune a Violin

A violin is one of the hardest instruments to tune. You must have a trained ear for music and pitch, or you won't be able to tune a violin on your own.

⊙ Steps

1   Decide on the kind of tuner to use. A chromatic tuner helps tune the violin and also has chromatic scales for practice. A violin tuner or pitch pipe can be used to find the right notes.

2   Get familiar with the tuning devices on the violin. At the top of the instrument are the pegs (usually black) that stick out, two on each side, just under the scroll. A fine tuner, or string adjuster, is located under the bridge on the E string (it looks like a tiny screw). Beginner instruments often have fine tuners on other strings.

3   Attach the chromatic or violin tuner to the bridge. Play the G note on the tuner, then pluck the G string. The light on the tuner indicates if the note is flat or sharp.

4   Use the fine tuner for a slight adjustment on the string. Turn it slightly, then listen again.

5   Turn the peg on the scroll of the violin to make a larger adjustment, or if there is no fine tuner, on the string. Gently push the peg in and turn slightly. Check the pitch and adjust as necessary.

6   Repeat the process for the D, A and E strings of the violin.

✳ **Tip**

Always tune the violin before you start playing each session. It does not take much for a violin to go out of tune. Humidity, bumps, faulty strings and many other things will cause strings to fall out of tune even while playing.

⚠ **Warning**

Never tighten the strings too much. Once a string is stretched too far, it takes away from the quality of the string and is essentially ruined.

Become an Opera Snob   **42**

Opera can easily seem intimidating, even to someone with a general interest and knowledge of classical music. It takes a lot of time and effort to develop a knowledge of this genre.

☉ Steps

1. The best way to sound like you know something about opera is to learn something about it. You cannot do this in a weekend. It will take months or years, depending upon how much you apply yourself. Pretending to sound like an expert, even if you are pretty good at improvising, will only make you look like a fool.

2. Start with the better-known works, as you will get more mileage from them when interacting with others. Works by Mozart, Verdi and Rossini are all good starting places.

3. Look into composers whose orchestral work you already know and like. This will make the whole process much more palatable. If you are a big Beethoven fan, then give *Fidelio* a whirl. If you love Tchaikovsky, then try *Eugene Onegin* on for size.

4. Go to live performances. A live performance is much more dramatic than listening to a recording or watching a DVD.

5. Get yourself a good opera reference book, such as the *New Grove Book of Opera*. Before heading out to a performance, review the plot. If you hear someone talking about a work you don't know, look it up later.

6. One of the reasons some people get intimidated by opera is that the works are in so many different languages. Although many opera aficionados pretend to know these languages and love to refer to individual arias in the original language, very few of these people speak the languages in question. Any languages you have studied or know to any degree will help you. However, the truth is that if you are serious about opera, you will probably spend quite a bit of your time enjoying operas in languages you do not understand. While some companies do offer performances sung in English translation, the standard is that they should be sung in the original. Most recordings you will buy include a full libretto with an English translation. Get used to it. It is just part of the tradition of opera.

✻ Tip

If you are a student or a senior citizen, most opera houses will you offer a discount on tickets. Matinee performances are also usually cheaper than evening performances.

⚠ Warning

Unless you know the people with whom you are speaking well, avoid sounding overly enthusiastic about Puccini. He is one of the most famous opera composers, and his works are dramatic and entertaining. However, some snobbier opera-goers look down on Puccini and often group his works in almost the same category as musicals.

Write a Movie Script   **43**

Every year thousands of people write movie scripts hoping to get them produced and make a lot of money. However, very few scripts are actually bought. If you are interested in dabbling in movie writing, then follow these steps.

☉ Steps

1. Select a genre and come up with a story idea. Use story creation techniques like brainstorming, headline fishing or sound boarding. Before you can do any writing, have a solid direction for your script.

✻ Tip

Pacing and arrangement of the scenes must be concise to keep a screenplay at a good length. Each scene must contribute to the progress of the plot and the development of the characters.

2　Familiarise yourself with the story "rules" for your movie genre. For example, if you want to write a horror script then include a hero who has a flaw and a fear. Your "monster" needs to be truly evil, and you need to include several "false alarms" during the second act to increase tension. You also need to isolate your hero so that he or she has no escape from the movie's monster, and at the end of your script, indicate that the monster is not really gone.

3　Outline your story idea. Break up your outline into three acts. The first act of your script needs to have a hook (opening scene), it needs to introduce the hero of the story, introduce the problem the hero has to overcome and introduce the supporting cast as well as the antagonist for the story. The second act needs to move the protagonist of the story into the heart of the problem that they have to face. By the end of the second act, have your characters at a point of no return. The final act needs to bring the hero of the story to a point when all seems lost or hopeless. Then you need to include the final confrontation and resolve the problem.

4　Conduct research for your story. Look for information that can help you flesh out your characters, locations and events.

5　Format your movie script. The industry standard is 12-point Courier single-spaced. The header needs to be right-justified and include the title of your script and the page number. The header should not appear until the second page of the script's body. Do not number the cover page or the first page of the script. The cover page needs to include the title of the movie script, the author's name and a note that your script is copyrighted by you, centred. Space down and left-justify to add your contact information.

6　Open your movie script with FADE IN and end your movie script with FADE OUT.

7　Allow your characters to speak by tabbing in four or five times and then spelling out their name, hard return. Then tab in three times, and type out the dialogue. Keep the dialogue block within a two-tab width space. If your dialogue spills over to a new page, end one page with CONTIN-UED ON NEXT PAGE, and then start the next page with CONTINUED. When referencing a speaking character, spell their name in all caps.

8　Keep the voice of your movie script in the present tense. For example use descriptions like, "Jason moves towards the axe, breathing heavily and dragging his leg" instead of "Jason moved towards the axe, as he breathed heavily and dragged his leg."

9　Label scenes. For example, if you are about to write a love scene, then your scene label might look something like this: INT. BEDROOM – NIGHT. On the other hand, if you are writing a car-chase scene, then your scene label might look like: EXT. HIGHWAY 6 – DAY.

✳ Tip

Tie each character to the plot line or moral of the story. This helps round out your movie script and create a better overall movie.

⚠ Warning

Unless you are going to be the director, do not include acting directions or shot directions. The director and actors can add these later on.

Relax in an Audition

44

If you don't seem confident in the audition, the casting people will think that you won't be confident on set or on stage.

Steps

1 Be prepared. Casting directors will generally provide you or your representation with your audition material a day or two before your audition. Go over your lines until you feel comfortable with them. Research the production for which you are auditioning. If it's a television show, try to watch an episode beforehand. If it's a film, familiarise yourself with the writer or director's other work. If it's a theatre audition, read a synopsis of the play.

2 Arrive at the audition early. Nothing will amp up your nerves like rushing to get there. Don't put yourself in a bad situation. Leave plenty of time to find the audition location.

3 Warm up before your audition. Perform tongue twisters to loosen your facial muscles and sharpen your diction. Sing a song loudly in the car to exercise your voice. Dance around before you enter the building. Essentially, release any pent-up tension you're holding inside.

4 Avoid caffeine and excess sugar before your audition. Both can make you jittery and manifest as nerves.

5 Breathe deeply and slowly as you wait to be called. Slowing your breath can have a very calming effect on your entire being. If you feel nerves overtaking you, close your eyes and slow everything down.

6 Keep your audition sides with you at all times, even if you've memorised your lines. You may forget a line or two in the audition room and you don't want to disrupt the entire audition to ask for it. A professional actor will always hold his or her sides during an audition and simply refer to them if he or she finds it necessary.

7 Bring a water bottle with you to the audition. You may experience a dry mouth due to nerves.

8 View your audition as a fun time to act in front of people. Try not to think of the end result. You may get or not get the role for a variety of reasons, many of which are out of your control. Aim to just do good work and have fun.

✳ Tips

Feel good about the preparation you've done. Self-confidence really reads to a room, so walk in feeling good.

Always greet everyone in the audition room warmly.

If you don't receive the sides beforehand, arrive at the audition a bit earlier than you normally would to work on them before your audition time.

⚠ Warning

Don't beat yourself up after an audition. It's hard to be objective about your own work. View every audition as a learning experience.

Become an Actor or Actress

45

Although being an actor is extremely rewarding, finding work can be a challenge. The profession requires great commitment and fortitude.

Steps

1 Decide whether you want to be a professional actor or an amateur. If you want to be a professional, read on.

✳ Tips

Acting is a tough business; make sure your personality is suited for the ups and downs. If not, amateur theatre is also a good way to practise your craft.

2   Move to a major city. Eventually, Los Angeles will be your destination, but as you build your CV of experience you can work in other major areas that have good theatre or film communities.

3   Enrol in an acting class. Good actors study their entire lives. To choose a good class, ask trusted, successful professionals for references.

4   Get a headshot.

5   Compose a CV of all the work you have done so far. As your body of work grows, drop the less professional work (such as school plays) from your CV.

6   Send your headshot and CV with a brief covering letter to all the casting directors and agents in your area. Follow up with postcards every four to six months, updating them on your current acting projects.

7   Read the trade papers regularly as well as online publications as appropriate. Know what is being cast where, and send headshots and notes directly to directors and producers whenever possible, requesting auditions.

8   Always accept invitations to industry events and parties, and meet industry professionals whenever possible. Who you know is extremely important in the acting business.

9   Persevere.

⚠ **Warning**

Be sceptical of shady services offered to actors; there are many scams that prey on the dreams of actors.

46 Be an Extra in a Movie

Finding work as a movie "extra" is an informative entry experience into the film industry.

◎ **Steps**

1   Go to your local theatre bookshop and buy a guide that lists the casting directors and agencies who deal specifically with extras.

2   Send your headshot and CV with a brief covering letter to the casting directors and agencies.

3   Follow up with a phone call. Enquire about their interview days.

4   Attend an interview day, when the agency holds an open call for prospective extras. They will take an instant-developing photo of you, plus statistics about your height, weight, hair colour and age. Fill out all necessary information, and behave in a polite and professional manner.

5   Be prepared to be called to show up on a movie set to work with only a day's notice if the casting director or agency accepts you. Know in advance how you can be free and/or get time off work to go.

6   Show up 15 minutes early for your "call time". Immediately find the staff person in charge of the extras. Fill out all forms and sign in.

7   Stay in the areas allotted for the extras; behave professionally, as you would on any important acting job.

8   Thank the staff member at the end of the day and request that you be brought back to work on the movie again.

❋ **Tips**

Bring several changes of clothes to the set; the staff in charge of extras may want to choose the best outfit for you.

Bring a book to read and be prepared to wait around for hours.

Make lots of friends; everyone on a set may move up the ladder and become important in the industry one day.

⚠ **Warnings**

Never wander around on the set; stay where you are placed.

Listen to instructions and be easy to work with.

Never make noise while the cameras are rolling, unless instructed to do so.

Don't disturb the director or take pictures of the stars.

Become a Contestant on a TV Game Show | 47

While many viewers are content to watch a TV game show from the comfort of their homes, some yearn to become a contestant. There are a few ways of putting your name forward.

⊙Steps

1   Gain an overview of the application and audition process for a variety of shows. Some TV game shows require elaborate application materials, while others simply require patience for standing in queues.

2   Watch your favourite TV game show through the end credits to learn about contestant applications. Game shows typically point viewers to a website or postal address where they can enquire about casting.

3   Locate the studio or network website of the TV game show you want to attend. These sites often have updated information on taping schedules, what to wear to the taping and other important notices.

4   Show your creativity and unique personality on TV game-show applications. Game shows that require a video from the applicant are looking for compelling characters to put on the air.

5   Apply to become a TV game-show contestant with friends and family. Some game shows have special episodes where relatives or best friends can compete together. Other game shows require teamwork on a regular basis, making a close relationship beneficial.

6   Check your application materials to make sure every area is completed. Incomplete applications are often discarded because producers are looking to narrow their applicant field in any way possible.

⚠Warning

Appreciate the slim odds of becoming a contestant on a TV game show. Game-show producers receive thousands of applications for a limited number of positions.

Become a Reality TV Star | 48

Anyone who has watched a reality TV show has thought, "I could do that!" And you really could, as long as you know how to play the game.

⊙Steps

1   Portray a stereotype. Reality TV loves stereotypes, so be a dumb blonde, a backstabber or maybe a nerd.

2   Be controversial. No one wants to watch you if you're boring, so spice it up by picking fights with everyone you come in contact with, then when confronted, cry. That way, people will feel sorry for you and want to keep you around longer.

3   Have a strategy. You want to become an important part of the show's plot, so don't get whisked away early on in the series. Make friends in the beginning and form alliances, then when people start to trust you, turn on them.

✳Tip

Be attractive. It isn't a prerequisite, of course, but when has being attractive hurt anyone?

⚠Warning

Don't pick sides in arguments. Stay clear of hot topics like religion and politics. You can get others to spill the beans and annoy viewers, but don't say a word to incriminate yourself.

4   Give a good back story. Nobody cares about the girl next door who grew up in the suburbs with loving parents; we want to root for the poor girl who had to grow up in foster care and work her way to fame and fortune. So be poor, beaten and illiterate.

5   Sleep with someone. Everyone loves reality romances, so strike up a romance with a fellow cast member or maybe even the host. When the show ends, let the tabloids see you locking lips with as many famous people as you can find. When all else fails, "leak" a sex tape to the media; that will buy you a few more minutes in the spotlight.

6   Develop a skill. Whether the reality show requires it or not, you need to be good at something in order to keep your TV fame going after the show is over. So learn to sing, dance or write. Standing in one place without falling over could lead to a career in modelling.

49   Enjoy a Romantic Comedy

A typical first date may include dinner and a trip to the cinema, and most guys are willing to endure a romantic comedy in the hope of impressing his date.

⊙ Steps

1   Pay attention to the dialogue. A little way into the film, you will almost certainly figure out what's going to happen. The plot rarely changes in a romantic comedy, but plot is not the point. Film students learn that romantic comedies are never concerned with the plot, but rather with the dialogue.

2   Take notes. This isn't to say what happens in romantic comedies will happen to you, but something similar might. This way, you'll know what to say or do when it does.

3   Laugh. That is, after all, the point of the film. Yes, romance is involved but the way the characters handle the situations in which they find themselves is what makes the film interesting. At least, that's what the director hopes.

4   Relax and have fun. These types of films aren't designed for you to figure anything out. They are made for pure entertainment purposes nd for you and your significant other.

5   Enjoy a romantic comedy DVD night. Forget your boyfriend who doesn't like romantic films anyway and invite your friends over for a pyjama party. Ask them to bring their favourite romantic-comedy DVDs.

6   Hold a romantic comedy DVD hen party. Instead of going out to a bar, stay in and watch wedding-themed comedies with the bridesmaids and other friends of the bride.

✷ Tip

If you're seeing a romantic comedy on a date, try to find one that balances the romance with other elements. *Jerry Maguire* is a good example – there's sport for him and romance for her.

Choose a Classic Film Noir

If you like gritty urban settings and hard-boiled, jaded heroes battling shady characters and deceitful women, then you should love this film genre. Finding the best film noir titles takes a little effort, but the rewards are always terrific.

⊙**Steps**

1   Read about film noir in film history books. This will give you a clearer sense of the genre and its roots.

2   Do a little online research on film noir.

3   Start a list of film noir classics based on your reading and the results of your online searches.

4   Be sure to include such must-see standards as *The Maltese Falcon* (1941), *This Gun for Hire* (1942), *Double Indemnity* (1944), *Murder, My Sweet* (1945), *The Killers* and *The Postman Always Rings Twice* (1946), *Out of the Past* and *Desperate* (1947), *The Lady From Shanghai* (1948), *D.O.A.* (1949), *The Asphalt Jungle* (1950), *On Dangerous Ground* (1952), *The Big Heat* (1953) and *Kiss Me Deadly* (1955).

5   Remember to add newer films to your list as well, such as *Chinatown* (1974), *Body Heat* (1981) and *L.A. Confidential* (1997).

6   Look for local video stores that carry a good selection of film noir titles.

7   Watch for films on your list when you check television listings.

8   Consider buying the titles you can't find. Here again, online sources will be helpful.

✴ Tip

Make friends with other film noir buffs, in person and online. You'll find film noir clubs and forums in cyberspace.

⚠ Warnings

Watch out for remakes. Sometimes they can be major disappointments – the original version of *Cape Fear* sticks to the gritty tradition of true film noir, but the remake with Robert DeNiro goes right over the top.

Wait for new releases to pass muster with the critics before you don your gangster outfit and head to the cinema.

51 Start a Franchise

Starting a franchise is a big decision and it takes quite a bit of time and money to set things up. Once operating, though, a franchise can be rewarding.

⦿ Steps

1 Choose a business. There are several different franchise companies available for purchase – do your research and find one that interests and excites you.

2 Obtain funding for the franchise. The start-up costs for beginning a franchise can be quite high. Determine the costs and be prepared with a business loan or other means of funding the franchise.

3 Find a location and proper equipment. In most cases, you must buy land, a building or a vehicle. Some franchisers will allow you to lease a building from which to operate the business. Various types of equipment must be purchased.

4 Obtain your opening inventory. Every franchise is different with regards the amount of inventory that is required. Check with the franchiser.

5 Advertise and display outside signs. There is usually a set fee for advertising and this is an advantage when deciding to operate a franchise, because the advertising is done for you. Although you will probably be required to purchase a sign package, you may need additional signs depending on the location.

✳ Tips

A good franchise organisation conducts research prior to selling an outlet. Study this research to know if there is a demand for the service and/or product.

Do your own research. Explore different franchises available and talk to others in the business or that have previously owned a franchise before deciding to start one yourself.

⚠ Warning

Do not expect to turn an immediate profit or double your income. Because of the high start-up costs, a profit may take a longer time than anticipated to achieve.

52 Start a Pub

Running a pub may be a lifetime dream, but make sure you follow the rules so it doesn't become a nightmare.

⦿ Steps

1 Decide on what type of pub you want. Do you want to include pool or darts in the fun, for example? A TV screen to show sporting events? Or do you want a straight drinking establishment?

2 Sketch out the basic requirements for space that will accommodate your needs. How much square footage will you need?

3 Find a commercial location for your pub. You'll want a pub that is relatively easy to find for the public, with high visibility for drive-by traffic. Also consider the parking needs of your future patrons.

4 Contact a commercial estate agent to help you find a leasable space.

5 Check local ordinances and zoning to make sure a pub will be allowed and appreciated in the area.

6 Get information from the city or county department that grants business licences and apply for one. Ask if there are any other requirements for starting a business in the area.

✳ Tips

Provide a unique atmosphere to attract customers – something comfortable and inviting.

Make sure a pub will measure up to local zoning requirements and ordinances before signing the lease.

⚠ Warning

Determine how you will handle rowdy and/or drunk customers.

7   Apply for an alcohol licence.

8   Research costs for a bar, seating and kitchen items.

9   Determine if you will serve food and what type. Will it be bar snacks or do you want to offer a full menu?

10 Sign the lease. The most common leases are those in which the tenant (you) pays all the operating and maintenance expenses, as well as taxes and insurance for the business and property.

11 Remodel the location for your particular needs. You will need to consult an architect and contractor.

12 Buy or lease kitchen and pub equipment.

13 Advertise the business. Send out leaflets, put advertisements in the local newspapers and related magazines, and do direct mailing to let people know when you're up and running.

14 Have a drink on the house.

Consolidate Business Debts   53

Having too many loans, bills and credit cards can hinder the success of any business; it may be wise to consolidate all the debts and send out only one collective payment each month.

◎ Steps

1   Select a debt-consolidation company. Ask for referrals from friends and acquaintances. Look in the local newspaper for companies that offer consolidation services. Call credit unions and banks in your area that specialise in consolidating business debts. Search the Internet for business debt-consolidation programmes.

2   Research several companies to compare their services. Carefully read each company's terms and conditions before signing up. Review the terms and plan to negotiate to get good deal.

3   Look for a programme that offers the best possible solution for large and small debt situations. Choose a plan that covers all your high-interest credit cards and lowers the interest rates on the overall payment.

4   Stay away from programmes that use a home-equity line of credit. Only use your home as collateral in an extreme case. A programme should let you use the saved capital in your business as collateral rather than asking you to risk your home.

5   Discuss all aspects of the consolidation programme with a representative. Go over different options that sit well with your business and let you use the resulting saved capital in your business.

 Tip

Always weigh the risks before signing up for a business debt-consolidation programme.

⚠ **Warnings**

A consolidation can't take away your debt, it only shifts the debt around in a way that is easy on the pocket.

Do not use a consolidation programme and then add more debt to your business.

Never opt for a business-loan consolidation with a long-term plan. This increases the interest rate in the overall scenario.

54 Cold Call

Cold calling, the process of contacting a prospective customer without prior warning or permission, is often an important step in the sales cycle. Cold calling is a difficult task that can be made easier by following a consistent process.

action

Cold Call by Phone

- Develop a script. Identify the value that your product or service offers, and write a script that allows you to communicate this value quickly and conversationally. Be prepared to deviate from this script during calls.

- Procure a list of phone numbers. If you own your own business, research and locate a reputable list vendor for your industry. If you work for a company, your marketing department may have a list. Make sure it includes the right contacts and is up to date.

- Research your prospects. Go to the company's website, read local trade journals, or look for the company in a business index.

- Establish targets. From your list and your script, determine how many calls you can reasonably expect to complete in a day. Also, determine the purpose for each call. This can be to close a sale, set up an appointment or make an initial contact. Make sure you leave enough time for other aspects of your sales process, such as appointments and paperwork.

- Make the calls. Try to keep each call warm and friendly, and don't push a prospect to talk. Give every prospect the option of talking at another time or in another venue, such as a personal appointment or via email. If you get voicemail, don't leave a message on the first try. When you do leave a message, make it short. Leave just enough that the prospect will be tempted to return the call. When making repeat calls, vary the time of day.

- Record the results. Evaluate how your script is performing and whether your target number of calls is reasonable. Make adjustments as necessary.

Cold Call in Person

- Identify your target geography. If you have an assigned geographic territory, use that as a starting point. If not, then use a map to draw concentric circles around your office. Start with the locations closest to you and work out from there. In particular, identify business complexes and industrial parks to increase the number of prospects within easy walking distance.

- Prepare for the visits. Make sure you can discuss the value that your product or services offers cogently and conversationally. Put together a packet of brochures and other sales materials to hand out.

- Establish targets. Determine how many visits you can reasonably expect to complete in a day. Also, determine your purpose for each visit, which can be to close a sale on the spot or to set up an appointment with a key decision-maker. Make sure you leave enough time for other aspects of your sales process, such as appointments and paperwork, too.

- Make the visits. Be respectful of any signage prohibiting solicitations, and always be courteous and friendly. Hand out the brochures and other material that you've taken with you whenever possible. If your target contact isn't available when you visit, ask for a business card and call back later.

- Record the results. Evaluate how your visits are going and whether your target number of visits is reasonable. Make adjustments as necessary.

Sell Products or Services on the Internet 55

Got something good to sell, or simply want to get rid of some old stuff that's lying around the house that might have some value? Try going online.

Steps

1 A good place to start is an online auction site. There are many specialised and unspecialised auctions on the Internet that can be found via Internet searches.

2 Many Internet service providers (ISPs), Internet directories and search engines feature classified ads that can be used to sell things to other online subscribers.

3 Find message boards and newsgroups that specialise in the item(s) that you're trying to sell and post a message containing your ad.

4 If you maintain a private website or home page, advertise your item(s) on your site.

5 Take pictures of everything you want to sell – it will drastically increase your chances of selling them.

* Tips

Some online auctions only allow their members to bid, rather than sell. Before you register for an online auction, make sure its policies suit your needs.

Include your email address and URL in your online ad, but not your address and phone number.

Outsource Services Effectively 56

Outsourcing tasks can effectively get projects completed without hiring more employees.

Steps

1 Identify which components of your business are candidates for being outsourced.

2 Determine whether your needs in these areas are temporary and thus warrant outsourcing.

3 Try to identify what it currently costs to operate these areas.

4 Ensure that choosing the outsourcer is a cost-effective and viable solution to your immediate needs.

5 Interview several outsourcers before making a selection.

6 Prepare a written contract and review with legal counsel if you feel it is necessary. Ensure that the contract has performance metrics that outline the level of service or production expected of the outsourcer.

7 Be willing to negotiate as needed.

8 Schedule regular meetings with those who work outside the company.

9 Review performance on a regular basis.

* Tips

Select someone who fits with company culture and has experience in the industry.

Be clear about confidentiality.

Determine whether there will be a notice period for termination on either end.

57 | Write a Personable Email

Staying in touch for business means using email as a means of communication – sometimes the only way to confer. Here are some tips to give your email a personal and professional touch.

Steps

1   Choose your words. You know how things can get taken out of context in an email, so make sure your message is clearly readable and friendly. While you can convey discontent in an email, you should always include a warm closing statement at the end. Short phrases and one-word replies can appear snide and rude – when it comes to business, clients need to feel special and that they can talk to you, even over email.

2   Name it. Include a greeting and the recipient's name. And if you're writing back and forth, try to include a greeting in each reply. Who knows who you're addressing when you start off an email with the first word of a sentence? In addition, use a salutation and sign your name, even just your first name if you're comfortable enough with a client or supervisor.

3   Enable contact. It's very important that someone can contact you in a way other than email, so have your phone number in a signature to your message. While some people don't agree with releasing this information, if you're in business you can't hide behind a computer. Giving business associates your phone number shows that they can reach you should they wish to talk instead of using email alone.

4   Chit chat. While you don't want to recap details of your weekend, you can include a personal note. It's never bad to tell someone you hope they had a nice time on their holiday after you ramble on in a message about business.

* Tip

If you're contacting someone who doesn't know you, be sure to include how you got their contact information, and give a brief introduction of yourself.

58 | Buy Small Business Insurance

With few employees and limited assets, buying all types of business insurance can be extremely expensive. Buying the right insurance can save a small business a lot of money.

Steps

1   Analyse the different types of assets and liabilities affecting your small business. These include business volume, salaries and rental costs, equipment, overheads, changing trends, and impact of the local economy. Make a clear statement of your insurance plan and the objectives for the firm.

2   Estimate potential losses. You can lose money from a fire or theft, employee action, damage to personal property, and loss due to economic hardship. Estimating your losses will help you decide on the level of cover you need.

3   Ensure that you have a good cover for your property. Low premiums provide low cover. Assess the true risk potential and make sure the high-risk factors are insured through your policy.

* Tips

Conduct regular appraisals for your property and assets. This will help you adjust your premium payments annually.

Designate a person/business partner who will be responsible for handling issues of insurance and claims processing.

4 Choose a high deductible depending on what you can afford.

5 Shop around for quotes from multiple insurance carriers.

6 Consider comprehensive coverage. You could buy group health insurance, group life insurance, vehicle insurance (if your business involves transport), flood insurance and disability insurance individually – or go with a bank that offers comprehensive coverage.

7 Choose an insurance agent, if possible. Apart from price, having a good insurance agent is the next most critical aspect of the insurance you choose.

8 Check the insurance company's financial strength. Various organisations publish financial ratings for companies, which are useful in determining the stability of the insurance company. Your insurance agent may also be helpful in assessing an insurance company's credibility.

Cut Business Expenses   59

If you own a business, you know how draining some expenses can be. To save money you must be frugal and avoid shelling out for unnecessary items.

◉ Steps

1 Buy from a wholesaler. When you need any kind of office equipment, check out wholesale companies to see if they have any products you can use. Ask for a discount when making large purchases.

2 Shop around for telephone services. Many companies offer new customers discounted phone plans.

3 Lease office equipment instead of buying it. Be aware that this may cost you more money in the long run, but you will be able to save some money in the short term.

4 Check with insurance companies about competitive rates. You can cut business expenses by switching insurance companies.

5 Cut back on all unnecessary items. For example, if your company gives the employees mobile phones, consider only keeping a couple to be shared by the group.

6 Downsize the staff. If you need to lay off workers because of poor earnings, you should not be afraid to do it.

7 Don't be afraid to be frugal in all business aspects. Every pound that you save will help your business survive.

⚠ Warning

Don't put out money for overtime pay. Make sure that all business tasks are completed within normal working hours.

60 | Overcome a Setback in Business

If you're a business owner, sooner or later you'll face either a difficult financial situation, a crisis within your business or even a business failure. The trick is learning how to come out on the other side stronger and wiser for the experience.

⊙ Steps

1 Believe and trust in your ability to overcome whatever problems come your way. That's the key to getting through any crisis.

2 Seek counsel from someone you trust – preferably someone in an industry like yours who has built his or her business from the ground up. The chances are he or she will have encountered and overcome the same problem you are facing.

3 Evaluate the situation and determine if it will have a negative impact on your cash flow or cash reserves. If you find that you will be short of cash to meet salary and other financial obligations, look for ways to reduce your everyday expenses. If your cash is seriously affected, consider temporary lay-offs of non-essential employees.

4 Keep a positive, upbeat attitude. If you look more worried than usual, your employees might get nervous and start looking for employment elsewhere.

5 Advise vendors of your situation if it is certain you will be late with payments. Before you contact them, however, be prepared to discuss a payment plan. When asked when payment can be expected, your answer shouldn't be "I don't know". Avoid telling people that the cheque's in the post if it isn't – you're only postponing the problem, and causing greater issues.

6 Review your current business plan. Change your plan as necessary to help reverse the setback and to prevent the same situation in the future.

7 Relax and unwind. Take a drive, see a film or steal away for a short nap. Getting your mind off your worries, if only for an hour, will allow you to come back to the problem and attack it with a clear head.

✳ Tips

Do everything in your power to pay your bills on time. If you make a payment arrangement with a supplier and can't meet it, call your supplier before he or she calls you.

Try not to hide from the problem by postponing critical meetings or not returning phone calls. This kind of behaviour is unprofessional and will raise red flags with business associates.

Try not to take the situation too personally. Heated words from suppliers who are owed money or from employees you had to lay off are just that – words.

⚠ Warning

Under no circumstances should you make promises for payments you can't make. Do not release cheques until the money to cover them is in your account.

61 | Decide When to Sell a Business

Selling a business, particularly one you've built by yourself, can be a traumatic experience. Here are some key points to consider in making a decision about whether to sell.

⊙ Steps

1 Check your motivation. Reasons may include disability, death and burnout, desire for greater profits, relocation, other interests, divorce and disinterest in the business model, family pressure or a sheer lack of skill at the business.

✳ Tip

If family is involved in this business, bring in a family business consulting firm to help inform your decision.

2 Check your timing. You may plan for a long time to sell the business, working for years to achieve one that is attractive and saleable, someone may make you a great offer out of the blue, or a family or personal crisis may drive your timing.

3 Consider selling the business but arranging to continue working there, if you still have your heart in the business but simply don't want to run it any more.

4 Decide whether you want to sell, and if you do, meet with your accountant, lawyer and spouse, individually or together, to determine the best time and process for selling.

⚠ Warning

No one can be objective about their own business. Hire a business broker to help you value your business objectively.

Price Your Product   `62`

Setting the right price for your product or service is a delicate situation. You must find a price that will reflect your production costs, as well as the value that your customers will place on your product.

⊙ Steps

1 Consider your production costs. These costs consist of both the fixed and variable expenses to manufacture or offer your product or service. Fixed costs include rent, salaries, property taxes – any expense that doesn't change often. Variable costs fluctuate depending on the amount of goods produced or services provided. They include raw materials, hourly wages and sales commissions.

2 Analyse your market. How much are customers willing to pay for your product? Conduct market research to test your pricing strategy. See what competitors are charging. You may price your product higher than the norm if you offer better service than your competitors.

3 Evaluate your product's uniqueness. See how closely your product resembles a competing product. Consumers will be reluctant to pay higher prices for your product if they can pay less for a competing brand of similar quality.

4 Determine your product's price elasticity, determined by whether price changes result in changes in demand. For example, if slight changes in price results in significant changes in demand, your product is considered to be elastic. However, if there is little change in demand even with significant price changes, your product is inelastic. The greater the price elasticity, the closer you should price your products to your competitors' products.

✳ Tips

Vary your pricing depending on your goals. For example, you might charge a lower introductory price for a short period of time to attract a large number of new customers.

If in doubt, price on the high side. It's always easier to discount prices than to raise them.

⚠ Warning

Beware of undercharging. Lowering your price far below that of competitors will create the wrong image for your product.

63 | Make a Candidate Comfortable During a Job Interview

Job interviews can be stressful for both a candidate and the person conducting the interview. When you make sure the candidate is comfortable, you set the tone for the entire interview.

⊙ Steps

1 Make sure you have the candidate's CV or application ready and read it before the interview starts. You look really unprepared and uninterested when you have to take time to look for paperwork or don't even know the candidate's name.

2 Hold all calls or interruptions until the interview is over. If you know you will have to take a call from your boss, tell the candidate in advance.

3 Think of a short welcoming statement to help put the candidate at ease. The most common one is about the weather, but you could comment on the traffic or note something the candidate has written about their hobbies and interests on their CV. The more you use the statement the more natural it will become. You can also think of more than one statement if you conduct a lot of interviews.

4 When a candidate is really nervous, let them know it's normal to be nervous during a job interview. Offering a glass of water or other drink may also help. Try not to say "Calm down" or "Relax" as these can come across as being condescending.

5 Thank the candidate both when they come in and at the end of the job interview. Whether you hire them or not, you want them to have a good impression of you and your company.

✳ Tips

If you can't pronounce the candidate's name, ask them how to say it before you mess it up.

Don't assume the person likes to be called a common nickname instead of their full name.

⚠ Warnings

Avoid controversial topics for your welcoming statement. Politics should absolutely be avoided in a job interview.

Don't keep candidates waiting a long time for job interviews. If a candidate arrives too early suggest that they take a walk or get a snack. If you are running just a few minutes late make sure the candidate is told.

64 | Write a Reference

Today's business and personal mores dictate that you always give someone a reference letter if they ask for it. Only positive things are written about a person or company – it can be dangerous (and illegal) to write negative things.

⊙ Steps

1 Confirm that the person worked for you, the range of dates they were employed and possibly their salary, if this is to be a reference for a new position. Talk about their job description and what tasks they performed for the company. Depending on how talented they were, you can write with enthusiasm and mention that they were an asset to your company, or you can keep the comments about their performance toned down.

2 Talk about the length of time you have known a person and describe the situation that created the relationship if you are giving a personal or character reference. This is one situation where if you have nothing good to say, say nothing at all.

⚠ Warning

If you are writing a character reference at the request of a lawyer, be careful that what you say is accurate as you may be asked to appear in court.

3 Recommend the excellent service a company provides if you are asked to write a reference for a business. Discuss the consistency and quality of their workmanship, their professionalism and their timely payments and good credit standing if the letter of reference requires that information. Again, keep your comments to minimum basic facts if you don't have anything good to say.

4 If you receive a phone call checking for reference information and are uncomfortable being put on the spot, tell the caller politely that your company has a policy of not discussing personnel information over the phone. Ask them to send your personnel director (or you) a letter requesting that information. This gives you time to think over what you wish to say.

Write a Rejection Letter   65

Conducting interviews and saying "no" to applicants doesn't always have to be stressful. You can almost always find something good to say about a candidate, even when you're not offering them the position.

⊙ Steps

1 Use formal letterhead when typing your letter. Do not hand write a rejection letter.

2 Address your candidate by name.

3 Thank the candidate for the time, effort and interest in the firm.

4 Write a supportive sentence about the candidate's qualifications, experience or, at very least, enthusiasm or motivation.

5 Make it clear that the reason you didn't hire the candidate was because you found someone else with better qualifications and experience.

6 Describe your company's procedures. For example, the company keeps CVs on file and notifies potential candidates about job openings.

7 Wish the candidate good luck in his or her career development.

8 Close the letter formally with "Sincerely" or "Best wishes".

9 Sign your name, including your title.

✳ Tip

Keep it nice and short, unless a special relationship exists between the candidate and the interviewer.

66 Create an Employee Handbook

Employee handbooks create a consistent, fair environment for employees. In addition, well-written, legally correct procedures can protect employers in many instances from legal liability. Companies of all sizes are well advised to write an employee handbook.

checklist

Preparation

❑ Write down your current employee policies. After you have put them down on paper, ask for input from supervisors at all levels.

❑ Ask for employee input. There may be policies that have developed among employees that you're not aware of. Some policies developed among departments may be useful and should be added to the written handbook.

❑ Recruit the appropriate professional team to create your employee handbook. Large companies may have the necessary writing and legal resources in-house. Small companies may be able to hire a writer and have their handbooks checked by the company's lawyers.

Contents

❑ Harassment (in all its forms)

❑ Drug and alcohol abuse

❑ Smoking

❑ Safety

❑ Use of company property

❑ General policies that apply to everyone, such as company holidays

❑ Standards of dress, discipline and attendance

❑ How employees should register complaints or report abuse or fraud

❑ Company benefits

❑ Legal sections as directed by your lawyer

Usage

❑ Distribute the handbook and verify that your employees have read the information contained in it.

❑ Periodically have meetings with your employees to explain new policies and reiterate old policies so everyone knows where they stand and what is expected of them.

❑ Ask employees to hand in a tear-out page from the handbook specifying that they have read, understood and will abide by the company's policy.

❑ Make the employee handbook part of every employee's hiring package. It should be read before the employee begins work.

Bear in Mind...

❑ Depending upon the size of your company, you may need to include equal employment information as well as other legally mandated policies. Companies that do not necessarily have to include these pages may want to do so to preclude having to update the handbook immediately after a growth spurt.

❑ Be aware that an employee handbook is considered a legal document. The entire book should be vetted by a professional who specialises in employment law.

Plan a Successful Company Event 67

Whether the event involves 50 people or 1,500, many of the preparations are the same – with a plan in your hand, you can't fail to plan a successful event.

⊙ **Steps**

1   Start with an announcement to round up your volunteers. Make this an open invitation to all employees. This will get a few folks moving but you will probably have to do some individual campaigning for support.

2   Have a kick-off meeting that includes refreshments. At the meeting, have a tight agenda where you delegate as much work as you can to others. At the kick-off, set up a follow-up meeting schedule and get consensus on dates, times and details.

3   Keep the decision-making for the food, activities and budget until later. This part you might want to keep to yourself or gradually give pieces of it to your coordinator if they are capable of handling it.

4   Attend meetings and assess progress. Provide feedback and give praise to those who are on target with their objectives for the event. As needed, meet with others, such as the caterers and entertainers, to finalise plans. Keep line managers in the loop on when and where the party will be held.

5   Notify employees and send invitations to the event at least six weeks before it if possible. If RSVPs are needed, include the date to return responses. Have your staff coordinator devise a mechanism for collecting this information. Use administrative staff as much as possible for the grunt work.

6   Conduct your final planning meeting one week before the event. Finalise counts, decorating tasks and other last-minute duties with your group.

7   Enjoy yourself at the event. Find time to search out your volunteers and thank each individually for all their help. Socialise as much as possible with your management team and get feedback from people on how they liked the event as well as suggestions for improvement.

8   Send out thank you letters to all the volunteers and have copies placed in their personnel files after the event concludes.

✻ **Tip**

The key ingredients of any successful event are food, music, entertainment or activities, and company communications or message.

Make Friends and Influence People 68

Be it in a business or a social setting, being liked and respected is an important part of our day-to-day lives. Read on for a few tips to help you win friends and influence people.

⊙ **Steps**

1   Be polite and smile. This – along with a positive attitude – helps people to feel at ease; criticising and complaining will push people into a defensive position. When in a defensive frame of mind, people tend to be less receptive to other's ideas.

✻ **Tip**

Don't sit on the sidelines and wait for people to come to you. Be bold and reach out first.

2 Use the person's name when talking to them. People like the sound of their own name and feel more comfortable when you address them by it. By using their name you will appear more personable.

3 Listen to others when they speak, encourage them to open up about themselves. When allowed to open up and share, people tend to feel closer to the person they have shared with. This will also give insights into the person's personality, wants and needs.

4 Talk to the person using what you have learned while listening to them speak. Make sure the things you say relate to your audience rather than trying to make your audience relate to you and your view of the world.

5 Make others feel appreciated by saying thank you and sincerely letting them know how much you appreciate their efforts.

69 Give an Effective Employee Evaluation

Evaluating an employee's performance isn't easy, but it can be a valuable process for both of you.

⊙ Steps

1 Be sure that your employee has been given a job description and knows what he or she is being evaluated against.

2 Let the employee see a blank copy of the evaluation form and ask him or her to fill out performance ratings to get an idea of how they view their own performance. This can often be quite different from your own view of their achievements and failings.

3 Set up a time and place to meet that will allow you both peace and privacy to conduct the evaluation without interruption.

4 Set aside at least an hour for the evaluation, even though you might not need it.

5 Outline your goals for the evaluation – to improve the employee's performance, reward good performance, establish new performance expectations, receive feedback or other goals.

6 Avoid doing all the talking. Ask questions and let the employee tell you how they feel and what they need.

7 Offer the employee the option of writing an alternative point of view for his or her file in case of disagreement.

8 Do your best to put the employee at ease, or anxiety will keep him or her from hearing what you say.

9 Avoid focusing only on areas that need improvement. Every employee wants and needs to be praised, so spend just as much, if not more, time describing what he or she is doing right.

✱ Tips

If the employee gets angry at something you say, let him or her vent while you listen. Don't become defensive and argue.

Even if you and the employee disagree on a point, you can both express your opinions.

⚠ Warnings

Be careful about what you say, and make sure you have consistent expectations of all your employees without regard to sex, colour, age or disability.

The performance review should not be a shock in and of itself, nor should it be the first time the employee hears about a particular problem.

Fire an Employee 70

Most – if not all – managers will say that their least favourite responsibility is dismissing an employee. Whether the reason is below-par performance, restructuring or downsizing, there are ways to keep the situation as professional as possible.

Steps

1 Document problems as they occur. When issues arise, give the employee a reasonable opportunity to improve and let them know clearly that their employment is in jeopardy if they are unable to improve.

2 Read and thoroughly understand your company's policies and procedures manual, and adhere to guidelines the company has already established regarding dismissals.

3 Check any contracts – written or oral – your company has reached with the employee. Adhere to contractual provisions regarding termination.

4 Decide who will do the firing and what will be said – and not said – at the final meeting. Plan to be courteous but firm.

5 Prepare a written statement explaining the reasons for and conditions of the termination. Detail the severance package, if any, that the employee will receive.

6 Call the meeting, making sure that it is conducted in private, attended only by the person doing the firing, the employee and a witness. Have the final pay cheque ready before the meeting.

7 Explain your decision. Allow the employee a chance to offer feedback about the company.

8 Collect keys, ID cards and other company property that may be in the employee's possession.

9 Ask that the employee signs the termination statement. Present the final pay cheque and details of the severance package.

10 Escort the employee from the building.

✳ Tips

Be consistent. If you fire one employee for constant lateness, be prepared to fire others for the same reason.

Try to give at least two weeks' notice, especially if the dismissal is being done in connection with a downsizing or restructuring.

⚠ Warning

Wrongful-termination lawsuits are becoming commonplace. Protect yourself by making sure you have carefully followed the terms of any employment contracts and the company's policies and procedures manuals.

Manage Staff Turnover 71

Keeping your workforce stable is a challenge for any manager. Here's how to encourage your employees to stick around.

Steps

1 Realise that money isn't everything. Although financial incentives will encourage employees to stay over the short term, over the long term they need opportunities for growth.

2 Offer a solid foundation for growth at your company. Let employees know specifically where they can go in the company and what they need to do to get there. Don't be ambiguous.

✳ Tip

Remember, training a new employee can be much more expensive than paying more to keep an established one. Don't be pennywise and pound-foolish.

3   Praise employees when they've done a good job.

4   Create a good working relationship with your employees. People are less likely to leave if they feel they're a valued member of a team.

5   Provide or pay for training. Although workers no longer expect lifetime employment at one company, they do want to be employable throughout their lives, and this means keeping their skills current.

6   Make certain your company has career plans for various departments for those who want to move upwards in the company.

72 Hire an Assistant

As businesses grow, professionals often find themselves in an overwhelming position. An overworked person can feel unable to catch up and almost powerless to try. A capable assistant or secretary can turn the situation around.

Steps

1   Hire before it's too late. The quality of training you are able to provide declines when you react to stress and overwork inappropriately. The time to find and train your perfect counterpart is before you reach a crisis point.

2   Use the grapevine. Tell colleagues you know and trust that you are looking for a competent assistant (or secretary). Ask if they have any recommendations. They may know someone who is right for the job or have inside information that may assist you. Input from business associates can be a valuable tool in your search for the right assistant.

3   Define the position. You cannot effectively hire someone if you do not have a clear job description. A worthy applicant will request an in-depth job description. Be prepared to provide one.

4   Interview, interview, interview and interview some more! In the beginning, an assistant spends a tremendous amount of time working with a superior. You must be certain the person you hire is someone you can tolerate for long periods. This person also represents you and your business to the world. Choose wisely.

5   Pay for quality. Cheap labour may not produce good labour, and a disgruntled assistant may spell trouble for a small business. Realise that this person is an important asset to you and your business, and pay them accordingly.

6   Hire your mirror image, not your clone. Professionals often try to hire someone who reminds them of themselves. This is a mistake. An assistant should stand out in areas where you have shortcomings. If both of you excel in public relations and neither of you can balance an office budget, you're still in trouble. Working together, the two of you should cover all the bases.

 Tip

Hiring an assistant is much like starting a new relationship. Until you start working together daily, you won't know if your styles mesh. Consider hiring your new personal assistant for a three-month probationary period.

Avoid Employee Theft

73

Most theft in the workplace is done by employees. Eighty per cent of employees will steal only if they are positive they can get away with it. Ten per cent of employees will never steal. And 10 per cent will always steal.

⊙ Steps

1 Pay your employees a fair wage. Employees who feel they are getting fair compensation are less likely to steal. Ensure that the job they perform is appropriate for the pay they receive.

2 Install security cameras. It is impossible for you to monitor all employees at all times. Security cameras can be reviewed quickly and at any time. The camera does not have to be operational as long as your employees believe it to be.

3 Install a time clock. One major form of employee theft is stealing time. Set up a system by which the employee cannot manipulate their attendance record.

4 Require proof of purchase. Be sure all employees can provide proof of purchase for any new item in their possession.

5 Reconcile sales transactions. Make sure that employees' sales transactions balance with your own records of the transactions.

✳ Tip

Let your employees know what security measures are in place.

Prevent a Strike

74

Strikes can be devastating for both employees and management, so it's best to avoid them altogether if possible.

⊙ Steps

1 Keep communications open. Always be willing to sit down with union representatives.

2 Stay on as friendly terms as possible with shop stewards and union representatives. Invite them out socially and pay attention to what they say. The stronger a relationship you cultivate with them, the more likely it is that they won't fight you on smaller issues.

3 Understand and clearly state management's position. Remember that bargaining in good faith means keeping the lines of communication open – it does not, however, mean that you have to give in to all the union's demands.

4 Point out the downside of striking to employees. Note that in many cases they will not be able to collect unemployment benefits, nor will they have health coverage. In addition, striking workers can be permanently replaced. Be careful, however, not to say anything that could be perceived as a threat.

✳ Tip

The best way to prevent a strike is to make sure the work situation never becomes that antagonistic in the first place. Cultivate shop stewards and front-line supervisors and get wind of any growing dissatisfactions.

⚠ Warning

Make sure you do nothing that could be construed as a threat or retaliation at striking workers.

75 | Handle Angry Customers

A satisfied customer is more likely return to your business. Maybe it is not necessarily anger that is causing the customer's unhappiness – they could just be frustrated from lack of good customer service.

⊙ Steps

1 Determine why the customer is angry. Frustrations with product returns, refunds or exchanges can cause a customer to become angry.

2 Listen to the customer's complaint. Let the customer know you will work to ensure satisfaction and are interested in resolving the problem.

3 Ask the customer what can be done to resolve the problem. Quickly resolve the issue by offering an equitable solution to the problem. If you are not allowed to give the customer their money back, consider offering store credit.

4 Be aware of negative body language. Always be attentive to the customer's concerns. Do not turn your back to them, fold your arms or place your hands on your hips. This can be viewed as authoritative behaviour. A customer may be more prone to become angry if they think you are not interested in good customer service.

5 Assure the customer that their business is always appreciated. Not all customer-service problems can be resolved, but the trick is to make the customer feel that everything possible has been done within company policy to ensure their satisfaction.

⚠ Warning

Always avoid promising a customer what cannot be delivered. Saying what the customer wants to hear just to get rid of them will backfire.

76 | Work Effectively in Groups

Working in groups is almost unavoidable today; specific and clear communication is the key to success in these scenarios, whether for short-term or long-term projects.

⊙ Steps

1 Get to know each other. If you're going to be working in a group with other people for any extended period of time, spend a few minutes talking at the outset of the first meeting. Introduce yourselves if you do not already know one another.

2 Assign roles if the project requires working together in a group for an extended period of time to reach a specific goal. For example, you might designate one person the group leader or facilitator and another the scribe or note-taker.

3 Exchange contact information to enable group members to communicate effectively outside scheduled meetings if the project is long-term.

4 Identify the group's goal. For example, perhaps a professor has asked you to accomplish a specific task within your group, or your company has asked you to research specific information and report back. Discuss and document the group's goal to make sure you all agree on the primary goal of the group's work.

✱ Tips

You may want each member to explain a bit about schedules or other commitments in the first meeting for long-term projects.

Even if you're working together just for a short time, make sure everyone in the group introduces themselves if people do not know each other.

Depending on the type of conflict, it may be dealt with between members privately or collectively through discussion. Keep personalities out of the picture when dealing with conflict and avoid negative attacks on individuals.

5   Divide tasks into steps and assign each member a specific task to attack long-term projects. This is often easier if people volunteer for tasks they would like to do.

6   Listen to and encourage each other. Make sure everyone in the group is heard and offer encouragement when others contribute a good idea or perform a task effectively.

7   Deal immediately with conflict if it arises. Although difficult to deal with, conflict or discord in a group can undermine the objectives. As quickly as possible, address any conflicts to keep the group members focused on the ultimate goal.

Brand a Business   77

Branding a business is key to its success. You want everyone to recognise your business logo; recognising your business brand will draw in customers.

⊙ Steps

1   Design a business logo. Make sure it reflects a style that is representative of your line of work. For example, a nursery should have a logo that looks kid-friendly. On the other hand, a spa should have an elegantly styled logo.

2   Use the same logo on every advertisement you produce. Your brand should never change. Consistent use of a brand will promote business recognition amongst your consumer base.

3   Order marketing materials that will reinforce brand recognition. Whether you distribute pens, t-shirts, baseball caps or mugs, your customers will see your logo.

4   Find ways for your business logo to be seen by the public. Buy advertising space on television, radio or the Internet. For smaller businesses, public visibility may be comprised of distributing flyers or hanging banners. Whatever you choose, make sure your logo is easily seen to create a recognisable brand.

✳ Tips

Be creative and unique. Part of the fun of having your own business is knowing that the sky is the limit.

When you get to the point of working out how you introduce yourself and what you will say both in person and in writing, make sure that you use the right words. This will help draw the right customers to your business.

Develop a Marketing Plan   78

Any potential lender or investor will want to see a marketing plan for your new product before making a commitment. Developing a marketing plan also gives you the opportunity to organise your thoughts and your strategy.

⊙ Steps

1   Describe your product in detail. What are its most significant features? Is the product still in development, or is it ready to roll?

2   Identify your target market. Who will this product appeal to most? Include all market research, including historical figures for sales of your type of product.

 ✳ Tip

Marketing plans can be just a few pages or as lengthy as novels. Keep in mind that the more thorough you are in supporting your plan with research, detailed information and financial projections, the more likely you will be to gain support from investors

3 Size up the competition. Who are your major competitors? How does your product compare to theirs? How strong a foothold do they have in the market? Look at the methods they use to market their products and learn from them.

4 Detail your marketing strategy. How will you advertise and market your product? Which features of the product will you focus on? What will be the product's price and why?

5 Describe your operations. Include any plans you have for customer service, proposed credit and sales terms, the qualifications and achievements of your management team, and the physical location of your business.

6 Prepare financial statements based on projections of sales, operating costs and expenses. Include cash-flow projections, profit and loss reports, and income statements for at least three years.

79 | Conduct Your Own Market Research

Market research is critical to understanding your customers and competitors. Here's how to conduct your own market research to plan a successful business.

◎ Steps

1 Determine your goals and objectives in conducting market research. What do you want to find out? What is your target population?

2 Give clients and suppliers a brief questionnaire to get the necessary information.

3 Follow up with phone calls. Ask for additional information and enquire about specific likes and dislikes.

4 Create a focus group of customers or suppliers to give feedback on what they want from your business.

5 Talk to your employees who man the frontlines, listening to customers. Encourage them to capture customer comments, opinions and ideas. Reward your employees for doing so.

6 Delegate a job of summarising customer comments in one report on a regular basis.

7 Examine sales records to see where popular selling regions are and what customers are buying.

8 Review questionnaires, interviews and focus-group results to determine particular trends.

9 Prioritise changes you wish to make based on feedback.

10 Decide who is responsible for making changes, and how.

✳ Tip

Ask questions rather than telling people about your business.

⚠ Warnings

Don't ask for feedback if you don't plan to use it.

Make sure that your results aren't biased. Ensure that they come from a broad cross-section of your customer base.

Write a Press Release
80

Ready to spread your news with a press release? Here are some tips for success.

Steps

1 Determine what the news is. Before you start writing anything, make sure you have something current to use as the plug in the headline and lead paragraph. Press releases are dependent on time-sensitive news, so choose your topic and give it a recent slant.

2 Take a glance at some other press releases on the Internet.

3 Format your press release. Generally, you will want to include a logo and contact information on the release. Next, create a headline (and a sub headline to get more information up front in large lettering under the headline). Then give your release a date and location notation.

4 Write the release – generally no longer than a page or two. At the bottom, include relevant websites or phone numbers, and you can note a name of who to contact regarding the news. Most people end their releases with "###" to show that it is officially the end of the message.

✳ Tips

Write like a journalist – use a punchy headline and include a verb in the header and sub-header lines.

If you don't feel comfortable writing your own release, hire a professional.

⚠ Warning

Make sure the release announces news in the headline and first paragraph. Don't include any fluff or you are likely to lose the reader's attention.

Design a Business Card
81

Making a business card can be both fun and challenging. A business card should be a visual representation of your business and yourself.

Steps

1 Think about the brand for which you are going to be creating a business card. What is this company all about? Check out the feelings the company puts out to its customers, as well as the colour pallet used by the brand. You will want to incorporate this into your business card.

2 Try using a dominant graphic element, such as a logo or stylised brand colours. You'll want to create a style that fits in with the brand. For example, if you have a flower shop, don't have jagged black and red lines that create an aggressive feel.

3 Start with a sketch pad and pencil – there are always things you can only put down on a sketch pad. Start sketching out business cards using different layouts, trying various graphic elements and perhaps some different (but still similar) colour ideas.

4 Once you have some ideas down on paper, look through them and start pointing out certain things you like. Take all the elements that you like and try putting them together in a new business card.

5 Once this is together, take the one design that has all the elements you like and try sketching it out in new ways with subtle things changed. Try moving one aspect from the left to right or adjusting size.

6 Put your card on the computer and design it using a program such as Adobe InDesign or QuarkXpress.

✳ Tip

The back of your business card is an opportunity to add more content.

⚠ Warning

While there is a lot of clipart available free online, you may not be the only person who chooses a particular design. If you want to distinguish yourself from the competition, hire a graphic designer to give you something fresh and original.

82   Choose Effective Colours for a Business Logo

Your logo is the first thing that strikes customers on your marketing materials, in your ads, on your website and on your products, so make sure you don't have a colour scheme that puts people off.

◉ Steps

1   Decide on the overall image you want your company to convey. This should be reflected in all your marketing materials, starting with your business logo. A laid-back software company will use different colours from a financial adviser who wants to gain the trust of big investors.

2   Research the logos of competing businesses. You don't want to pick a colour scheme that's too similar to any of your competitors. And you don't want to use bright colours when other companies in your sector are using subtle tones.

3   Pick a particular element in your logo that can stand out. You may have a catchy name or your graphic designer may have created a first letter or design element that you want people to associate with your company.

4   Choose a bright, warm colour for the element you want to stand out on your logo. Red is an aggressive colour and suitable for a company name or other critical design element. Orange is less severe than red, but still bright enough to attract attention.

5   Use blue to denote authority and stability. It can get boring, though, if you don't offer a contrasting bright colour or an interesting design element. Blue goes well with red and orange, though a logo with dark blue and white can also be effective.

6   Incorporate green into your logo if your business is associated with health. It has a calming, healing effect. Healthcare-related firms, alternative therapists and even athletics businesses like health clubs can greatly benefit from using green in their logos.

7   Go with colours like pink and purple if your customer base is female. It makes women feel the company understands their needs. Cosmetics, skin-care products and women-oriented fitness centres commonly use these colours in their business logos.

✳ Tips

Yellow can make your business logo look tacky so it's best to use it only for accent.

Grey works best as a supporting colour due to its association with depressing weather.

⚠ Warning

Avoid letting white or black dominate your logo colours.

83   Get the Most Out of Trade Shows

Trade shows are a place where top salespeople get new leads, make contact with current prospects, research new products and do some networking.

◉ Steps

1   Find the shows that will give the most return for your investment. It's important that you thoroughly research each show before attending to make certain the audience or the exhibitor base is right for you.

2   Look through published exhibitor lists for shows you plan to attend. Then get online and research individual companies.

✳ Tips

Use flags to mark pages in your show guide for easy reference.

Wear comfortable shoes and clothes. You want to concentrate on the show, not the blisters on your feet.

3   Arrive the day before the show and rest up. Plan to spend an entire day at the show; prepare for a lot of walking.

4   Try to attend a show during the middle of its run, when you will have the best chance of speaking with representatives. On the first day, exhibitors are usually swamped and have little time to talk to prospects; on the last day, some exhibitors are already packing up.

5   Get to the show early and take a little time to study the guide and floor plan. Formulate a plan of attack with emphasis on aisles that warrant special attention, as well as specific booths and product demonstrations you want to catch.

6   Take along a small notebook or dictaphone to make notes as you go.

7   Translate your notes as soon as possible to make certain you remember and record important details.

Find Free Advertising   84

The key to free advertising is to give something of value in exchange for what you want.

⊙ Steps

1   Look for partners to share their advertising in exchange for your goods or services. For example, if you are in property you may find a mortgage broker who is willing to place an ad featuring your business if you refer some of your business in exchange.

2   Find complementary goods or services that are already advertised and create a promotion whereby your product is included in exchange for free advertising.

3   Promise goods or service in exchange for free advertising. Find local newspapers that may be willing to take some of your products or services in exchange for free advertising.

4   Search the Internet for sites that could use your product. For instance, a women's health website might be interested in your low-fat recipes. Consider offering to write articles in exchange for a free link to your business's website.

5   Contact people or companies that need your goods or services and make a deal for advertising. For example, if you offer day care, contact large companies in your area and ask to be a part of their corporate newsletters, offering a discount rate to new clients.

6   Make a deal for free advertising in return for something else of value, such as your time, a consultation, or secondary goods or services.

7   Find an unconventional place for your advertising. Smaller websites, companies and papers are often more willing and able to make trades for services or goods.

✱ **Tips**

Always get any agreement in writing.

Consider all sources, even people or places that you wouldn't necessarily think of for advertising.

⚠ **Warning**

If it sounds too good to be true, it probably is.

85 Attract Advertisers

If you run a website, newspaper, newsletter, magazine or blog, you'll want to attract advertisers. Below are some tips for attracting the kind of advertising you or your business will need.

◎ **Steps**

Advertise to Attract Advertisers

1 Advertisers have to know you exist. Whether you run a blog or an ezine, you need to let potential advertisers know that you need them, so you need to advertise to advertisers.

2 Present your rates, specifications and contact information to attract advertisers. This information needs to go in the most logical place. If you run a newspaper, for example, put it on your website, in any extra space in the paper and in the mast-head.

3 Cross-promote yourself with your service providers. Give free space in your publication to your email newsletter software company, for example. The return on investment will be valuable, as they can give you leads, and in return you will send customers their way.

Give Them Something for Their Money

1 Advertisers need a reason to buy space in your publication. What are the benefits of doing business with you: high web traffic, large circulation, relevant articles?

2 Attract advertisers with evidence. Provide information about how many unique visits your website gets a day. Provide a current readership survey if you have one.

3 Provide competitive advertisement rates. Research your competition and adjust your rates accordingly.

4 Get testimonials from your readers and other advertisers. Give the potential advertisers something to gain.

Find Leads

1 To find advertising leads, you will have to do some legwork. What works best for your market? Get out there and conduct some market research.

2 Read the trade publications relevant to your industry. Put a contact form on your website. Look at who is advertising in similar publications.

3 When you get a lead, it is important to immediately follow up with the appropriate form of communication. Whether this is a phone call, an email or an old-fashioned letter, let the potential advertiser know you want their business.

Create a Media Kit   86

A media kit, or press kit, is a package of news and background information that is distributed to members of the media to build buzz about your product, service or event. The information in this kit will help give a reporter story ideas.

⊙ Steps

1   Describe your product, service or event in a concise press release. Don't forget to answer the following questions: who, what, when, where, why and how. Consider the question the editor will ask: "Will my readers find this interesting?"

2   Provide enough background information about the product, service or event and, if appropriate, a biography of key personnel. For example, a book author or public speaker would include a biography about his or her achievements in the relevant area.

3   Include a fact sheet listing bullet points with specific information and key facts. This is not the same thing as the background information.

4   Include a photo in your media kit. If it's a professional-quality photo, it will be more likely to run with your press release and get more attention in the publications.

5   Place any previous clips referring to you, your product, service or your company in the press kit. This adds credibility to your release.

6   Write a covering letter that ties the package together by explaining why your press release should be considered for publication. In your letter, suggest article topics and list yourself as an expert source for future interviews on those topics.

7   Answering questions in the form of a Q&A sheet could also be helpful to the journalist when he or she is considering an angle for your story.

8   Include a review copy of your book or a sample of your product if appropriate. If it's not feasible to send a sample, explain the item thoroughly and let the media know where it is available.

✳ Tips

Writing press releases in journalistic style will help reporters. The less editing it needs, the more likely it is to be printed.

Creating a press kit that is downloadable in PDF format is less expensive than sending it through the post.

⚠ Warnings

Do not include random clippings that don't pertain to you, badly photocopied clips, brochures or sales material. Journalists usually don't have time to read them and they get thrown out.

If it isn't newsworthy, it probably won't get published. Make sure your press kit has a hook to current events to make it topical.

Write a Jingle   87

Whether you're a songwriter who needs extra income or an entrepreneur who needs to advertise your business, knowing how to write a catchy jingle can come in handy.

⊙ Steps

1   Know the ins and outs of the product you're trying to sell. This helps you write a jingle that is accurate and informative, which makes buyers more familiar with what makes the product different from – and better than – the competition.

✳ Tips

Draft at least 10 different concepts to make sure you cover all angles.

Always have back-up lyrics and save music that you initially discarded. They can be used to inspire new ideas.

2   Write lyrics that use catchy literary devices. Puns, rhymes and onomatopoeia are all great ways to catch the listener's attention and draw him or her into your advertisement.

3   Make sure you include the name of the product and the business in the lyrics. A buyer can't buy a product if he or she doesn't know or remember what it is.

4   Write sentences that are strong, bright and filled with verbs. Avoid sentences that feel sloppy or awkward by weeding out the passive voice and any complicated phrasing.

5   Write a tune that's memorable. It doesn't have to be cutesy, happy or set in a major key, but it absolutely must stick easily in the listener's memory. Using arpeggios and scales to build your melody keep it simple and focused, and make it much easier for the buyer to remember.

88 Read a Company Report

If you're looking to invest in a new firm you need to get as much information as possible about the company. When you examine a company's financial report you discover how a company is faring and whether its outlook is positive or negative.

◉ Steps

1   Familiarise yourself with the types of statements and terminology one finds in a company financial report.

2   Read the letter to shareholders, which is typically found at the beginning of a company financial report. This letter, which the CEO usually pens, is a general statement regarding the state of the company and its financial performance in the past quarter or year.

3   Look over the overall business review next. This portion includes the company's objectives, recent developments and any trends.

4   Sift through the financial review, which includes vital information such as cashflow, profits, losses and taxes. Items such as the balance sheet, income statement and footnotes are included in the financial review.

5   Compare the company's report with other reports of firms in the same industry. Measuring up and comparing items such as debt, depreciation, sales and inventory will give you some insight on where your company stands.

6   Evaluate the information in the company financial report. A prospering company should have plans to build on its current growth, and a company that is not performing well should have concrete, convincing plans to improve in future quarters or years.

✳ Tip

Contact the company's corporate compliance or corporate communications office if you have any questions about the information presented in the company report.

Follow an Agenda   89

While business meetings have a reputation of being boring, or even unnecessary, a clear and concise agenda can help all involved realise the purpose of such meetings while assuring that maximum progress is achieved.

⊙ Steps

1 Decide what specifically needs to be accomplished at the particular meeting you're going to schedule. Let the actual needs of the moment dictate the items you include in your agenda.

2 Consult with the colleagues in your department some days before the meeting, if possible. This gives everyone a chance to participate in the process of the meeting, thus helping everyone feel involved. The more involved each meeting participant feels, the more likely it is that the meeting will run smoothly and stay on track.

3 Distribute the agenda in preliminary form, and allow department members to make suggestions. Again, this serves to give more collective ownership to the process. Allocate a specific amount of time for each item; make sure that you have enough time in the meeting to cover each item adequately.

4 Stick to the agenda as much as possible once the meeting has started. Follow the plan item by item. Invite conversation, commentary and debate on issues that warrant such an approach, but be ready to politely get people to move on to the next item when necessary.

5 Keep in mind that you can table certain discussions until the following meeting if you must. Be flexible, and know what items need to be finished up in that particular meeting, and which can be moved to the next meeting without negative repercussions.

✳ Tip

As the leader of the meeting, be ready to interject when necessary to move things along, or to allow everyone to participate. Sometimes one or two people can monopolise the meeting to air their grievances or express their points of view.

Relocate a Business Abroad   90

Some businesses relocate abroad to take advantage of lower raw material and labour costs, while others do so in order to meet an increased demand for their product or service.

⊙ Steps

1 Visit the country of choice before the move. Visiting the country and the specific area to which you want to move will allow you to familiarise yourself with the area and to check out local competitors.

2 Investigate all legalities. Make sure you can legally work and own a business in the country of your choice.

3 Apply for the proper visa and/or work permit. Types of visas and work permits vary greatly from country to country. Be sure you are applying for the proper one.

4 Learn the regulations and laws of the foreign government to ensure that you don't inadvertently face legal issues.

✳ Tips

Consider converting currency as you need it instead of all at once. Many banks will allow you to convert currency as it is withdrawn or deposited. Converting all at once may lead to losses due to market fluctuations.

Consider an offshore bank account. This may lessen your tax burdens and implications.

5   Seek out a local estate agent. Many countries restrict property ownership for non-residents. A local estate agent can guide you through the
process of leasing or buying property for both personal and business
needs. Hire a lawyer, too, because there are many intricate legalities
involved in leasing and buying property abroad. This process is best left
to a professional.

6   Open a business bank account. Keep in mind things such as the value
of your native currency against the foreign currency and the tax requirements of the foreign country as well as in your native country.

7   Reserve enough funds to support yourself and your business for at least
one to two years.

⚠ **Warning**

Know the tax implications and
burdens of both your native
country and the country in which
you are relocating. You may have
to pay taxes in both countries.

91 | Appear Wealthy

As the saying goes, "Money talks". Learn to keep up with the
high rollers by appearing wealthier than you are.

◎ Steps

1   Learn to talk the talk. The wealthy often discuss money or topics that
require loads of it. Do your homework by reading issues of magazines
such as *Forbes*. It won't hurt to brush up on topics like yachts, fine food,
boating and polo.

2   Dress like a million dollars. Purchase a few high-end suits, tailored
clothing items and other dressy pieces at outlets or clearance sales
rather than creating a wardrobe full of Gucci and Armani.

3   Be polished. Don't forget the small details. You should smell nice and
look good. Routine hair cuts, dental upkeep, manicures, pedicures and
a sophisticated perfume or aftershave show the importance of taking
care of yourself.

4   Carry a money clip instead of a wallet if you're male. If female, carry a
minimalist bag rather than a bulky handbag.

5   Don't forget your manners. Always treat others with respect, never
forgetting a please or thank you. Manners are tied to traditional
standards of the upper class.

6   Reduce talk of personal finances. Those who have it don't necessarily
flaunt it. The only time it's acceptable to discuss money is when referring
to the stock market.

7   Volunteer. A common activity for those who don't have to spend the
majority of their time at a job, volunteering will also let you rub shoulders
with the wealthy.

✳ **Tip**

Consider shopping at charity
shops if you really need an item,
otherwise budget for it over
several months.

Fill Out an Online Job Application 92

Whether you apply from home or in person, most employers today offer the option of an online job application.

⊙ Steps

1 Create one sheet of paper with all your personal information. Have this handy when you fill out the online application at home or bring it with you when you apply in person.

2 Read all the instructions. Pay special attention to the boxes and lines that are required. When you leave required spaces blank, the application will be sent back, which can take a lot of time and be confusing.

3 Check each page before you click on the Next button. You may not be able to go back after you get to the next page of an online job application. Use spell check if you can or check spelling very carefully.

4 Save the application and go back to it at another time. Many online applications have this feature, which is useful if you get interrupted or need some more information to complete the application.

5 Be prepared for tests and questions in the middle of an application. Read them carefully – if you answer them quickly you may rush and answer them incorrectly.

6 Read all the small print at the end of the application so you know what you are "signing" before you submit the completed online job application. This can include statements that references and credit will be checked, a pre-employment drug test is required and that all your answers are truthful.

✳ Tip

Have your CV open so you can cut and paste if the application asks for parts of it.

⚠ Warnings

Don't leave any questions blank – your application may be automatically rejected.

Don't try to guess or play tricks to figure out an application; answer all questions truthfully.

Email a Prospective Employer 93

Email is a major communication tool and can be used to your benefit during a job hunt.

⊙ Steps

1 Make your subject line compelling to get attention and a quick response.

2 Use an abbreviated, but fairly conventional, business-letter format: date, address, name, job title and salutation.

3 Mention how you heard about the job opening in the first sentence.

4 Make the enquiry or statement brief and concise.

5 Expect to be judged on attitude, spelling, grammar and your ability to meet deadlines.

6 Close every email with your contact information.

7 Remember that while email can feel impersonal, there is a human being reading it at the other end. Keep the tone friendly but professional.

8 Send a brief reminder email if you hear no word for two weeks. Employers are inundated with CVs after an initial posting and might be more receptive once things calm down.

✳ Tip

If you send your CV as an attachment, consider cutting and pasting it into the body of the email as well. That way, if the recipient can't open the attachment, he or she can still view it. Keep in mind that you may lose some of the formatting when you do this.

⚠ Warning

There is no expectation of privacy with work email accounts.

94 | Dress for a Job Interview – Men

Your interview attire is more important than you think. It's an opportunity to make a good first impression with a potential employer or future boss.

Steps

1   Know the company you will be interviewing with, and research the industry that it's a part of to familiarise yourself with the universal dress code. Ask a friend at the company or stake out the front door to find out what current employees wear to work.

2   Go in a suit and tie to any company that's part of a more formal industry, such as banking or law. Choose a basic black, dark grey or dark navy suit, a matching tie and black leather lace-up shoes. Borrow anything that you may be wary of investing in well in advance to ensure that it's clean and fits well.

3   Opt for dressy casual attire for a company that you know doesn't expect suits. An ironed button-down shirt, a belt and leather loafers will serve you well.

4   Match the belt to the colour of your shoes. Choose black if your outfit consists of dark grey, navy, brown or black. Opt for dark brown if you'll be wearing tans, muted pastels or medium-toned colours.

5   Polish or clean your shoes the night before your interview. Scuff marks on your shoes reveal a lack of forethought and attention to detail.

6   Keep interview accessories professional. Take a briefcase or nice leather- or vinyl-bound portfolio to carry your CV, references or other pertinent documents. Leave tatty folders at home.

7   Avoid aftershave that may overpower the interviewer.

8   Place your watch in your pocket once you make it to the front door so that you're not tempted to look at it during the interview.

✳ Tips

Check your appearance before heading into an interview. Ensure your tie is straight, your teeth are clean and your hair is groomed.

Let your talent and personality get you noticed, not your clothes. Save the bright colours, wild prints and trendy fashions for another occasion.

95 | Dress for a Job Interview – Women

Perfect grooming is your first assignment when you interview for a job, whether you want to be a CEO or an entry-level factory worker.

Steps

1   Call the receptionist or secretary at the prospective employer's office for tips on what employees there wear.

2   Consider the job's location. If it's a library, you can wear a jumper and trousers. At a corporate office, wear a conservative business suit. A trouser suit with a jumper or blouse is appropriate for an informal office.

3   Choose between closed-toe shoes or smart heels. If you are wearing a skirt, tights are a must.

4   Avoid miniskirts, tight sweaters, sloppy overalls and sandals with straps.

✳ Tips

You have one chance to make a first impression; it's better to dress too formally than to dress too casually.

Trendy is fine, as long as you keep your style subtle. Clothes make a strong statement about you. What do you want to say?

5　Check your outfit for holes, tears, stains, scuffs or wrinkles.

6　Tone down the use of makeup, hair spray, perfume and jewellery. One nose ring is one too many and may cost you the job of your dreams.

7　Inspect your hair, nails, hems and the shine on your shoes.

8　Wear a silk scarf and carry a nice briefcase or portfolio. Leave the over-sized, disorganised handbag at home.

Dress on the First Day of Work　　96

Do first impressions on the first day of work really matter? Do you want to blend with the office protocol or do you want to stand out as the new kid on the block?

⊙Steps

1　Arrive early when you go for your job interview so that you can spend a few minutes observing how the other staff members dress. When you are taken to the interview room, survey as much around you as possible without looking dubious.

2　Ask questions. First days often see the new employee with a mentor, so ask questions on dress code, coffee breaks and lunch breaks and general do's and don'ts of the office. Don't assume anything.

3　Wear an outfit that can be dressed up or down. Women might wear a skirt and jacket with simple top. If the jacket is too much, it can be taken off. A man might wear a two-piece suit where the jacket can be taken off if it is too formal.

4　Wear comfortable dress shoes, nothing outstanding in fashion. You can always elaborate in the future if you see it's appropriate.

5　Keep your makeup and hairstyle simple but elegant. Again, you can always elaborate as time goes on.

6　Don't wear strong perfumes or aftershaves as they can leave a negative lingering effect if they aren't accepted well.

✳ Tip

The important thing is to not cause offence or leave a negative effect at the end of your first day.

Make Decisions　　97

Making decisions can be intimidating and time-consuming. And while there's no easy way to just make them, the following tips can help you be more decisive.

⊙Steps

1　Mark out the parameters of the decision clearly. What choices do you have? Are there more than two?

2　Gather as much information as you can about each alternative – talk to the appropriate people, solicit advice from friends and family, and research by reading books and magazine or newspaper articles.

✳ Tips

Critically evaluate your decision from time to time – if you don't like how things are progressing, try something else.

If all else fails, try going with your gut feeling.

3   Get the experience that will help you make an informed decision. For example, if you're trying to decide whether to become a doctor or not, first volunteer at a hospital or clinic.

4   Jot down a list of pros and cons for each decision. Prioritise which considerations are very important to you, and which are less so.

5   Recognise that there are no right reasons for making a particular decision. The fact that a particular path is important to you, regardless of what others think, legitimises it.

6   Think honestly about any fears, motives or biases guiding your thinking. Recognise them for what they are.

7   Brainstorm alternatives. Can you synthesise the available alternatives into a compromise that maximises the pros and minimises the cons? Look for ways to have your cake and eat it too.

8   Put an end to collecting information about your decision. Avoid thinking that with just a little more time and information you'll be able to make the one perfect decision. You could go on forever thinking in this way – and still never make a decision.

9   Recognise that you might learn things in hindsight that would have changed your decision had you known about them earlier. This thought is normal, and should not be allowed to stall your decision-making.

10   Make the decision.

⚠ **Warning**

Keep one eye on the clock; avoid endless delays in making a decision out of fear that you don't know enough or will make the wrong choice.

---

98   Improve Your Concentration

Improving your concentration will help you to accomplish more in a shorter period of time.

◎ Steps

1   Create a space designated solely for work. If that space is your desk in a work office, for example, use it only for work – step away from it when taking breaks or eating.

2   Form a strong association between working and your desk to make concentrating easier.

3   Remove surrounding distractions. Turn off the ringer on your phone and, if possible, shut down your computer if you will be tempted to surf the Internet.

4   Assemble all the materials you will need (books, paper, charts). You want to avoid getting up to retrieve materials and distracting yourself.

5   Set a specific production goal and give yourself a manageable chunk of time (perhaps one or two hours) in which to achieve this goal.

6   Create pressure by scheduling meetings or other interruptions to force yourself to work more effectively during a shorter period of time.

7   Reward yourself after each period of intense concentration with a short break.

✳ **Tips**

Work at a time of day when you know you are alert.

Work with another person nearby to encourage yourself to concentrate more fully.

Try to stop work at a natural breaking point or after some sort of accomplishment.

⚠ **Warning**

Avoid expecting to work with maximum effectiveness for long, unbroken stretches of time, as there are limits to anyone's powers of concentration.

Organise Your Workspace `99`

Organise your workspace to encourage maximum productivity.

⊙ Steps

1 Place your computer monitor directly in front of you if you want to discourage people from interrupting your work.

2 Position your desk so that you can see people who approach your door.

3 Avoid leaving spare chairs around your desk to minimise distractions.

4 Keep important papers or equipment within reach. Your phone, computer, filing cabinet, fax machine and printer should be within reach if you use them frequently.

5 Post a calendar and clock close by. Try using a large calendar that can be posted on your wall and written on with erasable markers.

6 Have papers and materials only for the task at hand on your desk.

7 Establish a filing system, keeping current files in your deep desk drawer or a filing cabinet within reaching distance of your desk. Store papers you need only periodically somewhere else.

8 Label file names clearly, and try colour-coding your folders for better organisation. File alphabetically.

9 Set up an inbox and outbox – one to receive incoming papers and another to hold assignments you've completed before forwarding them to the appropriate person.

10 Read incoming paperwork with a highlighter in hand, marking important deadlines or phone numbers. Deal with urgent papers immediately, set aside those that aren't urgent, and throw away the ones that aren't important or relevant.

11 Tidy your desk space at the end of the day, noting what you need to work on tomorrow.

✳ Tips

Give computer documents logical names for faster recall.

Regularly review your filing cabinets, desk and hard drive to throw out old materials.

⚠ Warnings

Sticky notes often fall off or get lost, so avoid using them.

Avoid stacking papers on your desk – you will inevitably misplace important documents.

Manage Your Time `100`

Computers and the Internet were supposed to make life easier; instead, people are busier than ever. Learn to manage your time to get as much as you can out of each day.

⊙ Steps

1 Create a schedule or to-do list. Write down deadlines for accomplishing certain tasks.

2 Plan to tackle difficult projects at the times of day when you are most alert.

3 Schedule time for people, including yourself. Create some personal time by waking up half an hour earlier or going to bed half an hour later than usual; plan a weekly date with your spouse, or arrange to have lunch with friends.

⚠ Warning

Sometimes being too efficient can make you lose track of why you need extra time in the first place. Don't be so intent on scratching things off your to-do list that you don't make time for fun.

4   Prioritise what you need to accomplish. "Pareto's principle" states that 80 per cent of your accomplishments come from 20 per cent of your efforts, so think strategically: locate and isolate this valuable 20 per cent, then focus your efforts on the tasks that promise the greatest rewards.

5   Delegate as many chores as you can. Hand out projects to subordinates at work, recruit your children to help around the house, hire a gardener to maintain your lawn.

6   Learn to say no to non-essential demands on your time. Don't volunteer for a committee if you don't have time, and decline invitations to events you don't have time to attend.

7   Overcome procrastination.

8   Avoid perfectionism. Don't waste time obsessively perfecting a task when that time could be better spent on something else.

101　Reduce Paperwork

Papers can pile up quickly, leaving your desk cluttered and you feeling overwhelmed. Reduce paperwork in the office with the following tips.

⊙ Steps

1   Try to handle incoming letters, memos and notes immediately; don't put them to the side and assume you will look at them later.

2   Deal with a piece of paper only once. Once you pick up a piece of paper, do something to help you get rid of it: take the necessary action or copy information to the appropriate place, then throw the paper away.

3   File only what is essential. Review your files periodically and clean out the ones you no longer refer to.

4   Cancel subscriptions to magazines or journals you no longer read.

✷ Tip

"Paperwork" can include virtual paperwork, such as email messages. As with notes and memos, deal with the email message right away. Copy down dates or numbers, then delete it.

102　Use Technology to Save Time

Use technological advances to communicate more quickly, reduce paperwork and improve efficiency.

⊙ Steps

1   Assess your computing needs and get a personal computer that meets your needs. You might need software for word processing, spreadsheets, presentations, desktop publishing, personal-information management, accounting and virus protection.

2   Organise a filing system on your computer, with descriptive document and folder titles. Review stored documents periodically and remove the ones you no longer need.

3   Keep your email messages short and direct. Send documents as attachments.

⚠ Warning

Although the Internet enables quick and easy communication and research, it also has some features that can waste tremendous amounts of time, such as online chat rooms and aimless Internet surfing.

4   Limit your email volume by screening messages by subject header, giving out your address only when necessary and stopping spam (unsolicited junk mail). To do this, type "Remove" as the subject header and send an email to the auto responder address at the bottom of the spam you receive.

5   Make the most of your telephone. Consider caller ID (which displays the sources of incoming calls) to screen your calls, and a headset if you need to use your computer while you talk. Ask your phone company about services that route calls to your voice mailbox or another phone, such as your secretary's.

6   Designate one or two times in the day for returning email and calls. Cut down on phone ping-pong by leaving messages that include the best times to reach you.

Keep Email Private at Work   103

Keeping your email private at work is essential to keeping your private life private. Your email at work can be used against you and even give someone the information to steal your identity.

☉ Steps

1   Set up a password for your work email that will not be easily guessed. Your password should be at least eight characters long and should include both letters and numbers.

2   Keep your email account minimised on your screen when you are working on something else. A nosey co-worker can easily look over your shoulder and read your work email subjects.

3   Place a password on your screensaver for when you must leave your desk during the day. This password should not be the same as your work email password but follow the same conditions for a password as outlined in Step 1.

4   Set your computer to your screensaver before you walk away from it to keep your emails private. Even one minute away from your computer is enough time for someone to snoop at your work email.

✳ Tip

Change all your passwords for your work email monthly to keep them private.

⚠ Warnings

Using the names of loved ones is not a good idea for work email passwords as they can easily be guessed by co-workers.

Never write down your passwords for your work email. Someone will find them.

Reduce Stress While at Your Desk   104

Everyone gets stressed out during their day at work. Deadlines, workflow and other pressures are going to hit you all day. Don't feel guilty about taking a short break from your work if it's going to help you complete the job on time.

☉ Steps

1   Ask yourself why you are stressed. The simple act of acknowledging that there is a problem gives your mind a second to process it without worry, and then tackle the obstacle.

✳ Tip

Keep your desk organised – a messy space is a stressful one.

2   Take a five-minute walk. Getting up from your chair and walking once around the floor of the office building gets the blood flowing and loosens up the leg and back muscles. Sometimes it's all you need to get focused again and release that stress.

3   Get out your iPod. Some offices have rules about not playing music or listening to your iPod while working, but a quick three-minute song can give you stress relief that can last all day.

4   Look at a picture. Keeping a picture of a special place or person can generate the feeling of being away from your desk. Try a photo of your favourite holiday destination or put up a photo of people you care about.

5   Find a friend – you can share your concerns or take your mind off things by listening to a friend talk. It always pays to network around the office; having a friend in the workplace can help it seem brighter.

6   Remember what matters. At the end of the day, the thing that is stressing you out probably won't affect you on a long-term basis.

105 | Polish Your Presentation Skills

As the workplace becomes more complex, the need to communicate ideas effectively grows exponentially. A presentation requires great content, but at its heart, it's a performance.

◎ Steps

1   Research your audience. Knowing the background and interests of the people to whom you'll be presenting helps clarify your content and approach.

2   Think about last things first. Define – clearly and concisely – the results you want from the presentation. Remember that a presentation is a call to action: an appeal for investment, a solicitation of sales or an attempt to have specific information incorporated into future actions.

3   Clarify your story. Define the essence and the excitement of your product, project or service.

4   Connect with your audience emotionally – find a hook and introduce it early in the presentation.

5   Stress benefits rather than features. Remember that your audience members care more about positive solutions to their problems than about how the solutions occur. Emphasise how much your solution will cut costs, increase profits or better serve clients, for example, rather than detailing the many steps leading to these results.

6   Arrange a logical flow of content from beginning to ending. The type of structure does not matter – chronological or geographical, modular or matrix; use any form that fits the material. Choose just one, however, and stick to it throughout the presentation.

7   Keep the presentation as brief as possible while still covering the essential material. It's more important to be compelling than to be all-encompassing. Avoid piling on too many details lest you confuse members of your audience – or send them to sleep.

✳ Tips

To handle a heckler, try to diffuse the emotion by simply repeating his or her question in calmer language. Then either answer it or ask the questioner to speak with you later.

Finish your presentation earlier than the time stated on the agenda. You'll feel an aura of gratitude emanating from your audience.

⚠ Warning

Many presentations rely too heavily on PowerPoint. Be careful that yours does not fall victim to slide-overkill syndrome.

8   Plan the audiovisual aids. Decide whether to use PowerPoint slides, video clips, flip charts, handouts or a combination.

9   Borrow the storyboard technique from filmmakers. Before creating any slides, write your core ideas on cards or sticky notes. Experiment and rearrange them to get the most persuasive order.

10   Create an ending that circles back to the beginning. Your moments of strongest impact are the first few minutes of a presentation and the last few. Make sure they work together.

Take Control of a Conference Call   `106`

A conference call lets you remain at your desk rather than having to attend a meeting. It also provides a great opportunity to get the opinions and concerns of the entire team heard.

⊙ Steps

1   Volunteer to set up the call so you can assume the role of moderator. Confirm that everyone has both the dial-in and conference code numbers, as well as the correct time if calling from different countries.

2   Poll the other participants in advance about the items they want covered in the call. Develop a written agenda with a specific time allocation for each item on the agenda. Better yet, email the agenda to all parties before the call.

3   Take charge of gathering and disseminating the printed background material, numbering pages clearly and prominently. Nothing creates conference-call chaos faster than a chorus of "Where are we?" or "I don't seem to have that chart".

4   Refuse to discuss major agenda items until everyone is on the line. Bringing latecomers up to speed on important issues wastes time and irritates those who were prompt.

5   Monitor the clock closely. Be prepared to intervene with "Excuse me, we have to move on – we've run out of time for this topic." Stay polite but firm throughout.

6   End the call with a synopsis of conclusions reached and future actions required. Send out a written summary of these conclusions and action items to all participants promptly.

✳ Tips

Use a handheld phone on a land line rather than a mobile phone or speakerphone. Your voice will be clearer, with minimal background noise. Use an office where you can close the door to further reduce noise.

If more than two other people are participating in the call, keep a written list of names beside your phone so you can be sure you are getting everyone's input.

Pay Off Student Loans Quickly   `107`

Student loans are typically better than private loans because they have low interest rates. However, student loans still represent a debt burden for recent graduates.

⊙ Steps

1   Budget your finances. It is essential to create a budget so you can keep track of how much money is coming into your bank account, and how much money you are paying to cover expenses.

✳ Tip

Student loan debt is much better than other forms of debt (e.g. credit-card debt), so try to focus on paying off the most expensive debt you have.

2 Identify areas in which you can cut back on spending. Look at your budget and focus on areas in which you spend a lot of money. Consider ways to spend less. For example, if you spend most of your money on food, try to buy budget items for staples.

3 Consolidate your student loans. Contact your loan provider, financial institution or bank and ask if you are eligible to consolidate multiple student loans. Streamlining your student loans makes payments easier. It also helps to combine interest rates to take advantage of lower rates and save money on loan payments in the long run.

4 Ask for student-loan payment deferrals if you are unable to make your payments on time. Individuals who have lost their job or are undergoing economic hardship can sometimes defer student-loan payments.

5 Focus on paying off your student loan sooner rather than later. The longer you plan to pay off your student loan, the more you end up paying in interest. You may be paying less per month in student-loan repayments, but an extended loan repayment plan means you end up paying much more in interest.

6 Check to see what tax benefits you can get from paying your student loan. This can help you save more money and devote more of your budget to getting rid of student-loan debt. Depending on your tax bracket and job, you may be able to deduct your student-loan payments from your income. Consult a financial adviser or tax preparer to determine your eligibility.

108 | Separate Your Professional and Private Life

It's important to keep your private life out of the office and to leave personal problems at home when you go to work.

⊙ Steps

Keeping Your Professional Life Out of Your Private One

1 Break down a large task into its simplest elements. This way you won't be so overwhelmed at home by what you didn't get done at work.

2 Make daily to-do lists that include some of these elements.

3 Reward yourself for completing the small tasks instead of pushing to finish a large project without breaks.

4 Avoid falling into a permanent guilt mode, particularly if you work from home. Just because you *can* keep working doesn't mean you *should*.

5 Make time for a private life – even if this means that you need to put personal matters on your to-do list.

Keeping Your Personal Life Out of Your Professional One

1 Maintain a professional demeanour at work. While you may be upset over a failed romance, crying all day at your desk interferes with your productivity and that of those around you.

⚠ Warning

If you're more concerned about your personal life than your job while at work, the company will pick up on this and it will be a short-term relationship.

2   Keep discussions of personal problems with supervisors to a minimum. They should only be brought up if they are affecting your job performance.

3   Make calls to friends or family regarding personal matters during your lunch hour if the calls can't wait until you are home. Avoid using the business phone for personal calls.

4   Remember, your employer is more concerned with how well you do your job than what sort of person you are.

Come Out to Your Co-Workers   109

If you're tired of feeling left out of the "what I did last weekend" conversations around the office because you're a lesbian or a gay man, maybe it's time to come out to your co-workers.

⊙ Steps

1   Take stock of your situation. If you're concerned about a person or group who might find out about your sexuality from a co-worker, it might be best to come out as a homosexual somewhere other than the workplace to avoid difficult situations.

2   Consider how coming out will affect your immediate future at work, and bear in mind that not every coming out has a happy ending. On the other hand, a few days of discomfort may be better than years of lying, and often people surprise you.

3   Try coming out naturally rather than making a big announcement. Bring in a picture or two of you on a date or on holiday, or of your partner if you're in a long-term relationship.

4   Start giving a few more details of your activities when having personal conversations with colleagues. "I saw that film with my friend Harry last Friday. We loved it."

5   Participate actively in lunchtime discussions about your home life, foibles of mates and other personal (but not intimate) topics.

6   Answer the question "Oh, are you gay?" with a simple "Yes".

7   Take one or two good work friends aside and tell them you're gay, if you're not comfortable coming out naturally. They'll let others know and it can be easier this way.

8   Be considerate. Share only appropriate information.

9   Change the subject if people appear uncomfortable or if the conversation seems to die. People may not be ready to discuss your circumstances as soon as you tell them about it.

10   Be prepared to listen. In many cases, co-workers want to tell you about friends or family members who are gay.

 ✱ Tip

Not everyone needs to know you're gay. Remember, it's only one part of who you are.

110   Say No to Colleagues

Over-commitment on the job can be draining. If you're absolutely strapped, learn to say no to supervisors who suggest more projects, potential clients who want your services or colleagues who ask for favours.

Steps

1. Recognise that you have the right to refuse a request.

2. Say no politely but directly and firmly. If you cannot offer help, don't mislead the person by hedging with "maybe" or "I'll think about it".

3. Offer to help the person in another way that is more feasible for you, if you can.

4. Ask if a deadline can be extended, if time constraints are the problem.

✳ Tips

You don't have to provide a reason for saying no. Offering a reason might only encourage the asker to challenge your reason and ask again.

Think about why you are unwilling to say no. Do you fear anger or rejection from others? Are you reluctant to say no because you like feeling indispensable?

111   Work With a Person Who Has Body Odour

Body odour can be very funny – when you're not the person who has to smell it. You should not have to inhale eau de armpit all day.

Steps

1. Be mature. While it might be tempting to vent about your co-worker's body odour to colleagues, gossiping only makes the situation worse. Even if your friends laugh with you when you complain, they might grow to think of you as cruel and petty – and this won't do much for your career.

2. Limit the time you spend in close proximity to your smelly co-worker, if possible. If he or she works in the cubicle down the hall from you, stay at your workstation and just grin and bear it for short meetings or encounters in the canteen.

3. Keep pleasant-smelling items at your workstation, such as scented soaps, unlit candles and air fresheners. Inhale whenever you need a deep, cleansing breath.

4. Consider telling the co-worker about the problem. If they are emotionally stable, you're on friendly terms with them and are a tactful person, you can gently bring up the issue.

5. Talk to your human-resources department if you don't want to bring up the subject yourself. If you can't escape the body odour – if you must work next to the person for extended periods of time – it's not fair that you should be expected to tolerate such working conditions. Dealing objectively and compassionately with issues like these is part of being a human-resources professional.

✳ Tips

You don't have to provide a reason for saying no. Offering a reason might only encourage the asker to challenge your reason and ask again – leading to more discussion and trouble than you anticipated.

Think about why you are unwilling to say no. Do you fear anger or rejection from others? Are you reluctant to say no because you like feeling indispensable?

Complain About a Co-Worker

Smelly food, messy work spaces, body odour and lots of other big and little things can make work unpleasant. Complain in the right way and you can fix the problem with minimum fuss.

⦿ Steps

1. Identify the problem and separate facts from emotions. Make sure you identify the situation or behaviour that's bothering you and don't label the co-worker.

2. Think of possible solutions. If a co-worker never writes down telephone messages does he or she know how to transfer a call to voicemail? Ideas to solve the problem will help resolve it quickly and keep any conversation positive.

3. Talk to your co-worker. He or she may not know that what they are doing bothers you. Clearly state the facts and explain how the behaviour affects you.

4. Begin statements with "I" not "you" when you describe the problem. This helps keep emotions and labels out of the conversation. "I can't get the meeting started when you are late" will get a better result than, "You are so slow and lazy that our work can't get done."

5. Tell your supervisor or manager. If talking to the co-worker didn't work or it's a sticky situation then you have to take the complaint to your boss or human resources. Clearly state the problem using only the facts. Tell your boss about any possible solutions. Keep personal opinions out of the description.

6. Thank the co-worker when his or her behaviour changes. Unless the problem was a difficult one about personal hygiene your co-worker will appreciate hearing a thank you.

7. Move forward and don't keep complaining once a problem has been resolved. You'll get along better with co-workers if you don't refer back to the time that they bothered you or created a problem.

8. Don't use the problem as an opportunity to spread gossip. Complaining about a co-worker to lots of other people will only hurt your relationship with the co-worker. The gossip could get back to them. It won't help solve the problem and it could also get other people upset.

⚠ Warning

Don't respond with a quick email to avoid talking to the person or to your boss. When a co-worker reads an email it's easy for them to misinterpret your words.

113 Get a Job with the BBC

The British Broadcasting Company is the biggest broadcasting company in the world, but vacancies are predictably oversubscribed, and you'll face stiff competition for each place. However, it is possible to land that dream job.

Research

- Decide which area of the BBC you'd like to work in. As you'd expect in a company of this size, there is a multitude of roles available, from sales and marketing positions to more creative jobs in television-production teams and even on-screen opportunities in areas such as newsreading and TV presenting.

- Check the BBC's website as regularly as you can for advertisements of job openings. They have a page especially dedicated to recruitment, where you can also find out what it's like to work at the BBC and what benefits you are likely to receive.

- Consider taking an educational course to prepare yourself for a career at the BBC. Although not strictly necessary, most paid jobs at the BBC will require you to have some kind of experience in the field, and practical media courses are now offered at many universities and colleges around the country that will give you a preview of life in the media.

- Try getting a foot in the door by securing a work-experience placement or internship with the BBC. However, don't think it will be easy – the BBC receives over 20,000 applications for work experience alone each year, so make sure you can prove you know exactly what you want to do, what you can offer the company and why they should hire you.

- Prepare a list of all your qualifications, education and your work experience for the online application form you'll have to fill out through the BBC Jobs website. Try to match your experience and qualities to the requirements of the job.

Application

- Visit the BBC website to sign up for an online account and set up your application. You'll have to enter your basic details, your education history, qualifications, career history and some equal opportunities information. There's also a section called "Application Questions", where you'll need to write a personal summary of why you think you would be a good fit for the job.

- Complete and submit your application as soon as possible, and make sure it's before the deadline. Once submitted you should expect to wait at least a couple of weeks to hear back from the BBC.

- Don't be tempted to exaggerate your achievements on your application. You'll invariably be caught out. Be aware, too, that employers are allowed to request copies of your exam certificates.

- Don't panic if you're asked to go to the BBC for an interview or assessment day. Try writing down any questions you think you could be asked on the day, and get someone to practise them with you. Have answers prepared for any question you think the interviewer might want to ask.

- Be on time! You definitely won't make a good impression if you are late to the interview. Plan your journey in advance and check travel websites to see if there's likely to be any delays to your journey.

- Be persistent! It's rare to find someone working in the media that hasn't had to work hard to get where they are, and it's inevitable you'll face rejection at some point. If you haven't been successful this time, don't be disheartened, but instead ask for feedback on your application to help you make your next one even better.

action

Become a Tree Surgeon 114

A tree surgeon is involved in all aspects of tree care, including trimming, planting, pruning and treating diseases. Unlike logging or other tree-removal occupations, tree surgeons are interested in the protection and care of trees.

⊚ Steps

1 Enjoy working outdoors. Be physically fit enough to climb trees and work with hand and power tools, such as chainsaws, at various heights.

2 Take college courses in forestry, agriculture and arboriculture. Though there are no formal educational requirements to become a tree surgeon, you should study the characteristics of all types of trees.

3 Gain experience with the tools of the trade and get used to working outdoors by working as a landscape gardener or by volunteering for outdoor work for community services.

4 Apprentice with a tree surgeon for hands-on training. If you don't have a formal education, hands-on training is the best way to become a tree surgeon.

5 Join the local chapter of an association for networking. Continue your education and earn certification as a Skilled Tree Worker. Earn other special certifications, such as for working around power lines.

6 Adopt a conservation mentality. Tree surgeons are interested in saving trees, or cutting down only those that have been damaged by disease or weather. Work to preserve trees whenever possible.

✳ Tip

Don't think that because no formal qualifications are required this is an easy career choice – you'll need to be familiar with many different disciplines.

Become a Professional Referee  115

If you are a huge sports fan with detailed knowledge of the rules and regulations of a particular sport, you could become a professional referee.

⊚ Steps

1 Learn as much as you can about your favourite sport. You must know all the rules of the game whether it's football, basketball, boxing or whatever sport you enjoy. Become an expert in that field.

2 Take classes in communication, management, leadership and motivation. To become a professional referee, you must be an excellent leader who communicates well when you supervise athletic events. You must be able to make quick decisions.

3 Volunteer to be a referee in your community. Start at small events. Youth sports teams in your community or the local gym that trains boxers are good opportunities. Some towns have football youth programmes that provide free classes to train referees. Take advantage of as many different training classes as possible.

✳ Tip

Take advantage of as many clinics, training sessions, classes and meetings for referees as you possibly can in your community.

4   Have someone make videos of you as you referee. Study those videos, compare them to professional game videos and learn where you need to improve. Ask experienced referees to evaluate your game videos. Ask for advice on your performance.

5   Work your way up from volunteer work to paid community referee. From there, you can work up to school referees, then college. If you do exceptionally well at university or college level, the professionals will notice and doors will open up for you.

116 Become an Astronaut

Only the most highly skilled applicants enter NASA's space programme, and fewer still make it into space. Depending on their background, astronauts may train as pilots or as mission specialists.

◉ Steps

1   Know that you must be between 5 ft 4 in and 6 ft 4 in tall to be a pilot and between 4 ft 10.5 in and 6 ft 4 in to be a mission specialist. You also need to be in top physical condition and have great stamina.

2   Maintain an excellent academic record in your undergraduate and postgraduate studies. Many astronauts have doctoral degrees.

3   Although NASA does not specify "ideal" undergraduate degrees for its candidates, it may help to choose a scientific field for your bachelor's degree that you can use if you become an astronaut. Possibilities include subjects such as medicine, biology, chemistry, physics, aerospace engineering and mathematics.

4   Make certain you have at least three years of work experience in your field before applying as a mission specialist. An acceptable substitution might be a two-year graduate degree with one year of experience.

5   Have at least 1,000 hours of pilot-in-command time in jet aircraft, preferably with flight-test experience, if your ambition is to be a mission pilot.

6   Send for an application package (see Tips for the address). You'll have to pass the strict NASA physical as a basic qualification, but that really is only the beginning...

7   Realise that if you're accepted as an astronaut candidate, you're committing yourself to a training period of to two years in Houston, Texas, without a guarantee that you'll ever go into space. Training will be intense and often in low-gravity conditions. It will include land and sea survival training and scuba diving.

8   Prepare to remain with NASA for at least five years if you pass the training period and are accepted as an astronaut.

✳ Tips

You can obtain an application package by writing to NASA Johnson Space Center, Astronaut Selection Office/AHX, 2101 NASA Parkway, Houston, Texas 77058, USA, or by looking online.

If you're claustrophobic, don't apply to be an astronaut. Your problem will definitely be discovered.

⚠ Warning

You must be a team player at all times. Lives will depend on you.

Become an Aerobics Instructor 117

Teaching aerobics or group fitness classes can be a wonderful way to earn extra income, meet new people and get a workout – all at the same time.

☺Steps

1 Get experience in different forms of aerobic exercise, including step aerobics, high- and low-impact aerobics, kickboxing, water aerobics and sports conditioning.

2 Enrol in a CPR and first-aid training class. Most certifications require these skills.

3 Take courses or read books on anatomy, exercise physiology, kinesiology and motivational techniques. A basic understanding of fitness-related topics is recommended before pursuing a certification.

4 Seek certification by a nationally recognised organisation.

5 Practise cueing, or giving verbal instructions. Many certifying organisations offer classes on how to design and teach fitness classes, which include the techniques of cueing.

6 Seek opportunities to gain teaching experience. Organise a class for friends or family members in which you can act as instructor.

7 Team-teach with another instructor. Start by teaching a small portion of the class and gradually increase the amount of class time you teach.

8 Choose music that is professionally mastered for smooth transitions and even counts.

9 Check out teaching opportunities at local gyms, corporate health clubs, recreational clubs and hospitals.

✳ Tips

Most instructors are paid on a per-class basis depending on level of experience, background and participant feedback.

Most health clubs offer a free gym membership to instructors.

⚠ Warning

Be sure to adhere closely to the safety guidelines set forth by your certifying organisation and place of employment.

Become a Proofreader 118

If you have patience, a great eye for detail and a passion for reading, you may enjoy proofreading.

☺Steps

1 Begin in school and university by taking as many English and literature classes as possible.

2 Consider that a good education in a broad array of subjects will also serve you well. General knowledge about a vast number of subjects is invaluable to a proofreader.

3 Work for your school's newspaper or literary magazine; even if you're not proofreading, it's useful to learn about the process of putting together a newspaper, magazine or other publication.

4 Read books that inform you about editing and the publishing process.

✳ Tip

If you have an area of expertise other than editing – perhaps you speak Spanish, understand quantum mechanics or once attended cooking school – look for publishers that specialise in that field. This gives the publisher an added incentive to hire you, even if you aren't the most experienced proofreader applying.

5   Take a course in proofreading (many are offered through colleges or distance learning). Here you'll learn concrete skills such as proofreading notation and different methods of book production.

6   Decide whether you are most interested in proofreading books, magazines, newspapers or websites.

7   Decide whether you'd like to work for a single publisher or for several; some proofreaders work in-house for a single employer, while others work on a project-by-project basis for various publishers.

8   Apply for proofreading jobs that you find in local job listings. If you've taken a proofreading course, you might be hired without experience if you can pass a proofreading test.

9   Ask for feedback on the proofreading tests that you have taken; learn which types of errors you're most likely to miss.

10 If you haven't been hired for a full-time job, or if you'd rather work as a freelancer, look for companies that need freelance proofreaders.

⚠ **Warnings**

Proofreading is not a well-paid profession. People who are successful at it typically do it for the love of working with words rather than for the love of money.

Many people think that all it takes to succeed as a proofreader is a good knowledge of grammar, but this is far from true. You need training to learn how publications are put together and practice to develop your ability to catch inconspicuous errors.

119 Become a Book Indexer

Although some publishing and legal firms have a staff of in-house indexers, most indexers are freelancers and work with a variety of publishers.

◉ **Steps**

1   Indexing is a form of technical writing with its own set of methods, practices, rules and standards, which you'll need to learn. You have choices in how you learn these things: self-taught, formal indexing course, private lessons or apprenticeship.

2   Once you've familiarised yourself with indexing methods and rules, start practising straight away and looking at the indexes you see in books with a critical eye. Can you spot errors? Are there entries that you would write differently to make them more useful? Start with short samples of text to practise on – even brochures. Work your way up to longer works, until you can index a 200-page book. You'll need at least two practice indexes to show as samples when you start marketing yourself.

3   If you prefer to take an indexing course, look online for the best one for you. Most are distance-learning courses, but you can sometimes learn indexing in a classroom setting if you're lucky enough to live near a library school; occasionally their indexing classes are open to non-library students.

4   Once you have learned how to index a book, you'll need to find work. There are probably as many ways to market yourself as there are indexers. Try word of mouth, cold calling, sending letters on spec or creating a good website. Or join to the Society of Indexers and post your profile on their website.

5   It can take a couple of years until you have a large enough client base to earn a living from indexing. Many indexers started out moonlighting and give up their day jobs later on. Try not to get discouraged.

✳ **Tips**

Always manually check the alphabetisation when you have finished – the computer's "sort" function isn't infallible.

The Society of Indexers' website has a host of invaluable information. See www.indexers.org.uk.

Become a Flight Attendant 120

The main responsibility of flight attendants is to make sure that airline safety regulations are carried out on board an aircraft.

Steps

1 Search for flight attendant open-house listings in the newspapers of larger cities, or check online with individual airlines for job opportunities and requirements.

2 Understand that your competition will have at least a two-year college degree and customer-service experience, and that many airlines now require both.

3 Learn at least one foreign language if you plan to work for an international airline.

4 Accept that you may have to relocate to another city at the beginning of your career.

5 Be prepared to live on a reserve status for at least one year after your initial four- to six-week training period. You will need to be available as an on-call person, often on short notice. Advancement into regular assignments results from seniority, and the competition is fierce.

6 Expect to fly 75 to 85 hours a month and to also work on the ground. But realise that you will be paid for flight time only.

Tips

Learn to be on time for every event in your life before you begin this career. Your job will definitely depend on arriving before your assigned schedule.

Set aside time for annual training in emergency procedures and passenger relations.

Warnings

If you have problems standing for long periods of time, this is not the career for you.

Consider the possibility of medical problems brought on by irregular sleep, poor diet, stress and breathing recycled air.

Become a Museum Curator 121

Museum curators acquire, organise and oversee collections of art and valuable historical items. The competition for jobs in this field is tremendous.

Steps

1 Become familiar with the field by researching online career information, education requirements and colleges offering related courses.

2 Work in a museum as an intern while you're in college. You'll gain invaluable experience and contacts. Be aware that internships are highly competitive, even those that are unpaid.

3 Obtain an undergraduate degree in art history and a Master's degree in your area of specialisation. Ideally, your Master's will be in the specialism of the museum in which you hope to work.

4 Work towards receiving a PhD if you want to be a curator in any natural history or science museum.

5 Consider getting two Master's degrees, one in museum studies, the other in a speciality, to really stand out from most of the competition.

6 Be prepared to work your way up the curatorial ladder after you have your Master's degree. If you are fortunate enough to get a job in this competitive field, you may have to begin as an assistant curator or associate curator and do mostly administrative work.

Tips

Make certain your overall writing skills are superb.

Become proficient in the use of computer databases. You will need to catalogue your museum's collections.

Take a course in grant writing. You will be required to participate in fundraising for the museum.

Warning

Be prepared to travel if you work as a curator for a large museum. You will always be on the lookout for new additions to your museum's collections.

How to Do More of *(Just About)* **Everything**

122 Become a Fashion Designer

Fashion designers create the designs for clothing and accessories in shops around the world. However, few designers become as successful as Armani, Karan or Versace. Most work for mass-market manufacturers, designing basic pieces.

Steps

1 Be honest with yourself about your ability to sketch and your eye for design and detail. The competition is fierce in this field, and you'll need a strong inner drive to succeed.

2 Increase your chances for success by obtaining a two-year or four-year degree in fashion design. Expect to show samples of your sketches as part of your application.

3 Take as many marketing and business courses as possible, in addition to design courses. Knowledge of the business end of the fashion industry is vital to your career.

4 Develop a working knowledge of a variety of design-related software programs to stand out from the crowd when applying for jobs.

5 Put together a portfolio of your own designs. It must show how creative you are and convince potential employers that you would be an asset to their business.

6 Set up an internship as quickly as possible. You will gain valuable experience, and it might lead to your first job after graduation.

7 Make as many industry connections as you can while you are at college. Include people in design-related fields, such as advertising. You never know when such contacts will come in useful and it's never too early to start networking.

8 Regularly read fashion bibles such as *Vogue* to remain current on trends and future trends.

✳ Tips

Expect to work long hours at a low salary at first, doing relatively obscure design work.

Learn how to use a sewing machine. Your designs will be more impressive if you can show prospective employers the finished item, along with the sketch.

⚠ Warning

The dropout rate in this field is high, because of the low pay and the poor opportunity for advancement.

123 Become a Sportswriter

If you like sports, digging up information and writing, sports writing can be a rewarding career.

Steps

1 Take as many writing courses as possible in school and university because strong English skills are essential. Work on your school or college newspaper, too.

2 Bear in mind that, as in other branches of journalism, every subject will come in handy: history, political science, biology, etc. Study journalism only if the journalism department gives you time to take lots of outside courses.

3 Learn to type. Very few sportswriters learn shorthand, which is a mistake; they miss a lot in interviews, and tape-recording and then transcribing is too slow.

✳ Tips

Sportswriters must be neutral, objective and fair. Keep opinions out of news stories, but if you're a columnist, be prepared to praise or blast teams and athletes, depending on the circumstances.

If you're going into the profession for free tickets and other freebies, forget it. Journalism ethics, enforced at most publications, forbids the accepting of gifts.

4 Learn about sports: what constitutes a 300 game in bowling, how to do a box score in baseball, what three events make up the Triple Crown in horse racing. Watch and read about as many contests as possible.

5 Remember that apart from school newspapers, a great place to start is to cover school sports for a local paper. Most papers are anxious to find people willing to stalk the sidelines of Friday-night football matches; it might result in only a three-paragraph story, but it's a foot in the door.

6 Become a better sportswriter by reading good writers – and not just in the newspaper sports sections and sports magazines. Most of the best sportswriters read widely: mainstream novels, mysteries, articles on politics, etc.

⚠ Warnings

Athletes, coaches and managers are usually easy to deal with, because they are a) doing something they love and b) want recognition. However, they can also be difficult after losing or being criticised.

Sports' writing is not as glamorous as some imagine. Deadline pressure takes its toll and the money isn't great.

Become a Film Critic   124

You'll need to have substantial prior experience before a large paper or TV station will consider hiring you as a film critic, but here are some tips to get you started.

☉ Steps

1 Enrol in a college or university that has a well-known school of journalism or broadcasting, depending on your desired career.

2 Set up informational interviews with possible future employers. Find out what their minimum qualifications are for film critics and plan your education strategy accordingly.

3 Gain experience by writing reviews of plays, concerts and other productions for your college newspaper or radio station. You'll gain experience and polish your skills at the same time.

4 Take courses about the entertainment industry. You'll need to have some knowledge about its history to write effective reviews.

5 Become familiar with all the arts. Smaller publications or stations might require you to write reviews on all forms of entertainment before you can specialise in just one.

6 Obtain an internship with a local paper or station during your college years. It can lead to an entry-level position upon graduation, even if it doesn't initially involve writing reviews.

7 Consider working as a freelance critic for small publications to gain experience for your CV.

✳ Tip

Make certain that your writing skills are excellent and that you can write objectively. Take extra writing classes or workshops if necessary.

125 | Become a Cowboy

It's easy to recognise a cowboy – just look for well-worn boots and jeans, an oversized belt buckle and that unmistakeable 10-gallon hat.

Steps

1 Work on a ranch to learn everything you can about cattle. You'll feed the cows, give vaccinations, look out for health problems, help with calving and much more. Buy a ranch in a country like the United States or Australia if you can afford it, and can handle all kinds of uncertainty, from bad weather to sick cattle to fluctuating markets.

2 Select promising bulls for breeding and rodeo riding. Castrate the others and raise them for meat or for steer wrestling at the rodeo. Decide whether you'll use the females for birthing or beef.

3 Learn some rodeo skills at bull-riding or rodeo school, and develop other skills on the ranch. You rope a calf to give it medicine the same way you rope one to bring it down in the rodeo.

4 Buy cattle feed, or raise your own if your ranch is big enough. If it's really big, grow enough grain to sell to other people. Grass-fed cattle require a pasture consisting of high-energy grasses and clovers.

5 Mend fences and maintain farm buildings and equipment. Learn about machinery – a lot of ranch work, including branding and vaccinating, is now mechanised.

6 Feed and take care of your horses.

7 Be a savvy businessperson. You have to buy grain, sell animals and balance the books to make a success of being a cowboy.

8 Get someone to watch the ranch while you ride in the rodeo. Many cowboys work their ranches Monday, Tuesday and Wednesday and compete Thursday through to Sunday. (Some cowboys are only ranchers, some are only in the rodeo and some do both.)

9 Pay a rodeo entry fee and hope to place high enough to take some prize money home. Top rodeo cowboys earn a good living on the circuit, but many others barely scrape by.

10 Enjoy being outdoors, working with animals and keeping a quintessential way of life alive.

11 Buy an original Stetson.

✳ Tips

Get in shape – ranching and rodeo skills take a lot of strength and endurance.

Along with hands-on experience, many ranchers get agricultural-related degrees.

How to Do More of *(Just About)* **Everything**

Buy a Luxury Car 126

Buying a luxury car should be fun, so take your time. If you're spending a lot of money, you should be able to get exactly what you want.

Steps

1 Determine what you want to spend. Luxury cars start at about £20,000, and prices can go into the stratosphere.

2 Decide what's most important to you: safety, performance, value, handling, comfort, reliability, dealer service, looks, interior room, quietness, prestige.

3 Make a short list of the makes and models you want to consider. Do some research to determine how they stack up in terms of your priorities. Most luxury cars today excel in most if not all areas. However, some place comfort over handling and performance, or vice versa. Read magazine reviews to get a clearer picture.

4 Review the crash-test data for various cars.

5 Consider resale value. You may be surprised to find quite a bit of variation here. In general, German and Japanese luxury cars have the highest resale values.

6 Talk to friends who own similar cars. They may have some good advice.

7 Compare insurance premiums for different cars you are considering.

8 Test-drive the two or three cars on your shortlist. Don't worry about the dealers now. Focus on the cars. Do you feel comfortable in the car? Does it drive the way you want it to? Don't commit to any car or salesperson yet. Go home and think about it.

9 Rank the cars according to your priorities. Then rank them by price. You should be able to narrow the choice down to one or two cars. If the choice still isn't clear, test-drive the cars again.

10 Collect pricing information for the car you want, decide on colours and option packages, and get your loan together.

✳ Tips

Many luxury cars come with different engine, transmission and suspension options. Be sure to test-drive the cars with the options you want.

Consider cars with a sports package if you enjoy driving on twisty roads. But expect the ride to be harsher.

Buy a Sports Car 127

Modern sports cars can be quite practical and reliable. Who says you can't have your cake and eat it too?

Steps

1 Determine what you want to spend.

2 Decide how much room you need. Enough for two people and a spare toothbrush? Or do you need small back seats?

3 Consider a convertible. Modern convertibles often have safety features that the old ones didn't, like three-point seat belts and roll bars. Also, the tops have improved; they have fewer leaks and less interior noise.

✳ Tip

Consider colour carefully if you expect to sell the car in a few years – red will be much easier to sell than brown or beige.

4   Consider the various transmission options. Do you need five speeds?
    Six? If you drive in traffic a lot, you may prefer an automatic that gives
    you the option of switching to manual.

5   Think about engine performance. Do you want lots of horsepower and
    gobs of torque? Or do you prefer a high-revving engine? In general,
    muscle cars will be more fun around town, whereas the small displace-
    ment sports cars will excel out in the twisties.

6   Consider layouts. Do you like the horse in front of the carriage? Or would
    you rather have a rear or mid-engine? Mid-engine cars tend to sacrifice
    space and comfort for handling.

7   Don't forget resale value. You may be surprised to find quite a bit of
    variation here.

8   Compare insurance premiums on different cars you're considering.
    Realise that sports cars can be quite expensive to insure.

9   Test-drive some cars. This is the fun part. Realise that car salespeople
    tend to expect to make a lot of money on sports-car sales. Try to keep
    a cool head. Don't commit to any car or salesperson yet. Go home and
    think about it.

10 Rank the cars according to your priorities. Then rank them by price.
    You should be able to narrow the choice down to one or two cars.
    If the choice still isn't clear, test-drive the cars again.

11 Collect pricing information on the car you want, decide on colours
    and option packages, and then get your loan together.

12 Return to the dealer and tell the salesperson what you want.

128 | Buy an Eco-Friendly Car

While most of us are aware of the damage that cars do to the
environment, the push for greener car choices is still in the
preliminary stages. Here are some tips on the specifics of
green car buying to make the choice a little easier.

◉ Steps

1   Look for a hybrid. The best-known name in eco-friendly cars thanks to
    the past few years' marketing push in this direction by many car compa-
    nies, the hybrid offers a lot to the potential consumer. These cars
    capture potential energy in their batteries whenever the car stops.
    They get great mileage and they are quiet and run on traditional petrol,
    so they can be refuelled like normal cars, although less frequently. This
    being said, there are few choices for this type of car, so selection is
    minimal at best and the prices can be a lot higher than traditional models.
    The battery life, which prolongs the MPG ratio, is also debatable.

2   Try biodiesel fuel. If you want a traditional car model, but still want to do
    better for the environment, then try biodiesel fuel. A blend of traditional
    diesel and vegetable oil, it can be fluctuated in your tank with regular
    petrol if you are not near a biodiesel fuelling station. Biodiesel gives off
    lower emissions, can be used in a lot of car models and costs little more

❋ Tip

Check out the Green Car
website online to find out
more about eco-friendly cars.

than traditional fuels. The cons mainly lie in the after-effects of the fuel choice – you may have to change your oil filter more often and they can still cause smog. Cold weather can affect performance depending on the vegetable-oil content in your fuel and there are limited SUV and truck options that use biodiesel fuel.

3   Consider ethanol. A wheat-based fuel additive, E85 is the most popular form of this fuel, meaning that it is 85 per cent ethanol and 15 per cent petrol. Ethanol increases the octane in your fuel, decreases emissions and costs less that traditional petrol. The models that use ethanol are versatile, E85 can be swapped with traditional petrol and there are several vehicle choices. However, the locations of refuelling stations for E85 are few and far between in the UK. Look online to see where they are and find out if it's worthwhile taking advantage of the benefits of this fuel.

Inspect and Buy a Classic Car   129

Inspecting old cars is always a bit tricky. But if you're patient and careful, you can avoid the lemons and find a car that makes you happy for years.

⊙ Steps

1   Create a list of questions.

2   Call the owner and fire away. How long has he or she owned the car? What is the owner history? What repairs have been done recently? What is the car's condition? Is there rust? What repairs are needed? If you are satisfied by the answers to these questions, arrange for a test drive.

3   Call your mechanic. Tell him or her you may want to bring in a car for a pre-purchase inspection. Make a tentative appointment.

4   Inspect the car carefully before you drive it. Check for rust and body damage. Check the fluids, the belts and the hoses. Look for leaks.

5   Test-drive the car. Was the car started before you got there? Ask the owner to start the car and watch what comes out of the exhaust pipe – blue or black smoke isn't good. During the drive, be aware of any sway in the front end. Does the transmission shift smoothly? Does the car have power? Does it pull to one side when you use the brakes?

6   Ask to see repair records and all documentation. Be suspicious of an owner who can't provide any records.

7   Take the car to your mechanic, who will often find things that you have overlooked. This will give you added leverage when it comes time to make an offer. Consider the purchase carefully if the car needs a lot of work.

8   Make an offer in line with the price guide. Keep in mind that this car is for fun. You don't need it. Be prepared to walk away if the owner won't make a fair deal.

✻ Tip

Don't let your emotions take over. Unless you are looking at a racing car, you should be able to find another in as good or better condition.

130 Buy a Car at Auction

Buying a car at auction is a great way to save money and get a good deal.

Steps

1 Bring a copy of a good car-value guide with you. You'll want to know the fair market value of the car to make sure you get a good deal and not pay too much. The guide will list the value of the car along with prices of recent sales.

2 Get to the auction as early as possible and stay until the end. You never know exactly what will turn up on the auction block and the best deals are usually found at the beginning of the day and the end of the day. Getting there early also gives you the chance to look over all the vehicles before they go up on the auction block.

3 Ask about the history of any cars you're interested in and see if it's possible to run your own independent background check. Most car auctions now offer buyers the chance to run a check and often have stands set up for this purpose. This will let you find out about any accidents or major damage the car may have had in the past, which may affect its value or what you are willing to pay for it.

4 Check the premium added to the price of the car. This premium is a specific amount of money that goes back to the auction house for its services; it ranges from a set price to a percentage. The premium can make your good deal a little too expensive and you won't know it until you go to pay.

5 Bid what you feel comfortable bidding. The value guide shows you exactly how much the car typically sells for, but you may feel uncomfortable bidding a high amount. Keep in mind your own budget and only bid what you can afford to spend.

✳ Tip

Don't pay too much for a car just because you want to keep bidding, but keep in mind what the value of the car is according to your price guide. You may be tempted to spend quite a bit more on the car in front of you than its actual worth.

⚠ Warning

Don't buy any vehicle at the auction unless the title is there and ready for you. If you don't get a title it might be an indication that the car has been stolen or that the owner is hiding the car's history.

131 Buy a Motorcycle

Choosing the motorcycle that's right for you is not an easy undertaking. Your height and riding ability must get just as much consideration as the price of the bike and your bank balance.

Steps

1 Stay with a smaller cycle – no more than 250cc – until you have ridden several hundred miles. Don't try a big bike until you have been riding for a year or more.

2 Make sure the motorcycle fits you. Your feet should reach the ground when you're sitting on the seat.

3 Be sure the headlight and taillight, the front and rear brakes, the turn signals, the horn and at least one rearview mirror are working properly before making a purchase. Note that you need mirrors on both sides to survive in traffic.

✳ Tip

If you're not sure of the engine size, look for an identifying sticker on the frame, below the handlebars.

4   Remember that it's also a good idea to have reflectors along the sides of the motorcycle.

5   Be aware that new motorcycles and equipment should meet all safety standards. Check your equipment and be certain it's up to appropriate standards, especially if you are importing your motorcycle or buying a second-hand bike.

6   Make sure your motorcycle has an adequate muffler, keep it properly maintained and do not modify it to make it louder.

7   Display your licence plate on the back with a sticker showing the latest month and year of registration. Keep the licence plate clean and clearly readable at all times.

Buy a Motor Home   132

If you're in the market for a motor home or a recreational vehicle (RV), here's how to shop around to get the best buy for your recreational money.

⊙Steps

1   Determine what type of motor home suits your needs, desires and budget. Consider such factors as size, price, usage (weekend trips or extended travel), motorised versus towed models, and space requirements.

2   Attend an RV show to view a wide selection of motor homes. Talk to different RV dealers.

3   Get recommendations on suggested features and models by talking to current motor-home owners, such as friends and family members.

4   Narrow your selection by viewing features of different models on RV Internet sites or by subscribing to RV magazines.

5   Rent an RV for a weekend or a few days to "test drive" the type of motor home that you're considering.

6   Consider where you will store or park your motor home when you're not using it. Check out storage costs, parking regulations and parking-space availability in your neighbourhood. Remember that these vehicles take up much more space than a car, and you don't want to annoy your neighbours by having your RV sitting unused outside their house for months on end.

7   Examine your finances and arrange for financing through an RV dealership or a lending institution.

8   Make an offer on your final selection.

⚠ Warning

New recreational vehicles, like cars, depreciate rapidly during the first few years of use.

133 Buy a New Boat

If you're looking for a boat with the longest possible life span, buy it new rather than second-hand.

⊙ Steps

1 Look for boat review articles in sailing magazines. Libraries in areas in which sailing is popular may have back issues. Check websites.

2 Find the right boat style, size and equipment for your needs and budget. There's no better place to do this than at a boat show.

3 Introduce yourself to dealers who sell the boats that appeal to you most.

4 Explain your interest in buying a boat, and the dealer or the dealer's representative should provide you with more than enough information.

5 Ask about production schedules. Deliveries often lag as much as a year behind orders.

6 Study brochures and sales materials.

7 Make your best deal. Most dealers offer boat-show specials, which can range from discount prices to extra equipment. Be aware that these offers can sometimes be confusing.

8 Submit a credit application to the dealer's recommended lender.

9 Contact other lenders, including your own bank, to research the best deal.

10 Prepare yourself financially and emotionally to become a boat owner.

✱ Tips

Companies that sell new boats are called dealers, and those that sell used boats are brokers. Some companies are both dealers and brokers.

The best time to shop for a boat at a boat show is on an off-peak day, such as a weekday.

⚠ Warning

Boat salespeople push hard for a contract and payment on the spot. Get your deal in writing. Take time to evaluate the offer and compare it to other available offers. Come back later. You may find some leverage you didn't have during your first meeting.

134 Buy a Boat Trailer

Once you've purchased a boat, you'll need to buy a boat trailer. Not only is a trailer necessary for transporting your boat, but it also makes storage much easier.

⊙ Steps

1 Find out how much your boat weighs and estimate the weight of any gear and extras that you'll be transporting in the boat while it's on the trailer. Find a trailer that has the capacity to support this weight.

2 Buy a trailer with larger tyres; they last longer because they rotate less.

3 Consider purchasing a drive-on trailer. This type of trailer is simply backed into the water so the boat can be driven on to it. Make sure all the trailer lights are waterproof, as they'll definitely get wet.

4 Remember that you get what you pay for. Don't make the mistake of buying a cheap, poorly constructed trailer to haul around your expensive boat. Look for a high-quality trailer that will last a long time.

5 Think about buying a used trailer if money is an issue. However, take extra care to inspect the trailer thoroughly. Look for rust or corrosion, as well as cracks or any major damage to the frame. Look closely at the tyres – you'll have to replace them if they are worn. You should also hook the trailer up to your vehicle and make sure all lights are working properly.

✱ Tip

Larger tyres will further the life of your wheel bearings.

Write an Effective Used-Car Ad 135

It's not hard to write a good ad for your car – just be honest, describe the car accurately and keep it short.

⊙ Steps

1   Give the car's year, make, model, colour and current mileage.

2   Describe the car's condition in a word or two. "Reliable" indicates exactly that; "clean" means no dents and good interior. "Running project" or "mechanic's special" means it needs restoration but has potential. "Beautiful" means exceptionally clean and appealing. Be creative but clear.

3   State if the car has always been garaged.

4   Identify recent repairs or overhauls: new clutch, 6,000 miles on rebuilt engine, new tyres, service every 30,000 miles.

5   Identify any cosmetic details, negative or positive: no dents, dent in left front bumper, new paint, upholstery worn and new red paint.

6   If you are the first or second owner, state that.

7   State any interesting details that might drive up the price: convertible, roomy, rare.

8   Name a price. If the price is negotiable, add ONO, meaning "or nearest offer". If you do not want to bargain, add "firm".

9   Give a phone number where you can be reached and a time when you will be there.

✱ Tip

Don't understate damage or overstate positives. Heightened expectations mean a lower final sale price.

⚠ Warning

If you have anything major to declare about the car, such as the need for a new gearbox, say that in the ad. It's going to come out, so you might as well screen out those for whom it's a deal-breaker up front.

Negotiate the Sale of Your Used Car 136

Don't try to take anyone for a ride, but don't just dump the car to get rid of it, either.

⊙ Steps

1   Confirm that the interested party has decided to buy the car.

2   Ask him or her, pleasantly, to make you an offer.

3   Keep your bottom-line price in mind, but do not state it.

4   Wait before making a counter-offer if the buyer's offer is too low.

5   Explain your hesitance briefly, mentioning repairs or the possibility of receiving better offers. Judge the buyer's interest as you speak.

6   Make a counter-offer.

7   Leave your counter-offer on the table if the buyer rejects it, suggesting that you will continue to show the car.

8   Offer the buyer, pleasantly, an opportunity to call later if he or she reconsiders the counter-offer.

✱ Tips

Don't be too stubborn – just stubborn enough to indicate that you're holding to your bottom line.

Your counter-offer should not be too high unless the buyer's offer was unusually low.

Several rounds of offers and counter-offers are usually not necessary if both parties keep fairness in mind.

137 Service a Car

Your car should receive a service every two years or 30,000 miles, whichever comes first. During this service your car will receive some new parts that will hopefully keep it out of the garage for a while. A service isn't a cure-all, but if carried out regularly, it can prevent a host of expensive problems. Whether you do it yourself, or get your mechanic involved, here are the key things to check to keep your car safe and roadworthy.

checklist

- ❏ Replace the fuel filter. If you have a fuel-injection system, regular cleaning isn't necessary unless the injectors are clogged.
- ❏ Change the spark plugs (unless they're platinum, in which case you have 30,000 more miles to go).
- ❏ Examine the spark-plug wires and replace as needed. A new set of high-quality wires is worth the cost.
- ❏ If your spark plugs are permanently attached to the distributor cap, you may need to replace this as well.
- ❏ Replace the distributor cap and rotor if your car has them (some newer models with distributor-less ignition don't).
- ❏ Change the points and condenser if you have an older car (roughly 1978 or older) that doesn't feature electronic ignition. You'll actually want your points changed, or at least adjusted, every six months or so (if they're changed, check the ignition timing as well).
- ❏ Check the ignition timing and adjust as needed (this is rare for a car with electronic ignition – post-1980 – and some cars don't allow this at all).
- ❏ Adjust the valves as needed (unless your car has hydraulic valves).
- ❏ Replace the valve-cover gasket as well, especially if you see evidence of oil on top of your engine.
- ❏ Check the belts and replace them if they're worn.
- ❏ Check the fluids under the bonnet and replenish as necessary.
- ❏ Change the oil and oil filter if it's been 3,000 miles since the last oil change.
- ❏ Replace the air filter. In fact, this should be changed between services – every 15,000 miles – as well.
- ❏ Adjust the clutch.
- ❏ Service the battery, adding distilled water (if required).
- ❏ Clean the terminals and cable ends.
- ❏ Replace the PCV (positive crankcase ventilation) valve. This can make your car run rough or stall if it gets clogged, and it's cheap and easy to replace.

Prepare your Car for a Road Trip `138`

Whether you're heading for the mountains or the beach, it's crucial that your car is in good working order. There's nothing worse than having a holiday ruined by car trouble.

⊙ Steps

1 Make an appointment with your mechanic at least a few weeks before your road trip to do a pre-trip inspection. Bring a checklist of things to ask your mechanic to review.

2 Check all fluids.

3 Check belts and hoses.

4 Look for any leaks.

5 Check and fill all tyres, including the spare tyre, and make sure they're in good condition.

6 Perform a four-wheel brake check (if not done in the last six months).

7 Check the condition of the exhaust system.

8 Flush the cooling system (if not done in the last year).

9 Pressure-check the cooling system to inspect for leaks.

10 Load-test the battery to test its ability to hold a charge.

11 Check the alternator output to make sure that the charging system is working well.

12 Replace the spark-plug wires if they are more than two years old.

❋ Tip

Don't wait until the day before you plan to leave to make any big repairs or get a service.

Troubleshoot Your Brakes `139`

Have your car's brakes checked at least once a year; if you wait until you hear grinding noises coming from the brakes, you'll be spending extra money on your next brake job.

⊙ Steps

1 Make sure you're not driving with the hand brake on.

2 Get the brakes checked if you hear a high-pitched squeak that goes away when you step on the brakes. This noise comes from a brake-pad sensor – a soft piece of metal that scrapes against the brake rotor when the brake pads need replacing.

3 Check the brake-fluid level.

4 Take your car to a mechanic for a brake check if the brake master cylinder is consistently low on brake fluid. If you need to add brake fluid more than once every few months, there is probably a leak in the system.

5 If the pedal slowly sinks down to the floor when you brake, you may have a bad brake master cylinder.

⚠ Warning

You should not drive for more than a short distance if the brake light has come on. Check the brake fluid and make an appointment to have the brakes checked as soon as possible.

6　If the pedal feels soft and mushy but gets harder when you pump up and down, ask your mechanic to bleed the brake lines to remove any air pockets in them and check for a faulty brake master cylinder.

7　If the brakes pulsate when you step on them, your car may have warped rotors, which can affect stopping ability. Ask your mechanic to check them properly.

8　If the brake pedal sinks to the floor or gets soft when you're using the brakes on a long, steep downhill grade, the problem could be brake fade. This occurs when the brake fluid gets so hot that it boils. Your mechanic may not find anything wrong with your brakes because the problem disappears after the brake fluid cools down, so be aware of this potential problem.

140　Clean Spark Plugs

A spark plug is one of the tiny but crucial parts of a car's engine. Thankfully, you don't have to be a trained mechanic to clean your car's spark plugs.

⊙ Steps

1　Park your car in a safe and well-lit area. Have all your tools handy before you get to work, then open the bonnet and secure it in place.

2　Find your spark plugs. They're usually located at the terminating end of the fat rubber wires you see running throughout your engine. Depending on the type of engine you have, the spark plugs may be located in one of several different places. For exact directions, you'll need to consult your owner's manual.

3　Remove the wires that connect your spark plug to the engine. You may have to jiggle the spark plug in place to loosen it.

4　Use a wrench or ratchet set to unscrew the spark plug from the engine. Remove it completely.

5　Inspect the spark plug for any signs of corrosion or dirt accumulation. A little filth is normal, but if you see white or oily substances on the spark plug, it could be a sign of something more severe.

6　Spray a brake parts cleaner on to the spark plug.

7　Agitate the cleansing fluid with a wire brush. Scrub gently to remove dirt. Pay careful attention to the metal threads around the spark plug's tip. Spray the spark plug again to blow away any dirty you've loosened.

8　Use a fine diamond file to clean the contact end of the spark plug. Re-gap the plug following manufacturer specifications.

9　Insert the clean spark plugs back into the cylinder, tighten and reattach the wires.

⚠ Warnings

A row of spark plugs are meant to fire in a specific order. For this reason, it makes sense to clean or change your spark plugs one at a time.

When disconnecting the wires of a spark plug, make sure you follow the directions in the instruction manual.

Disconnecting a wire directly from the spark plug's "boot" can cause irreparable damage.

Replace Your Air Filter `141`

Changing the air filter should be part of any major service, but if you drive on dirt roads or in other dusty conditions, you will need to replace it more frequently. On most cars, this is a fairly simple procedure.

 Steps

1 Pop the bonnet and find the air-filter housing. It will be either square (on fuel-injected engines) or round (on older carburetted engines) and about 30 cm (12 in) in diameter.

2 Use a Phillips screwdriver to remove the screws or clamps that hold on the top of the housing.

3 Take out the old air filter and clean any dirt and debris from the housing with a clean rag.

4 Put the new air filter in.

5 Screw or clamp the lid of the air-filter housing back on.

✳ Tip
Remember to have your new air filter, a rag and a Phillips screwdriver at the ready,

Locate Hard-to-Find Parts `142`

New, original and reproduction car parts – even the most obscure – can be found with some detective work.

 Steps

1 Know the exact specifications of the part you are searching for. Ask yourself what kind of shape the part needs to be in for you to buy it, and how much you're willing to spend. If you can't find original parts, rebuilt or remanufactured parts could save you money and may also be the only replacement parts you can find.

2 Assuming you've already checked with your local car-parts dealer, browse the classified sections in both paid and free local newspapers. Some sellers (who advertise in the papers but aren't listed in the phone directory) offer cars for parts.

3 Root around a local scrap yard for a forgotten gem (look under "Salvage" in the Yellow Pages).

4 Check with local shops that work on your model car and that might be able to recommend a source for the elusive part.

5 Speak to local dealers who sell your car's make and model, if it's a new car.

6 Swap stories with car-club members who own your model. Read the classifieds in speciality magazines.

7 Scour Internet auction sites, online search services and bulletin boards. Check back often, as new items are listed frequently. An Internet auto parts locator service will put you in contact with dealers and private sellers for a fee.

8 Find out if you can use parts from another model car on yours.

✳ Tip
Original parts (commonly known as OEs) from car aficionados or dealers probably cost more, but are in better shape and guaranteed to work.

⚠ Warning
Saving money shouldn't be your goal for every replacement-part purchase. Some parts are vital to the safe operation of a vehicle, like rims, tyres and brake parts.

143 Clean Insects off a Car's Exterior

Everyone has experienced the annoyance of getting home after a drive on the motorway and finding the windscreen covered in insects. Here's how to get rid of them.

⊙ Steps

1 Mix one litre of hot water with three tablespoons of household cleaner. For a less chemical alternative, try a paste of baking soda and water.

2 Wipe and scrub headlights, bumpers or windows with a soft cloth. Alternatively, use a plastic mesh bag or a sponge covered in mesh – it is abrasive enough to remove the insects but soft enough not to scratch the glass.

3 Try a degreaser, such as WD-40, if the residue is particularly sticky.

4 Pre-clean bug splats, tar spots or bird droppings on the car's exterior with undiluted car-wash solution and a clean cloth or wash mitt. Then wash the car conventionally.

✳ Tip

Remove tree sap with a soft cloth soaked in olive oil or other vegetable oil. Rub in a circular motion until the sap is removed. Rinse.

⚠ Warning

Avoid using anything on the car's paint job that could remove or scratch the paint. Double-check by reading the car's manual about how best to clean the car's exterior.

144 Pimp Your Ride

You love your car, but you want it to be different from the Jones's car. It takes time and money, but there are many ways to pimp your ride.

⊙ Steps

1 Change the body panels on your car. Take off your fender, bumpers and lower side panels to prepare your car. Purchase an aftermarket fabrication kit to make your car stand out. This is an easy way to change the look of your car without having to make your own mould for these parts.

2 Paint your car. Pick your favourite colour combination and two-tone the vehicle. Put on extra clear coats and buff the paint until you see your reflection clearly. You may need to sandblast the car before painting it, depending on the kit that you use.

3 Pimp your tyres or rims to get a new look for the wheels of the car. Buy larger tyres or add alloys with seven spokes. Accent the rims with a dark, low-profile performance rubber. You could also choose to leave the rims and use whitewall tyres.

4 Install entertainment systems. A pimped-out car offers its passengers extra amenities. Install large monitors in the back of the front seat head rests. Modify your dashboard to hold a DVD player. Add a game station to your centre console. Connect the entertainment systems.

5 Tint your windows to finish your pimp. You want the windows to be noticeably darker, but you should check the law about what level tint is allowed and on what windows.

⚠ Warning

You'll need to reuse the screws, so be careful not to strip them when you take off parts.

Cool Down an Overheated Car

If your car overheats and damages the engine, you have no one to blame but yourself. Keep your eyes on the temperature gauge and never let the needle move into the red.

⊙ **Steps**

1 Turn off the engine and wait. If the engine is steaming, don't open the bonnet. Pull the bonnet release lever under the dashboard to open the bonnet when the car has cooled completely.

2 Check the coolant reservoir tank first. This is a plastic jug that has a small hose running to the radiator. The reservoir can be filled when the engine is hot (except on German and Swedish cars, the plastic reservoir is also under pressure, so don't open when the engine is hot).

3 Open the radiator cap with a rag. Remember: open it only after the engine has completely cooled. If you're not sure, don't open the cap. If you open the cap while it's still warm, you may burn yourself with steam or hot coolant. Open the cap slowly.

4 Examine the radiator. Look inside and see if there's coolant left. If needed, fill to the top of the radiator. Put the radiator cap back on.

5 Check to see that the upper or lower radiator hose, or any of the heater hoses, hasn't burst.

6 Restart the engine. Watch the temperature gauge obsessively.

7 Understand that you can continue driving a high-temperature vehicle if you're far from a phone or a service station and the car does not need coolant (or does not respond to these instructions). However, drive only as long as you stop and turn off the engine whenever the gauge gets close to the red, and let the engine cool down until you drive again.

✳ **Tips**

Overheating can be caused by factors other than low coolant level (thermostat stuck closed, blocked radiator, malfunctioning fan or failed water pump). If the coolant level isn't low, it's time to visit a mechanic.

It's okay to add just plain water or antifreeze in an overheating emergency situation. When routinely adding or changing coolant, always use a 50/50 mixture of water and antifreeze.

Start a Stalled Car

If your car won't start due to a dead or low battery or a broken starter, you can push-start it in just a few minutes.

⊙ **Steps**

1 Determine if your car has a dead battery or a bad starter. If the engine cranks your problem lies elsewhere. If the engine is silent or you only hear clicks when you turn the key, then your battery or starter is probably dead, and a push-start may be just what you need.

2 If your car isn't on a hill, ask a couple of friends or passers-by for help.

3 Turn the key to the on position and release the handbrake.

4 Push down on the clutch pedal and put it into second gear.

5 Keeping the clutch pedal depressed, either shout to your friends to start pushing or let the car roll downhill.

6 When the car is rolling as fast as a person running, slowly release the clutch pedal while giving the engine a little acceleration.

⚠ **Warning**

The car may jump forwards when you release the clutch. Make sure there are no people or obstructions in front of the car.

147 Free a Car Stuck on Ice or Snow

Drivers living in snowy regions quickly become pros at manoeuvring cars through deep snow. The rest of us may need a little help freeing a car that gets stuck in snow.

⊙ Steps

1   Put the transmission into four-wheel drive (if your car has it).

2   Shift into the lowest gear available.

3   If the car won't go forwards, put it into reverse and try backing up.

4   Turn the steering wheel slightly and try driving in a different direction.

5   Grab your spade and remove as much snow as you can from in front of all the wheels.

6   Determine which wheel(s) are slipping. Place sand, salt, dirt, cat litter or a piece of old carpet in front of the slipping wheel(s).

7   Ask friends or passers-by to push while you slowly depress the accelerator. Make sure nobody is standing in front of the car. Be careful – accelerating too much makes the tyres spin and heats up the snow underneath, turning it into ice.

8   Be prepared to steer and brake after your wheels gain traction.

⚠ Warning

Establish clear signals between the people pushing the car and the driver to avoid dangerous misunderstandings. You don't want to accidentally hit someone.

148 Replace a Car Battery

You don't need to be a mechanic to know how to replace a battery. It's probably one of the simplest repairs you can do.

⊙ Steps

1   First make sure your car is off. Open the bonnet and locate the battery.

2   Using a small adjustable spanner, disconnect the negative terminal (marked with a "-" symbol) then disconnect the positive terminal (marked with a "+" symbol). Always disconnect your battery in this order.

3   Look at the side of the battery tray (the thing your battery is sitting on). You'll see a small metal piece held down with a bolt. Remove the bolt then remove the metal hold-down. Your owner's manual should have illustrations to help with this.

4   Pick your battery up out of the car. Remember that a car battery is pretty heavy, so be careful.

5   Place the new battery on the tray. Install the battery hold-down the same way you removed it, by first placing the hold-down in the correct spot then installing the bolt. Make sure the bolt is tight. Reconnect the positive terminal first then the negative terminal.

⚠ Warnings

Battery acid is extremely corrosive. Don't let it splash out. Take care not to spill any on your hands, body or clothing, or on car paint.

Make sure you're connecting the wires to the right battery terminal otherwise you can cause damage to your vehicle.

Replace a Car Fuse

Car fuses are safety devices that protect wiring and components from excessive damage if a short circuit or overload of amperage occurs.

⊚ Steps

1 Purchase spare fuses from any shop that carries car accessories. Buy a few different sizes for spares. Some fuse panels have specific sockets in them for spare-fuse storage.

2 Locate your car's fuse panel. Most fuse panels are around, on or under the dashboard panel on the driver's side. Other locations include the glove compartment or under the bonnet. Some cars have more than one fuse box. If the fuse you are looking for is not in the first fuse box you find, look for a second box.

3 Use the manufacturer-provided fuse-pull tool or a pair of needle-nose pliers to grasp the burned-out fuse on the sides. Pull it straight out of the socket.

4 Push the new fuse into the empty socket. You can use the fuse-pull tool or the needle-nose pliers to do this if it is difficult to get your fingers into the fuse panel. Be sure that the new fuse is the same ampere rating as the fuse you removed.

⚠ Warning

Replace fuses with the same amp rating as the dead fuse. A larger ampere rated fuse will not protect the circuit correctly and could cause further damage to the circuit and wiring. A fuse that is too low in amperage will fail if the flow exceeds its rating.

Repair a Car Dent

Dents can be annoying and costly to fix. Fortunately, there are a couple of things that you can try at home that are inexpensive and relatively simple.

⊚ Steps

1 "Suck out" the dents with a plunger. This is an old and pretty reliable method. Place the plunger over the centre portion of the dent and push in, just as you would for a clogged toilet. Often, this will not work on the first try, so keep at it. This works better for smaller dents and dents in places where it is impossible to get behind the dent. This method carries no guarantee of saving the paint job, though!

2 Use dry ice. Dry ice is pretty cheap and can be found at most hardware or DIY shops. Simply put the block of ice over top of the dent. Gradually, the ice will pull the dent out. Keep repeating the process until the dent has gone. Be sure to wear protective gloves. It may be called ice, but it can cause severe burns to the skin. Usually, this method will not damage the paintwork.

3 Battle the dent with household items. Heat the dent with the hair dryer for about a minute, then immediately spray the entire area with an air duster. The hot/cold combination creates a suction and within a few moments the dent will pop out. Damage to the paint job is minimal.

⚠ Warning

Always use protective gloves and eye wear, as well as a breathing mask. If using chemicals, be sure to work in a well-ventilated area.

4   Bang out the dent. You can attempt to bang the dent out with a hammer, as long as you can reach behind the dent. Denting the car stretches the metal so it's best to attempt to soften the metal before using the hammer. For a chrome surface, use an acetylene torch to heat the area or an inexpensive propane torch. Don't get the metal too hot, though – just heat it a little bit. For non-chrome surfaces, use a hairdryer instead. Once the area is heated, lightly bump the dent out from the other side. It is best to use a rubber mallet, not a metal hammer, as this will be gentler on the car.

151 | Change a Hubcap

Parallel parking too close to the curb is not only bad for your tyres but can also damage or dislodge hubcaps. Fortunately, a hubcap is one of the easiest things to replace on a car.

◉ Steps

1   If a hubcap is missing, look at the other wheels to see how the hubcaps are attached to the car. Some screw on and off, some pop on and off, and others are held on by the wheel lug nuts, which you must remove before putting the hubcap on or taking it off.

2   If your car has the screw-on type, remove the screw that holds the hubcap on. It may be under a small plastic cover that you can pry off gently with a screwdriver. (If the hold-down screw is missing, remove a screw from another wheel and match it up at a car-parts shop or a hardware store.) Place the new hubcap on the wheel and reattach the hold-down screw.

3   If your car has the push-on type, remove the hubcap by prying around the rim with a screwdriver. Push on the new hubcap and gently tap around the rim until it stays on by itself. Then use a rubber mallet or the bottom of a shoe to hammer it until snug (a normal hammer will dent the hubcap).

✳ Tips

Hubcaps, especially the push-on kind, sometimes cause wheels to squeak when driving. Remove the hubcap and test-drive the car to diagnose whether this is the source of the squeak.

Be careful around live wires. They carry a significant charge and can give painful shocks. Touch only the insulation and wear insulated gloves.

152 | Hot-Wire a Car

Hot-wiring a car is generally done as an illegal activity. However, there are times when there is a legitimate need to start your vehicle without using the key.

◉ Steps

1   Locate the ignition tumbler – the spot where you normally put your key. Remove the covers and panels around the tumbler.

2   Examine the ignition set-up. There should be a panel with five to eight wires clipped to the rear of the tumbler. Remove the panel and try to manually turn the ignition switch using a screwdriver. If you can do this, then you are done! When you turn the ignition switch (usually with a key),

⚠ Warning

Remember that just because the car is running, the steering wheel may not operate. Many cars have the steering wheel lock hooked into the ignition tumbler as an antitheft measure, so you cannot unlock the steering wheel without the key.

it rotates a pin or lever on the back side of the tumbler. The panel is essentially a switch with four positions: off, accessories, full on and ignition.
The different positions of the key correspond to each of these positions.

3   Research the colour coding of the ignition wires for your specific car
     model. If you are not able to manually turn the ignition switch with a
     screwdriver, you will have to strip wires to hot-wire the car.

4   Locate the "on" positive and negative wires in the steering column.
     They should run up to the ignition tumbler and be colour-coded.

5   Pull those wires from the ignition, strip a portion of each and twist them
     together. The car will now be on and ready for ignition. This is where you
     truly hot-wire a car. These wires carry a charge, which is why they are
     called "hot".

6   Find the starter wires and pull them from the ignition tumbler as well.
     Strip the ends and touch these wires together briefly. This should
     activate the starter, firing up the car. If you have done everything
     properly, your car will now be running. Do not leave these wires
     touching each other once the car is running.

7   Cover up any exposed wires to avoid painful electric shocks. Drive away
     and have your ignition repaired or a new key made so you do not have
     to hot-wire the car regularly.

Avoid Being Ripped off by Your Mechanic   153

Cars are not as simple as they used to be, which gives
mechanics more of a chance than ever to add fraudulent
or unnecessary charges to your repairs.

⊙ Steps

1   Before allowing work to be done on your vehicle, ask for an estimate
     in writing. Don't agree to allow work to be done without your approval
     because it's then much harder to dispute anything you do not agree
     with. Make sure you ask questions if something doesn't seem right.

2   If the mechanic explains something but it still doesn't seem to fit, feel
     free to call around for other estimates. You aren't signing a contract by
     bringing the car there – don't feel any obligation.

3   Don't pay for anything until you understand every item on the bill. Ask
     why this part or work was necessary and use your manual as a guide. If
     the manual says you don't need to change your plugs for 20,000 miles
     and the garage wants to change them every time you come in for an oil
     change there is something wrong. Pay with a credit card if possible so
     you can dispute charges later if necessary.

4   Used parts can be a great way to save money. However if you agree to
     go that route ask for the old part back. Don't keep it – just make sure
     they changed the part.

✳ Tip

There's no need to pretend you
are a car expert, just let them
know you won't blindly pay for
unnecessary things just because
the mechanic says so.

154 Stay Alert While Driving

Driving drowsy is as dangerous as driving drunk. Follow these tips to stay alert on the road.

◎ Steps

1 Get a good night's sleep, and plan around your body clock so you drive at the times of the day when you are most alert.

2 Take a 10- to 15-minute break to exercise, stretch or walk briskly after every two hours you drive.

3 Let someone else do a share of the driving. Divide the driving into blocks of no more than about four hours for each driver.

4 Eat regularly to keep blood-sugar levels even, but be mindful of what you eat. A chocolate bar won't help much once the initial sugar buzz wears off. To stay alert, the body requires good nutrition.

5 Drink coffee or tea (or another form of caffeine) for a temporary fix. Keep in mind that caffeine does not take the place of adequate sleep.

6 Don't drink alcohol.

7 Avoid medicines that make you drowsy, including antihistamines, some antidepressants, cold and cough medications, and some prescription medicines. If the label warns "Do not operate heavy machinery" you are being told not to drive a car.

8 Learn to recognise drowsiness. Among the signs: you keep yawning, your head nods, your mind wanders, you feel eyestrain, or your eyes want to close or have trouble staying focused.

9 Take a nap if you're sleepy, even if you can't get to a bed. You'll have to judge your surroundings, but you're probably safer napping for half an hour in a locked car pulled over to the side of the road than you are driving drowsy.

✳ Tip

Some drugs cause drowsiness for the first few days, so take extra care when you start taking any new medicine.

⚠ Warning

If you ignore signs of drowsiness when driving, you not only put yourself at risk, but also your passengers and everyone else on the road.

155 Make a Three-Point Turn

It's not always easy to turn your car in a narrow road. Here's a step-by-step guide.

◎ Steps

1 Make sure the street has no traffic.

2 Turn the wheel all the way to the right and drive across the street.

3 Put the car in reverse, and turn the wheel all the way to the left, and back into the street.

4 Put the car in drive, and steer slightly right to straighten out the vehicle direction.

⚠ Warning

This should only be done on a street with NO traffic in either direction.

Make a U-Turn   156

Are you driving the wrong way? Have you taken a wrong turn somewhere? You should be going the opposite direction, right? Make a U-turn and correct the problem.

⊙ Steps

1 Switch on the indicator to show your intention of turning.

2 Check for oncoming traffic.

3 Make sure that a U-turn is not illegal in this location. U-turns should not be made across chevrons or where signs indicate that they are against the law.

4 Make sure that you have enough room to make the turn without hitting the curb or any parked cars.

5 Press the accelerator lightly while turning the steering wheel as far as it will go in the direction you want to turn.

6 Lift your foot off the accelerator and coast through the turn. Give acceleration as needed.

7 Enter your new lane and begin driving.

⚠ Warning

Be sure to watch for and avoid pedestrians, cyclists or anyone getting out of a parked car while you're completing your turn.

Handle Brake Failure   157

Thanks to a number of mechanical checks and balances, brake failure rarely occurs. But even though most drivers will never have to experience it, it doesn't hurt to be prepared.

⊙ Steps

1 Size up the traffic situation and base your decisions on the whereabouts of other vehicles, crossroads or steep hills.

2 Look for a safe place to steer your car and quickly downshift to low gear (this applies to both manual and automatic transmissions).

3 Build up your brake pressure by pumping the brake pedal fast and firmly. It should take three or four pumps to get the brakes to work. Don't pump anti-lock brakes – press down hard on them instead and plan on taking longer to stop. It is normal to feel pulsation at the brake pedal if you have anti-lock brakes.

4 Use your hand brake if the pumping solution is ineffective or not recommended. Release it quickly if the car starts to skid.

5 Don't forget to steer. Swerve only if it's absolutely necessary – doing so can cause you to lose control of the car.

6 Throw your car into reverse if all else fails. Note that this can cause serious damage to your gearbox, though.

✳ Tips

Sounding your horn and flashing your headlights will warn other motorists of brake failure.

Turn on your hazard lights straight away once you've come to a complete stop.

⚠ Warning

Do not drive for any long period of time with the brake light on. Add brake fluid and go and see your mechanic.

158 | Install Tyre Chains

For many motorists, installing tyre chains can be an intimidating, if not chilling, experience. Following these simple steps can make the job much more bearable.

⊙ Steps

1 Determine whether your car has front-wheel drive or rear-wheel drive. Tyre chains always go on the driving wheels.

2 Check your owner's manual for any reference to "class S" or limited clearance for tyre chains. If your tyres need a limited-clearance product, consult the manual for additional instructions, as traditional chains aren't recommended for your car.

3 Pull completely off the road and out of the way of traffic. Installing chains in the road can be dangerous to you and other drivers.

4 Make sure your hand brake is on and the car engine is off before you climb under the car. Passengers can stay in the vehicle or wait in a safe place away from traffic.

5 Lie the chains flat on the ground so each side is parallel. Make sure there aren't any twists in the links.

6 Drape the chains over each back tyre, keeping the "speed hook" (or "J hook") fastener on the inside. The other side of the chains has a lever fastener with a "keeper" link.

7 Make sure the smooth side of the cross-member end hooks is lying against the tyres. You'll be able to recognise these parts when you see the chains.

8 Reach behind each tyre and fasten the speed hooks by inserting the J hooks through the third link from the other end of the chain. Pull the slack towards the outside edge of the tyre.

9 Pull your car forwards several feet and pull the rest of the slack towards you.

10 Insert the lever fasteners through the third links from the opposite ends of the outside chains and pivot the levers back on themselves, then fasten them under the keeper links.

11 Drive forwards several feet, then pull all the slack out of the chains and refasten them as tightly as possible. There should be about the same number of loose links on each side of the chains.

12 Secure these extra links with zip ties, or remove them with bolt cutters.

13 Add rubber tighteners to lengthen the life of the chains.

⚠ Warning

Drivers should not exceed the maximum speed that's suggested on the tyre chain box or in the instructions.

Deal with Road Ragers `159`

Violence on the roads has become a serious problem, as more and more motorists are acting out their aggressions.

⊙**Steps**

1 Be aware that many drivers get angry if you follow them too closely. Allow at least a three-second time interval between you and the car ahead.

2 Don't slam on the brakes if someone's tailgating you. Instead, signal and pull over to let them pass.

3 Clarify your intentions by using your indicators and brake lights. If someone cuts you off, slow down and give the car room to merge.

4 Don't offend other drivers. Make sure you have plenty of room when you want to merge.

5 If you are in the right lane and someone wants to pass, move over to the left and let him or her by.

6 Keep as much distance as possible between yourself and another driver who wants to pick a fight. Motorists you might have offended can snap at any time, and it's better to be a live chicken than a dead macho man.

7 Give the other motorist the benefit of the doubt. A driver who's speeding or constantly changing lanes may be a doctor rushing to a hospital or an undercover policeman.

8 Allow more time for your trip. Listen to soothing music or a book on tape. Adjust your attitude and forget about winning. For too many motorists, driving becomes a contest.

⚠**Warning**

Although many drivers involved in road rage incidents are men between the ages of 18 and 26, anyone can get aggressive if they let their anger take control. Studies show that anyone can drive aggressively if they're in the wrong mood or circumstances.

Use Hybrid Cars Efficiently `160`

After purchasing a hybrid car there are many things you can do that will allow your car to run its best.

⊙**Steps**

1 Know that a hybrid car can drive up to 25 km per litre (60 miles per gallon) compared to non-hybrid vehicles that drive 9–12 km per litre (22–28 miles per gallon).

2 Accelerate slowly and smoothly. The engine is usually only functioning when you press the accelerator pedal, so avoid sudden acceleration to save as much petrol as possible.

3 Minimise braking and coast to a stop instead. This will extend the life of the brakes and not engage the petrol engine as often.

4 Maintain your vehicle according to manufacturer standards. Regular oil changes, services and other preventative maintenance will extend the life of your car and save you money in the long run.

5 Use cruise control when driving on the motorway. This will engage the engine appropriately, saving you as much fuel as possible.

✱**Tips**

Make sure that your tyres are inflated properly.

Park at the first available parking spot. Driving around looking for a spot will only make you lose fuel.

Don't use fuel with an octane rating higher than your care requires.

Choose a hybrid car with tinted windows. Air conditioning drains your car's engine power.

161 Choose a Motorcycle Helmet

It is against the law – not to mention dangerous – to drive a motorbike without wearing a helmet.

Steps

1   Select helmets that fit snugly all the way round.

2   Find helmets with strong straps with two rings to fasten them. Snap fasteners can unsnap in an accident.

3   Buy a helmet that's a bright colour such as red, white, yellow or orange.

4   Consider a helmet made of a reflective material or one that has reflective tape on the back and sides.

5   Purchase helmets that are free of defects such as cracks, loose padding, frayed straps or exposed metal.

⚠ Warning

Always fasten your helmet firmly. A loose-fitting helmet is just as dangerous as no helmet at all.

162 Stop Quickly on a Motorcycle

All motorcyclists have to make quick stops every now and then, no matter how careful they are.

Steps

1   Apply both brakes simultaneously to stop abruptly. Grip the front brake as fully as possible without locking the front wheel. Don't just grab at it.

2   Release the front brake and reapply it if it starts to lock up. Press down on the rear brake at the same time.

3   Keep the back brake locked until you're at a complete stop if you start to skid. Even with a locked rear wheel, you can control your bike as long as you're still upright and moving in a straight line.

4   It's hard to keep your motorcycle upright when you have to stop quickly on a curve. Apply both brakes and ease off on the throttle to reduce your leaning angle. As you slow down, you can apply more brake pressure. Straighten your handlebars in the last few metres of stopping.

⚠ Warning

Motorcycling is an inherently dangerous activity that can result in serious injury or death. Always seek proper training and equipment before attempting this activity.

163 Avoid an Accident on a Motorcycle

Blame is irrelevant when people are killed or injured in motorcycle accidents. The reality is that it's up to you to avoid them.

Steps

1   Wear highly visible clothing (especially at night) and use your headlight, even in daylight.

2   Communicate with drivers in other vehicles by using the proper signals, your brake light and lane position.

⚠ Warnings

Never tailgate another vehicle.

Rainy conditions increase road hazards for motorcycles.

3   Keep an adequate space cushion when following, being followed, sharing your lane, passing other vehicles or being passed.

4   Scan your course of travel 10 to 15 seconds ahead so you can identify and avoid potential hazards.

5   Remain alert, and always be prepared to avoid a crash.

Drop an Anchor   164

It can take years to perfect the sailing techniques used by professional sailors and members of the Royal Navy. Here are basic guidelines for dropping an anchor.

◉ Steps

1   Drop and furl your sails if you're on a sailing vessel.

2   Select your ideal anchoring spot and proceed steadily but slowly towards it. Look for an area that's at least 30 m (100 ft) away from other boats. Remember that your vessel will swing around its anchor point, and the last boat to drop the hook is responsible for moving if it's anchored too close for comfort.

3   Free the anchor from any bonds that connect it to the roller.

4   Check to see if the rode (anchor line) will run free when released.

5   Make sure the bitter end (the tail end of the rode) is secured to the boat.

6   Turn the bow of the boat into the wind.

7   Stop the boat in the water. Release the anchor over the bow slowly until you feel it touch the bottom.

8   Let out an additional length of rode equal to one-third the depth of the water.

9   Wrap the rode around the deck cleat and travel in reverse gear to set the anchor. You'll feel the anchor "take a bite", and you may hear the line ring like a guitar string. Don't try to hold the rode with your hands as you do this step, or you may experience rope burn.

10   Release the wrap on the cleat and continue releasing the rode as you motor backwards slowly.

11   Release enough rode so that it's equal to at least four times the water's depth in calm conditions, and seven times the water's depth in wind or current.

12   Stop the boat and wrap the rode around the cleat. Secure with a cleat knot.

13   Travel in reverse until the boat swings around and the anchor is set.

14   Take a mark on the shore by lining up two stationary objects, such as lamp posts or trees. If one of the marks moves away from the other, your anchor is dragging and you need to reset.

✳ Tips

Avoid throwing an anchor over the side. Although this is a common practice, the chain and rode may catch on the flukes of the anchor and cause it to drag.

If the boat turns sideways to the wind, you're dragging anchor and need to reset.

⚠ Warnings

Keep yourself and other crew members away from the cleat while the boat is moving, as the cleat may get pulled out of the vessel.

Make sure you're properly trained in all aspects of sailing before you venture out into the waters on your own.

Wear a life jacket when working on the foredeck.

165 | Upgrade Your Computer's RAM

To increase the random-access memory (RAM) of your computer, you must know the type of RAM it uses, how the RAM is configured and how many open RAM slots are available.

⊙Steps

1 Check the owner's manual or motherboard manual to determine if RAM is parity or non-parity. The website of the company you purchased the computer from will usually tell you what kind of memory your computer needs as well.

2 Find out the speed of the RAM (for example, 60 nanoseconds).

3 Determine whether the computer uses single in-line memory modules (SIMMs) or dual in-line memory modules (DIMMs).

4 Find out whether the computer uses regular, FPM, EDO or Synch DRAM.

5 Determine the number of pins on the motherboard: 30, 72 or 168.

6 Remove the cover from the machine to find the number of open RAM slots. Look for between two and eight same-sized parallel sockets on the main circuit board. Usually at least two of those sockets will contain RAM – ruler-shaped circuit boards with chips on one or both sides.

7 Purchase additional RAM that matches existing memory specifications.

✲ Tips

You usually have to install SIMMs in pairs.

If you don't know how much RAM you have installed currently, check your My Computer properties in Windows or choose About This Mac from the Apple menu.

166 | Clean a Computer Keyboard

It's easy to clean a computer keyboard, and apparently good for your health, as bacteria can accumulate where there is dirt.

⊙Steps

1 Hold the keyboard upside down and gently shake it to release any debris caught under the keys. If a large particle seems stuck, press the key a few times while the keyboard is upside down to dislodge it.

2 Spray a can of compressed air on the keyboard, again while you hold the keyboard upside down. Use the straw nozzle on the can of air to reach underneath the keys and in between the crevices.

3 Dip a cotton swab into either a computer cleaning solvent, alcohol or a solution of water with a drop or two of washing-up liquid. Dab the swab on a towel to remove any excess liquid and wipe the edge of each key. Make quick work of this by going across each row then zigzagging down between each key.

4 Place cleaning solution on a soft, lint-free cloth and wipe the top of each key and around the entire keyboard. White computer keyboards will show more dirt, but look closely at black or grey keyboards. They contain the same amount of dirt; it's just not as visible.

5 Finish with an antibacterial wipe. Clean each key top and the surrounding keyboard, disinfecting the entire keyboard.

✲ Tips

Wipe down the keyboard weekly or even daily with an antibacterial wipe.

Carry a small packet of antibacterial wipes if you are in contact with many public keyboards. Clean it with a quick swipe over the keyboard and most of the infectious germs are history.

⚠ Warning

Always turn the computer off before you clean the keyboard. It's always good to avoid the mixture of liquid and electrical currents, and this also ensures that random keys aren't pressed.

Buy a Basic Video Card

Businesses and ordinary users alike employ basic video cards. They are inexpensive and a cinch to buy if you know what to look for.

Steps

1 Choose the type of video card you want based on the type of slot your motherboard has. An AGP slot offers options up to 8x, while a PCI Expert (PCIe) slot is available in 1x, 4x, 8x, 16x and 32x. PCIe is considered to be superior to an AGP card because a PCIe motherboard can support multiple PCIe slots but only one AGP. Multiple PCIe slots enable you to load two graphic cards. If you use advanced image-editing or audio-editing applications, a PCIe card is ideal for you.

2 Understand processor clock speed. This is a measure of a processor's power – but not the only one. A higher clock speed does not guarantee faster processing but certainly helps to increase the processing speed. A basic video card generally has a clock speed ranging between 240 MHz and 300 MHz.

3 Understand memory size. The memory size of a graphics card refers to the extent to which it can support graphics operations without tapping into the PC's memory. The more memory it has, the faster it works. A basic graphics card generally has a memory ranging up to 128 MB.

4 Understand memory bandwidth. Memory bandwidth refers to the speed at which the graphics processor communicates with the graphics memory. A higher memory bandwidth enables faster rendering.

5 Learn about fill rate. This refers to the number of pixels that can be reproduced on the screen per second. A good fill rate would result in the faster loading of the image on the screen.

6 Consider the following options: a model with the TV-out facility, which enables you to watch your PC video on a TV screen; a model with DVI that would enable you to watch PC video on DVI monitors; or a dual-head graphics card that enables you to connect two monitors together on one graphics card.

7 Compare prices of video cards online as well as in computer shops. Look at various buyers' guides to understand features, pricing and versions of different video cards.

8 Buy your preferred graphics card online. You can log on to any reliable online retailer or go to the preferred brand's website and shop online.

9 Buy your graphics card from a local retailer.

✻ Tips

Browse through product reviews on the Internet before you settle for a particular graphics card.

Browse through blogs and discussion forums for gamers and advanced graphic designers. These are good sources of information about what types of video cards are required for different applications.

Check compatibility with your computer. Although video cards are compatible with most computers, they may require advanced configuration.

168 | Set Up a Web Cam

Web cams are extremely popular, especially for those that spend a lot of time on the Internet. Here's how to set one up.

⊙ **Steps**

1 Purchase the web cam. Look for one that allows a high rate of frames per second. This will allow you to see the other person more clearly and without choppy pictures. Look for one with high resolution as well.

2 Download the software that comes in the package. This will be a CD that was included with the web cam. If one was not provided, you can try downloading Microsoft Windows Media Encoder version 9, which is available free online.

3 Shut down your computer once the software is installed and restart it. Connect the web cam to the back of the computer. It will have a USB cable connection.

4 Join Yahoo, MSN or AOL messenger. If you have an email account with one of these three then you can sign up on their messenger service. The person you plan to view on the web cam will need to be signed up to the same messenger service as you in order for you to be able to see each other.

5 Situate the web cam where you want it. You can hook it on top of the computer screen or place it next to it. Most web cams are made to be able to attach to the computer screen. Sign on to the messenger and select the person on your chat list. Select Contacts in the chat window and then Contact Options and View Web Cam.

✱ **Tip**

Do not connect the camera before downloading the software. Some software will react badly and it could damage the system.

169 | Change the Default Printer on a Mac

If you have more than one printer, or if you're connected to a network with multiple printers, you'll want to make one of them the default or automatic selection.

⊙ **Steps**

1 Click on the Apple menu and select Chooser.

2 If the printer driver is installed, you should see an icon for your printer model on the left of the chooser. Click on the icon.

3 If you want to use a printer directly connected to your computer, choose the port (printer port or modem port) that the printer is connected to.

4 If you're on a network, make sure that AppleTalk is active. Find the printer you want on the network and click on it.

5 Click to turn background printing on or off.

6 If you don't see your printer's icon, either the driver (the instruction file your Mac uses to recognise and operate your printer) is not installed, or it is installed in the wrong place.

7 Search your hard disk for the word "driver" or for your printer model name to see if the driver for your printer is there.

✱ **Tips**

If you select the modem port for your printer, you cannot use your modem at the same time.

If you turn on background printing, you can print while doing other tasks and working on other files, but the printing will either slow down your work or be slower itself.

How to Do More of *(Just About)* Everything

8   If your driver is not on your hard disk, find the disk that came with your printer and install your printer driver.

9   If your driver is on your hard disk but in the wrong place, drag the driver icon into your System Folder.

10 Click on the close box for the Chooser.

Change Laser Printer Cartridges   `170`

Most laser printers deliver thousands of pages before the toner cartridge runs out, but when those tell-tale streaked pages start showing up, it's time for a switch.

☉ **Steps**

1   Turn off the printer and disconnect the power cord.

2   Remove any paper trays.

3   Open the cover on the printer. If you're not sure how it opens, consult the manual that came with your printer or the directions packaged with your replacement cartridge.

4   Rest one hand on top of your printer. With the other hand, grasp the toner cartridge and pull upward until the cartridge unlocks and releases.

5   Set the cartridge aside and open the bag that contains the replacement toner cartridge.

6   Install the replacement cartridge in the printer, following the instructions that were packaged with it.

7   Place the old cartridge in the bag and box that the new one came in so you can post it back to the manufacturer for recycling. Many manufacturers will pay the postage for returning used cartridges.

8   If your new toner cartridge starts out printing lightly or unevenly, you can speed the break-in process by printing a couple of pages of solid black (to do that, draw a black box in Microsoft Word or another application).

✹ Tip

If your toner cartridge starts to die in the middle of an important job with no replacement on hand, you can squeeze out a few more good pages by removing it and gently rocking it back and forth to redistribute the remaining toner powder.

⚠ Warning

Toner cartridges are sensitive to light, so don't leave a new one sitting in a pool of sunlight while you make a sandwich.

Clear a Printer Paper Jam   `171`

A jammed printer is the digital-age equivalent of a flat tyre. Sooner or later it happens to everyone, so here's how to get things moving again.

☉ **Steps**

1   Turn the printer off and on to see if it can automatically clear some or all of the jam. Many printers provide an error-code listing on the front panel display for the area where the jam has occurred. If your printer shows an error code, make sure you check the printer manual to see if that identifies the area of the printer where the jam has occurred.

2   Turn off the printer.

✹ Tip

If you get toner or ink on your clothing, wipe it off with a dry cloth and then wash the clothing in cold water.

3   Remove any paper trays. Inspect them for wrinkled or damaged paper.

4   Open any other doors that give access to the printer's paper path and to the toner or ink cartridge.

5   If necessary, remove the toner or ink cartridge. Place it in a bag or away from light to avoid damaging it.

6   If you find a piece of jammed paper, remove it by holding it with both hands and pulling firmly. The goal is to keep the paper from tearing. If several pieces are jammed together, try pulling out the middle piece first to loosen the jam.

7   If the paper does tear, try rotating the roller gears manually to free the paper. Don't force anything, though.

8   Replace the toner or ink cartridge and paper trays, close any doors you opened and turn the printer back on.

9   If the printer paper jam message still appears, then there is still some paper in the printer. Reinspect the paper path.

⚠ **Warning**

Watch out for loose toner or ink on jammed paper, and do your best to avoid spilling it on yourself or the printer.

172   License Software

A software licence both imposes restrictions and grants certain rights to the end user. Using the software outside the terms of the licence is considered an infringement and gives the owner the right to sue.

❋ **Tip**

If you decide to create your own licence, consider having a legal professional check the final document for accuracy.

⊙ **Steps**

1   Obtain a free software licence. This licence gives users the ability to modify the software how they want to and to distribute it in any way they choose. Copyrighted software prohibits users from redistributing or making any modifications to the software.

2   License your software with a copyleft licence. Unlike a copyright licence, users are free to modify, reproduce and redistribute software with a copyleft licence. The only requirement is that users pass on the copyleft freedom when redistributing the software.

3   Use a Creative Commons licence for your creative software, especially if you plan to release it on the Internet. A Creative Commons licence helps owners share almost all their creative rights with users of the software and allows them to build upon it.

4   Try Open Content licensing. This type of licence makes your work available in a way that is easily accessible by anyone to copy or modify at any time.

5   Make your source code available for modification with an open-source licence. Under this type of licence, your name and original copyright statements might be preserved, but you will not receive payment for the software.

6   Create your own licence by making a list of what you want future users of your software to be able to do with it. Draw up a document containing this information, and include statements to inform users that using the software in other ways will violate the terms of the licence.

⚠ **Warning**

If you're developing your own software, don't get a software licence confused with a companion commercial licence. This is especially important if you plan on distributing your software in shops or online for profit. Whereas a traditional software licence dictates the terms for using your software, a commercial licence details exactly how and when you will be compensated for the use of your software.

7   Discuss your licensing needs with a copyright lawyer. Your licence
    should state what the user is allowed to do with the software. The lawyer
    will be able to draw up a copyright licence that will incorporate this infor-
    mation, while taking special care to limit your liability and protect your
    program from illegal use.

Create a Mail Merge   173

Mail merge is an easy way for businesses to create official
correspondence and marketing materials to send to clients
and business partners. The following steps walk you through
creating mail-merged letters using Microsoft Word.

⊙Steps

1   Create data sources. Open a blank Microsoft Word document. Click
    Tools, Letters and Mailings, then Mail Merge Wizard.

2   Under Select Document Type choose Letters. Then click Next: Starting
    Document.

3   Identify the type of document you will merge under Select Starting
    Document. Choose from Use the Current Document, Start from a
    Template or Start from Existing Document.

4   Select data sources. Click Next: Select Recipients at the bottom right of
    the pop-up box on your computer screen. Identify the data source you
    will use for the merge under Select Recipients. Click on the relevant
    button to Use an Existing List, Select from Outlook Contacts or Type a
    New List.

5   Load an existing recipients' data source list by clicking Browse under
    Use an Existing List. Locate the file of recipients on your computer, then
    click OK to upload the file.

6   Create the letter. Click Next: Write Your Letter. Click Enter on your
    computer keyboard to leave space for the merged items at the top of
    your merge letter template. Type the date. Click Enter six times to leave
    enough room for the recipient's address and a greeting. Type the body of
    your letter. Click Save.

7   If you have previously created the letter, locate the template on your
    computer. Click OK to upload the letter you will use in the merge.

8   Select Greeting Line to insert a greeting at the top of each letter. Click
    Address Block to insert each recipient's address into the merged letters.

9   Set the document to print. Click Next: Preview Your Letters then click
    Next: Complete the Merge. Select the printer to send the letters to then
    click OK.

✳ Tip

The Microsoft Word mail merge
function also works in conjunction with some of the other
Microsoft programs. For example, when creating the merge,
designate an Excel spreadsheet
as the data source document.

174 Add Figures in Microsoft Excel

You can add figures in Microsoft Excel even if you have no previous experience using spreadsheets.

⊙ Steps

1 Open up Microsoft Excel to create a new file where you will enter the figures.

2 Click File then Save on the top menu and give your Excel document a name. The File menu is located all the way at the top left-hand corner of your screen.

3 Enter your figures in the cells in a column format. Use your down arrow or enter key to move to the next cell. The active cell always has a black box surrounding it.

4 Highlight the entire column at once by clicking and dragging your mouse from the top of the column to the bottom. Do not let go of the mouse.

5 Click the Auto Sum button on the top of the Excel worksheet. You will want the total to appear just below all the figures. Click Bold on the top menu while still on the figure total to make it stand out more.

6 Highlight the column once more and click the £ sign on the top menu to make your figures appear as pounds.

7 Click the Save button once again to save your file. Remember the file name so you can recall your figures later.

✳ Tip

If you get lost or enter something incorrectly, click the Undo icon on the top toolbar menu.

175 Effectively Use PowerPoint

PowerPoint has quickly become a staple of business and educational presentations; it can combine text, images and media in a professional, organised manner.

⊙ Steps

1 Begin using the Outline View. The most important part of any presentation is content. In structuring content in a way that best communicates those messages to your audience, the Outline View is key. Set up the structure of your presentation in Outline View before doing anything else.

2 Use contrasting colours for texts, backgrounds and other elements. For viewers to be able to read your slides there must be a lot of contrast between the text colour and the background colour. A dark background with light text seems to be the most readable combination. Be sure to test your presentation on a projector before using it, since most projectors make colours duller than they appear on a screen.

3 Use large enough fonts. In many cases, when being read from a distance on a large screen, any font size less than 24 point is too small to be reasonably read in most presentation situations. Titles should be 36 to 44 point size. If you are using a small screen in a large room, your font will look smaller, because the image will not be as big as it should be. If you can't get a larger screen, use a wall instead of a screen to project on to,

✳ Tip

PowerPoint provides a place for lecture notes so you can keep all the information you need in one place. Use Notes View to record your lecture notes.

move the chairs closer to the screen or remove the last few rows of chairs.

4 Don't animate text too much. You want your audience to read the text, and then rely on the presenter to deliver the message. Text that is flying in, spiral or zooming makes it harder for the audience members to read. It also shifts their focus away from the message and presenter.

5 Turn off the pointer. During a presentation, it's very annoying to have the pointer (the little arrow) come on to the screen. It causes movement on the screen that distracts the audience. To prevent this from happening, after the slide show view has started, press the Ctrl-H key combination. Doing so prevents mouse movement from showing the pointer.

Use Basic Tools in Photoshop 176

If you're new to Photoshop, you may need a crash course to start using the basic tools.

⊙ Steps

1 Use the tool bar to the left of your monitor screen. It comes with a navigator window that allows you to zoom in and out of the image you are viewing. It also has history buttons, action buttons, various layers and channel paths to explore.

2 Start with the rectangular marquee tool, which makes various rectangular shapes, and the elliptical marquee tool to make elliptical selections. The lasso tool allows you to draw designs on shapes and selections. The magic wand moves selections and images. The selection brush tool lets you draw using a variety of brushes.

3 Create professional effects using your crop tool to take away the edges of an image, an eraser tool to erase part of your image, the blur tool to blur sections of your image or the smudge tool to smudge part of an image. Many of these tools are similar to photography tools.

4 Choose different colours using the eyedropper tool. You can even change the background and foreground colour.

5 Write with the notation tool – a basic tool available so you can make notes on your Photoshop file for yourself or someone else.

✱ Tip

Most graphic designers use pixel measurements when working with images, but if you are going to be making a hard copy of the image, you may prefer to use inches or centimetres.

⚠ Warning

When sizing an image, bear in mind it can become distorted if Constrain Proportions is not selected.

Create a Compilation CD in iTunes 177

If you have iTunes on your computer, you can make a compilation CD using any of the songs in your iTunes library.

⊙ Steps

1 Open up iTunes.

2 In the lower left-hand corner, locate the Create a Playlist button and click it. This is the button with the plus sign on it.

✱ Tip

Don't worry about adding too many songs. iTunes won't begin burning the CD if there are too many songs for the CD to hold.

3   When you click the button, you'll notice that a new icon pops up under Playlists on the left-hand side of iTunes. Next to the icon, you will see the words Untitled Playlist. This is the blank playlist to which you will add songs in order to create your compilation CD. Note that you can rename it anything you want.

4   Click on your iTunes music library and simply drag the songs you want on to the new playlist you've created.

5   Once you've added all the songs you want, click on your new playlist. In the bottom right corner of iTunes you'll see a button that says Burn Disk. Insert a blank CD into your computer and then click the button.

6   Wait a few minutes while iTunes burns your playlist to the CD. Once it finishes, you can take your new compilation CD and play it in on any CD player.

178 | Chat with a Friend on Skype

Have you ever wanted to chat with a friend, family member or co-worker without making any noise? Now you can – on Skype.

⊙ Steps

1   Go to www.skype.com and download the application free of charge. Follow the installation instructions given onscreen to install Skype on your computer.

2   Open your Skype application: click on Start then Programs then Skype if you're using Windows. If you are a Mac user, click Applications then Skype.

3   Log into your Skype account with your username and password, if you aren't automatically logged in when you start up Skype.

4   Click Contacts in the horizontal text menu at the top of your Skype window.

5   Select Add a Contact from the drop-down menu. Fill in the field with your friend's Skype name, email address or real name and click on the Search button.

6   Look through the results of your search for your friend. You can sort by Full Name, Skype Name, Country, City or Language by clicking the field headers.

7   If you believe you've found your friend, double-click his or her name, and click Add Contact.

8   Right-click the name of the contact you'd like to chat with. This will prompt a pop-up window to appear.

9   Click Start Chat from the menu. There is a light-blue talk bubble next to the menu option. A new chat window will open offering a number of chat options. Choose which one you want – and chat away!

✻ Tips

In your new chat window, you'll see a blue circle encasing a talk bubble with a plus sign, which allows you to add more people to the chat.

Pressing the red "X" will permanently remove you from that chat, but you'll still be logged into Skype and any other chats you have going.

You can create a new chat with current participants by clicking the white talk bubble with lines in it.

Save Files in Different Formats   179

You can save a file in a different format so that people can read it even if they don't have the application you used to create it.

⊙Steps

1   Open the file you want to change by double-clicking on it.

2   Click on File.

3   Click on Save As.

4   Type a new name for the file, if you want to rename it, in the File Name box.

5   Hit the arrow next to the Save As Type box and choose the format you want to save it in.

6   Choose a location for the new file.

7   Click the Save button.

✱ Tips

The list of formats will vary depending on what kind of file you're trying to save and the application you're using.

Save pictures as jpegs if you want to keep them on a disk, so you can fit more of them on it.

Change the format of a Word document so it can be read in different versions of Word and on different programs. RTF, or Rich Text Format, can be read by many different word processors, and it retains formatting.

Add an Item to the Start Menu   180

Instead of opening an application by finding its icon and double-clicking it, you can add an application shortcut to the Start menu. These instructions work for Windows 95 or 98.

⊙Steps

1   Click the Start button, which is often located in the bottom left-hand corner of your screen. A menu will appear.

2   Scroll up to Settings and click on Taskbar and Start Menu. A small window will appear.

3   Click Start Menu Programs, then click Add.

4   Type the path to the application (something like C:\Programs\MyProgram\Program.exe) in the command line, or click Browse to find the program by navigating through folders.

5   After you've located the application with Browse or typed in the path, click Next.

6   The folder and subfolders that appear next represent the Start menu and its submenus. Click the folder where you want your new shortcut to appear, or click New Folder to create a new subfolder. Then click next.

7   Type in a name for the new item (such as My Program) in the text field that appears. Then click Finish.

8   Your new item is now added to the Start menu in the submenu that you selected. Test it to be sure it works properly.

⚠ Warning

Be sure to select the correct executable file, or your software will not run from the Start menu shortcut. If you have made a mistake, you can correct it using the Remove option instead of the Add option.

181 | Use Keyboard Commands Instead of Menu Commands

Many computer commands can be accomplished by using keyboard commands instead of mouse commands. Using the keyboard is a much faster method once you have memorised the commands.

⊛ Tip

The keys marked F1 to F12 perform specific functions. Check your user's manual for details.

⊙ Steps

1 To find a complete list of keyboard commands, use the online help on your computer. Search for "keyboard shortcuts".

2 Many software applications, such as Microsoft Office, show the keyboard commands next to their equivalent menu commands. The keyboard commands appear to the right of the menu commands.

3 To use a keyboard command, hold down the first key listed, and then press the second key. In Windows, the first key is usually Control. On the Mac, the first key is usually Command. Some common keyboard commands follow.

4 To copy selections, press Control and C (commonly abbreviated Ctrl+C) in Windows. On a Mac, press Command and C (commonly abbreviated Command-C). Your selected material will be copied into the clipboard.

5 To paste material from the Clipboard, use Ctrl+V in Windows and Command-V on a Mac.

6 To cut selected material, use Ctrl+X in Windows and Command-X on the Mac.

7 To print the active file, use Ctrl+P in Windows and Command-P on the Mac.

8 To save a file, use Ctrl+S in Windows and Command-S on the Mac.

9 To select an entire document, use Ctrl+A in Windows and Command-A on the Mac.

10 To use the Undo command, press Ctrl+Z in Windows and Command-Z on the Mac.

11 To restart your system without shutting down completely, use the Control, Alt and Delete keys simultaneously in Windows. On a Mac, press the Power key.

12 To display the Start menu in Windows, use Ctrl+Escape.

13 To switch to another application in Windows, hold down the Alt key while repeatedly pressing Tab.

Customise Macintosh Desktop Icons   **182**

With a Macintosh, it's quite easy to use your own pictures for any icons – document, application, folder or whatever.

⊙ Steps

1 Create, copy or scan an image file into a paint program.

2 Copy the image to the clipboard by pressing Command-C.

3 Select the icon you want to use the picture with.

4 Open the File menu and choose Get Info, or press Command-I.

5 Click in the box at the upper-left corner of the Get Info dialogue box.

6 Press Command-V to paste the image into the box, and your new image will be used for the icon picture.

✱ Tip

Mac icon images are 32 x 32 pixels. You can attempt to use a larger image, but it might get shrunken in a strange way.

Set Up a Computer Network   **183**

Do you have more than one computer and want to share files, a printer, an Internet connection, or other computer resources between them all? If so, then you need a computer network.

⊙ Steps

1 Get a network adapter for each computer that does not already have one. Every computer on the network will need one of these. Network adapters come in many forms – some connect to your computer by using USB (this is the easiest type to install), some use a 9- or 25-pin serial port. The type of network adapter most people use is an ethernet adapter. Most modern computers have an ethernet adapter already installed from the factory.

2 Get Category 5e cables. This is the type of cable that is used to connect computers using ethernet adapters. Usually category 5e cable is a thick blue cable with plugs on the end that are similar to telephone plugs, except they are wider.

3 Get a network router or switch. This will be at the other end of the category 5e cable from each computer. Only one is usually needed for a network of four computers or less. A router is simply a switch that allows one network to be linked to another network through Network Address Translation technology (NAT); you will probably need a router if you are using your network to share a single Internet connection.

4 Make sure your network adapters are installed on all computers. If all ethernet adapters are installed, plug in the category 5e cables to the router or switch. If you have a switch, then you simply plug in one end of each cable to a plug in the switch, and the other end into the plug in the ethernet card of each computer. However, if you have a router, it is important to determine which plug should be used. Cables that are going to the ethernet cards on the computers need to plug into one of the plugs on the router that is labelled LAN or Local or Network. If you are sharing an Internet connection, make sure you have a Cable or DSL modem that has an ethernet output.

✱ Tip

Kits with a hub, two ethernet cards and cable are available.

5   When you find the ethernet plug on your cable or DSL modem, plug in one end of a category 5e cable to that plug, and the other end to your router. The cable or DSL modem needs to connect to the plug on your router that is labelled Internet or WAN or Uplink.

6   Restart each computer on the network.

---

184   Copy Internet Settings to Another Computer

If you want to access your ISP somewhere else, what do you do? In Windows, you'll have to manually transfer Internet settings from one computer to the other.

⊙ **Steps**

1   Starting with the computer you want to copy settings from, open the Start menu, choose Settings and then choose Control Panel.

2   Double-click on the Internet Options icon.

3   Select the Connections tab.

4   Click the Settings button next to the Dial-up menu.

5   Click the Properties button in the new Settings window.

6   Select the Server Types tab. Note the type of server listed in the Type of Dial-Up Server menu.

7   Click the TCP/IP Settings button towards the bottom of the Server Types panel.

8   Write down the IP address and any server addresses that appear in the TCP/IP settings window.

9   Click OK in each window to close them.

10 In the target computer, access the Connections section of the Internet Options control panel as described above.

11 Create a new Connection file by clicking the Add button next to the Dial-up menu. Follow the instructions for setting up the new file. This will involve entering your login name, password and other information provided by your ISP.

12 Once the Connection file has been established, click on the connection you just made in the Dial-up menu and click the Settings button.

13 Access the TCP/IP Settings section and input the information that you wrote down from your old computer, including the IP address and any server addresses.

14 Click OK in each window to close them.

⚠ **Warning**

Note that many ISPs use server-assigned IP and server addresses. In this case, the only thing to copy down will be to click the Server-Assigned radio button.

Upload Files to Another Computer with an FTP Program

With File Transer Protocol (FTP), you can upload software, music files or any other type of digital information from one computer to another.

⊚ Steps

1   Select this option if you are uploading files to a remote computer that does not permit web-browser uploads. This is often the case if you are uploading files to a website for which you have purchased storage.

2   Open your FTP program. Enter the host address in the space provided.

3   Enter your login ID and your password. If the remote computer is configured to allow Anonymous FTP, you may be able to login without a password or by using "guest".

4   Click Connect.

5   You will see two windows containing a list of folders and files when the connection is established. The window on the right represents the folders on the remote computer. The window on the left represents the folders on your hard disk.

6   Move around in the left-hand window until you have located and opened the folder in which your uploaded file is to be stored.

7   Move around in the window in the left-hand side until you have found and selected the file that is to be uploaded.

8   Drag the selected file over to the window on the right. Most FTP programs will allow you to upload this way. If your FTP software doesn't allow this, consult the help file for uploading instructions.

9   Check that the file is listed with the other files on the right-hand side when the file is uploaded.

✱ Tip

The time required for the upload varies. It depends on the size of your file, the speed of your Internet connection and the amount of traffic on the Internet during the time of the upload.

⚠ Warning

It is illegal to distribute software programs, music, graphics or other content unless you are licensed or legally entitled to do so.

Connect to Wi-Fi

There are many places that offer free wireless connections, but how do you connect once you get there?

⊚ Steps

1   Some computers connect automatically. The only thing that you have to do is make sure the wireless in your computer is turned on. There should be a button with an indicator light near your keyboard. If you have trouble locating it, refer to your user manual for the location.

2   For older computers more steps are needed. With a computer running Windows, open your Start menu and find Network or Internet Connections. There should be an option for Wireless that you can click. Your computer will search for wireless connections and you will be offered a list of options. Find the connection in the list for the location that you are at. Once you click it you will be connected.

3   For wireless connections that have passwords, the wireless wizard is your best option. It will allow you to first enter the SSID – the name of

✱ Tip

Double check your computer to make sure you have a firewall and antivirus software configured before connecting to a free or unsecured network.

⚠ Warning

Never use a connection that you don't have permission to.

the network. Usually the SSID and password are posted in locations where the access is free. The SSID is the name of the network. Keep clicking Next through the screens and enter the user name and password in the indicated fields.

187 Transfer Contacts with Bluetooth

Bluetooth is a great tool if you have a new mobile phone and don't want to untertake the tedious task of manually inputting all your contacts.

⊚ Steps

1. Pair your computer and mobile phone. Every device is slightly different, but it should be self-explanatory – go to the Bluetooth menu on your phone and select Add New Device and go from there. You will need to activate the devices to make them discoverable. Follow each device's instructions to do so.

2. Once you have them paired, go to your phone's contacts list. This may be found via Options then Send Name Card, or something similar. Click Via Bluetooth and you can then select multiple name cards to send to the PC. These name cards are contact information stored in a format that electronic devices, like your computer and mobile phone, can read and understand.

3. Click Send and the transfer of contacts will begin. You will probably have to accept the transfer on the PC. Store the name cards in a folder. You can then transfer them to another device if necessary.

Tips

Make sure you back up the PC files too.

Follow each device's instructions to set up the Bluetooth link.

188 Password-Protect Your Computer

Security-conscious – or just want to ensure your files are private? You can prevent others from using your unattended computer by creating a password to use Windows or quit your screen saver.

⊚ Steps

Password-Protect Your Computer

1. In Windows 98, click Start.

2. Click Settings and then Control Panel.

3. Double-click on Passwords.

4. Click Change Windows Password.

5. Follow the additional onscreen instructions.

Password-Protect Your Screen Saver

1. Right-click on your desktop.

2. Click Properties and then Screen Saver.

⚠ **Warning**

In these days of fraud and identity theft, protecting your computer using passwords is more important than ever.

3   Click Password-protected and then click Change.

4   Enter a password.

5   Click OK.

6   Click Apply and then OK.

7   Enter your password when prompted to return from the screen saver to your Windows desktop.

Clean a Virus-Infected Computer 189

Computer viruses are insidious, sneaky and constantly mutating. If you think your computer has been infected, the only safe course of action is to use a good anti-virus program.

Tip

There's no substitute for prevention. Good anti-virus software more than pays for itself as long as you keep it up-to-date.

Steps

1   As soon as you suspect that your computer has a virus, remove your computer from any networks it might be on, as well as from the Internet, so that you don't inadvertently spread the bug to others. Unplug your network cable if you have to.

2   If you have virus-scanning (anti-virus) software installed, run it.

3   If you don't have anti-virus software, you'll need to obtain some. If you can't get it from a network administrator or download it from an uninfected computer, you can mail-order it from a retailer.

4   Start your computer (still not connected to a network) and follow the instructions that came with the anti-virus software.

5   Keep running the virus-scanning software until your computer comes up clean.

6   Reconnect your computer to the Internet and check with the anti-virus software's publisher to make sure you have the latest updates. If not, download them now.

7   After updating the anti-virus software, run it again until your computer comes up clean.

⚠ Warning

Never open an attachment from someone you don't know, and be suspicious of odd attachments from people you do know (a virus may have mailed itself to you from their computer).

Restore a Deleted File 190

Have you ever pressed the delete button, said OK and then wanted those files back? Just follow these few steps to retrieve files you've inadvertently deleted.

Tip

While the file is in the Recycle Bin you will not be able to click on it and read any of the information. You must first restore the file before you can open it again.

Steps

1   Understand that when you click Delete to throw away a file, you aren't actually deleting that file in the normal sense. What you're doing is simply placing the file in the Recycle Bin. Files will remain there for a specified time and eventually they will be completely gone. While the file is in the Recycle Bin you can still retrieve it.

2   Double click the Recycle Bin folder that usually sits on the desktop.

3   Arrange the information so that you can find the title. If you know the name of the file you can click on the Name column to alphabetically sort the items by name.

4   Once you have found the file you wish to recover, highlight it.

5   Right click and then choose Restore. This will retrieve the file and put it back in the folder that it was in before it was deleted. If you can't remember where it was before you deleted it you can always perform a Search for the file name.

⚠ **Warning**

Once the file has aged out of the Recycle Bin it is gone forever (in most cases).

---

191 | Organise Directories on Your Computer

Organise the folders, also called directories, on your computer to keep all your programs and documents where you can easily find them.

⊙ Steps

1   Use the Windows-created My Documents folder as the "root" or base-level folder for your documents, or create a new folder with a different name for the root file folder.

2   Create folders within the My Documents folder for the various categories of documents you work on: for example, photographs, letters, databases, web pages and so on.

3   Create subfolders within the category folders, going as many levels deep as you need. For example, in the Photographs folder, you might have a folder for each of your children, with subfolders for each year.

4   When you save documents, make sure you change the save location so they are filed in the appropriate folder.

5   Change your backup program to back up the My Documents folder and all its subfolders, rather than tracking down personal files all over your hard disk.

6   Make a directory on your root drive called Web Downloads for Internet downloading.

7   Change the default save location on your web browser to Web Downloads.

8   Create subfolders under Web Downloads for the different files commonly downloaded, such as image files, shareware programs, sound files or upgrades. This allows you to do fast checks with your anti-virus software on just one directory and easily back up downloaded files that you don't have a physical installation disk for.

9   Install new programs into the Program Files folder, automatically created by Windows when it's installed.

✻ **Tip**

Create a text file where you record the name, revision number and date of any programs that you download, to quickly determine whether you need upgrades later.

⚠ **Warning**

Don't move previously installed program directories around to organise your hard drive. Windows may not be able to find the files it needs to run a program once it's been moved.

Practise Zen 192

Zen meditation, also known as Zazen, has been practised by Zen Buddhists for centuries as a way to forget the self, opening the mind to the oneness of the universe and achieving enlightenment.

⊙ Steps

1. Wear loose clothing and remove your shoes. The ideal Zen pose is called the "full lotus" position. In this position you sit with crossed legs on the floor with each foot positioned on the opposite thigh. An easier position for most is the "half lotus" position, seated with crossed legs on the floor with both feet touching the ground.

2. Hold your spine upright, positioned in a slight S shape. To do this, tuck in your chin, push your chest out slightly, and cast your gaze down. Drop your arms and shoulders. They should be completely relaxed. Your hands should rest in your lap with the palms facing up.

3. Touch your lips together while holding your tongue lightly to the roof of your mouth. Relax your eyes, holding them slightly open. Allow them to relax until the focus blurs and you see nothing.

4. Breathe in through your nose, filling your diaphragm. Then breathe out through the nose. In order to reach a Zen state, try to become aware of the thoughts and feelings you are experiencing at that moment. Try to experience them without amplifying or suppressing them. Try not to be attached to them, just allow them to come and go freely.

✳ Tip

Specially composed music can aid practitioners of Zen meditation with their ability to concentrate.

⚠ Warning

Zen meditation should not be used as a substitute for any conditions for which you have been prescribed treatment by a health professional. Though practitioners often report heightened physical and mental health, you must consult your doctor before ceasing any medical treatments.

Conduct a Japanese Tea Ceremony 193

Becoming a skilled host of a Japanese Tea Ceremony requires years of practice, during which spiritual growth accompanies acquisition of skill.

⊙ Steps

1. Prepare the tea room for the tea ceremony by bringing in the following items: stoneware tea set, stoneware jar or *mizusashi*, *tana* or wooden stand, *namagashi* or sweet appetisers, *hachi* or bowl in which you will serve your sweet appetisers, *chaire* or bowl to store powdered tea, *kakemono* or scroll painting, *kama* or kettle, *furo* or portable hearth, *shifuju* or fine silk pouch to cover the *chaire*, and *tatami* mats for kneeling.

2. Invite guests to enter room. This is done using a gong during the day or a bell in the evening.

3. Allow your guests to purify their hands and mouths using fresh water from a stone basin, or *tsukubai*. You can do this by standing at the entrance and showing the guests the stone basin. After guests have cleaned their hands, guide them to their mat.

4. Leave the room and return with the *chawan*, or tea bowl. In your tea bowl you should have the *chasen* (tea whisk) and the *chakin* (tea cloth). The *chashaku* (tea scoop) should rest across the top of the bowl. Serve your guests sweets, such as *namagashi*.

✳ Tip

When conducting the tea ceremony, remember that the water represents the Yin and the fire represents the Yang.

5   Leave the room again to retrieve the *kensui* (waste water bowl), the *hishaku* (bamboo water ladle) and the *futaiki* (green bamboo rest for the kettle lid). When you return to the room with these items, offer your guests some sweets.

6   Use the *fukusa* (fine silk cloth) to cleanse the tea container and scoop.

7   Ladle hot water into the tea bowl and then rinse the whisk. Once finished, empty the tea bowl and wipe it with the *chakin*.

8   Place three scoops of tea per guest in the tea bowl using the *chaskaku*. Be sure to lift both the scoop and tea container when doing this.

9   Ladle hot water from the kettle into the tea bowl. You should add enough water so that you create a thin paste with the whisk.

10 Whisk the paste into a thick liquid. Add water if necessary and then return any unused water to the kettle using the ladle.

11 Pass the bowl to the main guest. The guest should bow when accepting the bowl and then rotate the bowl to admire it. Finally, the guest should drink some of the tea, clean the rim of the bowl and then pass the bowl to the next guest.

12 Receive the bowl after all guests have tasted the tea. Rinse the whisk and the tea scoop. Finally, clean the tea container and offer it to the guests to admire.

194 | Become a Guru

A guru is a spiritual master in Hinduism, Buddhism and Sikhism who is able to transmit the wisdom of spiritual study and meditation to others.

⊚ Steps

1   Survey the spiritual studies of Hinduism and Buddhism. Although many feel that a self-improvement book will do the trick, Buddhism and Hinduism are among the oldest philosophical and spiritual systems in the world. You should know a bit about each system, and something about "sister" systems such as Sikhism and Jainism, so you can take your first step in the right direction.

2   Study the Vedas. The Vedas are the nearly endless orthodox texts of Hinduism. They contain the first ideas about becoming a guru as well as many of the seeds of wisdom and teaching that led to the development of Buddhism and the advent of Eastern wise men and spiritual masters.

3   Decide to devote yourself to Hindu or Buddhist spiritual practice. As much as any other ancient religion, Hinduism and Buddhism prescribe ways of life that help a devotee get closer to a heightened spiritual state. Taking this step require lots of patience and devotion, so be sure of it before you take the plunge.

4   Find your own guru. Before you can become a guru, you need to be taught by a guru of your own. You can travel to distant locations like India or Nepal to seek out a native guru, or you can contact a local Hindu, Buddhist or Hari Krishna cultural centre to get information about a guru who can start you on the path to becoming a master.

✳ Tip

Study with an open heart and be willing to share your experiences with anyone who seeks your advice.

5   Be prepared to test yourself. A devotee must pass rigorous spiritual tests before being considered a guru. The *Maitrayaniya Upanishad*, one of the sacred Vedic texts, speaks specifically about the need to test potential gurus for spiritual purity and devotion, so be prepared for a potentially long and difficult testing process before you become a guru.

Make a Rakhi   195

A Rakhi is a traditional Indian bracelet made by a sister to show her love for her brother, and to wish him good luck, prosperity and a long life.

⊙ **Steps**

1   Cut the threads in strands about 50–75 cm (20–30 in) long. Gather all the threads together in a neat bundle and fold the bundle in half.

2   Tie a knot with the cotton thread about one quarter of the way down from the folded edge. Make sure the knot is secure. The shorter section will be the rakhi, and the longer section will go around the wrist.

3   Snip the ends off of the shorter, folded end, so you have no loops.

4   Hold the knot firmly and vigorously brush the threads on the short end with a toothbrush until they become very fluffy.

5   Divide the longer section in half and plait each half. Tie a knot at each end and brush the cut ends with the toothbrush until they are soft and fluffy.

6   Decorate the centre area above the knot (the rakhi) with sequins, beads, artificial pearls or any embellishments you desire. Use craft glue to attach the embellishments and allow the finished piece time to dry.

✳ **Tip**

Include a few strands of golden silk thread to give your rakhi an especially elegant appearance.

Things You'll Need

❑ Several strands of brightly coloured silk or cotton thread

❑ Scissors

❑ Sequins, beads, artificial pearls or other embellishments

❑ Craft glue

❑ Hard-bristled toothbrush

Make a Dream Catcher   196

Dream catchers were originally made by the Ojibwa (Chippewa) Native Americans to protect their children from nightmares. Bad dreams were trapped in the web and burned away with the first light of the sun.

⊙ **Steps**

1   Soak the twig or grapevine in water to make it supple. Bend it into a circle no less than 7.5 cm (3 in) and no greater than 20 cm (8 in) in diameter. Take some of the wire and use it to tie the twig ends together.

2   Tie a loop of sinew to the top of the circle. Continue to loop the sinew around the circle, spacing the loops evenly (about 2.5–5 cm/1–2 in apart). Make the loops snug but not too tight, since that will bend the dream catcher out of shape. You want it to be able to lie flat.

3   Finish the first set of loops. Start a second row of loops by threading the sinew between the first and second loop. Evenly space the second round of loops inside the first row of the dream catcher.

✳ **Tips**

Use a metal hoop about 13 cm (5 in) long if you can't find a suitable twig or vine. Wrap the hoop in suede lacing. Approximately 1.2 m (4 ft) of lacing should cover the hoop.

Although it is not traditional, you can also decorate the feather with a small metal concho for a nice accent.

4   Thread one of the pony beads on to the sinew during the third or fourth row of loops. This bead is a symbolic spider, whose web will "trap" the bad dreams.

5   Tie a knot in the bottom of the round when the hole in the circle gets small and it is difficult to tie more loops. Let the sinew dangle from the knot and trim it to about 20 cm (8 in) in length.

6   Add pony beads to the end of the sinew and thread feathers between the sinew and the beads. Glue carefully into place and allow the dream catcher to dry.

Things You'll Need

❏ Twig or piece of grapevine

❏ Real or artificial sinew

❏ Small packet of pony beads

❏ Two or more feathers

❏ Thin wire

---

197   Join a Nudist Club

To the naked eye, nudist clubs have always operated under the radar. However, thanks to the Internet, it's now easy to access a wealth of information on the concept behind nudist clubs, where they can be found and how to join one.

✳ **Tip**

Nude club members are also called naturists.

◉ Steps

1   Find a chapter based in your local area by searching the Internet. Most chapters have a website that explains a bit about them and their activities so you can see if it might be right for you.

2   Call or email the contact person for more information on the particular chapter, as each chapter is as unique as its members are.

3   Call ahead to schedule a first visit. During this call, feel free to ask as many questions as you like. Some issues you may want to touch on are whether the club operates a clothing-optional or clothes-free policy, whether they permit children and if they do what activities are available for children, and if they have a singles policy. Also enquire about bringing pets along to activities, if desired.

4   Know what to expect on your first visit. Most clubs allow first-timers to remain clothed during their fist visit, at least until they become comfortable going nude, but make sure you know your club's policy.

5   Understand that people of all ages are probably going to be present – from infants through to the elderly. Body types and sizes range across the board, but nobody cares because going nude is about freedom and enjoyment and is not viewed as something sexual.

6   Follow through with the chosen club or chapter according to their requirements. Some clubs may require a paid subscription to their newsletter before you can continue with the application process. From there, you may need to obtain a specified number of signatures from members at three different activities. You'll probably owe annual fees. This is all to show that you have an interest as a contributing member, rather than being someone who simply wants to see what it's all about before disappearing.

Study the Bible | 198

Studying the Bible should not be difficult and it definitely shouldn't be boring. Here are some tips on how you can draw inspiration from your Bible.

✳ Tip

The best method of studying the Bible is simply to read it, prayerfully, every day.

◉ Steps

1 Begin with a plan. You will get the best results when you work your way through the Bible systematically rather than randomly. By studying the Scriptures in this way, you will also become familiar with the whole counsel of God's Word.

2 Before you begin your Bible study, spend time in prayer asking the Lord to reveal Himself to you through His Word. Ask the Holy Spirit to help you see Jesus today.

3 Reread a passage a number of times and thoughtfully consider what it is saying. Meditate upon the meaning of the text and how you can apply it to your life.

4 Write down one application based on the insights you have discovered through your study of the text. Writing your thoughts down will help you to fully think them through and make them easier to remember and apply. It has been proven that writing promotes memory and helps you to express what you have learned more clearly to others. Remember to make your application personal, practical and provable.

5 On a small piece of paper write down the verse that impacted you the most from your study, and carry it with you throughout the day. Occasionally, pull the card out and read the verse. This will help you recall what you studied and keep those truths fresh in your thoughts. You might also want to use this system to begin memorising Scripture.

Convert to Christianity | 199

The overriding message of the Christian faith is that God loves you and wants to have a relationship with you. You have to willingly make the choice to become a Christian.

✳ Tip

Finding another Christian to talk to about your newfound faith may help you learn more about living a Christian life.

⚠ Warning

Be wary of people who expect you to perform specific tasks, give money or pray very specific prayers. God does not require any of this for you to become a Christian.

◉ Steps

1 Understand that God loves you and wants you to have an eternal life after you experience physical death. This message is found throughout the Bible, but you can read it briefly in the Book of John, Chapter 3 Verse 16.

2 Realise that everyone has done bad things, also known as sin. Because of these sins, you are separated from God now and will be forever separated from Him when you die. The Book of Romans says that the wages of sin is death (Romans 6:23).

3 Discover that you can be forgiven your sins because Jesus lived a perfectly sinless life as a man and died on a cross. Jesus suffered death so that we can live an eternal life. You can read about Jesus' life and death in the Books of Matthew, Mark, Luke and John (the Gospels).

4   Imagine Jesus standing at your front door and asking to come in. You don't have to answer the door. He wants to come in but will wait patiently until you ask Him to enter your life.

5   Receive Jesus into your life. You don't have to do any special tasks or give anyone any money to let Him in. God's forgiveness and love are free gifts to you; this is known as God's Grace.

6   Commit to learning more about God. Read your Bible and, if possible, find a church you feel comfortable attending.

200 Receive Communion in the Catholic Church

Receiving the sacrament of Holy Communion in the Catholic Church is an act that requires knowledge and reverence, and allows you to receive many graces in your spiritual life.

⊙ Steps

1   Become a member of the Catholic Church.

2   Take First Reconciliation classes and make your first confession.

3   Receive Holy Communion in a state of grace. This means that no mortal sin has been committed. If you are unsure, talk to a priest and/or go to confession before receiving the Eucharist.

4   Prepare yourself mentally during the Consecration for the reception of the Eucharist. The Consecration is the moment when the bread and wine are transformed into the Body and Blood of Christ. Be thankful for the gift you are about to receive.

5   Bow or bend the right knee and make the sign of the cross when you reach the priest to receive Holy Communion.

6   Receive Holy Communion on the tongue or by hand. If you are receiving it on the tongue, tilt your head back slightly and extend your tongue far enough so there is no danger of the Host falling. If you receive it in your hand, place one hand on top of the other, palms up; receive the Host with one hand and place it in your mouth with the other.

7   Make the sign of the cross after you have received Holy Communion. Return to your seat and kneel in prayer or meditation to show your respect to Christ.

⚠ Warning

Do not let the Host fall to the ground. If it does, pick it up quickly and either consume it or let the priest know.

201 Obtain Permission for an Exorcism

Many people believe that demonic possession and exorcism are archaic beliefs and practices, but recently many priests, ministers, clerics and laity have begun to see evidence that demonic possession is becoming more common.

⊙ Steps

1   Schedule a visit with a psychiatrist and your medical doctor. Many of the signs exhibited in a possession are also symptoms of certain

⚠ Warning

Because of the dangerous nature of exorcism, all religions clearly warn against lay or inexperienced people performing this rite.

psychological disorders, or even physical illness, that need to be ruled out before proceeding with an exorcism.

2 Make sure you go to a priest who is has some knowledge about satanic possession, or who will be able to refer you to someone who has. A priest must have the permission of his bishop to perform an exorcism.

3 Remember that exorcism is a very serious matter and a bishop will not give his permission unless he is absolutely certain that some or all of the signs are present.

4 Find out if the victim is able to understand or speak in languages previously unknown and never heard or studied. This is one common sign, along with what may appear to be dual personalities and vocalisations in voices not belonging to the subject. Often there will be more than one – possibly many – voices using the body of the person.

5 Watch for what appears to be nearly inhuman strength in the person. It often takes a number of strong men to restrain a child or small adult. Victims of demonic possession are known to have the ability to levitate or lift heavy objects without being near them. They also lose control of their bodily functions and are able to twist their bodies and faces in horrific contortions.

6 Pay attention to what the victim tells you. Often they can accurately foresee events in the future, usually in dreams. Many know deeply hidden secrets about those around them and scream accusations during the exorcism in an attempt to disrupt the process. They may know of situations that are happening elsewhere in the world, or things that happened in the distant past.

7 Remember that the most intense and ever-present sign of demonic possession is complete and utter hatred of anything sacred. Those who are possessed spew blasphemous words, demonstrate obscene gestures and are usually unable enter holy places.

Practise the Five Pillars of Islam   202

The foundations of Islam are the Five Pillars of Faith. Every Muslim is obligated to perform each pillar except *Hajj*, the pilgrimage to Mecca, which is only required if one is physically and/or financially able to do so.

⚠ **Warning**

The only acceptable way to read the Qur'an is in the original Arabic.

◉ **Steps**

1 Proclaim "There is no god but God, and Muhammad is his Prophet". The First Pillar, Profession of Faith – *Shahadah* – affirms in the face of temptation that only God is worthy of worship and that Muhammad, a human being, brought God's message.

2 Pray five times a day at particular times. Prayer, *Salat*, reminds Muslims of their global community, as all Muslims pray at the same time. Those who pray are directly linked to God. Call to Prayer occurs at dawn, noon, mid-afternoon, sunset and nightfall.

3 Perform financial obligation, *Zakat*. Muslims are called to set aside calculated portions of their earnings for those less fortunate among them. This is in direct response to the Prophet Muhammad (PBUH),

who prescribed, "'Charity is a necessity for every Muslim". Offering *Zakat* also purifies what a Muslim retains.

4   Fast during Ramadan, *Sawm*. During the month of Ramadan, all who are able to must fast daily from dawn to dusk. During this time, Muslims abstain from food, drink and sexual relations. Those who are excepted from *Sawm* are people who are ill, those who are travelling, women who are menstruating and the elderly. Fasting during Ramadan serves as purification and as self-restraint. *Sawm* is an edict of Allah, as shown in the Qur'an.

5   Make a pilgrimage to Mecca, *Hajj*. All Muslims who are able to, in the twelfth month of the lunar year, must make *Hajj* to the holy city of Mecca in Saudi Arabia once in their lifetime. The pilgrimage involves special clothing, visits in prescribed manners to locations including the Ka'bah, the hills of Safa and Marwa, the plains of Arafat, Mina and the festival, the Id al Adha.

203   Behave Inside a Mosque

In the mosque, Muslims recreate the divine presence on Earth. As a visitor, you should adhere to the required behaviours and styles of dress.

⊙ Steps

1   Get permission. If you are not Muslim and want to enter a mosque, ask the Muslims who attend it for permission. Know that men and women pray separately, either at different times of the day, or in different locations inside the mosque. Look for separate entrances for males and females, although not all mosques have them, and enter as appropriate.

2   Wear appropriate clothing inside a mosque. Men can wear ordinary clothing but it must be loose. On Fridays choose your best clothes and adorn yourself with perfume. Wear a long, loose cloak if you are a woman. In conservative mosques women wear veils, but a hood or headscarf may be acceptable. Consult with other women who attend the mosque and follow their lead.

3   Perform *Wuzu*. If you are male, perform the ceremonial washing before prayer. Most mosques offer facilities for performing the ablutions, which must be conducted in a specific way. Watch how this is done, and respectfully follow the process yourself.

4   Enter the prayer section inside a mosque barefoot. Leave your shoes at the shoe-storage area near the entrance. Step inside with your right foot first and recite a blessing for Muhammad and his family as you cross the threshold. Speak softly once inside.

5   Participate in *Namaz*, the ritual prayer of Islam, hallmarked by a series of standard movements.

⚠ Warning

Most Muslims attend mosques frequented by others of the same creed, although many mosques are neutral and open to all creeds.

Be Respectful When Visiting a Hindu Temple 204

A visit to a Hindu temple can offer an insight into a culture and religion that may be very different from your own, but always show respect in your new surroundings.

☉ Steps

1 Dress appropriately. In accordance with religious beliefs, avoid showing too much flesh. Make sure that shirts and tops have sleeves and that shorts and skirts fall below the knee. Women should avoid wearing low-cut blouses and fasten all buttons. Don't wear clothes that have offensive slogans or sexual overtones.

2 Behave. It may seem obvious, but many people don't understand how offensive their behaviour can be. Be sedate and respectful, and avoid loud conversation and laughter. Don't make comments criticising the religion or culture. Always bear in mind that the temple is a sacred space for those who are there to worship.

3 Leave habits outside. Extinguish cigarettes before entering and don't eat or drink anything once inside the temple. Don't chew gum loudly and always dispose of rubbish in a bin. Turn mobile phones and pagers to silent or off completely.

4 Follow the rules. Every temple is different and will have different rules and guidelines that you are expected to follow. Only enter during visiting hours. Even though worshippers may be there all the time, you are only a visitor. Know what is out of bounds – innermost sanctums are only accessible to priests and Hindu followers. Some temples may require you to leave bags and outerwear at a security office before entering.

✷ Tip

Remove shoes and socks and enter the temple barefooted.

⚠ Warning

Taking video or photos is not allowed, and you may have to leave cameras at the door.

Become a Rabbi 205

Being a rabbi means having the prestige and responsibility of being a spiritual and civic leader, as well as being a scholar and a therapist.

☉ Steps

1 Be Jewish or convert to Judaism. Conversion is a multi-step process, with different requirements for the different branches of Judaism.

2 Be a good speaker and a good listener. Your success as a rabbi hinges on interacting well with people to gain their confidence.

3 Decide which branch of Judaism you want to serve: Orthodox, Conservative, Reform or Reconstructionist. (Orthodox Judaism ordains only male rabbis.) Format and rituals can even vary within one branch.

4 Get a college degree. Seminaries look for qualities that will make you a successful spiritual leader. They weigh your academic success, volunteer work, psychological makeup and more.

✷ Tips

Brush up on your Hebrew and Jewish studies before you enter a seminary, or you might spend an extra year there preparing for the regular course of study.

Rabbis' earnings vary greatly, according to where they practise, the branch of Judaism to which they belong, and the size and finances of the congregation.

5   Gain substantial life experience. Many lawyers, doctors and business people become rabbis as a second career. They view their religious calling as a way to give back to the community.

6   Complete a four- or five-year seminary programme. Each branch of Judaism has its own requirements, but you can usually expect an academic programme plus internships and field training.

7   Graduate as a rabbi with a Master's degree in Hebrew letters. Or you can study longer and earn a doctorate in Hebrew letters.

8   Get hired by a congregation and receive direction from your congregation's board of trustees. There is no religious hierarchy in Judaism, so rabbis don't report to a superior such as a bishop or a pope as is the case in other religions.

9   Expect to start small in your first job. Competition is stiff for large congregations. You can become an assistant rabbi, a leader of a small congregation or a chaplain in the military.

206 | Practise Shamanism

Shamanism is a mystical religion that believes that the spirit world can be controlled. A shaman believer puts faith in the idea that healing the spirit will also heal the body.

⊙ Steps

1   Research the history of shamanism through Joseph Campbell, an author highly regarded for his written information on shamanism.

2   Investigate shaman schools. Although some cultures believe you cannot train to be a shaman, others support the philosophy.

3   Learn more about shamanism and your ability – or lack of ability – to practise it by visiting www.tengerism.org, an organisation that educates people about and preserves the practices of Siberian and Mongolian shamanism. Under Tengerism belief, you cannot become a shaman without being born with the gift.

4   Enrol in a training facility to receive certification as a shaman, if you believe it is possible to train to practise shamanism.

5   Learn the principles of shamanism if you are only interested in practising shamanism in private.

6   Set up a shamanism practice. If you are interested in using your shamanism training to help others on a public basis, setting up a practice is one of the best ways to make your services available.

7   Decide whether or not you plan to charge people for your services when you heal. Some shamans do not charge for their healing services.

8   Contact the training programme that you have completed to get the word out regarding your certification as a shaman.

⚠ Warnings

Do not rely solely on the healing of a shaman. If you have trouble breathing or feel you are having a life-threatening crisis (like a heart attack), seek medical help.

Before you start any alternative medical technique, be aware that many have not been scientifically evaluated. Often, only limited information is available about their safety and effectiveness.

Achieve Nirvana 207

While the path to Enlightenment isn't easy, there are a few things that you can do to help you achieve Nirvana and learn the meaning of life and everything around you.

⊙ Steps

1   Realise that you don't belong to yourself. You're a part of the energy and matter that make up the universe. You're one with the trees, the river and the sky. You are but one single entity, moving along the cosmic path to Enlightenment. This idea is one that is strengthened on your path to achieving Nirvana.

2   Come to terms with the fact that you own nothing. Personal possessions mean nothing to you, as you realise that you're one with the universe. The longer you study Buddhism, the more you'll begin to understand that mental concentration is the key to everything.

3   Give up your possessive emotions. Ideas like greed, hatred and jealousy all stem from the idea of self. Once you let go of your ideas of self and your worldly possessions, you will no longer feel the need for such emotions.

4   Let go. The last stage to achieving Nirvana has to do with letting go completely. You're surrendering to the higher power, the universe and all that it represents. It's no longer about you and what you want, but rather about the world as a whole. Negative and positive things hold no emotions, since they're all part of the flow of energy.

❋ Tip
Buddhists believe that everyone can achieve Nirvana if they open up their minds and hearts, but it can be a long process.

Identify Cults 208

As diverse as cults may be in their teachings and individual creeds, there are undeviating similarities that identify them as cults.

⊙ Steps

1   Watch for changes in an individual's personality and a growing estrangement from or even hostility towards family and friends. Cult members are discouraged from remaining in contact with former associates who might cause them to doubt the teachings and practices of the cult. Members are indoctrinated to distrust anyone who criticises the cult or leader(s).

2   Be aware. Cult members are often convinced to contribute all their money and goods to the cult as a sign of their commitment. They spend much time recruiting other members, which they do by preying on their emotions.

3   Recognise the lack of control over the member's private life. Cult leaders monopolise the member's time and relationships, cultivating complete dependence on themselves and the cult. Members are taught to distrust anyone outside the cult and are discouraged from reading any material except that provided or approved by the cult.

❋ Tip
If the group your loved one has joined meets the characteristics of a religious cult, seek support groups online where you can share your ideas and fears with others in the same situation.

⚠ Warning
Never use the word "cult" when talking about the group with someone who has joined it. This will only make them defensive, and they will not be able to hear what you are saying.

4   Note that cult members are discouraged from thinking for themselves. They are given little or no time alone and are constantly engaged in physical or group activities. They are engaged in mind-altering behaviour, such as chanting, denunciation of selves and others, and they are encouraged to report suspicious behaviour in other cult members, including their own families.

5   Notice the unquestioning dedication that cult followers exhibit towards their leaders. They learn to rationalise this behaviour even if it contradicts previously held beliefs or common sense.

6   Keep in mind that forcing or coercing a member to leave a cult can cause psychological and emotional damage. They have been programmed to believe God will punish them if they leave, and threats are used to force them to maintain silence about cult activities. It is necessary to get help from a professional deprogrammer, and ensure that they are kept away from other active cult members.

---

209 Get Involved in a Political Campaign

You can easily become involved in supporting the candidate of your choice by devoting some of your free time to whatever campaign work is needed in your area.

⊙ Steps

1   Consider joining a political party. Examine each party platform and decide which one comes closest to your own beliefs.

2   Write or email your representatives and local MPs for a list of the issues they support and oppose.

3   Remember that in addition to national candidates, those in your local community also need campaign workers.

4   Call the local offices of the individuals you choose to support. Volunteers are always needed for a variety of tasks during a campaign.

5   Realise that all campaign work is necessary, even basic duties like handing out flyers or making phone calls.

6   Check your chosen party's website to see if you can offer your help online, especially if your spare time is scarce.

❋ Tip

Try to get your friends to become involved in volunteering their time as well.

---

210 Write a Petition

Writing a petition is not as difficult as you might think. Save yourself time by following the regulations set forth by your local council.

⊙ Steps

1   Contact the administrative office of your local council.

2   Verify that your cause for petition falls under its jurisdiction. Ask the office to direct you to the department that handles matters related to your cause.

❋ Tip

A typed summary looks more professional and is easier to read.

3   Request petition guidelines. Find out how many signatures you need and whether your petition needs approval before being circulated.

4   Use the guidelines to write a short summary of your cause. People won't stick around to read something long, so make it simple and to the point.

5   Read over your summary carefully. Make sure it a) describes the situation, b) suggests what is needed and c) explains why it is needed.

6   Divide the petition page, with the summary at the top, into four columns with a ruler. Label the columns: Name, Address, Phone Number and Signature. Allow plenty of room for the Address column.

7   Label more pages accordingly or make copies of your original. Make sure you have enough pages for the number of signatures you need.

8   Secure the papers to a clipboard. Attach a pen to the clipboard.

9   Go out and get those signatures! Make sure all signers are registered voters. When you have enough signatures, submit your petition.

Organise a Boycott   211

Nothing speaks louder than lost revenue, so an effective boycott can get a CEO's or board director's attention quickly.

⊙ Steps

1   Identify who or what you want to boycott. The beauty of a boycott is that you can have a major effect on a seemingly impenetrable multinational corporation by calling attention to how it conducts business. Keep the message simple yet emotionally appealing.

2   Research to death the product or group that you are interested in boycotting. Consider boycotting both the consumer and the seller. PETA, in its boycott of fur coats, intimidates the seller, the maker of fur coats, and the people who buy and wear them.

3   Warn the company early on of your plans to boycott. Sometimes just the threat of a boycott does the job.

4   Spread the word via word of mouth, email and a website dedicated to the cause. Get a petition going.

✳ Tips

Keep up the momentum. Sometimes a boycott takes years before it effects change. Don't give up.

Consult a lawyer about how to boycott effectively without risking a slander or libel lawsuit.

Rescue a Hostage   212

Hostage situations are very unstable, and for both sides they are hard to control. Anything can happen at any time.

⊙ Steps

1   Clear the surrounding area. Rescue personnel, spectators and reporters need to be kept well back. The more noise and activity, the higher the stress level for everyone and the less controlled the environment.

2   Identify a negotiator and prevent anyone except that person from communicating with or gaining access to the perpetrators.

✳ Tip

Seek assistance from people respected by the perpetrators. Parents, religious figures or political leaders may be helpful. These people can be put in touch with the perpetrators once you're assured of their support.

3 Attempt to establish communication with the perpetrators. They undoubtedly have demands and are anxious to talk.

4 Ascertain exactly how many perpetrators there are. This may be easy to do if they are making demands for transportation, as you can reasonably ask what capacity vehicle they need. If shooting starts, you need to know how many targets to track.

5 Establish the number of hostages taken. Determine if there is a way to evacuate all of them quickly.

6 Get a list of demands. Concede to some of them if possible in exchange for the release of some hostages.

7 Utilise high-tech tools to track the perpetrators' movements. Infrared sensors and listening devices can yield clues about perpetrators' numbers and plans.

8 Position sharpshooters in as many locations as possible. If there's only one perp and you get a good shot, take it.

9 Proceed slowly and recognise that the perpetrators don't hold all the cards. A perpetrator's threat of violence is therefore somewhat muted by his need to keep the negotiation moving.

10 Plan any intervention to occur at a transition point. If hostages and perpetrators are being driven to the airport, the move from car to plane may offer an opportunity.

11 Station additional sharpshooters and personnel at the intervention site. Assign targets to your team members and instruct them to shoot at your signal.

⚠ Warnings

Agreeing to a terrorist's demands may be tempting, but it is, perhaps literally, a dead end. You are almost guaranteed to be targeted by additional groups.

Use extreme caution when placing tracking equipment, to avoid infuriating the perpetrators.

---

213 | Introduce People

Want to meet new people and improve your social graces? Here's how to make proper introductions at parties, dinners and other social situations.

◉ Steps

1 Introduce individuals to each other using both first and last names.

2 If you're introducing someone who has a title – a doctor, for example – include the title as well as the first and last names in the introduction.

3 Introduce the younger or less-prominent person to the older or more prominent person, regardless of the sex of the individuals. However, if a considerable age difference lies between the two, it is far more courteous to make introductions in deference to age, regardless of social rank.

4 If the person you are introducing has a specific relationship to you, make the relationship clear by adding a phrase such as "my boss" or "my wife". In the case of unmarried couples who are living together, "companion" and "partner" are good choices.

5 Use your spouse's first and last name if he or she has a different last name to you.

6 Introduce an individual to the group first, then the group to the individual.

✳ Tips

If you've forgotten a name, you'll seem impolite if you try to ignore the need for the introduction. It's less awkward (and better manners) to apologise and acknowledge that the name has escaped you.

If your host neglects to introduce you to other guests, feel free to introduce yourself, but make your relationship to the host clear in your introduction.

⚠ Warning

Formal etiquette censures repeating names and adding phrases such as "a pleasure", as it may appear insincere.

Shake Hands

214

Historically used to show that both people were unarmed, the handshake today is a critical gauge of confidence, trust, sophistication and mood.

⊙ Steps

1 Extend your right hand to meet the other person's right hand.

2 Point your thumb upwards towards the other person's arm and extend your arm at a slight downward angle.

3 Wrap your hand around the other person's hand when your thumb joints come together.

4 Grasp the hand firmly and squeeze gently once. Remember that limp handshakes are a big turnoff, as are bone-crushing grasps.

5 Hold the handshake for two to three seconds.

6 Pump your hand up and down a few times to convey sincerity (this gesture is optional).

7 Make eye contact when shaking hands. This shows sincerity and honesty. If you avoid making eye contact you may be perceived as lying, inferior, or possibly nervous.

✳ Tip

A two-handed handshake is not for first meetings. It is a sign of real affection, and you should reserve it for friends and intimates.

⚠ Warning

Handshakes are not appropriate in all cultures. Investigate local customs if you will be visiting a foreign country.

Remember Names

215

Many people have difficulty remembering names, but it is important in many cultures. The ability to remember the names of people you meet will always serve you well in social situations.

⊙ Steps

1 Pay attention when you are introduced to someone. A few minutes after you meet the person, say his or her name to yourself again. If you have forgotten it, talk to the person again and ask for their name, apologising that you have forgotten.

2 Write down the new name three times while picturing the person's face; do this as soon as possible after meeting someone.

3 Ask how to spell a difficult name, or glance at the spelling on the person's business card, if it's offered. If you know the spelling of a word and can picture it in your mind, you'll remember it better.

4 Connect a name to a common word you will remember. For example, the name Salazar could sound like "salamander", "bazaar" or "sell a jar".

5 Make a connection to the person's hobby or employment. "Bill the pill" might help you remember the name of your pharmacist, for example.

✳ Tips

Writing down new names is generally a very successful memorising technique that doesn't require a lot of work.

For a memory boost, check out a book about using mnemonic devices or strategies.

216 | Accept a Compliment

Receiving a compliment can be somewhat embarrassing, but knowing the correct way to accept to a compliment is important to avoid offending the person who has offered it.

⊚ Steps

1   Look the person in the eye when they are speaking to you. Even though it can be embarrassing to receive a compliment, it is more respectful to the person who is giving you the compliment to look at him or her while they speak.

2   Recognise that someone has taken the time to notice something about you that they appreciate or admire. You can do this by saying something like, "I really appreciate that you noticed that". A simple comment like this lets the person know that you understand, appreciate and believe their compliment.

3   Say "Thank you" with meaning. Often people feel that the proper way to accept a compliment is to try to water it down with disqualifying comments. This is both rude to the person giving the compliment and unappreciative.

4   Understand that you do not have to give a compliment in return. If you would like to return the compliment, that's fine, but trying to rush a quick compliment without much thought will be obvious. The person will realise that you are just trying to be polite and that your compliment probably isn't sincere.

⚠ Warning

Don't laugh at the person giving you a compliment. The person may already be nervous about complimenting you; don't make it worse for them.

217 | Apologise Creatively

Apologising is an art form – and remember that etiquette demands that serious offences require serious apologies. Read on to learn how to apologise creatively.

⊚ Steps

1   Hire a performer to sing, act or dance an apology. If you'd rather do the performing and risk embarrassment, rent a costume to apologise in and give the performance of your life on his or her doorstep or while they are out eating dinner with a friend. Making a fool of yourself or having someone else make a fool of themself on your behalf is a great way to break the ice.

2   Think of the things you have told him or her you hate to do but that they love to do. Set up a date and time to do exactly that, but keep the event a surprise. When you arrive at the event, apologise for whatever misunderstanding or offence happened and put it all behind you by participating in one of their favourite activities.

3   Make something simple and handmade. Create a collage from newspaper or magazine clippings that spells out your apology. Leave clues, like for a treasure hunt, to lead to your apology. Leave a big poster board in their car that admits your wrongdoing and ask them to drive around with it. Write a poem or a song for them. Colour a page in a colouring book that fits the reason for your fight.

✱ Tips

Flowers and chocolates have become standards for apologies. If you want to be creative, do something different.

Keep the actual words that you say simple. Let the creative expression you decide on be a celebration of good times and a putting of the incident behind you.

How to Do More of *(Just About)* **Everything**

4   Make a photo album of great moments you've had together. For the last photo, take a picture that's a re-enactment of your infraction, and incorporate "I'm sorry" into the picture. This focuses the attention on more important things and shows the strength of your relationship, while acknowledging the wrong you've done in a light and humorous way.

Propose a Toast to Your Host   218

An expression of gratitude and admiration, a toast can be the highlight of your host's evening if delivered correctly. Keep it short, sweet and complimentary.

⊙ Steps

1   Time your toast to be delivered directly before or directly after the meal is served. If you wait until after the meal, make sure that every guest has finished eating before you begin.

2   Tap delicately on a glass, if necessary, to get everyone's attention.

3   Ask everyone but the host to rise.

4   Raise your glass and begin speaking.

5   Make your toast personal or humorous, depending on the occasion. Always make sure you include your gratitude for the invitation.

6   Compliment the host on one or more attributes or an accomplishment that everyone is there to celebrate.

7   Use a personal anecdote to support your compliments.

8   Finish the toast by inviting guests to drink in the host's honour.

✳ Tips

Keep it short and sweet. The worst toasts are those that drag on unnecessarily.

Make a few notes to yourself prior to the toast to remind yourself of everything you would like to say.

Leave a Party Graciously   219

Arriving at the party is the easy part. When you are ready to leave, exercise tact and always thank the host or hostess before you depart.

⊙ Steps

1   Wait until the host is not in conversation or caught in the middle of cooking or serving duties.

2   Express your gratitude for the invitation, and compliment the host on one particular aspect of the party.

3   Make a tentative reference to the next time you will see each other. For example, saying "We should get together for drinks soon" takes the emphasis off your departure.

4   Acknowledge everyone in the room, if possible. If the party is too large to permit this, express a parting gesture to those guests with whom you spent time talking.

5   Make your parting words short and sweet in an attempt to let everyone else get back to the festivities.

✳ Tips

Avoid long and effusive apologies. Others will look upon your departure negatively if you insist on apologising for it.

If the party invitation included an ending time, don't stay too long after the time indicated.

220 Tip a Waiter

Food servers receive a low hourly wage because of the income they receive in gratuities, or tips. Follow these guidelines for tipping at a restaurant or café.

⊙ Steps

1   Tip 15 per cent of the overall bill, minus the VAT, in most cases. Depending on the service, 15–20 per cent is the common range.

2   Tip an extra 5 per cent (a total of 20 per cent) if the restaurant is a highly rated establishment or if a large party is dining and the gratuity is not automatically added to the tab.

3   Add the gratuity to the overall bill, which includes alcohol but does not include VAT.

4   Consider scribbling a note on your bill if you wish to acknowledge someone on the staff who went out of their way for you.

5   Leave a lesser tip if you are unhappy with the service. A word with the server is also appropriate.

✳ Tip

The word "tip" was originally an acronym for the phrase "to insure promptness".

221 Eat Lobster

The shell is a small obstacle to that rich, tender lobster meat. Here's how to get at your dinner.

⊙ Steps

1   Allow the lobster to cool after cooking.

2   Remove the large claws from the body by twisting them off at the joints.

3   Crack the claws. A nutcracker works for this, but so does the back of a heavy chef's knife, a small hammer or even a rock.

4   Bend the body back from the tail – it will crack and then you can remove the tail. Break off the small flippers on the tail.

5   Push the tail meat out of the tail. It should come out in one piece. Remove the black vein in the tail and discard it.

6   Dip the lobster meat in melted butter and enjoy. Repeat as you unshell more meat.

7   Find the tomalley (the lobster liver; it's green) and discard it – unless you like to use it in sauces.

8   Note that the coral-coloured roe in a female lobster is also edible, though you can discard this, too.

9   Crack the body apart to find the meat in four cavities where the small legs join the body.

10 Look for meat in the small walking legs, too, if you have a lobster weighing more than 1 kg (2 lb). Push a skewer into the legs to get the meat out.

✳ Tip

Some people eat the coral and tomalley; you can also mash them up, add a little stock or cream, and use the tomalley as a sauce.

Be Politically Incorrect

222

Many people like to find relief from the oppressive regime of political correctness by indulging in offensive, inappropriate and completely insensitive behaviour.

⊙ Steps

1 Speak of women as sexual objects and refer to men as witless Neanderthals.

2 Find out about various stereotypes and make offensive jokes out of them. There are many stereotypes to choose from, including those dealing with race, ethnicity, gender, religion and sexuality.

3 Consider physical and mental disabilities as fodder for sarcastic comments and other types of jokes.

4 Include large amounts of sexual innuendo in your speech.

5 Flee in terror from politically correct witch-hunters.

⚠ Warning

This type of humour is best carried out good-naturedly and among people who understand you're simply making a statement about the extremes of political correctness. Be aware of anyone who might be genuinely offended by your comments.

Write a Sympathy Card

223

The best way to write a sympathy card is to be genuine and simply say what you feel – thus, you should send your condolences as soon as you hear the news of the death.

⊙ Steps

1 Use personal stationery and a pen with blue or black ink.

2 Address the letter to the deceased's closest relative, such as the widow or eldest child, if you knew the deceased well but did not know the family well.

3 If you did not know the deceased, write to the relative with whom you are acquainted and express your wish to give comfort, even if he or she is not the closest relative.

4 Express sympathy for the family and acknowledge their loss: "Please accept my sympathy for the terrible loss of your father."

5 Include a personal memory and/or acknowledge the character and accomplishments of the deceased. If you did not know the deceased, you can simply say, "It must have been wonderful to have him (or her) in your life."

6 Offer support and assistance in any way needed if you know the person to whom you are writing.

✳ Tips

Avoid dwelling on the details of the death.

Avoid euphemisms or dramatic conclusions such as "It's all for the best", which may seem to skirt the issue of the death or the suffering of the bereaved.

224 | Plan Your Own Funeral

Planning your own funeral ahead of time can save your family members a great deal of stress, anxiety, emotional upheaval and financial burden in the event of your death.

⊙ Steps

1 Determine whether you'd like a traditional funeral, a funeral that celebrates your life rather than mourning your death, a more casual memorial service without your body present or even a party.

2 Let your loved ones know if there is anything in particular you'd like included or avoided at your funeral. For example, if you don't want an open casket, a 20-minute-long eulogy or people to dress in black, make this known. If you would like a certain song played or sung, a poem read or a slide show of certain photographs, make this known as well.

3 Come up with a short list of locations and venues you'd prefer. Have a first, second and third choice.

4 Choose whether you'd like to be buried underground in a grave, entombed in a mausoleum or cremated.

5 Pick your preferred cemetery site.

6 Choose your casket ahead of time. Pick one that will fit your body, that suits you in terms of style and that won't break the bank. This will save your loved ones a lot of hassle.

7 Buy an appropriate burial site for you and your other family members ahead of time to ensure where you'll be buried and to save your family the financial and emotional burden of buying one for you.

8 Find out if you are eligible for death benefits.

9 Establish a funeral fund to cover the expenses if death benefits are not allowed or if they won't cover the entire costs involved.

✳ Tips

Only buy a burial site if you're sure you won't be moving far away for the rest of your life.

Every time you make an extensive move before you die, pull out your funeral plans and arrangements and see if any adjustments need to be made, particularly with the funeral location or venue, burial site and funeral home.

Make your funeral plans in collaboration with your loved ones.

225 | Choose a Hymn for a Funeral

Choosing a hymn for a funeral can seem overwhelming, but it doesn't have to be. The hymn selection is a wonderful way to celebrate and reflect the character or beliefs of the deceased.

⊙ Steps

1 Look through the hymnal to find fitting titles. These songs can be old favourites of the deceased or songs that express spiritual beliefs about death and the afterlife. Choosing an appropriate hymn is a matter of taste.

2 Talk to family members and friends. They may be able to give more insight into the deceased's favourite music. Speak to members of the church, temple or synagogue for more ideas.

3 Arrange for a musician, if one has not already been booked. Find someone who is familiar with the style of music and if possible the hymn itself.

✳ Tip

Not all pianists or organ players are familiar with every hymn. Check early to make sure that they are familiar with your choice or give them time to get to know the hymn.

4   Determine the appropriate time for the hymn to be played. Many funerals have music at different points throughout the ceremony.

5   Choose your hymn. Base your decision on what you know and have learned about the deceased; also consider any special requests.

Plan a Wake   226

The wake traditionally involved a period of time when friends and relatives literally stayed awake with the body of the deceased until it was taken to the church for the funeral or to the cemetery for burial.

⊙ Steps

1   Inform friends and family that a loved one has passed away, and let them know the date, time and place of the wake. This can also be done by placing an obituary in the local newspaper with the same information.

2   Let the funeral home know when you wish to have the wake. The home will prepare the body for viewing, and will see that any flowers sent will be displayed during the visitation.

3   Display a guest book for people to sign as they come in. This is often provided by the funeral home, or you can purchase your own.

4   Bring some pictures of the deceased to put on a table in the room, if desired. People will appreciate seeing the person as he or she appeared in life.

5   Plan to be present during the visitation to greet friends and neighbours who come to pay their respects to the deceased and to the family.

6   Plan an old-fashioned wake for the deceased away from the funeral home, if that is your preference. You can reserve a pub or restaurant, or hold the wake in your home.

7   Provide beverages, food, disposable cups, place settings, napkins and plates if the wake is held in your home. Alcoholic beverages are usually considered appropriate.

8   Greet guests, lay out the food and drink, and spend the time toasting or otherwise remembering the deceased.

✱ Tips

Visitors usually bring food to a wake if it is held in a home. The food is eaten by guests, and any remaining food is left with the family of the deceased.

Old-fashioned Irish wakes consisted of drinking, game playing, wrestling, dancing and singing. Use your best judgement about what is appropriate.

Write an Obituary   227

An obituary is usually written in paragraph form and charts the life of the deceased in chronological order.

⊙ Steps

1   Check with the newspaper to see if there are any restrictions on length before you write the obituary.

2   Give the deceased's full name and date and place of death.

✱ Tip

Consider sending the obituary to newspapers in other cities where the deceased formerly lived or worked.

3 Recount the main events in the person's life, beginning with his or her birth and birthplace.

4 Include a list of schools they attended, degrees received, their vocation and hobbies.

5 Acknowledge any survivors, including parents, spouse and children.

6 Announce when and where the funeral, burial, wake and/or memorial service will take place.

7 Conclude with a statement regarding where memorial contributions can be sent, if applicable.

8 Time the publication of the obituary so that it runs a few days before the memorial service.

⚠ **Warning**

Most newspapers charge by the word or by the line to publish obituaries. Keep it brief if money is an issue.

228 | Hunt a Dragon

Whether you're under contract by a local king or you're a big-game hunter looking for a new challenge, learning how to hunt a dragon is crucial to your success.

◉ **Steps**

1 Before you can kill a dragon, you must find a dragon. Believe it or not, dragons are not very stealthy beasts. When they walk, the Earth trembles. When they exhale, entire villages are fireballed. If you're looking for a dragon, stop, close your eyes and listen. The screams of murder you hear? Those are a good place to start.

2 Once you know where the dragon has been, you can see where it's going. Follow the trail of blood, limbs and bones. The dragon will knock down everything in its path – houses, trees and mountains. Above all else, you don't want to confront a dragon when it's ravaging a village, you want to track it to its lair.

3 Dragons usually build nests in caves; however, it takes a large cave to house a dragon. Once you track your dragon to the mountain it calls home, you will need to navigate the internal network of tunnels and underground rivers to find its nest. Luckily, dragons do more than eat villagers – they steal their fortunes, too. The dragon's lair will be filled with gold, treasures and weapons.

4 When you're ready to slay the dragon, you want to make sure your weapon is ready. Hopefully you've brought along a big sword, or at least a heavy mace or lance. Attacking a dragon with a butcher's cleaver is the stuff of tragedy. Once you've evaluated the size and strength of the dragon, if you believe your weapon is not up to par, look around his lair. He probably already stole a better sword from a better warrior.

5 Since killing the dragon is your ultimate goal, everything up to this point will be worthless if you don't come out of this alive. In his lair, the dragon will have less mobility than he would outside; however, you still need to avoid his tail, claws, teeth, wings, fire and poisonous spit. A dragon's scales are also usually impenetrable, so you'll have to aim for his soft underbelly or throat. A hard, fast stroke or stab is all it takes. Hacking away will make you look like an amateur.

⚠ **Warning**

Dragons are big and tough, and when you go up against the beast, only one of you will come out alive. Remember, the chances are it won't be you.

6   Claim your trophy. Most kings will require proof of a dead dragon, and if you're hunting for your own pleasure, a dragon's head is better than any antler rack or mounted bass. Other dragon body parts may be worth money, depending on their medicinal properties, so before you embark on any dragon hunt, you should check the local market.

Trap a Yeti 229

This hairy beast is quite elusive, and trapping one is very challenging. If you dare to tangle with this giant creature, it's best to be prepared.

⊙ Steps

1   Strike out to the Himalayas. If you're after an actual Yeti, it's said that this is where he makes his home. If you'd be just as satisfied with his cousin Bigfoot, then you may not have to go as far.

2   Set a bait trap. There are so many tales about Yetis you'll find different references as to what they like to eat. Some references may indicate that Yetis are carnivores, so rabbits might make good bait.

3   Use live human bait. This method was made popular by several B movies in which a human, usually alive, is used to lure the Yeti into a trap. But this is only going to work if the Yeti is indeed a carnivore.

4   Restrain the Yeti. Some say a Yeti can't be trapped or even killed, but you can restrain one. The trick is to lure it with a beer-like substance called Chang, which the beast finds irresistible. Once the Yeti falls into a drunken sleep, you can then restrain him with some extremely strong chains.

5   Give up on finding the real beast. If you don't want to go to the trouble of travelling to the Himalayas, tracking and then trying to trap a real Yeti, try playing "The Rampaging Yetis". In this video game one quest, "The Yeti Hunt", allows you to trap and kill a fictional Yeti with the help of a character named Zho.

✳ Tip

Ride Disney's Animal Kingdom ride, "Expedition Everest". No, you won't get to trap a Yeti, but you will get to see one on this unique rollercoaster ride in which a Yeti tears up the tracks and sends you plunging back the way you came with the beast hot on your tail.

Ghost Hunt 230

You can ghost hunt with little more than an open mind and a willingness to conduct research, as long as you follow a few careful steps.

⊙ Steps

1   Research the site where you intend to conduct your ghost hunt. You want to know as much as possible not only about the site, but about the ghost said to frequent there, the ghost's identity and history in life, previous supernatural incidents and the form that any past manifestations have taken.

2   Scout out the location and get a good feel for it before you begin a ghost hunt. If the property is privately held, approach the owners politely and

✳ Tip

Dress appropriately whenever you wish to hunt a ghost, especially if it's in an outdoor locale such as a cemetery. Wear warm clothes to protect against the chill and a pair of good sturdy shoes to help you move quickly if need be.

ask for permission to visit there. You should also check the area for any dangerous spots such as deadfalls or loose floorboards, and make sure you and anyone with you knows about them before you go stumbling over them in the dark.

3   Determine the best time to hunt for your ghost. Specifics vary according to individual hauntings. Most ghosts will appear at night, but some come at all times of the day, and certain experts also claim that the "magic hour" at dusk or dawn is most conducive for spirits to enter our world.

4   Gather any equipment you may need. Theoretically, you need only warm clothes and an ability to observe, but if you are serious about hunting your ghost, you may want to include devices to help detect it, such as EMF meters and digital thermometers, as well as cameras and audio recorders to collect evidence of manifestations. A few torches couldn't hurt either, especially if you're conducting your hunt after dark.

5   Arrive in time to set up your gear and to find the best place to wait for the ghost. If you are recording, you should set up your cameras to capture as wide an area as possible, and if you have more than one person along, you can split up to make sure someone is watching anywhere the ghost might appear. Make sure you cover every spot where the ghost is likely to manifest.

6   Stay quiet and keep your eyes open. When you hunt a ghost, you need a great deal of patience. It might not appear for many nights, if at all. Wait quietly while you keep vigil, but stay alert and watch for any signs of the ghost's presence.

7   Keep a diary of everything you see, even if it seems incidental. Write down the time and date of any sounds, visions or incidents, and try to describe them as objectively as possible.

8   Record anything that appears, be it with the cameras, audio recorders or electromagnetic detectors. Tangible evidence is the ultimate goal of any ghost hunt, and the more solid information you can retain and present, the easier it will be to prove the existence of a ghost.

231 | Locate Atlantis

Atlantis exists, but people are looking in the wrong places. Inject science into legends for the best way to find Atlantis.

◎Steps

1   Study all the information that you can about Atlantis. Look for materials that talk about its end. Plato's *Critias* is one place. Other cultures around the world talk about continents sinking beneath the waves.

2   Notice common trends. Different theorists propose different Atlantis locations, when it went under and how it went under. They also advance common trends despite their stories' differences, such as volcanic eruptions, floods and earthquakes.

3   Look at the results from a scientific perspective. Plato placed Atlantis's end 9,000 years before his time. That's a little over 11,000 years ago,

✻ Tip

Divers found underwater structures on our continental shelves; our ancestors built these structures when their areas were still on dry land. Humans tend to live by the water; as the waters rose they moved further inland, abandoning their constructions.

towards the end of the last ice age. Large ice sheets aren't the only thing that happened during the ice age. Those ice sheets held what's mostly ocean today. Our water levels were lower, exposing large land masses off the coast.

4   Obtain a global map showing underwater topography. Compare that to land masses exposed during the last ice age. Find a land mass that exceeded Libya and Asia as seen by the ancients. Understand that their interpretation of the Atlantic Ocean was different from ours. To them, the Atlantic Ocean encircled the Earth. Look for such an underwater land mass.

5   Figure out what part of the world would have supported double harvests, suggesting a warm climate, during the last ice age. Look to lands in the Equator area and zero in on the underwater continental shelf connecting Southeast Asia to the Asian mainland. That area was exposed during the last ice age, and lies right on the Equator.

6   Read about geographical, geologic and meteorological changes that take place at the end of an ice age. Understand that when the ice sheets melt, the pressure points shift, causing volcanic eruptions, earthquakes and rising sea levels, activities associated with the "sinking" of Atlantis.

7   Search for Atlantis in the waters in Southeast Asia.

Tell if a Space Alien Means Harm   232

In the movies, it always seems easy to tell if a space alien has good or bad intentions. But if you were to encounter one here on Earth, how could you gauge if the alien is a potential friend or foe?

⊙ Steps

1   Determine the alien's mood if you can. If he is attempting to be friendly, the chances are good that the alien means no harm.

2   Notice how the space alien is treating you. If it is trying to comfort you, that is a far more positive sign than if the alien is coming after you with a weapon or other instrument to hurt you.

3   Find out exactly what the alien means if it is using English to communicate with you. Their understanding and interpretation of a phrase may not be the same as yours.

4   Note how the alien treats other Earth creatures. If it is willing to hurt or maim animals, the chances are it won't be gentle with you.

5   Reassure the space alien that you don't mean to harm it. Remember, it has come from millions of miles away, and probably doesn't know what to make of you and your behaviour either.

6   Trust your instincts. If for some reason you feel uncomfortable around the alien, see if you can gracefully get away from it. Try to convince it that you need to check something out with your leader before you attempt to represent the entire human race, if necessary.

❋ Tip

You may wish to observe the alien before introducing yourself if you can.

⚠ Warnings

Don't brandish weapons at your first meeting if you can avoid it. It is hard to convince other humans that you mean no harm that way, so it could be difficult to convince a completely different species that you come in peace if you are armed.

Don't rely on the outward appearance of the alien to determine if it is friendly. People have reported encounters with kind but ugly aliens.

233 Give the Evil Eye

The evil eye is a powerful communication technique, one that can inspire fear or guilt in those who are in its range.

◎ Steps

1   Find the person to whom you want to give the evil eye. Make sure that you are not seeking too hard or in any doubt about the identification of your recipient, because this takes away from the effect of the gaze.

2   Recall the event or reason you are giving this person the evil eye. This will increase the meaning and power behind your gaze. Focus on your intent as you prepare to launch the evil eye.

3   Squint your eyes slightly while thinking of the offence committed by your victim. The evil eye is evil, after all, so you want to make it intimidating but not silly.

4   Raise one eyebrow slightly whilst squinting. This gives the eye a more evil appearance and increases the malice that comes through in the gaze. It should feel like you could set fires with the power of your evil eye.

✱ Tip

Turning your head sharply away at the end of your evil eye can add tension and a level of disgust to your evil eye that is very effective.

⚠ Warning

Do not give the evil eye to someone who could possibly beat you up. Make sure you size up your evil-eye recipient accurately before giving it.

234 Sponsor a Child Overseas

Sponsorship provides consistent support for a child in a developing nation by providing basic needs like food, shelter, healthcare and education.

◎ Steps

1   Get information about sponsorship programmes. There are many organisations that manage sponsorship of children overseas, including the Salvation Army and WorldVision. Search online.

2   Decide how much you want to spend and choose an organisation. Sponsorships are usually priced by month and vary in cost and services provided. Be sure to ask how much of the money goes directly to the child's needs and how much covers the organisation's costs of operations.

3   Sign up to be a sponsor. Many organisations let you sign up online. You can usually choose the country, age and gender of the child you want to sponsor. Some websites post pictures of children who need sponsors. If you prefer to post a form and check or arrange the sponsorship by phone, look at the organisation's website for information on how to do this.

4   Determine a payment schedule. Many sponsorship organisations allow you to pay yearly, monthly or quarterly. You may also be able to pay lump sums twice each year.

5   Start paying for the sponsorship. Typically you can use direct debits, cheques or debit cards. Contributions are tax deductible.

6   Review the welcome kit that the organisation sends you. Get to know the child you are sponsoring and his or her country and circumstances.

7   Receive photos, updates and other information on the child's progress. How often you get this information depends on the organisation.

⚠ Warning

Sponsoring a child is a big commitment – make sure you're prepared to be involved for a number of years.

Join Amnesty International 235

Amnesty International is a worldwide organisation of people who campaign for internationally recognised human rights.

⊙ Steps

1   Check to see if an Amnesty International group exists at your college or university. Call the campus operator for a phone number or browse a list of active groups and clubs at your student centre.

2   Visit the Amnesty International website. Click the Act Now button at the top of the home page to learn more about current campaigns and political action opportunities.

3   Click the Join Now button on the right of the Act Now page to join Amnesty International. Enter your country of residence to begin the registration process.

4   Fill in the application. It asks for your name, contact information, the type of membership you wish to purchase and your credit-card number. After completing the form, select the Donate button at the bottom of the form to submit your application.

5   Contact your local Amnesty International office for information about volunteer opportunities, local chapters and other regional information.

✳ Tip

To find information about a specific issue, visit the website and choose from the Select an Issue drop-down menu or the Choose a Country drop-down menu in the What's Going on Where box.

Donate Your Body to Science 236

Donating your body to science is the ultimate rare event – a once-in-a-lifetime opportunity to benefit medical teaching and research.

⊙ Steps

1   Register your donation with a local medical school or university. You'll be given a registration packet that covers policies and procedures; read it very carefully.

2   Sign a consent form stating your desire to donate your body, and put a copy of it with your will and other personal documents. You won't be listed as a donor until a completed form has been returned and acknowledged. Cancel your decision at any time by notifying the medical school or university in writing.

3   Arrange for the medical school or university to be notified when you die, so that your body can be properly transported and prepared. When your corpse is delivered to the medical institution, it will be embalmed and refrigerated until it's needed for study.

4   Check with the college to see what its policies and procedures are regarding your body after it has been studied. Most institutions will respectfully cremate your remains at their expense and give your ashes to your loved ones. Don't expect to get paid for your donation pre- or post-mortem. By law, medical schools are not permitted to purchase anyone's body.

⚠ Warning

The mistreatment of donated bodies is not uncommon so be very careful in your choice of institution.

237 Use a Dictionary

This perennial bestseller is something we take for granted, but its features are numerous. Read on to take full advantage of all your dictionary has to offer.

⊙ Steps

1   Read the introductory or front matter of the dictionary. You'll understand the various features and how they're set off using typefaces (bold, italic, etc.), numbering, lettering and punctuation.

2   Pick an entry or two to review, referring back to the introduction. Find the parts of speech and related words, and look up the abbreviations used.

3   Find several etymologies (word histories) and use the list of abbreviations to decipher them.

4   Check the pronunciations of some words you know, using the pronunciation key to become familiar with the conventions used in your dictionary. Then look up a word that you do not know how to pronounce and see whether you can figure it out.

5   Consult your dictionary about finding words if you don't know the spelling. Often, good suggestions are offered in the explanatory material.

6   Note special features such as quotations or examples of use. These are intended to help you find the exact meaning you're seeking. Try substituting the word in a sentence to test it.

7   Use the dictionary to hunt around for synonyms of words. Although it's not as handy as a thesaurus, you will find plenty of related words by doing multiple look-ups using the words in definitions.

✳ Tip

Consider investing in specialised dictionaries: unabridged, foreign language and special subjects, for example. Not all words are in any one dictionary.

⚠ Warnings

There are variant spellings and pronunciations. The first listing is not necessarily correct but preferred.

Remember that the dictionary is not an unquestionable authority. It is written by trained professionals reporting on the real use of words and phrases by the general public.

238 Use a Thesaurus

A thesaurus helps you avoid repetition in your writing and assists in finding words for any idea you have in mind.

⊙ Steps

1   Read the introduction to your thesaurus. There are two main kinds: a Roget-type, which has a categorisation system, and an A-to-Z thesaurus. Both may also contain antonyms, word lists and other interesting features.

2   Get to know the features of your thesaurus. By understanding what changes in typography mean, you will grasp the nuances of the reference book's text.

3   Become familiar with the categorisation scheme if you have a Roget-type thesaurus. And in an A-to-Z thesaurus, you may also benefit from the definitions for each entry.

4   Look up a word in a Roget-type thesaurus in the index. The index will probably have the meanings listed under each word. Don't limit your search to one category; also look at the categories just before and after the one you first look up.

✳ Tip

Use the thesaurus to avoid repeating words within a sentence and avoid beginning successive sentences or paragraphs with identical words.

5   Examine the offerings in all parts of speech in the category of interest. You might find something you can use by broadening your search.

6   Choose synonyms carefully. You will soon recognise that few words are exactly interchangeable. Use the thesaurus in conjunction with a good dictionary whenever selecting an unfamiliar word or phrase.

Use Apostrophes Correctly   239

Apostrophes have three basic uses: to replace missing letters or numbers, to show plurals of lower-case letters and to indicate possession. They are not used for most plurals – the most common form of misuse.

⚠ **Warning**

Do not use contractions in formal writing, such as school essays or business reports.

⊙ **Steps**

Missing Letters or Numbers

1   Use an apostrophe to indicate missing letters. This occurs when you are writing a contraction, such as don't (do not), wouldn't (would not) or it's (it is).

2   Use an apostrophe for "it's" only when you are writing a contraction of "it is". When writing the possessive "its", do not use an apostrophe.

3   Use an apostrophe to indicate missing numbers. This generally occurs when you are abbreviating the year, such as "it happened back in '99".

Plurals of Lower-Case Letters and Single Capitals

1   Use an apostrophe to indicate the plural of lower-case letters, such as "my typewriter won't make n's".

2   Apostrophes can be used to indicate the plural of a single upper-case letter, such as "she gets all A's in school", although omitting the apostrophe is acceptable.

3   Do not use an apostrophe for the plural of upper-case acronyms (MREs) or numbers (the 1980s).

Possessives

1   Use an apostrophe to indicate possession. If the noun is singular, such as girl or dog, put an apostrophe after the last letter and add an s (the dog's ball) – even if the singular noun ends in s (James's car).

2   Add an apostrophe after the s if the noun is plural and ends in s, and do not add another s (girls' ribbons).

3   Add an apostrophe and an s to plural nouns that do not end in s (women's toilets).

240 | Write a Book Report

Writing a good book report requires summarising a lot of information in a very small space. Your job is to extract the main ideas of a book and analyse it, then type it up into a presentable report.

⊙ Steps

1 Take thorough and careful notes as you read the book. Use sticky notes to mark pages that contain important passages or quotes.

2 Gather your reading notes and the book and have them by your side as you write your report.

3 Ask yourself, "What would I want to know about this book?"

4 Look through your notes and decide, based on the length of the book report and your answers to the above question, what is essential to include and what can be excluded.

5 State the main point of the book: why did the author write the book? Or for fiction, give a brief plot summary.

6 Outline the plot or main ideas in the book, or for fiction describe the story and key dramatic points.

7 Follow your outline as you write the report, making sure you balance the general and the specific. A good book report will both give an overview of the book's significance and convey enough details to avoid abstraction.

8 Summarise the overall significance of the book: what has this book contributed to the knowledge of the world? For fiction: what does this story tell us about the author's take on life's big questions?

✳ Tips

Make sure you proofread your book report carefully before turning it in.

Type your report on a computer.

241 | Work Out a Percentage

The percentage is the fraction of the whole that is made up by one particular aspect of it. It is easy to work out a percentage using basic algebra skills.

⊙ Steps

1 Calculating a percentage is based on a simple algebraic equation: Is = Per cent X Of. Begin by filling the appropriate values into the equation. (Example: to calculate the percentage of 16 that is made up by 4, the equation would read, 4 = Per cent X 16.)

2 In an algebraic equation, you can shift numbers around. When two numbers are being multiplied, you can move one of them to the other side of the equation by dividing both sides by that number. By doing this, you can work out the percentage. (Example: (4) / 16 = (Per cent X 16) / 16 becomes 4 / 16 = Per cent).

3 Reduce the remaining equation to determine the decimal value of the percentage. (Example: Per cent = 4 / 16 = .25)

4 Multiply this final value by 100 to determine the final percentage.

✳ Tip

You can use the same concept to manipulate and reduce any algebraic equation.

Convert Temperature Measurements | 242

Several different temperature scales exist – the Celsius scale sets freezing and boiling points of water at 0 and 100, while the Fahrenheit scale sets them at 32 and 212.

⊙ Steps

1   Multiply the Celsius temperature reading by 9/5, and then add 32 to get the temperature in Fahrenheit: (9/5 °C) + 32 = °F.

2   Subtract 32 from the Fahrenheit temperature, and then multiply this quantity by 5/9 to get the temperature in Celsius: (°F - 32) x 5/9 = °C.

3   Add 273.15 to the Celsius temperature to get Kelvin temperature (the scale used in thermodynamics calculations). To convert from Fahrenheit to Kelvin temperature, first convert Fahrenheit to Celsius using the formula above, and then add 273.15 to the Celsius temperature.

✳ Tip

An easier way to remember temperature conversions is to use estimates, such as 2 for 9/5. For example, multiply temperature in Celsius by 2, and then add 32 to get the approximate temperature in Fahrenheit.

Remember Important Dates | 243

Mnemonic devices and good old-fashioned date books can pave the way to a more productive and efficient memory.

⊙ Steps

1   Invest in a sturdy and accurate date book with plenty of room for multiple entries and details.

2   Train yourself to check the date book every day, first thing in the morning.

3   Use mnemonic devices – whole-brain memory techniques. For instance, utilise a rhyming technique, such as "On June 28, Bill and I have a date".

4   Visualise each week and month as a virtual calendar in your head. By imagining the impending event within this virtual calendar, you will have a visual "memory" of it before it even occurs.

5   Carry your date book with you at all times. When you make a date with someone, record it immediately in your date book.

✳ Tip

Keep a wall calendar or separate mini-calendar on hand to remember birthdays and anniversaries. Train yourself to check the calendar every week to plan for impending events, such as buying gifts or writing cards.

⚠ Warning

Don't rely on sticky notes and cluttered bulletin boards: it's too easy for these scraps of paper to get lost or buried.

Help Your Children Manage Homework | 244

Homework shouldn't throw the household into a nightly uproar. Here are some common-sense guidelines to help your children take responsibility for their own homework.

⊙ Steps

1   Help your children organise the three S's: space, stuff and schedule. Disorganisation will turn 40 minutes of maths, history and science into two hours of blood, sweat and tears.

2   Ask your children to review their assignments with you every so often, especially as they get older when coursework must be managed over time. Be sure your children plan the work and work the plan.

⚠ Warning

Don't fall into the trap of doing your children's homework for them. Process is as important as product, and it doesn't help your child that you know how to reduce fractions to the lowest common denominator.

3   Emphasise that your children's schoolwork is the top priority. Continued participation in extracurricular activities, a part-time job, and/or leisure pursuits are to be worked in around completion of regular homework and other assignments.

4   Check your children's work – not every night, but often enough that they know you might do so (and that you care).

5   Insist that they redo sloppy work, but don't correct mistakes. Teachers need to know what students don't know.

245   Help Your Child Cope with a Bully

Parents today worry more than ever before about the possibility of their children becoming victims of school bullies. Here's what you can do to protect your child.

⊙ **Steps**

1   Look for signs. Many children will not complain about being bullied at school, but rather will express a desire to avoid certain activities or even to avoid school altogether. This can take the form of psychosomatic illness or dropping out of previously favoured activities.

2   Take your child's concerns about bullying seriously. The need to prevent school violence must be paramount.

3   Assess the severity of the situation. If your child has been physically harmed or even threatened with physical harm, notify the school immediately and insist that staff there take action to protect your child from violence.

4   Work with your child to brainstorm ways to deal with less severe bullying directly, and help them make a plan. The more you can empower your children to manage their own affairs, the greater their self-esteem will become.

5   Explain the dynamics of bullying to your child. Help them understand that bullying comes from the bully's low self-esteem.

6   Bolster your child's confidence. Despite their behaviour, bullies are basically cowards and gravitate towards easy marks. Encourage your child not to react to a bully's taunts, enrol them in a martial arts class, or otherwise make your child a less attractive target. Don't, however, enourage them to fight back physically – violence like this is never the answer to bullying.

7   Keep a close eye on the situation. If things don't improve, or if your child begins to express concerns about their personal safety, don't hesitate to contact the school and demand a resolution.

⚠ **Warning**

Resist the temptation to contact the bully or the bully's parents directly. Usually this only serves to expand the conflict and escalate the bullying.

Select a Gift for a Teacher 246

Winter holidays just around the corner? End of the school year fast approaching? Here's how to select just the right gift for your child's teacher.

⊙ Steps

1 Check with the school to be sure you understand its gift policy. Some schools forbid gifts altogether; others discourage them or set a limit on their value.

2 Check with your child to make sure he or she wants to give a gift. If your child doesn't, but you do, make it clear that the gift is from you.

3 If your child does want to give a gift, involve him or her in the selection process. Start by asking your child what the teacher might like.

4 Shop with the idea that the gift is a token of your child's appreciation for the teacher's efforts. Think small and inexpensive.

5 Encourage your child to make a gift. Even a Year 1 pupil can frame a picture with lolly sticks, and those are the types of gifts teachers treasure long after they've eaten the last box of chocolates.

6 Shopping at the last minute? Personalise that "World's Greatest Teacher" mug with a hand-made card from your youngster.

✳ Tips

Be sensitive to diversity issues and avoid gifts associated with specific religious observances, such as Christmas decorations.

Remember, it's the thought that counts!

Learn Key Phrases in French 247

Although the French have a reputation for being critical of foreigners who butcher their language, it's largely undeserved.

⊙ Steps

1 Use *bonjour* (pronounced bohn-ZHOOR) for hello and *au revoir* (oh ruh-VWAR) for goodbye.

2 Introduce yourself by saying *Je m'appelle* (zhuh muh-PELL) and then your name.

3 Make copious use of *s'il vous plaît* (see voo PLAY) and *merci* (mehr-SEE) to say please and thank you.

4 Say *oui* (WEE) for yes and *non* (NOH) for no. Of course, nodding or shaking your head works, too.

5 If you're looking for something, say *où* (OOH), which means "where".

6 You can use *je voudrais* (zhuh voo-DRAY), which means "I would like", in many situations. Just point to whatever you want, remembering to tack on a *s'il vous plaît* at the end.

7 If all else fails, ask *Parlez-vous anglais?* (PAHR-lay voo zahn-GLAY), which means "Do you speak English?" If your new French-speaking friend doesn't, he or she can probably find someone who does.

⚠ Warning

The phonetic spellings given here are only approximations of the French pronunciations. If you pronounce these words while pretending to be Pepe Le Pew, you'll probably be pretty close.

248 | Learn Key Phrases in Italian

Even if you don't speak a word of Italian, it will only take a few minutes to learn some basic phrases that will help you communicate in this elegant language.

⊙ Steps

1 Use *ciao* (pronounced CHOW) for both hello and goodbye – it's a handy multi-purpose word that's easy to remember.

2 Introduce yourself by saying *Mi chiamo* (mee key-AHM-oh) and then your name.

3 Make copious use of *per favore* (pehr fa-VORE-ay) and *grazie* (GRATS-ee-ay) to say please and thank you.

4 Say *si* (SEE) for yes, and *no* (NOH) for no.

5 Say *dove* (DOH-vay), which means "where" if you're looking for something.

6 Use *vorrei* (vohr-RAY), which means "I would like", in many situations. Just point to whatever you want, remembering to tack on a *per favore* at the end.

7 If all else fails, ask *Parla inglese?* (PAHR-lay een-GLAY-say), or "Do you speak English?"

✻ Tip

If you carry around a small phrase book or dictionary, you can look up words you don't know – and even point to them if you can't pronounce them.

249 | Learn Key Phrases in Spanish

Spanish is one of the most-spoken languages in the world, so understanding a few phrases will help you get along in many different countries.

⊙ Steps

1 Use *hola* (pronounced OH-la) for hello and *adios* (ah-dee-OSE) for goodbye.

2 Introduce yourself by saying *Mi nombre es* (mee NOME-bray ess) and then your name.

3 Make copious use of *por favor* (pore fah-VORE) and *gracias* (GRAH-see-ahs) to say please and thank you.

4 Say *sí* (SEE) for yes and *no* (NOH) for no. Or just nod or shake your head.

5 Say *donde* (DONE-day), which means "where", if you're looking for something.

6 Use *yo quisiera* (yo kee-see-YARE-uh), which means "I would like", in many situations. Just point to whatever you want, remembering to tack on a *por favor* at the end.

7 If all of the above fails, ask *Habla ingles?* (AH-bla een-GLASE), or "Do you speak English?"

✻ Tip

Use the power of body language: pointing, drawing, gesturing and pantomiming will all help you get your point across.

Learn Key Phrases in German

Even if you don't speak a word of German, make the effort to memorise a few basic phrases to impress the locals.

◉ Steps

1 Use *guten tag* (pronounced GOOT-en TAK) for hello and *auf wiedersehen* (owf VEED-uh-zain) for goodbye. Or utter *servus*, which means hello or goodbye.

2 Introduce yourself by saying *Ich heisse* (ikh HEYESS-eh) and then your name.

3 Make copious use of *bitte* (BIT-eh) and *danke* (DAHNK-eh) to say please and thank you.

4 Say *ja* (ya) for yes and *nein* (neyen) for no. Of course, nodding or shaking your head works, too.

5 Say *wo* (voh), which means "where", if you're looking for something.

6 Use *Ich möchte* (ikh MERKH-teh), which means "I would like", in many situations. Just point to whatever you want, remembering to tack on a *bitte* at the end.

7 If all of the above fails, ask *Sprechen Sie Englisch?* (SHPREKH-en zee ENG-lish), or "Do you speak English?"

✱ Tip

Remember – most people will appreciate even the most rudimentary attempts to speak their language.

Learn Chinese

Chinese is a difficult language: it doesn't use the 26-letter alphabet and fluctuations of the voice can make a word mean different things.

◉ Steps

1 Immerse yourself in the Chinese culture. Move to China. Go alone without another English speaker so you are forced to learn the language. Interact with people at the local markets and on the streets.

2 Rent a flat in London's Chinatown. Get a job in the Chinese portion of town, shop there, eat there and make friends there. Be bold and speak the language.

3 Get Rosetta Stone Chinese language kits. Choose between Mandarin or other Chinese languages that Rosetta might have available. Check your local library for a free subscription. Follow the lessons. Study and talk out loud to your computer. Part of learning a language is hearing yourself speak it. Learn to fluctuate your voice.

4 Use flashcards. Write a word on one side of the sheet and the interpretation on the other side. Or write the word in Chinese and pin it up next to that object. Study with a friend. A native speaker can listen to you and let you know how you are doing as well.

5 Watch Chinese films and ignore the subtitles, then watch them again and read the subtitles.

✱ Tip

As China becomes one of the world's leading economies, more and more people are choosing to study the language.

252 Survive Your A Levels

A levels will be the death of you, as any former A leveller will gladly affirm. That is, they would be the death of you without the correct preventive measures to ensure you gracefully weather the combined storms of stress, exams and pending results. So, don't panic – here's how to survive your A levels.

CHOOSE YOUR SUBJECTS WISELY

Many students fail to thoroughly think through their choices. Merely liking a subject or having an interest in it will not guarantee you do well at it.

- Consider your GCSE results.
- Look up the relevant subject syllabuses.
- Ask any A levellers you know for their opinion on your potential subjects.
- Check university preferences/entry requirements.
- Select a subject combination that you can work with.
- Hold your breath and hope for the best.

ATTEND YOUR LESSONS AND TAKE NOTES

If you want to stand a chance of achieving a decent pass in your A levels, attending all your lessons and taking good notes is a no-brainer.

- Keep track of your notes – make sure you've got them all, and don't lend them out.
- Have notes in a format you can easily revise from.
- Investing a little time in your notes will really pay off when it comes to the exams, since you'll be less stressed and more focused on killing your exam papers.

KEEP TRACK OF YOUR WORK AND/OR COURSEWORK

It's essential to keep on top of your coursework.

- Deadlines were put in place for a reason, so work to them, as this is where you can pick up more points.
- Aim to get a high mark for your coursework units, as this significantly increases your chances of getting a good overall grade.
- Do your homework and essays – because practice does make perfect.

DON'T FORGET TO CHILL OUT

Relaxing is an important part of A-level survival.

- When it gets a bit too much, take deep breaths. Or run away.
- Take exercise and spend time with friends.
- As long as you have everything under control on the academic front, it's fine to party and have fun.
- Re-energise and then return to conquering your A levels!

EXAMS, EXAMS AND MORE EXAMS!

Within these two years, you will be sitting many very important exams. Good exam preparation is key for success.

- Make sure you are organised and start your revision early.
- Become familiar with the exam content and any relevant websites for your course
- Know what exam boards you are with and attempt all the practice exam papers available (whilst looking at the mark schemes).
- If you mucked up on your revision, play it strategically. You are entitled to retake, just decide which subject and plan accordingly.

chart

Visit Prospective Colleges · 253

Choosing a college or university is a big decision. By taking a tour of prospective colleges, you can get a better idea of the quality of life and activities offered by any particular college.

Steps

1. Make appointments in advance to meet with college advisors and to take a tour of the campus. Ideally a tour would take place in the autumn or spring, when life there is in full swing.

2. Arrive at your appointments early. This will allow some extra time before the appointment to wander around campus and browse through any books and brochures available in the administration offices. Take this time to observe how the staff and students interact.

3. Ask plenty of questions. Find out about class sizes. Ask if classes are taught primarily by professors or teaching assistants. Is the campus diverse? How is the social scene? What activities are there to do on and around campus? Find out if having a car is necessary or if you can get by without one. How are the food and the meal plans?

4. Pick up as much information as you can: financial-aid forms, course catalogues and any brochures that you can get your hands on.

5. Look at campus notice boards and calendars. Read the local newspaper. These items will give you a good idea about the everyday activities on campus, and will also give insight to the extras like concerts or parties.

6. Enquire about campus jobs. If you intend to work your way through college, get a good feel for the types of employment available on campus. If nothing looks promising on campus, check out the town.

7. Look into extracurricular programmes such as sports and societies. Arrange to attend a training session, game or competition so that you can get a good feel for the programme.

✳ Tip

By interacting with students and staff, you can get a sense of how you will be treated while attending college and what activities will be available to you. In general, if you do not feel comfortable during your visit, you will probably not feel comfortable spending three or four or years there.

Improve Your Chances of Admission to College · 254

Getting into a good university is tough, but if you plan early and work hard, you can reach your lofty goals.

Steps

1. Study hard. This is the foundation of a good school record and will also endear you to your teachers.

2. Participate in extracurricular activities. Colleges and universities look for well-rounded students who do more than just get good marks.

3. Do community service. This will make your application even more well-rounded.

4. Take difficult classes. Colleges want to see that you won't shy away from academic challenges.

5. Study for standardised tests long before you take them. The more you're prepared for the actual test, the better you'll do.

✳ Tip

Don't spread yourself too thin: instead of being slightly involved in lots of different extracurricular activities, limit yourself to one or two activities that you can really focus on.

6   Cultivate good relationships with your teachers, who will be writing recommendation letters for you.

7   Spend a lot of time thinking about and writing the essays on your college applications, as these are weighed heavily by admissions committees.

8   Be as natural as possible during any admissions interviews you might have to undergo: colleges are looking for human beings, not robots.

255 Get a Scholarship

More scholarships are available than you may think, and it's worth the time and effort to seek out relevant scholarships and apply for them.

◎ Steps

1   Start looking for scholarships at least one year before entering college or university.

2   Consider whether you are a member of an underrepresented group, in financial need, or interested in certain fields of study. Scholarships are available for those with special talents in many areas, including sports, art, science and music.

3   Think about applying for a fellowship – a scholarship for graduate students – if you want to do a postgraduate degree.

4   Recognise what you can expect from a scholarship when you apply for it. Some offer to pay all your expenses, while others only pay for room and board.

5   Be prepared to answer general questions such as name, address, national insurance number, date of birth, citizenship status and marital status.

6   Provide any necessary financial information such as total family income, number of children in your household and number of children in college.

7   Supply information about the talent required by the scholarship for which you are applying.

8   Post all the paperwork to the address listed on the application.

✳ Tip

Talk to your school college advisor; he or she is paid to help you make decisions about your future.

256 Use Distance Learning for Graduate Courses

Taking courses online gives you the freedom and flexibility to choose the colleges and subjects that interest you. This method of learning is becoming extremely popular.

◎ Steps

1   Consider earning your degree from a college or university you know well. If your old college offers distance education for graduate courses, you may feel most comfortable working within that environment.

✳ Tips

Consider price and prestige when choosing a distance-learning college. In general, registration fees for distance learning are the same as those for on-site learning.

2 Think about other places that offer courses and degrees that interest you. You may start by choosing a college you like, then going online to see if it offers distance-learning courses, or you might elect to choose a graduate course of study and then find out what colleges offer it.

3 Read through the course offerings and make sure you can earn the degree you want from that institution.

4 Check to see if you have the appropriate computer equipment before registering. The website will tell you what type of computer and equipment you need.

5 Fill out the online registration form, or call and register. Admissions committees will consider your academic and professional experience and how well their programme suits you.

6 Purchase any textbooks, DVDs, CD-ROMs or other materials required for the class. You can do this online as well.

7 Read your professor's lectures (via the web, email or conventional mail) and participate in classroom discussions in online chat rooms, on message boards or both.

8 Do your homework online and take tests. Consider all feedback, and contact your professor by email or phone if you have questions.

A fast Internet connection will make your interaction with your classmates and professor more pleasant and productive.

⚠ Warning

If you're not the self-motivated type, you might not do well with distance learning, which happens without direct interaction with other students or professors. Be realistic in assessing the likelihood that you'll be disciplined and focused.

Decide to Study Overseas   `257`

Studying overseas provides a unique opportunity to learn a new language, see the world and understand other cultures.

⊚ Steps

1 Visit your university's education office to see what colleges are available for exchange programmes. Make a list of your top choices.

2 Find out whether the colleges you like offer the right courses for you, so that you don't get behind in your studies, and whether they will be taught in English or another language.

3 Talk with the education abroad adviser about the programmes that interest you to determine how difficult it is to be accepted on them.

4 Make sure you have the necessary grades to study abroad.

5 Determine how many letters of recommendation you'll need, and think about which professors you can ask. Plan ahead.

6 Check exchange rates and living costs in the country where you want to study, and decide whether you can afford it.

7 Find out whether your current financial aid, if any, can be transferred to the education overseas.

8 Think about how living arrangements will be while you're gone. Do you have someone to sub-let your accommodation? Will your landlord or college waive your fees during the time you're overseas?

9 Determine if you have to withdraw from your university before leaving. This means you'll have to reapply when you return.

10 Prepare by brushing up on the history of the country you'll be visiting.

✳ Tips

Consider the knowledge, confidence and experience (not to mention the great addition to your CV) you'll gain from studying abroad.

Try applying with a friend if you don't think you can go it alone.

⚠ Warning

Be sure that you can be away from your family and friends for a term or year.

258 | Choose a Topic for a Dissertation

Dissertation topics are notoriously difficult to figure out, since the possibilities seem endless. Follow these steps to nail things down.

◉ Steps

1 Make a habit – as early as possible in your graduate career – of jotting down ideas for research while sitting in lectures and doing your reading. Particular findings can point to new and interesting questions.

2 Weed out ideas as the time to choose draws nearer. Consider such issues as level of interest (how excited do you get when you think about it?), practicality (too broad or too narrow?), and how significant a contribution it will make to your discipline.

3 Consult with fellow students: they may offer great ideas.

4 Ask your advisor and other professors what they know about work that's already been done on the topics that remain after your weeding-out process.

5 Find this work, and see how similar or different it is from your own ideas. If it's too similar, you've just eliminated another possibility.

6 Choose whichever of the remaining topics interests you the most.

7 Keep in mind that your topic is a work in progress, and allow yourself to be flexible. It's inevitable that some aspects of your topic will change as you progress in your research and writing.

✳ Tips

Keep your topic ideas in a central location, preferably a computer file that you can easily back up.

Consider setting yourself a deadline for finding a topic.

259 | Write a Rough Draft

In a rough draft, you get all your ideas on paper and flesh them out. You will add and delete material several times before you're satisfied that your work is complete and you're ready to write your final draft.

◉ Steps

1 Write your thesis statement and a summary of your objective at the top of a clean sheet of paper. This will become your topic paragraph after revision.

2 Approach your rough draft in sections; there's no need to concern yourself with the overall flow of the paper just yet. Each section will be a paragraph or group of paragraphs in your final draft.

3 Start with the first item on your paper outline. Write the title of this item on a sheet of paper and write all relevant ideas beneath it.

4 Write the title of the next item of your outline on a separate sheet of paper with all its relevant ideas beneath it.

5 Continue this process with all sections of the outline.

✳ Tips

Consider triple-spacing your draft. This will give you extra space between lines to write in comments or revisions.

After completing your rough draft, wait a while before returning to revise it, if possible. This will give you a fresh approach to the paper.

⚠ Warning

Don't be afraid to change your original statement completely should your paper arrive at ideas different from those you began with. Writing is discovery.

6   Tie together each item on your outline in a brief conclusion at the end of the draft. This will become the concluding paragraph after revision.

7   Spend a little time brainstorming before beginning your rough draft. Write these ideas on a sheet of paper.

8   Organise your ideas by "clustering" them. Write each idea in the centre of a page and circle it.

9   Arrange related ideas around each idea, trying to place ever-more-detailed pieces of information close to one another on the paper. This will give you some idea of how to structure your paper: if you find you have many ideas clustered in one area, you may want to focus there.

10 Make an informal paper outline to provide guidelines for the format and flow of your paper. At first, you can just list points in order. Later, you may want to arrange your information in standard outline form.

11 Do some brief, preliminary research. Consider which authors, books or quotations might offer you good supporting evidence. Save your in-depth research for draft revision.

Take Research Notes   260

Take organised research notes now, and you'll thank yourself later when writing your research paper.

⊙ Steps

1   Write down all the bibliographical information – author's name, publisher, date and place of publication – on a 3 x 5 index card when you find a source for research material you would like to use. This is your source card. Number each one.

2   Skim through each source for information on your subject.

3   Write down the information you wish to note on an index card, called an information card. Write only one piece of information per card, using a direct quote, a paraphrase or anything that will help you remember the information.

4   Jot down the page number of the source from which you got the information on the information card.

5   Number each information card to correspond to the source card of the work from which it comes so that you can always refer back to the source.

6   Organise your information cards according to subject matter. For example, if you are writing a paper about mountain wildlife, separate the cards about bears from the cards about eagles. This way, you avoid searching through the cards when writing the paper.

✳ Tips

Paraphrase information as often as possible to cut down on the number of citations you'll have to make.

Use pen rather than pencil when writing on index cards. Index cards are usually stacked and rub together, so pencil tends to smudge and become illegible.

⚠ Warning

Be scrupulous about citing your sources. If you use someone else's ideas or exact words without giving proper credit, you will be plagiarising and may be punished.

261 | Write a Research Paper

Writing a good research paper is a tough challenge, but breaking it down into smaller pieces helps a lot.

⊙ Steps

1 Choose a topic that is broad enough to be interesting but narrow enough to be manageable.

2 Find your sources. Start with three or four, check their bibliographies for additional sources, and repeat the process until you have enough material to work with.

3 Reserve one index card for each source. Record the bibliographic information for the source on its index card, and number each card for ease of future reference.

4 Take reading notes on index cards, writing down only the material that is most relevant to your project. Write the source number on each card.

5 Organise your index cards by topic and sub-topic.

6 Write an introduction that grabs the reader and plots out the trajectory of your argument.

7 Write the body of the paper, following the structure you created in your outline. Make sure you correctly cite your sources.

8 Write the conclusion, reviewing how you've made your points.

9 Come up with a title after you've written the paper, not before: you don't want the content of the paper to be hamstrung by an inappropriate title.

10 Read your paper at least twice to be sure your argument makes sense and is presented logically.

11 Proofread carefully – teachers hate typographical errors.

✱ Tip

Don't leave such a difficult task to the last minute. Start early, and work gradually.

262 | Understand Quantum Physics

As more than one notable scientist has observed, anyone who thinks he understands quantum physics really doesn't. With that proviso in mind, here's a quick introduction to this abstruse discipline.

⊙ Steps

1 Know that particles can be both "solid" and "wavy". You might think of a proton (one of the components of the atomic nucleus) as being like a snooker ball, but it in fact has a tenuous "wave" component, just like light. Physicists have shown that beams of protons or electrons will interfere with themselves, proving that these subatomic particles aren't "solid" and have some wave-like properties.

2 Know that you can't measure a particle's momentum and position with arbitrary accuracy. Known as the Heisenberg Uncertainty Principle, this law dictates that the more accurately you measure the location of, say, an electron, the more its momentum (and hence its energy) will increase, and

⚠ Warning

Quantum physics is one of the most interesting branches of science, but it takes time and patience to understand it.

vice versa. This doesn't reflect a limitation of our ability to measure particles; rather, quantum physics itself places limits on what can be measured.

3   Know that distant particles can be "entangled". A particle light years away can instantaneously "know" what a companion particle on Earth has done, without light having had time to convey the information. This property – which has given physicists and philosophers fits for decades – has been experimentally demonstrated, and is known as "entanglement".

4   Know that there's an innate element of probability. Unlike classical physics, in which you can, at least theoretically, calculate the future state of a system from the present configuration of all its particles, quantum physics has improbability at its very core. For example, it's impossible to predict exactly when an atom of a radioactive isotope will decay (which is a quantum process), only the probability that this will happen in any given time.

5   Understand that quantum physics is weird, but it isn't mystical. Despite all those bestselling books you see, quantum physics does not open some kind of "back door" to telepathy or reincarnation. In other words, just because scientists don't understand everything about quantum physics doesn't mean that it's somehow "beyond science".

Set Personal Goals   263

We all have different things we want to accomplish during our lifetimes. Whatever it is you hope to achieve, it's a good idea to keep a list of these objectives.

⊙ Steps

1   Start off by writing down some long-term goals. These should be things you hope to accomplish sometime down the road, perhaps 20 to 25 years into the future. The exact nature of these goals will be determined by your age. Somebody under the age of 20 may list items such as "having a family and a great career" as personal goals. A person over the age of 40, on the other hand, may write down "be retired" as one of his or her long-term goals.

2   Map out each of your long-term goals. List goals you will need to achieve through the years in order to reach your overall objective. For example, if one of your long-term goals is to have X amount of money saved, write down things you will need to do in the next five, 10 and 15 years.

3   Think about a few things you want to achieve in the present and list those as your short-term goals. Getting in shape is a common example of one of these objectives. Every item on this list should be a goal that can be achieved in the next six months. Map out different things you will need to do in order to reach these goals.

4   Write down different obstacles that may prevent you reaching your goals. These could personal weaknesses, such as fears or your (lack of) work ethic. Obstacles can also be practical things, such as money or time. Be honest with yourself when listing these items. Only then will you be able to overcome them and achieve your goals.

✱ Tip

List personal goals in different categories. Examples could be "financial goals", "academic goals" and "career goals".

⚠ Warning

Don't put a timetable on goals regarding your personal life. It's fine to say that you want to be married and have a family 20 to 25 years down the road. However, stating that you want to be married and have kids by the time you're 25 and no later is unrealistic.

264 | Find a Job While in College

Having a part-time job while you are in college will give you greater financial independence and real-world experience.

Steps

1 Determine your available hours and the minimum salary you need.

2 Prepare your CV before you even begin to look for a job. You will then be able to apply immediately when you find a job opening.

3 Check the student centre for a list of part-time jobs on campus, including clerical, bookshop and cafeteria positions.

4 Ask the managers of shops near your campus about possible job openings. Consider working for establishments where you can get food or clothing at a discount.

5 Go through the classified employment ads of your college paper and the local paper.

6 Consult with your departmental advisor about any available paid internships. Many degrees require internships anyway, so it makes sense to combine part-time work and experience in your future field. But be aware that many internships are unpaid.

⚠ Warnings

Be aware that on-campus jobs generally pay low hourly wages. However, they offer the convenience of being close to your lectures.

Don't wait until well into the term to look for a job. The good ones will get snapped up early.

265 | Find Cheap Textbooks

Textbooks can cost a lot of money, but you don't have to pay a lot. Take some time to look around and you're bound to find some good deals.

Steps

1 Find out as early as possible which textbooks you'll need for your course.

2 Ask older friends who may have taken the course in recent years if they've kept the old textbook or books.

3 Look for used textbooks at your campus bookshop. They should be clearly marked "Used"

4 Check out other bookshops with used collections and scour them for the books you need.

5 Visit used-book websites and buy from them.

6 Be patient, and don't expect to find all your books in one place. That's the nature of bargain hunting.

✳ Tips

Start looking early. It can take some time to find the best deal.

The Internet is a great resource for cheap books; the proliferation second-hand book sites has made finding inexpensive textbooks much easier than it used to be.

Decide Whether to Live On or Off Campus

266

Many factors can influence your decision to live on or off campus. Consider the following carefully before committing to a housing choice.

⊙ Steps

1 Determine your budget for your monthly rent and compare the options. If finances are the issue, your choice will usually be dictated for you.

2 Decide which would benefit you more socially, intellectually and/ or physically.

3 Think about the ages of those who would likely live around you, and whether you have similar interests.

4 Consider your transport options, taking into account relevant expense and convenience.

5 Figure into your decision any work and family concerns.

6 Evaluate each environment to make sure it meets your standards for noise, pollution, security and safety.

✳ Tip

Make the extra stretch to live somewhere you like. It's important to go home each day to a place in which you feel comfortable.

⚠ Warning

Don't sign a lease that leaves you no escape clause. You always need an out in case something awful happens.

Overcome a Lack of Academic Confidence

267

One of the scariest things about starting college or university is the sense that everyone is cleverer than you.

⊙ Steps

1 Realise that most people who seem overly intelligent aren't any cleverer than anyone else. It's often just a matter of presentation.

2 Recognise that you have your own kind of intelligence, which might not be measured well by standardised tests or "normal" marking criteria.

3 Tell yourself that you're not going to be intimidated by people who appear, in your eyes, to be more intelligent than you.

4 Take the high ground: if someone tries to make you look stupid, realise it's probably that person's insecurities coming through and has nothing to do with your intelligence.

5 Study – your feelings of intellectual inferiority may stem from being less prepared than your fellow students, not less intelligent.

6 Contact your school's academic counselling office. The professionals there have a wealth of advice for you.

✳ Tips

Remember that you're not alone. People often feel stupid in the world of academia, but it rarely has anything to do with intelligence.

Keep in mind that standardised tests and normal marking criteria don't measure your potential or how hard you tried.

268 | Make a Speech Memorable

Speaking at an event is an honour, whether you're delivering an educational discourse or a corporate lecture. Employ several public-speaking strategies to connect with audience members and help commit the most important points of your speech to their memory.

⊙ Steps

1   Determine one point you'd like the audience to remember and build around it. Discuss it immediately in the introduction and again during your conclusion. Try to limit your other essential ideas to three so the speech will be easier to organise, write and follow.

2   Include humour, personal experiences or powerful anecdotes with which audience members can identify.

3   Consider the age and background of your audience as you write. You want your speech remembered for the right reasons, not because of its abundance of off-colour jokes or inappropriate anecdotes.

4   Reference touching or humorous stories from books and films, or borrow effective snippets from historical speeches if they fit with your subject. If you found them memorable, so will your audience. Remember to give credit to the original source.

5   Encourage audience participation to keep the crowd involved. Ask them to repeat key words or finish popular phrases. Ask questions with predictable answers that can help emphasise your point.

6   Devise a catchphrase, buzzword or creative last line that the audience will remember and repeat to others.

7   Use hand gestures. Body language is an important part of speech-making.

8   Practise until your voice, tone, hand gestures and facial expressions are relaxed and natural. Memorise anecdotes so you can deliver them without reading the cue cards.

9   Recite your speech in front of friends and family before you speak in public. Discuss which points they consider most memorable. Rework any sections that don't have as much emotional impact as you'd like.

✳ Tip

Acknowledge that everyone experiences some anxiety before public speaking and do it anyway.

⚠ Warnings

Don't picture people naked to control nerves. You could get a case of the giggles.

Don't make a speech on a topic that you are not prepared to answer questions on. Your audience will know.

Open with a joke only when it is appropriate, and use a tasteful joke.

Buy an HDTV

269

HDTV, or high-definition television, uses digital signals broadcast by television networks and stations. If the digital signal is received by the right product, the result is great picture and sound quality.

☀ Tip

Some of the best deals are available online, but check out your favourites in a shop first.

◉ Steps

1　Determine if the HDTV signal is being broadcast in your area.

2　Consider the cost. Initially these products may cost as much as £5,000.

3　Decide if you want to buy a product that has a digital decoder. This decision will depend on whether you want to purchase accessories. If you buy a decoder, you can connect it to your present television, but it will not get HDTV-quality pictures. Or you can buy the whole shebang and still receive the standard television signals being broadcast by stations in your area.

4　Purchase a set that has full Dolby Digital Surround Sound, an electronic programme guide, and automatic switching that will allow you to go back and forth between HDTV and SDTV.

5　Select a rooftop aerial that is compatible with HDTV. If you own a satellite system, you will have to buy another one that's designed for use with HDTV.

6　Ask the salesperson to demonstrate a few sets for you. Then take the remote yourself and work the sets.

Choose a Screen Size for a Plasma TV

270

One of the main considerations when shopping around for a plasma TV is its screen size. If the size is inappropriate, you might regret it for years to come.

☀ Tips

Selecting a screen size that is too large for your room may not be a good decision. As time goes by, the pixels on the screen become more prominent when viewed from shorter distances.

Remember that screen sizes are measured diagonally and not horizontally.

◉ Steps

1　Measure the dimensions of the room where you plan to put your TV. Depending on the viewing distance you may decide that one size is better than another. Use the following as a guide:

Viewing distance / Suggested screen size

1.8–2 m (6–7 ft) / 30 in

2–2.4 m (7–8 ft) / 35 in

2.4–2.7 m (8–9 ft) / 40 in

2.7–3 m (9–10 ft) / 45 in

3–3.3 m (10–11 ft) / 50 in

3.3–3.6 m (11–12 ft) / 55 in

3.6 m (12 ft) and above / 60 in or 65 in

2   Check the availability of space in the area where you are going to place your TV. Don't crowd yourself. However, if you happen to be a party person and like to invite friends over every weekend, you may want to opt for a larger screen size even if there is a space constraint.

3   Plan your budget carefully when you buy a plasma TV. Bigger screen sizes can cost much more than the smaller ones.

4   Determine the alternative uses of your plasma TV. If you plan to conduct presentations via computer or play interactive games, the size of the screen could matter even more.

271 Fix a Remote Control

A couch potato without a remote control is like a king or queen without a sceptre, but what do you do if the sceptre is broken?

⊙ **Steps**

1   Open the remote and confirm that the batteries are there.

2   Assuming the batteries are present and not caked in acid (a bad thing), double-check that they are inserted correctly. Someone could have dropped your remote and hastily scooped up the batteries, then surreptitiously reinstalled them the wrong way.

3   While you're checking the battery installation, make sure that the contacts for the batteries aren't corroded or bent. You can clean them with a pencil eraser followed by a nail file. If necessary, gently bend them back to their correct position.

4   Try a fresh pair of batteries. Be sure to put them in the right way.

5   If your remote is a universal model that can be programmed to control multiple devices, consult the manual to find out how to reinitialise it. Maybe it has forgotten its codes.

6   Check to see if the problem is with the TV or another component that you're trying to control. Try unplugging it for a minute and plugging it back in. Some VCRs have a "parental" mode that locks a remote and/or "timer" modes that shut down a remote until the mode is turned off.

7   Test to see if the remote is getting interference from other electrical devices in the room. To do this, turn off absolutely everything except the device you're trying to control.

✳ **Tip**

Remote controls are so attractive to dogs that they might as well be bone-shaped. If Spot ruins yours, consider replacing it with a programmable model.

272 Fix Cable TV

Even if you have no experience with or knowledge of electronics, it may be possible for you to fix your cable TV by following some simple steps.

⊙ **Steps**

1   Make sure all connections are set up correctly. No cables should be loose or broken, outlets should be hot (working properly) and all connections

✳ **Tip**

Turning the box off will not work as a replacement for rebooting the system. You need to cut all connections to the system.

should be coming in and out of the proper outlets and hook-up plugs. Unplug and replace cables to make sure they are hooked up correctly.

2   Reboot your cable TV box if you get an error message or if the image freezes for longer than a minute. The easiest way to reboot your cable TV is to unplug the box from the electrical outlet and then wait about 60 seconds before plugging it back in.

3   Look in your cable manual to see if there are specific issues that can be related to the cable box itself. Depending on the model, your cable may produce error messages when connections become loose or split, or when the signal is weak.

4   Don't do anything if you get an error message related to the signal or if you experience small problems such as the sound coming on and off. These issues are probably due to technical difficulties within the cable company itself, rather than a problem with your personal set-up.

5   Replace your coaxial cable if it has become bent or open. This may cause loss of signal, which can affect the quality of the image or cause it to disappear completely. Coaxial cable is available for sale at any electronics shop, and replacing it should be an easy task, even for those who have no experience with electrical appliances.

Set Parental Controls on a DVD Player   273

The parental-control settings are password-protected on a DVD player so that children can't access the content.

⊚ Steps

1   Press Setup on your remote control to go to the system settings menu on your TV screen. Use the left or right arrows on your remote to go to the Preference page.

2   Scroll down the menu with the up or down arrows until you get to Parental. Choose this option using the right arrow button on the remote. This will take you to the parental settings menu on the screen.

3   Use the up or down arrows to choose a setting for your DVD player. Hit OK to confirm that the DVD player is preset to Level 8 for adults.

4   Change the parental levels whenever you play a new disc. Go back to the Preference page from your remote. Use the down arrow to go to Parental, and then choose the right arrow again to select the parental option.

5   Choose your rating level from the right side of your TV screen. Using the up or down arrows on your remote, pick 1 for Kid Safe, 4 for PG-13, or 6 for R. Press the OK button on your remote to confirm your new setting.

6   Enter a six-digit password so that children can't access the DVD. Type in any numbers from 1 to 9 using the alphanumeric keypad on your remote. Select the OK button to confirm your password. Press Setup to exit the Preference page, and then the Setup main menu to start watching your DVD.

✳ Tip

Write your password on a piece of paper and put it in a safe place because this password cannot be changed.

✓ 274 Troubleshoot a DVD Player

Although DVD players may look like their CD-playing cousins, they're run on a very different kind of optical technology. And thanks to the audio and video demands of movies, they're also more complicated to set up. Use these points to identify and resolve your DVD problems.

INTERMITTENT OR NO SOUND, WEAK VOLUME, POOR SOUND QUALITY

- Check the audio connections to make sure they're secure.
- Replace the cable connecting the DVD unit to your receiver.
- Clean the contacts on the player and receiver with electronics-grade contact cleaner, which can be bought at most electronics outlets.

VIDEO IMAGES BREAKING UP OR FREEZING

- Make sure the DVD is clean and unscratched. DVDs can be cleaned in the same way that CDs can, but they are more fragile and more sensitive to scratches than CDs are.
- If your disc is smudged simply wipe it over with a soft, clean cloth.
- Small scratches can be improved by wiping, but a seriously scratched DVD should probably be ditched altogether – there's little you can do to solve the problem.

DVD DISC NOT RECOGNISED AFTER LOADING

- Check that the disc is loaded the correct way.
- Check that the disc is encoded for your geographical region. A disc from North America (Region 1) won't play on a European (Region 2) player.
- Turn off the player with the disc inserted. Unplug the player from the wall outlet and then plug it back in and switch it on.
- If your player has a transportation lock (usually a plastic screw on the bottom of the unit), make sure that it is not engaged.
- If you have an older DVD player, check with the manufacturer to see whether an update to the firmware is available. Many newer DVD titles with lots of special features are well-known for causing problems on older players, so you may need an upgrade.

OTHER TECHNICAL DIFFICULTIES

- If films are playing with the subtitles on, go to the disc's menu and turn off the subtitles (this setting is usually found somewhere in the main menu page). Some players will let you turn off subtitles by pressing the Subtitle button on the remote and then pressing 0 or Clear.
- If your picture is squished, check the player's setup menu to make sure it's not set for a wide-screen TV if you don't have one.
- If the CD-R disc isn't recognised after loading, be aware that most DVD players can't read CD-R discs, even if they can play normal CDs.
- If your picture quality alternates between light and dark, this can sometimes be caused by the Macrovision copy-protection scheme, and may result from copying the DVD video to VCR or if you hook up a DVD to the TV by way of your VCR.

chart

Clean a Slot-Load DVD Player — 275

You've had your DVD player for a while and suddenly the films don't want to play or they keep skipping. What do you do?

Steps

1   Get a blank CD and rub some rubbing alcohol on it; insert the CD into the DVD player.

2   Open the door and blow into it. You can also use a hairdryer for this.

3   If that doesn't help, take a screwdriver and open the top of the DVD; carefully remove the lens cover. Make sure the player is unplugged before you do this.

4   Take a cotton swab with a bit of alcohol and pass over it. Put the cover back on the DVD player.

⚠ Warning

Opening the DVD player has its risks and it is always best to try to find alternative ways to clean the player.

Play a DVD on Your Computer — 276

It's simple to play a DVD on your computer, as long as you have a DVD drive and the appropriate software.

Steps

1   Check the compatibility of your drive with the DVD. You must have a drive that supports the DVD format. If not, then get a DVD drive installed on your computer.

2   Insert the DVD in the drive. A menu will appear on your desktop asking to play the DVD video using Media Player or a similar media software program. Click the option available. If you get a message saying Format Not Supported you may need to download and install a DVD decoder.

3   Surf online to get a decoder, if necessary. Google or Yahoo search engines will help. Download and install a compatible DVD decoder. For Windows, software like PowerDVD or WinDVD can be used. If you use a Mac OS X, then VLC media player/Videolan is adequate for the task.

4   Select the full screen option once the film starts playing. Learn the different keys and shortcuts to enhance your DVD viewing experience.

5   Adjust the brightness, colour and contrast to suit your requirements.

6   Check all the settings and new options in order to have a perfect picture.

7   Scroll and explore the menu by right-clicking on the DVD screen.

8   Fine-tune the volume by clicking on the speaker icon from the task bar on your desktop.

✳ Tip

If you plan to get a new DVD drive, buy a DVD/CD RW combo drive. These are reasonably priced and provide you with the added functionality of burning CDs.

⚠ Warning

Install anti-virus in your machine prior to inserting any disc.

277 Install a DVD Burner in a Home Computer

Installing a DVD burner in a home computer is a task that can be undertaken by anyone with a simple understanding of electronics assembly.

⊙ **Steps**

1 Ensure that the computer is completely off, discharged and unplugged.

2 Open the computer case by removing the screws at the rear corners or the thumbscrews on the rear side. Each case may be different. Obtain entry into the case enclosure.

3 Remove the ribbon cable from the rear of the existing CD or CD recorder. Leave the ribbon cable attached to the computer motherboard if the DVD burner's manufacturer has not supplied a new ribbon cable.

4 Disconnect the power cable from the existing CD or CD recorder. This will be a four-wired connector, usually at the left rear of the component.

5 Remove any CD audio cable from the rear of the existing component. This cable is usually located at the right rear.

6 Remove any retaining screws or brackets from the existing component. Slide the unit out of the computer.

7 Insert the DVD burner into the open slot.

8 Connect the ribbon cable to the rear of the DVD burner.

9 Connect the DVD audio cable to the rear of the DVD burner.

10 Connect the power-supply cable to the rear of the DVD burner.

11 Install any DVD burner drivers or software provided with DVD burner unit.

✳ **Tips**

Refer to the DVD burner's manual for the best results.

Wear a protective ESD (electrostatic discharge) strap when working with electronic components.

⚠ **Warnings**

Ensure that the computer has no power to the unit.

Connect all cables correctly and replace any frayed or damaged cables.

278 Buy a Blu-Ray Player

Blu-ray discs have become the new standard for home entertainment. When replacing your DVD player with a blu-ray player, what should you look for?

⊙ **Steps**

1 Consider purchasing a Sony PlayStation 3. This gaming system includes excellent blu-ray disc-playing capabilities.

2 Visit your local electronics store to see what is available. Ask a sales associate to explain the differences between players and features, and why some players are more expensive than others.

3 Look for well-known brand names when selecting a blu-ray player. Sony is considered the leader in blu-ray technology, but other well-known brands also make a good product. You get what you pay for.

4 Search online for product reviews when you narrow your selection to a few blu-ray players. The Internet is a great resource to find reviews from both experts and consumers.

✳ **Tip**

Decide what options are essential for you. If you have a very good quality HD television and will spare no expense for the best clarity possible, you're looking at spending a lot of money.

5 Understand that the crisp picture and quality sound for which blu-ray discs are praised are only evident when supported by high-quality equipment. If you have a HDTV with surround sound, you will definitely notice a difference between a blu-ray and a DVD. However, a blu-ray player is unlikely to improve your media experience if you have a tube television.

Buy a State-of-the-Art Sound System | 279

If music is important to you then having the best-quality sound may be your top priority. Here's how to splash out on the very best...

Steps

1 Let your listening habits and desires be your guide. You should assemble a system that sounds great to you, not a salesperson.

2 Assess your living and work spaces. A system that sounds incredible in a small demonstration room might sound poor in a large, high-ceilinged living room.

3 Take your own music with you when you shop. You'll know the nuances of that music better than the demo CDs designed to highlight an audio system's strengths.

4 Listen to systems without regard to price range, at least at first. You want to hear why prices vary so much. Try to listen to various components in isolation. If you're comparing two amplifiers, use the same CD player, CD and speakers during your test.

5 Select a system with separate components (including amplifiers and preamps). Each component should have its own power supply to reduce electrical interference between components. Get a power conditioner to further reduce interference.

6 Splurge on speakers if you're making budget trade-offs. Crank up the music as loud as you're likely to play it at home.

7 Shop for a digital audio receiver if you want your stereo to play Internet-based music or MP3s from your computer. Digital audio receivers are a new and varied breed of component. Some connect directly to the Internet via your broadband connection; others connect via your computer and can access MP3s on your hard drive. They require a network connection in addition to stereo cables.

8 Buy high-quality cables. It makes little sense to connect top-end audio components with pound-shop cables.

9 Link your high-end audio system into your whole-house media and control systems.

✱ Tips

If you want to provide more power to your speakers, purchase a pre-amplifier.

Ask the stereo salesperson for advice on the best sound equipment for the size, shape and building materials of your particular room. A rough estimate of the room's dimensions should be fine.

✓ 280 Set Up a Home Entertainment Centre

This feature explains how to set up a home entertainment centre for all your audio-visual entertainment needs. It discusses all the key elements of a home theatre and how they come together to create an entertainment room that will blow everyone away.

The Components

- The centre of any home entertainment centre is the TV. If you already have a good-sized TV you may want to hang on to it for now, but older televisions cannot compare to the brightness and clarity of today's high-definition models. Alternately you may want to consider a projector as a replacement for your TV.

- A surround-sound receiver (the amplifier that everything hooks into) is essential to a home theatre. You will want one that has high-definition outputs and has an input for every device in your home theatre. This means that if you will have a DVD player, a gaming system, a cable box and a CD player you will need at least three video and audio inputs and one audio only.

- You will also need speakers to go with your stereo. These include front left and right, a centre channel, rear/surround left and rights, and preferably a subwoofer.

- You may want to consider a media centre computer for your entertainment system. These allow you to have your whole music collection at your fingertips, watch movies via the Internet on your big screen, play DVDs and computer games on your home theatre, listen to Internet radio through your stereo and surf the Internet from the comfort of your sofa.

- Now come all the basic components – DVD player, VCR, cable box, CD player, gaming systems, etc.

- You will probably want a piece of furniture to house everything. If you have a projector, then all you really need is a small shelf for all the components to sit on and maybe a wall or ceiling mount for the projector.

Setting Up

- Taking stock of what A/V components you already have can help you figure out what you need to make your home entertainment centre complete. Deciding on a budget for your home theatre is also important, since you don't want to blow all your money on just one component.

- Take a look at the space where the entertainment centre will reside. There needs to be plenty of space for the TV and front speakers as well as a stack of all your other components like the receiver and DVD player. You need an outlet close by to power everything. Take some measurements of the space so you know how much room you have when you buy a shelf for everything to go on.

- Now it's time to set everything up. Put all your components on the opposite side of the room and put your shelf in place, leaving plenty of room behind it to hook everything up.

- Now put all the components in their place. To avoid confusion do not hook any wires up until everything is where you want it to be.

- Now interconnect all your components. Try and use the highest-quality connections for each item, here is a guide starting at the best quality: VIDEO: high definition, S-video, RCA component, coaxial; AUDIO: fibre optic, SPDIF coaxial, shielded RCA, headphone-type plugs. If you need any extra wires make sure you measure how long they need to be and make a list.

- Finally, plug everything in to a surge protecting power strip. This will protect both you and your equipment from power surges.

reference

Buy Wireless Headphones   281

Offered in a variety of styles and a range of prices, wireless headphones are manufactured by most major electronics brands and can be bought in most electronics stores.

⊙ Steps

1   Set an appropriate budget for wireless headphones. The major electronics brands offer wireless headphones that fit most budgets, although the more expensive sets offer greater range and better reception.

2   Decide what kind of wireless headphones you'd like to buy depending on how you plan to use them. There are two basic types of wireless headphones: infrared and radio frequency. Infrared headphones require the user to be in the line of sight of the transmitter, limiting roaming capability and range. Although roaming is limited, the reception of infrared wireless headphones is superior. If you plan to use wireless headphones in the same room as your electronics, infrared headphones are a great option. Radio frequency wireless headphones offer great range and the capability for use on different floors in a building; however, the reception can be sub-standard.

3   Try on the wireless headphones that appeal to you. Ensure that the fit is comfortable, that the headphones are adjustable and that they are lightweight.

4   Test the wireless headphones before you purchase them. Many electronics stores offer product testing, so take advantage of this. If buying on the Internet, attempt to find the same headphones in a shop near you so you can test the sound quality.

5   Ask about refund and return policies before you buy to insure your investment. Try the purchased wireless headphones at home to ensure proper working order.

✴ Tip

As with most electronics equipment, bear in mind that with headphones you generally get what you pay for. It's usually worth shelling out those extra few pounds.

Clean a Vinyl Record   282

Are your vinyl records getting dusty? Let your records spin well into the future by keeping them clean.

⊙ Steps

1   Acquire all the materials you need: a record-cleaning pad or carbon-fibre record brush and record-cleaning fluid. Optionally, get an anti-static gun and record-cleaning machine.

2   Clean the stylus first, if necessary.

3   Place the record on the turntable, handling it by its edges and label area.

4   Use an anti-static gun if you have one to neutralise dust.

5   Dry-clean the record if it is not very dusty and has been cleaned regularly.

6   Follow the manufacturer's instructions for applying fluid if you decide on wet-cleaning.

Things You'll Need

❑ Anti-static gun

❑ Record-cleaning machine

❑ Record-cleaning pad

❑ Record-cleaning brush

❑ Record-cleaning solution

❑ Turntables

❑ Vinyl records

7   Hold the ends of a brush or pad between your fingers. Manually rotate the platter in a clockwise direction while pressing the cleaning brush gently into the grooves.

8   Sweep the brush up and away to lift dust from the record surface.

9   Use a brush holder, credit card or similar object to scrape dust off the brush – do this away from the turntable.

10 Repeat until you can't see any dust on the record.

283 | Buy an MP3 Player

An MP3 player is the perfect tool for people on the go who have moved their music collections on to their computers. The Apple iPod is undoubtedly the most popular, but there are many others.

⊙ Steps

1   Shop for price. MP3 players range from £40 to £300.

2   Get a player with as much storage as you can afford. The more storage, the more music it can hold. One minute of MP3 music takes up about 1 megabyte (MB) of memory, so a 128 MB MP3 player can hold about two hours of tunes.

3   Make sure any potential purchase works with your computer. Many MP3 players don't work with Macintosh computers.

4   Try the controls. Less-expensive players often have control panels that can charitably be described as "minimalist". Make sure they make sense to you.

5   Pick up the unit to gauge its size and weight. Would it be comfortable in your pocket or on your belt? How about when you're moving around?

6   Check out the player's advertised battery life. Manufacturers' claims aren't exact, but they can be used for comparison.

7   Choose a unit with USB or FireWire, rather than a parallel connection to your computer. USB and FireWire are fast and flexible.

8   Look for a player with an FM radio receiver. Some models can record music from the radio, and will identify the artist and title the next time you connect the player to your computer. Some also double as digital voice recorders.

9   Look for expandable storage, especially on units without much built-in memory. CompactFlash, MemoryStick and SecureDigital media are common choices. Newer models with more storage have internal hard disks that can store computer data.

10 Have a listen. MP3 players use standard stereo headphones. If you don't like the headphones that come with a player, there are a variety of styles you can purchase.

✳ Tips

A few high-end MP3 players have built-in FM transmitters to send music wirelessly to a car stereo. You can do the same with a pocket-sized FM transmitter.

Some MP3 players double as portable CD players, so you can burn your MP3 files to a CD and pop it in the player.

⚠ Warning

The legalities of MP3 music-swapping are constantly changing, but please respect the work of the artists.

Find out the Generation of Your iPod   284

Before you buy any accessories for your Apple iPod, you will
need to know which generation it is. This is easily done by
looking at a few key features.

⊙ **Steps**

1   Check whether your iPod has a scroll wheel or a touchpad. First-
    generation iPods have a mechanical scroll wheel that actually moves
    around. In all later generations, there is simply a touch-sensitive pad.
    If you have a moving scroll wheel, you have a first-generation iPod

2   Check to see if the Menu, Play/Pause and Skip buttons form a ring
    around the scroll pad. On a second-generation iPod, the scroll wheel is
    touch-sensitive and the Menu, Play/Pause and Skip buttons form a ring
    around it but are not actually attached to the pad.

3   Check to see if the Menu, Play/Pause and Skip buttons are arranged in
    a line just under the screen. This is a characteristic of a third-generation
    iPod. Additionally, these buttons are touch-sensitive and do not click in
    when pressed.

4   Check to see if the Menu, Play/Pause and Skip buttons are part of the
    scroll wheel itself. The fourth-generation iPod has the Menu, Play/Pause
    and Skip buttons on the scroll wheel itself. iPod Minis are also counted as
    fourth generation. Most devices that work for the larger fourth-generation
    iPods work for the minis as well.

5   Check your screen. The iPod video is the fifth generation and it has a
    colour screen and comes in 30 to 60 GB sizes.

6   The sixth generation is the iPod Classic, and doesn't look much different
    to the 5G, but comes with larger memory options.

7   Check the accessories to see if they work with iPod Nano. The iPod Nano
    is in a class of its own and only accessories that say they work with the
    Nano are guaranteed to do so.

❋ Tip

The iPod was launched in 2001
and has since gone through six
'generations' – online charts can
help you identify your iPod using
visual references.

⚠ Warning

Bear in mind that other iPods
exist, including the iPod Touch
and the Shuffle. These have their
own set of generations.

Reset Your iPod   285

Resetting the iPod is similar to rebooting a computer, as all
songs and data stored on the device stay there, and only
temporary information is reset.

⊙ **Steps**

Click-Wheel iPods

1   Toggle the Hold switch to the On position, then Off. The Hold switch is
    the small sliding switch on the top of the iPod. Move it to the On position
    to show an orange rectangle. Move it back to the Off position to show a
    white rectangle.

2   Hold the Menu and Centre buttons. Press the buttons at the same time
    for between eight and 10 seconds. Your screen will go blank and then

❋ Tip

If your iPod is under warranty,
you can have it serviced through
AppleCare. If your iPod is not
covered under warranty, other
repair service providers may be
able to fix the error.

boot up with a dark Apple icon. The icon eventually turns bright and brings you back to your main menu once the reset is complete.

3   Check your iPod to make sure it plays properly. If the iPod still does not work, repeat the reset process.

Scroll-Wheel and Touch-Wheel iPods

1   Move the Hold switch from On to Off.

2   Press the Play/Pause button and the Menu button at the same time. Press both buttons together for approximately six to eight seconds. This initiates the self-running reset process.

3   Make sure the reset was successful. If problems persist you may need to perform the reset process once again.

iPod Nano

1   Move the On/Off switch to the Off position that shows the green strip. Leave the iPod Nano in this position for five seconds.

2   Move the switch back to the On position.

3   Use your iPod Nano to make sure the reset worked properly and all your music is intact.

286 Sync Calendar Events to Your iPod

Follow the steps below to sync your schedule to your iPod so it is right there at your fingertips when you're on the go.

⊙ Steps

1   Connect your iPod to your computer using the iPod's USB connector cable (supplied with the iPod).

2   Open iTunes if it doesn't automatically launch.

3   Select your iPod under Devices on the left-hand menu in iTunes.

4   Select the Contacts tab in the main iTunes window. This should be the second tab from the right.

5   Select Sync iCal Calendars. This is the only calendar option, located beneath the options for Contacts.

6   Click Apply in the bottom right-hand corner.

7   Eject your iPod from iTunes.

8   Disconnect your iPod from your computer when it is ready. All your calendar dates should now be on your iPod.

✳ Tip

As long as the Sync iCal Calendars option is selected, new calendar events will automatically be added to your iPod whenever you connect it to your computer.

⚠ Warnings

Update the software on your iPod. Sometimes, even slightly out-of-date iPod software can cause problems with newer versions of iTunes.

Be sure you have enough extra space on your iPod to hold the calendar information.

Add Album Artwork to Songs in iTunes   287

Knowing how to add album artwork to songs in iTunes helps you keep your music folders, libraries and playlists as organised as possible.

⊙ Steps

1   Locate the iTunes icon on your computer's desktop or on one of the icon toolbars on the bottom of your screen. Open iTunes so that you can take the following actions.

2   Scroll through the songs in your music library. When you find the song that you would like to edit, highlight it with the mouse.

3   Go to the File menu and choose the command Get Info. This allows you to access the identification information for that particular song.

4   The info screen for that particular song will now appear. This screen will have several text boxes to record the song's information. At the top of this screen are five tabs. Click the last tab, which says Artwork.

5   You'll see a window that shows artwork already stored with this song, or the window may be empty if no artwork is available. Click on the Add button at the bottom of the screen to browse for more artwork to add to this song. When you find the picture you like highlight it and hit Enter.

6   When you have finished with this screen you can click OK to apply all the new management changes or you can click Cancel to exit without applying any of the changes you may have ticked.

✳ Tips

You can choose any picture file from your computer to symbolise a song.

Files that you download through iTunes already come with correct ID3 tags and album art.

⚠ Warning

Depending on the settings of your iPod's automatic organisation features, changing the ID3 information of a song may have an effect on where iTunes chooses to store that particular song.

Use a Digital FM Transmitter   288

To use your MP3 player in your car or on your home stereo system you can use a cost-effective FM transmitter, which broadcasts a short FM transmission of the songs playing on your MP3 player.

⊙ Steps

1   Purchase a digital FM transmitter for your MP3 player.

2   Plug in your MP3 player.

3   Set the transmission frequency on the FM transmitter to a non-used station (most transmitters suggest an ideal frequency).

4   Tune your FM receiver to the FM transmission station.

5   Listen to your MP3 station.

⚠ Warning

Not all transmitters are compatible with all MP3 players. Verify that your MP3 player is listed as a compatible device before buying the transmitter.

289 | Sync an iPhone

An iPhone can carry much of the information you have on your computer, especially your contacts, and music and videos from your iTunes library. Your iPhone can also collect your calendar items, photos, email and Safari web browser bookmarks.

⊙ Steps

1   Connect your iPhone with its USB2 connector to a computer that has iTunes. iTunes will show a window with several tabs for syncing your iPhone. A capacity bar at the bottom of the window lets you know how much space is available.

2   Select the contacts you want synced with your iPhone under the Info tab in iTunes. You can sync all contacts or just selected groups.

3   Choose which iCal calendars you want to sync under the Info tab. iTunes will also let you sync calendars from Entourage on a Mac or Outlook on a PC. Under the Info tab, you can also choose to sync email accounts and Safari bookmarks

4   Pick whether you want to sync all songs or just selected playlists under the Music tab. Check whether you want to include music videos.

5   Check which photos you want to sync to your iPhone under the Photos tab. You can choose to sync all photos from iPhoto or just selected albums.

6   Identify which podcasts and videos you want to sync under the Podcasts and Videos tabs respectively. Under each tab, you will have the option to sync all podcasts and videos or just ones you haven't heard or seen yet.

7   Click on the Sync button at the bottom of the window once you have determined what information you want on your iPhone.

✳ Tip

The sync feature is especially helpful with podcasts and audio books, because the iPhone will automatically remember the point in the track where you last finished and start playing again from that position the next time you listen.

290 | Make Custom iPhone Ringtones

With a little bit of trickery you can create ringtones from any one of your non-DRM songs in your iTunes library easily, and for free.

⊙ Steps

1   Open iTunes and find the song that you want to make into a ringtone.

2   Listen to the song and find the part of it you want to use. The chorus may be a good place to start.

3   Write down the start and stop times of the clip.

4   Right-click the song and select Get Info.

5   Click the Options tab.

6   Type in the start time of your ringtone in the text box next to Start Time in the minutes:seconds (i.e. 2:01) format.

7   Type in the end time of your ringtone in the text box next to Stop Time. Make sure the ringtone is no more than 40 seconds long. Click OK.

⚠ Warning

This will not work with songs bought at the iTunes store or that have DRM (copy-protection). Your best bet is to use a song that you have imported from a CD.

8   Right-click your song again and select Convert Selection to AAC. Wait for iTunes to convert your song. It will create a duplicate version.

9   Right-click the ringtone and select Delete.

10 Click on the Keep Files button.

11 Find the file. It's usually in your User folder under Music > iTunes > iTunes Music and under the band's name. It will have an extension of m4a.

12 Replace the m4a extension of your ringtone with m4r. You can either double-click slowly to re-name your file, or right-click and select Get Info on a Mac or Rename on a Windows PC.

13 Click Use .m4r or the PC equivalent when the system warns you that the change may affect the use of your file.

14 Double-click the ringtone file. iTunes will automatically add it to the ringtones folder in your iTunes Music Library.

15 Connect your iPhone and sync your ringtones.

Open Email Attachments on a Blackberry   `291`

Viewing email attachments on your Blackberry is a snap, as the device is extremely versatile.

⊙ Steps

1   View your message list by using your track-wheel to click on Messages from the home screen.

2   Check to see if an incoming email has an attachment. If so, it will have a paper-clip icon next to its listing in your message list.

3   Scroll to an email that has an attachment and press the Enter key to open the email.

4   Press the track-wheel while viewing the open email and select Open Attachment.

5   Use the Table of Contents or Full Contents option to allow you to view enough information about the attachment to determine if it is supported by Blackberry. This will ensure that you wish to retrieve it and that it is not a threat to your Blackberry security.

6   Select the Full Contents option and use the track-wheel to click on Retrieve. Depending on the size and format of your incoming attachment, only part of your document may appear.

7   Scroll through the document to retrieve the rest of it.

8   Return to the main body of your message after viewing an attachment by pressing the ESC key. Your Blackberry server generally does not save the attachment to your device unless you have installed third-party software to edit and re-use the attachment.

9   Return to the message list to view other messages and attachments by pressing the ESC key again.

⚠ Warning

Always handle attachments with care and ensure that they will not threaten your system security before you retrieve them. Unknown email attachments are among the most common carriers of computer viruses, worms and malware.

292 Condense Text Messages

Text messaging is quicker than writing an email and can serve as a form of entertainment. However, it can take a long time to punch out a message and respond to it. Learn how to condense your text messages with these tips.

⊙ Steps

1 Examine your mobile phone. Get to know its capabilities and settings. Text messaging can be made easier when you learn the extent of your phone's SMS messaging functions.

2 Learn your texting parameters. The last thing you want is for your text to be broken up into two or more separate texts. That means your message is too lengthy and it may throw off the receiver.

3 Learn to abbreviate key words. Some commonly abbreviated words include doctor, because, same here, okay, please, thank you, minutes, be right back, among others.

4 When writing sentences, remember that you don't have to! Texting isn't a lesson in grammar or word fluidity. Its purpose is to send a quick message that is easy to respond to. Keep it that way.

5 To get your point across in a text message, you can leave out words. Don't worry about being proper or eloquent. Chances are, whoever you're texting knows you well enough.

6 Use symbols such as "@" to substitute for the actual word. If someone makes you laugh, imply it with a smiley face. It's more fun and leaves no doubt what you mean.

✳ Tip

Use pre-programmed text messages provided by your phone. They often include common texts.

⚠ Warning

Don't overdo texting. Unless you know someone fairly well and know they enjoy text messaging, limit your messages.

293 Dispose of an Old Mobile Phone

It's exciting to get a new mobile phone, but what do you do with your old one? You can either recycle the phone, donate it, resell it or dispose of it.

⊙ Steps

1 Recycle your phone. Mobile-phone manufacturers as well as service providers and non-profit groups have programmes to recycle old phones. Look on the Internet for national organisations – they'll often send you an envelope to return the phone to them.

2 Donate your phone. Look for local charities that are interested in small electronics, if you decide to donate your mobile phone.

3 Sell your phone. Try the Internet or the local newspaper if you decide to resell your mobile phone.

4 Remember that mobile-phone batteries should never be put in the bin because they are harmful. If you decide to dispose of your old mobile phone, check with your local council for the proper instructions on how to dispose of the battery safely.

⚠ Warning

Before you do any of this, remember to remove all private or sensitive information stored on the phone.

Practise Pager Etiquette 294

Some people become so enamoured with their pagers that they begin to misuse them, often to the irritation of others.

⊙ Steps

1 Leave your pager at home if you're going somewhere where you know it will be disruptive. The cinema, theatre and churches are examples of places where pagers don't belong.

2 Set your pager to vibrate whenever possible.

3 If you're waiting for an important page at an event, sit near an exit so you'll disturb as few people as possible on your way out.

4 Avoid taking your pager along on a romantic evening. Your date won't be impressed; he or she is more likely to feel neglected and unimportant.

5 Decide whether or not to respond to a page immediately by judging how important it is. Avoid getting into the habit of running to the phone every time your pager goes off.

6 Avoid giving your pager number in place of a telephone number. This can send an array of confusing signals, such as you can't afford a phone.

7 Avoid getting carried away with pager codes and other pager uses. These things can grow tiresome very quickly.

⚠ Warning

Pagers can still be heard when set to vibrate. All though the low rumbling is less disruptive than the alternative, it can still be irritating in a quiet environment.

Take a Good Picture 295

By following a few simple rules, even a beginner photographer with a basic camera can take beautiful pictures.

⊙ Steps

1 Be aware of how you are framing your picture. Is the subject where it should be (generally in the centre of your frame)?

2 Be sure there are no unwanted objects or people in the background of your picture.

3 Adjust the lighting as necessary. Flash does not necessarily make for a good picture. Try to achieve the desired light without using the flash. Natural light is the most flattering.

4 Be aware of the distance between you and your subject. If there is too much distance, you may not be able to make out fine details in the photo. If you are too close, you may be cutting out important aspects of the frame.

5 The best portraits look natural. Try to catch your subject is a casual moment, when they are engaging with another person or looking away from rather than towards the camera.

✱ Tip

When shooting in the wilderness make sure you leave the area how you found it.

⚠ Warning

Make sure your equipment is fully charged before setting off.

296 | Take Digital Photos Outdoors

Taking digital photos outdoors requires a little more planning, skill and finesse than taking photos inside a building. Success is largely dependent on how well you can control the sunlight. That is sometimes difficult, but not impossible if you follow these few tips.

Steps

1 Use automatic exposure for most outdoor scenes.

2 Override automatic exposure when the scene is much lighter or darker than middle grey.

3 Increase exposure to lighten a scene; decrease exposure to darken a scene.

4 Override automatic exposure when the sun is behind or on one side of the scene to be shot.

5 Override automatic exposure when light reflects off bright surfaces such as sand or snow.

6 Experiment with overriding the automatic exposure when shooting high-contrast scenes.

7 Use a light meter to determine the appropriate aperture setting and shutter speed.

8 Adjust the aperture setting and shutter speed in small steps.

9 Shoot a picture and preview it to evaluate settings. Adjust as necessary and shoot again.

10 Try shooting from several angles; you can delete the worst choices on the spot.

11 Avoid low-light situations whenever possible, or use a fill-in flash.

12 Avoid direct sunlight or shooting directly into the sun.

13 Avoid shooting harsh shadows.

✳ Tip

If your camera does not allow manual adjustments, you may be able to compensate with image-editing software..

297 | Choose Photo-Editing Software

With the increasing popularity of digital cameras and photo-enabled mobile phones, many photography enthusiasts require photo-editing software.

Steps

1 Evaluate your current digital camera features and photo-editing software capability. Some cameras perform many editing functions internally. Consult with your camera manual for instructions. Give your current photo-editing software a decent trial and determine which features you do and don't like, so that you know what to look for.

✳ Tip

Basic programs are often bundled with scanners and digital cameras.

2 Set a budget for digital photo-editing software. A low budget will eliminate many digital image products, but don't despair. Good budget photo-editing software is available. Additionally, consider online auctions, online classifieds and reseller websites for savings. Look for "academic software" versions if you are a student.

3 Determine the purpose of your photos and how you intend to display them, including print, digital photo frame or on the Internet. If this is the primary household camera it is important that a photo-editing software contains fixes for red eye, basic adjustments (brightness, contrast and hue) and solid print adjustments.

4 Decide how much effort you wish to put into navigating the photo-editing software. Generally, the more features the product has the more of a learning curve the software requires. If you like a mainstream product but find it too complicated, look for a scaled-down version the company may offer or seek an alternative.

5 Don't pay for unneeded features but recognise those that are important to you. To better organise your photos, select photo-editing software that offers a "media manager". Enjoy special effects? Stick with leading manufacturers to accommodate photo special-effects packages known as plug-ins.

6 Take advantage of trial versions of photo-editing software before you make a purchase. The more photo software products you try the better your level of satisfaction will be. While you may fall in love with one product, a similar one may be available at a reduced cost or with better features.

7 Don't overlook open-source or free photo-editing software. Some like GIMP are quite popular. For simple photo-editing, free online photo editors such as Picasa may be sufficient.

8 Remember, complex, professional programs, such as Adobe Photoshop, are immensely powerful but are also difficult to use and expensive. If you're just going to be scanning photographs of your children and cleaning them up for a website, you're better off with a cheaper, simpler program.

✓ 298 Edit Digital Photos

Digital photos have become the preferred method of photography, especially with the affordability of digital cameras. The advantage of digital photography is that you can edit and print your own photos from your computer.

Store and Edit Digital Photos

- Keep up with your digital photos before and after editing with two basic computer programs: photo-catalogue software and a database of where files are stored. Your camera usually comes with a catalogue-type software, but it can be cumbersome and unreliable.

- Do not store photos on your computer's hard drive. You need a backup storage device such as a dedicated hard drive (external or internal) or CDs or DVDs to ensure the safety of digital photos. Create a database of your photo names and locations, such as an Excel spreadsheet.

- To edit digital photos you need a photo-editing program. Programs range from free basic programs to professional photo-editing software such as Adobe Photoshop.

Photo Sizing

- Photo-editing capabilities vary across programs, but there are some basic features common to all programs. The first step in editing photos is to look at image size. Correlate the image size to the medium you will publish to – print or the web. Make sure you click the "maintain aspect ratio" control for an undistorted image.

- Maintain the size of the original photo if you need to use it again. Enlarging a smaller photo causes distortion. Choose the Save As option for the resized photo.

- To cut out unnecessary parts of the photo, use the Crop feature in your editing software. Select the Crop option from your toolbox. Create a box around the photo. By dragging in or out on the corners, you will cut everything out beyond the box.

Colour and Light Controls

- Familiarise yourself with the numerous controls in your photo-editing programs to change the brightness and contrast of photos, usually operated by slider bars.

- Play with the colour output to adjust the colour balance of your photos. Most basic programs use red, green and blue channels, or RGB. Some of the more advanced programs use other channels such as cyan, magenta, yellow and key (CMYK). For basic editing purposes, the RGB channels are fine. Professional printers use CMYK.

- Know that different programs have different filters. Filters can change the photo's finish to something that looks like paintings or drawings.

Correcting Errors

- Use photo-editing software for common errors in digital photos. Cropping, for example, can remove some errors and straighten edges.

- Use the red-eye feature. Red-eye is one of the most common errors in digital photography. Most editing software has a feature to reduce red-eye. This feature takes a sample of the area around the red-eye and replaced the redness with a layer of these same pixels as the surrounding area.

- Adjust the colour saturation of your photos by using slider bars to add more or less of one of these colours. You can work with the colour balance and saturation to produce colour photos that look great.

Reduce Red-Eye in Photos   299

Red-eye can ruin both digital and print photos, and without Photoshop it can be difficult to do anything once this happens. Learn how to prevent red-eye before it happens.

⊙ **Steps**

1   Use the red-eye mode. This may sound simple but it is a step many people overlook. Most cameras today have red-eye reduction settings. Normally the icon for this mode is an eye. This will cause a few small flashes before the picture is taken, which makes the subject's pupils smaller and thus reduces the reflection that causes red-eye.

2   Try to take your pictures in a bright area. Outdoors is best, or near a natural light source inside. If you are taking pictures at night, turn on lights to reduce red-eye. The reflection from the flash against the back of your eye causes the red-eye, so to minimise this you need to minimise that reflection by having the smallest difference in brightness between the flash and the lighting in the space.

3   If your flash is removable, move it so the flash is pointing directly into the subject's eyes. Try to reflect it off the ceiling or a wall to reduce the risk of red-eye. If the flash is attached to your camera, make sure the subject isn't looking directly into it.

4   If you do have a great picture and find out you have red-eye, you can use the red-eye reducer in most photo-editing software. You can also ask a technician to help if you are having your photos printed for you.

❋ **Tip**

If you do end up with red-eye in your photos, it can be removed. Digital photos can be retouched on the computer with photo-editing software. Film photos or photos already printed out can be touched up with a special red-eye reduction pen. The pale blue ink counteracts the red, making the eye darker.

⚠ **Warning**

Red-eye in pictures of humans is different to pet-eye. Pet eyes tend to glow white, light blue or transparent. Since their eyes are different from humans', these techniques won't necessarily work on pet pictures.

Troubleshoot a Digital Camera   300

Digital cameras have brought more fun to photography than anything since the first Polaroid, but there's a little more to making them work than point and click.

⊙ **Steps**

Taking Pictures

1   If the image quality is poor, check the lens to make sure it's clean. Learn how to focus or pre-focus your model of camera. Check the manual to see what resolutions your camera supports and make sure you know which one is selected. Higher resolutions give better pictures but take up more digital space. If using a flash, make sure you're close enough to the subject.

2   Having problems locating the pictures you've taken? Look for Playback or Review mode on the camera to view the pictures. Use the arrow buttons to scroll through the pictures. Make sure the battery is attached properly and that the camera is powered, to confirm pictures were actually taken. Make sure the correct memory card is in it in case you have more than one.

❋ **Tip**

Short of dropping the camera into a lake, most of the problems you'll encounter can be fixed using these guidelines.

3   If the camera won't let you take pictures, check that it is not set to Playback or Review mode. Make sure the memory card is in the camera and that the card is properly formatted. The memory may be full, so try downloading the images to your computer or deleting them. Check the batteries to make sure they aren't flat and replace them if necessary. Check the flash, as it may simply be recharging.

Technical Difficulties

1   If the camera won't switch on, check the batteries. Connect the camera to an AC adapter. Remove all the batteries, disconnect the AC adapter, wait a minute, reinsert the batteries and reconnect the adapter. Turn on the camera again.

2   If the camera gets wet, turn it off if it's on. Remove all batteries and media. Let it dry completely for at least 24 hours before reinserting the batteries.

3   If the camera is burning through the battery too fast, minimise your use of the camera's built-in LCD if it has a viewfinder you can use instead. The LCD is the biggest power drain on your camera. Use only heavy-duty batteries – ordinary alkalines won't cut it. Look into upgrading to rechargeable NiMH batteries. If you have or can get an AC adapter for your camera, always use it when downloading photos directly to your computer. If your camera uses PC Cards or SmartMedia cards, get a card reader that will connect to your computer. This will save battery life and improve data-transfer speed. If the problem occurs during very cold conditions, warm the batteries in your pocket or hand just before inserting them into the camera and taking the picture.

4   If the the screen keeps turning off, check the message display for an explanation such as focus or lighting. If it says the battery is low, replace or recharge it. Some cameras have a Power-save mode that shuts down after a certain amount of time not being used, so make sure this isn't what's happening. In some models, you may be able to take non-flash pictures with a low battery. The battery may also be too cold if the screen keeps switching off. Warm it to room temperature.

5   If the camera won't let you connect it with the computer, make sure you're using an AC adapter. Check with the camera manufacturer (try its website) to make sure you have the latest version of the necessary software drivers. If your camera connects via a serial (COM) port, check for serial-port conflicts. If you're using a FireWire cable to connect to the computer, turn the computer on, turn the camera on and then connect the cable between the two. Don't turn off the camera while the cable is still attached. If the camera won't recognise the media, make sure the media is inserted correctly and check to see if it's been write-protected.

6   If the flash doesn't work, the first thing to check is that batteries are fresh. If the batteries are okay, check that the camera hasn't been set to No-flash mode. Give the flash time to charge before pressing the shutter.

Locate Your GPS Position on the iPhone

301

The iPhone application's ability to locate your GPS position is quite impressive and, perhaps even more importantly, extremely user-friendly.

⊚ **Steps**

1   Tap on the Maps icon on the home screen of your iPhone to open the application. Next, tap on the Directions button. You will see two fields labelled Start and End, as well as a keypad where you can type in addresses. Make sure you include postcodes if possible to ensure the accuracy of the directions provided.

2   Type your current address or starting location into the Start field. If this is a primary address from where you will regularly seek directions, you can create a bookmark for this location by tapping the Bookmark icon at the top of the iPhone's screen. This address will be labelled as Current Location and will be stored in the iPhone.

3   Select the Satellite icon at the bottom of the map by tapping on it. There will be two other icons next to this one – the Map icon, which shows you a road map of your route once you enter in a destination, and the List icon, which displays a step-by-step list of driving directions to your destination. The Satellite icon utilises GPS to map out your location using coordinates from nearby towers, displaying it on the map.

4   Enter the address of your final destination into the End field displayed above the map. Now tap on the Route icon at the bottom of the screen to see your driving route mapped out on the iPhone map.

5   Track and locate your GPS position as you drive towards your destination by tapping on the icon that looks like a target. A purple circle will appear on the screen outlining your current GPS position on the map, and will continue to track your position as you drive.

⚠ **Warning**

Remember that the iPhone's GPS application is not capable of tracking your exact location and instead makes an estimate of your position.

Select a GPS Car Navigation System

302

GPS car navigation systems can show and even tell you how to get to any destination, using a host of satellites to determine where you are.

⊚ **Steps**

1   Decide how often you intend to use the system. Inexpensive systems simply plug in to your car's cigarette lighter and are small enough to store in your glove compartment, but they're not as user-friendly.

2   Consider the layout of your car. Some systems come with a monitor that displays a map. The monitor is usually installed on the dashboard or on a pedestal extending from the dashboard. In some cars, such an installation may block air vents or make it somewhat uncomfortable for a passenger to enter or exit the vehicle or sit in the passenger seat.

3   Select a system that features multiple ways of getting to your destination. This can include by address, by a personal address book or via a location selected directly from the map.

⚠ **Warnings**

Manufacturers of GPS car navigation systems warn that, if the product is installed by a consumer or an unauthorised dealer, the company will void the warranty.

No matter how fancy your GPS is, there are instances where it can malfunction or not get reception. Always have a paper map back-up.

4   Look for a system that gives you vocal as well as graphic directions. The systems that use a map and monitor include arrows that show you the direction of a turn and also indicate where your car is on the map in relation to the destination. Other systems use the head unit or radio to display the name of the street on which you are to make a turn or on which you are travelling. Both these systems also give you verbal directions as you approach a turn.

5   Select a system that includes point of interest data. Most GPS systems include locations of airports and other transportation services, for example.

6   Consider installation time if you are working on a tight budget. Systems that rely on maps displayed on monitors are more complicated and take longer to install than other types of systems.

7   Once all specifications have been identified for your GPS system, price out different units. Most retailers will have demo units in-store that you can see, touch and experience. You can always check online retailers for a better price. Don't forget about eBay.

303 | Buy a Handheld GPS System

Forget a compass, which only shows you north, south, east or west. A handheld GPS device can tell you where you are and what route to take to get to a destination.

✱ Tip

Purchase and carry extra batteries for use when needed.

◎ Steps

1   Consider the size of the unit. Do you want to slip a unit into your pocket? If so, you'll want something relatively small and compact. Various carrying cases are available for larger models.

2   Choose a system that has multi-parallel channels. This ensures that several satellites are tracking you at one time rather than just one. You get faster fixes in difficult conditions.

3   Select a system that can store 100 or more way points. These are geographic points that can be used as markers.

4   Pick a system that can give the distance and direction of a point from your current position and that can store several routes.

5   Pick a system that is capable of using UTM grid data maps or local grid maps. Make certain that the system can use the common datums used worldwide.

6   Make sure the unit is rugged and waterproof, and that it has a backlit display. This is essential if you intend to do your hiking or bike riding at night.

7   Make certain that the battery life of the unit is sufficient for your travels.

8   Ask the sales representative to show you how to work the unit and then work it yourself.

Install a Car Stereo

If you're on a tight budget but want a better sound system in your car, install a stereo yourself.

⊙ Steps

1   Purchase a new stereo. Make sure you get one that will fit properly into the slot for your old one.

2   Disconnect the ground (negative) cable from your battery. Never work on the electrical system of your car with this connected.

3   Remove the dashboard panel that covers your stereo. Unscrew and slide out your old head unit. There will either be one single plug with lots of wires that connect to the back of it, or a bunch of individual wires. If there are lots of single wires going into the back of the stereo, do not detach them yet. You'll want to do them one at a time to avoid confusion and remember where they all go when reconnecting.

4   Connect the positive wire from each speaker to the positive connector on the back of the stereo first. Then connect the negative wire from each speaker to the negative connector on the back of the stereo. If there is only one wire coming from the speakers, the speakers are grounded at the chassis. In this case you will need to install new speaker wiring.

5   Connect the ground wire (-/black) of the stereo to a screw or bolt near where the radio is mounted in the dashboard. Make sure the wire is attached to metal, not plastic or fibre glass.

6   Connect the 12 constant and ignition power wires (both +/red) to the new stereo. Refer to your stereo's installation manual to make sure these go to the correct places. You should have a nice single connector that hooks up to all the proper wires in your car.

7   Slide your new stereo into the mounting bracket that came with it. In some rare cases you may have to use the bracket from your old car stereo.

8   Plug the harness connector into the back of your new stereo. There should be only one lone wire left from your old stereo now. This is the antenna. Plug it into your new unit. There may also be a power antenna wire that you will need to connect.

9   Slide your new car stereo into the slot in the dasboard. Don't screw it in yet; you'll need to test it first.

10 Reconnect the negative cable of your car to the battery.

11 Turn your car on and power up your new stereo. Put some music on and listen to all your speakers to make sure everything works.

12 Screw your new car stereo into place and put the dash cover back on.

✱ Tip

The most common reason a newly installed stereo does not turn on is a bad ground. If you have this problem, find some other piece of metal that you can attach the ground to in your dash and try again.

⚠ Warning

Never work on the electrical system of your car with the ground wire attached to the battery. You can damage yourself and your equipment.

305 | Add Surround Sound to Your Car

Surround sound has become all the rage in home entertainment and cinemas. Now some car-audio manufacturers are offering surround-sound components specifically designed for cars.

⊙ Steps

1 Consider your car. Is it a two-seater? If so, the rear speakers may have to be too close to the listeners. Is it a convertible? If it is, you won't be able to achieve the proper staging for a true surround-sound effect. If you are putting surround sound in a two-door or four-door sedan, you need to consider the size of the car. The rear speakers may be too close or too far away from the listeners in the front seats, and passengers in the back seat may not get the true effect of the centre channel.

2 Select a head unit that can wire into a surround-sound processor. Because the processor is digital, the head unit needs to supply a digital signal. Usually, fibre-optic cables are used to transmit digital signals between components. If your head unit cannot supply digital signals, include a CD changer with fibre-optic connection and connect the processor to the CD changer.

3 Include a high-end CD changer and/or DVD unit that can play the software that carries the surround-sound signals.

4 Purchase a five-channel amplifier that can serve the front speakers, the rear speakers and the subwoofers. You are feeding sound to the four corners of the car, plus the subwoofers. Each corner and the subwoofers are separate channels.

5 Include a mid-range speaker and tweeter to serve as the centre channel. This speaker combination needs to be in its own enclosure and should be placed in the centre portion of the dashboard.

6 Select an amplifier to run the centre-channel speakers. A modest two-channel amplifier played bridged mono will suffice.

7 Include an electronic crossover. The crossover can be outboard, or it can be built in to the amplifiers.

8 Speaker locations should be in the four corners of the car. Some cars have speaker locations that are well-placed for a surround-sound environment. You may have to add a tweeter high on the door or pillar at about shoulder height, while placing the mid-range speaker in the factory-made opening in the door. Use a passive crossover to compensate for the distance between the mid-range speaker and the tweeter.

9 Set the electronic crossover. When setting up the crossover point for the centre channel, keep in mind that you don't want to play it full range. Set the crossover point for the centre channel at about 80 Hz and up.

10 Adjust the system once everything has been installed. Set the processor's adjustment in the middle, and first play with the amplifiers' gains. Turn the gain up until you just start to get distortion, and then turn it down just a little. Once the amplifiers' gains are set, you can fine-tune the system by setting the surround-sound processor.

⚠ Warning

Always take extra care when working with electrical wiring. Take care to avoid electric shock!

Set a Three-Way Electronic Crossover for Car Audio   306

An electronic crossover routes frequencies from your stereo to the proper speakers.

☉ Steps

1   Set the high-pass crossover point at the tweeters' spec recommendation and up. If, for example, the specs show the tweeter can play down to 4,000 Hz, set the crossover's high-pass at 4,000 Hz and up.

2   Listen to the tweeters. If you want the tweeters a little louder, cross out the lower frequencies and set the high-pass crossover point a little higher. Listen to the tweeters at the volume level you would normally listen to your system.

3   Adjust the crossover high-pass a little higher if you hear distortion.

4   Set the mid-range or band-pass adjustment to the tweeters' lowest frequency at the top end. Set the bottom end of the band-pass at 150 Hz and up.

5   Listen to music and adjust the setting until the mid-range and tweeters blend.

6   Set the low-pass for the subwoofers at the bottom frequency of the band-pass.

7   Listen to music and adjust the low-pass crossover point to your liking.

✳ Tip

Three-way simply refers to the array of drivers a speaker uses to produce sound. The three-way configuration incorporates a woofer for low frequencies, a tweeter for high frequencies and a mid-range driver.

Choose the Best Phone System   307

There's no one-size-fits-all solution to phone systems, so you should choose a combination that's right for you.

☉ Steps

1   Log your calls for a month or two to analyse your calling patterns, the number of minutes you use and how often you call long distance.

2   Consider your voicemail needs. Voicemail that's included in your phone service usually costs a few extra pounds a month. For your home phone, an answering machine may be a more cost-effective option. Either way, you want to be able to access messages easily from any phone line – home, mobile or external.

3   Look for packages. Bundling long-distance and local phone service can be good deals if you make a lot of calls from one place, such as a home office. Find out if your broadband Internet provider can bundle your telephone and Internet service.

4   Go totally wireless if you're not home much and you don't need a fax, modem or other wire-dependent service. Make sure your provider has good coverage in both your home and workplace.

5   Keep a wired phone around the house for emergencies. When the power goes out, cordless phones go dead because their bases are plugged in, but a wired phone will still work.

✳ Tip

Cordless phones that use the 2.4 GHz frequency can interfere with wireless computer networks, and vice versa.

308 | Use a Satellite Phone

If you are in an area that needs a satellite phone – or find yourself caught in a disaster without a mobile phone – here's how to use one.

⊙ Steps

1   Before you buy or rent a phone, fully evaluate why you need one. Phones are company specific. You cannot use one company's phone with any other satellite service, so choose wisely. A few countries, like Burma, make the possession of satellite phones illegal as they cannot censor or wiretap them easily. Do your homework before you lock into a company.

2   If you need a satellite phone, be aware there may be a slight delay and sound quality is not as good as your mobile-phone service.

3   Cost is between £700–£1,500 for most satellite phones. Air time is about £1 a minute. Plans vary and packages are available. Texting and data transfer are possible and differ from plan to plan and between companies. Again evaluate your needs and see what companies fit your use. If it is for one trip, consider renting a phone.

4   You usually need to be outdoors or near a window facing the satellite for good reception. There are two types of satellite phone services. LEO is Low Earth Orbit. LEO uses orbiting satellites and should have continuous coverage – as one satellite goes over the horizon another should be coming into range. They are lower to the Earth and may have bad reception in low valleys or against steep cliff walls. Geosynchronous satellites are a system in which the satellites are higher up. They appear in a fixed position and rotate at the same speed as Earth. That means four satellites can cover the globe except for the extreme poles. They have better global coverage, but an LEO system may be better for use in specific areas.

✳ Tip

Don't confuse Global System for Mobile Communications (GSM) mobile phones with satellite phones that offer mobile service. GSM phones don't use a satellite network.

309 | Use a Digital Answering Machine

Digital answering machines have been created with features that help to make life a little easier.

⊙ Steps

1   Study the diagram of your answering machine in the manual. This helps you easily locate and identify all the buttons on your digital machine.

2   Locate the On/Off button and turn on the answering machine.

3   Adjust the volume. Look for the volume-control buttons on the machine to adjust the speaker volume. The machine will beep when you have reached the highest or lowest setting.

4   Set the clock so you can get a time stamp for each message. Press Change then Clock to begin to adjust the time. Use the Skip/Scan and Repeat/Scan buttons to change the day and increase or decrease the hour and minute. To make sure you have the right setting when you have finished, press the Clock button. The machine will announce the current day and time.

✳ Tip

If you receive a lot of calls, consider purchasing an answering machine with a larger than average memory to avoid running out of space for messages.

5   Decide how you want to use your answering machine. You can use your machine to just give recorded messages to callers or you can use it to record messages from callers.

6   Assign mailbox numbers. Some answering machines have multiple mailboxes that allow you to share the system with other members of your household. Decide who will have each mailbox and assign numbers accordingly.

7   Record your outgoing message. Make sure you include information on who has what mailbox and what the caller should do to leave a message for a particular person. Otherwise, all messages will be recorded in the first mailbox.

8   Record special greetings. Some answering machines give you the option of recording special messages for calls coming from particular numbers, calls from people who have blocked their name and number, and calls from areas where the caller ID feature is not available. These callers will hear the messages you have designed for them instead of the general outgoing message.

9   Follow the instructions in your user guide to set a remote-access code. This code will allow you to call in and check your messages while you are away.

Beat Automated Phone Systems   **310**

Automated phone systems are used by many companies to increase their overall efficiency and save costs. These systems use interactive voice response (IVR) technology designed to route customers through a series of phone menus and voice prompts, often leading to lengthy waiting times for the caller.

 Tip

Get a headset so that you can be free to multi-task while on hold.

⊙ Steps

1   Enter 0. You may be able to beat the automated phone system by doing this as soon as you begin to hear the phone menu. If nothing happens, or if the menu starts over again, enter 0 twice.

2   Give it the silent treatment. By simply not speaking or entering any numbers, the system may be designed to conclude that you are calling from a rotary phone. If this is the case, the system will automatically route you to the next available operator, thereby greatly reducing your waiting time.

3   Be incoherent. If the system is not able recognise key words or if you mumble, the result may actually be quicker service.

4   Stay busy. If you've tried everything you can think of and still can't get in touch with a live person, increase your own efficiency by reading your post or catching up on paperwork while you wait. Chances are the time will go by much faster and you'll have less to do later on.

5   Go online. In addition to increasing their use of automated phone systems, many companies are now turning to the Internet. By visiting the company's website, you can check accounts, pay bills or even have your questions answered online.

311 Buy a Telescope

The best telescope is not the most expensive or the biggest – it's the one you'll use most.

◎ Steps

1. Read astronomy magazines – one of the best places to get an expert opinion on the type of telescope you should buy.

2. Measure the area where you plan to place the telescope.

3. Purchase a telescope you can transport and assemble with minimum difficulty. You don't want something too unwieldy.

4. Determine a telescope mounting that meets your needs. The less money you spend on the mounting, the more money you can spend on optics.

5. Ask yourself if astronomy will be a lifelong pursuit or just a passing hobby. This is particularly important if you're buying a telescope for kids.

6. Determine what you want the telescope for. Ask yourself if you want to view the planets in this solar system or do deep-sky viewing.

7. Research the size of the aperture you need, which will determine how much light the telescope can gather and the clarity of the image.

8. Find out whether the telescope dealership will collimate, or align, the telescope's internal optics.

9. Determine how much money you want to spend, as this will have a large impact on the quality of the telescope you buy.

✳ Tips

There are three types of telescopes: refractors, reflectors and a combination of the two.

Find out from the shop whether your telescope is under warranty and for how long. You might want to buy insurance if you intend to travel with your telescope.

312 Choose Binoculars

Binoculars come in many sizes and shapes, and prices vary from less than £25 to well over £1,000.

◎ Steps

1. Determine the purpose for which you will use the binoculars. Binoculars taken to an occasional sporting event do not need to be as finely crafted as binoculars for birding.

2. Handle a variety of brands and models. Note how heavy and comfortable they are in your hand, and how easily and finely they focus. If necessary, ask whether they can be used by people who wear glasses.

3. Take several pairs outside, if permissible, and try them in various levels of light, including full sun and shade.

4. Focus binoculars as far as you can in both directions, and check the clarity of objects in the short and long view.

5. Ask about warranties.

6. Shop around for a good price once you have decided on the binoculars you want. Expensive binoculars can often be found at discount camera or optical shops for hundreds of pounds off the suggested retail price.

✳ Tip

With binoculars, the "formula" is made up of the numbers that tell you the magnifying power and the diameter of the objective lenses. Thus, 7 x 35 indicates that the binoculars magnify seven times and that the diameter of the front lenses is 35 mm.

⚠ Warning

Binoculars with straps worn around the neck can cause neck pain.

Appear Younger

Ageing is surely not a punishment – it actually looks really good on some people. However, there are times when you may want to reduce the effects of ageing on your body.

⊙ Steps

1   Act younger – you're only as old as you act and if you keep yourself young at heart it will pay off.

2   Drink cocoa. Hot cocoa contains flavonols, which help repair sun damage. Aim for one mug a day. Cocoa also contains phenylethylamine, a compound that boosts production of serotonin and dopamine. It highers oxytocin as well, which helps you relax.

3   Eat cinnamon. As we age, our lips tend to thin. Cinnamon helps the tiny blood vessels to dilate, smoothing out fine lines, so cinnamon plumps lips instantly and naturally.

4   Use soy products. Soy-based products increase collagen production, which can help decrease sagging and wrinkles.

5   Drink water. Our bodies are made up of 70 per cent water, and it is vital for our well-being.

6   Moisturise. Moisturising skin on a daily basis locks in moisture and makes your skin smoother.

7   Get enough vitamin C. This is a potent antioxidant that helps protect against the destructive effects of free radicals. Vitamin C can also help reverse damage already caused. You can take a supplement or eat foods rich in vitamin C, such as citrus fruit, cabbage and tomatoes.

8   Sleep on your back. When you sleep on your stomach or your side, it makes your face wrinkle as you sleep.

9   Eat nuts. These are good for many reasons, including helping with circulation. Sunflower seeds and almonds in particular are loaded with vitamin E. Without enough vitamin E you may suffer poor circulation, so adding these nuts to your diet is good for you and your body.

✳ Tip

If eyes are bloodshot there are various products that can help. Be aware that they should not be used every day, though.

Prevent Premature Wrinkles

Learn how to keep your skin looking fresh and wrinkle-free for many years to come.

⊙ Steps

1   If you're young, it is important to start warding off premature wrinkles now. Already experiencing wrinkles? Then it's time to beef up your anti-ageing skincare routine and use quality products made for your skin type that target wrinkles and fine lines.

2   Sunscreen is one item that can make or break whether you'll age well or terribly. The key to avoiding premature wrinkles is early prevention. If you're not using quality sunscreen with SPF, you'll pay the price when you get older.

✳ Tip

Always do a patch test before trying out new skin care or anti-aging products.

3   The key to sunscreen is reapplication! Follow the rule of thumb and reapply at least every two hours if you plan on being in the sun for a long period of time. If you're playing sports, swimming or doing physical activity that will result in excessive sweating, you may want to reapply more often than every two hours.

4   Don't like slathering sunscreen on your face? Search for skincare products that already contain SPF. There are also makeup products like foundation and powder that are formulated with SPF.

5   Dry skin is the most prone to premature wrinkles so moisturise, moisturise, moisturise! Even if you don't have dry skin, the chances are your skin has dry patches. Make sure you apply moisturiser during your skincare regime in the morning as well as before bed. The more moisturised your skin is, the harder it will be for fine lines and wrinkles to penetrate.

6   Stop smoking! Smoking can cause your skin to look slack and dull – not to mention that you can easily develop "smoker's lines" on your upper-lip area. These types of fine lines are extremely hard to get rid of.

7   Want to protect your eyes from those crow's feet? Go out and buy good-quality eye cream. If you currently don't have the onset of any fine lines or wrinkles around your eyes, it's still a good idea to use an eye cream regularly that moisturises, soothes tired eyes and fights against dark circles, puffiness and bags.

8   Do not use a strong anti-ageing eye cream if you do not have "mature" skin – in fact, do not use anti-ageing products if you don't need them yet. Using normal versions of such skincare products will do more than its share of preventing premature wrinkles.

⚠ **Warning**

Darker-skinned individuals need sunscreen, too! Just because you don't burn as easily as someone with fair skin does not mean you are immune to skin cancer and wrinkles.

315 Wear Clothes That Make You Look Slimmer

With a little fashion savvy, you can learn to make your clothes work for you, showing off your best features and minimising the not-so-flattering ones.

⊙ **Steps**

1   Choose clothing all in one colour to give yourself a long, lean look.

2   Wear black. It gives a look that is especially slimming.

3   Try to avoid shapeless clothing. No one is fooled, and loose clothes often make you appear wider or heavier.

4   Avoid tight clothing that will emphasise your heavy areas.

5   Choose softly tailored pieces that define but don't constrain.

6   Steer clear of horizontal stripes, which make you appear wider, but consider vertical stripes, which make you look longer and leaner.

7   Wear blocks of colour that draw the eye away from less-than-perfect areas. Wear a red or royal blue jacket, for example, to draw attention away from your legs.

8   Wear wide necklines to balance wide hips.

✳ **Tips**

Stand up straight. Good posture always enhances your look.

Whether your style is conservative or daring, wear your chosen clothes with confidence and you'll always look good.

9 Choose trousers that have narrow or tapered legs to hide a large midsection. Flat-fronted trousers and side or back zips will flatter your figure, while pockets, pleats and tight trousers will only draw attention to your midsection.

Give Yourself a Manicure   **316**

You don't have to journey to the local beauty salon to pamper your hands. Do it yourself at home.

⊙ Steps

1 Remove old nail polish thoroughly.

2 Soak hands in warm water for 10 or 15 minutes. Dry hands.

3 File nails in one direction only. Avoid using a seesaw motion.

4 Push back cuticles. Use a cuticle moisturiser if they do not push back easily after soaking.

5 Massage your hands. Use a moisturising lotion. Use an exfoliating lotion if your skin is dry and/or roughened.

6 Apply a base coat. Allow it to dry.

7 Apply nail polish. Clean any stray marks with a cotton swab dipped in nail-polish remover.

8 Add a second coat for deeper colour.

9 Finish the manicure with a top coat of clear polish.

✳ Tip

Plunge your hands into a basin or sink full of cold water if you need your nails to dry in a hurry.

⚠ Warning

Avoid cutting your cuticles with scissors or nail clippers.

Paint Your Toenails   **317**

Application of bright polishes can be tricky. Here's how not to look like you've been finger-painting with your feet.

⊙ Steps

1 Trim those talons girls! Clip your toenails short and straight across.

2 Wipe toenails with nail-polish remover to clean the nails and strip away any oils.

3 Put on open-toed shoes or sandals. If you're wearing your shoes while painting your toenails, you can head straight out afterwards.

4 Apply a clear base coat. The base coat works as a filler at the edge of the nail. Then when you apply the coloured polish later, it won't be running out of your nail beds and looking messy. Let the base coat dry for five minutes.

5 Apply a coloured polish – two coats. You should notice that it goes on more easily over the base coat without streaking.

6 Clean up any bobbles by dipping a cotton swab in nail-polish remover and erasing the errant polish.

✳ Tip

Apply a topcoat to make polish last longer and look smart.

318 Shape Your Eyebrows to Work for Your Face

Having the correct shape to your eyebrows can not only make you look younger but more awake and modern as well.

Steps

1 Know it is always easiest to groom any type of hair after showering or at least steaming the area of concern. So begin by either showering or placing a very warm, damp flannel over your eyebrow area.

2 Stand in an area with good natural light. Make sure you have a mirror in front of you as well as a handheld mirror nearby. Gently brush your eyebrows from the inside corner to the outside corner.

3 Take a pencil or brush and place it vertically along the right side of your nose. The tip of the brush should run up slightly past your eyebrows. This will show you approximately where your eyebrows should begin on the inside corners. Anything that is past the pencil or makeup brush will need to be plucked with tweezers.

4 Pluck the hairs that fall past the pencil or brush, then place it on the opposite side and follow the same steps again. Once finished, you will need to focus on the outside corners of the eyebrow by placing the pencil or brush at the tip of your nose and then line it up at an angle to the outside corner of your eye.

5 Define your eyebrow arch. The arch of the eyebrow should lie naturally above your pupil when you are looking forwards. You can use the pencil or brush once again to find this, or you can look in the handheld mirror and find it by looking straight ahead. Most people will have a definite arch already formed, so you should only need to clean up the area slightly. Do this on both sides of your eyebrows.

6 Take the handheld mirror and look for any stray eyebrow hairs that may be sticking out, and pluck them.

✳ Tip

Always pluck the hairs in the direction of growth.

⚠ Warning

Remember not to over-pluck. If you are nervous, only pluck a little at a time until you get the right amount removed.

319 Make Your Lips Look Fuller

Who doesn't want beautiful lips that can stop traffic from a mile away? Here's how to make your lips appear full and big.

Steps

1 Your lip liner should be a shade that is comparable to the lipstick or lip gloss you have selected. Once you have chosen the colour of the lipstick, buy a lip liner that is just a shade darker.

2 If you don't have a v-line (the middle of your top lip that goes inwards, forming a v-shape), then take a white lip liner and gently trace a vertical line starting from the brim of your nose to the top of your upper lip. Make sure that the vertical line you make is faint. It has to be in line with the middle of your upper lip. Use the brim of your nose to direct you.

✳ Tip

Avoid using colours that are too dark or too light as it hampers the look of a fuller lip.

⚠ Warning

Be cautious when you are applying lip colour – it must not go outside the lip-liner line you have drawn.

3 Take the white lip liner and trace your actual lip line. Make sure your lip liner is soft. It has to easily roll off of the pencil. Be very light in the tracing. This will become your foundation line.

4 Now add the colour. Make sure your coloured lip-liner pencil is sharpened, then reline your lips slightly above the natural lip line you have created with the white lip liner, using the of colour of your choice.

5 Make sure you don't overlap or trace over the base line (white line) you created earlier. Pay careful attention to the v-line. Remember, the v-line should be faint. This allows you a place of reference that is easily erasable.

6 Now apply the lip gloss in the centre of your upper and lower lips. Do not spread it completely towards the edges. This will create a fuller effect that will focus on the middle portion of the lips.

7 Finally, add your lipstick.

Exfoliate Your Body **320**

By removing the top layer of dead epidermis cells, you will make your skin appear smoother and less wrinkled. Here are a few steps to help you achieve healthy-looking, clear skin.

⊚ Steps

1 Brush dry skin before getting into the shower. You can use either a loofah, exfoliating gloves or a body exfoliating brush. Start at the soles of the feet and work your way up.

2 Get into the bath or shower and wet your entire body.

3 Apply exfoliating cleanser to your loofah or exfoliating brush or gloves.

4 Scrub your body with it, using gentle, circular motions.

5 Opt for grainy types of cleansers to clean the skin, rather than soap. Choose exfoliating cleansers that contain ingredients such as oatmeal, ground almonds or even sea salt. The grainy texture exfoliates the skin.

6 Use a flannel for mild exfoliation.

7 Rub rough spots, such as heels, with a pumice stone or stick.

8 Apply lotion containing alpha or beta hydroxy acids after you exfoliate. This will continue the exfoliating process because the acids further remove dead skin cells.

9 Make sure you use body moisturisers at least once a day. Regular exfoliating is extremely drying to the skin and will do more harm than good unless the skin is rehydrated liberally with lotions.

✳ Tip

Some products are more abrasive than others. If your skin is very sensitive, use as little friction as possible and stick to the least abrasive products.

⚠ Warning

Never over-exfoliate with excessively abrasive exfoliating cleansers, or you run the risk of bursting the delicate blood vessels under the skin.

321 | Conceal Blemishes

Instead of feeling uncomfortable with how you look, keep a few basic makeup supplies on hand to conceal blemishes.

Steps

1   Wash your hands before handling your face. Dirt and oils on your hands will only aggravate the blemish.

2   Choose a concealer appropriate to the colour and type of blemish you wish to hide. Pick a yellow-tinted concealer to hide red blemishes; choose a concealer a little lighter than your blemish if you want to hide darker marks.

3   Choose a masking cosmetic (thicker than concealer and with added pigment) to hide more prominent blemishes, such as small scars left from pimples or skin irregularities.

4   Apply the concealer or masking cosmetic over the blemish using your finger, an eye-shadow brush or a sponge.

5   Blend the edges with the surrounding skin, using a circular motion.

6   Set the masking cosmetic with a special setting powder, then apply oil-free foundation and powder on top.

✱ Tip

Try a cover stick, which is a stick version of a concealer. These contain a high proportion of wax to add body and thickness.

⚠ Warnings

Using too much makeup to cover blemishes may make skin look blotchy. Start conservatively and add as needed.

Cover sticks aggravate acne, so use them sparingly if you're prone to spots.

322 | Reduce Stretch Marks

Stretch marks are an inevitable result of pregnancy or rapid weight loss or weight gain for some men and women. Many people are self-conscious about their stretch marks.

Steps

1   Brush your skin with a loofah or skin brush when you shower to stimulate circulation.

2   Massage cocoa butter into the stretch marks.

3   Use vitamin E oil on your stretch marks. Massage it into your skin after a shower.

4   Talk to your doctor about using tretinoin cream on stretch marks. This is available by prescription only.

5   Eat foods high in vitamins A, E and C, or take supplements in addition to your diet. However, pregnant women should avoid taking more than 25,000 IU of vitamin A.

6   Add foods or supplements to your diet that are high in zinc, which is good for the skin, and silica, which helps form collagen, the supporting fibres in the skin.

7   Eat foods that contain essential fatty acids, which help make cell walls. Essential fatty acids can be found in many vegetables, vegetable oils and fish oils.

✱ Tip

Lasers have shown some promise in reducing the appearance of stretch marks. They seem to work best on stretch marks that are still fairly new and are red or purple in colour.

⚠ Warning

Always consult your doctor or a medical professional before making changes to your diet.

Make Perfume `323`

How would you like to have your own signature scent that lingers in a room or in the mind of that special someone long after you've taken your leave? Making your own perfume is easier than you might think.

⊙ **Steps**

1 Choose the right essential oils. You will need some to be your perfume's base, middle and top notes. You will also need an essential oil to act as a bridge or binder for the other three. The base note is the strongest and longest-lasting, while the top note is the lightest and first to dissipate. When selecting your essential oils, you can use as few or as many as you like, but the use of three separate fragrance layers with a binder is the generally accepted structure for building a perfume.

2 Place eight drops of your base-note essential oil, followed by eight drops of your middle note and finally eight drops of your top note into 70 g (2.5 oz) vodka. Ultimately, your fragrance should follow the following formula: 15–30 per cent essential oil, 70–80 per cent pure-grain alcohol (vodka works best) and 5 per cent distilled water.

3 Add a few drops of binder oil to the mixture if your selection of essential oils does not already include some.

4 Let the mixture sit for at least 24 hours. The longer the mixture stands, the stronger the fragrance will be. Let it stand for as long as you need to in order to achieve the right combined fragrance of the oils.

5 Add two tablespoons of distilled water to the essential oil-vodka mixture. Mix well.

6 Add a few drops of glycerin as a fixative to help the fragrance last longer. Mix well.

7 Before the mixture can settle, pour it into a perfume bottle through a coffee filter. The filter will act as a strainer for any particulate matter left behind from the oils and extraction process.

✳ **Tip**

Your sense of smell can sometimes seem overwhelmed when sampling multiple essential oils. To cleanse the nasal palate, hold coffee beans or coffee grounds approximately 15 cm (6 in) from your nose and breathe in several times. The coffee clears the nasal cortex of scents it has absorbed.

Things You'll Need

❑ Essential oil(s)

❑ Vodka

❑ Glycerin

❑ Distilled water

❑ Perfume bottle

❑ Coffee filter

Avoid Spots `324`

Most people suffer from spots at some point in their lives, but some have them worse than others. Spots can't be prevented without a good skin-care regime.

⊙ **Steps**

1 Wash your face two or three times daily.

2 Use a gentle, water-soluble cleanser and tepid water.

3 Apply a medicated cream, such as benzoyl peroxide, to potential problem areas.

4 Use non-comedogenic moisturisers and makeup.

5 Avoid over-moisturising the skin. Use the lightest-weight moisturiser you can.

✳ **Tips**

Drink plenty of water to flush out impurities.

Keep your hands and hair away from your face.

⚠ **Warning**

Using too many medicated products may dry out skin.

6   Use a mud pack on your face once a week to clean out pores.

7   Try a medicated refining mask that cleanses and corrects problem skin.

8   Wash makeup brushes and sponges frequently to minimise dirt and bacteria.

325 | Apply Moisturiser

Moisturiser helps keep your skin smooth, soft and looking youthful. You should use moisturiser on a daily basis to help keep your skin soft and supple.

◉ Steps

1   Wash your hands and face as usual.

2   Put a small dollop of moisturiser on your hand.

3   Spread the moisturiser in your hands.

4   Wipe your face with your hands, rubbing the moisturiser all over your face. Use firm, upward strokes, particularly around the neck and jawline.

5   Keep rubbing your face gently until the moisturiser has been absorbed into your skin.

6   If you are applying moisturiser to other parts of your body, follow the same steps.

✻ Tip

Moisturiser can make your face look oily, especially if you already have oily skin. Choose the right kind of moisturiser for your skin type – for oily, dry or normal skin.

326 | Make a Herbal Facial

You can make a herbal face mask from ingredients you already have around the home. Using a face mask regularly can help remove dead skin, unclog pores and help to prevent lines and wrinkles.

◉ Steps

1   Cleanse your face thoroughly before you begin, making sure all makeup is removed.

2   Combine 1 egg white, 1 tbsp dry milk, 1 tsp honey and ¼ tsp of a herb such as camomile flowers, fennel, parley, lemongrass or mint leaves, in a bowl.

3   Whisk or blend the ingredients at low speed for two minutes, or until the mixture is creamy.

4   Apply to your face and throat.

5   Let the mask set for 15 minutes. Sit back and relax.

6   Rinse the mask off entirely with warm water.

✻ Tip

You may want to steam your face first to eliminate toxins. Steam for eight to 10 minutes and then apply the mask.

Things You'll Need

❑ Dried herbs

❑ Mild facial cleansers

❑ Blender or wire whisks

❑ 1 tsp honey

❑ 1 tbsp dry milk

❑ 1 egg white

Give Yourself a Home Facial 327

Here's a way to bring that turquoise-walled, tinkly-pianoed, ocean-scented spa experience to your own home.

Steps

1 Fill your biggest saucepan with water and bring to the boil. After it begins to bubble, put the pot in your sink and turn the stove off. Lean into the steam and breathe in. Your face will become flushed, hot and moist.

2 After you've steamed and opened your pores, swirl on a face-mask. If you have oily or problem skin, use a mask that has the word "clarifying" in its name. If you tend to be dry and crinkly, use something more "moisturising". Or, if you can find it, use a "rolling peel mask". This is a cross between a mask and a scrub – you smear it on, but then flake it off the moment it dries.

3 Take a long, hot shower to cleanse and remove your mask. Gently swirl and buff away the mask with a smooth flannel. Slather yourself with your finest cleaning products while showering, just to extend the process of luxuriating. Don't use any of your normal facial cleansers, however – the mask is enough.

4 Immerse your face in a basin of iced water. This tightens your pores and closes them to prevent overactive sebaceous glands, which can lead to spots.

⚠ **Warning**

Don't over-steam – two minutes should do it.

Get Rid of a Tattoo 328

We all have regrets, and tattoos top many people's lists. But no matter how misguided or foolish our misspent youth was, tattoos don't need to be the permanent reminder that they used to be.

Steps

1 Discuss it. Make sure you go through all your options with a doctor. The more you understand the risks and advantages of each technique, the better your final decision will be.

2 Rub it away. "Fade away" creams break down the ink into smaller particles, which are then absorbed by the body. This is a very slow process, and there is not much clinical data to support the manufacturers' claims.

3 Peel it away. Chemical peels should be conducted by trained doctors. A chemical compound is applied to the skin, which will cause it to eventually peel off.

4 Cut it away. Surgical excision removes the tattoo by cutting away the skin. This is only effective on smaller tattoos, or if done in steps on a larger tattoo. A skin graft (using a patch of skin from elsewhere on your body) may be needed.

5 Grind it away. Dermabrasion is essentially sanding away the tattoo. The tattoo area is either numbed or sprayed with a chemical that freezes it. A tool with a spinning, abrasive surface is used on the tattoo. Salabrasion

✱ **Tips**

Talk to your tattoo artist for recommended removal service providers. Chances are good that they already have a network of trusted doctors and clinics.

Many tattoo-removal procedures are done in stages, with steps that need to be repeated over time to fully remove a tattoo.

⚠ **Warning**

No tattoo removal technique is perfect. In almost every case, some scarring or discolouration will occur.

is an older, specific technique. The tattoo area is numbed, and a solution of tap water and salt is applied and rubbed in. No power tool is used.

6   Zap it away. Laser tattoo removal is the newest innovation in the field of tattoo removal. Lasers are used to penetrate the skin and to break up the tattoo ink below the surface. The body then absorbs the smaller particles and the tattoo fades.

329   Get Rid of Dandruff

Most dandruff is caused by a disorder of the oil-secreting glands known as seborrhea. Read on for various steps you can take to reduce or eliminate this condition.

⊙ Steps

1   Mix eight tablespoons of peanut oil with the juice of half a lemon. Rub the mixture into your hair, leave on for 10 minutes and then wash as usual.

2   Add three drops of tea tree oil, a natural antiseptic, to a small amount of shampoo and then wash your hair.

3   Rinse your hair with a solution of vinegar and water.

4   Use an infusion of the herbs chaparral or thyme as a hair rinse.

5   Add flaxseed oil, primrose oil or fish oil to your diet.

6   Use kelp as a seasoning.

7   Take selenium, vitamin B complex, vitamin E and zinc supplements. Do not exceed 100 mg of zinc a day.

8   Take vitamin C and a bioflavonoid complex.

9   Add lecithin granules or capsules to your diet.

10   Make at least 50 per cent of your diet raw food.

11   Avoid or decrease your intake of fried foods, dairy products, sugar, chocolate and nuts.

✳ Tip

Seborrheic dermatitis is a condition that causes severe dandruff. It requires prescription medication to help reduce the symptoms and clear the rashes.

330   Straighten Hair with a Blow Dryer

Want to calm the frizzies or straighten your curls for a day? It's really not that hard to do.

⊙ Steps

1   Begin by shampooing, conditioning and towel-drying hair.

2   Apply a heat protectant product to your hair, paying special attention to the ends.

3   Place a dollop of straightening balm in your palm. Rub your palms together to distribute the product over your hands, then massage it evenly through your hair.

✳ Tips

Always point the dryer downwards as you blow-dry hair; blowing hair upwards can make it frizzy.

Tame flyaway hair with an anti-frizz serum. Place a few drops in your hand, rub gently, then apply it your hair.

4   Comb through your hair with your fingers while gently blow-drying it on a low setting. This removes excess water.

5   Pull your hair into three sections, two at the sides and one at the back. Clip the two sides up. Select a small portion of the hair from the unclipped section to straighten.

6   Using a thick, round brush and beginning at the roots, gently pull the brush through the hair to the ends while blow-drying it. Pull the hair away from your head, stretching and straightening it as you go.

7   First pull the brush through the underside of your hair so that you expose it directly to the heat of the dryer. Once that area is mostly dry, switch to the top of the hair.

8   Keep the tension consistent and evenly distribute heat over the section of hair you're working on. This ensures uniform hair texture and prevents overdrying of certain areas. Once that portion of hair is straightened, continue selecting and blow-drying small portions until that section is dry and straight.

9   Repeat the process on the two other sections to straighten your entire head of hair.

⚠ **Warning**

As with all electrical devices, be cautious when using blow-dryers around water and/or children.

Dye Hair with Coffee   331

Coffee is not just good for waking you up in the morning, it can provide a much-needed wake-up call for your hair as well. Here's how to brighten your hair with coffee.

◎ Steps

1   Make up some coffee using granules and boiling water. Pour it into a basin. If you have not let the coffee cool, do so now. You may wish to place the basin in a sink in case of sloshing.

2   Brush your hair thoroughly. A rinse like this one is easiest to apply to clean, tangle-free hair.

3   Dip your head in the basin. Use the cup to thoroughly saturate your hair with the coffee. Work the coffee through your hair from the roots to the tips using your fingers or the hairbrush.

4   Rinse your hair with the coffee 15 times. Use a cup to scoop the coffee out of the basin and pour it through your hair. This will take about 15 minutes.

5   Wring out your hair. Make sure you do this over the sink so that you do not stain your carpet or tile floor.

6   Allow the rinse to set for 15 minutes. If you wish, you can clip your hair up to prevent dripping. Do not wrap it in a turban or the towel will absorb the coffee.

7   Rinse your hair and then dry and style it as usual. You will notice that greys have disappeared and that any reddish tints you had before are brighter and more vibrant.

✳ **Tip**

If you do not see as marked a difference as you hoped for with your coffee rinse, repeat the rinse process for several days in a row. Sometimes natural dyes have a more subtle effect and can take multiple applications to achieve the desired look.

⚠ **Warning**

If you are a platinum blond, the effect of a coffee rinse can be instant and dramatic. Test the rinse on a clipping of your hair before treating your entire head.

332 Avoid Hair Loss

An estimated 95 per cent of hair loss is genetic, but other factors, such as nutrition, overall health, hormone deficiencies, over-colouring of hair and emotional stress, can be controlled to keep your hair healthy and in place!

Steps

1 Wash your hair regularly in warm water and use a deep conditioner every time.

2 Make sure you eat a balanced diet. Nutritional deficiencies, eating disorders and excessive amounts of certain vitamins, such as A and E, can cause hair loss.

3 Take care of your health. Chronic illness, high fevers and infections can contribute to hair loss.

4 Stay away from harsh chemicals – permanent hair colour and perms are the most damaging – and avoid colouring your hair more than once every six to eight weeks.

5 Avoid hairstyles like ponytails, which stretch and pull hair.

6 Keep in mind that it's normal to lose between 50 and 100 hairs a day.

7 Consult your general physician or dermatologist regarding concerns about hair loss.

✳ Tips

Because of hormonal changes in their bodies, nearly 50 per cent of women experience hair loss after pregnancy. Normal hair production will eventually resume, though it can take as long as six months.

Some methods of preventing hair loss are merely old wives' tales. These include massaging your scalp, standing on your head to increase blood flow to hair follicles and vigorous hair brushing.

⚠ Warning

If you experience a sudden hair loss not related to pregnancy, age or other such factors, contact your doctor.

333 Stop Biting Your Fingernails

Nail-biting is a common habit and one that's not easy to kick. However, following these steps may help you quit, and give you the long, strong nails you desire.

Steps

1 Purchase a bitter-tasting formula made expressly to stop nail-biting. Choose the worst-tasting solution you can find.

2 Wash your hands every morning with soap and water and towel dry.

3 Apply a liberal amount of the solution to the nails, cuticles and surrounding skin.

4 Continue to reapply the solution throughout the day as it wears off.

5 Reapply the solution at bedtime. Make sure the bitter taste is always present on your nails.

✳ Tips

As nails begin to grow, coat them with a polish made for strengthening nails.

Make sure you have regular manicures to maintain your nails.

Choose a Toothbrush 334

You'll come across toothbrushes with just about every imaginable variation: tapered heads, boxy heads, angled heads, neon handles, handles with bending rubber. Which is best for you?

⊙ Steps

1 Bristles are the most important consideration when buying a toothbrush. Choose soft nylon bristles, which will last a long time and won't hurt your gums even after vigorous brushing.

2 Select a brush head that is small enough to access hard-to-reach areas.

3 Keep in mind that there is no evidence that electronic toothbrushes work more effectively than conventional ones. However, people who are handicapped or who wear braces may prefer them.

4 Replace your toothbrush once every three months or whenever it becomes worn.

⚠ Warning

Change your toothbrush after recovering from an infection during which bacteria in your mouth and saliva might have transferred to your toothbrush.

Control Perspiration 335

Perspiration, or sweating, is your body's way of regulating its temperature and responding to stress. But it can also lead to foul odours and damp clothing.

⊙ Steps

1 Use a product that contains both deodorant and antiperspirant. The deodorant only helps control odours, whereas the antiperspirant helps block sweat.

2 Sprinkle talcum powder in problem areas to absorb moisture.

3 Dress in layers so you can control your temperature, thereby reducing your body's need to sweat.

4 Wear a white or light-coloured hat to reflect sunlight on hot days, since your head is an important temperature-control point on the body.

5 Wear natural fabrics such as wool, silk and cotton that allow air to circulate around your body easily.

6 Drink plenty of fluids and stay fit. Fluids and a fit body help regulate your temperature and reduce sweating.

7 Relax as much as possible using regulated breathing, yoga or meditation. This can reduce stress, a perspiration trigger.

✱ Tip

Cotton socks and foot deodorants can minimise foot sweat.

⚠ Warning

If you perspire even when you're relaxed and the temperature is cool, see your doctor – it could be a sign of an underlying health problem.

336 | Clean Hard and Soft Contact Lenses

Cleaning your contact lenses is an important process that will help you avoid eye infections.

◉ Steps

Soft Contact Lenses
1 Wash your hands.

2 Remove the right or left contact lens and place in the centre of your palm.

3 Add three or four drops of multipurpose cleaning solution to the surface of the lens.

4 Using the index finger of the opposite hand, gently rub the solution into the lens for about 30 seconds.

5 Rinse the lens with multipurpose cleaning solution, place the lens in the case and then fill the case with cleaning solution.

6 Repeat the process for the other contact lens.

Hard Contact Lenses
1 Wash your hands.

2 Remove your right or left contact lens and place in the centre of the palm.

3 Add two to four drops of hard contact lens cleaning solution to the surface of the lens.

4 Using the index finger of the opposite hand, gently rub the solution into the lens for about 30 seconds.

5 Carefully rinse the lens thoroughly with fresh tap water, then place it in the case and fill the lens case with hard contact lens conditioning solution.

6 Repeat the process with the other contact lens.

⚠ Warning
Cleaner will irritate eyes unless rinsed thoroughly. If cleaner does get into your eyes, immediately remove the lenses and flush your eyes with water.

337 | Care for New Body Piercings

Post-piercing care is a must to ensure proper healing. In addition to the aftercare list provided by your piercer, consider the following useful alternatives.

◉ Steps

1 Rinse your mouth after eating or drinking anything but water to keep your tongue stud free of debris. Use an antiseptic mouthwash or a sea-salt and water gargle twice daily to kill germs.

2 Dilute three drops of tea-tree oil in a cup of distilled water and use it as an antibacterial rinse twice daily for any external piercings. Substitute a capful of isopropyl alcohol when tea-tree oil is unavailable.

3 Twist or rotate your jewellery gently after applying a rinse. This action allows the antibacterial agents to penetrate the piercing.

4 Blot areas crusted with pus with a warm-water compress. Dab a small amount of antibacterial ointment where you notice trace amounts of blood.

✳ Tips
Keep your hands away from your new piercings. Constant fiddling will prolong the healing time.

Healing times for various body piercings range from a few weeks to a year. You will need to wait at least six weeks and up to 10 months before considering a jewellery change.

⚠ Warnings
Seek immediate medical attention if you experience

5   Keep soap, facial astringents or toners, treatment creams and moisturiser away from the pierced area. Take care that flannels and towels do not snag on your jewellery.

6   Wear loose-fitting shirts and low-rise trousers until a belly-button piercing has healed and the tightness surrounding the area has subsided. Be careful not to catch facial piercings on clothes you pull over your head, on your bedding or on any protective facial gear.

7   Take a multivitamin that includes zinc and vitamin C. This will help the body fight off infection and promote healing.

8   Consult your piercer if you have any aftercare questions.

throbbing pain, prolonged swelling, lasting heat spots at the piercing point or prolonged redness.

Never remove your nose ring if you suspect infection, unless under a physician's recommendation. The bacteria causing the infection may get trapped in your system as the hole begins to seal.

Wax Leg Hair   `338`

Waxing your legs is a simple process that can produce finer, smoother hair. Follow these steps to do it correctly.

⊙ Steps

1   Purchase a wax kit that is specifically designed for leg hair, and that contains washable waxing strips – these can be bought separately if necessary.

2   Read the wax kit's instructions, paying particular attention to the heating instructions.

3   Heat the wax according to the instructions. Test the wax on the hairless part of the back of your hand to ensure that it is not too hot.

4   Sit down on a clean, uncarpeted surface. Moving in the direction of hair growth, spread a thin layer of wax over a section of your calf that is smaller than your waxing strip to test for sensitivity.

5   Quickly place the waxing strip over the warm wax and press down firmly. Allow the wax to cool slightly before moving on to the next step.

6   Use one hand to pull the skin taut, swiftly pull the fabric strip up and in the opposite direction of the hair growth.

7   Allow the skin a chance to settle down by placing a cool, slightly damp flannel over the waxed area. Move on to a new, possibly larger section when you are certain your skin is not sensitive to the product. Repeat the process until finished.

✳ Tips

Legs should be clean and dry before you wax.

Regularly exfoliate your legs using a scrub or loofah to prevent ingrown hairs.

The faster you pull off the strip, and the tighter you pull the surrounding skin, the less pain you will experience.

⚠ Warnings

Never use wax that is too hot, and always follow heating instructions exactly.

Do not wax if you have diabetes, circulatory problems, varicose veins, warts, moles, haemophilia, acne, irritated or sunburned skin, or are prone to infection.

Do not continue to wax if your first attempt leaves skin sore or extremely sensitive.

Trim Nostril Hair   `339`

You could probably figure this one out on your own, but a few quick tips might spare your nose a bit of discomfort.

⊙ Steps

1   Stand in front of a mirror with a pair of small scissors in your hand.

2   Lean your head back slightly and tug up the edge of one nostril.

✳ Tip

You can use electric nose-hair trimmers instead of scissors.

3 Carefully clip away any extraneous hair with the scissors. Clip the hair close to its base, if possible.

4 Look in the mirror and inspect your work. Touch up as necessary.

5 Repeat with other nostril.

6 Wipe your nose and wash the scissors.

⚠ **Warning**

Avoid putting the scissors too far into your nose.

340 | Avoid Razor Burn

If you dread shaving your face because of the nasty red bumps that always ensue, take heart. A few simple steps can minimise your discomfort and improve your appearance.

◉ Steps

1 Put a new, sharp blade in your razor. Shaving with a dull blade will inflame your skin.

2 Shave carefully, applying only as much pressure as necessary.

3 If you're shaving off a beard or several days' growth, change blades.

4 Rinse off the shaving cream with cold water.

5 Apply aftershave or another alcohol-based product.

6 Dry your face well.

7 Use moisturiser on any dry patches.

✳ **Tips**

Certain shaving lotions and creams are designed to prevent razor burn.

The use of electric shavers may cut down on or eliminate razor burn.

341 | Prepare for Electrolysis

Electrolysis is a way to permanently remove unwanted hair. It requires many sessions, in which hairs are destroyed with an electric current then plucked out.

◉ Steps

1 Plan on having electrolysis every six weeks for one to three years to achieve the best results.

2 Be prepared to spend anywhere from £15 to £75 per hour of treatment. Factors that affect total cost include which parts you want treated, the amount of hair you have, additional skincare for problems that may result afterwards, and medication for pain relief.

3 Remove all makeup in the places where you will be having electrolysis.

4 Avoid showering or getting hairs wet for several hours before electrolysis. Water softens the hair shafts, causing them to droop. Hairs will be easier to remove if they are upright.

5 Take a mild analgesic 30 to 60 minutes before electrolysis. It will help ease the discomfort caused by the procedure.

6 Use only reputable electrolysis salons. Make sure conditions are clean and that fresh electrolysis probes are used for each client.

✳ **Tip**

Before electrolysis, your electrologist will remove your makeup.

Accessorise an Outfit 342

If you want to spice up a basic outfit, adding some well-chosen accessories can do the trick.

⊙ Steps

1   Liven up a neutral sweater and skirt outfit with strands of long gold chains and coloured beads to make your look more arty and original.

2   Layer on bangles and cuff bracelets.

3   Look for belts and jewellery with metallic finishes.

4   Mix silver, gold and bronze-toned pieces.

5   Select accessories that have a common colour but different finishes to make your outfit appear more interesting.

6   Buy clothing with the accessories already built in, such as tops decorated with jewelled pieces and jeans with tiny silver sparkles in the weave.

7   Wear opaque black tights to turn a basic dress into something more modern and fashionable.

8   Use coloured shoes and a handbag that contrast – rather than match – your outfit. For instance, a simple outfit of jeans and a black top will benefit from the pop of a bright-green shoe.

9   Find one-of-a-kind pieces at art shows or antique shops.

10 Change the look of a dress by adding a patterned scarf around your neck or a wool cape over your shoulders.

11 Realise that glasses come in a wide range of shapes and colours today and can instantly up your style quota.

12 Pull back your hair with a jewelled barrette or clip for the perfect finishing touch.

✱ Tips

Trade in your shoes for boots to change the look of your outfit in one easy step.

Remember that a deep lipstick colour can also serve as a nice accent to brighten your look.

⚠ Warning

Avoid wearing too many accessories at once. Check yourself in the mirror before leaving the house and when in doubt, remove one item before you go out.

Avoid Fleeting Fashion Styles 343

Though you don't have to avoid all fads, try not to be a slave to fashion – you'll end up looking just like everyone else.

⊙ Steps

1   Develop and keep your own style. Trust your instincts about what looks best with your colouring, habits, personality and place in the world.

2   Adopt what you truly like, but recognise that it may not be the last word in fashion forever.

3   Understand the process. Be aware of why, as well as when, a trend is cooling. Fashion trends and fads can happen because a style is cool (heavy-soled shoes) or fun (temporary tattoos) or even shocking (lingerie as outerwear).

4   Adapt the style you want to adopt. For example, is everyone wearing short shorts but you just can't? Add a piece of fabric or ribbon to your hems so you can wear them short but not as short as everyone else.

✱ Tip

Realise that a stylish woman with purple hair can carry it off if she's confident.

⚠ Warning

Impulse buys are for gratification in haste and repentance at length.

5   Mix trendy pieces with classic ones.

6   Break some rules and simply bend others. If fashion are catered towards large breasts and you're not so well-endowed, get a push-up bra and avoid the more radical surgery route. If straight hair is in this season, use large rollers and blow-dry your hair before you chemically straighten your ringlets.

7   Develop confidence: take a course in fashion, read fashion magazines, take lessons in how to apply makeup or go to a department store and ask a representative on one of the cosmetics counters to show you your best colours and how to apply them.

8   Learn about fashion, style, tips and tricks, then go out and make your own fashion news.

344 Make Your Breasts Look Fuller

Even if you weren't born with an ample bust, with the right bra and a little manoeuvring, you can look spectacular.

⊙ Steps

1   Buy a Wonderbra, Miracle Bra or other padded push-up bra. These are made for enhancing the look of your breasts.

2   Insert foam pads into your bra. Place them in special pockets built into the bra, or place them in the cup under the breast.

3   Choose a material that hugs and draws attention to the bustline.

4   Apply blusher, a shade darker than your skin tone, between your breasts to suggest shadows and cleavage. A touch of glitter on top of each breast will highlight the rounded top and make it appear fuller.

5   Wear a tight Lycra top over your bra and under your shirt or jumper to add an extra layer.

6   Stand up straight.

7   Do exercises that strengthen the pectoral muscles and lift your breasts.

✳ Tips

The next time you're in a lingerie department, ask the salesperson which enhancing bras are the bestsellers. If you are unsure what size to get, ask for advice.

Do a little experimenting with padded bras or tight tops, and have a friend give you an honest opinion on how it looks. It's not always easy to be objective.

⚠ Warning

Too much padding or blusher can be obvious. Go for the subtle, almost subliminal approach.

345 Match Shoes with Your Outfit

To put your best foot forward in the right pair of shoes every time, just follow the tips below.

⊙ Steps

1   Pair a long skirt with ankle- or knee-high boots, flat shoes, ballet slippers or backless slip-ons.

2   Wear conservative heels of medium height with skirts for work. Shoes with a rounded or square toe and a stacked or slightly tapered heel look professional.

3   Choose platforms or chunky loafers with some heel with a casual skirt.

✳ Tips

Wear shoes with ankle straps only if you have long legs. Straps make your legs look shorter.

If you're shopping for shoes to match a specific skirt or pair of trousers, wear the article of clothing while you shop.

4   Don stylish footwear with a dressy skirt. Try high sandals for skirts that graze or just cover the knee, or pointed-toe shoes with Sabrina heels to give yourself a leggy look.

5   Zip up some knee-high boots with a miniskirt if your legs are long enough to get away with it.

6   Ground your jeans or cords with boots, chunky-soled shoes or trainers.

7   Slip on open-toed flats or espadrilles with soft, looser trousers.

8   Choose oxfords or loafers that are flat or have low to medium heels if you're wearing business trousers.

9   Wear boots with long, dressy trousers, or high, strappy sandals with straight, glamorous trousers in sleek fabrics.

10 Put on platforms or open-toed mules with capri trousers, or nosebleed-high sandals for daring nights out.

⚠ Warnings

Avoid shoes that don't feel comfortable the minute you put them on, no matter how great they look.

Be careful with platforms, as it's easy to twist an ankle in these.

Wear High Heels Without Feeling Pain   346

High heels are worn to complete an outfit, make legs appear longer and leaner, and to give a little sass to our step. To avoid foot and leg pain, follow these steps when wearing high heels.

⊙ Steps

1   When purchasing high heels, make sure that there's enough room in the front of the shoe to not cramp your foot. Shop for heels in the afternoon, when your feet are a little swollen from being on them a few hours.

2   Look for a shoe with ample padding in the soles.

3   Purchase and insert a pair of gel pads in the front of each shoe. Again, your toes are not cramped.

4   Before wearing your high heels, make sure that your toenails are trimmed enough to not push against the front of the shoe.

5   When wearing your high heels, maintain a good posture. Standing up straight will give you better balance and prevent awkward strain on your legs and feet.

6   When you get the chance, take a seat. If you are wearing heels for hours on end, it's important to give feet a rest and take weight off the ball of your foot. Wiggle your toes while you sit, and rotate your ankles.

7   If you've followed every instruction, your feet may be feeling fine. There is always the chance, however, that no tips can do the trick and your feet will simply hurt after hours in high heels. In this situation, pull out those emergency flats and slip them on.

⚠ Warning

Beware of wearing heels the day after a night of drinking alcohol. Alcohol tends to make us swell, and your once-comfortable shoes may feel too snug if you've had a few drinks.

347 | Choose a Flattering Swimsuit

A flattering swimsuit makes the most of the proportions of a woman's figure. It's all about a careful mixing of colour, print, and the right lines and silhouette.

⊙ Steps

1   Use blocks of colour to divert attention from wide hips or a belly bulge. Wear one-piece suits with a dark-coloured, solid lower half and a lighter-coloured or printed bodice.

2   Choose suits with at least 15 per cent spandex to minimise flabby areas. If you have wide hips, opt for styles that cut across the hips rather than hanging below them.

3   Enhance a small chest with a lightly padded halter top or a demi cut with an underwire; the demi cut resembles a bra, but it's not a full cup. Also look for suits that offer texture, like ruffles or smocking, and material with a small print – these are guaranteed to deflect attention from your bust.

4   Minimise a full chest with a dark, monochromatic bodice that has a high or square-cut neck. Make sure the suit offers your bust ample support to resist drooping or sagging, and choose a wider-cut bottom to balance your overall look.

5   Elongate a petite frame with a one-piece suit that has thin vertical stripes. Lend short legs length with a suit cut high on the hip.

6   Give a square or boyish figure the appearance of a waist with a one-piece or tankini (a bikini with a top shaped like a tank top) that has a darker colour from the crotch to the middle ribs and a lighter colour over the chest. Consider a skort – a combination short and skirt – to conceal and divert attention away from a too-round bottom.

7   If you have toned legs and sexy shoulders, flaunt them in a string bikini or cutout one-piece swimsuit.

❋ Tips

Nowadays, you can essentially create your own two-piece suit. Look for companies that offer a variety of mix-and-match, coordinated tops and bottoms.

Wear your swimsuit with a long sleeveless blouse, print sarong or wraparound skirt if the thought of walking around in your swimsuit makes you uncomfortable.

⚠ Warning

You generally can't return bathing suits. Check restrictions prior to purchase.

348 | Dress for a Nightclub – Women

Every girl wants to get noticed when out on the town. Here's how to dress to attract attention on the dance floor.

⊙ Steps

1   Think smokey eyes and lush lashes. Play down lip colour if you plan to go heavy on the eyes, or spare the eyeshadow if you want to coat your lips in a dark, smashing red.

2   Experiment with shine. Smear on lip gloss, or dust strategic parts such as your collar bone with body glitter.

3   Try clipping small, sparkly barrettes in your hair.

4   Wear touchable fabrics that won't mind sweat: nylon and polyester blends.

5   Colours should be simple, solid and uninvolved; no frilly patterns. Try clothes with a bit of shimmer or sheen instead.

❋ Tip

Wear comfortable shoes if you're planning on a marathon-length dancing session.

6   Anticipate getting hot from dancing. Wear a sweater or long-sleeved jacket that can be peeled off to reveal something sexy underneath. Consider a spaghetti-strap top, or maybe something cropped.

7   Leave jeans and khakis at home and opt for dressier trousers or skirts in varying degrees of shortness. A short, simple black dress is also nice.

Tie a Bow Tie   349

With practice and a little dexterity, you won't need to rely on a pre-tied bow tie any longer.

⊙ Steps

1   Adjust the tie's length so it fits your neck size.

2   Lift up your collar and put the tie around your neck so the ends hang down in front. One end should hang about 4 cm (1.5 in) lower than the other.

3   Bring the longer end across, behind and over the shorter end, forming a simple knot. Pull the knot snugly around your neck.

4   Fold the shorter end where the hourglass shape begins to narrow (the widest point of the shorter end), forming a bow shape. The bow shape should be in front. Hold the bow in a horizontal position at your neck.

5   Bring the longer end over and in front of the shorter end.

6   Fold the longer end where the hourglass shape begins to narrow, forming a second bow.

7   Bring the second bow under the first bow.

8   Tuck it into the space behind the first bow.

9   Adjust the shape of the two bows.

✱ Tip

This is one of the trickiest of all men's accessories – don't get disheartened if you don't get it right first time.

Wear a Kilt   350

Wearing a kilt requires the right accessories and the right attitude. Here's how to pull it off like the Scots.

⊙ Steps

1   Understand the difference between a "great kilt", which is not sewn but draped, and a Scottish (or English) kilt, which wraps on with sewn pleats. These steps are for the sewn or "small kilt".

2   Close the kilt by taking the right apron through the hole of the left buckle and fastening it to the left buckle.

3   Fasten the left apron to the right; the fringed edge and kilt pin should be to the right.

4   Make sure that your kilt falls to the centre of the knee, sitting exactly on the natural waist.

✱ Tips

A plain white shirt looks best with a kilt, unless you wear the traditional waistcoat.

Choose a tartan, or research your clan's tartan if you're Celtic.

Even in Scotland, kilts are usually reserved for weddings, funerals and special events.

5   Make sure pleats are at the back of the kilt.

6   Strap on the sporran about three fingers below your waistcoat or belt. The strap fastens at the back.

7   Wear kilt hose folded two to three fingers below the kneecap.

8   Place the flashes on the outside of the leg, covering the strap with the fold of the sock top.

9   Lace the ghillie brogues in the following way: cross the laces and pull into a simple knot. Twist them three times and pull tight again to create a thong. Pass the laces around the back of the ankle, bring to the front and tie a bow, letting the laces and toggles hang in front.

⚠ **Warnings**

Unless you're brave or a nut for so-called authenticity, wear underwear under there. Research suggests that even the ancient Scots wore something like boxer shorts under their kilts.

Kilt pins were not worn until the seventeenth century, but are useful to keep your modesty during high winds.

351   Dress if You Are Tall

Being tall is a blessing, but if you prefer to downplay rather than embrace your height, follow these quick tips to "shorten" your look.

⊙ Steps

1   Try wearing a longer top to help visually shorten your legs.

2   Wear trousers with cuffs to ground and truncate your legs.

3   Choose horizontal stripes over vertical ones; avoid pinstripes, for example, which will elongate your figure.

4   Mix light and dark shades. Pairing a dark shirt with light trousers, or vice versa, will shorten your body.

5   Put on flat, rather than heeled, shoes.

✱ **Tip**

Pick clothes that have larger details – wide lapels, buttons and other features. Delicate details such as small collars will make the body look large by contrast.

⚠ **Warning**

Avoid dressing all in one colour, which enhances height.

352   Dress for a Nightclub – Men

These days, it's no longer acceptable for men to roll out for a night on the town dressed in dirty jeans and an old t-shirt. Here's how to dress for success on the dance floor.

⊙ Steps

1   Make sure your hair looks clean and groomed. Gel it if necessary.

2   Try a tight shirt that hugs your curves as you groove to the music and check out the scene. Or put on a nice button-down shirt.

3   Keep in mind that billowing silk shirts and white tank tops have no place on the club scene.

4   Wear khakis or darker-toned trousers. Avoid tapered trousers, white jeans and anything stone-washed or acid-washed.

5   Remember that shoes should be comfortable and a darker colour. Leave the old trainers at home.

✱ **Tip**

Avoid heavy gold chains or tufts of chest hair peeking out from beneath an open shirt. No matter what 1970s' TV series suggest, this is not attractive.

Patch Jeans 353

If ripped or hole-ridden denim just isn't your style, use one or more of the following steps to easily mend the damaged area.

⊙ Steps

1. Make repairs to denim before the rip, tear or hole becomes too large or the edges become too frayed. Patches can be applied as reinforcement to high-stress areas before worn spots turn into holes.

2. Cut any loose threads from the edges of the rip, tear or hole.

3. Use the zigzag setting on your sewing machine to make a satin stitch along the length of a very clean cut or tear. This option is a good one if appearance is not important.

4. Position an iron-on denim patch on the underside of the fabric. The patch should be large enough to completely cover the damaged area. Press the patch with an iron to fuse it to the fabric.

5. Look for products that let you fuse your own fabric patch to the damaged area. With these products, a denim patch is cut from similar fabric. The patch is then fused to the fabric via a liquid or powdered substance and an iron.

6. Use liquid and powdered substances for a stronger bond than that provided by an iron-on patch.

7. Use decorative patches to cover very large holes. Hand or machine sew them into place on the right side of the garment.

✱ Tips

Sturdy cotton is a good choice for patches.

Some people like to use decorative patches of a variety of other fabrics, such as velvet, and add some embroidery, beadwork or sequins.

Fold a Sweater 354

Sweaters can be bulky and take up a lot of space in drawers and suitcases. The trick to folding sweaters is avoiding big bulges, thus allowing for more storage space.

⊙ Steps

1. Lie the sweater face-down on a flat surface.

2. Bring in one side lengthwise to just before the neckline. Flatten out this fold.

3. Fold one sleeve down so that it lines up vertically with the length of the fold.

4. Repeat on the other side.

5. Fold up the bottom of the sweater halfway.

6. Fold up again, this time to the top of the sweater.

✱ Tip

To safeguard your folded sweater against moths and other pests, store it in a chest of drawers made of cedar. Cedar deters most insects.

355 | Stretch Shoes

On average, you take several thousand steps every day. So if the shoe doesn't fit, try stretching it.

⊙ Steps

1 Purchase a professional-quality shoe stretcher from your local shoe repair shop. For ladies' shoes, the stretchers go by shoe size and are designed for both low-heel and high-heeled shoes, with bunion attachments.

2 Get a bottle of liquid shoe stretch to spray on your shoes while using the wooden shoe stretcher. If your shoes are leather, you'll have greater success.

3 Consider taking the shoes to a professional shoe-repair shop to have them stretched. They often use a stretching machine to apply specific pressure and heat precisely where the shoe hurts – including length, toe raise, instep stretching and so on. On occasion, they'll speed up the process with a leather softening agent.

❋ Tips

Purchase shoes at the end of the day, or after work or playing sports, to make sure you get the best fit.

Measure both feet, as no two feet are the same size. Buy shoes for the larger foot.

Walk around the shop to ensure a comfortable fit before buying, and always try on shoes with the socks or hosiery with which you will wear them.

356 | Remove Grass Stains from Clothing

A grass stain is one of the hardest stains to remove. Try these tips to remove the stain, then wash the garment according to the instructions on the label.

⊙ Steps

Washable Fabrics

1 Sponge washable fabrics with water. Then sponge the stain with rubbing alcohol and let it dry. Do not use alcohol on silk or wool. Dilute the alcohol a lot (three parts water to one part alcohol) for acetate.

2 Sponge with cool water, then work a liquid detergent into the stained area. Rinse with water and leave to dry.

3 If the stain remains, soak the fabric in a mixture of warm water and one tablespoon of a stain-removing enzyme product for 30 to 60 minutes. Rinse thoroughly and re-launder in hot water, with a bleach that's safe for the fabric.

4 Bleach with hydrogen peroxide as a last resort.

Dry-Cleanable Fabrics

1 For the best results, take the garment to the dry cleaners as soon as you can. Point out where the grass stains are.

2 If you need to remove the stain yourself, sponge with white vinegar, then water. If that doesn't do it, apply a paste of enzyme product – but not to silk or wool. Leave on for 30 minutes, then blot with a warm, wet sponge.

3 Try applying a paste of baking soda and water to the stain. Work in a little white vinegar with a sponge. The bubbling of the chemical reaction may work to get the stain out.

⚠ Warnings

Don't use alkalis such as ammonia, degreasers or alkaline detergents on grass stains. They interact with the grass and can permanently set the stain.

On some fabrics, a grass stain cannot be removed, not even by a dry cleaner.

Chlorine bleach may change the colour of the garment or cause irreversible damage. Check for colourfastness before using. If the stain does not come out within 15 minutes of bleaching, it cannot be removed by bleaching.

Keep Eggs Fresh 357

Eggs are both versatile and good for you, but keeping them fresh is an important part of maintaining their taste and nutritional value.

⚠ Warning

Avoid stacking eggs.

◉ Steps

1 Always choose fresh eggs in the shop or supermarket.

2 At the checkout, pack the eggs up with any frozen items you have chosen or ask the cashier to wrap the eggs in special refrigerating bags.

3 Check your refrigerator's temperature. Eggs need to be stored at 4°C (40°F) or lower to retain their freshness.

4 Clean off the middle of the refrigerator rack so that you will have space for the carton of eggs. Put cooked foods on a separate shelf.

5 Check the carton for any breaks. Whole cartons help protect eggs from absorbing unwanted smells or tastes from surrounding food. Consider replacing the carton if big cracks or tears are present.

6 Proximity to cooked foods may speed up spoilage. Putting the carton in the middle of a fridge rack ensures that the eggs will remain a uniform temperature.

7 Eat the eggs before their expiry date. Expiry dates are carefully calculated using the date of laying, transit times and the expected time that the eggs will remain on the shelf in the shop or supermarket.

Poach an Egg in a Microwave 358

You don't need pans of hot water on the hob to poach an egg any more. You can poach and serve gourmet eggs in a matter of minutes using your microwave.

✳ Tip

Make sure that you remove the egg from the water as soon as possible, as the egg will continue to cook in the hot water.

◉ Steps

1 Fill a small glass cup or dessert bowl one-third of the way to the top with clean, fresh water. Add a splash of white vinegar or apple cider vinegar, depending on your taste.

2 Crack an egg carefully and drop it into the water. Leave the egg as it is if you would like the yolk runny, or use a toothpick to poke a small hole in the yoke if you prefer the egg cooked through. Cover the dish loosely with a piece of plastic wrap and place it in your microwave.

3 Set your microwave for one minute on medium heat and listen carefully. Depending on the wattage and type of microwave, poaching may take more or less than one minute. You will know the egg is done when you begin to hear popping noises.

4 Remove the bowl using oven gloves and remove your poached egg from the water carefully with a slotted spoon. Serve the poached egg immediately, seasoning with a bit of salt and pepper.

359 | Make Puff Pastry

Flaky puff pastry is a staple for any well-equipped baker, and can be used in many mouth-watering recipes.

⊙ Steps

1 Combine the flour and salt in a mixing bowl, and add the sliced butter. Mix until the butter slices are coated with the flour. Add the water and mix with a wooden spoon.

2 Place the pastry dough on to a lightly floured surface and knead it into a loose ball. Form the dough into a rectangle. Roll it flat and fold the dough into thirds, then turn the dough and fold it again to create nine layers.

3 Wrap the dough tightly in plastic wrap and let it cool in the fridge for 20 minutes. Remove the dough and repeat Step 3 twice more. Re-wrap the dough and place it in the refrigerator for another 20 minutes, then remove and slice it into equally sized pieces.

4 Place the pastries on to an oiled baking tray. Leave ample space between each pastry to prevent them from sticking together. Bake the puff pastries in the over at 200–220°C (400–425°F) until they're golden, puffy and appear dry.

Things You'll Need

- ❏ 2 cups all-purpose flour
- ❏ ½ tsp salt
- ❏ 1 cup cold butter (sliced
- ❏ 5/8 cup ice water
- ❏ Oil

360 | Bake the Perfect Cake

Making a cake can be a fun and rewarding experience, unless of course your cake comes out of the oven looking like a flying saucer. Simple but important steps need to be taken in order to produce successful results.

⊙ Steps

1 Read the recipe and make sure you have all the ingredients to bake your perfect cake. Set refrigerated items out to arrive at room temperature (eggs no more than 30 minutes ahead of your baking time).

2 Make sure you have the correct pans. Improper sizes cause unattractive, overcooked or undercooked cakes. Grease the insides using butter or shortening. Flour the pans, then dump out any excess. Set aside.

3 Preheat the oven to the temperature specified in the recipe.

4 Measure all ingredients accurately using dry measuring cups and a liquid measuring cup. Combine the dry items in a mixing bowl. Slowly add the wet ingredients and beat with an electric mixer according to speed and time specified.

5 Fill the cake tins two-thirds of the way up and tap the tins on the kitchen counter. This forces air bubbles to the surface.

6 Place in the oven and set the timer. A good rule of thumb is to set the timer eight minutes less than the time in the recipe. Insert a toothpick into the centre to check the batter consistency. If clean, the cake is done. If wet, set the timer for four more minutes and check again.

✱ Tips

When you bake, always use high-quality aluminium pans for the best results.

If you substitute self-raising flour for all-purpose flour, eliminate the baking powder.

7 Remove the cake from oven and set on a rack to cool for 20 or 30 minutes. Run a knife around the sides of pan to loosen. Holding the rack over the top of the cake tin, invert to remove the cake. Cool completely.

Make Blueberry Muffins 361

This classic breakfast muffin can be made all year round with frozen blueberries. This recipe makes about a dozen muffins.

⊙ Steps

1 Heat the oven to 190°C (375°F).

2 Generously butter a standard 6.5-cm (2.5-in) muffin tin or line it with greaseproof paper.

3 Sift the dry ingredients into a bowl, then stir together and form a well in the centre.

4 Beat the egg and milk together in another bowl, then beat in the butter.

5 Pour the wet ingredients and the blueberries into the flour and stir the mixture together slowly only until everything is combined. The mixture should still be lumpy, not smooth.

6 Divide the batter between the muffin cups, filling each one about three-quarters full.

7 Bake for about 20 minutes or until the tops turn golden.

8 Let the muffins cool in the tins for about five minutes, then remove them to a rack to finish cooling. This is important, because they'll steam when they leave the oven and this steam helps moisten them. However, too much steam will make them soggy, so remove them while they're still hot and finish cooling them outside the tins.

Things You'll Need

❑ 450 g (16 oz) all-purpose flour

❑ 1 tbsp baking powder

❑ 60 g (2 oz) sugar

❑ ½ tsp salt

❑ ½ tsp allspice

❑ 1 egg

❑ 170 g (6 oz) milk

❑ 120 g (4 oz) melted butter

❑ 340 g (12 oz) fresh or frozen blueberries

Peel a Mango 362

Peeling a mango isn't as easy as peeling many other fruits. Once you get the first few strips of skin off, the mango becomes extremely slippery and is difficult to keep in place.

✱ Tip

Peeling a mango can be messy, but it's worth the effort!

⊙ Steps

1 Peel the mango when it's ripe. The mango should give a little when you apply slight pressure to the side of the fruit with your thumb. It shouldn't feel firm nor should it squish; it should just move a little. If it's not ripe yet, put it on your kitchen counter or in a paper bag, which will help it ripen more quickly.

2 Cut one side of the mango with a serrated knife, leaving about two-thirds of the fruit uncut. Mangoes have tough centres and you avoid cutting that deep this way. Slice the "cheek" off the other side as well.

3 Use the knife to slice the pieces right up to, but not through, the skin. This is called "scoring". Score the pieces horizontally, then vertically.

You'll end up with mini squares as you do. Push on the skin side of the mango to invert the mango upwards.

4   Take the knife and run it along the inside of the mango pieces to take off the skin from the squares. Push the already-cut squares to the side.

5   Remove the pit by cutting around it with the knife. Take the skin off the pieces that are left following the same process as in Step 2. This time, chop the pieces up into squares after removing the skin.

363 | Bake Bread

If you thought baking bread was difficult, give this recipe a test-run and see for yourself how easy it is.

◎ Steps

1   Put 2½ teaspoons of bread yeast and 0.7 litres (3 cups) of bath-temperature water in a large bowl. Let it sit until the yeast dissolves.

2   Add a dash of olive oil, four teaspoons of salt and 450 g (5 oz) of all-purpose flour. Mix on a low speed with hand mixer, scraping down the sides until bubbles appear on the surface when the mixer is turned off. Add 525 g (17.5 oz) of flour and hand mix with a large wooden spoon until the dough separates from the sides of bowl.

3   Sprinkle a clean surface with flour. Pour the dough on to the surface and sprinkle flour on top.

4   Using your hands, pat down the dough and fold it over itself. Press and fold the dough (knead), adding a little more flour when it becomes sticky. Knead until the dough has a uniform texture and an indentation made with your finger pokes back out quickly (about five minutes).

5   Spray the large bowl with cooking spray, place the dough back in the bowl and spray the dough on the top and sides. Loosely cover the bowl with clean kitchen towel and set on the counter until it has doubled in size (about an hour).

6   Turn the bowl upside down and let the dough fall on the counter. Press down on the dough until all air bubbles are removed and the dough looks relatively flat and circular. Cut it into two equal pieces and fold one in half. Fold in two sides of this piece and shape it to form loaf. Press the seams together if needed. Do the same to the other piece. Spray a baking pan with cooking oil and place the two loaves on it. Cover the baking or loaf pans with a clean tea towel and let them rise until almost double the size (20 to 30 minutes). Preheat the oven to 220°C (425°F).

7   Remove the tea towel from the loaves and place in them in the oven. Fill a drinking cup half full with water and quickly dump the water on to the inside bottom of the oven (being careful not to pour it on the loaves). Repeat this step again in five minutes. Repeat again after another five, then set the oven to 175°C (350°F). Bake the loaves for another 20 minutes. The bread should smell done (not yeasty). The crust will turn brown, and when done the loaves will sound hollow when tapped on the bottom. Remove them from the bread pans and leave on a colling tray. The bread is ready to eat when warm – not hot.

⚠ Warning

Make sure dough doesn't rise too long the second time around – if it sinks in the oven you'll know it rose a little too long.

Make Toast   364

Most nutritionist agree that breakfast is the most important meal of the day, and there's nothing better for breakfast than a slice or two of perfectly made toast.

Steps

1   Get two slices of bread.

2   Place the slices into a toaster.

3   Remove the slices once the bread has browned. Many toasters have a preset timer that you can adjust depending on how brown you want your bread to be.

4   Choose a spread. You can use only one spread or use multiple spreads, but there's a whole range to choose from – from sweet jams to crunchy peanut butter.

5   Take a butter knife and scoop up a spread. Smear the spread across the bread. If you would like the spread warm and melted, smear the spread while the bread is still warm. If you would like your spread to be chilled or at room temperature, smear the spread once the bread has cooled.

6   Eat the toast by biting into it while holding it with your fingers. You can also cut it into little squares to be eaten as a small finger food.

✳ Tips

Do feel free to experiment with a variety of breads and spreads. Remember, the two slices do not have to be the same bread or spread.

Warm beverages such as coffee or hot chocolate are perfect additions to toast.

⚠ Warning

Don't let your bread turn black. This means it has burned and the taste will be altered.

Make French Toast   365

Home-made French toast is both delicious and easy to make. Let the kids help in the kitchen when making this comforting and tasty breakfast.

Steps

1   In a bowl, combine two eggs, half a cup of milk, a pinch of sugar, a splash of pure vanilla extract and enough cinnamon to cover the top of the mixture. Whip the ingredients together with a whisker.

2   Heat a skillet or griddle, and allow a tablespoon of butter to melt in the pan. This will prevent the French toast from sticking.

3   Dip a piece of bread in the egg mixture. Make sure both sides are evenly coated. Place the slice of bread in the heated pan. Repeat this process with each piece of bread.

4   When the bread is golden brown, flip it over and cook the other side. The bread should no longer be soggy when it's done. When both sides are cooked, sprinkle with a little more cinnamon and serve. If you like powdered sugar, sprinkle some on the top before serving. Otherwise, butter each piece of French toast before adding syrup.

Things You'll Need

❏ White bread
❏ Eggs
❏ Milk
❏ Sugar
❏ Cinnamon
❏ Pure vanilla extract
❏ Butter
❏ Syrup

366 | Make a Basic Omelette

Omelettes made in the French style are actually fairly easy to make, and are a delicious and quick meal if you don't have much time.

⊙ Steps

1   Combine the eggs, water, salt and pepper in a medium-sized bowl. Beat with a fork until the ingredients are combined but haven't become too frothy.

2   Melt a little butter (1 or 2 teaspoons) over medium-high to high heat.

3   When the butter stops foaming, pour the egg mixture into the skillet, and without moving the skillet, allow the eggs to set on the bottom (this should only take a few seconds).

4   As the eggs set, take a spatula and push the edges of the egg mixture inwards, allowing the uncooked eggs on top to flow underneath and make direct contact with the skillet. This is to ensure that all parts are properly cooked. Repeat the procedure at various spots around the edge of the setting egg mixture.

5   When the eggs are set but still shiny, remove the omelette from the heat. The whole process of cooking your omelette should take no more than two or three minutes.

6   Fold the omelette in half and slide it on to a warm plate.

✳ Tips

Practise with plain omelettes before you try filling them.

To make a low-fat omelette, prepare using one whole egg and two egg whites, instead of two whole eggs.

Things You'll Need

❑ 2 eggs

❑ Butter for the pan

❑ Dash of black pepper

❑ ⅛ tsp salt

❑ 1 tbsp water

367 | Make a Green Salad

When you make a green salad, the most important thing is to dry the leaves completely before tossing. You don't want extra water to dilute your dressing.

⊙ Steps

1   Select crisp, fresh greens with no bruised spots on the leaves or streaks of brown near the roots.

2   Use a variety of greens. Vary dark with light, and crisp with tender.

3   Remove any broken or damaged outer leaves.

4   Wash and drain the greens thoroughly. Use a salad spinner to dry the greens quickly, or you can wrap the greens in a towel.

5   Make sure the greens are cold and dry before making your salad.

6   Gently tear the greens into bite-size pieces.

7   Make sure your additional ingredients, if you use any, go well with each other. You don't need to add anything else if your greens are interesting enough. Possible additions include sliced radishes, chopped scallions, sliced carrots, crumbled bacon, cut-up apples or pears, or whatever suits your fancy and your greens. Usually just a few additions are best.

✳ Tips

Try red and green leaf lettuce; bronze lettuce; Romaine, Boston and Bibb lettuce; curly endive and escarole; spinach; watercress; dandelion; and beet or mustard tops. Many supermarkets now sell "spring mix" or "mesclun", a pre-mixed batch of interesting greens.

Store greens in a plastic bag or container in the refrigerator to ensure crispness.

8   Add dressing at the last minute. Use just enough to coat the leaves lightly, and toss gently.

9   Garnish with toasted nuts, croutons, tomato wedges or sliced olives.

Make a Potato Salad   368

Wow your friends with "real" potato salad at your next barbecue. It's a simple but delicious side dish.

⊚ Steps

1   Boil whole, unpeeled potatoes for 15 minutes, or until just tender. Don't overcook the potatoes or they will fall apart when you cut them.

2   Peel and dice the potatoes while they are still warm.

3   Add the mayonnaise and diced eggs, and stir until the potatoes are moist.

4   Add salt and pepper to taste, plus any of the ingredients listed opposite.

5   Mix all the ingredients thoroughly.

6   Place the finished salad in a large salad bowl and garnish with sliced egg, chopped parsley and paprika.

7   Refrigerate or keep on ice until ready to eat.

Things You'll Need

- ❏ Yellow or red onions
- ❏ 5 hard-boiled eggs
- ❏ 1.3 kg (3 lb) russet potatoes
- ❏ Mayonnaise
- ❏ Cucumber, celery and peppers
- ❏ Parsley
- ❏ Paprika
- ❏ Cider vinegar
- ❏ Celery seeds
- ❏ Sweet pickle

Make Carrot and Coriander Soup   369

This is a simple and delicious soup – its fresh taste is perfect all year round. It can be served as a starter at a dinner party, or it makes a healthy meal in itself.

⊚ Steps

1   In a large saucepan melt the butter over a medium heat and cook the onion and garlic until soft, without colouring. Covering the saucepan during cooking helps prevent colouring.

2   Add the roughly chopped carrots, vegetable stock and nutmeg. Cover and bring to the boil. Then turn down the heat and simmer until the vegetables are tender.

3   Cool the soup a little, then puree in a blender (or with a hand-held blender). Transfer the soup to a clean saucepan if you need to keep it warm for a while, or a serving bowl if you plan on serving it immediately.

4   Stir in the grated carrots, coriander and cream. Season with salt and pepper. If you don't have fresh coriander it's possible to use dried, but be careful as a little goes a long way.

Things You'll Need

- ❏ 2 tbsp butter
- ❏ 1 medium onion, finely chopped
- ❏ 1 garlic clove, crushed
- ❏ 450 g (1 lb) chopped carrot
- ❏ 100 g (¼ lb) grated carrot
- ❏ 800 g (28 oz) vegetable stock
- ❏ Pinch of nutmeg
- ❏ 1 tbsp fresh chopped coriander
- ❏ 110 g (4 oz) whipping cream

370 | Eat Caviar

Though considered a luxury, those salty fish eggs are easy to prepare and serve.

⊙ Steps

1 Serve caviar in a crystal, glass or porcelain bowl on a bed of crushed ice, or in a special caviar server with a tiny spoon that is neither silver nor stainless steel (these metals can give the caviar a metallic taste). Traditionally, a mother-of-pearl or gold spoon is used, but you can use horn, wood or glass. Plastic would be gauche.

2 Put about one teaspoon of caviar on your plate.

3 Spread the caviar over dry or lightly buttered toast points or unsalted, bland crackers.

4 If you like, squeeze a drop of fresh lemon juice over the caviar.

5 Eat it plain or choose your garnish: typically crumbled, hard-boiled egg, chopped onion or crême fraiche.

6 Drink champagne, ice-cold vodka or chilled white wine with the caviar.

7 Try a very traditional Russian recipe of caviar on whole-wheat pancakes (blini) with a dab of sour cream.

❋ Tips

Etiquette dictates taking only a small portion of this treat.

Eat the whole tin at once. If you must store opened caviar, wrap it tightly in plastic and turn the tin over so the oil is always evenly distributed.

Use unsalted butter on the toast points, as the caviar itself is salty.

371 | Cook Salmon

Salmon is one of the healthiest foods you can eat. Baked salmon is easy to prepare and cooks fast.

⊙ Steps

1 Preheat your oven to 175°C (350°F).

2 Check the salmon for stray bones. If you find bones, remove them immediately and discard.

3 Place the salmon on an oven tray lined with baking foil so it will be easy to clean after cooking.

4 Smear the salmon with butter, getting into all cracks and crevices. Soften the butter in a microwave if necessary.

5 Sprinkle the salmon with lemon pepper and dried parsley. Squirt a little bit of fresh lemon juice on the salmon.

6 Place the salmon in the preheated oven and cover it loosely with aluminium foil.

7 Bake the salmon for approximately 12–15 minutes. This will vary depending on the size and thickness of the fillet; more cooking time may be needed for larger thicker salmon cuts and less cooking time may be needed for smaller or individual salmon fillets.

8 While the salmon is baking, zest the lemon and set aside.

Things You'll Need

❑ 450 g (1 lb) salmon fillet

❑ Butter

❑ Lemon pepper

❑ Dried parsley

❑ Fresh lemon wedges

❑ Lemon zest

❑ Tartar sauce

9 After eight minutes of cooking time, check the salmon to see if it is cooked. Stick a fork in the thickest part of the salmon to test for flakiness. If the salmon is still a bit tough or raw, continue cooking and check in two-minute increments thereafter. If the salmon is tender and flakes when you stick the fork in it, it's done.

10 When the salmon is properly cooked, remove from the oven and sprinkle lemon zest on top. Serve with fresh lemon wedges and tartar sauce.

Prepare Traditional Roast Beef 372

Preparing roast beef may seem intimidating at first, but really there's little more to it than putting the roast in the oven and pulling it out when it's done.

◎ Steps

1 Heat the oven to 230°C (450°F). Remove the roast from its packaging and place it in a sturdy roasting pan.

2 Rub the roast lightly with the oil. Try not to get any oil in the bottom of the roasting pan.

3 Rub the roast with enough salt and pepper to lightly season it.

4 Place the roasting pan in the oven.

5 After 15–20 minutes, turn the heat down to 160°C (325°F). Test it using an instant-read thermometer. For rare meat, remove the roast when the internal temperature reads 55–57°C (130–135°F). For medium rare, remove at 60–62°C (140–145°F). And for medium, remove at 68°C (155°F) or above. A large rib roast takes two to four hours to cook.

6 Let the roast beef rest at room temperature, without carving or cutting into it, for 20 to 30 minutes.

⚠ Warning

Always let roasted meat rest before cutting it. Residual heat will continue cooking the meat for up to 20 minutes after it comes out of the oven.

Things You'll Need

❏ 4.5–7 kg (10–15 lb) prime rib roast

❏ Cracked black pepper

❏ Salt

❏ Olive oil (not virgin)

Roast Lamb 373

Roasting a leg of lamb isn't as hard as you might think. It's worth the time and effort since it's absolutely delicious.

◎ Steps

1 Take the leg of lamb shank and place in a roasting pan.

2 Spear the lamb and insert the garlic cloves into the roast. Place in a preheated 200°C (400°F) oven and cook for half an hour. Reduce the heat to 175°C (350°F).

3 Place the potatoes and onions in the roasting pan with the lamb. Salt and pepper the potatoes. Cover the whole roasting pan with foil if you don't have a lid. Cook for half an hour, uncover and turn the potatoes, then recover the pan. Potatoes and onions should be added to the roast approximately 1½ hours before the roast is done.

4 Cooking time for the leg of lamb is approximate and it's best if you use a meat thermometer.

Things You'll Need

❏ 1.8–2.7 kg (4–6 lb) leg of lamb

❏ 6 white potatoes (peeled and cut into quarters)

❏ 2 onions (peeled and cut into quarters)

❏ 2 garlic cloves

❏ Salt and pepper

374 | Make Fish Cakes

If you're looking for a new way to prepare an old favourite, delicious fish cakes are quick and simple to make, and are a healthy and nutritious meal.

⊙ Steps

1 Scrub, peel and boil the potatoes. Once soft, strain the water and mash the potatoes until creamy.

2 Poach 450 g (1 lb) of your favourite fish – cod, salmon or trout work best for fish cakes – in a shallow pan or a frying pan. Keep the fish whole and don't allow the water to come to a boil. The fish is done when you can flake pieces off easily.

3 Drain the excess water from the fish and carefully remove the bones and skin. Add the cooked fish to your mashed potatoes. Salt to taste and gently fold the fish into the potatoes. Taste the mixture and add extra salt or seasoning if needed.

4 Place the potatoes and fish in the refrigerator until chilled; this will help to hold your finished cakes together. Once chilled, form the mixture into cakes.

5 Fry your finished fish cakes in hot oil, cooking for four or five minutes on each side. Serve with your favourite sauce.

Things You'll Need

❏ 450 g (1 lb) potatoes

❏ 450 g (1 lb) fish

❏ Salt

❏ Oil

375 | Serve Cheese Fondue

Serving cheese fondue is a time-honoured tradition that can make a big impact on your next party or get-together.

⊙ Steps

1 Prepare the cheese fondue according the recipe 30 minutes before your guests arrive. While there are different variations, a cheese fondue recipe typically consists of two different kinds of cheese, a little bit of white wine or beer and some flour for thickening.

2 Transfer the mixture to a lit fondue pot once the cheese is melted.

3 Arrange various dippers on a tray and place it next to the fondue set. Good dippers for cheese fondue are crusty French bread, vegetables, cooked meat, potatoes and any other savoury item you can think of.

4 Instruct guests on how to spear a piece of bread, dip it into the fondue and then twirl to remove any excess.

5 Explain the fondue etiquette rules to your guests. The rules include not allowing their lips to touch the fondue fork, not double dipping and not dropping any food into the fondue pot. Give guests a separate plate and fork on which to transfer over their food while it cools.

6 Keep track of the dippers and fondue supply, and replenish as needed.

✳ Tips

Serve your guests a nice white wine to help wash down their cheese fondue.

Make sure your dippers are all bite-size pieces.

⚠ Warnings

Check your cheese fondue often to make sure that it isn't burning. A little stir or an adjustment of the heating element will usually solve the problem.

Tradition says that if you or a guest drop a piece of food into the fondue pot, you have to either buy the next bottle of wine or plant a kiss on someone of the opposite sex.

Grill Vegetables 376

Grilled vegetables can be an easy accompaniment to other grilled foods or the centrepiece of a vegetarian meal.

⊙ Steps

1 Choose vegetables that take well to grilling, such as peppers, aubergine, tomatoes, corn on the cob, button mushrooms and summer squash.

2 Clean and trim the vegetables. Cut large ones into halves or slice them into large sections.

3 Parboil small, waxy potatoes until tender before grilling. Remove silks from corn but leave the husks on, and soak in water for about one hour before grilling.

4 Marinate vegetables for 15 minutes before grilling. Or just brush them lightly with oil so they don't stick to the grill, if you won't be cooking them in a foil pouch or vegetable basket.

5 Prepare a medium-hot fire in the charcoal or gas grill.

6 Put the vegetables directly on the grill grid, on skewers or inside a foil pouch or vegetable basket. Begin with the vegetables that take the longest to cook – denser vegetables such as potatoes or peppers will take longer than moisture-filled ones such as tomatoes.

7 Turn the vegetables often, brushing on more marinade as needed.

8 Remove the vegetables when they can be easily pierced with a fork.

✱ Tips

Marinades can be made the day before and stored, covered, in the refrigerator. Try this basic marinade: Combine 2 parts olive oil and 1 part lemon juice with 1 peeled and crushed garlic clove.

Flavoured butters, such as chilli butter and herb butter, are delicious with grilled vegetables.

Make Vegetable Chilli 377

Chilli is a perpetual favourite – particularly on cold winter evenings. But you don't need meat to make a good chilli.

⊙ Steps

1 Chop the vegetables and mince the garlic.

2 Coat a non-stick skillet with cooking spray and place over a medium-high heat until hot.

3 Add the onion, green pepper, carrot and garlic, and cook until tender.

4 Combine the vegetable mixture in a Dutch oven with the vegetable broth, kidney beans, pinto beans, whole tomatoes, undrained and chopped, tomato paste, chilli powder, cumin, oregano, cinnamon, hot sauce, jalapeno pepper and bay leaf.

5 Bring to the boil.

6 Reduce the heat and simmer uncovered for around 45 minutes, stirring occasionally to prevent burning.

7 Remove the bay leaf.

8 Ladle the chilli into individual bowls and top with a dab of non-fat sour cream and sharp cheddar cheese.

Things You'll Need

- ❏ Olive oil
- ❏ 1 large chopped onion
- ❏ 3 garlic cloves
- ❏ 1 tin tomato paste
- ❏ 1 tin pinto beans
- ❏ 1 tin kidney beans
- ❏ 2 green peppers
- ❏ 4 carrots, peeled and cut
- ❏ 3 fresh tomatoes
- ❏ Cumin, oregano and cinnamon
- ❏ Vegetable broth
- ❏ Chilli power and jalapeno

378 Go Green Vegetarian Style

Our meat-based diet contributes to world hunger and is a primary cause of deforestation. A vegetarian approach to a green lifestyle can improve your health while enhancing the lives of everyone in the world.

Go Vegetarian

- To avoid craving the meat dishes you grew up on try some meat substitutes, like dishes made with garden burgers or smart dogs (made with soy or wheat gluten) instead of hotdogs. Eating healthily can be good for the world and fun and delicious.

- Include raw fruits and veggies in your diet. Cooked foods lack essential enzymes needed for digestion. Try a salad with nuts and use Thai sauces to make dishes fun.

- Keep healthy fats in your diet, such as avocado and nuts. Studies show that when people crave meat in their diet, they are actually craving fat, not protein.

- Invest in a vegetarian cookbook.

- Take time to taste food rather than swallowing it just to feel full.

Remain a Meat-Eater

- Even if you can't give up that bacon sandwich, you can still go green vegetarian style. For example, switching to organic and free-range meats is much greener than eating meat raised on intensive farms.

- Try almond, soya or rice milk rather than hormone-laden cow's milk. If you're concerned about getting enough calcium, eat green leafy veggies and exercise. Exercise can prevent osteoporosis even in dairy-free diets.

- Explore international foods. Expand beyond meat and potatoes to discover the world of yellow curry and sweet and savoury vegetarian meals. Travel the globe on your dinner table. Make every meal an adventure rather than a chore. Enjoy every moment of your meal.

Green Growing and Buying

- Find out about the treatment of animals that are raised for consumption. You don't have to become a right-on activist, but everyone should understand what they're eating and make an informed decision about whether or not they're happy about it.

- Look for foods that have not been grown using artificial fertilisers or pesticides, which are damaging to the environment.

- Choose foods that come in green packaging to have minimal environmental impact. If you have to buy food that doesn't come in already recycled packaging, then make sure you'll be able to recycle it afterwards – avoid plastic packaging, which uses up oil reserves and is harder to recycle than paper, glass or cardboard.

Green Lifestyle

- Get involved in energy conservation in your area. Hold elected officials accountable for the environment in your area. Write letters and be proactive. Ask them for more and safer cycle paths, sustainable public transport, and tax breaks and incentives for sustainable home energy use.

- Lead by example. Walk or ride your bike and use public transport.

- Recycle all your food and other packaging. Almost everything can be recycled these days so make sure you're doing your bit. Divide plastic packaging into its different types, as well as paper and cardboard. Make compost from food waste and any leftovers – this natural fertiliser is great for your garden.

reference

Make Stuffed Peppers   `379`

The bell pepper is a vegetable ready-made for stuffing. The stuffing here is a well-seasoned paella-style rice pilaf, but you can use many different kinds of stuffing.

⊙ Steps

1   Heat the olive oil in a saucepan or sauté pan over medium heat.

2   Add the onion and cook for about two minutes, stirring occasionally.

3   Add the garlic and stir it in well.

4   Add all the dry spices and continue cooking until the onion is soft – another minute or so.

5   Add the tomato, cook another minute, then add the rice and stir everything together.

6   Add the stock and bring to a boil, lower to a simmer, then cook, uncovered, for 10 minutes.

7   Add the corn and cook, covered, for 10 to 15 minutes more or until the rice is just becoming tender. Some liquid should still be in the pan.

8   While the rice cooks, heat the oven to 175°C (350°F).

9   Cut the tops off the bell peppers, scoop out the seed pods, and reserve.

10 Lightly grease a baking dish and prepare an aluminium foil cover.

11 When the rice is almost fully cooked, scoop the mixture into each pepper. Place the peppers in the baking dish, cover and bake for 30–40 minutes.

Things You'll Need

- ❏ 110 g (4 oz) olive oil
- ❏ 2 garlic cloves
- ❏ 1 medium onion
- ❏ 2 small tomatoes
- ❏ ¼ tsp turmeric
- ❏ ½ tsp garlic powder
- ❏ 4 red or green bell peppers
- ❏ ½ tsp chilli powder
- ❏ ¼ tsp ground cumin
- ❏ 660 ml (3 cups) chicken stock
- ❏ 1 ear fresh or frozen corn
- ❏ ½ tsp dried marjoram
- ❏ 220 g (8 oz) long-grain rice
- ❏ ½ tsp black pepper

Make Vegan Nut Roast   `380`

Please the vegans at your dinner table with this hearty roast.

⊙ Steps

1   Preheat the oven to 200°C (400°F).

2   Heat the oil in a saucepan over medium heat and cook half the onion and the garlic in the saucepan until tender.

3   Add the cashews and half the bread cubes to the onion. Add vegetable stock, salt, pepper, nutmeg and lemon juice.

4   Place half the bread mixture in a small non-stick loaf pan. Set aside. Toast the remaining bread cubes in the oven for 10 minutes or so.

5   Combine toasted bread cubes, margarine, the remaining onion, celery, thyme, marjoram, sage, parsley and salt to taste in a mixing bowl. Put this mixture on top of the mixture already in the pan.

6   Add what's left of the first mixture to the loaf pan so that there are three layers of mixtures. Put the pan on a baking sheet and bake for 30 minutes, or until the top is browned.

7   Let the roast cool for five minutes, then turn out on to a serving platter.

Things You'll Need

- ❏ 1 kg (36 oz) cubed bread
- ❏ Raw cashews and celery
- ❏ 3 tbsp chopped fresh parsley
- ❏ 5 minced garlic cloves
- ❏ 2 tbsp lemon juice
- ❏ 2 tbsp melted margarine
- ❏ ½ tsp marjoram and nutmeg
- ❏ 3 finely chopped onions
- ❏ ½ tsp sage and thyme
- ❏ 2 tbsp vegetable oil
- ❏ 220 g (8 oz) vegetable stock

381 | Dress a Salad the Healthy Way

If you're trying to eat more healthily, salads can be a great way to go – but beware, hundreds of empty calories may lurk in the dressing.

⊙ Steps

1   Request your dressing on the side when ordering out. Dip your fork or each individual bite of salad lightly into the dressing. This method packs in a punch of flavour with every bite, and you may find over half the dressing left in the bowl.

2   Coat your salad lightly with dressing just prior to serving. Don't drown your vegetables.

3   Create your own dressings. Lemon juice, olive oil and vinegar are classic salad-dressing ingredients, but anything is possible. Try them with different combinations of Dijon mustard, fresh garlic or ginger, soy sauce, honey, fruit purees or salsa. For a creamy dressing, use low-fat yoghurt instead of sour cream.

4   Add a little salt and pepper to home-made dressings to brighten the flavour. Fresh herbs also make a great addition.

5   Use a ratio of one part acid (lemon juice, vinegar) to three parts oil when mixing salad dressings. If mixing in a blender or with a whisk, combine all ingredients and stream the oil in last. If combining dressing ingredients directly on your salad, add the acid before adding the oil to allow the flavour to soak into the leaves a bit.

✳ Tip

Try different kinds of vinegar in your dressing mix. Balsamic, tarragon, champagne and red wine vinegars are all delicious options.

382 | Make Lemon Meringue Pie

Use this recipe to make an old-fashioned lemon or lime meringue pie.

⊙ Steps

1   Make or buy shortcrust pastry.

2   Sprinkle a little flour on to a work surface and roll out the ball of pastry.

3   Transfer to the pie pan by rolling the crust around the rolling pin, then unrolling in the pan, or by folding the crust into quarters, then unfolding in the pan.

4   Trim the edge to a 2.5-cm (1-in) overhang; fold the edge under to make a rim. Use your fingers to crimp the edge of crust decoratively and then place in the refrigerator for 20 minutes.

5   Preheat oven to 200°C (400°F).

6   Use a fork to prick the dough repeatedly.

7   Crumple a sheet of greaseproof paper and cover the piecrust with it. Place pie weights or dry beans inside the piecrust.

8   Bake for 12 minutes then take out the paper and weights.

Things You'll Need

- ❏ ¼ tsp salt
- ❏ 340 g (12 oz) sugar
- ❏ 3 eggs (separated)
- ❏ 2 tbsp butter
- ❏ ¼ tsp cream of tartar
- ❏ 6 tbsp cornflour
- ❏ ½ tsp vanilla
- ❏ ½ cup fresh lemon juice
- ❏ 4 tbsp icing sugar
- ❏ 1 tbsp lemon zest

9   Bake for another six to eight minutes or until the crust has turned golden.

10 Whisk together the granulated sugar, cornflour and salt in a saucepan over a low heat and gradually blend in a little cold water and the fresh lemon juice.

11 When the mixture is smooth, gradually add in three well-beaten egg yolks and butter. Whisk constantly while slowly adding 340 g (12 oz) boiling water. Slowly bring the mixture to a full boil, whisking gently. As the mixture thickens, reduce the heat and simmer for one minute.

12 Remove from the heat and stir in the lemon zest.

13 Pour the lemon mixture into the pie crust and spread evenly.

15 Preheat the oven to 175°C (350°F).

16 Beat two egg whites and the cream of tartar with an electric mixer in a chilled mixing bowl until the mixture forms stiff peaks. Beat in the icing sugar one tablespoon at a time. Add the vanilla.

17 Cover the filling completely with meringue. Make sure you spread the meringue all the way to the edges of the crust so it is sealed to the edge when it bakes.

18 Bake for 15 minutes. The top of the meringue should be browned and crisp, but the insides soft.

Make Rhubarb Crumble   `383`

Rhubarb is a forgotten treasure for many of us. Rhubarb crumble is an easy dessert to make, bake and serve either warm or cool.

⊙ Steps

1   Preheat the oven to 175°C (350°F).

2   Cut the rhubarb stalks off the plant. These stalks look like red pieces of celery. Rinse to remove any of the soil and strip them of any of the stringy pieces. Cut them into 2.5-cm (0.5-in) pieces. Put them into the pie pan.

3   Toss one cup of granulated sugar and two tablespoons of flour into the pie pan. Stir to mix all the ingredients.

4   Mix one cup of granulated sugar, one cup of flour, the oatmeal, salt, cinnamon and baking powder in a small bowl. Stir until all these ingredients are thoroughly combined.

5   Crack the egg into another small bowl and use a whisk or egg beater to beat the egg until it begins to expand in the bowl and turn a lemony yellow colour. Add the beaten egg to the sugar-flour mixture in the other small bowl.

6   Spread the sugar-flour-egg mixture (this makes the crumble or crust) over the top of the rhubarb pieces that are in the pie pan. Shake the pan to make the crumble settle into the rhubarb.

7   Melt the butter and drizzle it over the top of the rhubarb crumble.

8   Bake in the oven for about 40 minutes. The rhubarb crumble will brown on top and you will see evidence of a thick sticky syrup underneath the crumble. Serve warm or cold.

⚠ Warning

Do not eat any other part of the rhubarb plant other than the stalks.

Things You'll Need

❏ 570 g (20 oz) rhubarb

❏ 550 g (16 oz) granulated sugar

❏ 2 tbsp flour

❏ 55 g (2 oz) oatmeal

❏ 150 g (5 oz) flour

❏ 1 tsp baking powder

❏ 1 egg

❏ Dash of salt

❏ 1 tsp cinnamon

❏ ½ stick butter

384 | Make Custard

Learn to cook custard on the stove, in the oven or microwave, and make it a popular menu item for your household.

◉ Steps

1 Heat the milk for two or three minutes in the microwave. Whisk the eggs until smooth and add them to the milk.

2 Add the sugar, salt and vanilla. Stir this mixture into the milk and egg mixture until dissolved.

3 Run the whole mixture through a strainer and stir again. This will give you a smooth, sweet, pudding-like treat.

4 Pour the custard into small custard dishes, a casserole dish or a pie dish. Sprinkle the top with ground cinnamon or nutmeg, if desired.

5 Bake your custard at 160°C (325°F). It's done when a knife or toothpick inserted into the centre comes out clean.

6 Vary the flavour of your custard by scooping caramel sauce, sliced berries or syrups on top. If your family enjoys pies, place the custard mix into a pre-baked pie crust for a quick treat.

⚠ Warning

Baking custard too long may result in it curdling. Not cooking long enough may result in thick custard that didn't set.

Things You'll Need

❑ 880 ml (4 cups) milk

❑ 6 large eggs

❑ 150 g (5 oz) sugar

❑ ½ tsp salt

❑ 1 tbsp vanilla extract

385 | Make Dark Chocolate Sauce

This dark, sweet sauce is heaven on vanilla ice cream – and it's not too bad for you, either!

◉ Steps

1 In a heavy saucepan, heat water with the sugar over moderate heat.

2 Whisk until the sugar is dissolved.

3 Add the cocoa powder and salt, and whisk the mixture until smooth.

4 Add the butter and vanilla, and whisk until the butter is melted.

Things You'll Need

❑ Pinch of salt

❑ 60 g (2 oz) cocoa powder

❑ 85 g (3 oz) of dark brown sugar

❑ 2 tbsp unsalted butter

❑ Vanilla extract

386 | Make a Hot Fudge Sundae

Hot fudge sauce and cold vanilla ice cream: an unbeatable combination. For the best sundae, make your own hot fudge, ice cream and whipped cream.

◉ Steps

1 If you haven't made your own sauce, heat 50–100 g (2–4 oz), depending on how decadent you want to be, of prepared sauce in the microwave.

2 Put two or three scoops of vanilla ice cream into a bowl.

3 Pour the hot fudge over the top of the ice cream.

4 Top with whipped cream, a few cherries and nuts.

✽ Tips

You can use other ice-cream flavours, but the combination of vanilla and fudge is a winner.

Toast the nuts to bring out their flavour.

Make Crème Brulée   387

There's nothing more delicious than crème brulée, an
enormously popular dessert served in fine restaurants.

☉ Steps

1   Heat the oven to 135°C (275°F).

2   Scald the cream and vanilla extract by heating them in a non-reactive pan
    over a low heat until steaming.

3   When the cream is hot, whisk together the egg yolks and sugar until
    well blended.

4   When the cream starts to steam, shut off the heat.

5   Pour a little cream into the egg yolks while whisking quickly. This will
    slowly heat the yolks, reducing the chance of them curdling.

6   Remove the whisk from the eggs, start whisking the cream, and steadily
    pour the yolks into the cream while whisking quickly.

7   When thoroughly mixed, divide the mixture into oven-safe individual
    ramekins.

8   For the best results, an optional step is to chill the filled ramekins
    overnight before cooking.

9   Place the ramekins in a tall-sided baking pan. Pour simmering water into
    the pan about halfway up the sides of the ramekins.

10 Bake for 35–45 minutes.

11 Cover and chill for at least two hours.

12 When ready to serve, sprinkle the top of each serving with a thin, even
    layer of sugar.

13 If you have a propane kitchen torch, heat the sugar with the flame until it
    begins to brown. Stop when it reaches a golden colour. It should not get
    too dark.

14 Without a torch, use the oven's broiler setting to caramelise the sugar.
    Broil for 20 to 30 seconds within an inch of the flame or heating element.

⚠ Warnings

In an electric oven with a top-
heating element, place a sheet
pan on the top rack to protect
the custards from direct heat.

Watch the ramekins very carefully
when they are under the broiler to
avoid burning the sugar.

Things You'll Need

❏ 70 g (2.5 oz) sugar

❏ 4 egg yolks

❏ 1 pint heavy cream

❏ 1 tsp vanilla extract

Make Gingerbread Men   388

Continue the gingerbread man tradition throughout the year with
a favourite recipe and a little creativity.

☉ Steps

1   Mix and refrigerate your favourite gingerbread recipe. Cold dough is
    firmer and easier to handle.

2   Preheat the oven to the temperature specified to bake in your
    gingerbread recipe. Set the oven rack in the middle of the oven.
    Placing the oven rack too low in your oven creates men with
    burnt bottoms and undercooked tops.

✳ Tips

Freeze the dough for several
weeks to prepare it in advance.

Use the gingerbread dough
scraps to make other shapes
like stars.

3   Prepare the baking sheets by lining them with parchment or greaseproof paper. Restaurant or bakery supply shops sell precut parchment paper the size of standard baking sheets and pans.

4   Roll the dough out on a floured counter or between two pieces of greaseproof paper to prevent the dough from sticking as it warms to room temperature. Roll the dough to around 0.5–1 cm (0.2–0.4 in) in thickness depending on the size of your shape cutter.

5   Cut the gingerbread man or woman shape out of the rolled-out dough. Put a little flour on the cutter to prevent the dough from sticking. Move the cut shapes to the lined sheets. Decorate the men with raisins or turbinado sugar for buttons and bow ties. Use a knife to carve a face. Put a lollipop stick under some of the shapes to have the option to make a gingerbread bouquet.

6   Bake the biscuits according to the recipe. Underbake them a bit and allow them to finish baking on the sheet for a couple of minutes when you take them out of the oven to avoid overcooked, hard biscuits.

7   Prepare royal icing for further detailed decorations such as outlines and buttons. Substitute meringue powder for raw eggs. Also cut gingerbread or other decorative shapes out of fondant.

389 | Make a Basic Risotto

Risotto is a creamy Italian rice dish. You can add a multitude of things to this delicious basic recipe to give it your own personal touch.

⊙ Steps

1   Put the broth in a saucepan and heat to a gentle simmer on the stove.

2   Heat half the butter and the oil in a large heavy-bottomed saucepan over medium heat. When the butter has melted, add the onion and cook for three minutes.

3   Add the rice and stir to coat the grains well with the butter and oil. Cook for another minute while stirring gently.

4   Set your kitchen timer to 18 minutes.

5   Add the wine, stir and let it cook until the wine is almost completely absorbed by the rice. Add quarter of a cup of broth and stir frequently until it is almost completely absorbed.

6   Continue adding the broth, a little at a time, until it is gone. You should be adding the last of the broth around the time when the timer goes off.

7   Taste the rice. It should be tender yet firm to the bite, rather like *al dente* pasta. If it's too hard, keep adding broth or water until it's done.

8   With the last addition of broth, also stir in the remaining butter, salt, pepper and cheese.

9   If you run out of broth before the timer sounds, add more broth or water until you hear the timer.

✳ Tip

Do not rinse the rice prior to cooking. The starch is essential to ensuring a creamy texture in the risotto.

Things You'll Need

❑ 1 tbsp olive oil

❑ 1 small onion

❑ 2 tbsp unsalted butter

❑ Parmesan cheese

❑ White wine

❑ 440 ml (2 cups) heavy cream

❑ 880 ml (4 cups) chicken or vegetable broth

❑ 400 g (14 oz) Arborio rice

❑ Pinch of salt

❑ White pepper

Cook Thai Green Chicken Curry $\qquad$ 390

Thai green curry gets its name from the colour of the dish. The main ingredient, green curry paste, is made from a combination of spices ground together.

Steps

1 Heat the oil in a wok skillet then stir in the green curry paste for about two minutes.

2 Stir in the coconut milk, brown sugar and fish sauce and bring to a gentle boil on medium heat for about eight to 10 minutes.

3 Add the chicken pieces and red bell-pepper strips, cover the skillet and let it simmer on a medium-low heat for about 30 minutes or until the chicken is cooked.

4 Lower the heat and stir in the Thai basil leaves, Kaffir lime leaves and lime juice, and let it simmer for three to five minutes.

5 Serve in bowls poured over jasmine rice or a rice of your choice.

Things You'll Need

- ❏ 2 tsp green curry paste
- ❏ 1 tin coconut milk
- ❏ 1 tbsp brown sugar
- ❏ 2 tsp fish sauce
- ❏ 450 g (1 lb) boneless diced chicken breasts
- ❏ 1 large red bell pepper
- ❏ Chopped Kaffir lime leaves and Thai basil leaves
- ❏ 2 tbsp lime juice

Make Fajitas $\qquad$ 391

Classic Tex-Mex fajitas consist of juicy strips of steak combined with colourful bell peppers and onions, all wrapped up in a warm tortilla.

Steps

1 Slice the sirloin steak into thin strips, cutting across the grain of the meat. Cut any long slices in half.

2 Place the strips in a sealed bag and add the jalapeño pepper and rice vinegar. Close the bag and turn it to make sure the meat is completely coated. Refrigerate the meat overnight or for at least three hours.

3 Remove the meat from the refrigerator and take it out of the bag. Discard the marinade.

4 Heat the canola oil in a heavy skillet over a high heat, and cook the meat for about four minutes, until it's just barely pink in the middle. Move it to a plate and set it aside.

5 Place the bell-pepper strips, thinly sliced, in the skillet with the onion and garlic, and cook the mixture over high heat for three or four minutes, or until the vegetables are slightly tender. Sprinkle Mexican seasoning or fajita seasoning over the top.

6 Put the cooked steak back in the skillet and cook just until the strips are heated through.

7 Spoon the fajita mixture into warm tortillas, and serve with salsa, sour cream, grated cheese or other toppings.

Things You'll Need

- ❏ Boneless top sirloin steak, well-trimmed
- ❏ Rice vinegar
- ❏ Fresh jalapeño peppers, seeded and minced
- ❏ Canola oil
- ❏ Yellow, red and green bell peppers
- ❏ 1 onion, cut into wedges
- ❏ Garlic cloves
- ❏ Fajita seasoning or Mexican seasoning
- ❏ 4 tortillas

392 | Make Pizza Dough

Pizza dough is made with yeast so it does take a little advance planning, but it's easy to handle and can be frozen.

Steps

1 Sprinkle the yeast in a medium bowl containing the warm water and stir until the yeast dissolves.

2 Add half the flour and stir until blended. Then add the rest of the flour and blend until too stiff to stir with a spoon.

3 Turn the dough out on to a floured surface and knead it for 10 to 15 minutes until the dough is smooth and elastic.

4 Place the dough in another bowl, greased with a small amount of oil. Turn the dough once so that the top is oiled. Cover with plastic wrap and put it in a warm place for about 45 minutes.

5 Preheat the oven to 260°C (500°F).

6 Dump the dough back on to the floured surface and punch it down, getting rid of any bubbles. Divide the dough in half and let it rest.

7 Roll each half into a circle. It will puff slightly when baked.

8 Transfer the dough to an oiled pizza pan or baking sheet, or, if you have a baking stone, to a cornmeal-sprinkled wooden pizza peel for transfer directly to the stone.

9 Add sauce, cheese and toppings as desired. If you like, brush the exposed edges of the crust with olive oil.

10 Bake each pizza for 15 to 20 minutes, or until the crust is nicely browned and the cheese is melted.

✻ Tips

If the water is too cold or too hot, the yeast will either not activate or be killed.

To freeze the dough, form it into a ball, wrap it in plastic wrap and then in foil, and freeze. To defrost, put it in the refrigerator in the morning before you go to work, then take it out for an hour or two before you plan to bake. It should be room temperature when you roll it.

Things You'll Need

❏ 275 ml (1¼ cups) warm water

❏ 1 tsp salt

❏ Vegetable oil or olive oil

❏ 600 g (20 oz) sifted flour

❏ 2 packages dry yeast

393 | Make Sushi

Sushi is not only delicious, it's beautiful and good for you, too. If you're interested in making this delightful Japanese dish, you're in for a treat.

Steps

1 Measure out the rice and rinse it with water repeatedly.

2 Cook the rice in a rice cooker with the water. If you do not have a rice cooker, cook the rice in a saucepan on the stove with the same amount of water. Bring the rice and the water to a boil, then reduce it to a gentle simmer. Cover and cook for 10 minutes. Remove it from the heat, and let it steam for 20 minutes.

3 Spread the cooked rice in a large dish using a spatula so that it cools down. Cool the rice completely.

4 Combine the rice vinegar, the sugar and salt in a saucepan and heat until the sugar and salt dissolve completely.

Things You'll Need

❏ 400 g (14 oz) Japanese short-grain rice

❏ 400 ml (2 cups) water

❏ 2 tbsp sugar

❏ 1 tsp salt

❏ Ingredients for fillings (raw or cooked fish, vegetables, eggs, sesame seeds)

❏ Nori sheets

❏ Gari (pickled ginger)

5   Add the vinegar mixture to the rice using a wooden spoon or spatula. Be careful not to press or mash the rice kernels.

6   Decide what ingredients you want in your sushi. Some of your options are smoked salmon, cooked prawns, fresh raw tuna or salmon, tofu, crab, eggs (made into omelette and cut into thin strips), toasted sesame seeds, avocado, carrots, cucumber, mushrooms, snow peas and daikon radish. Cut your ingredients into thin strips.

7   Toast the nori (seaweed) sheets lightly in a pan over a low heat.

8   Put the rolling mat flat on an even surface and place a nori sheet on the mat.

9   Spread a cup of cooked rice on the sheet evenly using your hand. Leave an empty patch, about 2.5 cm (1 in) wide, at one end on the nori sheet. This will help to hold the roll together.

10 Add wasabi to the rice. Smear it in a straight line near the centre of the roll.

11 Place the filling on the rice in a straight line in the centre. Roll the sheet up using the mat.

12 Gently squeeze the mat to ensure that the sushi roll is tightly packed.

13 Open the mat and take out the sushi roll. Cut the roll horizontally into equal pieces and serve with soy sauce, wasabi and gari.

- ❏ 55 ml (¼ cup) rice vinegar
- ❏ Wasabi paste
- ❏ Soy sauce
- ❏ Sushi rolling mat

Make Jamaican Jerk Chicken   394

Jerk is a method of cooking pork and chicken where you make holes in the meat and stuff it with a variety of spices.

◉ Steps

Preparing the Rub/Marinade

1   Seed and finely chop the peppers.

2   Chop the onions and garlic.

3   Combine all the ingredients (excluding the chicken) in a blender.

Preparing the Chicken

1   Chop the chicken into four pieces.

2   Season the chicken with the jerk seasoning rub.

3   Cover and marinade in the refrigerator for a least an hour.

Cooking the Chicken

1   If you are using your oven, broil the chicken on each side for about five minutes. Bake on one side for 30 minutes then 30 on the other.

2   If you choose to grill, slowly grill the chicken until it's cooked, turning it regularly.

3   Baste occasionally with the remaining marinade.

4   Once cooked, chop the chicken up in smaller pieces before serving.

Things You'll Need

- ❏ 1.5 kg (3.5 lb) chicken
- ❏ 6 sliced scotch bonnet/ habanero peppers
- ❏ 2 tbsp thyme
- ❏ 2 tbsp ground pimento
- ❏ 8 cloves garlic, chopped
- ❏ 3 medium onions, chopped
- ❏ 2 tbsp sugar
- ❏ 2 tbsp salt
- ❏ 2 tsp ground black pepper
- ❏ 1–2 tsp ground cinnamon, nutmeg, ginger
- ❏ 110 ml (½ cup) olive oil
- ❏ 110 ml (½ cup) soy sauce
- ❏ Juice of one lime
- ❏ 220 ml (1 cup) orange juice
- ❏ 220 ml (1 cup) white vinegar

395 | Shop at a Farmers' Market

In an era of waxed fruit in supermarkets and fast food, fresh, organic, locally grown fruits and vegetables are in demand.

⊙ Steps

1 Keep your eyes open. Farmers' markets can be found in a variety of places. They often spring up on an open lot where space has been cleared after a building has been demolished.

2 Get up early. Many farmers' markets open early in the morning. Some remain open all day throughout the weekend, others close by afternoon.

3 Check websites. Many farmers' markets are part of non-profit cooperatives.

4 Support a local farmer. Small, family-owned farms are a vanishing breed. Shopping at a farmers' market helps keep locally grown produce available.

✳ Tips

Don't buy too much at one time. Since these foods are fresh, their shelf life is limited. Only buy what you can use within the next day or so, unless you are planning to tin vegetables yourself.

Learn new recipes for fresh fruit and vegetable dishes. Having a plan to do something new with fresh food makes the trip that much better.

396 | Keep Coffee Beans Fresh

Few things make for a better cup of coffee than using the freshest beans possible.

⊙ Steps

1 Avoid grinding the beans when you purchase them at the shop. Keeping the beans intact and only grinding what you need each time ensures a longer life for your coffee.

2 Keep coffee beans stored in an airtight container.

3 Keep the coffee beans in a dark place. Light and heat can quickly diminish the shelf life of coffee beans. The fridge is ideal.

4 Factor the amount of coffee consumed in your household before purchase. Even in the best storage conditions, it's recommended that your coffee should be used within three to four weeks of buying.

5 Be mindful of the skins on the coffee beans. Their purpose is to maintain the essential oils of the beans, so the oils will deteriorate quickly once the skins are broken.

⚠ Warning

While roasting your own coffee is the most ideal process for the freshest beans, it should only be undertaken by those with at least some degree of know-how.

397 | Make Iced Tea

Summer's perfect drink has been a favourite for generations. For the best results, use whole-leaf loose tea and good water.

⊙ Steps

1 Place the sugar and half the water in a serving jug and stir to dissolve the sugar, then chill.

2 Bring the remaining water to boil in a non-reactive pot.

✳ Tip

Pouring the hot tea into the cold water helps keep the tea clear.

3   Remove the water from the heat as soon as it boils and add the tea.

4   Cover and steep for five to eight minutes.

5   Strain the hot tea into the sugared water.

6   Add lemon slices or mint sprigs if desired, or place them in serving glasses as a garnish.

7   Fill serving glasses with ice and pour the tea in them to serve.

Things You'll Need

❑ 2 heaped tbsp orange pekoe or black whole-leaf tea

❑ High-quality water

❑ 220 g (8 oz) sugar

❑ Lemon slices or mint sprigs for garnish (optional)

Make an Irish Coffee   398

Irish whiskey and a dollop of whipped cream elevate this cup of coffee from the everyday to the sublime.

◉ Steps

1   Pour the whiskey into an Irish coffee mug and add sugar.

2   Fill the mug with hot black coffee.

3   Stir until the sugar dissolves and top with whipped cream.

Things You'll Need

❑ Hot coffee

❑ Whipped cream

❑ Irish whiskey

❑ Sugar

Make a Bloody Mary   399

You'll get a kick out of the bloody Mary, a familiar mix of vodka, tomato-based juices and some zesty spices.

◉ Steps

1   Put ice in shaker with V-8 or tomato juice, lemon juice, ground black pepper, vodka, Worcestershire sauce and Tabasco sauce. Shake six to eight times.

2   Strain the cocktail from the shaker into a chilled, old-fashioned glass.

3   Garnish with a celery stick or lime wedge.

✱ Tips

For a sweeter drink, add a few more drops of Worcestershire sauce.

Use tequila instead of vodka, and lime juice instead of lemon juice for a bloody Maria.

Make a James Bond Cocktail   400

Yes, the spy always ordered a martini "shaken, not stirred", but the martini was already named the "martini", so you can't go naming the martini the "James Bond" can you?

◉ Steps

1   Drop your sugar cube into the champagne flute.

2   Pour two or three dashes of bitters on to the cube, soaking it.

3   Pour in your vodka.

4   Fill the glass with champagne.

5   Voila! A licence to kill your own brain cells with a classy cocktail!

What You'll Need

❑ 35 g (1¼ oz) vodka

❑ Champagne

❑ Bitters

❑ Sugar cube

❑ Champagne flute

401 | Build a Home Distillery

The simplest version of still to build at home is the pot still, which is actually still used to make most Scotch and virtually all Irish whiskey today.

⊙ **Steps**

1 Buy or convert a sealed copper boiling pot. Remember that this pot is where your substance to be distilled goes. The size of it will determine how much you can distil at once. If you are making your own pot, you will find that the simplest design involves a clamp-and-seal lid, much like that of a kitchen pressure cooker. Either way, you will need to closely monitor the temperature of the heat source, to make sure it is boiling the alcohol and not the water.

2 Consider how you intend to heat your pot. The simplest version of a copper pot still involves putting the boiling pot on stone blocks or metal stilts, and burning a fire underneath it to provide heat. Industrial stills involve circulating steam through the bottom of the copper pot in pipes. You might need to do this if you plan to run your still indoors, but overall your heating system need only be as complicated as you make it.

3 Run a condensation coil from the boiling pot to the collecting pot. These tubes are where the alcohol will condense and collect, and it should slope downwards to the collecting pot.

4 Buy or convert a collecting pot. This also needs to be sealed, and will fit into the other end of the condensation coil. These are usually smaller than the boiling pot, but if you want to put multiple distillations into the same pot without having to disconnect and empty it, it ought to be as big or bigger.

⚠ **Warning**

Building a home distillery from scratch is beyond the capabilities of a person who does not already have an intermediate grasp of plumbing and welding.

402 | Make Wine

Making wine at home can be a fun and rewarding experience. Though the entire process takes more than a month, depending on the type of wine you are making and the recipe you are using, any wine connoisseur will learn a lot from the process.

⊙ **Steps**

1 Gather the ingredients you need to make wine.

2 Separate the grapes from the stalk. Wash the grapes.

3 Crush the grapes with your hands and place them in an earthen jar.

4 Whip the egg whites well.

5 Add 1.8 kg (4 lb) of sugar and all the other ingredients to the crushed grapes.

6 Cover the jar with a well-fitting lid to prevent any dust or insects from entering the jar.

7 Open the lid and stir the contents once a day for 21 days. Ensure that you replace the lid properly after stirring.

✳ **Tip**

You can reduce the amount of sugar if you do not want your wine to be very sweet.

What You'll Need

❑ 3.6 kg (8 lb) sugar

❑ Food colouring

❑ 100g (4 oz) yeast

❑ 2.2 kg (5 lb) blue grapes

❑ 11 litres (3 gallons) water

❑ 450 g (1 lb) wheat

❑ 2 egg whites

8 Add the remaining 1.8 kg (4 lb) of sugar to the jar after 21 days.

9 Keep the container for another 21 days without opening.

10 Open the jar and carefully strain the clear wine on top using a nylon cloth.

11 Add colour if you want. Remember that artificial colours are very strong, though, so add it drop by drop.

Preserve an Open Bottle of Wine 403

If you find yourself unable to finish a bottle of wine in one go, follow these steps to preserve the quality of the wine.

⊙ Steps

1 Keep the cork. You can purchase plastic bottle stoppers, but this is unnecessary if you can keep the cork.

2 Buy a spray preserver or vacuum pump, which protect the wine from the air in the bottle – wine essentially turns into vinegar as it comes into contact with oxygen. The vacuum pump sucks the air out while the spray forces some of the air out and leaves a blanket of inert gases to coddle your bottle during the night. Buy the spray at any wine retailer.

3 Stand the bottle up in a cool, dark place. The fridge is fine; just don't freeze your wine – 55° is ideal.

4 Revisit the wine within a day or two. Don't let it sit all alone on a shelf next to items such as milk or fruit juice. Drink it within a week.

⚠ Warning

Do not lie the bottle on its side after opening. Side storage is good for unopened bottles because it preserves the cork. But the cork's day is almost done and what you need to focus on is reducing the surface area of the wine exposed to any elements in the remaining space of the bottle.

Taste Wine 404

Wine tasting can be intimidating, but it shouldn't be, since the only thing that really matters is if you like it or not.

⊙ Steps

1 Look at the wine. Is it clear and clean or cloudy? The former is usually an indication of good wine while the latter might indicate the opposite. Young white wines are usually pale, while older ones can be straw-coloured or more golden. Young red wines are dark or purplish, while older red wines can take on a red brick or amber colour.

2 Smell the wine. Does it smell mouldy or have a strong vinegar smell? This first sniff is simply to make certain the wine has not gone bad. If the wine passes this first sniff, inhale deeply in order to let your nose experience all the various nuances of the wine.

3 Take a sip of the wine and hold it on your tongue, breathe in to help release the flavour of the wine. The weight of the wine in your mouth will tell you whether it's light, medium or full-bodied. It also tells you how much sweetness, acidity, alcohol and tannin it contains.

4 Swallow the wine. The "finish" of a wine describes the sensations after the wine is swallowed. It will often be different to how the wine came across on the palate, so take note.

❉ Tips

If you are at a wine tasting and multiple wines are to be sampled, spitting out the various samples (while not as much fun) will help to keep your senses clear.

Don't let others influence your decision on whether you like a wine or not – the ultimate decision is yours!

405 Drink Responsibly and Safely

Do you want to find that balance between drinking too much and not drinking at all? This list will help you keep yourself in check by not drinking too much, but also not depriving yourself of that delicious drink you crave.

At Home

- When you are home alone, don't drink a lot. One beer or glass of wine is okay, but don't take it beyond that. This is for two reasons: because you should not be drinking much alone, and for safety reasons. If something were to happen to you when you drink alone, there is no one there to help you.

- When drinking with friends at home, have fun, but drink in moderation. Make sure that at least one person will be lightly drinking or not drinking at all for safety reasons. Drink to get a fun buzz, if you'd like, but once you feel yourself losing control, stop drinking immediately. Make sure you have snacks and water on hand so you can keep yourself full and hydrated.

Out and About

- When drinking at a restaurant, stick to a few drinks. You don't want to become loud or sloppy at a restaurant, especially a fancy one. Think to yourself: "Will I be embarrassed if I get loud or sloppy? Am I getting to that point?" This should help to keep you in check.

- When drinking at a house party, make sure to have a designated driver with you, or make sure you can sleep over at the party. Also, if you will be drinking, make sure that you know people at the party. You need to have someone who will make sure that you are safe. Go ahead and have some drinks, but keep the drinking under control, and never put your drink down. Keep it in your hand at all times.

Safety First

- When drinking at a club or party at a venue, always have a designated driver or enough money to pay for a cab ride home. Never let your drink out of your sight. Drink enough to make dancing fun, but never more than that. You do not want to pass out at a party like a wedding – it's embarrassing and disrespectful.

- When drinking in any situation, if you start to feel negative or unhappy, stop drinking. If you begin to feel sick, stop drinking. If you can't find your designated driver or friend, stop drinking. You do not want to find yourself in a situation where you can't get home or are too drunk to know what is going on around you. At the first sign of being left alone – just stop!

Stop and Think...

- Drink slowly! Get a drink and take your time over it. Drinking responsibly is easy when you get a glass of your favourite beverage and hold on to it, savouring it all. This way, you do not need to be self conscious if everyone around you has a drink, because you will too.

- Think about your friends. If it seems as if all your friends are getting drunk, you should stop in case they need you to help them. It may not be fun being the only sober person in the group, but your friends will be incredibly grateful when you save them from any sticky situations that they may find themselves in. Take it in turns to be the responsible one!

reference

Recognise a Heart Attack 406

Heart attacks are not always sudden; there can be signs for days or weeks that indicate trouble. Seeking medical help early dramatically increases your chances of surviving an attack.

⊙ Steps

1. Heed the first warning signs of discomfort or pain in the chest. This is the holy grail of symptoms. It might feel as if an elephant is sitting on your chest, or possibly a squeezing or fullness in the centre of the chest.

2. Remember that pain in other parts of the upper body may signal a heart attack. This might include the arms (particularly the left arm), jaw, back, shoulders, neck or stomach. It may feel more like discomfort.

3. Recognise that being short of breath after physical activity is normal, but if shortness of breath occurs after walking a little way, climbing a flight of stairs or even lying in bed, see your doctor immediately.

4. Watch out for nausea, light-headedness or cold sweats. Feelings of anxiety or nervousness may accompany these symptoms.

5. Take note of any increased heart rate. That, coupled with any of the symptoms described above, may indicate an impending heart attack. Some heart-attack sufferers even experience feelings of impending doom.

❋ Tips

Speak to your doctor about your risk-level for a heart attack and what you can do to prevent one.

Have regular physical examinations and cardiac stress tests to detect any problems before they turn serious.

⚠ Warning

High blood pressure, high cholesterol, smoking, lack of exercise and obesity can increase your heart-attack risk.

Tell if Someone Has Had a Stroke 407

A stroke is a life-threatening event caused by loss of oxygen to the brain. With each minute that passes, more brain cells die. The way to remember what to do is to think FAST.

⊙ Steps

1. Check for numbness or weakness in the face (the F in FAST) by asking the person to smile. If one side of the face droops or the person can't smile, it may mean a stroke. Strokes cause weakness or numbness to the face, usually limited to one side.

2. Look for muscle weakness. Ask the person to raise both arms (the A in FAST). If one arm drifts down or can't be raised, it may suggest a stroke has occurred. Strokes cause muscle weakness or numbness in the arms or legs, usually limited to one side. The person may also have trouble walking or keeping balance.

3. Ask the person to repeat a simple sentence. If the speech (the S in FAST) is slurred or hard to understand, or the person has trouble remembering the words to repeat, it may suggest a stroke. Strokes cause difficulty with speech and comprehension, as well as dizziness and confusion.

4. Get help immediately if you or someone else experiences any of the signs of stroke. Call 999 or get the person to a hospital. Tell emergency medical personnel you're dealing with a possible stroke, so they can start proper treatment right away. Time (the T in FAST) is the most important factor in helping someone survive a stroke or limiting its effects.

⚠ Warnings

Don't die of embarrassment! It's better to err on the side of caution, so if you or someone you know experiences any of the signs of stroke, get help immediately.

Don't drive yourself to the hospital if you've experienced any of the signs of stroke. Call 999 or have a family member get you to the hospital immediately.

408 | Diagnose Mumps

Since schools have required the mumps vaccine, the disease is not as common as it used to be. However, if a child misses the vaccine, the virus is still around and mumps is still possible.

⊚ Steps

1   Realise that mumps is a virus. It is spread through respiratory droplets like other respiratory viral infections. Its most common symptom is inflammation and swelling of the parotid gland, which is the body's largest salivary gland. The gland is located in the side of the face, just under and in front of the ear.

2   Know the symptoms of mumps. Just before a person develops the full-blown symptoms of mumps, they may run a low fever and have muscle aches. The incubation period for the disease from time of contact until these early symptoms is two to three weeks. When full-blown symptoms begin, the patient may have abdominal pain, swollen testicles, pelvic pain or a very bad headache in addition to swollen cheeks.

3   Be aware that other conditions may cause the same symptoms as mumps. These include a blockage in the duct that drains the parotid gland, a bacterial infection and other viruses. Some of these conditions require antibiotics and occasionally the duct that drains the gland must be surgically opened.

4   Go to the doctor. Understand that a child or adult who has definitely been vaccinated against mumps stands a very low chance of ever getting the disease. If these people have inflammation of the parotid gland, it is probably not caused by mumps and should be checked by a doctor.

5   Get a blood test – the only definitive way to diagnose mumps.

✳ Tips

If testicles become swollen, or if you have abdominal pain, seek medical care. Also seek medical care if the body temperature reaches 39°C (103°F) and cannot be reduced by medication or any other measures.

Mumps is entirely preventable by vaccine. The vaccine is part of the MMR series (measles, mumps and rubella).

409 | Treat Chicken Pox

Chicken pox is a viral infection that causes a blister-like rash on the skin; some people even get pox inside their mouth and under their eyelids.

⊚ Steps

1   Place cool, wet compresses on the rash or apply calamine lotion to relieve the itching.

2   Take a bath in oatmeal, which is very soothing to the skin.

3   Trim a young child's or baby's fingernails so he or she doesn't scratch the rash. Consider putting mittens on a baby's hands.

4   Use acetaminophen to reduce fever, aches and pains.

5   Eat soft foods and avoid acidic juices if there are pox inside your mouth.

6   Stick to a nutritious diet to boost the immune system.

✳ Tip

Chicken pox is considered contagious until all the pox are crusted over. It usually runs its course within two weeks.

⚠ Warning

Keep infected children away from frail elderly people, newborn infants and pregnant women.

Treat a Broken Arm 410

By immobilising your arm properly and following through with your doctor's treatment plan, recovery should just take a few weeks, depending upon the severity of the break.

⊙ Steps

1 Place an ice pack on the suspected area of the fracture until you can get medical assistance. Keep the ice on the area for 20 to 30 minutes at a time. Avoid placing the ice directly on your skin by wrapping a clean towel around your arm first.

2 Immobilise your arm further by making a sling out of a towel or shirt and then tying it around your neck. You can also immobilise your arm by rolling a thick newspaper around it and taping it closed.

3 Get medical assistance as soon as possible in order to evaluate the severity of the fracture. X-rays will determine the type of fracture and the subsequent treatment.

4 Determine which type of immobilisation will be required for the arm to heal. A splint or a partial cast will usually be applied for fractures to the radius and ulna (the two bones that make up the forearm, below the elbow). An upper arm (humerus) or shoulder break may just require a splint.

5 Expect hospitalisation for more serious types of arm fractures, such as compound fractures (where the bone breaks the skin), multiple fractures, dislocations of the elbow or shoulder, or fractures where there is nerve or blood-vessel damage.

6 Continue to apply ice packs once you get home to treat the swelling. Your doctor may prescribe medication to further reduce pain.

7 Keep your cast or splint clean and dry at all times.

8 Keep your arm elevated, preferably above the level of your heart, to help reduce swelling.

9 Follow up with your doctor after the recommended period to see if the arm has healed and if it's time to remove the cast or splint.

⚠ Warning

A compound fracture – where the bone actually breaks through the skin – will require emergency medical help and possible hospitalisation, since the victim will be bleeding and may go into shock. Stabilise the arm and apply gentle pressure to stop the bleeding. Call 999.

Prevent Skin Yeast Infections 411

To protect your skin against candidiasis or yeast infection, apply the following preventative measures.

⊙ Steps

1 Cleanse your whole body by taking daily baths or showers. Make sure you dry yourself well after taking a shower, especially around the groin, skin folds, anal area and armpits.

2 Control the use of antibacterial agents when it comes to washing the skin, mouth, genitalia or the anus. It is much better if you use it alternately with clean water every other day.

✱ Tip

Good personal hygiene can limit the chances of getting a skin yeast infection.

3 Maintain proper hygiene in specific areas of your body. Brush your teeth, floss and use a mouthwash to cleanse your mouth daily. During menstruation, change tampons or sanitary towels regularly. Wipe the anus properly from front to back after defecation.

4 Wash and change towels as often as possible. Avoid using the same towel for a long period of time. Avoid sharing towels with others.

5 Do not take antibiotics or steroids unless it's necessary for you to do so. These types of drugs may suppress the body's immune system, causing increase in the growth of fungi.

6 Wear clothes and underwear that allow your skin to breathe. Overly tight clothing or underwear will only increase moisture and humidity around the areas of the skin and genitalia, making it an ideal place for fungi to settle.

7 Change soiled and wet clothes immediately. After doing your exercise or after swimming, change your damp clothes or swimsuit immediately to protect your skin against fungal attack.

8 Eat well. Add yoghurt in your diet because it contains good bacteria known as *lactobacillus acidophilus* that keeps the body healthy and prevents invasion of fungi or candida. Eat a lot of fruit and vegetables to keep your immune system strong. Decrease your sugar and alcohol intake, because this only promotes the growth of yeast.

9 Keep your body lean and healthy. Skin folds are an ideal place for fungi.

10 Try taking garlic extracts. These contain a substance known as allyl alcohol that inhibits or prevents the growth of candida.

412 | Treat Impetigo

Impetigo is a highly contagious bacterial skin infection that occurs most frequently in children. It is characterised by red and blistery sores that usually appear around the mouth and nose, as well as on the arms and legs.

◎ Steps

1 Avoid scratching the blisters. Rupturing the blisters can spread the bacteria to other parts of the body and other people.

2 Clip fingernails (especially children's) to help minimise scratching.

3 Wash infected areas gently several times a day with an antibacterial soap and cover infected areas loosely with gauze after washing them.

4 Avoid sharing towels, clothing or razors with anyone with the infection.

5 Change clothing daily and launder it in hot water.

6 Apply over-the-counter antibiotic ointment. Remove crusted areas by soaking them gently with warm water and a flannel.

7 Notify your doctor if sores do not begin to heal or if they worsen after 24 to 48 hours of self care. Your doctor may prescribe oral antibiotics or a stronger ointment.

8 Keep infected children home from school while sores are weeping. Infected people are contagious until the sores are all crusted over.

✳ Tip

A person is no longer considered contagious after two days of oral antibiotic treatment.

⚠ Warning

A serious side effect of impetigo is a rare kidney disease known as glomerulonephritis. Seek medical care if you or your child experiences headaches, high blood pressure and brown-coloured urine.

Avoid Getting Cold Sores   413

Cold sores are caused by the herpes simplex type I virus, and once you are infected with it, the virus stays with you forever.

⊙ **Steps**

1   Stay out of the sun, or at least limit exposure. Overexposure to the sun can trigger outbreaks. Wear sunscreen if you are out in the sun.

2   Drink alcohol in moderation.

3   Stay out of the wind as much as possible.

4   Protect your immune system. Other viruses, such as the flu, can trigger outbreaks of the cold-sore virus.

5   Make sure you eat a healthy diet with plenty of fresh, unprocessed foods. Reduce your consumption of processed foods, fizzy drinks, sugar and caffeine, which may increase the chance of an outbreak.

6   Take a good, high-potency multivitamin.

7   Keep in shape, get enough sleep, do things you enjoy and drink lots of fluids.

8   Don't share a drinking glass, food utensils or a toothbrush with someone who has a cold sore.

9   Avoid intimate contact such as kissing someone on the lips when that person has a cold sore.

✱ Tip

Herpes is contagious and your best bet is to avoid close contact with a person who has an outbreak.

Fight Hay Fever   414

Hay fever (allergic rhinitis) can cause itchy eyes, a runny or stuffy nose, headaches and coughing, and in the summer months it can cause extreme discomfort to sufferers.

⊙ **Steps**

1   Close windows and doors, and stay inside when the pollen count is high.

2   Change filters in heating and air-conditioning systems often. Use an indoor air filter if necessary.

3   Wear a surgical mask when in the garden or cleaning the house.

4   Avoid smoking and stay clear of second-hand smoke. Minimise other air pollutants in your home.

5   Buy a vacuum cleaner with a HEPA filter and use it often.

6   Avoid wall-to-wall carpeting. Carpeting traps pollen, animal hair, dust and other allergens.

7   Talk to your healthcare provider about getting tested for allergies to trees and grasses that you come into contact with.

✱ Tips

Saline-solution nose spray can help loosen secretions. It is not a drug and can be used as often as you want.

If you don't want to spray water in your nose, opt for a hot shower. The steam will help to loosen mucus secretions.

⚠ Warning

Read labels carefully if using over-the-counter antihistamines or decongestants. Many make you drowsy. Avoid alcohol when taking them.

415 Treat Varicose Veins

Varicose veins are raised and blue veins in the legs, and are caused by leaky valves inside superficial leg veins.

⊙ Steps

1   Wear lightweight compression tights for small varicose veins and heavier elastic support stockings for advanced varicose veins not being treated by a surgeon.

2   Consult a certified dermatologic or vascular surgeon about your varicose veins and find out about treatments.

3   Have an outpatient duplex scan or ultrasound of your legs to rule out deep vein and/or circulatory disease.

4   Talk to your doctor about sclerotherapy, a popular treatment.

5   Explore laser treatment. No injections or surgery are required. One vein generally requires four to six treatments, lasting 15 to 20 minutes each.

6   Evaluate vein stripping. With this surgical procedure, a vascular surgeon makes an incision in your leg, often in your groin, locates your varicose vein, ties it off and sometimes removes it. Stripping requires general anaesthetic, and is usually performed in a hospital. Be aware that after vein-stripping surgery you will wear a firm bandage from foot to mid-thigh for two to three days. You will be asked to rest and keep your leg elevated.

7   Ask about ambulatory phlebectomy. With this procedure, your surgeon inserts a small hooked instrument into tiny incisions he has made on the underside of your skin to collapse your veins.

✤ Tips

Forty-one per cent of women aged 40 to 50 suffer with varicose veins, and 72 per cent of women aged 60 to 70.

Twenty-four per cent of men aged 30 to 40 have varicose veins.

⚠ Warning

Avoid wearing elastic bandages for home treatment of varicose veins. It's too easy to wrap these types of bandages too tightly, especially around the calf, which produces a tourniquet effect.

416 Treat Hyperventilation

Hyperventilation occurs when an anxious person breathes so rapidly that he or she cannot get enough carbon dioxide. The person will feel like they are suffocating.

⊙ Steps

1   Look for any of these signs and symptoms of hyperventilation: high anxiety, rapid and deep breathing, rapid pulse, a feeling of suffocation, dizziness or faintness, dry mouth, numbness in the hands and around the mouth, a feeling of paralysis in the hands, stabbing chest pain.

2   Calm the person down by identifying the source of anxiety and addressing it. Hyperventilation is often triggered in wilderness settings by a fear of heights, by equipment failures or by a minor injury that causes anxiety.

3   Communicate continually with the injured person: explain that even though he or she feels a need for more oxygen, the problem is that he or she is getting too much of it, and that the symptoms will go away as breathing calms down.

4   Have the person breath into a bag if one is available, covering both the nose and mouth with the bag. This will increase the amount of carbon dioxide in the blood.

⚠ Warning

If the person does not respond to treatment within 20 minutes, the ailment may be something other than hyperventilation. Other possibilities are asthma, heat exhaustion and heat stroke.

Diagnose and Treat Hypothermia · 417

Signs of the onset of hypothermia include feeling cold (in the hands and feet in particular), slurring speech, shivering and a loss of balance and coordination.

⊙ Steps

1 Understand that when serious hypothermia sets in, shivering stops because the victim can no longer get warm without help.

2 Watch for signs of the victim becoming irrational and angry, no longer being able to stand, becoming listless or appearing to be dead.

3 Find shelter and change into dry clothes to treat mild hypothermia.

4 Get into a sleeping bag and drink hot and sweet drinks, avoiding coffee and tea (caffeine can make dehydration worse).

5 Fill hot water bottles, wrap them in clothing and put them in the sleeping bag with the person.

6 Begin rescue breathing to treat serious hypothermia, and then find shelter and do everything as outlined above. Re-warming may take 24 hours or more, so prepare for a wait.

7 Zip together two or more sleeping bags and put warm, dry rescuers in the sleeping bag with the victim.

8 Evacuate the victim by helicopter if possible.

⚠ Warning

If symptoms persist or if you have specific medical conditions or concerns, contact a physician. This information is not intended as a substitute for professional medical advice or treatment.

Prevent Alzheimer's Disease · 418

Paying attention to your lifestyle now can do a lot to minimise the chances of having to deal with senile dementia in old age. Here are some steps you can take.

⊙ Steps

1 A daily crossword can be like press-ups for the brain, keeping the synapses active and helping stave off diseases like Alzheimer's. People who do four crossword puzzles or more a week are much less likely to develop dementia than those who do only one.

2 Regular exercise is good for just about everything in life, so it's no surprise that it can help in forestalling mental decline.

3 What's good for your heart is also good for your brain. Eat lots of vegetables, fish, an occasional glass of red wine, and keep away from too much fat, sweets and junk food.

4 Social interaction is also a wonderful exercise that contributes to a brain that works better for longer. So visit friends, join a club, volunteer or do anything else that gets you out and about and mixing with others.

5 Our understanding of Alzheimer's is increasing, as is the range of prevention and treatment options. There are some interesting drugs in development that may one day make a big difference in dealing with senility.

✳ Tip

There's some evidence that tumeric, a spice commonly used in curry, can act to protect nerve cells in the brain. A little vindaloo now and then certainly can't hurt.

419 Live with Diabetes

Diabetes is a disorder that requires self care and a willingness to take personal responsibility for its control on a daily basis. It's not always easy to live with diabetes, but understanding a few basic guidelines can help.

Steps

1 Speak with a dietician about a diet that you can follow. Discuss the foods you like and dislike, any religious or ethical restrictions, and so on. If you don't speak up, the dietician won't be able to best assist you. Buy low-fat cookbooks, sugar-free cookbooks and cookbooks written specifically for diabetics.

2 Lose weight if you are overweight. Losing weight can make a big difference in your treatment plan. Many people are able to eliminate or reduce the amount of medication needed – or to avoid needing it in the first place – once they take the weight off.

3 Join a gym, join a rounders team, sign up for karate: exercise and activity are essential for all of us in keeping healthy, and extremely important for a diabetic. Find a sport or exercise that you enjoy, something that will motivate you to keep at it.

4 Make your life more active. Get up and walk around at work if your job is sedentary, climb the stairs, walk to the shops.

5 Wear a medical alert bracelet. It is vital that you be identified as a diabetic in case of a medical emergency.

6 Speak to your doctor if you are planning a long trip. Crossing time zones can throw your medication/eating schedule out of kilter. Diabetics can travel safely without restrictions, but first learn how to best to handle it.

7 Be prepared. Always carry a snack with you.

8 Keep a separate blood-glucose meter at your place of work or school. This will make it easier to monitor your blood sugar when you are away from home. Keep the meter strips in their original container, where they are less likely to deteriorate.

9 Feel free to eat out in restaurants, but watch what you are eating. Avoid huge portions. Share a dessert rather than eat a whole one yourself. If food is late in coming, or there is some other delay, eat a snack if you have taken insulin.

10 Drink a glass of wine if you enjoy it, but don't overdo it.

11 Avoid smoking and second-hand smoke. Diabetics have twice the risk of heart disease as the rest of the population and can't afford the extra risk of smoking.

12 Speak with your doctor if you are diligent about your diabetes programme, but your blood sugar is still fluctuating beyond your set parameters. Modifications may be necessary.

❈ Tip

With few restrictions, you can live a normal life with diabetes. For the majority of diabetics, their quality of life depends on how much responsibility they take for their own care.

Live with OCD

If you suffer from OCD (obsessive compulsive disorder), you already know how frustrating it can be. However, it is possible to learn how to live with OCD in a productive way.

Steps

1 Recognise that you are not alone. Nearly 2.5 per cent of people in the world live with OCD.

2 Get a good book about OCD to help you manage your symptoms.

3 Join a support group for people who suffer from OCD. Being able to talk openly about your condition with other people who have it too can be extremely beneficial.

4 Find a good psychologist who specialises in cognitive therapy. Cognitive therapy involves talking your way past obsessions and compulsions through subtle retraining. It has been shown to be very effective in helping OCD patients manage their symptoms and sometimes overcome them.

5 Consult with a psychiatrist if your symptoms are severe. You may need medication. Psychiatrists specialise in knowing what medications to prescribe for mental disorders such as OCD.

✳ Tip

Understand that having OCD does not mean you are crazy. OCD is an anxiety disorder, not a psychosis.

⚠ Warning

Don't try to fight your obsessions and compulsions through sheer force of will. This rarely works and will probably end up causing you more stress.

Cope with Dyslexia

A neurological disorder that hinders reading and writing, dyslexia can plague children and adults. Learn to cope with dyslexia to minimise frustrations and enhance the quality of your life.

Steps

1 Understand that there are different forms of dyslexia and varying degrees of the disability. Some people have trouble writing and reading, while others find mathematics a problem.

2 Learn to organise your thoughts. For students and adults who are dyslexic, use a technique called a Mind Map to create structure when writing or studying. Draw a large circle in the middle of a piece of paper with the main topic inside. Extending from the circle, draw lines with circles on the end; place subtopics inside these circles. Be as specific as you need to be in order to have organised thoughts.

3 Pair up with a person who is not dyslexic at school or in the work-place. This person can help you take notes, fill out forms and perform reading tasks.

4 Break up large tasks into smaller projects. Dyslexic individuals become overwhelmed with large, general tasks. Smaller, specific goals are easier to achieve.

5 Ask to take tests orally instead of doing written exams.

✳ Tips

Try to start working on projects in the morning, when the brain functions at its highest level.

Be involved in the workplace and at school. People who participate in discussions and get involved retain more of what they learn.

422 Deal with Vertigo

Vertigo is not just feeling dizzy, but a feeling of movement when you are still. A vertigo attack can also cause nausea and vomiting. Causes of vertigo can be inner ear problems, head injuries, migraines, viral infections and drug interactions. Vertigo can be temporary or long-term from more serious conditions. If you suffer from vertigo, it's important to know how to deal with an attack and alleviate the symptoms.

SYMPTOM	DESCRIPTION	TREATMENT	SAFETY
Feel out of balance suddenly.	You may feel as though the floor is rising up to you and your balance will be out of sync. You can lose your balance and fall.	Move slowly if an attack hits suddenly; get to a sofa or bed safely while your balance is off.	Remove obstacles from walkways and paths; make sure there are no electrical cords to trip over, remove raised thresholds, pick up throw carpets and tack down loose carpeting.
Feel as though your body is spinning or whirling, even though you are still.	This will cause your balance to be off and cause difficulty in walking safely.	Lie down slowly, keep your head elevated by propping yourself up. Lying flat tends to make spinning sensations worse.	Place handrails in hallways and stairways; if you feel that you are losing your balance it will be a safety measure to grab on to. Install grab bars inside your shower and next to the toilet. Place non-skid mats inside the shower.
Feel like you are tilting or have falling sensations.	These sensations will cause difficulty in walking or standing and may cause a fall.	Keep your head still to reduce the feelings of motion and deal with an attack of vertigo.	Keep a torch and fresh batteries at your bedside. Also keep a cordless phone on your bedside table in case of emergency.
Sudden sensations of nausea of dizziness.	A common symptom of vertigo, you may feel a churning in your stomach and that you will be sick.	Lie down and have a bowl and tissues handy, in case you have vomiting.	Install remotely operated lights and switches; this will save you from having to reach for them if feeling nauseous.

chart

Fight Fatigue 423

Fatigue can be caused by anxiety, illness, a poor diet or a sleep disorder. Identifying the source of the problem can solve it.

⊙ Steps

1 Make an appointment with a counsellor to find constructive solutions to stressful problems or depression.

2 Sign up for a stress-management class or a relaxing activity such as meditation or yoga. Anxiety can exhaust you.

3 Exercise a few times a week to improve your overall energy and reduce stress or anxiety.

4 Improve your sleeping conditions. Buy a new mattress if yours is uncomfortable, and make sure your room is a comfortable temperature, dark and quiet.

5 Maintain a diet that supports steady energy levels. That means eating several small meals a day (including a breakfast that includes complex carbohydrates and protein) and avoiding refined sugar and caffeine.

6 Drink at least eight glasses of water a day; dehydration can cause fatigue.

7 Make sure you're getting enough calcium and potassium.

✱ Tip
If you wake up in the morning as tired as you were when you went to bed, or have trouble sleeping through the night, you may be suffering from a sleep disorder.

Treat Snake Bites 424

Because a snake bite has the potential to be fatal, it's important that you know in advance what to do if you are bitten.

⊙ Steps

1 The first thing to do is always call emergency services, but while you're waiting, here are some tips on how you can help the snake-bite victim.

2 Make sure you and the victim are away from the snake. If you don't know where it went, make sure you're sitting somewhere you can keep an eye out for it. However, don't waste time looking for it to kill the snake or take its picture; most trained emergency personnel can identify the snake by the bite patterns.

3 Don't elevate the bitten area. Keep it below the level of the heart, and wash the bite with soap and warm water if it's available to you. This can help keep potential bacteria out of the puncture sites. Keep the victim calm by having them sit down, instead of wandering around.

4 Most snake bites occur on an extremity, such as the arms or legs. If the victim is wearing any sort of constricting clothing or jewellery, remove it to prevent tissue death in case of swelling. If professional help is more than half an hour away, bandage the limb 5–10 cm (2–4 in) above the bite. Make sure the bandage doesn't cut off blood flow from an artery or vein.

5 Follow basic first aid while waiting for emergency personnel to arrive. Watch the victim for signs of shock. Don't cut the bitten area or try to suck out the poison; this can do more harm than good.

✱ Tip
Prevent snake bites by wearing long trousers and high boots when outdoors. Also, don't stick your hand anywhere that a snake might hide, unless you've already checked to make sure the space is empty.

425 | Care for Sensitive Teeth

If you have sensitive teeth, you may feel pain when your teeth are touched or exposed to hot or cold foods.

⊙ Steps

1 See your dentist first. He or she might seal the sensitive area with a bonding agent or prescribe a fluoride gel, which can be rubbed into gums after brushing.

2 Use a toothbrush with extra-soft bristles, and do not brush horizontally, which exposes tooth roots.

3 Switch to a toothpaste formulated especially for sensitive teeth.

4 Avoid stimuli that trigger pain. Hot or cold foods like ice cream and coffee, sweet or sour foods such as lemons and sweets, and acidic foods such as wine and grapefruit juice commonly cause problems for people with sensitive teeth.

✱ Tip

If you grind your teeth, consider stress-reduction techniques such as exercising.

⚠ Warning

It is important to visit your dentist first to determine the underlying cause of hypersensitivity, which could be cavities, abscesses or other problems.

426 | Floss Your Teeth

Regular flossing reduces decay, gum disease and bad breath by helping to remove plaque that forms along the gum line.

⊙ Steps

1 Take 30–45 cm (12 to 18 in) of floss and grasp it so that you have a few centimetres of floss taut between your hands.

2 Slip the floss between your teeth and into the area between your teeth and gums as far as it will go. Floss with eight to 10 vertical strokes to dislodge food and plaque.

3 Try to floss at least once a day. The most important time to floss is before going to bed. Floss before or after brushing – either is fine.

✱ Tip

Remember to floss all your teeth, including behind the molars at the back.

⚠ Warning

You may experience some bleeding at first. Don't worry; this is normal.

427 | Gargle

Gargling is a great way to kill bacteria in your mouth. It also helps to give you fresher breath.

⊙ Steps

1 Pour the mouthwash into a clean cup. If you pour it into the cup attached to the top, you'll run the risk of contamination.

2 Slide the mouthwash quickly over your tongue.

3 Throw your head back and stop the mouthwash right before it hits your epiglottis (the cartilaginous flap in the back of your throat). You'll know the mouthwash is resting in the right spot if you feel as if you're going to gag or swallow.

⚠ Warning

For children under eight, check with your doctor. Children who are too young to understand how to gargle should not be given mouthwash.

4   Make the mouthwash bubble and gurgle for at least 45 seconds. Pull your tongue back a little and blow air through your throat slowly.

5   Drop your head back down and spit the mouthwash out. Repeat.

Stop Grinding Teeth at Night
428

Grinding (bruxism) can be caused by stress or an unconscious attempt to smooth out a poor bite. It wears down and may fracture teeth, and it can lead to gum and jaw problems.

⊙ Steps

1   Make an appointment with your dentist, who will make a custom mouthpiece for you to wear at night. This will prevent further damage to your teeth and may reduce your tendency to grind.

2   Ask your dentist to file down your "high spots", which are any teeth that interfere with a comfortable, aligned bite.

3   Hold a warm, damp cloth next to your face for 10 minutes before you go to bed to help calm your jaw muscles.

4   Relax before bedtime by meditating, taking a hot bath or stretching.

5   Reduce alcohol and caffeine consumption.

6   Learn to reduce stress. Take stress-management classes and learn relaxation techniques.

✳ Tip

Researchers are investigating the use of periodic injections of botulinum toxin (BTX) to treat severe teeth grinding. Ask your dentist for more information if you're interested.

⚠ Warnings

If you wake up with headaches, ear pain, pain in your jaw or if your teeth look misaligned, call your dentist.

If symptoms persist or if you have specific medical conditions or concerns, contact a physician.

Stay Healthy Through Personal Hygiene
429

Taking the time to properly groom yourself will help you avoid illness as well as help you achieve social acceptance.

⊙ Steps

1   Bathe daily. Use soap to cleanse your body and shampoo to cleanse your hair. Body odour is offensive and daily bathing will eliminate it.

2   Brush your teeth a minimum of twice a day. Brushing your teeth helps promote healthy teeth and gums as well as defeating bad breath.

3   Groom yourself as needed. Keep your hair neat and tidy, trim your fingernails and toenails, and shave or wax regularly.

4   Apply deodorant daily. You may not notice your body odour, but others do, and it's not acceptable.

5   Get plenty of rest. You can erase dark circles, minimise wrinkling and be in a better state of mind by getting plenty of rest.

6   Drink the recommended amount of water each day. Hydrated skin has a healthy glow to it that can not be duplicated.

7   Dress in clean and well-fitting clothing. Cleaning yourself just to put on dirty clothing is not acceptable. Undergarments need to be clean and well-mended as well as your outer garments.

✳ Tip

It sounds obvious, but personal hygiene is the simplest way of staying healthy.

430 | Use a Thermometer

Temperatures can be taken in several ways. These instructions are for taking the temperature orally.

⊙ **Steps**

1 Shake down the thermometer until it reads below 35.5°C (95.9°F), if you're using the glass-mercury type.

2 Turn on the thermometer if you're using the digital type. Insert the thermometer into the mouth, under the tongue.

3 Leave the thermometer in place for three to five minutes if you're using the glass-mercury type. For the digital type, wait until the thermometer signals that the process is complete.

4 Read the thermometer where the line of mercury ends, or read the display on a digital thermometer.

✳ **Tips**

Clean a glass thermometer with soap and water. Sterilise it by soaking it in alcohol.

Clean a digital thermometer by following the manufacturer's instructions.

431 | Check Your Own Pulse

Developing the habit of taking your pulse can help determine if you are at risk of developing heart problems, such as tachycardia and atrial fibrillation.

⊙ **Steps**

1 Place your index and middle finger around the back of your wrist. Use the hand with which you feel most comfortable.

2 Use your index and middle fingers to find the radial artery in your wrist. If you place your fingers correctly, it will be very easy to find.

3 Apply light pressure so you can feel your pulse. Count the number of heartbeats you feel in 30 seconds.

4 Multiply the result by two so you can calculate your pulse or number of heartbeats per minute.

5 Repeat the procedure so you can compare your two results.

✳ **Tip**

Morning is the ideal time to take your pulse.

⚠ **Warnings**

If you notice irregularities, such as pauses or lack of pauses or skipped beats, let your doctor know. These could be signs of problems with your heart.

For people suffering from heartbeat irregularities, it is important to take the pulse for the full minute

432 | Prevent Scarring

Scars from acne, abrasions and surgery are difficult to prevent and don't fade immediately. If you start your battle plan soon after the injury you can lessen the severity of most scars.

⊙ **Steps**

1 Consult your doctor about how aggressive to be in managing any wound and ask about the likelihood of scarring.

2 Let your skin breathe. When damage to skin is new, do not aggravate it by putting anything such as bandages or ointment on the area.

✳ **Tips**

Raised acne scars also respond to silicone sheets. You can wear the sheets at night if desired.

Prevent acne scars by keeping hands and nails away from blemishes.

3   Use an antibacterial soap to make sure the skin stays clean.

4   Apply a small amount of aloe vera to the area daily as the wound is healing.

5   Once the damaged area has healed and you are left with a scar, put vitamin E oil on the scarred area every night.

6   Apply a light moisturiser with sunscreen to the area every morning.

7   Exfoliate the area very gently. This should only be done after the skin has completely healed.

8   For a thick, raised scar, try using silicone sheets. The silicone encourages hydration and softening of the scar. Wear a sheet for a prolonged period of time to reduce the raised nature of the scar.

⚠ **Warnings**

Silicone sheets may cause sweat rashes or irritation.

Pregnant women and women trying to conceive should avoid vitamin A products, as they may cause birth defects.

Spot Signs and Symptoms of Dry Drowning — 433

Dry drowning is when someone cannot breathe in enough oxygen for a number of reasons. Here are the basic signs.

◎ **Steps**

1   The first step in preventing a dry-drowning episode is close observation. Remember, dry drowning can be caused by muscular paralysis or only a small amount of liquid, so it doesn't necessarily have to be from a pool.

2   Monitor the person's breathing. Difficulty breathing, painful breathing or shallow breathing are all red flags that a person is at risk of dry drowning. Count the number of respirations for 15 seconds and multiply by four. Over 20 respirations per minute could be a sign of dry drowning.

3   Check for persistent cough, pain in chest and mood or mental status change. Lethargy or increased agitation when lying flat, sweaty skin or colour changes such as pale, or blue/greyish colour are all signs.

4   Dry drowning usually occurs between one and 24 hours after the incident.

✳ Tips

If it is caught early, dry drowning can be treated.

Call 999 or take the person immediately to A&E if there are signs or symptoms indicating risk of a dry-drowning episode.

Use a Home Pregnancy Test — 434

If you suspect you are pregnant, you might consider using a home pregnancy test, which can be bought at most major pharmacies or supermarkets.

◎ **Steps**

1   Wash your hands with soap and hot water.

2   Remove the test stick from the foil wrapper.

3   Sit on the toilet. Place the test stick in your urine stream with the "result window" facing up.

4   Urinate on to the test stick for at least five seconds.

5   Place the stick on a flat, dry surface with the "result window" facing up.

6   Wait for the amount of time specified until results appear.

✳ Tips

Home pregnancy tests can be accurate any time past the first day of your missed period.

Instead of urinating on to a stick, you can collect your urine in a cup and plunge the stick into the urine.

⚠ Warning

Consult a doctor if the test reads positive.

435 Write a Birth Plan

Some women enjoy dimmed lights during labour. Others like gentle music. Trying to tell your birthing team your preference during mind-altering contractions, however, can be difficult. Birthing plans are a way to get your preferences down on paper before the big event so that everyone who will be part of the experience can make it as pleasant as possible. Use the following guidelines to create a birth plan. Be flexible and realistic about your expectations. Giving birth is a very unpredictable process, and you must accept that there will be some things that are simply beyond your control.

PLAN YOUR SURROUNDINGS

❏ Consider who you want to be in the room. Some women invite family and friends to be part of the birthing experience, while others prefer a more private experience with only their significant other or birthing coach. Neither decision is wrong, and you are allowed to change your mind.

❏ Envision your ideal environment. Indicate whether you'd like music playing, the lights dimmed or photos to be taken.

MEDICAL ISSUES

❏ Write down what you'd like to happen upon arrival at the hospital or birthing centre. This includes things like whether or not you want an enema or to receive a routine IV for administering intravenous fluids should you need this later.

❏ Indicate your preferences for any interventions the medical staff may make. This includes episiotomy, Caesarean section, foetal monitoring, labour induction and forceps or vacuum extraction. Let them know under what conditions you would consider these procedures.

LABOUR AND DELIVERY

❏ Think about the actual labour and delivery. Indicate whether you want access to a shower or bath, whether you'd like food and drink, who you would like to cut the umbilical cord and when you will be able to hold and feed your baby.

❏ Mention any postpartum concerns you may have. This will include things like whether the baby is to be exclusively breastfed or allowed a dummy, whether a boy baby will be circumcised, and whether the baby will room in with you or stay in the nursery.

BE PREPARED

❏ Make lots of photocopies of your birth plan. Pack them in your hospital overnight bag, give them to your birthing partner, midwife, doctors and anyone else who will be part of your birthing experience.

❏ If you prefer to have a more private experience, nurses and other hospital staff can be great allies in keeping out armies of excited grandparents-to-be and other well-wishers until you are ready for them. Make sure your birth plan or partner is clear on your preference.

❏ Expect the unexpected. Remember that in many cases, birth doesn't happen as you plan or hope. You should feel comfortable changing your mind about any of your plans during labour and delivery, and don't feel you have failed if you do so.

checklist

Improve Your Self-Esteem 436

Everyone suffers from low self-esteem at one time or another, for all sorts of reasons. Here are some tips for dealing with it, and feeling better about yourself.

Steps

1 Take stock of your strengths. Review what you are good at and tasks you excel at.

2 Think of things you can do or projects you can undertake that use and develop these strengths.

3 Reflect honestly on your weaknesses – but instead of dwelling on how lazy, mean, disorganised or passive you are, commit to change. Brainstorm specific things you can do to overcome the flaws you believe you have.

4 Survey your environment. Is a friend, family member or co-worker criticising you unjustly? Distance yourself from this person or resolve not to let his or her opinion affect you.

5 Act confidently. People will sense your self-confidence and respond positively to you, strengthening your image and self-image all at once.

✳ Tips

The key to positive self-esteem is to remember that you have control over your situation: When feeling glum about a character flaw, remind yourself that you can take action to change yourself and shape your future.

Try not to base judgements of yourself on others' perceptions, which can be fickle.

Cope With Anger 437

We all feel angry at times, but it's important to learn how to curb this anger to avoid flying off the handle and doing something you might later regret.

Steps

1 Take slow, deep breaths and count to 10 when you feel a hot surge of anger. Use the time this takes to keep yourself from doing something rash or regrettable.

2 Try to consider the offensive situation from all perspectives, not just your own – maybe the offending parties had no choice but to do what they did. Consider whether your anger is justified.

3 Think about the object of – and the underlying reason for – your anger. Go beyond easy scapegoats and focus on what specifically triggered your temper.

4 Take positive action to improve the situation once you're in a more controlled state of mind. For example, if you feel your boss has treated you unjustly, collect yourself first and then approach him or her with your concerns. Refrain from venting and taking it out on your subordinates or colleagues.

✳ Tips

Feeling tired can make you more irritable and prone to anger. Make sure you're getting enough sleep and eating a healthy diet.

Establish a regular exercise programme to physically let out tension and lingering aggression.

If you're aware of specific issues that provoke your anger, avoid encountering them to the extent you're able.

Running late or feeling behind may trigger your temper more easily. Schedule your day with cushion time for commutes, projects at work and the other things you have to do.

438 | Wake up Revived

Waking up groggy and unrefreshed is often due to lack of sleep or the inability to sleep soundly. A change in sleep patterns is often all that is needed to end morning drowsiness.

⊙ Steps

1 Assess how many hours you sleep each night. Most people need between seven and nine hours per night.

2 Notice how long it takes you to fall asleep at night. If you are still awake after 30 minutes, either you're going to bed before you're tired or you may be suffering from insomnia.

3 Lengthen your sleep time if you are not getting enough. Do it in 15-minute increments until you feel rested in the morning.

4 Check out your bed. If you wake up aching and sore, it may be time for a new mattress.

5 Block out the light. Hang curtains or draw the blinds tightly. Wear an eye mask. Light disrupts the normal circadian rhythms and signals to the body that it's time to wake up.

6 Keep out the noise. If necessary, wear earplugs. Or use "white noise" such as a fan to block out irritating sounds.

7 Set the temperature. Optimal sleep happens in rooms that are cool – neither hot nor cold.

8 Ask your bed partner if you snore. Or if you live alone, have a friend spend the night with you. If you snore very loudly and wake up feeling very tired, you may be experiencing sleep apnea. Consult your doctor if this is the case.

9 Avoid drinking alcohol late at night, especially if you find yourself waking up several times during the night. Alcohol may help us fall asleep faster, but it can disrupt sleep patterns.

10 Avoid heavy meals late at night. They can interfere with digestion, which may keep you awake and restless.

11 Seal up your mattress and pillow. Allergies to dust mites can leave you feeling groggy in the morning. These covers are sold in shops, online and through mail-order catalogues.

12 Stick to a regular sleep schedule. Go to bed and get up at about the same time every day, even if you don't have to go to work. You will sleep better and feel better in the morning.

❋ Tips

If you are able to wake up without an alarm clock and feel refreshed and rested, you are probably getting enough sleep.

Relax before going to bed. Drink a cup of herbal tea, take a hot bath, do light exercise, read a good book.

Cut down on or eliminate caffeine. Caffeine is present in coffee, tea, many soft drinks and chocolate. Too much caffeine can affect your sleep. People who need coffee to wake up in the morning tend to be groggier than those who don't.

Examine your overall health. If you feel tired and lack energy no matter how well you sleep, there may be another health problem going on. Speak to a health professional.

Get Over Heartbreak 439

Heartbreak is painful and terrible, but it happens to everyone. That depressed, defeated feeling is enough to scare off even the most optimistic of lovers into closing themselves.

⊙ Steps

1 Let go. Realise the relationship is truly over. You cannot begin moving on until you completely give up on that person. Discard the last shred of hope that you may get back together.

2 Come to terms with the relationship. Once you have accepted that it is over, you are ready to make amends with yourself. Forgive yourself for mistakes you may have made.

3 Stay busy. Keep your mind occupied, and if you can't keep your mind occupied, keep your body occupied. Try not to be alone. Go out with friends, play sports, take up a new hobby. Try to avoid the routines you used to follow during the relationship.

4 Seek new experiences. The best way to forget the old is to embrace the new. Now is a good time to broaden your horizons. Find out for yourself that there is more to life than that one lost love.

5 Break the habit. You may have had daily rituals that involved him or her. Avoid situations that remind you of their absence. Now you have to find other activities to fill the void.

6 Find a healthy outlet. Write in your diary or talk with friends. Get out all those nasty feelings.

✳ Tips

Know the balance between repressing negative emotions and letting them rule you. Don't spend all day crying in your room and hating the world, but don't become a bitter, unfeeling husk of a human being either.

Employ daily affirmations. Remind yourself where you stand, how you are feeling, how you felt and how you want to feel.

⚠ Warning

Beware of false hope. Don't misread signs and go back to thinking things can work out with your lost love; that will only set you back in the long run.

Help a Depressed Person 440

It takes patience and time to help a depressed person, but the effort is worth it when you see them smile again.

⊙ Steps

1 Research the symptoms of depression. Try to understand how the person is feeling. Learn about the side effects of medication.

2 Talk to the person about the effects of the depression on relationships. Speak in a caring way, and don't accuse.

3 Seek aid from friends and family. Repeatedly remind the person that you are all supportive and available to help.

4 Seek professional help from a therapist, psychologist or psychiatrist.

5 Offer the person a place to stay. People with depression may have trouble coping on their own.

6 Stay focused, and don't give up. A depressed person may experience mood swings and may feel like giving up. Set a great example by showing how nothing is impossible.

7 Be patient. This is the most important point to remember. Don't let the person feel they are an inconvenience.

✳ Tips

Talk to the person about where and from whom to seek treatment. Go with them to meet the professional who will be caring for them.

Do activities together. Make the person feel they belong.

⚠ Warning

Never force the person who is depressed into social interactions. Let them decide when they want to become socially active.

441 Be Healthy, Wealthy and Wise

Everyone has heard the old adage, "Early to bed, early to rise, makes a man healthy, wealthy and wise." But is this sleeping routine enough to achieve the perfect lifestyle? Here are some real, easy tips to living the dream.

Be Healthy

- Make sure that you are getting at least 30 to 60 minutes of physical activity a day. This can be accomplished by playing with your children, throwing a frisbee with a friend or your spouse, walking or running – any activity that gets your heart rate up and gets you moving.

- Make sure that you are eating a healthy diet full of fresh fruits and vegetables. There is no better food for you than fresh produce. It is packed full of fibre and vitamins, and will give you pure, boundless energy to deal with life.

- Make sure that you are drinking plenty of filtered water. Pure water is the best type of fluid that you can put into your body. It regulates your body's functions and keeps you full of energy and health.

Be Wealthy

- Make sure that you are living debt-free. Stop using any type of borrowed money, such as credit cards. Pay off debt and use a cash-only manner for buying the things you need.

- Save money. Put aside a little every month and you'll be surprised how quickly it grows.

- Challenge yourself in the workplace. Pick a job that you love but that will constantly challenge you. People who enjoy their work are always more successful and often wealthier than those who simply work to live.

- Make sure you rise early in the morning and write down a plan for the day. People who make lists are wealthier and get more accomplished than those who do not.

Be Wise

- Make sure you meditate or pray at least once every day. Praying and meditating relax the spirit, the body and the mind. They clear your head and allow you to focus on what you truly want out of life.

- Read! Get your hands on books, newspapers, magazines – even information available online. Try to learn something new every day.

- Listen to those older and more experienced than you, and learn from their stories and advice. Accept that you don't always know best – be humble.

- Open your mind to all cultures, beliefs and opinions. Move away from seeing life in black and white, and instead embrace its various shades of grey.

Live the Dream

- Seize the day. Wake up in the morning determined to take every opportunity that comes your way. Don't be afraid of new challenges – they often lead to the most rewarding results.

- Value your friends and family, and always make time for them. Life without people close to you is no life at all.

- Travel. See the world and all it has to offer. Every country and culture will teach you something new. Get into the great outdoors and admire the beauty of nature.

- Work out what you want from life and pursue it relentlessly. Don't give up at the first hurdle. Plan how to achieve your aims and accept that setbacks are part of the rich tapestry of life.

Use Aromatherapy for Headaches 442

Aromatherapy is an alternative treatment that uses the highly concentrated essential oils that are extracted from plants to treat symptoms and assist in the healing process. Fresh scents are useful for alleviating tension and therefore aid in relieving headaches.

⊙ **Steps**

1 Use lavender and rosemary oils in a blend to relieve the stiff neck so often associated with a headache.

2 Apply your massage-oil blend to the temples, forehead and to the base of the skull using circular pressure with your fingertips.

3 Massage your neck and shoulders, face and scalp as you apply an aromatic oil blend.

4 Apply a cold compress with two drops of peppermint oil added to the forehead.

5 Blend lavender and marjoram oils to enhance their soothing and quieting effect.

6 Apply lavender oil to the temples to relieve a headache.

7 Put a drop or two of lavender oil on your pillow to calm and quiet your mind.

8 Blend camomile and geranium oil for their ability to calm and ease anxiety, as well as reduce stress-related headaches.

9 Relieve a sinus headache by inhaling a few drops of marjoram from your handkerchief.

10 Use rose oil in your next facial oil to calm your nerves, lift your spirit and relieve your headache.

⚠ **Warnings**

Avoid peppermint if using homeopathic remedies.

Avoid marjoram and rosemary oil if you are pregnant.

Avoid rosemary oil if you have high blood pressure or epilepsy.

Consult your physician and an aromatherapist prior to using essential oils if you are pregnant.

Check each essential oil for specific precautions prior to using them.

Things You'll Need

❏ Camomile essential oil

❏ Geranium essential oil

❏ Lavender essential oil

❏ Peppermint essential oil

❏ Rosemary essential oil

❏ Rose essential oil

❏ Marjoram essential oil

Use St John's Wort 443

St John's wort has been used for centuries to treat a variety of illnesses, including respiratory problems, dysentery, worms, jaundice and gastrointestinal disorders.

⊙ **Steps**

1 Choose a St John's wort product that says it has a standardised 0.3 per cent hypericin content. The higher the hypericin content, the higher the potency will be per milligram.

2 Make sure you buy a brand that has a standardised concentration. Since herbs are unregulated, this is a way of ensuring you are getting a quality product.

3 Buy St John's wort in capsules, as a tincture or as a tea. Use according to product directions.

✳ **Tip**

Consider seeking therapy if you are depressed.

⚠ **Warning**

Possible side effects with St John's wort include fatigue and gastrointestinal upset . However, side effects are generally mild.

4   Take at least 900 mg a day. That is the amount usually needed to be effective. The usual dose comes in 300 mg capsules, taken three times per day.

5   Use sunscreen when taking St John's wort. It has the potential to increase photosensitivity, although studies have found side effects to be rare.

6   Don't expect an instant cure when taking St John's wort. It works more slowly than prescription medication, so you may need to take it for several weeks before noticing the benefits.

444   Do Self-Hypnosis

Self-hypnosis is a good way of releasing yourself from the stresses of the day and calming you if you are feeling anxious. So sit back and relax. You are getting very sleepy...

⊙ **Steps**

1   Recognise that to be hypnotised is to enter a trance state. You will be very focused, but will also be aware of what is happening around you.

2   Sit in a comfortable chair or recline on a couch in a quiet place. Be sure that your clothes are loose and comfortable and that the temperature is not too warm or cool.

3   Turn down the lights so that it's not too bright. It doesn't need to be dark.

4   Relax. You can have your eyes open or closed, whichever is most comfortable for you. Feel every muscle go limp. Feel your mind slow down.

5   Breathe deeply and hold it. Feel all your stress and worries sucked from your body and your head into your lungs. Blow them out slowly and watch them swirl away from you.

6   Notice the different colours of each concern. See them float away and dissolve in the air. You are feeling more and relaxed with every breath.

7   Feel your heart. It is strong and slow. You can feel it beating, slowly, slowly. Each time you exhale, your body relaxes more. You are calm and safe. You can feel your heart. It's beating so slowly.

8   Feel your toes. They feel empty and light. They want to float away. That lightness is spreading up your legs, through your hips and into your back. Your body is so empty that you can see through it.

9   Feel your arms. They feel empty. Your shoulders are empty. Your neck is empty. Your head is floating, weightless. You feel calm.

10   Feel liquid begin to fill your body through your navel. It's deep blue. It feels cool and comfortable. Watch it fill up your body. Cool blue. When you are full, you will feel calm and completely at ease.

11   Now open your eyes fully and sit up. Your cool, blue feeling will stay with you for some time.

✳ Tip

Remember that hypnosis is a skill that, like any other, must be practised.

Improve Your Posture

445

Good posture can keep the spine aligned and healthy, and can help you avoid back problems later in life.

⊙ Steps

1   Examine the areas that need improvement. Do your shoulders hunch, or are you swaybacked?

2   Sit in a chair that is ergonomically designed to support the back and the natural curves of the spine.

3   Sit all the way back in a chair so the elbows are at a 90-degree angle. Adjust the chair height if necessary.

4   Keep feet flat on the floor whenever you sit in a chair for long periods. Consider a foot stool to raise the feet off the floor. This may also relieve pressure and stress on the lower back.

5   Stand and walk with your shoulders back and head straight. This may take some time to get accustomed to.

6   Drive in a position where the headrest supports the middle of the head. Your back should also rest against the seat for proper support.

7   Sleeping habits may also need to be corrected to improve posture. Mattresses should be comfortable, but firmer mattresses offer better support. Side sleeping and back sleeping are healthier for the back than stomach sleeping

8   Consider learning yoga. Many yoga movements stretch and invert the spine to relieve many of the forward-sloping or slumping positions such as sitting in an office chair.

9   If you sit for long periods, get up and move around.

⚠ Warning

Be careful when lifting heavy objects. Using the knees to lift will help protect your back muscles.

Reduce Fat in Your Diet

446

Whether you want to lose weight or just trim the fat, the following steps will help you achieve your dietary goals.

⊙ Steps

1   Decrease or eliminate animal products that are high in fat. This includes red meat, poultry and some dairy products, such as whole milk, cream and butter. If you do eat meat, choose the leanest cuts of meat, poultry and fish available.

2   Check healthy cookbooks for tasty new recipe ideas.

3   Increase the amount of fresh vegetables and fruit in your diet. Eat them raw whenever possible.

4   Change your method of cooking. Broil, bake, steam or poach rather than fry.

5   Use vegetable cooking sprays rather than fat or oils when you cook.

✳ Tip

You need to have some fat in your diet. The ones that are best for you are monounsaturated and polyunsaturated fats, which come from plant sources like peanuts and olives.

⚠ Warning

If you have any questions or concerns, contact a physician or other healthcare professional before engaging in any activity related to health and diet.

6   Select low-fat or non-fat alternatives when they're available. Choose non-fat yoghurt over regular, for example.

7   Eat low-fat cheese and drink skimmed milk.

8   Remove the skin from chicken or turkey.

9   Reduce the amount of nuts, nut butters and olives that you eat. All are high in fat.

10 Snack on fresh fruit, crisps that are baked rather than fried, or air-popped popcorn.

11 Watch labels. Low-calorie does not always mean low-fat.

447   Eat More Iron

It's easy to get enough iron in your diet without gulping down loads of spinach like everyone's favourite cartoon sailor, Popeye.

⊙ Steps

1   Eat chicken, fish, egg yolks and red meat.

2   Feast on dark green, leafy vegetables such as chard, kale, spinach, endive, and mustard, collard and turnip greens.

3   Snack on high-iron dried fruits such as prunes, apricots, dates, figs, peaches and raisins.

4   Start off your day with iron-fortified cereals and breads for breakfast.

5   Eat iron-rich foods in combination with foods that are high in vitamin C to better absorb the iron. For example, have spinach salad with orange slices, or eggs with grapefruit juice.

6   Eat foods that are naturally high in both iron and vitamin C, such as broccoli and bok choy.

7   Cook in cast-iron pots. Iron will be absorbed into the food, especially acidic foods such as tomato sauce.

8   Drink tea between meals, not with them. Tea contains tannin, which blocks the absorption of iron. Herbal tea is a good alternative.

✱ Tip

Keep in mind that iron deficiency has become fairly common, especially among young women and children.

448   Buy Vitamins

It's hard to get the Recommended Dietary Allowance (RDA) of all the vitamins you need, even when you're eating well. Find out what you're missing and how to close the gap with supplements.

⊙ Steps

1   Pinpoint any special needs you have. Vegans need extra vitamin B-12, pregnant women need extra folic acid, those who don't eat dairy and women over 50 need plenty of calcium, and people who aren't exposed to much sunlight need additional vitamin D.

✱ Tip

Try taking supplements with food for better absorption. Take fat-soluble vitamins (A, E, D and K) with foods containing fats, and water-soluble vitamins with any foods.

2   Visit CyberDiet and fill out a nutritional profile. A list of the vitamins and
    minerals you need and estimated amounts will be generated for you.

3   Ask your doctor whether any medication you take interferes with vitamin
    absorption, and what you should do about this.

4   Buy a combination of generic multivitamins and additional supplements
    that covers the list you compile. Generics are just as effective as
    brand names.

 Warning

Avoid vitamins that deliver more
than 100 per cent of the RDA,
because some can be toxic in
large doses.

Give Up Coffee   449

**Millions of people around the world begin their day with a cup of
coffee, believing that they cannot wake up without it. However,
there are other ways to get going in the morning.**

 Tip

Having an occasional cup of
coffee will not get you hooked
on the coffee habit again.

Steps

1   Motivate yourself to give up coffee. Keep in mind that coffee drinkers
    tend to be more groggy and sleepy in the morning than non-drinkers.
    You will eventually feel more awake and energetic than when you needed
    coffee to start the day.

2   Wean yourself slowly, especially if you drink several cups throughout
    the day. Caffeine is addictive, and you may have withdrawal symptoms
    if you stop too abruptly. Symptoms are usually mild to severe headaches,
    fatigue, nausea and depression.

3   As another approach, gradually replace your caffeinated coffee with
    decaf. Drink the same number of cups, but increase the decaf and
    decrease the regular coffee until you are drinking 100 per cent decaf.

4   Get enough sleep at night. Most people need between seven and nine
    hours a night to feel rested. Maximise your sleep. Keep your room dark
    and cool, eliminate or minimise noise, and sleep on a comfortable bed.
    Speak to your doctor if you have problems with insomnia or other sleep
    disorders. Not sleeping soundly will keep you feeling groggy and tired in
    the morning.

5   Open the curtains and turn on the lights when you get up in the morning.
    Bright light signals to your brain that it's time to wake up.

6   Eat a high-protein breakfast. Some researchers believe that protein will
    wake you up and keep you energised. Avoid sugary pastries. They give
    you an energy surge and then a rapid slump.

7   Work out in the morning. Exercise will give you more energy.

8   Drink green tea if you still want some morning caffeine. It contains a
    much smaller amount than coffee, particularly drip coffee, and is a potent
    antioxidant and an all-around healthful drink.

450 | Build Stronger Bones

Bone strength is vital for the condition and health of the entire body. Make sure your diet and exercise habits promote it.

⦿ Steps

1   Eat a diet high in calcium and vitamin D. Some good foods are dark-green leafy vegetables, broccoli, sardines, salmon, kelp, oysters and dairy products.

2   Try not to eat whole grains and calcium-rich foods at the same time. Whole grains contain a substance that binds with calcium and prevents proper absorption.

3   Enjoy foods that contain sulphur. Good ones are garlic and onions.

4   Pass on phosphate-containing foods such as soft drinks. Phosphorus causes the body to excrete calcium.

5   Limit or avoid high-protein animal foods. A diet high in protein causes calcium to be excreted from your body.

6   Decrease caffeine consumption.

7   Exercise daily if possible. Weight-bearing exercise, such as running, weightlifting or dancing is best for bone health.

8   Add supplements of calcium, magnesium and vitamin D if you aren't sure that you are getting enough in your diet.

9   Supplement your diet with silica; it helps your body absorb calcium.

10 Add bone-building herbs to your diet. Alfalfa, barley grass, dandelion root, nettle, parsley and rosehip are a few good ones. Take as a tea, tincture or tablets.

11 Studies have shown that walking and running are better for building strong bones than other activities, including working out on step-climbing machines or stationary bikes.

✳ Tips

Any age is a good time to build healthy bones, but the younger you are when you start, the better your chances of avoiding osteoporosis.

It is always appropriate to consult your doctor before adding supplements or herbs to your diet.

Read a Novel 451

Reading novels is great for building your vocabulary and enhancing your own writing abilities. It's also a pleasant way to pass the time when travelling.

⊙ Steps

1 Read the "blurbs" on the inside and outside covers of any book to familiarise yourself with the subject and the author of the novel.

2 Glance through the table of contents to determine how many chapters there are and how long each one will be, especially if you are reading for a class.

3 Write a list of all the characters as they appear in the story, since relatively unimportant characters often resurface at the end of the book. You can do this on the inside cover of the book or on a small card that you can also use as a bookmark.

4 Read with a highlighter or pen in hand, marking particularly interesting, important or repeated points.

5 Look for points at which the narrator is making some sort of evaluation or judgement about the characters. It's important to note whose "side" the narrator is on – it may not be the side you would take.

6 Pay attention to dialogue: characters reveal many things about themselves in their conversations with others.

7 Make notes on what characters actually do in comparison to what they say. They may reveal their vices or virtues through actions that don't match their words.

✳ Tips

Keep your novel handy so that when you find yourself with a few minutes of time (on the bus, waiting for a friend, eating lunch) you can get back to the story.

For a "good read", gather provisions such as snacks and cold or hot drinks, put on your most comfortable clothes, kick off your shoes and recline somewhere quiet.

Choose an eBook Reader 452

Books used to come in two styles: hardback and paperback. Then they went digital and reading became a whole new ball game.

⊙ Steps

1 Think about where you read the most and where you're most comfortable doing it. Some formats will confine you to your desktop, whereas others will work with handheld devices.

2 Consider the hardware you already own. Some ebook readers are offered as downloadable software, others are sold as part of a handheld device.

3 Keep your eye health in mind. Take into consideration the size of the screen you'll be reading on and whether or not it is backlit. Reading digitally displayed words puts a different strain on your eyes.

4 Check prices. Some ebook reader software programs, such as Adobe Reader or Microsoft Reader, are available as a free download. Handheld reader devices, palm PDAs and pocket PCs range up to £300 or more.

5 Compare the features. Some ebook readers support multiple formats such as HTML, PDF and DOC, some offer text-searching features, bookmarks, a way to add notes and touch-screen menus.

✳ Tips

Make sure you check system-compatibility requirements before you choose any ebook reader.

Try before you buy. Download free software to your computer first to make sure you like reading digital versions of books.

⚠ Warning

Don't expect reading an ebook to be the same as reading a traditional hardback or paperback. It's a different experience, and one that may take some getting used to.

453 | Build a Model Railway

One of the most enjoyable aspects of this is the planning and building of a railway that mimics an actual railway system.

◉ Steps

1   Get inspired by visiting model-railway shows, hobby and model shops, and friends who have model railways.

2   Research the various styles, gauges and brands of model trains. Consider how much you want to spend and what you want the overall layout to look like. Check out trains, buildings and scenery on eBay and model train websites and catalogues.

3   Select the area in your home where you will build a model railway and measure the space.

4   Plan the track layout, scenery and buildings. Start by sketching out ideas and possible track layouts. Overestimate the space requirements and allow for future growth of the model railway. Decide whether you want a particular theme, such as a model of the town where you live or a specific rail line. Search the Internet for layouts and ideas.

5   Construct a platform. Plywood is a good choice for building a platform because it's easy to cut and drill. Make sure that the platform is sturdy and braced to avoid swaying.

6   Design and begin to install landscaping and scenery. Valleys, rivers and mountains should be in place first. They can be constructed of wire mesh moulded over wooden supports, and covered with plaster or papier mâché. Many speciality products are available to aid in scenery construction. Take time to make landscaping as realistic as possible.

7   Lay out tracks before attaching them. Decide whether to glue or pin the tracks in place. Clip the sections of the track together and glue or pin them securely until the whole railway is laid out. Allow the track to sit overnight until the glue is set.

8   Add sidings and stations, houses and buildings. Construct these from plans or kits. Remember that you are developing a community and countryside, and all buildings should have a reason for being where they are. Add cars, people and other accessories.

✱ Tips

Make sure the platform is the right height for a realistic viewing angle.

Compare the different gauges available before you purchase and build your model railway. "N" is one of the smallest gauges. "G" is a large scale often used outdoors in garden railways.

454 | Build a Plastic Model Aeroplane

Model building is a rewarding and relaxing hobby, enjoyed by people of all skill levels and ages.

◉ Steps

1   Remove the parts from the box and compare them to the direction sheet to ensure there are no missing pieces.

2   Separate the pieces by colour and paint. To make painting the smaller parts easier, leave them attached to the frames.

✱ Tip

Allow plenty of time to build your model. Glue takes time to dry completely, so plan accordingly.

3   Hold the wheels with a toothpick to paint them.

4   Trim the pieces before gluing to remove the casting sprues. A small craft knife such as an X-Acto works well for this.

5   Assemble your model in the order dictated in the direction sheet. Use the smallest amount of glue possible. The point of a round toothpick makes a good applicator. Use only a high-quality model cement or crazy glue.

6   Finish your model by touching up areas where paint was not possible to apply before assembly. Apply decals and let dry.

⚠ **Warning**

Some model cements are toxic; use carefully and in a well-ventilated area.

Build a Rocket   455

There are several methods of building a rocket, ranging from buying a rocket kit to designing and building your own rocket from scratch.

◉ Steps

1   Draw out your design. If this is your first attempt at making a rocket, keep the design simple. A cylinder for the body, a nose cone, three fins and an engine are really all you need. Don't forget the recovery method or you'll just have to build another rocket. Now you need to gather the materials and cut them to the size in your plans.

2   Attach the nose cone to the body, with the parachute attached to the back of the nose cone. Plastic cement should be used; wood glue won't bond with plastic. Superglue can also be used, but it's easy to glue yourself to your rocket, so be careful.

3   Sand the fins. The goal is to make the entire rocket as smooth as possible to aid in aerodynamics. Air will move more easily over smooth fins than rough, helping avoid unwanted drag. Balsa wood is the most commonly used material for fins. If you're making your own fins you'll need to make a fin template. Place this template on a piece of balsa wood and trace the shape; use a craft knife to cut the shape out of the wood.

4   Attach the fins after they have been sanded. Use plastic cement if you're using a plastic body, if you're using cardboard then wood glue will work fine.

5   Attach the engine mount. This will slide into the bottom of the rocket, just under the fins. Use a cotton bud to apply glue to the outside of the engine mount. This will hold it securely to the body of the rocket.

6   Paint the rocket. A good paint job will consist of several light coats, and will make the entire rocket move through the air more smoothly. If you want different colours on your rocket the easiest method is masking. Paint the entire rocket in one of your colours. Mask the areas you want to stay that colour, then pain the rocket again. Once the paint is dry, peel the tape off and your rocket is ready to launch.

✳ **Tips**

Draw out your design from scratch, including measurements of the cylinder, fin size and any other design specifications before you build.

Decide what materials you want to use. Cardboard is usually used for the body of the rocket, but plastic can be used as well. Plastic is the best choice for nose-cone material; it is tough and resilient.

⚠ **Warning**

Never try to make your own rocket fuel. You can be killed.

456 | Operate a Ham Radio

Ham-radio enthusiasts operate primarily via voice and Morse code. Each has unique characteristics, requires skill and provides its own enjoyment.

◎ Steps

1 Check frequencies. Each band offers different communication possibilities depending on atmospheric conditions and time of day.

2 Make sure you are within the proper frequency allocation permitted by your licence.

3 Tune the band to find a clear frequency.

4 Tune the transmitter into dummy load.

5 Monitor the frequency for a short period to make certain you will not interfere with another conversation.

6 Begin your first transmission by asking if the frequency is clear.

7 Call CQ.

8 Monitor the transmitter and antenna performance while transmitting.

9 Exchange routine information with your contact.

10 Speak naturally but relatively slowly and distinctly.

11 Make your transmissions relatively short to ensure continuous contact.

12 Allow appreciable pause when turning over transmission to another party so that parties on other frequencies might have a chance to join in the conversation.

13 Remember to identify your station with your licence-call letters every 10 minutes or sooner.

14 Sign off smartly when the conversation is over. Don't draw out your goodbyes.

✳ Tip
Practise your sending off the air.

⚠ Warning
Expect to be nervous during your first few contacts.

457 | Start a Bird-Watching Club

Bird watching, like any passion, is more fulfilling if you can share it with others.

◎ Steps

1 Research other clubs. Talk to members of other bird-watching clubs and see how they organise their meetings and membership. Choose the methods that appeal to you.

2 Write a constitution. Every organisation needs basic rules of conduct. You may want to include the club's name, objectives, membership guidelines, dues, officers, election guidelines, meeting times and places, committees and the steps needed to dissolve the club.

✳ Tip
Many bird-watching clubs have websites that might give you some ideas for your own.

3   Find a meeting place. Look for a location where you can be either indoors (for meetings) or outdoors (for bird watching.)

4   Set a schedule. Decide how frequently you want to meet and what time of day will work best for your prospective members.

5   Advertise. People need to know your club exists in order to join. Use word-of-mouth advertising among enthusiastic bird watchers for the most effective advertising.

6   Get together and find those birds. The point of the club is to see more birds and learn about them. Now is the time to start doing what you love.

Press Flowers   458

Preserve the beauty of flowers rather than letting them wither.

⊙ Steps

1   Select flowers, grass, moss and a background material such as construction paper or tracing paper.

2   Gently squeeze the centre of the flowers with your index finger and thumb to flatten. Thin out mosses and grasses.

3   Use tweezers to arrange the plant material into the desired design. Try to use plant material of the same thickness to avoid uneven pressure.

4   Glue the plants to the background material.

5   Place the arrangement between blotting paper.

6   Place newspaper underneath and on top of the blotting paper.

7   Place flat, heavy objects such as a phone book on top of the newspaper.

8   Let it sit for two weeks.

Things You'll Need

❏ Blotting notebook papers

❏ Phone book

❏ Flower press

❏ Fresh flowers

❏ Fresh plant materials

❏ Eyebrow tweezers

❏ Old newspapers

❏ Paper glue

Make Candles   459

Candles set the mood. Whether you want romance, soft lighting or eerie effects, you can take even more pleasure in candles when you make them yourself.

⊙ Steps

1   Choose your wax, mould and wick.

2   Melt the wax in a double boiler until it reaches pouring temperature.

3   Tilt the mould and pour the wax smoothly down the sides. Fill the mould to within a few centimetres of the top.

4   Gently tap the mould to release air bubbles in the wax.

5   Poke a skewer or chopstick down along the wick occasionally to release air bubbles forming there.

6   Watch for the candle to shrink as it cools. Top off the wax to the original level.

✳ Tip

The wick can be inserted after the wax is poured. It's a matter of personal preference. This is done by sinking the wick tab in the hot wax.

7   Put the cooled candle and mould in the refrigerator for 10 minutes or so.

8   Turn the mould upside down over a clean towel. The candle should slide out easily.

9   Hold the candle by the wick only and polish the candle using a nylon stocking or pair of tights, or spray it with candle spray or clear shoe-polish spray.

10 Untie the wick and trim it to 1 cm (0.4 in) above the top of the candle.

11 Even out the bottom of the candle by heating it on a warm skillet or hot plate and letting it melt until the base is level.

⚠ **Warnings**

Keep small children and pets out of the candle-making area.

Wax is flammable at high temperatures and should never be left unattended.

Use a fire extinguisher or baking soda rather than water if you have a wax fire.

---

460 Crochet

Crochet is a fun and relaxing way of passing the time – you can do it while watching TV or listening to music, and you'll end up with something pretty that you've made yourself, too!

◉ **Steps**

1   Hold the crochet hook in whichever hand is most comfortable.

2   Make a slip knot on the hook with your yarn. Bring the yarn over the hook from the back to the front then grab it with the hook.

3   Draw the hooked yarn through the slip knot and on to the hook. This is one chain stitch. Repeat this step until the crochet length is as long as you want it.

4   Insert the hook into the centre of the second chain stitch.

5   Draw the yarn through the chain stitch and on to the hook. There will be two loops on the hook.

6   Bring the yarn over the hook from the back to the front, then draw it through both of the loops on the hook. This is one crochet stitch. Repeat for each of the remaining chains. Once you've finished, this is one row of crochet.

7   Make one chain stitch at the end of the row, then turn your work anticlockwise. Leave the hook in the chain.

8   Make a new row and work in the stitches of the row you have just created. Continue until the block is as big as you want it.

9   Cut the yarn around 15 cm (6 in) from the block when you have finished. Draw the hook through the last loop on the hook, then detach the hook.

10 Thread yarn into your yarn needle, then weave the yarn back and forth through the stitches to keep the end secure.

✳ **Tips**

Experiment with different yarn weights and hook sizes to get different crochet effects.

If you find it difficult to get a good grip on a crochet hook, wrap a rubber band around the handle.

Knit Your Own Robeez

If your kids love their Robeez shoes, here's how to save some money by knitting your own.

⊙ Steps

1   These are made in four parts: the top flap, heel, sole and embellishment (in this case, a flower). When increasing (inc), knit into the front and back of the next stitch. When decreasing (dec), simply knit two stitches together (k2tog). When working stockinette stitch (stst), knit one row, purl one row, repeat. When working garter stitch, knit all rows.

2   Top flap
Cast on 7 sts. Purl one row.
ROW ONE: k1, inc1, k across to last two stitches, inc1, k1
ROW TWO AND ALL EVEN ROWS: purl across
ROW THREE: k1, inc2, k across to last three stitches, inc2, k1
FIVE: k1, inc1, k across to last two stitches, inc1, k1
SEVEN: k1, inc1, k across to last two stitches, inc1, k1. Repeat this row until you have 27 stitches on your needles.

Work in stst for 10 rows, then bind off.

3   Heel
Cast on 40 stitches with size 5 needles and pink yarn.
Beginning with a knit row, work in stst for seven rows. Switch to size 1 needles and purl one row with white yarn.
Work a k1, p1 rib tightly for 9 rows.

Bind off in rib.

4   Sole
With size 5 needles and brown yarn, cast on 7 stitches.
ROW ONE: k1, inc1, k across to last two stitches, inc1, k1
ROW TWO AND ALL EVEN ROWS: knit across
ROW THREE: k1, inc2, k across to last three stitches, inc2, k1
FIVE: k1, inc1, k across to last two stitches, inc1, k1
SEVEN: k1, inc1, k across to last two stitches, inc1, k1
You should have 17 stitches on your needles now.
Work in knit rows for 40 rows (20 garter ribs).
DECREASE ROW ONE: k1, dec1, k across to last two stitches, dec1, k1
EVEN ROWS: knit across
THREE: k1, dec2, knit across to last three stitches, dec2, k1
FIVE: k1, dec1, knit across to last two stitches, dec1, k1

Bind off.

5   Embellishment

With a crochet hook, cast on 3 sts with brown, join to form a loop. Work six dbl crochet sts in the loop. Attach white, and in the top of every dbl crochet, work ch2, 2dbl crochet, ch2, slip stitch to the next loop.

6   Stitch the finished flower to the top flap. Stitch the heel flap to the sole using a yarn needle. Stitch the top flap to the sole. Note that the sides of the top flap will overlap the heel flap 0.75–1 in.

7   Using the strand of yarn from the ribbing bind-off, tie the tops of each corner of the ribbing together, and stitch to the underside of the top flap.

❋ Tip

If you can't knit the ribbing tight enough, you may want to knit in some elastic thread.

462 Make a Kite

While kites are inexpensive to buy, making one adds to the fun. You'll be especially proud when your diamond-shaped creation takes to the sky.

◉ Steps

1 Cut two lengths of dowel rod, one 40 cm (16 in) long and another 60 cm (24 in) long.

2 Measure each cut piece with a ruler. Mark the shorter piece at half its length and mark the longer piece at a third of its length.

3 Position the two rods at right angles, one on top of the other so that the marks touch. The two rods should form a cross shape.

4 With strong, thin string, bind the two rods together where they meet. Tie a secure knot and cut off any excess string.

5 Use a utility knife to cut a small notch into the ends of both rods. These notches will hold the string that gives the kite its shape.

6 Place some string in the notch at the top of the kite frame and wind it around the top of the rod.

7 When the string is well-secured at the top of the rod, draw it tightly around the edge of the frame. Make sure it fits securely into each notch in the rods.

8 When you return to the top of the frame, secure the string by tying its ends together in a tight knot.

9 Place the finished frame on top of a large piece of paper.

10 Using the kite frame as a template, cut the paper with scissors or a utility knife. Leave an excess of about 1 cm (0.4 in) when cutting around the sections of string.

11 Smear glue along the outside edges of the paper and fold it over so that it encloses the string and secures itself to the paper inside the frame as well. Make sure you use enough glue and spread it evenly enough to attach the paper both to the string and itself.

12 Tie a length of string to each end of the shorter rod. The string should be a bit longer than the rod.

13 Tie another length of string to each end of the longer rod. Again, the string should be a bit longer than the rod.

14 Pick up the two strings with one hand, finding the point at the front of the kite where they overlap. Using a bit of extra string, tie them together. This is the point at which you will attach the kite string when it comes time to fly.

15 To make a tail for your kite, secure several ribbons to the bottom of the kite using strong glue.

⚠ Warnings

Paper kites are particularly delicate and may not be strong enough to endure high winds or falls.

Always avoid power lines when flying kites.

Things You'll Need

❑ 2 dowel rods

❑ Ruler or yardstick

❑ Utility knives

❑ Strong string

❑ Construction paper

❑ Glue

❑ Scissors

❑ Ribbons or strips of cloth

Make a Ballerina Costume   463

These instructions will help you make a ballerina costume for a fraction of the price that you would spend on a completed outfit at a shop.

⊙ Steps

1   Measure the waist and hips of the person who will be wearing the skirt. Measure how long you want the skirt to be. If making a long skirt, have the person take a large step and measure the space between the legs. The finished skirt needs to be as wide as that space. Draw the body outline of the subject. Draw the skirt shape that you want over the body using the measurements. Add 1 cm (0.4 in) to allow for seams. Cut out the skirt shape.

2   Purchase twice as much tulle as the pattern shows. Buy more if you want the skirt to be really puffy. Buy a length of elastic that is the same size as the subject's waist measurement. Purchase thread in a coordinating or matching colour. Buy the slippers and leotard (if you don't already have these).

3   Fold the tulle in half. The folded edge is the bottom of the skirt. Pin the pattern to the tulle and cut out. You will need to cut out two of these. Pin the elastic 1 cm (0.4 in) from the top of the skirt.

4   Sew the 1 cm (0.4 in) of tulle down over the elastic band. You should have a tube that the elastic can slide through. Sew the two sides of the skirt together. Slide the skirt around the elastic until there is an equal amount of material on all sides. Make a couple of stitches to the elastic so that it won't slide around any more. Don't add too many, however, or the elastic won't stretch.

5   Decorate the skirt with sequins, beads or patches. You can also place similar coordinating items on the leotard to make a complete outfit.

✳ Tip

Tulle can often be found at discount prices at wedding shops after peak seasons.

⚠ Warning

Be careful when sewing the material so that you don't sew the skirt to together in places that you don't want to be together.

Things You'll Need

❑ Tulle

❑ Measuring tape

❑ Thread

❑ Sewing machine

❑ Elastic

❑ Tights

❑ Ballet slippers

❑ Leotard

❑ Beads or sequins to decorate the costume (optional)

Make a Hat Out of Paper   464

Making a hat out of newspaper is one of those projects that is so simple, yet most kids enjoy a great deal.

⊙ Steps

1   Lie the newspaper out in front of you on a flat surface, with the short sides of the newspaper at the top and bottom. The paper should be a rectangular shape with the typical newspaper fold already folded.

2   Fold the newspaper by bringing the top short edge down to the bottom short edge. Crease this fold well.

3   Fold the newspaper again by bringing the left side over to the right side. Crease this fold well then unfold.

4   Fold in the left corner diagonally until the corner reaches the middle crease made in Step 3. Crease this fold well.

✳ Tip

This is really simple, so show the kids how to do it, too.

5 Fold in the right corner diagonally until the corner reaches the middle crease made in Step 3. Crease this fold well. You should now have a point at one end of the newspaper.

6 Fold up the top layer of newspaper from the bottom edge several centimetres. Crease this fold well.

7 Flip the newspaper over so that the other side faces up.

8 Fold the top layer of newspaper up from the bottom edge again to match the fold made on the other side in Step 6. Crease this fold well.

9 Look at your hat and notice the four flaps that extend up from where you just folded up the bottom edges. Tuck these flaps in to the middle of the hat. These flaps can be taped to secure if you wish.

465 | Decoupage

Decoupage is the art of sealing paper cutouts to a surface, giving the appearance of a delicate inlay. Decoupage can add a creative and artistic touch to picture frames, lamps, furniture and dishes.

◉ Steps

1 Choose a surface to cover with cutouts. Wood, metal, stone and glass are all suitable materials for decoupage.

2 Make paper cutouts to place on the surface you've chosen.

3 Place the cutouts in their intended pattern on the surface, without using glue. This will help you figure out how to arrange the cutouts, how much area you'll need to cover and how much glue you'll need.

4 Apply a small amount of glue or decoupage medium, such as Mod Podge, to the area of the prepared surface where you want to place the cutout.

5 Smooth the glue out with a small foam paintbrush.

6 Apply a small amount of the same glue to the back of the cutout, and smooth with a small foam paintbrush.

7 Place the cutout on top of the freshly glued area.

8 Smooth out bubbles and wrinkles in the cutout using your thumb, being careful not to rip the cutout.

9 Apply the rest of the cutouts in the same manner. Cutouts can be overlapped to suit your taste.

10 Apply three or four coats of decoupage medium or clear varnish to the finished surface after it has completely dried. Allow the surface to dry between coats.

11 Apply a final coat of acrylic sealant to the surface after the varnish has completely dried.

❋ Tip

Wallpaper, greeting cards, wrapping paper and pictures from magazines all make good cutouts for decoupage.

⚠ Warning

Allow varnish to dry in a well-ventilated area to avoid fumes.

Things You'll Need

❑ Decoupage mediums

❑ Hobby paintbrushes

❑ Sponge paintbrushes

❑ Old cards

❑ Glue

❑ Varnish

❑ Manicure scissors

❑ Old magazines

Make a Piñata 466

Used today worldwide as a favoured party pastime, piñatas are typically made of straw, clay or papier mâché, and shaped as cartoon characters, animals or superheroes.

⊙ Steps

1 Gather your supplies on a newspaper and greaseproof-paper-covered flat working surface.

2 Tear 30 to 40 newspaper pages into sections that are 2.5 cm (1 in) wide and 15–20 cm (6–8 in) in length.

3 Stir in water with your papier-mâché paste in a large bowl. If you don't have papier-mâché paste, simply mix two parts white glue with one part water. Stir with a rubber spatula until well mixed.

4 Blow up your large balloon until full, tie it off and set it aside.

5 Dip the newspaper strips one at a time into the glue, covering them completely on both sides.

6 Spread each newspaper strip around the balloon until it is covered. Be sure to leave a space around the knot of the balloon that will later be filled with sweets. Allow this first layer to dry for several minutes.

7 Repeat the layering process two more times, allowing each new layer to dry thoroughly.

8 Pop the balloon with a pin once your newspaper has dried completely.

9 Decorate your piñata using paint, crêpe paper, stickers and whatever else your heart desires. Be sure to paint first, allowing the paint to dry before gluing on your streamers and other decorations.

10 Poke four holes in the top of the piñata near the sweet hole. Insert string into these holes and pull through to hang the pinata securely.

11 Fill your piñata with sweets and cover the hole with glue and crêpe paper or a piece of cardboard cut to fit the hole precisely.

✳ Tip

Personalise your piñata by adding wool hair, clothing and other items.

⚠ Warning

Make sure you cover your workspace well before you begin, as this process is typically very messy!

Things You'll Need

❏ Newspaper

❏ Water

❏ Papier-mâché paste

❏ Large balloon

❏ Paint, crêpe paper, streamers

❏ Cardboard

❏ Greaseproof paper

❏ Large mixing bowl

❏ String

Face Paint 467

Face-painting is a great activity for parties or other celebrations.

⊙ Steps

1 Place the model in a chair with a towel around his or her shoulders.

2 Tie back long hair so it doesn't get in the way.

3 Wipe the model's face clean with a moisture wipe or tissue.

4 Apply base paint with a makeup sponge so that it covers the entire face.

5 Paint details with makeup brushes according to package directions, putting lighter colours on first. Use a thin brush for fine lines.

6 Have the model look up when painting below the eyes. Have the model's eyes closed when painting above them.

✳ Tips

Always paint on clean skin and use clean brushes and sponges.

Mix paints to create your own colours.

⚠ Warning

Never use face paints on someone with a skin problem or allergy.

468 | Recycle Old Crayons

Instead of sending old crayons to the landfills, collect them in a bucket and recycle them.

⊙ **Steps**

1 Separate your crayons by colour and place them in waxed muffin cups in each section of a muffin tin. Melt them in the oven at about 120°C (250°F) and monitor them closely. After they melt, you will have round crayons that you can re-use, which are great for small hands to use.

2 Cover a skillet with aluminium foil and place different colours of peeled crayons on to the foil. Let them melt and lay a piece of folded construction paper on top of the melted crayons. Press and let it sit a few seconds, then lift the paper and set it to the side to dry to make a cute card to give to your friends.

3 Melt the crayons into a puddle on the aluminium foil. Dip the tips of matches into the melted crayons. This will damp-proof the match, making them great to use for camping trips.

4 Use old crayons to draw on your Easter eggs before colour-dying them. This will make interesting designs on your eggs because the dye can't penetrate the wax.

5 Create multi-coloured candles from your old crayons by melting them in a double boiler and dipping the wicks into the wax or pouring the wax into a jar over the wicks. Give them away as gifts.

✳ **Tip**

Ask your friends with kids to let you have their old crayons if they're not going to recycle them themselves.

469 | Make Potato Prints

You can make potato prints with your family and have fun decorating pictures, gift bags, cards and photo frames.

⊙ **Steps**

1 Slice the potato in half. Cut more to create more stamps. Each potato makes two stamps.

2 Draw a design on a piece of paper. Make simple shapes that stamp well. Consider drawing circles, hearts, stars, letters and a four-leaf clover. You can draw more intricate designs if you're good at carving.

3 Cut out the shape from the paper. Place the shape against the potato on the flat side. Trace the shape on to the potato using a fine-tipped pen. Create an indentation by pressing firmly as you trace the shape.

4 Carve from the perimeter of the shape outwards, leaving the shape intact. Remove all the area around the design about 1 cm (0.4 in) deep. Your shape should stand out from the rest of the potato.

5 Pour paint into a container wide enough to fit your potato. The container needs to be shallow. Use several containers for different colours.

6 Dip your potato into the paint. Let excess paint drip off. Press your potato against the surface you want to print on.

✳ **Tip**

Keep your paper flat so the paint doesn't run.

Start a Stamp Collection   470

Stamp collecting, or philately, is a fascinating way to chronicle the history of the world. Here are some tips on how to begin your collection.

Steps

1   Go to the post office and purchase new stamps.

2   Take used stamps off your old post. Note that it's sometimes more valuable to collect the entire envelope rather than stripping off the stamp because of a unique postmark date.

3   Ask friends and family for their old stamps. Their saved envelopes can also be valuable.

4   Purchase stamps from dealers, who are often listed in newspaper classifieds and offer stacks of assorted stamps.

5   Order stamps through the mail or via websites, either by approval or by want list. "Approval" is when a dealer sends you assorted stamps and you choose which ones to keep. A "want list" is when a dealer checks his or her stock and quotes prices for specific stamps you want to collect.

6   Bid at stamp auctions or philatelic exhibitions. Take the time to look through the merchandise and make educated deals.

7   Trade with fellow collectors. Do this by meeting other stamp traders at shows, auctions and stamp clubs.

✳ Tip

Store your stamps where they will not be harmed. A simple shoebox will do for a beginner collector.

⚠ Warning

While some stamp collection can become extremely valuable, don't expect all your stamps to be rare collectors' items.

Collect Comics   471

While the majority of comic-book titles are superhero books, you also can collect comedy, drama, adaptations, children's, horror, fantasy, science-fiction, educational, mystery, adult, foreign-language and international comic books.

Steps

1   Put comics in a mylar sleeve that covers the book like a clear envelope and has a pressed-board backing to keep it straight.

2   Slide the backing into the mylar sleeve with the treated side facing front. (Backing boards are white on one side and grey on the untreated side.)

3   Slide the comic book into the sleeve, with the cover facing out.

4   Store comics in short or long comic boxes with the comics standing up.

5   Locate your local comic and speciality shops.

6   Browse the shop of choice. Look for comics with strong storylines and exceptional illustrations.

7   Collect what interests you or what you think will increase in market value. If you're lucky, you'll do both at once.

✳ Tip

Most comic speciality shops have saver programmes or subscriptions that allow you to have the books set aside for you as they are shipped to the shop.

472 Collect Seashells

Seashells, also known by biologists as the exoskeletons of creatures in the phylum *Mollusca*, are popular with collectors.

⊙ **Steps**

1 Get more out of your collecting by learning what animals lived in the shells you pick up.

2 Look for bubbling holes in the wet sand. This indicates mollusc burrows, which means there should be abandoned shells nearby.

3 Check out the rules concerning shell collecting in the areas that you are interested in. Some places don't allow collecting or allow it only at certain times of year. Some require permits. The local park service is a good place to start looking for information.

4 Use a piece of screen stretched on to a wooden frame to sieve out the sand. Be sure to use a type of screen that won't degrade from the water – brass is good.

5 Put things back if you move them. Rocks and driftwood may reveal a great find, but remember those places are also probably some creature's home.

6 Handle starfish and phylum *Echinodermata* carefully – they're very delicate.

✳ **Tips**

Don't limit yourself to sandy beaches, particularly ones with hard surf, which aren't good habitats for shell dwellers. You can find shells in mud flats and reef areas as well.

Walking along a beach after a storm is a good way to find empty seashells that have been washed ashore.

⚠ **Warnings**

Be careful. Don't get so wrapped up in your hunting that you lose track of time, the tides and your sunscreen.

Some areas prohibit the collection of all seashells.

473 Bid at Auctions

For a novice, it can be quite intimidating to enter the bidding fray, but with a few tips you'll be waving your paddle with the best of them.

⊙ **Steps**

1 Register. For most auctions, you will need to get bidding paddle with a number on it. To get this, you will have to register with the cashier and may have to show ID, or give a refundable deposit or leave your credit card. This is to ensure that you pay before you leave with your item and to show that you have enough money to participate.

2 Watch and listen. Each auctioneer is a bit different. Listen for a while before getting into the action to get used to the auctioneer. Otherwise you may end up bidding much more than you thought you were.

3 Buyer beware. Check out the goods carefully before buying. Most sales, such as for a car auction or collectibles, give a few hours before the auction to look over goods. If you come late, sometimes you can look among the unsold items during the auction.

4 Choose paddle movement. In most auctions, bidders do not wildly wave their paddles. Many bidders try to be discreet so as to keep people from running up the bid and making them pay more than necessary out of spite. The auctioneer learns to recognise the signals of regular bidders. It may be a paddle in front of the chest, a slight head nod, or raising the

⚠ **Warning**

Decide what your maximum bid will be and stick to it.

hand to shoulder level. Just make sure you are noticed and your bid taken.

5 Buying the lot. If the auctioneer is selling several like items, be careful to hear whether you are bidding one price for the whole lot, bidding on one item, or bidding for one item but buying the whole lot.

6 Stay within limits. Auctions are fast-paced and exciting. Auctioneers are skilled at trying to get the most out of an item for the seller. To keep your head, you need to decide ahead of time what your maximum bid will be and make sure you don't go above that.

Play Poker   474

Poker is a card game that can be played by two to 10 players. There are variations in this game such as draw poker, stud poker and community-card poker. The commonly played poker game is draw poker, so we'll focus on this.

⊙ Steps

1 Understand the various jargons associated with poker, such as bluff, aggressive play, conservative play, action and tell.

2 Keep the "token bet" in the pot. It could range from few pence to many pounds. Decide the amount before beginning the game.

3 Distribute five playing cards to each player. The dealer has to start from left to right while distributing the cards face-down. One card is given to all players. Give the second card in the second round and so on. Place the remaining deck of cards in the centre of the table.

4 Pick up the distributed cards. Make a bet. The first player to the left of the dealer starts the betting. The next player to bet is to the left of the first player, and so on. The dealer (if playing) is the last to bet.

5 Choose the option for the type of betting. It can be done in three ways depending upon the game: see, raise or fold. In the "see" option, the present player has to match the bet of the previous player. "Raise" means that you raise the amount of the bet. In "fold", you choose to pack up instead of betting on bad cards. Or else opt for "check", in which you choose not to bet. A check can be made only when any player has not bet in that particular round.

6 Note that you can open the betting if no one has bet money until your turn comes in the play round. Discard the cards you want to change. Pick up another card. The players can exchange up to three playing cards from the deck. The cards should be face down and no player except you should see your cards. Begin the betting for the next round.

7 Remember that a maximum of three rounds of betting is generally allowed in casinos. At the end of the round, each player shows his or her cards. The player with the highest hand is the winner and takes away the pot.

8 Begin another round of the game by repeating Steps 1 to 7.

✳ Tip
Take care that your opponents do not get any hint how good or bad your cards are. The main trick is to bluff intelligently and make everyone bet more.

475 | Bluff in Poker

In poker, one of the main objectives is to disguise your hand by using deceptive play. If you can do this effectively, your opponents will make more mistakes against you and you will win more money in the long run.

◉ Steps

1 In order to make an intelligent bluff, you have to set it up before actually attempting it. If you plan to bluff on the river, you should represent strength on a previous street by betting or raising.

2 In addition to sending your opponent signals, you should have an idea of your opponent's hand. At the least, you should have a feeling that your opponent is weak when attempting a bluff.

3 Usually, you'll want to bet an amount ranging from half the pot to the pot amount when bluffing on the river, although the decision about how much to bet is situation-dependent. In general, you want to bet enough to discourage your opponent from calling, but you also don't want the bluff to appear obvious. Again, this is where your read on the opponent is of prime importance.

4 One of the best times to bluff is when a scare card comes and you don't feel that it has helped your opponent. For example, if there are two spades on the board and a third spade comes on the river, you might try a bluff if you don't feel that your opponent has a flush.

✳ Tip

Generally, you should try to bet about the same amount on a bluff that you would with a real hand. This will make your bluffs harder to read.

⚠ Warning

You should rarely try to bluff a calling station. This is a player who will call down almost any bet. Against this type of player the best strategy is to wait until you have a big hand and extract chips from them.

476 | Count Cards

Counting cards is the method by which players can beat the game of blackjack.

◉ Steps

1 Learn the rules of blackjack.

2 Learn basic strategy for a six-deck blackjack game with standard Las Vegas rules.

3 Acquire and shuffle a normal deck of 52 playing cards.

4 Deal out the cards as you would see them in a normal blackjack game in which players try to get as close as possible to 21 without going over.

5 Notice the combinations formed and that cards often cancel each other out or make pairs.

6 Learn the values of the cards: aces and 10-value cards (kings, queens, jacks and tens) are worth -1; twos, threes, fours, fives and sixes are worth +1; and sevens, eights and nines are worth 0.

7 Make a chart (or flash cards) of the rules of basic strategy and memorise it so that it becomes second nature.

✳ Tips

To practise your skills, start first at a reputable online casino where you can hone your skills and increase your comfort level.

Take insurance only if the true count is at least +3.

Abstain from drinking while counting cards. Even one drink can impair your ability to add and subtract, multiply and divide.

⚠ Warning

Counting cards does not guarantee that you will win.

Gambling can be addictive. If you have a gambling problem, get help immediately.

8   Count down the deck until you can do it in 25 seconds or less. Pairing cards, so that they cancel each other out, will make this easier.

9   In the casino, bet when the true count is +2 or higher. Divide the count by the number of decks left in play to get the true count.

Play Solitaire   477

The object of this card game is to move all the cards to the four foundations.

⊙ Steps

1   Deal seven cards horizontally with the first card on the left face up and the rest face down.

2   Repeat the deal with six cards, skipping the pile with the face-up card. Again, the first card in the deal (the second pile from the left) should be face up and the rest face down.

3   Do this until you have dealt 28 cards. The last card on each pile should be face up.

4   Put the rest of the cards aside, face down in a stack. This is the stockpile.

5   Put any aces showing on the foundation piles. The foundations are built up in sequence by suit. In other words, the first card in each foundation pile is an ace, the next is a 2, and so on. One pile is hearts, one is diamonds, one is spades and the last is clubs.

6   Turn over the top card in the stockpile if you can't play any of the cards that are showing.

7   Build tableaux in descending order and by alternating colours. This means that the card played on a tableau must be the opposite colour of the card showing and it must be lower ranking. For example, if a 6 of spades (black) is showing, you can play either the 5 of hearts or the 5 of diamonds (the red suits) on it.

8   Put the card on the waste pile if you have no place to play it.

9   Move an ace to the foundation when you find one.

10 Turn the exposed face-down card over when you move a face-up card from the tableau.

11 Move a group of cards when you have an open tableau. If the face-up card on a tableau is a red king and you have another tableau with the sequence queen-jack-10-9-8, you can move the entire sequence to the king as long as that queen is black.

12 Place a king in an empty tableau space.

13 Win by using up all the cards and filling each foundation by suit with the ace to king cards.

❋ Tip

Many computers come with an electronic version of this game – it can be a pleasant way to spend your lunch break!

478 Play Bridge

Contract or rubber bridge is a partnership bidding game emphasising communication between two sets of two partners. The object of the game is to win the highest number of tricks.

Setting Up

- Agree upon partnerships. Designate who will be the scorer.

- Draw a cross in the middle of a piece of paper, and write the words "we" and "they" on either side of the cross at the top of the page.

- Seat partners at the table opposite from each other. North and South are partners versus East and West.

- Shuffle and deal in a clockwise direction a standard deck of 52 playing cards, starting with the person to the dealer's left, until each player has 13 cards.

- Sort your cards into suits.

- Evaluate your cards. Determine if you have a good or bad hand.

- Bid on your hand. The dealer is the first to bid, with bidding continuing in a clockwise rotation.

- Determine the declarer.

- Lay down all your cards face up on the table arranged in suits with the trump suit on the right if you're the declarer's partner. Make no further play of any kind during that round and allow the declarer to play the hand.

- Lay one card on the table if you're the person to the left of the declarer. Play the next card from the dummy hand, and allow each partner to lay one card on the table.

- Pick up the trick if you're the winner.

- Continue in this fashion until all 13 tricks have been played.

Scoring

- Score 20 points below the line, if you're the declarer, for each trick bid and made above book in clubs and diamonds.

- Score 30 points below, if you're the declarer, for each trick bid and made above book in spades and hearts.

- Score 40 points below, if you're the declarer, for the first trick bid and made above book in no-trump. Score 30 points for every no-trump trick bid and made after that.

- Score 20 for each unmade trick in clubs and diamonds, 30 for each unmade trick in spades, hearts or second no-trump, or 40 points each first unmade no-trump for your opponent below the line if you did not make your bid contract.

- Score 700 points above the line if you and your partner won the first two out of three games.

- Score 500 points above the line if you and your partner won two out of three games.

- Score 500 points above the line if you made a small slam while not vulnerable.

- Score 750 points above the line if you made a small slam while vulnerable.

- Score 1,000 points above the line if you made a grand slam while not vulnerable.

- Score 1,500 points above the line if you made a grand slam while vulnerable.

- A game is made when one side scores 100 points.

- Points scored above the line don't count for the game.

Set Pieces on a Chess Board　　479

Chess is a war game based on ancient battle scenarios transferred to a board with 64 squares and 32 game pieces, with the object of capturing your opponent's king.

⊙ **Steps**

1　Set the board between you and your opponent on a steady surface. Make sure that there is a white (or light) corner to the right of each player.

2　Learn the particulars of the board itself. The rows that go sideways are called ranks. The rows going top to bottom are called files, while the rows going diagonally are called diagonals.

3　Familiarise yourself with the five different game pieces. In each colour (black and white) you will have one king, one queen, two each of bishops, knights and rooks, and eight pawns.

4　Position the king and queen in the two middle squares of the rank closet to you. The black queen must be placed on a black square and the white queen must be placed on a white square (each player does this on his or her own side of the board).

5　Situate the bishops, knights and rooks on the same rank (or row) as the king and queen, with one of each on either side of the king and queen.

6　Place the eight pawns in a straight line across the chess board in the row directly in front of your other pieces.

✳ Tip

Although chess pieces come in all colours, the lighter colour is always considered white and the darker colour is always black. White always goes first.

⚠ Warning

Remember that not all pieces can move all ways. Bishops only move diagonally across the board in any direction. Knights can jump over other pieces, but must move three squares at a time. Rooks move backwards and forwards, side to side or up and down. Pawns move one space forwards. The queen can move in any direction, but cannot jump other pieces. The king can move in all directions, but only one space at a time.

Play Backgammon　　480

The object of the game is to be the first to get all your pieces off the board.

⊙ **Steps**

1　Throw a single dice to determine who will get to move first. Roll again if both players get the same number.

2　Move first according to the roll of the dice if you rolled the higher number, but keep in mind that you must use both dice to determine your first move.

3　Number points 1 to 24 starting with the point on the upper right-hand corner furthest away from you.

4　Both players move in an anticlockwise direction.

5　Move on to open points only; you aren't allowed to move on to points with two or more opposing pieces. Move pieces separately or in pairs.

6　Move all the pips shown on the dice. Play the larger number if you can only use one of the two numbers or as many of the doubles as you can.

7　Place your opponent's piece on the bar when you hit a blot.

8　Commence bearing off when you've moved all your pieces into the home board quadrant.

✳ Tip

Always sit facing your opponent, with the board between you.

481 | Play Roulette

Roulette is a game of chance. The object is to guess where the roulette ball, spinning on the roulette wheel, will land.

Steps

1 Scope out the available roulette tables before playing. Each table will have a sign showing its minimum and maximum bets. Look for house rules written on the table's surface.

2 Find a roulette table that has a minimum bet in your price range, sit down and ask the table attendant to change some money into chips for you.

3 Place bets by setting some chips on top of the number or numbers that you have selected. The attendant will call for all betting to end and then set the ball in motion. Any bets placed after the ball has been released will not be honoured.

4 Cash in your chips at the roulette table when you have finished playing. Roulette chips are usually different from the chips used at card games, so it is unlikely that you can use them elsewhere.

5 Learn about the straight-up bet, a bet placed on a single number. If you choose the winning number, you will be paid at 35 to 1 odds.

6 Understand the split bet, a bet placed on the line between two numbers. If either number wins, the bet pays 17 to 1.

7 Know the row bet, a bet placed at the edge of a row of three numbers. If any one of the three numbers wins, the bet pays 11 to 1.

8 Familiarise yourself with the corner bet, a bet placed at the intersection of any four numbers. It pays 8 to 1.

9 Understand the street bet, a bet placed at the edge where two rows of three numbers meet. It pays 6 to 1.

10 Learn about the column bet, a bet placed at the bottom of a column of 12 numbers. It pays 2 to 1.

11 Know that there are many bets on a roulette table that pay 1 to 1 (an amount equal to your bet). You can place these bets on either side of the numbered section. These bets include colour bets (red or black), odd- or even-number bets and bets on numbers 1 to 18 and 19 to 36. The individual sections for these bets are clearly marked.

⚠ Warnings

Though there are many strategies for winning roulette, the odds are really in the house's favour.

When choosing an online casino, stick to the reputable casinos that have been in business for several years.

482 | Solve a Sudoku

A Sudoku square has nine rows and nine columns, divided into nine sub-squares with nine individual boxes. Each row, column and sub-square must contain the numbers 1 to 9 without repeating any number within any rows, columns or sub-squares.

Steps

1 Start by looking for patterns that leave only one possible correct placement of a number.

✻ Tip

Sudoku puzzles are offered on a number of websites to play for free. You can also download more complex versions of Sudoku.

2 Focus on one number at a time for each of the major segments of the Sudoku square. Divide the sub-squares into groups and assess the possibilities for a number.

3 Use the numbers you fill in to lead to additional successful answers. When you fill in one number it affects the placement of the number in other rows and columns.

4 Focus on sub-squares that only have three boxes left to fill. Use the columns and rows that compose the sub-square to try to eliminate some possibilities.

5 Note what numbers are missing from a sub-square and find where those numbers are located in the columns and rows that compose the sub-square. If a missing number is in two out of the three rows or columns comprising the sub-square, then this tells you where the number should go.

6 Write down the numbers missing from a sub-square next to the Sudoku square. Note the possible locations of each number. This may help you eliminate some choices and enable you to place a number without seeing that number in any of the columns or rows that compose the sub-square.

7 Mark potential correct locations for a number around the edges of the box. Write them smaller than you would normally write the correct answer.

⚠ **Warning**

Don't make too many markings for potential correct spots for numbers. It is easy to make a mess and get confused.

Buy a Handheld Video-Game System   483

Handheld games may not have the resolution or large screen of a console-based system, but they are portable.

◎ **Steps**

1 Seek out the advice of video-game magazines. These magazines do reviews and previews of new products, including the hardware and software. This will give you an idea of what is out there and how much it costs.

2 Explore the Internet. There is a plethora of personal pages by video-game fanatics. These pages can give you a good idea about the products and what game titles are available that support them.

3 Consider brand-name systems. If the brand has built up a reputation over the years, it will probably be around for upgrades, and the manufacturer will ensure that plenty of game titles are released to support the system.

4 In the shop, compare at least three systems. Ask the salesperson to demonstrate each product, then play with them yourself.

5 Consider the audio on each system.

6 Determine which game pad is most comfortable for you to use. Some have two buttons to control play, and some have four. The two-button variety may not be able to work certain games while the four-button version can. Consult with your salesperson.

7 Ask about the library of game titles available for the systems. You will probably want to choose a system that has plenty of game titles to support it.

✳ **Tip**

There's no substitute for just going to a shop and trying out handheld devices – it's important to find one that works for you.

8   Consider the screens. Are the images crisp and clear?

9   Consider the power of the processor working the system. This determines how fast it works.

10 Ask about peripherals that are offered to support the products. Some systems will accept peripherals offered by manufacturers other than the one who made the handheld system you are considering.

484 | Use Wireless Controllers for PlayStation 3

PlayStation 3 is a revolutionary gaming system that utilises completely wireless, Bluetooth controllers. For some users, however, this leap in technology is a bit confusing.

⊙ Steps

1   Make sure that your PlayStation 3 is properly set up and connected to your television, and that it's functioning properly. If you can't get your PlayStation 3 to start and display its start-up graphics, something isn't hooked up right. You'll need to fix it before you can use your wireless controller.

2   Plug the power cord for the PS3 wireless controller into one of the USB ports on the front of the PlayStation 3.

3   Plug the other end of the power cord into the access port on the top of your wireless controller.

4   Allow the wireless controller to charge, leaving it plugged into the PlayStation 3 undisturbed for several hours to gain a full charge.

5   Disconnect the PS3 wireless controller from the power cord. Press the PS button to start up the PlayStation 3. The PS button is located in the middle of the controller. It is clear and displays the PlayStation logo of a letter P and a letter S moulded together into one shape.

6   Use the wireless controller to control the PlayStation 3, exactly as you would have with a corded controller for earlier PlayStations.

✳ Tips

Learn how to use the SixAxis elements of your wireless controller effectively.

If the red LED light on the PS3 wireless controller is flashing, this means that it's low on battery charge. When this occurs, save your game, and then hook the controller up to charge.

⚠ Warning

Remember to charge your controllers after each use. It's very frustrating to be in the middle of a difficult part of a game and suddenly have your controller's battery run out of juice, leaving you with no ability to control the system or the game until you've hooked the controller up to its power cord.

485 | Create a Wii Mii

To play several of Wii video games, you must create your very own Wii Mii. This character can be a duplication of yourself, someone you know or even a celebrity.

⊙ Steps

1   Turn on your Wii video-game system. When the main menu loads, the Mii Creator program will appear as the second icon in the top row. Aim your Wii remote towards this icon and press the A button on the remote.

2   Use your Wii remote to press the start button that appears on the next screen. This will officially bring you into the Mii Creator.

✳ Tip

It's great for all the family to have a Wii Mii that looks like them when playing together.

3   You will now enter the Mii Plaza. This is the area where all your Miis will explore and hang out. Look at the various icons to the left and find the one that features a smiley face and a plus sign. Aim your Wii remote at the icon and press the A button to load the creator.

4   You will be given two options: Start From Scratch and Create a Look-a-Like. Select Start From Scratch.

5   Select whether you want your Mii to be male or female.

6   Now you will be at the main panel to edit your Mii. The top of the screen shows different icons used to edit different sections of your Mii. The first section is the head shape and skin colour. Select one of the eight different-shaped heads and then aim your Wii remote to the colour panel at the right to select the skin tone.

7   Select the hairstyle for your Mii. There are several different styles on multiple pages and this is where you adjust the colour of the hair as well.

8   Select the eyebrow shape. This may not seem important, but the eyebrow shape can actually change the mood that your Mii appears to be in, so look through these carefully.

9   Select eyes for your Mii. Use your Wii remote to place the eyes at different heights of the head and also different sizes.

10 Choose a nose and mouth for your Mii. If you want a mouth to express some emotion, you can. You can always edit it later.

11 The last icon to the far right has different accessories you can add for the head, such as facial moles, glasses and hats.

12 Select the second icon from the left to adjust your Mii's height and weight. This can make a difference in games like Tennis and Bowling.

13 Select the first icon to create your Mii's profile. In the profile editor, enter in the nickname, gender, birthday, favourite colour and other settings.

14 Select the Quit button and your Wii Mii has been created.

Clear the Cache on Your Xbox 360   486

Has your Xbox been running sluggish lately? Clearing the cache may help.

⊙ Steps

1   Turn on your Xbox 360 and navigate to the system settings under My Xbox. Select this and then select Storage Devices and then highlight the storage device (hard drive or memory unit).

2   With the storage device highlighted, press Y for Drive Options. Enter the sequence X, X, LB, RB, X, X. The following message should appear: "Do you want to perform maintenance on your Xbox 360 storage devices?" Select Yes.

3   Sit back and wait while the system clears the files in the cache. It may take a few minutes for the process to be completed, especially if you haven't done this before or for a while.

4   Restart your console.

⚠ Warning

You will lose updates when the cache is cleared, but these can easily be downloaded again.

487 Win Space Invaders

To score big at Space Invaders, you must have quick hands and a winning strategy.

⊙ Steps

1 Take advantage of cheat-enabling double shots on the Atari console. Turn the power off and hold down the reset button. While holding down the reset button, turn the power back on. Let go of the reset button and start a game, and you can fire twice every time you press the fire button.

2 Shoot a narrow path in one of your barriers and then hide under it. You can continue to shoot through your path, and the barrier provides at least some protection as long as the opening is as narrow as possible. This strategy ends at level five, however, as there are no more barriers.

3 Prepare to beat level five before it begins. For the first five levels of the game, the space invaders start lower and lower on the screen and by level five they are as low as they can get. Hold the joystick to the right before the level begins with your finger on the fire button. Move quickly across the screen, stopping briefly at each space invader in order to shoot him to clear this dangerous, low row right away.

4 Repeat this movement for each subsequent level. All levels after level five are exactly the same. By clearing out the lower row immediately, you dramatically improve your chances to beat the game. If you move quickly you can even eliminate the lower two rows by holding in place slightly longer before moving on to the next space invader.

5 Get bonus points by shooting the motherships that cross the top of the screen. Concentrate on shooting the space invaders until you get down to two rows of four invaders. Then avoid the space invaders' fire and wait for motherships to pass, shooting them as they do. Be careful not to shoot any more space invaders, as the motherships will not pass if there are less than eight invaders on the screen.

6 Beat the game with 500,000 points. Although the game does continue infinitely, getting 500,000 points is the benchmark at which you beat the game.

488 Select Educational Software

Every software producer would like parents to think their programs are "educational". The question is, what exactly do they teach?

⊙ Steps

1 Consider your child's age, then add two years to determine which products are age-appropriate. (One exception: don't buy programs that require the player to read if your child is a pre-reader.)

2 Think about your child's interests. There are games devoted to almost every interest imaginable, and your three-year-old son is far more likely

to use (and therefore learn from) a program about dinosaurs than one that teaches how to count in Spanish.

3 Decide what you want your child to learn – and not learn. Some games, even for very young children, have violent or insensitive content you may not want your child exposed to.

4 Talk to your child's teacher. Since many schools now have computers in the classroom, your child probably has some favourite programs at school. His or her teacher can recommend similar titles for you to purchase to use at home.

5 Read some product reviews. Spending money on software is a total waste if your child can't navigate the program or loses interest after half an hour.

6 Try before you buy. Most toy shops have demo CD-ROMs and PCs set up for you to try a program you're considering for purchase. Unless it's a gift, you might want your child to try it out, too.

7 Look for patterns. You're bound to buy a few duds now and then, but look for similarities among the games your child really enjoys. It's your best guide to picking winners in the future.

Guess Someone's Astrological Sign   489

The ability to guess someone's astrological sign is a great way to impress a date or a group of friends.

⊙ **Steps**

1 Study the different astrological signs. You will have to know these well to be able to make any real guess at someone's sign. Pay attention to the character traits and personality qualities that are associated with each sign.

2 Examine the signs of the zodiac, and memorise these characteristics:

- Aquarius – Easygoing, creative
- Aries – Initiator, starts trouble
- Taurus – Materialistic but appreciative
- Gemini – Informative, likes trivia
- Cancer – Likes family and groups
- Leo – Reliable and strong
- Virgo – Analytical and scientific
- Libra – Works well with others, cooperative
- Scorpio – Emotional, likes challenges
- Sagittarius – Searches for meaning, philosophical
- Capricorn – Likes order and rules
- Pisces – Enjoys civil disobedience and the divine

⚠ **Warning**

Be mindful of what kind of company you are with when you're doing this. Some people are uncomfortable with astrology.

3   Look for blatant qualities in the people you are trying to guess. For example, if you are trying to guess someone who is loud and wants to fight, your first instinct might be to think Aries.

4   Study the person's appearance, looking for any characteristics that you can identify as associated with a particular sign. You may or may not find these, depending on the person you're looking at.

5   Familiarise yourself with the different elements, as they are associated with astrological signs. Fire, earth, wind and water make up the four elements and you should probably know all the characteristics associated with them before trying to guess someone's sign.

6   Continually observe your subject for a while and compile your data. Start trying to put the person into a category, perhaps narrowing it to two or three probable signs.

7   Make an educated guess based on all of the above information you have amassed about your subject. Believe it or not, you will actually get better over time.

490 | Read Palms

There are sceptics who will tell you palm-reading is nonsense. But for those who think there may be something to it, here are some basics.

⊙ Steps

1   Determine which is the active hand and which is the passive. For instance, if you are right-handed, the active will be the right hand and the passive the left. The passive hand should be studied more for inherited characteristics and the active hand to reflect changes.

2   Identify the three main lines in your palm: the heart line (or love line) is the top line closest to the fingers, the head line is the middle and life line is at the bottom.

3   Look at the heart line, which relates to emotions and love. If the line begins right under the index finger, you are more likely to be in a loving relationship. If it begins below the middle finger, you are more self-centred and tend to pull back from love. A line that begins between the middle and index finger signifies something in between.

4   A heart line that goes across the hand suggests a person who is more controlled or closed off emotionally. A line that curves upward towards the index finger indicates a more affectionate person.

5   Observe the length of the heart line. The longer it is, the more concerned you are with love. The shorter it is, the more interested you are in sex. If the heart line points downwards and touches your life line (at the bottom), then it's easy for you to have your heart broken. A line that is long and curvy indicates that you freely express your emotions and feelings. A heart line that is straight and parallel to the head line indicates that you have more of a handle on your emotions.

✳ Tip

Contrary to popular belief, the lines on your palm do not remain the same throughout your life.

⚠ Warning

Palm-reading is a not a form of fortune telling. It doesn't predict the future.

6   Observe the head line, which relates to the way you think. The space between the beginning of the head line and the beginning of the life line indicates how cautious you are. When these lines are joined at the beginning, you tend to have a more cautious and possibly fearful nature. The further apart, the more of a risk-taker you are.

7   Look at the length of the head line. The longer the line, the more emphasis you put on thought and intellect. A wavy line indicates that you have a shorter attention span and tend to avoid deeper thinking.

8   Study your life line (which begins at the edge of your palm, in between your thumb and index finger) and reflects the quality and length of your life. If it runs close to your thumb, it indicates that you have less energy. The more curvy the line, the more energetic and optimistic you are. If the line swoops around in a semicircle, you are extra strong and enthusiastic. If the line is straight and stays close to the edge of your palm, you are more cautious.

9   Observe the length and depth of the life line. The longer and deeper the line, the longer and healthier the life.

10 See if you have more than one life line. If you have two or three, this means you are very positive with a zest for life. If you have lines that extend up and beyond your life line, you are resilient and recover well from bad situations, but if you have lines that extend below your life line, you tend to dwell on the negative.

Read Tarot Cards   491

There are no hard-and-fast rules for the care and reading of your cards, but these are some suggestions to start you off.

⊙ Steps

1   Get a deck of tarot cards. Shop online or at bookshops, which often carry tarot decks.

2   Use a scarf or cloth and wrap your cards to create a safe and clean environment. You may also want to buy a special box in which to store your wrapped deck.

3   Season your deck of cards by sleeping with the wrapped cards next to your heart or under your pillow for a week. Now you're ready to read!

4   Concentrate on the question being asked, and shuffle the deck. You can mix the cards in a big pile using both hands, and then gather them up neatly and proceed with a regular card shuffle.

5   Cut the deck. If reading for someone else, have him or her ask the question out loud as he or she cuts the deck. If you do the reading for yourself, ask your own question as you cut.

6   Deal the cards using the tarot spread of your choice. A simple card spread is four cards in a diamond shape.

✳ Tip

In the four-card, diamond-shaped layout, the card at the top point of the diamond represents your romantic life. The next card, below card one on the right point, represents finances. The third card on the lower point of the diamond represents health and happiness. The fourth card, which is placed opposite card No. 2 on the left diamond point, represents career.

⚠ Warning

You should be the only one to handle your deck unless you want the person for whom you're reading to shuffle or cut the deck.

7   Look first at the design on the cards. Cards that look right side up for the reader are in a positive position; cards that look upside down for the reader are reversed. Reversed cards indicate conflict or blocked energy, or weaken the card's influence.

8   Look on the Internet for card meanings and learn these.

9   Come up with your own card meanings and descriptions to personalise your reading style. Don't be afraid to follow your instincts.

492 | Analyse Handwriting

A person's handwriting can say a lot more than their actual written words can. You can tell a person's mood, motive and character by their handwriting.

⊙ Steps

1   Look at how the letters connect. If they connect in a simple manner without using any unnecessary strokes then this is someone who thinks on his feet and sees the whole picture.

2   Notice the size of the letters. If they're large with very little space in between them, this person is friendly and likes to be around large groups of people. If the letters are small, this person is very shy and likes to be around just one or two friends.

3   Check out the slant of the letters. If they slant to the left this person is rebellious. If the letters slant to the right then he leans on other people for support. If the letters are straight up and down then she is genuine but very independent.

4   Take notice of the length of the upper loops in the letters of the handwriting when you analyse it. Tall upper loops means he is all talk but no action. Short upper loops mean she is all about getting things done.

5   Analyse the lower loops in the letters. If the lower loop is small, then this person says what he feels. If the lower loops are larger, than she is full of energy.

⚠ **Warning**

Keep your distance if the handwriting slants in all different directions – this means the person is really stressed!

493 | Raise Bees

Beekeeping is not for the faint of heart. Of course, with the right kind of protective clothing and tools it is quite safe once you get used to the fuzzy little guys.

⊙ Steps

1   Buy the right kind of equipment for protecting yourself from bees. There are various types of suits for this, but they all basically cover your entire body and are elasticated at the wrists and ankles. The bee helmet, or hat, has netting to cover your face and zips on to the suit. You will also need leather gloves and boots for protection.

⚠ **Warning**

Although the suit will keep you pretty safe, be prepared for a sting or two when dealing with bees.

2 Buy a brood chamber and supers to start your hive. The brood chamber is where the queen lays her eggs, which the workers feed and keep clean. The supers are frames with a hive-like, wax pattern on the bottom on which the workers will build honeycombs to hold the honey. Start with five frames.

3 Order your bees from a bee supplier. You will need a queen, workers and drones. The queen, who leaves the hive once in her life to mate, spends the rest of her life (two to three years) laying eggs. The workers do everything else, from feeding larvae, cleaning, guarding the hive and gathering nectar to make honey. Drones seem to serve only one purpose – mating, after which the queen kills them.

4 Feed your bees supplements in the spring to get them started. These include pollen supplements or sugar and water. These will give them nourishment until the flowers and trees begin to bloom. Then the workers will go out and collect nectar to bring back and store in the supers and wax cells they have built.

5 Wear a protective suit and use a smoker when working with the bees. Smoke calms them down and stimulates the feeding instinct; it also blocks the smell of the danger pheromone given out by the guards. This will allow you to remove full supers and check the bees in the brooding chamber without exciting them. Use moss, rotten wood or other fuels in your smoker.

6 Replace your queen if she dies or leaves with a swarm. A healthy hive will swarm two or three times a summer, when the queen and half of the colony leaves. Buy a new queen or artificially start a new colony by taking a frame containing workers and larvae. The workers will feed a nutrient-rich food to chosen larvae to create a queen.

7 Remove honey-filled supers any time for honey extraction, removing debris or bees from the honeycomb. Replace supers with empty frames, where the honeybees will create wax cells with secretions from their bodies and fill them with honey. When the cells are full and have matured they are capped with wax by the bees for future use.

8 Cover your hive in the winter, making sure you have left enough food for the bees until winter is over. The bees keep from freezing by forming a swarm around the queen in the lowest chamber. By shivering and moving constantly, they keep the temperature at approximately 27°C (80°F) and will not freeze unless it is a particularly long or cold winter.

494 | Wrap a Birthday Gift

Try to be as creative as possible when wrapping a birthday gift. Keep the gift recipient's age, likes and dislikes in mind when choosing the colours and types of materials used in your wrappings.

⊙ Steps

1 Choose a wrapping paper appropriate to the gift recipient. Is the gift for a child's birthday? Your grandmother's birthday? Does the recipient have a favourite colour?

2 Choose coordinating ribbon, and either purchase a pre-made bow or make your own. If you decide to make your own bow, purchase additional ribbon.

3 Gather your materials and lay them out on a flat work surface. A kitchen or dining-room table works best, but be sure not to scratch the table's surface when cutting the wrapping paper.

4 Use a string or a tape measure to determine the dimensions of your gift box. For a rectangular box, measure around the box as if you were measuring a waist. Add 5 cm (2 in) to this dimension, and jot down this number.

5 Measure the length of your gift box. Measure the height of the box, multiply that number by two and add the total to the length measurement. Write this number down.

6 Use a ruler to cut a piece of wrapping paper to the dimensions calculated and place wrapping paper face-down on your work surface.

7 Position the package, top down, on to the paper so that you are able to bring the lengthwise edges of the wrapping paper to the middle of the box. Centre the gift box.

8 Bring one lengthwise edge of wrapping paper to the centre of the box. Secure with tape. Turn the opposite edge of paper under and bring this to the centre of the box as well. The turned-under edge should overlap the first taped edge.

9 Position the box so that one short end is facing you. Grasp the left and right edges of wrapping paper and push the sides in so that top and bottom flaps are formed. Make sure that the edges are pushed in as far as they will go without ripping the paper. Secure the pushed-in edges to the box with tape.

10 Bring the upper flap down against the side of the box, making sure that the flap is sharply creased at its folds. Secure the flap against box with tape. Bring the lower flap up against the side of the box. Crease and secure as you did for the upper flap. Repeat for the opposite end of box.

11 Position the package so that the seamless side is up. Affix the ribbon and bow as desired.

✳ Tips

Consider using comics or newspaper to wrap your present; or stamp or paint appropriate designs on to plain white or brown Kraft paper.

Choose transparent tape for your gift-wrapping needs. This will give your package a more tidy appearance than can be achieved with other types of tape.

⚠ Warnings

Check the label on any package of gift-wrapping paper to make sure there's enough paper inside to wrap your gift box. If you are wrapping a very large box or several gifts, you may need to purchase more than one package.

Don't choose gift-wrapping paper that comes folded into precut squares. It has deep creases, which can give your package a crumpled, untidy appearance. Opt for paper that comes in a roll instead.

Receive a Bad Gift Graciously — 495

It's the worst gift in the world, but you have to be polite – time to beef up your acting skills, show your appreciation for every gift you get and make it look real.

Steps

1. Pretend that the gift is the best you've ever been given. Be enthusiastic about the gift, not just polite. The giver must never suspect that you really hate it.

2. Think of an adjective to describe the gift without offending the giver. Words like "unique" or "unusual" are good choices. No one will know that you plan to hide the gift in a dark corner when you get home.

3. Ask the giver where they got the gift. This is a good way to slyly discover where to return it, if the receipt is not included.

4. Smile as you think of an equally bad gift to give to them. Planning your revenge is the best way to receive a bad gift while maintaining a polite and gracious smile.

Tip

If the gift is not unusual, substitute an appropriate adjective, such as colourful or stunning.

⚠ Warning

Don't praise the gift too effusively or the giver might get you something similar for your next birthday.

Buy a Teenager a Gift — 496

Teens are hard to buy for; they're at an age where their interests are constantly changing and they're often in search of what is "cool". Learn the teen's personality and hobbies to buy a great gift.

Steps

1. Consider money. It isn't personal, but it will get them exactly what they want or need. Every teen has something he or she can spend money on.

2. Get technical. iPods and a host of MP3 players, computer gadgets and mobile phones are items teens are obsessed with.

3. Give them style for their bedroom or college room. Teens want their space to feel personalised. A trendy chair, lamp or other decorative detail can be a great gift that they'll use every day.

4. Get them tunes. A gift certificate to a music shop or an iTunes gift card show that you value their interest in music, while leaving the actual choice in purchase up to them.

5. Make a goodie basket. An uncommon gift, they'll love the creativity of unexpected surprises. Fill them with snacks and sweets, school supplies, decorative items, books, CDs, DVDs and clothing.

6. Be sporty. Are they active in an athletic sport at school or part of a club with a specific interest? Get them clothing related to the sport or a book about the sport. Better yet, a ticket to a match will be a hit.

7. Be practical. Ask if there is something he or she needs. Clothing, socks, shoes and school-related items are possibilities.

Tip

Bear in mind that not all teenagers are the same. Think carefully about whether they're sporty or book-loving before buying a birthday gift.

497 Give an Amazon Gift Card

An Amazon gift card allows the recipient to choose practically any gift they like – the perfect Christmas present for the person who has everything.

⊙ **Steps**

1 Visit the gift-card section of the Amazon.co.uk site.

2 If your recipient is in another location and has access to an email account, you can choose to simply email the gift card. When you select this option you will be prompted to enter the amount and the email address of the recipient. You can even include a personalised message that will be delivered with your gift card.

3 If you'd like to have something to personally deliver to the recipient, choose the Print at Home option.

4 If you would like an actual gift card delivered by post, choose that o ption from the Amazon gift-card home page. You'll provide the same information as above, along with an address, and a physical gift card will be delivered to your recipient.

5 If you are placing an Amazon.co.uk order, you can include a gift card (or several of them) to be delivered with your order.

✻ Tip

With any of these options, you will be allowed to select a design for your gift card.

498 Make Great Christmas Cards

Christmas cards help you express the love and joy of the season and well wishes for the coming year. Make the cards even more meaningful by creating your own.

⊙ **Steps**

1 Buy blank pre-cut cards or create your own by trimming and folding a piece of card stock to fit the envelopes you have on hand. Great colours for Christmas cards are silver, blue, white, oatmeal and the traditional red and green.

2 Cover the front of the card with an additional layer of coordinating card stock or patterned paper for added interest. Measure and trim the sheet so a narrow border of the card base will still be visible after the decorative paper is stuck on.

3 Trim an additional rectangle of card stock that will sit in the centre of your card and serve as the background for the main embellishment.

4 Decide what you'd like to use as an accent. Try stickers, small die cuts, rubber-stamped images or felt or foam shapes. You can also save money by trimming the images of Santa Claus, snowmen and angels from the Christmas cards you received last year.

5 Stick the accents to the small rectangle of card stock (use foam tape for added dimension) and affix that to the centre of your card.

6 Stamp a Christmas greeting along the bottom or inside the card along with your handwritten message.

✻ Tip

If you're running short on time, but still hope to create Christmas cards on your own, consider printing simple designs from the Internet.

Things You'll Need

❏ Blank cards

❏ Envelopes

❏ Card stock

❏ Scissors

❏ Patterned paper

❏ Glue

❏ Embellishments

❏ Rubber stamps and ink

❏ Recycled Christmas cards

❏ Pens

How to Do More of *(Just About)* **Everything**

7   Make cards personal by incorporating small photos into the design. If you're creating a tree-shaped card, for example, output photos the size of index prints and "hang" them from the branches like ornaments.

8   Add glitz by using a metallic ribbon bow, creating a card base from metallic or embossed card stock or "painting" specific sections of stickers or die cuts with glue and sprinkling with glitter.

❏ Photos
❏ Ribbon
❏ Glitter

Make Paper Chains | 499

Paper chains can be used for any number of occasions, but are a particular favourite at Christmas.

◎Steps

1   Cut the construction paper lengthwise into strips that are about 2.5 cm (1 in) wide. They can be of pretty much any length, keeping in mind that the longer the strip, the bigger each link in the chain will be.

2   Bend the first strip around to form a circle or loop.

3   Seal the open ends of the circle link with glue, tape or a stapler so that it stays connected on its own.

4   Take another strip and thread it through the first loop, forming a second, connected, circle.

5   Seal the second circle with glue, tape or a stapler so that you have two linked circles.

6   Repeat Steps 3 and 4 to make the chain as long as you like.

Things You'll Need
❏ Red and green construction paper
❏ Scissors
❏ Glue, tape or stapler

Make a Christmas Advent Calendar | 500

Making your own family advent calendar is a great opportunity to teach children about recycling and create a Christmas tradition that your children will remember.

◎Steps

1   Start with a 23 x 30 cm (9 x 12 in) sheet of construction paper. This will be the front of your "house". Draw a line down the centre, lengthwise, on the wrong side of the paper as a guide.

2   Measure down each side 10 cm (4 in) and draw a line from the point to the centre of the top. This will form the roof of the house. Draw in the chimney about midway down one side of the peak – the chimney is 3 cm (1.25 in) wide – and cut out from the same paper as the front of the house. The house will now be 23 cm (9 in) wide and 30 cm (12 in) tall at the centre of the peak.

3   On the right side of the paper, mark off the windows starting 7.5 cm (3 in) down from the top of the roof. All windows are 2 cm (0.75 in) square, except the three in the third row. These are 2.5 cm (1 in) tall and 2 cm (0.75 in) wide for variation. Leave 1.2 cm (0.5 in) between all windows and about 0.6 cm (0.25 in) between the rows. Centre your rows, leaving an equal amount of space on each side.

Things You'll Need
❏ 23 x 30 cm (9 x 12 in) coloured construction paper
❏ Red tissue paper or cellophane
❏ Used Christmas cards
❏ Pencil
❏ Ruler
❏ Scissors
❏ Craft knife
❏ Glue sticks
❏ Black marker (optional)

How to Do More of *(Just About)* Everything

4   The front door is centred on the front of the house and is 3.8 cm (1.5 in) high and wide.

5   Using a craft knife and a ruler edge, cut across the top and bottom of all windows and the door, then down through the centre of each window. Carefully bend back the "shutters". DO NOT cut down each side of the windows or you will lose the "shutter" effect.

6   Paste strips of foil from old Christmas cards to decorate the front of the house. You can also use coloured construction paper for trim. Don't forget to decorate the front door, chimney and roof. Use a glue stick, as it will not damage the construction paper and will dry clear.

7   On the back of the calendar, paste a lining of single thickness red tissue paper or cellophane. Use the glue stick to fasten the paper securely.

8   In each little window paste a tiny picture cut from old Christmas cards. Paste the cut-out on the red tissue paper or cellophane. Paste a Christmas tree behind the door. Close all the shutters and the door.

9   Starting on 1 December, one window should be opened each day until the 24th when the door is opened and there is the Christmas tree!

10 Once all the windows and door are opened, stand the calendar in front of a lamp. The light will shine through the red paper backing and your little house will glow!

501 | Make Bubble Bath

Bubble bath makes a great Christmas gift – but you don't need to splash out at the shops. Make it yourself!

◎ Steps

1   Warm 1 litre (4 oz) of distilled water. It doesn't need to boil but it does need to be warm enough to melt the castile soap that will be added and create a liquid soap.

2   Grate the bar of castile soap, using a cheese grater. If you are making a lot of soaps, candles or bubble bath, it is a good idea to have a separate grater reserved for these ingredients alone.

3   Combine water with the grated castile soap and stir until a liquid soap forms.

4   Add 1 litre (4 oz) of liquid glycerin to the liquid soap you have just created then stir all the ingredients together.

5   Select a fragrance and add it to the mixture. If stress relief, relaxation and unwinding are the goals, choose a soothing fragrance such as lavender or camomile, for example.

⚠ Warning

With essential oils, you only need a little bit to go a long way. A few drops of essential oil (no more than four) is all you need to make a batch of bubble bath.

Things You'll Need

❏ Distilled water

❏ Castile soap

❏ Liquid glycerin

❏ Essential oils

Use Mistletoe to Your Advantage **502**

A kiss under the mistletoe is one of the romantic images of the Christmas season. Be creative and use it to your advantage in unexpected places.

⊚ Steps

1 Make certain you and your partner will be uninterrupted for the evening.

2 Select music that puts you in a romantic mood.

3 Put artificial mistletoe over every doorway in your home.

4 Place a trail of mistletoe leading to a romantic setting.

5 Have your beverage of choice chilled.

6 Use your imagination!

✳ Tip

At a party, you can always lure someone under the mistletoe and steal a kiss.

⚠ Warning

Avoid standing under mistletoe with someone you would prefer not to kiss.

Plan a Christmas Dinner **503**

Planning a Christmas dinner isn't complicated, but the more forethought you give it the easier it will be.

⊚ Steps

1 Decide how many guests you'll have at least two weeks beforehand, and assess how much space you have, both at the table and in your home.

2 Compose your menu at least two weeks ahead of time as well. Organise the menu into to-do lists, including all preparation steps.

3 Clean out as much of the fridge as possible one week ahead. Be ruthless in your decisions about what to throw out. The more free space in the fridge, the better.

4 Make the big trip to the supermarket a week ahead. Most items, with the exception of salad greens and some fruit, will keep for a week.

5 Set the table and ready your home two days ahead, if seating people at a table for dinner. This will give you enough time to buy or borrow things you may need.

6 Consider serving the meal as a buffet if you want more guests than your table will seat. Set the table against a wall near the kitchen and use it as the serving area. For buffet service, make sure you divide all the food into small portions.

7 Peel and cut all vegetables two days before. Carrots and potatoes can be stored in iced water in the fridge; onions, celery and other vegetables must be kept dry and wrapped well.

8 Make as many dishes the day before as you can. Prepare and chill desserts, make seasoning mixes and make accompanying sauces.

9 Trim and ready your turkey for the oven. Place it in the roasting pan and chill until needed. Don't season it ahead of time, though.

10 Plan your guests' arrival to give you enough time to cook.

✳ Tips

Don't worry about having too little; most people's eyes are larger than their stomachs.

Don't worry about having too much, either – leftovers are good.

⚠ Warning

You cannot be too organised, but you can let it affect how much fun you have. Remember to enjoy yourself.

504 | Celebrate Chinese New Year

In Chinese families, the New Year celebrations can last for two weeks or more. Here's how to share in the fun.

⊙ Steps

1 Sweep the dust and dirt of the old year from your floors to make way for the new year.

2 Decorate your house in the traditional Chinese colours of wealth and good fortune: brilliant shades of red and gold.

3 Fill the rooms with flowers and blooming plants. They symbolise rebirth and new growth, and they ensure prosperity in the coming year.

4 Use peach or flowering quince branches, or bowls of fragrant paper-white narcissus, which bring good fortune.

5 Order a traditional New Year's Day dinner from a Chinese restaurant – either to eat on the spot or to bring home and serve at your own party.

6 Cook your own luck-drawing dishes. Include foods such as oysters, which represent good fortune and success, fish, representing surplus, and lettuce, representing wealth, riches and prosperity.

7 Ring in the new year with noisemakers to drive away evil spirits.

✳ Tip

Remember, the object is to have fun and bring light to the dark days of winter. Don't drive yourself crazy trying to be "authentic" or "accurate" in your celebrations.

505 | Keep Your New Year's Resolutions

If you're the type who likes to ring in the New Year with an engraved list of resolutions, read on for hints about how best to keep them.

⊙ Steps

1 Aim low. Most New Year's resolutions are easier said than done, and if you set the bar too high, you're doomed from the start.

2 Don't overload yourself. It's difficult enough for the average person to follow through on one ambitious New Year's resolution let alone three or four. Choose the most pressing issue at hand and concentrate on that.

3 Tell everyone you know. The more people to whom you announce your resolution, the more people there'll be to prod you along if you fall behind.

4 Reward yourself. Following through on a New Year's resolution is rarely easy, so a little Pavlovian conditioning goes a long way.

5 Wait until spring. Sometimes the best way to accomplish a New Year's resolution is to make it at a time of year of your choosing, rather than the one dictated by the calendar.

✳ Tips

Don't worry about the setbacks; persistence is the key.

Register with an email reminder service to keep you committed.

Stay Awake on New Year's Eve 506

Whether you set a goal to sing "Auld Lang Syne" or you're just trying to kick the old-geezer label, follow these steps to remain awake on New Year's Eve.

Steps

1 Spend New Year's Eve with family or friends. It's much easier to stay awake while interacting with others. The kids probably stay up later than you do anyway, so why not make a party out it?

2 Decorate for your New Year's Eve party, no matter what the size.

3 Eat party food. Since the New Year's resolution to diet begins the next day, eat to your heart's content the night before.

4 Stock up on games to play. Cards and board games work well at parties, but also plan games like charades that get you up and moving. Anything that stimulates your brain can keep you up.

5 Play your favourite music, as long as it's loud and dance-worthy.

6 Drink coffee when all else fails, but beware – just as everyone drifts off after the festivities, you'll find yourself too wired to sleep.

7 Count down loud and clear. Afterwards, pat yourself on the back for a job well done.

✻ Tip

Getting a good night's sleep the night before New Year's Eve can help you start the day fresh and keep you going into the evening.

Organise an Easter-Egg Hunt 507

Turn an ordinary Easter-egg hunt into a festive spring affair. With the right decorations and food, you can make it a hunt they'll never forget!

Steps

1 Send out colourful construction-paper cut-outs in the shape of ducks and rabbits as invitations to the hunt.

2 Fill plastic eggs with small toys, jellybeans, coins, stickers, beads, stamps, keyrings and sweets. Estimate about a dozen eggs per guest.

3 Decorate nearby tables with pastel-coloured tablecloths and streamers.

4 Stock the tables with punch and snacks for hungry hunters.

5 Set up the playing area according to age groups, either dividing the area by age group and marking the boundaries clearly, or by colour coding eggs (for example, blue and green ones for the older kids, yellow and pink for younger kids).

6 Hide eggs based on the age groups. Go easy on the younger ones, leaving eggs on low branches and open places; challenge older kids by concealing eggs in pipes, bushes and even gutters.

7 Station supervising adults in designated areas of the hunting site at the beginning of the game.

8 Start the game off with a whistle, and let the hunt begin!

✻ Tips

Be ready for anything. Prepare extra baskets for kids who forget to bring their own, as well as a first-aid kit for any unforeseen accidents.

To get the kids involved without the fear of competition, hide empty plastic eggs and have them trade them in for a bag of goodies at the end of the hunt.

⚠ Warning

Younger children can choke on such treats as jellybeans and small toys.

How to Do More of *(Just About)* Everything

508 | Sponge Paint Easter Eggs

This method of decorating Easter eggs is an easy one that the whole family can enjoy.

⊙ **Steps**

1 Assemble watercolour paints, hard-boiled eggs and sponges.

2 Cut the sponges into small triangles.

3 Hold an egg in one hand with your thumb on one end and index finger on the other.

4 Dip the tip of the sponge triangle into the paint and dab it on to the egg. Make sure you get a sponge texture by pressing lightly. You do not want to rub the sponge against the egg, as this will eliminate the textured look. Leave spaces between your sponge prints.

5 Allow the egg to dry after painting with one colour, then add another colour. Hold the egg in a slightly different spot so that the whole egg can be painted.

6 Sponge-paint light colours over light and dark colours for an interesting look. If you place a dark colour on top of a light colour, you will obliterate the light colour.

7 Let the eggs dry completely.

8 Store them in the fridge.

✳ **Tip**

Place eggs into cups used for soft-boiled eggs to make it easier for a child who cannot hold an egg and paint it at the same time.

Things You'll Need

❑ Sponges

❑ Hard-boiled eggs

❑ Egg cups

❑ Scissors

❑ Watercolour paints

509 | Disguise Yourself

There are many reasons to disguise yourself – attending a costume party, not wanting to be recognised by certain people, or just having fun at Halloween.

⊙ **Steps**

1 Apply makeup. If you normally wear makeup, try colours different from those you are used to. If you tend to wear a lot, try wearing less and vice versa.

2 Create a different hairstyle. You can add a wig for length or a completely new hairstyle. Cutting your hair is another way to go. If you decide not to wear a wig, change the colour and/or texture of your natural hair.

3 Add accessories. Wear a hat; this will repel attention from your face. Wearing glasses is a good way to veil your eyes.

4 Dress in clothes and accessories that are traditionally designed for the opposite sex.

5 Alter the appearance of your size. If you are thin, wear a fat suit. If the opposite is true, consider wearing clothes that appear to slim your figure.

6 Change the way you talk. If you have an accent that is indigenous to a particular geographical region, try to speak without it. If you do not have a distinct accent, add one.

✳ **Tips**

Be sure to adjust your talk, walk and mannerisms to reflect the change of dressing as the opposite sex.

Avoid conversations with people. By doing so, you will avoid giving them a chance to stare at you and realise you are in disguise.

Create a Ghost Costume   510

Here's a quick, easy-to-make Halloween ghost costume.
Remember to get creative with enhancements!

⊙ Steps

1   Get your hands on a white sheet that you don't mind cutting. Check
    charity shops for an old sheet, but remember to wash it before you
    use it.

2   Put the sheet over the person who plans to wear it, with the person's
    head in the middle of the sheet.

3   Draw two circles around each of the person's eyes with a crayon or other
    blunt marker.

4   Mark how much material has to be removed to keep the sheet off the
    ground when the person will be moving around, to avoid accidents, and
    then remove the sheet.

5   Cut the eyeholes in the sheet using cloth scissors, and cut the bottom off
    if needed.

6   Cut the sheet in a ragged fashion at the bottom for a more ghostly effect.

7   Brush glue on the hem and around the eyeholes to prevent fraying.

⚠ Warnings

Make sure there is complete
visibility from inside the costume,
especially if the ghost plans to go
trick-or-treating.

Do not use a pencil or pen to
trace around the eyes. One quick
move could mean an eye injury.

Things You'll Need

❏ Hobby paintbrushes

❏ Craft paints

❏ Glue

❏ White sheet

❏ Scissors

❏ Marker pen

Trick-or-Treat Safely   511

Trick-or-treating can be loads of fun for kids, but it can also
make them easy targets. Here are a few things for kids to
remember on All Saints' Eve.

⊙ Steps

1   Go in a group accompanied by at least one adult, and carry a torch.

2   Obey all traffic laws, cross streets only at pedestrian crossings and walk
    on the pavement at all times.

3   Visit only well-lit homes with porch lights and/or other exterior lights on.

4   Wear costumes that are flame-resistant, and make sure costumes do not
    drag or otherwise pose the threat of tripping you.

5   Put reflective tape on costumes to make them visible to drivers at night.

6   Make sure you can see where you are going if you are wearing a mask.

7   Stand away from lanterns that contain candles, and never go into a home
    unless you know the occupants well and the adult accompanying you
    goes in too.

8   Make sure everyone stays in the group and that stragglers don't get
    left behind.

✳ Tip

Consider going trick-or-treating
before dark.

⚠ Warning

Do not eat sweets while trick-or-
treating. Bring everything home,
inspect all the items and throw
away any previously opened or
otherwise suspicious treats.

512 | Celebrate Mexico's Day of the Dead

Having originated with the Aztecs or the Mayans, and later combined with the Catholic All Saint's and All Soul's Day holidays, the people of Mexico now celebrate the holiday on 1 and 2 November.

⊙ **Steps**

1 Place a candle or offering on an altar. If you're feeling up to it, you can build your own to honour a departed relative.

2 Leave sugar skulls on the altars. While they are edible, the amount of handling that goes into making each one doesn't make them the cleanest of treats. Instead of eating one, try your hand at making or decorating your own.

3 Shop at the local artisan's booths during Mexico's Day of the Dead festivals. You'll find a wide range of folk art depicting skeletons doing just about anything you can imagine. The skeletal bride is a popular motif in Mexico's Day of the Dead art.

4 Remain respectful even at the most tourist-friendly celebrations. Many towns in Mexico welcome with open arms thousands of strangers into their personal celebrations. As a visitor, you should observe cemetery proceedings from afar.

⚠ **Warning**

Make your plans well in advance if you plan on spending the Day of the Dead in Mexico. Hotels and tour groups fill up well in advance for this popular holiday.

513 | Celebrate Burns Night

Burns Night celebrates Scotland's favourite son, poet and balladeer Robert Burns, who is traditionally toasted on 25 January.

⊙ **Steps**

1 Start by "piping in" the guests. In a traditional Burns Supper this would be done by a live bagpiper, but recordings of traditional music will do. The music should play until the guests (or at least those at the head table) are ready to be seated.

2 Welcome the guests with the Chairman's Welcome. This is a warm welcome to the guests traditionally read by the host, or Chairman.

3 Recite the Selkirk Grace.

4 Ask guests to stand while the haggis is carried to the table by the chef, piper and person who will soon recite "To a Haggis".

5 Have the whisky-bearer refill all the glasses at the table.

6 Have the reader recite the Burns poem "To a Haggis" with great emotion, cutting the haggis open at the appropriate line in the poem. They should then triumphantly lift the haggis in the air, while guests toast it.

7 After-dinner entertainment should include readings from Burns' poetry or a speech on his life.

8 Thank everyone for attending and invite them to close the evening with a rendition of "Auld Lang Syne."

✻ **Tips**

There's more to a Burns Supper than the haggis. Other items on the menu might include cock-a-leekie soup, neeps and tatties, roast beef, steak pie, clootie dumpling, tipsy laird and of course liberal amounts of wine, ale and whisky!

Study up on your pronunciation before attempting to recite a poem by Burns. Listen to professional readers reading his poetry and songs.

⚠ **Warning**

Be sure to pierce the haggis before it is brought to the table to prevent it from spraying diners when it is cut open.

Celebrate Twelfth Night 514

Throughout the world, Twelfth Night (5 January) is a time for light-hearted fun, rowdy games and dressing up in outrageous costumes.

⊚ Steps

1 Throw a Twelfth Night fancy-dress party. Decree that your guests dress either as ancient Roman celebrators, as characters from Shakespeare's *Twelfth Night* or in any costumes that suit their (or your) fancy.

2 Serve lamb's wool, the traditional Twelfth Night drink in England and Ireland, made of cider or ale, sugar, spices and roasted apples.

3 Pour a little lamb's wool or cider on your apple trees if you have any; it's customary to bless them that way on Twelfth Night.

4 Serve a Twelfth Night cake, sometimes called a king's cake. The recipe and the accompanying game vary slightly from country to country, but everywhere the crucial ingredient is the same: a bean or a trinket baked inside the cake.

5 Find the piece with the token inside, and become king or queen of the party. Choose a consort, and together you'll reign over the festivities as absolute monarchs who direct your "subjects" to perform ludicrous tasks or behave in ways comically contrary to their usual natures.

✳ Tips

You can also put both a bean and a pea in your cake, and the people who find them become dual monarchs.

In Portugal, whoever finds the bean is not only crowned king or queen but also must make the cake the following year.

⚠ Warning

If you have any fears that a bean could get stuck in the throat of one of your guests, use a large coin or trinket instead. (In France the cake usually contains a small china doll.)

Celebrate Carnival in Rio de Janeiro 515

If you love to samba and want to party, don't miss the most unique Carnival celebration on Earth.

⊚ Steps

1 Plan ahead. Brazil requires a tourist visa even for short visits, so check out the nearest Brazilian embassy for instructions. Also, Carnival officially begins 40 days before Easter, so the dates vary from year to year. Check your calendar and be sure to book a flight and hotel far in advance, as this is peak tourist season in Rio.

2 Get your tickets early. The Samba School Parade held at the Sambadromo on Sunday and Monday of Carnival weekend is the highlight event of the Carnival season. Samba schools (or teams) compete in this all-night spectacle, which is a must-see.

3 Spend at least a week in Rio during Carnival season. There is so much to do and see, you won't want to miss a thing.

4 Watch a Samba school rehearse before the big parade. Rehearsals take place in the schools' respective neighbourhoods but are open to the public and easily accessible by taxi. Arrive any time after 11 p.m. and be prepared to dance!

5 Go to a street parade called a *banda* or *bloco*. It's free and a good way to burn some calories as you samba in the streets with all the locals.

✳ Tips

Samba schools are not schools at all; they are the organisations that compete in the parade and were formed by residents of the city's working-class neighbourhoods.

When in doubt, talk to the locals; they know best. They can give you tips on the best venues for Carnival balls, parties and bandas.

⚠ Warnings

Remember that Portuguese is the official language of Brazil and should not be confused with Spanish.

6   Buy an official *banda* T-shirt available only during the street parade. It makes an inexpensive and unique souvenir you can wear every day.

7   Visit one of the hundreds of Carnival Balls held on Friday, Saturday and Tuesday during the Carnival. Ticket prices are reasonable and sold at the door. Costumes are not required but many people do dress up, so be adventurous and creative!

Don't go it alone. All the festivities draw large crowds, and unfortunately, thieves take advantage of it. It's also advisable to leave any valuables at the hotel.

516 Celebrate Bastille Day

The French nation celebrates Bastille Day on July 14 to commemorate the 1789 storming of the Bastille.

☉ Steps

1   Prepare and enjoy a French meal reminiscent of the eighteenth century. Hallmarks of the French table relied on quality ingredients and included soups, pastries, game birds like pheasant and partridge, and fresh seasonal produce and pastries.

2   Study the history of the Bastille. Browse the library shelves for a good read, like Simon-Nicolas-Henri Linguet's account of his time in the prison. Explore a website like Chez Jim's Welcome to the Bastille that will introduce you to the landmark as if you were a prisoner.

3   Dance the night away as if you were at a café in Paris! Many Parisians celebrate Bastille Day with balls or with café and bistro dances. Let the wine and champagne flow.

4   Raise the French flag. The tricolor flag was introduced during the French Revolution. The blue panel is the colour of royalty and sports a gold *fleur-de-lis*. The red panel symbolises the kingdom and the white represents the French navy.

5   Sing France's national anthem "La Marseillaise", which was composed in 1792 and quickly became a revolutionary march. If you do not know the words or tune, watch the movie *Casablanca*, set during World War II when half of France was occupied by the Nazis.

✳ Tip

The best place to celebrate Bastille Day is, of course, Paris itself, but there's no reason why you can't decorate your own home with French flags and pretend you're there!

517 Celebrate St Patrick's Day

On 17 March you could take in your town's St Paddy's Day parade, and then wander down to the local pub for some green beer.

☉ Steps

1   Go to Ireland. Take in the St Patrick's Day Festival in Dublin if crowds don't bother you (the festival draws more than a million people each year). Otherwise, get out of town and explore the countryside.

2   Treat yourself to an evening at the theatre. Irish playwrights – from Synge, Shaw and Yeats to Brian Friel – have produced some of the world's best drama.

✳ Tip

Until 1996, when Dublin launched its annual festival, St Patrick's Day festivities in Ireland ranged from low-key to non-existent. Now the celebrations include a long weekend of parades, concerts, art exhibits and a "Monster Ceili" held on St Stephen's Green.

3 Delve into Ireland's pre-Christian past. Take a Celtic history course at a nearby university, or start your explorations at a good bookshop.

4 Sign up for Irish-dancing lessons. It's great exercise and a lot of fun.

5 Light a fire, pour yourself a glass of Irish whiskey and curl up with a good book. Much of the best literature ever written comes from Ireland. Whether your taste runs to ancient myths and sagas, rib-tickling humour, classic fiction or modern poetry, you'll have an evening well-spent.

6 Honour your Irish roots by planting a rose with a name reminiscent of the Auld Sod. Consider Irish Beauty, a fragrant salmon pink; Irish Mist, a profuse bloomer in orangish-salmon; or Dublin Bay, a clear red, large-flowered climber.

7 Have a party. Play Irish folk music, serve whiskey and stout, and dish up pub grub: cheese, soda bread, pickled onions and sausages.

⚠ **Warning**

Don't confuse Irish with Scottish Gaelic. They are separate, though closely related, languages.

Celebrate the Five Days of Diwali   518

Diwali, the Festival of Lights, is a five-day festival that celebrates the triumph of good over evil and hope for all mankind.

⊙ **Steps**

1 Find out the exact time of the five days of Diwali each year. Diwali is usually celebrated at the end of the Hindu month of Ashwauyuja, which is generally in October or November, exactly 20 days after Vijayadashami, another annual Indian festival.

2 Determine which version of Diwali you want to celebrate. Diwali is observed by Hindus, Sikhs and Jains in slightly different ways according to the specifics of their religious beliefs.

3 Celebrate the first day of Diwali, known as *Dhan teras*, by shopping for all the clothing, fireworks, lights and supplies for the festival.

4 Begin the second day, known as *Naraka Chaturdasi*, by waking before dawn and bathing. Then put on the new clothes you bought the day before and light lamps all over your home. Meet with friends and family, and light fireworks to ward off demons.

5 Note that the third day of the festival is the actual day of Diwali, the centre of the celebration, which occurs at the advent of a new moon.

6 Observe the religious aspects of Diwali during the fourth day of the festival, also known as *Annakut*, which celebrates Krishna defeating Indra. Mountains of food are prepared on this day.

7 Conclude the Diwali celebration on the fifth day, called *Bhayiduj*, by spending time with your brothers and sisters.

✳ **Tip**

Most of the Diwali celebration should occur just before dawn and just after sunset, when the lighting of the lamps is the most dramatic.

⚠ **Warning**

Before lighting any fireworks to celebrate the five days of Diwali, check to see if they are legal in your area. Note that in India, there are many campaigns to reduce or eliminate fireworks as part of Diwali, due to both safety and pollution concerns.

519 | Light the Menorah

The menorah is the centrepiece of the eight-day Festival of Lights known as Hanukkah. Here's the ritual used in lighting it.

◎ Steps

1 Place the menorah in a central spot in your home, where all who pass can see its glow.

2 Recite the following blessing at nightfall on the first day of Hanukkah before you light the candle on the far right: "Blessed are you, Lord our God, King of the universe, who has sanctified us with his commandments and commanded us to kindle the lights of Hanukkah."

3 Light the *shamash*, or service candle, and then use it to light the candle, or oil wick, on the far right of the menorah. As you do so, say the following: "Blessed are you, Lord our God, King of the universe, who performed miracles for our ancestors, at this season, in days past." Replace the *shamash* in its holder and let both candles glow until they burn themselves out.

4 Add the following *shehechiyanu* blessing only on the first night of Hanukkah: "Blessed are you, Lord our God, King of the universe, who gave us life and kept us and delivered us to this time."

5 Light two candles on the second night, keeping in mind that you always light from left to right using the *shamash*.

6 Continue with three candles on the third night in the same fashion, and continue doing this each night until, on the eighth night, all eight candles are burning brightly (nine, including the *shamash*). On each night, repeat the first two blessings quoted above.

✳ Tips

The menorah should be filled from right to left, but the candles lit from left to right.

The placement of the *shamash* can vary with different menorahs, but it will be set apart in some way. It may be in the centre of the menorah, or it may be raised above the others.

On Friday, light the candles before sunset to avoid lighting on the Sabbath.

⚠ Warning

As you do with all lighted candles, keep these ones away from inflammable objects and well beyond the reach of small children.

520 | Dress for Summer Solstice at Stonehenge

You have been invited to attend the most incredible sunrise wedding, the nuptials of Heaven and Earth. God, the Sun King, has asked the Goddess, Mother Earth, to take his hand in holy matrimony.

◎ Steps

1 Get a book about the Druids, and use it to figure out how they dressed.

2 Wear an accurate Druid costume. The typical outfit at Stonehenge consists of a long, white, flowing polycotton robe. It is covered with a white, ground-length tunic of a thicker material.

3 View a definite sprinkling of Summer Solstice attendees wearing tunics of black/brown/green, red/blue and silver/gold, representing ranks among the present-day Neo-pagan Druids.

4 Take a white hood, which attaches loosely to your robe. Wear sweatshirts and warm trousers under your white robe. This will help you stay warm when the sun goes down and it gets cold.

✳ Tips

Attend this event without cash-flow worries. Both parking and the festival are free of charge.

Observe the rules. Camping, dogs, fires, fireworks, glass bottles, large bags and rucksacks are not allowed. Also, revellers are not allowed to climb on the stones.

⚠ Warning

Don't plan on sleeping Friday night. Attendees stay up all through the night, chatting and celebrating.

5   Don a sprig of mistletoe and your Druid *sigil*. A Druid *sigil* is a circle, usually a wreath, with two lines running straight through it, in a parallel fashion. Wear your *sigil* in the form of a silver brooch and attach it to your robe, carrying mistletoe in your hands.

6   Dress in an elaborate costume. Revellers often dress in outrageous costumes decorated with crowns, helmets, breastplates, rings and a range of tools.

7   Dress as a pirate. This is a popular costume among men who celebrate Summer Solstice at Stonehenge.

8   Wear your normal clothes. You won't be turned away, as there is no official dress code for this event.

9   Put on comfortable shoes. You may be on your feet for much of the Stonehenge celebration.

Celebrate May Day 521

May Day, celebrated on 1 May, heralds the return of sunlight and fertility after the cold grey of winter. Ancient Europeans knew it as Beltane and honoured the occasion with rowdy celebrations. You can stage festivities tame enough for a two-year-old and have just as much fun.

◉ Steps

1   Throw an outdoor party for the whole neighbourhood.

2   Dance around the maypole, a classic Beltane symbol. To make a maypole, stick a pole in the ground – the taller the pole, the better. Fasten long, colourful ribbons to the top and let them stream down to the ground.

3   Have everyone grab the end of a streamer and skip merrily around the pole. (It helps to have some rousing dance music playing in the background.) As you dance in one direction you'll weave the ribbons into a colourful plait; turn and go in the opposite direction and the streamers will float freely again.

4   Have the kids make May baskets, a custom that survived in many parts of the country as recently as the 1940s and 1950s. Fashion baskets from colourful paper, or buy attractive wicker ones, and fill them with flowers, sweets and other small treats.

5   Sneak quietly up to the door of someone's house, hang the basket on the doorknob or leave it on the threshold, then ring the doorbell and run like mad.

6   Take a few May baskets to a nursing home, or give them to older friends and relatives who probably made them as children.

✳ Tip

Small children, toddlers and adults who turn giddy with the first breath of spring cannot fathom why these delightful customs have been left to languish in the closet of obscure folklore.

⚠ Warning

Teenagers may find maypoles and May baskets silly, embarrassing and totally uncool.

522 Celebrate St George's Day

St George is the patron saint of England, and St George's Day is England's national day. Increasing numbers of people are celebrating on 23 April, so here are some tips for getting involved.

◎ Steps

1 Read *St George and the Dragon* by Richard Johnson (1596), which tells of the great courage St George displayed when he rescued a princess from a terrifying dragon.

2 Wear a single red rose in your jacket lapel or give a rose to a loved one. As the national flower of England, the rose is a symbol of patriotic pride.

3 Do one of the 3 Cs. St George is associated with Courage, Charity and Chivalry. For Courage you could use the day to overcome a phobia (and defeat your own personal dragon). For Charity you could organise a sponsored pub crawl. And for Chivalry give your loved-one a red rose.

4 Fly the St George Cross flag. Many churches and official buildings fly the flag on St George's Day.

5 Visit one of the historical sites associated with St George, such as Coventry, Salisbury Cathedral and Westminster Abbey.

6 Visit http://www.stgeorgesholiday.com and sign the petition to make St George's Day an official bank holiday in England.

7 Send a St George ecard to friends and family wishing them a Happy St George's Day.

✳ Tip

St George's Day isn't as widely celebrated as many other saints' days. Make the effort to revive this celebration and revel in your Englishness!

523 Observe Ramadan

Each year, Muslims throughout the world observe the holy month of Ramadan, which falls during the ninth lunar cycle of the Islamic calendar.

◎ Steps

1 Recognise that Ramadan commemorates the month in which the Qur'an, the word of God (or Allah), was first revealed to the Prophet Muhammad. The Qur'an, which literally translates to "the recitation" in Arabic, is believed to be divine communication directly from God that was delivered to Muhammad over a period of 23 years.

2 Discover that Ramadan embraces the fourth of the five pillars or religious duties of the Muslim faith. As such, it is characterised by a period of fasting as a means toward self-purification of mind, body and spirit.

✳ Tip

Those who are travelling, ill, elderly and women who are pregnant or nursing during Ramadan are allowed to break the fast and observe an equal number of days of devotion at another time.

How to Do More of *(Just About)* Everything

3 Understand that fasting during Ramadan means more than abstaining from food and drink. During Ramadan, one must also avoid sexual activity, arguing, gossip, expressions of anger and envy. The purpose of these restrictions is to encourage self-discipline and devotion to prayer, elevating attunement with the divine.

4 Expect the practice of fasting from food and drink (even water) during Ramadan to be observed every day of the month from dawn until sundown. The fast may be broken when it is time to perform *Maghrib*, the fourth daily prayer at dusk.

5 Know that Muslims strive to read the Qur'an in its entirety during the month of Ramadan. Sunni Muslims hold to nightly recitations of *Tarawih* (extra prayers) with sections of the Qur'an being read each night for 30 days. Shiite Muslims practise a nightly prayer, known as *Salat al-Layl*, and encourage independent study of the Qur'an.

6 Be aware that the rising of the next new moon ushers in Eid ul-Fitr, the Festival of Breaking the Fast, and signals the end of Ramadan.

Write a Romantic Valentine 524

Love is in the air (and everywhere else) when you follow these tips for creating a romantic and personalised Valentine's Day greeting.

◎ Steps

1 Meditate upon the subject of your Valentine. Make a list of your sweetheart's unique attributes, and focus on them in your note.

2 Choose a writing style. Traditional poetry, haiku, free verse or letter format all constitute romantic methods by which to express yourself.

3 Choose words that are positive, complimentary, romantic and deeply personal. Now is not the time to be shy.

4 Suggest a romantic interlude, or reminisce about a past encounter with your Valentine. You can be discreet and seductive by weaving meaning into your words and asking your Valentine to read between the lines.

5 Compare your Valentine to a phenomenon that you find almost as stunning as him or her: a sunset, a rose, a waterfall.

6 Write with scented and coloured pens to add a mystical and luxurious element to the Valentine.

✳ Tip

The method of delivery can be as romantic as the card itself. Place your love note under a pillow or tucked between items on a breakfast-in-bed tray.

Things You'll Need

❏ Valentine's Day greeting cards

❏ Calligraphy pens

❏ Coloured ink pens

❏ Stationery

❏ Flower bouquet

❏ Acid-free tissue paper

❏ Perfume

525 Find a Valentine

The quest to find a Valentine can be lots of fun – just consider your personal safety, and remember that you can have lots of fun on Valentine's Day, even if you don't find a romantic partner!

⚠ Warning

If you're planning on ordering a gift online to persuade someone to be your Valentine, make sure you order well in advance.

⊙ Steps

1 Do something fun with a group of your single friends – you will almost certainly find other groups of singles wherever you end up.

2 Go to the supermarket and hang around the frozen foods aisle. You might find another lonely heart looking for comfort next to the frozen fish fingers.

3 Buy one perfect rose, and give it to the first interesting/attractive person who smiles at you.

4 Take yourself to a non-date type of film – alone. You never know who you may end up sitting next to.

5 Sign up for a class or seminar – you may or may not meet someone interesting, but at the very least you will learn something!

6 Call someone you know only as a casual acquaintance, and ask them to go out for coffee or lunch – perhaps a friendship, or even a future romance, might come from a friendly overture.

7 Go for a long walk with your dog, if you have one. Borrow one, if you like. Pets – the cuter the better – are great conversation starters.

8 Sit in a café reading an interesting or controversial book – the attractive person at the next table just might ask you a few questions about it.

9 Open your mind to new experiences. Take yourself hand-gliding, ballroom dancing, or whatever else you have always dreamed of doing. The right person may come along when you aren't even looking.

10 Be safe and trust your instincts, especially if something doesn't feel quite right about a person you meet. Take phone numbers rather than giving out your own, if possible, and make sure that first encounters take place – and remain – in a safe public area.

Enjoy Spring Cleaning

Giving your home a thorough clean after the sludge and doldrums of winter not only ensures a healthy environment for your family, but also ensures that the house is well-maintained.

⊙ Steps

1 Make spring cleaning part of your fitness routine. If you go to the gym, run, jog or exercise on a regular basis, consider substituting one of your fitness sessions for a spring-cleaning day.

2 Do it with friends. Cleaning is always fun when done with people you care about. Call friends and family and make spring-cleaning day a fun get-together. Don't forget to thank them for their efforts at the end of the day – perhaps by treating them to a takeaway!

3 Share the experience online. Almost everyone participates in online social networking. Make spring cleaning fun by sharing photos of "before and after" and videos of your housekeeping experience.

4 Donate to charity. Spring cleaning usually involves putting away your winter wardrobe. Why not help the underprivileged while clearing out space in your wardrobe?

5 Reward yourself. Before even starting your spring cleaning, think about what you will give yourself when you're done.

✳ Tip

Tasks like housekeeping and spring cleaning are more enjoyable when you work with your favourite music in the background. Choose upbeat and dance music to help keep your energy high.

⚠ Warnings

Never try to do too many things at the same time. Clean one section at a time so that you don't become overwhelmed and discouraged.

Stay hydrated. Nothing kills fun quicker than fatigue. Drink often and take breaks for meals and rest.

Clean Curtains

Curtains should be cleaned often as they tend to accumulate dust and dirt. And with a variety of cleaning options available, there's no excuse for neglecting them.

⊙ Steps

1 Take down your curtains and inspect the back side of the fabric for signs of sun-rotting by stretching and feeling. If the curtains are sun-rotted, don't bother cleaning them. Buy new curtains instead.

2 Wash unlined curtains according to the instructions provided on the label – usually these can be machine washed.

3 Have lined curtains professionally dry-cleaned to prevent ruining them.

4 Wash large curtains in the bath to prevent possible damage to your washing machine.

5 Boil rusty curtain rings in vinegar to rediscover their shine. Rub soap on old curtain rods to make them run smoothly again.

6 Toss your curtains into a tumble dryer for a quick job. Add fabric softener to an air-dry setting and you'll find you've got fresh-smelling curtains in half an hour.

✳ Tips

Odours can can collect in curtains, so clean them regularly.

Dust your curtains frequently using a vacuum attachment. This way, you'll keep them clean without having to periodically take them down and put them back up.

528 Clean an Oven

So your lasagna bubbled over and your soufflé exploded? Not to worry – cleaning your oven is not the all-day chore it used to be.

⊙ Steps

1 Remove the oven racks and place them in soapy water to soak.

2 Heat the oven to 200°C (400°F).

3 Turn the oven off and spray the inside with oven cleaner, then allow to sit for 10 minutes.

4 Wipe the cleaner and dirt away with a damp sponge, rinsing frequently.

⚠ Warning

Take care when working with a hot oven.

529 Remove Red Wine Stains from Fabric

From painstakingly washing the fabric by hand to simply throwing it into the washing machine, effective methods are available for getting rid of those dreadful red wine stains.

⊙ Steps

1 Blot the stain immediately with paper towels. If it is a dry-clean only garment do not pre-treat the stain and get it to the cleaners as quickly as possible. Pre-treatment of the stain can cause irreversible damage.

2 Mix one teaspoon of laundry soap or pre-treatment and one cup of hydrogen peroxide in a small bowl. Soak a clean sponge in the mixture, squeeze it halfway dry, then gently blot the stain.

3 Place a dry towel or flannel between the front and back of the garment if the stain has not penetrated through to the back of the fabric. This will prevent staining on the back of the material.

4 Review the washing instructions on the label of the fabric. Heed any special care instructions.

5 Wash in cool water and air dry if the fabric is machine-washable.

6 Wash gently in the sink with a mild detergent if the fabric is hand-wash only.

✳ Tip

Always use white paper towels, as coloured towels may stain.

⚠ Warning

Avoid scrubbing or rubbing the stain excessively. This can cause the stain to further penetrate the fabric.

530 Remove Mildew Stains from Tile

Nasty mildew doesn't have to ruin your bathing experience.

⊙ Steps

1 Remove as much mildew as possible by spraying the area with tile cleaner and scrubbing with a toothbrush or stiff-bristled brush.

2 Squirt persistent mildew with a solution of commercial bleach and water (one part bleach to 10 parts water is usually effective). Leave the room and allow the solution to work for five to 10 minutes.

3 Return and rinse with water.

✳ Tip

If, despite your efforts, mildew remains on your tiles, consider purchasing a commercial mildew remover containing sodium hypochlorite and sodium carbonate.

How to Do More of *(Just About)* Everything

Remove Odours 531

Foul odours can appear anywhere in your house or car. Here's how to eliminate the odour as well as any bacteria and dirt.

⊙ Steps

Organic Odours: Vomit, Urine and Others

1. Remove the source of the odour from the affected area either by clearing it away (in the case of solid matter) or blotting with paper towels.

2. Moisten a sponge with some bacteria/enzyme digester and blot the stain according to directions on its label.

3. Cover the stain with a plastic bag to help the digester retain moisture.

4. Allow the area to air-dry.

Cooking Odours and Smoke

1. Remove the source of the odour from the affected area.

2. Air out the affected area by opening windows or directing fans at it.

3. Apply an odour-neutralising spray to the area.

Things You'll Need

❏ Disinfectant spray
❏ Fan
❏ Sponge
❏ Bacteria/enzyme digester
❏ Odour-neutraliser
❏ Rubber gloves
❏ Plastic bags
❏ Paper towels

Clean Pet Vomit 532

Removing vomit from carpet or upholstery is tricky business, but with the right treatment you can minimise the stain and make your carpet or sofa as good as new.

⊙ Steps

1. Check the material of your carpet or sofa to see if it is safe to get it wet. Some materials are not water safe. If your material is not water safe, read the manufacturer's cleaning instructions. There are special cleaning solutions for wool rugs and carpets.

2. Act as soon as your pet throws up or you spot the vomit. Pick up the solid parts of the vomit using paper towels, a fabric towel or spatula. Do not press down on the vomit. Blot the damp spot with a sponge or paper towels once all the bulk has been removed.

3. Use a dishwashing liquid to prepare warm, soapy water. Take a new sponge and immerse it in the water. Rub the affected area until the stain has gone. Rinse the sponge a few times and repeat for effective cleaning. Use a hard-bristle brush if needed for a good scrubbing.

4. Do not scrub the vomit if it has already dried. Use a metal or plastic scraper to remove the sticky part and continue with the warm soapy water treatment in Step 3.

5. Use dry towels to absorb any remaining liquid. Let the area dry. Spread deodoriser on the spot and vacuum the area thoroughly.

6. Rent a steam cleaner if you need to a more thorough cleaning. Hire a professional service if your sofa or carpet is antique or valuable.

❋ Tips

An alternative treatment is to sprinkle baking soda or salt on the area and rub with warm, soapy water.

For stubborn stains, use a stain-removal product according to the manufacturer's directions.

533 Go Green with Candles

By replacing traditional candles with eco-friendly, natural ones you can protect your health at the same time as keeping the environment clean.

⊙ Steps

1 Try to discontinue the use of traditional candles that contain paraffin, which is a by-product of the petroleum-refining process. Paraffin-based candles cause pollution and may cause health problems.

2 Choose soy, beeswax, palm wax or vegetable wax candles. These are environmentally friendly, biodegradable, sustainable and renewable. They burn longer and offer a much greener alternative to traditional paraffin-based candles.

3 If you like aromatherapy candles, consider purchasing scented candles that use only 100 per cent pure, undiluted essential oils.

4 Look for candles that come without packaging or utilise recycled paper.

5 Always look for candles with wicks made of cotton, paper or hemp. Make sure wicks are chemical-free and lead-free.

✳ Tip

You could even try your hand at making your own eco-friendly candles.

534 Clean Wine Glasses

Though it may be time-consuming, wash stemware in the following manner to avoid damage.

⊙ Steps

1 Prepare by placing a rubber mat on the bottom of the sink and a rubber guard on the taps.

2 Wash the glasses one at a time using a very mild dishwashing detergent and water.

3 Rinse in warm water and dry each glass by hand immediately after rinsing using a soft, dry dish towel.

⚠ Warnings

Avoid exposing cut glass and crystal to high temperatures.

Do not wash stemware in a dishwasher.

Do not place stemware upside down to dry. Always dry by hand.

535 Shop on a Budget

Do you always seem to spend more than you want on food and other items in your weekly shop? Follow these steps to successfully shop on a budget.

⊙ Steps

1 Write down exactly what you need to get from the shop or supermarket. Make sure you include ingredients for recipes you have planned. Check for the basics such as milk, eggs, bread and flour.

✳ Tip

Shopping for just the food you want to eat that evening is a sure way to blow your budget.

2   Plan your meals for a month. Keep them nutritional with a lot of vegetables. Healthy meals end up being a lot less expensive than ready meals.

3   Make some of the basics from scratch, such as bread and muesli. The ingredients to make them are a lot less expensive than the finished product in the long run.

4   Eat before you go shopping. If you shop when you are hungry or craving something, you'll end up spending a lot more than your budget allows.

5   Map your way around the supermarket so that you only go down the aisles with the products that you need and you avoid trouble zones such as the chocolate aisle!

6   Leave the children at home if possible. Children have a way of sneaking items into your trolley or talking you into products that you do not need. If you must take them, then feed them first.

Childproof a Kitchen 536

Because parents spend so much time in the kitchen, small children will want to be there with them. To keep your little one safe, take the following steps.

⊙ Steps

1   Store matches, lighters, sharp utensils and household cleaners in a cabinet accessible only to adults.

2   Put child-safety latches on all lower-level cabinets.

3   Unplug appliances when not in use and make sure the cords are out of reach of children.

4   Never pour hot liquid near a child and never leave hot drinks within reach.

5   Use the back burners of the stove wherever possible and turn pot handles towards the back.

6   Purchase safety features that secure free-standing ovens to the wall.

7   Watch out for tablecloths – since small children enjoy pulling on the cloth, glasses and plates can fall off.

8   Keep stools and chairs away from counters and stoves.

9   Be sure to keep alcohol locked away from children.

10 Cook meat, eggs, poultry and shellfish thoroughly to prevent food poisoning. Always wash your hands with soap after handling meat or poultry.

11 Use a child-safety gate, if possible, in the doorway to keep children out of the kitchen completely when you are in another room.

❋ Tip

Since children enjoy "helping" in the kitchen, give them large plastic containers and wooden spoons to play with while you're cooking to keep them out of trouble.

⚠ Warning

Many kitchen accidents occur within seconds. It's best to keep small children out of the kitchen completely.

✓ 537 Save Money and the Environment

Going green saves the environment and money. It's actually quite simple to introduce environmentally friendly behaviour into your household – and the little things can make a big difference. Even just putting into action one of these points can help.

In the Home – Energy

- Use energy-efficient light bulbs.
- Turn off lights when leaving a room.
- Try to incorporate solar panels or solar lighting in your home.
- Consider a wind turbine in your garden to generate electricity.
- Install blinds in your home to prevent heat loss during the winter.
- Make sure windows are not drafty.
- Unplug all chargers when not in use.
- Don't leave your television or computer on standby – switch it off properly.

In the Home – Water

- Take showers instead of baths.
- Turn off the water while brushing your teeth instead of leaving it running.
- Don't waste drinking water – just use what you need.
- When washing clothes, make sure you have a full load, not partial, and rinse with cold water.
- Fix any leaking or dripping taps.
- Share bathwater with your partner or children to avoid refilling the bath.

In the Garden

- Plant a small garden of your own in your flower boxes instead of flowers or hedges.
- Have a compost heap and put all food waste on it.
- Grow your own herbs in beds or in window boxes.
- Have a vegetable patch to grow your own produce.
- Reuse water from the bath or washing up to water your garden.
- Have a rainwater tub.

At the Shops

- Buy organically grown foods, either in a supermarket or at a farmers' market.
- Buy seasonal fruits and vegetables so you don't encourage transportation of produce long distances.
- Don't buy more food than you need to avoid waste.
- Do not purchase aerosol products, use normal spray bottle products.
- Buy recycled paper.
- Buy rechargeable batteries.
- Walk or cycle to the shops.

Recycling

- Reuse plastic bags or buy cloth bags to do your shopping.
- Reuse the back of paper for notes or shopping lists.
- Refill your water bottle when you go to the gym.
- Look for recycled packaging on all food products.
- Take any unwanted clothes to the charity shop.
- Use a fake Christmas tree instead of a real one.

With the Kids

- Use cloth nappies instead of disposables.
- Don't use baby wipes, use reusable flannels instead.
- Give your kids reusable lunchboxes with reusable containers inside.
- Recycle old crayons by melting them down and letting them cool in moulds.
- Put the lids back on felt pens and markers after use.
- Instead of buying new toys, swap with your friends.
- Pass on outgrown clothes to friends.

action

Prepare Your Home for a Power Outage

538

Don't get left in the dark if a power outage strikes your neighbourhood. Take steps now to prepare your home.

◎ Steps

1 Gather emergency supplies, such as candles, matches, torches and batteries, a battery-operated radio, a manual tin opener and tinned food.

2 Know the location of the fuse box or circuit breaker in your home.

3 Learn how to reset the circuit if necessary or change a blown fuse.

4 Find out ahead of time how to manually override an electric garage door.

5 Turn your fridge and freezer to the coldest settings if you think an outage could occur. This will help keep the food cold longer.

6 Use a surge protector to protect electrical items such as your computer, TV and DVD player. This can prevent a sudden surge of electricity from damaging them.

7 Have blankets or cardboard handy to cover windows in the event that the heating goes off. This will help prevent drafts.

8 Identify the most insulated room in advance; that's where you and your family can gather if you need to stay warm.

9 Turn your thermostat to low and turn off the circuit breaker for your water heater to reduce a high demand for electricity once the power does come back on. This will help prevent an overload that can cause it to go off again.

10 Leave one light switch on so you'll know when the electricity has been switched back on.

✳ Tips

If you do have a power outage and want to try to save your food, put perishables like milk, cheese, pork, poultry and meat in the freezer to help keep them fresh. They spoil quickly at temperatures above 4°C (40°F).

Cover the freezer with a blanket to help keep the cold air in.

⚠ Warning

If you smell gas, do not use matches or flip switches, including torch switches.

Install a Smoke Detector

539

The carbon monoxide produced from smoke can cause people to go into a deeper sleep, so by waking you up, a smoke detector could save your life.

◎ Steps

1 Walk through your home and locate the areas where you want to mount smoke detectors. Detectors should be mounted only inside bedrooms, outside bedrooms and in hallways leading to bedrooms.

2 Grab your ladder and mount smoke detectors high – on a wall or on the ceiling, though the ceiling mount is preferable as they will go off sooner.

3 Smoke rises, so if you have an odd-shaped ceiling, opt for the highest point on the ceiling to place the detector.

4 Avoid mounting smoke detectors near windows or doors, where smoke can escape before reaching the detector.

5 Avoid mounting smoke detectors in kitchens, dining rooms or living rooms. Smoke and steam from cooking, fireplaces, candles and so on

✳ Tips

In hallways, take care that the detectors are not placed too near bathroom doors. Steam from showers and baths can set off alarms.

Test your smoke detector every month.

You may want to consider purchasing a combination smoke/carbon-monoxide detector. They are more money, but well worth it.

How to Do More of *(Just About)* Everything

can cause false alarms. Basements and garages should also be avoided. Water heaters, fumes from solvents, paint or gasoline and dust from forced air heaters can set off alarms.

6 Follow the directions on the package for mounting the smoke detector once you've chosen the area for the device. You'll probably need a drill and a screwdriver.

7 Make sure a qualified electrician mounts the device if you choose to go with a detector that will be hardwired to your home's electrical system.

⚠ Warnings

If a smoke detector goes off, you literally have seconds to respond. There is absolutely no time to gather possessions or pets.

Never go back into the house once you've escaped from a fire.

---

540 | Escape from a Burning Building

There are procedures to follow if you find yourself or someone else in a burning building. Be careful and aware of what is going on around you.

◉ Steps

1 Call 999. Find the closest phone and call your local emergency services. As you make your way through the fire, call out for other people who may be caught as well. Do not delay in contacting emergency services.

2 Stay close to the ground. Smoke is poisonous and can kill you. Stay as far from the smoke as possible, and if this isn't possible, put a damp cloth to your mouth and nose area. This will make it easier to breathe as you move your way through the burning building.

3 Touch doors with the back of your hand. When you come to a closed door only use the back side of your hand. Your palm is very sensitive and can burn easily. If a door feels warm, do not open it. Try to find an alternative route. Leave doors open after you have passed through. This will make it easier for firefighters to move through the building.

4 Move quickly through the burning building. Proceed to the nearest stairway. Move down to the ground floor and out of the building. Do not go up floors in a burning building. Never use lifts when you are trying to rescue a person in a burning building.

5 Use extreme caution. If you are unable to locate someone else promptly, leave the building and let the firefighters take over the search.

✳ Tip

Have an escape route in place in case of fire. Have a fire drill every few months so everyone in the building knows what to do in the event of a fire.

---

541 | Get Rid of Rats

Rats can be very destructive to your home and your health. They chew through walls and wires, spread disease and are generally a nuisance.

◉ Steps

1 Identify the problem areas around your home. Look for rat holes along the skirting boards, especially in dark corners and by sources of water. Rats can chew through very small openings, so don't discount a hole or crack thinking it's too small. Plug holes with steel wool – it will cut a rat's gums to chew through. Seal it with a squirt of spray foam.

✳ Tips

Glue traps are often not effective on full-grown rats, but will help with mice or younger rats.

If all else fails – get a cat!

2　Look for areas with rat droppings. Rats will congregate where food is present and available. Place unrefrigerated food in plastic containers to help discourage chewing through boxes. Pick up clutter around your home – the more open your floors are, the less rats will like to be there.

3　Decide if rat poison is a good choice for you. It is possible to safely use rat poison to get rid of rats when you have small children or pets, but you have to be careful in placement of poison. Rats are most comfortable moving along a wall or other tall object, so it's easy to place poison behind appliances to keep your children and pets safe. Make sure you use plenty of rat poison – if they only ingest a small amount it will make them ill, but then they will become poison shy and steer clear of it in the future.

4　Place a small dab of peanut butter on rat trap; this is far more effective than cheese at attracting rats. Wrap a small amount of dental floss or thread around the peanut butter. A lot of rats are quick enough to get the peanut butter and run before the trap snaps, but the dental floss gets caught in their teeth.

5　Use gloves when removing dead rats from your home. Make sure you disinfect the area where you find the dead rat, as they carry diseases.

⚠ **Warning**

Use great care in cleaning up rat faeces or urine – inhaling the dust that comes from either can cause serious illness and even death.

Make Sofa Covers　　542

You can change the look of your sofa without having to actually upholster it, by sewing a sofa slip cover instead.

◉ Steps

1　Choose a fabric based on your family's needs. If you have pets or children, you may choose a more durable fabric that's easy to spot-clean. If you don't have kids or pets, you could choose a more plush, elegant fabric to make your sofa cover.

2　To measure, drape the fabric over the sofa and let it hang down on all sides. Use the sewing pins to hold it in place as you measure and mark how much fabric you'll need. If you don't want to have to do a lot of tucking after the cover is finished, only measure enough fabric so that it will cover the front without a lot of excess fabric.

3　Remove the fabric from the sofa, leaving the pins where you placed them. This will help guide you when you cut and sew the pieces together. Now lay the fabric on a flat surface and cut off any excess from your measurements. Leave enough fabric for a 2.2-cm (0.8-in) seam allowance on all your pieces.

4　With the pieces right-side together, sew a seam across the inside back and arms where the back of the sofa meets the cushions. This is where you can create a more tailored look and won't have to do a lot of tucking. Sew seams down each back and front sides in the same way. Hem the sofa cover with a 1.5-cm (0.6-in) seam all around the bottom.

5　Put the sofa cover on the sofa and adjust and tuck it into the cushions until you're satisfied with the look. Take the spiral pins and pin the fabric to the sofa on the back outside and inside, as well as all around the bottom underneath the sofa. The pins will hold the sofa cover in place and will keep it from coming off when you sit on it. Add cushions.

❋ **Tip**

Sew matching cushions and curtain panels to add a whole new look to your room.

Things You'll Need

❏ Upholstery-grade fabric

❏ Thread

❏ Tape measure

❏ Sewing pins

❏ Spiral upholstery pins

❏ Sewing machine

How to Do More of *(Just About)* **Everything**

543 | Make Chair Cushions

Making your own chair cushions is a quick sewing project that can add a bit of colour and a personal touch to your living area.

⊙ **Steps**

1 If you want round or square cushions, measure the seat of the chair and decide what size you need. Use the ruler or compass to draw the correct size on a piece of paper. When you have the cushion shape, draw a second line 1.3 cm (0.5 in) outside the first. This will be the cutting line, allowing extra room at the edge for sewing.

2 Draw a rectangle about 7.5 x 30 cm (3 x 12 in) on paper. This will be the strap pattern.

3 Put the patterns on the fabric and cut out two pieces of the seat shape, plus four strap shapes for each cushion you want to make. Also cut one seat shape out of quilt batting for each cushion.

4 Sew the straps first. Fold each strap in half with the right side in, and sew along the long open edge and one end. Turn the straps right side out, using a pencil to push the fabric through if necessary.

5 Stack the pieces as follows: the batting, one right-side up fabric seat, the straps and finally the other fabric seat, upside down. For the straps make sure you do it in pairs, with the open ends at the edge of the cushion where they should attach and the rest of the strap folded up in the middle so it doesn't get sewn into other seams accidentally.

6 Pin this stack if you want and sew most of the way around the outside, leaving a gap of several centimetres.

7 Trim the edge of the batting layer as close as possible to the seam.

8 Turn the cushion right-side out. Fold the remaining raw edges in and carefully hand-sew the gap closed using an overhand stitch.

9 Attach the cushion to a chair using the ties.

Things You'll Need

❏ Fabric

❏ Quilt batting

❏ Needle and thread

❏ Sewing machine (optional)

❏ Scissors

❏ Pins

❏ Tracing paper

❏ Pencil

544 | Make a Quilt

To make a quilt, you can use scraps of material from other sewing projects or purchase fabric in bulk. A block-style quilt using just two colours is the most basic quilt pattern.

⊙ **Steps**

1 Search the Internet or fabric shops for a quilting pattern. While at the fabric shop, select the fabric you will use for the quilt. Pick fabrics that will not shrink or fade.

2 Batting is the filler of the quilt. The thicker and loftier the batting, the warmer the quilt. You will also need to buy backing material for the underside of your quilt. Depending on the pattern, it is possible to use a sheet for the backing. Make sure the backing material is 8–10 cm (3–4 in) bigger than your quilt size.

Things You'll Need

❏ Quilting pattern

❏ Needle and thread

❏ Fabric

❏ Batting material

3   Follow the instructions in the pattern to cut out the blocks for your quilt. Make sure you cut out the proper number of blocks in each colour or type of fabric.

4   Use a 0.6-cm (0.25-in) seam allowance. After you have the strips completed, sew them together to form the body of your quilt.

5   Place the backing material on the bottom. Follow with the top of the quilt (your sewn-together blocks) face-down on top of the backing material. Put the batting material on top.

6   Using a needle and thread (or a sewing machine), sew around three sides of the quilt completely. On the fourth side, leave a 0.6-m (2-ft) opening.

7   You will need to turn the quilt inside out, which will actually bring the top to the outside and put the batting in the middle where it belongs. After you have flipped it so that the layers are in proper order, baste the opening by hand to close the seam.

8   Using a matching or contrasting thread, start from the middle of the quilt and work your way out. You can quilt by hand or just use your sewing machine to sew from one end to the other of the quilt in straight or curved lines. Your quilt is now finished.

Hang Art   545

Hanging art is not a science, but sometimes it may feel that way. Here are a few tips for getting it right.

⊙ Steps

1   Most art should be hung 150–165 cm (60–65 in) from the floor to the centre of the art. Your line of sight should roughly be in the centre of the piece. Think about how the artwork will relate to everything else in the room, whether it is over a piece of furniture such as a table or a sofa, or on a blank wall.

2   If it is on a blank wall, such as in a hallway, you will probably want it a little higher, but if it's over a sofa or bed you will probably want it around 15–30 cm (6–12 in) above the back of the sofa or headboard. If you have someone who can help you, ask them to hold the artwork at the spot you think it will work and walk back to decide if you like it there.

3   If you are hanging a small piece, such as a small mirror, you will probably want to do groupings or find a smaller or more narrow wall so the piece doesn't get lost in the space or look too small. A grouping of four to six small paintings hung vertically or horizontally on a wall has a very modern appeal.

4   If you're hanging artwork by yourself, cut paper templates to size for each piece of art and attach the paper cut-outs to the wall with painter's tape. This will give you the option to stand back and see how the artwork's size relates to your room and your furniture. Move the template up and down to find the perfect spot prior to hanging the picture. Once you're ready to hang, make sure you put a small pencil mark where your nail will go. Place your nail or picture hanger and hammer away.

Things You'll Need

❏ Paper
❏ Pencil
❏ Tape measure
❏ Scissors
❏ Nails
❏ Hammer

546 | Make a Small Space Seem Bigger

Small spaces don't have to feel dark, dingy or cramped. There are simple ways to make small spaces feel brighter and roomier – from top to bottom!

☉ Steps

1 Create space and contrast by painting different areas to give each their own zone. Paint your hall and kitchen a fun colour. It will seem like you are creating more space within your space, instead of just one overall colour.

2 Repeat prints and motifs such as a contemporary border or metallic wallpaper in the kitchen and again in the hallway. This is a fun way to make a small space seem grander without being over the top.

3 Use light colours on floors. Whether you have hardwoods or carpet, try to keep it as light as possible. Hardwood floors can be stained white; use rugs that are white or light-coloured throughout your space. If you get good sunlight in your space, remember that sunlight tends to bounce off floors and will create a light and airy effect.

4 Incorporate artwork, stripes or curtains from floor to ceiling. The trick is to make the eye glance upwards, which makes any space seem larger. Wallpaper emphasises high ceilings, and hanging large pieces of art from the edge of the ceiling will bring the focus up.

5 Mix in one or two oversized pieces of furniture. This might seem counterintuitive, but having one or two large pieces of furniture can trick the eye by making the rest of the furniture seem smaller. Having one large, interesting conversation piece also takes the focus off the smallness of your space, because it's unexpected.

✴ Tip

It helps to use high-quality paint on your walls.

⚠ Warning

Keep in mind that dark colours cannot become light colours. It is very difficult to lighten them, so stay light – you can always add darker colours.

547 | Fix a Clogged Dishwasher

Dishwashers are one of the greatest modern inventions, but they aren't perfect. Sometimes the dishwasher drain can get clogged with food or debris and won't drain properly.

☉ Steps

1 Check the dishwasher drain to make sure it is not full of food and debris. If you see anything down there clogging up your dishwasher drain, take a paper towel and clear out the debris. If the dishwasher still won't drain, take a stretched-out metal coathanger and clear out some of the hard-to-reach draining holes.

2 If the dishwasher continues to stay clogged, pull out the bottom panel of the dishwasher and check the draining hose. There could be a fold, clog or kink in the hose that is keeping it from draining. Unravel the hose and try to get it as untangled as possible. If you see a clog in the hose, it may be time to replace it.

3 If you're still having draining problems, reach far inside the dishwasher with a screwdriver and unscrew the draining basket from the drain. You may have to clean underneath it to really get at the food and debris.

⚠ Warnings

Make sure you thoroughly rinse your dishes before placing them in the dishwasher to prevent a clog in the first place.

Be sure to unplug the dishwasher before using any tools.

Things You'll Need

❏ Wire coathanger

❏ Screwdriver

❏ Paper towels

Rinse the draining basket and remember to screw it back on.
It's important to keep the dishwasher from clogging in the future.

4   If you have tried all these steps and you're still having problems, it's time
to call a professional. Your local plumber will know exactly what you need
to replace to get your dishwasher working in no time.

Repair a Dripping Showerhead 548

A constantly dripping showerhead doesn't just waste water –
it can drive you crazy.

⊙ Steps

1   Unscrew the showerhead from the pipe coming out of the wall. This
can be done by hand but sometimes requires a crescent spanner or
large pliers. The head may be held on with a screw, which you'll have
to remove.

2   Look at the threads inside the showerhead where it screws into the pipe.
There should be a small washer made of plastic or a rubber O-ring.
Replace it if it looks even a little damaged or brittle.

3   Wrap the showerhead stem with Teflon tape or pipe sealer (pipe dope) to
seal the connection.

4   Remount the showerhead on the stem. Don't over-tighten. Hand-
tightening should suffice.

5   Turn the water on and off. Wait several minutes and check for drips or
leaks. If the showerhead is still leaking, you may have problems with the
shower's water-control valve and need to call an expert.

⚠ Warning

When working with chrome
or brass fixtures, protect the
surfaces from tools with a
piece of leather, heavy cloth
or duct tape.

Remove Wax from a Carpet 549

Although it may look like a permanent mess, spilled wax can be
removed from a carpet with the help of a warm iron.

⊙ Steps

1   Scrape away as much wax as you can.

2   Place a sheet of greaseproof paper, glossy side up, or a portion of a
brown paper bag on top of the wax.

3   Press the tip of a warm iron gently over the affected area until the wax
melts and attaches to the paper.

4   Lift the paper from the carpet.

5   Dab a small amount of denatured alcohol on to the stain if any candle dye
is left on the carpet.

6   Sponge with water.

✳ Tip

Try not to let the iron touch
the carpet, as it may leave
scorch marks.

550 | Change a Doorknob

Installing a new doorknob is easy using a few basic tools.
Most (but not all) door mechanisms are interchangeable.

⊙ Steps

1 Detach the trim (the ring of metal between both doorknobs and the door) by removing the two screws that hold it on. Sometimes the trim has to be gently prised off rather than unscrewed.

2 Remove two more screws under the trim. These are long screws that attach the two doorknobs on either side of the door. Pull the doorknobs apart and remove them from the door.

3 Remove the two screws that hold the bolt (the locking mechanism), which remains attached to the door, and extract the bolt.

4 Look at the metal strike plate attached to the frame around the door. If the strike plate is not loose and is the right colour, leave it there. Otherwise, detach it from the doorjamb by removing its screws.

5 Insert the new bolt into the door and screw it into place. Remember to face the slanted side towards the direction the door closes in.

6 Place a trim piece between one new doorknob and the door, and insert the doorknob. Insert the other doorknob and trim piece on the other side of the door, making sure they are aligned so that the long screws hold them together.

7 Tighten the screws gradually, alternating each one so that the doorknobs come together evenly.

✳ Tips

As you remove the various parts, put them back together in the same positions they were in, including screws. This will prove invaluable if when you're done the new doorknobs don't work well – or at all.

If you get in trouble, remember that there are plenty of other doorknobs around the house. Take them apart if you need to, just to remind yourself how they fit together.

If the new bolt mechanism or strike plate feels loose, replace the screws with longer ones.

⚠ Warning

Go slowly. Unless you've done this before, there are lots of little parts that can be confusing.

551 | Replace a Circuit Breaker

Circuit breakers are designed to interrupt the power to a circuit and protect your wiring. Here's how to fix a tripping breaker.

⊙ Steps

1 Purchase a new circuit breaker from a hardware store.

2 Take the panel cover off the panel box by unscrewing the face plate.

3 Notice the two wires feeding into the side of the breaker. Remember which one is in which position.

4 Loosen the screw holding the white wire first, just enough to get the wire out. Put a wire nut on the end of the white wire and bend it out of the way.

5 Loosen the other screw and do the same thing with the coloured wire.

6 Pull the old circuit breaker out and snap a new one into place.

7 Replace the wires in the same positions as they were on the old breaker – coloured one first, white one second.

8 Tighten the screws holding the wires and replace the face plate.

9 Turn on the power to the panel and then turn on the breaker.

⚠ Warning

Replace breakers with units of the same amperage. They are specifically designed for safety. If you use a higher amperage, you are overriding the safety feature.

Wallpaper Corners and Around Trim
552

Unless you're wallpapering a round room, you're bound to hit a corner eventually – and probably a window or door, too.

Steps

Corners

1 Use your trim knife to press the wallpaper into an inside corner and cut it with your razor, as though it were going against the ceiling or skirting board. Smooth down the whole strip, then peel back from the corner.

2 Draw a new plumb line on the adjacent wall with your spirit level, measuring out from the corner the width – minus 1 cm (0.5 in) – of a piece of wallpaper.

3 Line up the next piece of wallpaper to this plumb line and apply towards the corner matching the pattern, letting the extra paper flop over.

4 Using your trim knife again, cut the second strip of paper just a little bit wider than the corner and smooth the paper tight into the corner.

5 Lap the first piece over the second piece; this will ensure that if the paper shrinks, no gap will appear between the two strips.

6 Press down the paper and clean off any adhesive that has squeezed out.

Door and Window Frames

1 When you reach a piece of trim, smooth down the paper against the trim. Use a pair of scissors to cut off most of what flops over the trim, leaving only about 5 cm (2 in) to work with.

2 Where the trim makes a corner turn, make a diagonal cut in the paper, starting from where the paper touches the corner, and going out to the edge of the remaining few centimetres. This allows the paper to lie flatter.

3 Smooth down the paper again and cut the paper against the trim as you would against the ceiling or skirting board.

✳ Tip

Sometimes the next full-length strip after a window or a door does not quite match up with the smaller strips above or below a window, or above a door. You may have to "cheat" a little by lapping the strips over each other a bit. If that doesn't work, simply try to match the pattern at the most obvious place – eye level.

Things You'll Need

❑ Wallpaper

❑ Wallpaper paste

❑ Razor knife

❑ Trimming knife

❑ Scissors

❑ Spirit level

❑ Putty knife

Match Old Paint
553

You love the paint on your living room wall and you'd like to touch it up – but what colour is it and what kind of paint?

Steps

1 Cut out a 10 x 10-cm (4 x 4-in) piece of painted drywall from a corner of the room. Take this sample to the paint shop to be matched.

2 Determine what kind of paint you have by rubbing a small section of the surface with a clean rag saturated with denatured alcohol. If paint rubs off as a gooey substance, it's water-based. If it remains unchanged, it's oil-based.

3 Verify the paint type by dabbing a small amount of water-based paint on the surface. If it beads or separates, it's oil-based. If not, it's water-based.

⚠ Warning

Be absolutely certain of the type of pre-existing paint before you apply a new coat; water-based paint will not adhere to pre-existing oil-based paints.

554 | Conserve Water in the Home

Using household water more efficiently saves money and makes prudent use of a finite natural resource.

⊙ **Steps**

1   Check for and fix any leaking toilets or faucets.

2   Use low-flow showerheads.

3   Install shut-off valves to reduce flow while soaping and shampooing.

4   Catch the flow of cool water in buckets while you're waiting for it to heat up; you can use it later for gardening or cooking.

5   Insulate hot-water pipes.

6   Turn off the water while brushing your teeth or shaving.

7   Avoid washing dishes under a running tap – rinse them in a washing-up bowl instead.

8   Wait until you have a full load before running the dishwasher or washing machine, and use the shortest cycles.

9   Take shorter showers.

10 Avoid wasting bath water while waiting for it to warm up. Cold water will mix quickly with hot water to give you the temperature you want.

11 Clean driveways with a broom rather than hosing them down.

✳ **Tip**

You can reuse bath water or water used for washing up to water the garden.

555 | Conserve Electricity

With the cost of energy rising, it's important to conserve electricity as much as possible. Not only does this save money, but it helps the environment as well.

⊙ **Steps**

1   Unplug appliances when you're not using them. Using a power strip makes it easier to conserve electricity because you just have to unplug one cord instead of many. Also unplug any chargers that aren't in use because they still use electricity even when they're not actively charging something.

2   Set your thermostat at a reasonable temperature. Set it as high or as low as you need to be comfortable, but don't heat or cool excessively.

3   Use your appliances efficiently to conserve electricity. Refrain from opening your oven unnecessarily, because it has to work harder and use more energy to heat back up; only run the dishwasher when it is fully loaded; adjust the water level on the washing machine for smaller loads and clean out the lint filter in your dryer before every load.

4   Turn off the lights when you leave a room. If your lights have a dimmer switch, dim the lights as much as possible. Also use sunlight to your advantage during the day and turn off artificial lighting.

✳ **Tips**

Leave the thermostat on when you leave the house. The air conditioner or heater has to work twice as hard when you turn it back on.

Hang clothes on a clothesline instead of using a tumble dryer.

✓ 556 Negotiate with a Contractor

Once you've decided what kind of work you will have done it is always beneficial to seek bids from contractors that have a good reputation in your community. When hiring a contractor, it's important to ask the right questions to make sure you're going to get the work done properly.

❑ **Have you been clear about the scope of your work?**

Never leave things open to interpretation by the contractor. For example, if you're building a pool and the contractor is doing some demolition, make sure the price includes haul-away of the removed items and restoration of any damaged items not slated for demolition.

❑ **Have you asked for a line-item estimate from your contractor?**

This way you are able to revisit the contract if you choose to delete an item, and you will know what the exact credit for this item should be. Ask the contractor to list the brands of the materials he will be using, so he can't swap these for cheaper materials once he has started the job.

❑ **Have you been clear about the start and finish dates?**

If you want the job done by a certain date, ask the contractor if he is able to staff the job appropriately. Ask questions like "What will you do if you fall behind schedule?" If he doesn't say that he will make up the time by using more workers or working overtime, then this may not be the contractor for you.

❑ **Have you read the small print of the contract?**

Never sign a contract that has penalties only towards the owner. Some contracts are set up so that you pay extra in the event of delays by rain or other acts of God. Also never pay more than a 10 per cent deposit to start the work. Insist that this deposit be paid at the end of the recission period. If you pay when you sign the deal it may take weeks or months to get your money back if you decide to cancel.

❑ **Do you have a list of subcontractors?**

Check their reputations and licences as well. Tell the contractor that you want to be notified in advance of any changes to his subcontractors. Some contractors will begin to shop your project around after they sign your deal. This way they are able to find the cheapest prices for the subs' work and charge you the higher-priced sub prices.

❑ **Do you have a project schedule?**

This will ensure that you are paying the contractor for work that is completed in accordance with the schedule. The schedule should be detailed enough so that it is clear what items will be done by the milestone dates. Never pay for work not completed. Sit down with your contractor each time he asks for money and check off the items completed on the schedule.

❑ **Have you been given detailed estimates for any changes to the work?**

If changes are necessary to the work, make sure the contractor gives you a detailed estimate as well as proper credit for any work being deleted. Do not allow the change to revise your schedule unless you are adding significant work to the project. Do not negotiate additional work without getting it in writing. Keep things on a professional basis.

❑ **Are you happy with the end result?**

At completion make sure you walk the job with the contractor list all the deficient items. Do not make the final payment until these items are taken care of. Make sure that all the warranty manuals for the equipment and fixtures are handed over to you. Make sure there are no mechanics' liens or stop notices filed by your contractor's subcontractors.

557 Run Wires Through a Wall

Most serious home-repair fiends will probably be faced with having to run electrical wires through walls at some point.

⊙ **Steps**

1 Inspect your home. Go to the basement and to the loft to see how accessible the walls are from each location. Inspect the rest of your home if access to the loft or basement is limited.

2 Determine where you want to run the wires to and plan out the most direct route.

3 Working from the loft, drill through the top 2 x 4 to get into the wall. If working from the basement, drill through the bottom 2 x 4.

4 Run the wire along the skirting board and tack it down if you can't gain access to the walls through the loft or basement. To pass the wire on to the next room, drill a hole in the wall and run the wire through into the next room using the fish tape.

5 Avoid drilling within a few centimetres of the corners; there are always 2 x 4s at the corners and you don't want to drill into them.

6 Drill separate holes through the walls on each side. Measure from a common point to line up the holes. Make sure you are not drilling into other wires or pipes between the walls.

7 Continue until you reach the place where you intend to terminate the run.

⚠ **Warning**

Individual specifics of this job will vary greatly depending on the layout of your home. You will probably have to play around for a while and figure out the best procedure.

Things You'll Need

❏ Tape measure

❏ Drill bits

❏ Fish tape

❏ Variable-speed drill

558 Carve Wood

Carving wood is a great way to add decoration to plain wood – you can even make bigger projects such as carving a wooden door, ceiling mouldings or cabinets and bookcases.

⊙ **Steps**

1 Get a piece of wood. For starters you may want to choose soft types of wood like basswood, aspen or butternut.

2 Assemble a carving toolkit. Start with a knife, like a utility knife, a pick and wood chisel. Make sure that your tools are sharp.

3 Create a design. You can draw it directly on the wood using a pencil or use a graphite paper to transfer the pattern. If you are just starting out, make the design as simple as possible.

4 Start carving. You can start from the tip of the design using a small knife, such as an X-Acto. Then use a bigger utility knife, gradually upgrading to a more sophisticated carving knife. Use a wood chisel to carve deeper. Going with the grain is an easier way to carve out designs for those who are inexperienced.

5 Use a hammer to strike the top of the chisel to get deeper. Push the chisel slowly as you hit it with hammer bit by bit, making sure you stay along the lines of the pattern. Use caution so as not to injure yourself.

⚠ **Warning**

Always use protective gloves and eye goggles.

Things You'll Need

❏ Wood

❏ Carving tools

❏ Graphite paper

❏ Hammer

❏ Sandpaper

❏ Wood stain

❏ Tack cloth

6   Blow off or vacuum off the debris and then examine the carvings. Wipe out smaller lints with a tack cloth. Continue improving the carvings or details until you are satisfied. Use sandpaper to remove the splinters or sharp edges.

7   Add stain to protect your final piece.

Build a Staircase   559

Building stairs can be a daunting project even for an experienced builder. However, building a straight stairway to a porch or deck it is something that a competent DIY-er can take on.

⊙ Steps

1   Understand that stairs consist of three parts: the stringer, the riser and the tread. The stringer is the part of the structure that actually supports the stairs (one at each side). The riser (the rise) is the height of an individual stair, and the tread is the width of the stair.

2   Know that the total rise is the vertical height from the landing to a point level with the height of the upper floor. The total run is the horizontal length of the stairway, measured from the end of the staircase on the landing to the edge of the upper floor.

3   Put a 2 x 4 on the deck, then check that it's level with a spirit level. Measure from the bottom of the 2 x 4 to the ground.

4   Calculate the number of steps. Divide the total rise by 7.25. (7.25 in is generally considered a good riser height). Round up your answer to the next whole number to determine the number of steps in your stairway.

5   Calculate the total "run". Remember, on a stairway when you go up or down, the last step is either the ground or the deck surface, so you need one less tread than riser.

6   Calculate the exact height of the risers by dividing the total rise by the total number of risers.

7   Use a framing square to lay your stairs out on the 2 x 12 stringers. Using the numbers on the outside of the square, mark the long arm with a piece of masking tape. These are your rise and run calculations.

8   Position the long end of the framing square towards the end of the board and line up the two marks with the edge of the board facing you. Mark the outline of the square.

9   Slide the framing square up to the top mark, align the markings and again mark the notch. Continue marking and sliding up the length of the stringer.

10 Use a circular saw to carefully cut along the marked lines. Stop well back of the corner mark, and finish the cut with a handsaw. (If you cut all the way to the mark on the surface, the circular saw blade will cut past the line, weakening the stairs.)

11 Test-fit this first stringer in place to ensure your calculations and measurements are accurate, and then use this stringer as a template for marking the other stringers.

Things You'll Need

- ❑ Framing square
- ❑ 3-in nails or screws
- ❑ Circular saw and hand saw
- ❑ 2 x 6 lumber for treads
- ❑ 2 x 12s for stringers
- ❑ Masking tape
- ❑ Joist hangers
- ❑ Tape measure
- ❑ Spirit level

12 Attach the stringers to the deck by toe-nailing or using joist hangers attached to the deck framing.

13 Starting at the bottom, install the stair treads using 3-inch nails or screws to fasten them.

---

560 Restore Old Hardwood Floors

Have you just found hardwood floors hidden under an ugly carpet, or are your wood floors starting to show their age? Here's how to restore them.

◎ Steps

1 Remove any existing floor covering. Clean the floor with standard wood floor cleaner and let it dry thoroughly.

2 Reset the nails to below the surface of the floor and fill any holes with wood filler.

3 The floor now needs to be sanded or smoothed out. Using a commercial sanding machine improperly can leave tragic results. Hire a professional to sand the floor or rent a random-orbit floor sander, which is less risky.

4 If you go with the random-orbit floor sander, guide it in no particular pattern until all the finish is removed. Then, take a finer-grit paper and repeat the process. Finally, go to an even finer grit, 80 or 100, to smooth the wood before finish is applied. Be sure the surface is completely clean and wipe the floor of sawdust and surface contaminants.

5 Before applying the stain, test the colour on a piece of scrap wood. Stir the contents and, once you start, don't stop. Use a brush or a synthetic-based pad to apply. Don't use steel wool, as it can leave flakes and rust. Start staining on one side of the room and work your way across. If you stop in the middle, you will end up with an overlay mark.

�֍ Tips

Drying agents can be added to a stain to speed up the drying process.

Clean every two weeks with a cleaner made for wood floors.

Light-wood floors show dust less than dark wood floors.

⚠ Warning

Stay away from general-purpose or wood furniture type cleaners. These are harmful to the long life of your floor.

---

561 Hang a Door

Hanging a door has to be one of the easiest and most rewarding jobs in home improvements.

◎ Steps

1 Measure the width of the opening before ordering the door. The width needs to be 5–7.5 cm (2–2.5 in) wider than the door. More space in this area will give you room to fit the jambs and the shims into the door opening. For example, if your width measures 80 cm (32 in), then you need to purchase a 75-cm (30-in) prehung door.

2 Confirm the length of your prehung door jambs before installing. It may need to be trimmed to reduce the space under the door. Commonly, the door should clear the floor by 2 cm (0.75 in).

3 Check the floor to make sure it is plumb. This is important for cutting the bottom of the door. The jambs need to be cut, too, if the floor is not plum.

✖ Tips

The floors should also be checked to see if they are level and to compensate for proper installation of the door.

An accurate level is vital for this project. Make sure you plum your level before using it to ensure it is working correctly.

4 Install casing on one side of the door frame, using the pneumatic nail gun.

5 Put the pre-hung door into the door opening.

6 Shut the door, using the pneumatic nail gun to tack the hinge side of the pre-hung door to the door opening. It is important to keep the hinge side of the door tight to the door frame.

7 Confirm the reveal around the door and jamb to ensure that this is even all the way around. It is important to then shim the opposite side of the door jamb to the door frame.

8 Set the shims in place and tack the door casing to the door framing.

9 Recheck the reveal on the door.

10 Nail the opposite side of the door casing. Verify that the reveal on the door is even.

11 Make sure the gap at the bottom of door is 2 cm (0.75 in). If not, pop the hinges to release the door and trim the bottom so you have the gap.

12 Reinstall the door if necessary. Then caulk the door-frame casing and putty the nail holes.

Propagate from Cuttings and Leaves

562

Propagating from cuttings and leaves is an economical way to add to your plant collection.

Steps

1 Choose fleshy-leafed plants, like succulents, as food is stored in these types of leaves and will root.

2 Cut leafs from stems with shears or sharp knife.

3 Plant the leaf in moist sand, burying at least 2 cm (0.5 in). Place in warm shade and cover.

4 Check for root sprouts and keep the sand moist.

5 Transplant to the soil or soil/sand mix when roots are 2.5–7.5 cm (1–3 in) long.

6 Select roots a pencil width in diameter from healthy plants.

7 Using sharp shears or a knife, cut the roots into pieces 2.5–7.5 cm (1–3 in) long.

8 Fill a planting box or flat with potting soil and sand mixture up to 2.5 cm (1 in) from the top.

9 Place cuttings 5 cm (2 in) apart in a horizontal position on top of the soil.

10 Cover with 1.5 cm (0.5 in) of soil, and water thoroughly.

11 Cover with wet newspapers, cardboard or glass and place in the shade until root sprouts appear, then remove the covering.

12 Place in pots of the soil/sand mixture, thinnest end down into the soil.

Tips

Root-propagation plants include anemones, poppies, blackberries and raspberries and trumpet creepers.

Check moisture levels. Don't let root pieces dry out.

563 | Plant Hanging Tomato Plants

Tomato plants don't only have to be planted in the ground.
They can thrive hanging upside-down as well.

⊙ Steps

1   Purchase an empty bucket with a snap-on lid. Clean the bucket with
    warm, soapy water to prepare it for planting your tomato plant.

2   Cut a hole in the bucket using a drill or a utility knife. The hole should be
    right in the middle of the bottom of the bucket and about 5–7.5 cm (2–3
    in) in diameter. Cut several 1-cm (0.5-in) holes in the lid to allow you to
    water your plant.

3   Place several layers of newspaper in the bottom of the bucket, covering
    the hole. This will later be used to anchor the tomato plant. Fill the bucket
    with soil and put on the lid. Soils with vitamin additives are the best for
    growing tomatoes.

4   Turn the bucket over and plant the tomato seedling. Cut two slits in the
    newspaper at the bottom of the bucket to allow you to plant the tomato
    plant. Plant the seedling with only about 7.5 cm (3 in) of the plant coming
    out of the hole. Use extra soil to anchor it in the bucket.

5   Hang the bucket in a sunny area and water regularly. Tomatoes require at
    least 50 per cent sunlight. Move the bucket according to where the most
    direct sun is during the day.

6   Harvest the tomatoes as they ripen on the vine. The fruit should be red
    and firm before cutting from the plant.

❋ Tip

Check moisture levels. Don't let
root pieces dry out.

564 | Grow Lettuce

Lettuce is one of those versatile veggies that looks as good in
the garden as it does on the table.

⊙ Steps

1   Buy lettuce plants at the nursery for planting when night temperatures
    stay above 0°C (30°F). Otherwise, sow seeds outdoors in spring.

2   Choose a site that gets full sun in cool-weather areas, partial sun in
    warmer climates or for summer plantings.

3   Till the soil thoroughly, breaking up soil clumps and removing stones.

4   Dig in plenty of compost and well-cured manure to ensure the kind of
    soil lettuce needs: well-draining yet moisture-retentive, and rich in the
    nitrogen necessary for good leaf development.

5   Set plants 20–40 cm (8–16 in) apart, depending on the variety. Check
    the plant label or a comprehensive gardening book for mature size.
    When in doubt, err on the side of distance – crowded plants and poor
    air circulation invite disease and insect problems.

6   Keep the soil moist, but avoid watering in the evening: foliage that stays
    wet overnight is prone to disease. Mulch to conserve moisture and keep

❋ Tip

Keep plants well-watered,
and feed them every two weeks
with compost tea or a diluted
mixture of seaweed extract
and fish emulsion.

⚠ Warning

If slugs are a problem where you
live, avoid mulching lettuce; it's
like throwing an open house for
the slimy creatures. Instead,
simply weed diligently and
keep the soil cultivated.

the soil cool, and feed every three weeks with seaweed extract or compost tea.

7   Ensure a full season's worth of greens by making successive sowings 10 days apart, and by choosing heat-resistant varieties for late-spring plantings and cold-resistant ones for harvesting well into the autumn.

8   Begin cutting leaf lettuces as soon as they're big enough to use. Harvest heading types when the heads are firm and fully formed.

Grow Carrots   565

Carrots are good for you – chock-full of fibre and vitamins. They're beautiful too, with lacy, fernlike foliage that's perfect for containers and flower borders.

⊙ Steps

1   Choose a site that gets full sun (carrots will tolerate light shade but won't do as well). Soil should be light, with a pH of 5.8 to 6.8.

2   Dig to a depth of at least 30 cm (12 in), and remove all traces of rocks and other debris.

3   Add plenty of organic matter; this will lighten heavy soils and increase the moisture retention of sandy ones.

4   Sow carrot seeds directly two to three weeks before the last expected frost in cool regions; in warm climates, plant in autumn, winter or spring.

5   Speed germination, which can take 10 days or more, by soaking the seeds in water for six hours before you plant them.

6   Make early sowings shallow to capture warmth from the sun; sprinkle the seeds on the soil surface, tamp them gently and cover them with a thin layer of finely sifted compost.

7   Thin seedlings before the tops become entwined: either clip off the greens with scissors, or pull the roots very gently from the ground so you don't disturb the remaining plants. Allow 7.5–10 cm (3–4 in) between carrots.

8   Spray young plants once with compost tea to ensure good growth, and mulch with compost to deter weeds and retain moisture.

9   Begin harvesting carrots when they've turned deep orange.

✳ Tips

To prolong the harvest, you can make succession plantings every two weeks until the temperature reaches 27°C (80°F), then, when the temperature cools in the autumn, plant another crop for winter harvesting.

Like all root crops, carrots need lots of potassium. Boost your soil's supply by sprinkling wood ashes over the planting area before you sow the seeds.

⚠ Warnings

Carrots that are exposed to the sun turn green and bitter-tasting. To keep them orange and sweet, make sure the roots stay completely covered with soil.

Avoid manure and other fertilisers high in nitrogen; they'll encourage top growth at the expense of good root development.

Grow Strawberries   566

No garden should be without strawberries. They're beautiful, easy to grow and the first fruits to appear in the spring.

⊙ Steps

1   Buy strawberry plants at the nursery or order them from a catalogue for planting in early spring as soon as you can work the ground. Make sure the plants are certified disease-free; strawberries can carry viruses that will not only kill the crop but will also spread through your garden.

2   Choose a site that has excellent drainage, gets full sun and warms up early in the spring so blossoms aren't destroyed by late frosts. A gentle, south-facing slope is ideal. If your soil drains poorly, grow strawberries in raised beds or containers.

3   Till the planting bed thoroughly to a depth of at least 30 cm (12 in), removing all traces of weeds and grass, and dig in plenty of compost or well-cured manure to ensure the rich, fertile soil that strawberries need. The soil's pH should be slightly acid, from 5.5 to 6.5.

4   Dig a hole for each plant 13–18 cm (5–7 in) wide and deep enough to accommodate the roots. Set the plant into the hole with the crown just above ground level, and fill in the soil so that the roots are completely buried. Spacing depends on the planting method you choose.

5   Use the "matted row" planting method for the easiest maintenance. Set plants 46 cm (18 in) apart in rows 1–1.2 m (3–4 ft) apart. The plants will send out runners with abandon, with each runner producing a new little plant.

6   Keep the spaces between rows open by returning to the berry patch after each harvest and removing the outermost plants from both sides of each row. You can either snip the runners and dig up the attached plants, or simply run a mechanical tiller down the row.

7   Remove some of the original "mother" plants from each row at same time, leaving the newest plants, which will bear more vigorously the following season. Treat the crop as a biennial, ploughing the plants under after the first harvest and starting again the following spring.

8   Cut off all runners as soon as they appear. This way the plants direct all their energy into fruit production and should give you ample harvests for six years or more.

9   Make sure young plants get at least 2.5 cm (1 in) of water a week. Mulch to conserve moisture and deter weeds. A light material such straw or salt hay is ideal for both purposes.

10 Avoid letting any fruit develop the first year, regardless of which planting method you use. Instead, pick off each blossom as soon as you see it – forming and ripening even a berry or two will weaken a plant so much that the following year's production will be cut drastically.

11 Pick all strawberries the day they ripen, and eat or preserve them as soon as possible: overripe fruit spoils quickly on or off the vine.

567 | Transplant Flowers

At some point, many flowering plants need to be transplanted. Having to transplant flowers is usually a sign that you're doing something right and with a little know-how, it doesn't have to be a tricky process.

○ Steps

1   Choose the appropriate time of year. Any transplanting should wait until after the last frost of the year and, ideally, should be done on a warm,

✳ Tip

Many gardeners recommend transplanting after the flowers die. Doing this will avoid damaging the flowers while they're blooming.

cloudy day. Summer and early autumn are also good times for transplanting.

2   Decide where you'd like to put your transplants. If you're moving from one container to another, choose a new container that has room for growth, but will not engulf the transplanted flowers. In the garden, choose a spot that is ideal for your flowers and make sure it will give them room to grow.

3   Prepare the area that you'll be transplanting the flowers to. Dig a hole large enough to accommodate the plant's root ball, while leaving the stem of the plant above the level of the surrounding soil. Ensure that there are no large dirt clods or other debris in the hole and that the dirt is broken up and soft.

4   Dig up the flowers to be transplanted. Dig far enough out from the stem of the plant so that you can get the entire root ball. Gently lift the plant from the soil and move it to its new container or garden spot.

5   Place the flowers in the new spot and fill in around the root ball with soil. Place enough soil around the plant to completely cover the roots, but don't cover the stem of the plant.

6   Water thoroughly. Many plants will require frequent watering, at least every other day, until the new growth appears. Water once a week after the plants have established themselves.

⚠ Warning

Don't over-water the transplanted flowers. The soil should stay moist, but avoid standing water.

Pick Flowers for Hanging Baskets   568

A well-designed hanging basket can add beauty and colour to a home, and a custom-made basket allows you to select flowers that will complement the other elements in the surrounding space.

⊙ Steps

1   Select flowers with similar growing conditions for large hanging baskets. A variety of colour and texture is appealing but will soon become an unsightly mess if the plants don't all require the same light, water and soil conditions.

2   Choose the location for your hanging basket first and then pick flowers based on the amount of sunlight that will be available. Different species of flowers require different levels of sunlight, and if you don't choose plants correctly they won't thrive.

3   Consider the colour of the basket. The flowers should complement the colour of the container and items in the surrounding area.

4   Plant only one type of flower if the basket is small. If you only have room for two or three plants, the arrangement will be much more attractive if they are similar in size and shape. To add variety to the basket, mix the colours.

5   Mix trailing or vining types of flowers with an upright type of flower if your container is large enough to accommodate it. Placing the tall flowers in the centre and surrounding them by vines hanging down the outside of the basket adds an attractive dimension to the display.

✱ Tip

When selecting flowers for any container garden, consider the season. If you want early spring or late autumn colour, choose hardy annuals like pansies or ornamental cabbages, which thrive in cool weather. If you are planting in summer, go for the warm flowering plants like petunias that thrive in the warm sun.

569 Grow Roses

Roses have an undeserved reputation for being fussy, hard-to-care-for plants. Some roses do require more maintenance than others, but growing roses is something even a beginner can do. Follow these instructions for a perfect rose garden.

Pruning

- Prune roses in winter or early spring once the rose starts to show signs of new growth, usually in the form of tiny red buds.

- Cut out any obviously dead or damaged branches first. Then cut out all but four or five healthy main stems.

- Cut the stems back by a third to a half, depending on how tall you want the bush to be. Make these cuts right above an out-ward-facing bud. This directs the bud to grow up and out, leaving the centre of the rose bush open for a prettier shape and better air circulation.

- Deadhead. This simply means trimming off spent roses to encourage the bush to pro-duce more. While some roses bloom only in June, others are keep producing all season.

Fertilising

- Start fertilising roses regularly at the start of the growing season. Roses are hungry plants, demanding lots of nutrients for the best growth and flowering.

- Fertilise roses with a liquid fertiliser every three to four weeks during the growing season or according to package directions.

- Stop fertilising roses in early autumn, at least a month before the first annual frost. Fertilising too long into autumn encourages roses to produce tender new growth that will get nipped by the cold.

- Mulch. Roses need less weeding and watering and have fewer diseases if you lay down 2.5–5 cm (1–2 in) of organic mulch, such as wood chips, pine needles, grass clippings or other biodegradable material.

Watering

- Water diligently. Roses need a steady source of water during the growing sea-son, about 2.5 cm (1 in) a week from rain or watering. In arid regions consider installing a drip-irrigation system.

- Water early in the morning. Watering in the evening or overnight promotes disease.

- Keep water off the foliage of the rose bush. A drip irrigation system is recom-mended. You can use a water hose to water the base of the rose bush by turning it on slightly and allowing water to slowly seep into the soil.

- Read the label that came with your roses, or research your variety on the Internet or in a rose handbook. The label may have instructions on proper watering.

Protecting

- Spray. If your rose bush becomes dis-eased or has an insect infestation, you may want to deal with it by spraying. Trim off the affected part and take it to a reli-able garden centre, where the staff can prescribe the correct treatment.

- Protect roses as needed in late autumn, after the first hard freeze. In regions where temperatures don't fall below -7°C (20°F), no additional winter protection is needed. A simple mounding of several centimetres of soil over the base of the rose should suffice. In colder regions, mound to about 0.3 m (1 ft) about a month after the last average frost is expected; additionally, two weeks later, the entire plant should be wrapped in burlap to protect the upper parts.

reference

Grow Honeysuckle 570

Honeysuckle is known for its sweet, edible nectar and is relatively easy to care for given the proper conditions.

⊙ Steps

1 Find a good location to plant honeysuckle. Most species need full sun, although some may tolerate partial shade. The soil should have plenty of moisture and good drainage so that standing water does not accumulate.

2 Plant honeysuckle in early spring after the last frost. The plants should be placed about 1 m (3 ft) apart. Space them slightly closer together if they are to serve as ground cover.

3 Mulch the base of the plant heavily with a covering of leaves to allow moisture retention in the soil and shade the roots. Mulching will also protect the root system during the winter.

4 Water honeysuckle regularly after planting. Once established, it should only need additional water during dry periods in the summer.

5 Fertilise with a balanced fertiliser (10-10-10) at the beginning of the growing season and again in the middle of the blooming season.

6 Prune honeysuckle in late February to March when it is well established in about two years. Remove dead and weak stems to encourage new growth. Additional pruning throughout the growing season will vary according to the particular species.

✱ Tip

After pruning, always give the plant extra water.

⚠ Warnings

Be careful of poison oak or ivy. Honeysuckle tends to become entwined with other plants.

Never prune honeysuckle that is less than two years old.

After severe pruning the honeysuckle vine will often re-grow rapidly, but may fail to flower.

Propagate a Bay Tree 571

The bay tree, *Laurus nobilis*, is a large, attractive evergreen tree that gives us the culinary leaves known and loved by cooks everywhere.

⊙ Steps

1 The easiest method of propagation if you have a tree that has a lot of basal suckers is to dig the sucker growth with some roots attached, then transfer it to grow on separately in a pot until large enough to plant. The ideal time to do this is in the spring when growth is strong.

2 If there are no rooted suckers to take advantage of, take cuttings. Take a number of them to be sure you have enough successes to serve your needs. Not all are likely to make it.

3 Bay cuttings will fare best with bottom heat. If you have a heating mat, you will be able to control your heat. For purists who have the set-up for it, you can use hot compost under the pots or rooting trays.

4 Bay is susceptible to fungus and rot, which makes it a bit more tricky since your rooting medium should not be allowed to dry out. Rooting hormone powder should help, as it not only encourages the formation of roots, but has a fungicide mixed in. Dip your cutting in the hormone powder and press the end of the cutting into your moistened medium.

⚠ Warning

Not all bay leaves are safe to eat.

5   If you don't want to use rooting hormone powder, you can try using a tea made of dried willow leaves and watering with it. It is not fungicidal, but it will encourage rooting.

6   With bottom heat and high humidity (misting will help), your cuttings should start to root from 30 to 90 days in temperatures ideally in the 70s. They can, however, take up to a year, so if they are still green, don't give up on them.

7   When you see your cutting actively putting out new growth, you will probably have some good roots started. Wait until the plant has grown a few new leaves before planting in a larger container. Although your tree will grow reasonably quickly at this young age, it may be a year or two before it is ready to go into the ground.

8   You can try growing bay laurels from seed, but most seed tends to rot before germinating.

9   Layering is also a way to propagate this plant. Bend a branch gently until it lies on the ground. Make a nick in the branch where it touches the ground and hold it in place against the soil with a rock on either side, or use garden staples. You can also use hormone powder on the nicked area. This is a hit-or-miss method, but if your layering works, your plant is likely to grow a bit faster than a cutting.

572 | Build a Raised-Bed Garden

A raised-bed garden is ideal for the modern gardener, with yields double the traditional home garden.

◉ Steps

1   A raised-bed garden simply means the garden soil is above ground level. Understand that raised-bed gardens are ideal for city dwellers or anyone who has only a small space to devote to a garden. It is also good for anyone who just wants to raise fresh vegetables for home use.

2   A raised-bed garden should be no more that 1.2 m (4 ft) wide. Remember you will not walk in it so you will need to be able to reach at least half way across to weed etc. It can be as long as you have space. Choose a space where your garden will receive eight hours of sun a day.

3   Construct your bed out of pressure-treated lumber, redwood, cement block or brick. Avoid using creosote or pentachlorophenol-treated lumber. Note that cement block will raise the pH of soil over time and lime may be needed.

4   The bed should be raised 0.6 m (2 ft) or more. This will allow home owners that have low spots to use this space and still avoid ponding in the garden.

5   Cover with clear plastic to use as a hot box and start planting much earlier or use longer in autumn. You will also be able to have plants much closer together and increase production.

✱ Tip

If you like to sit in chairs while gardening, you can make raised-bed gardens 1 m (3 ft) high.

Lay a Path Through a Garden   573

No need to pay someone to lay a path through your garden. All you need is a little imagination, some elbow grease and strong legs to lift those stepping stones for the path.

⊙ Steps

1   Select the layout and design (or purpose) of the garden path.

2   Choose the look for the new garden path. You need to select large stepping stones that will be walked on, and then pick out the gravel that will surround it.

3   Dig out the grass and the top layer of soil to create the path. Dig down at least a few centimetres.

4   Line the dirt path with some sort of plastic lining to prevent weeds or grass from growing in the path.

5   Place a permanent border down each side of the dirt path.

6   Poor sand on to the plastic liner to serve as the foundation.

7   Place the stepping stones. Walk the path as you place them, making sure they aren't too far apart or too close together.

8   Pour the smaller gravel around the stepping stones to ensure their security and placement.

❋ Tip

If your path will be cutting across a lawn, keep the surface of the path on the same level as the surrounding lawn, so that you'll be able to mow right across it.

Plant a Hedge   574

Planting a hedge in your garden is one of those great landscape projects that not only adds beauty and shelters wildlife, but can also help reduce energy costs and require less maintenance than a traditional wood fence.

⊙ Steps

1   Choose a site for your hedge based on your need and the plant's requirements. Make sure your soil has adequate drainage.

2   Dig the planting trench the length and width of the desired hedge. The exact dimensions will be determined by the purpose, site and the plant that has been chosen. A general rule is that the trench should be at least 0.3 m (1 ft) wider than the plant root ball and of equal depth.

3   Fill the planting trench with water, and allow it to soak into the soil. This "watering-in" step ensures that water will reach the plant's roots and help prevent shock.

4   Place all plants in the trench at the appropriate spacing. Make sure the plants are straight. Any necessary trimming may be done at this stage.

5   Backfill the trench with the original soil. Gently tamp down soil and water deeply.

6   Spread a 5–7.5-cm (2–3-in) layer of mulch or other organic material around each plant and over the entire hedge area.

❋ Tips

Digging a planting trench is usually preferred over digging individual holes.

The plant spacing will be determined by the type of plant and the purpose or effect of the hedge. Be sure to check your plant tags for information.

⚠ Warnings

Plants for an untrimmed hedge should be spaced further apart than ones that are to be trimmed.

Be careful not to let the top of your hedge become wider than the bottom. A wider top will shade the bottom and weaken the plant.

575 | Make a Boxwood Topiary

Creating a topiary requires patience, technique and a steady hand.

☉ Steps

1. Gather supplies. Use a boxwood plant with a straight centre trunk that's the height of the desired topiary. Select a container at least one size larger than the pot or burlap ball.

2. Remove lower branches, working from the bottom up to form a well-defined trunk. Snip the branches with clipping scissors close to the trunk. Stop clipping approximately two-thirds of the way up the trunk.

3. Remove the boxwood from its original container and put in the new larger container. Fill in the gaps with topsoil first, and then a low-growing ground-cover such as moss or blue-star creeper as the top layer.

4. Stake a thin bamboo stick into the soil next to the boxwood's trunk. Support the trunk upright to the bamboo by tying together with raffia.

5. Groom the topiary regularly by pinching leaves, stems and branches with your fingers. New growth forms from those pinch points.

✳ Tip

Encourage vertical height or more vegetation by leaving 2.5–5 cm (1–2 in) of branch when removing the lower branches.

Things You'll Need

- ❏ Flower pot or container
- ❏ Clipping scissors
- ❏ Top soil
- ❏ Ground-cover plant
- ❏ Bamboo stick
- ❏ Raffia

576 | Water a Lawn

Proper watering is key to keeping a lawn healthy. It's best to water infrequently and deeply rather than often and lightly.

☉ Steps

1. Purchase hose-end sprinklers or install a below-ground automated system.

2. Test your sprinkler output and consistency of coverage. Place flat-bottomed cups or tins within the sprinkler pattern and measure the water over a given time. Make adjustments as necessary so the entire lawn is watered evenly.

3. Water early in the morning, or when the winds are calm and enough daylight is left to dry the leaves before nightfall.

4. Apply enough water to wet the root zone to 15–20 cm (6–8 in) deep with each irrigation, and let the soil dry partially between irrigations. To avoid producing runoff, run the sprinklers in cycles, turning sprinklers on for 10 minutes, turning them off to let the water soak in, then repeating.

5. Adjust the watering schedule depending on weather, seasons and rainfall. Grasses generally require more water during their active growing season than when they're dormant, though all grasses need an average of 2.5–5 cm (1–2 in) of water per week in summer; cool-season grasses can take more than this in winter.

6. Set automated timers so you don't forget to turn the water off.

7. Maintain sprinkler systems so they operate efficiently. Watch them run, and make adjustments and fix clogs or leaks as necessary.

✳ Tips

Your lawn will tell you when it needs water – two signs are when the grass changes from bright green to dull grey-green, and when footprints remain when you walk across the lawn.

To check how deep water is penetrating, probe the soil with a stiff wire or screwdriver. It will move easily through moist soil and be harder to push when it reaches dry soil.

⚠ Warnings

Frequent, shallow watering results in shallow roots and a weak lawn.

Applying too much water is wasteful and can cause lawn diseases and promote weed growth.

Buy the Right Garden Shed 577

Buying the right garden shed is important because these structures can last for years and often house important projects or equipment.

⊙ **Steps**

1 Decide if you want a pre-made shed or if you want to build one yourself. Pre-made garden sheds are easy to install and are ready to use. If you choose to build your own shed, plan on buying supplies and schedule enough time to build it.

2 Choose the size of your shed. Measure the area for the shed and decide what the shed will hold.

3 Determine the type of shed you need. For heavy-duty equipment or larger gardening supplies, a metal shed is the best choice. Wooden sheds are common because they are pleasing to the eye and reliable. Plastic storage sheds are used for smaller gardens and not for daily use.

4 Decide on your budget. Spending a little more money for higher quality pays off in the long run.

5 Visit your local hardware or DIY store. Browse through their sheds and find the one that meets your size, composition and budget requirements. If they don't have what you need, try a company that specialises in small metal buildings or sheds.

✳ Tip

Select a shed that complements your garden's style.

⚠ Warning

People in areas where high winds are prominent should not buy a wooden shed.

Build a Greenhouse 578

A greenhouse can be anything from a large-scale construction project down to a couple of afternoons' worth of work.

⊙ **Steps**

Planning Decisions

1 Consider what kind of space you have available. The greenhouse will need to fit in with your home's design and outside landscaping. You should also determine what, if any, zoning requirements and restrictions there are in your area, since this can impact the design of your greenhouse.

2 Decide on the shape of the structure itself. You can build greenhouses in all kinds of free-standing designs such as A frames, Quonset huts or even barn-like structures with Mansard (or sloping) roofs. Alternatively, they can be attached to the side of a house or shed as lean-tos or just mounted on a window.

3 Evaluate potential locations. A greenhouse needs to be located where it gets maximum sunlight. The optimum location is on the south or south-east side of a building, but any location where the greenhouse will get morning sun is usually fine. Large trees that provide shade from the heat of the sun during the afternoon are a bonus, but you don't want them shading the location in the morning.

✳ Tip

An alternative to building your own greenhouse from scratch might be buying a greenhouse kit (available at garden centres and DIY stores). Everything you need is in the kit, and all you have to do is read and follow the directions.

Coverings

1 Determine how your greenhouse will be covered. Glass is the traditional covering, and provides great light penetration. Tempered glass is a better choice, since it is more resistant to cracking. However, all glass can break, so a substantial frame and foundation is usually required.

2 An alternative to glass is fibre glass. This is available in clear or translucent options and is much lighter than glass, so the frame doesn't need to be substantial.

3 Consider clear plastic film if you want to build a small, light-framed greenhouse. It's very lightweight, easy to install and readily available. The major downside to plastic film is that doesn't last more than a few years and so needs to be replaced more frequently than glass or fibre glass.

Greenhouse Bases

1 A permanent glass or fibre-glass covered greenhouse will require a substantial foundation. Due to the weight of the structure, it will require concrete footings or even a poured concrete foundation.

2 Lighter-framed greenhouses (plastic film) can be installed on concrete pavers laid directly on the ground.

3 Cover the floors of any greenhouse with at least a few centimetres of fine aggregate gravel. The gravel will allow water to run off the surface while providing good footing on the damp floors.

Heating and Ventilation

1 Heating a greenhouse usually requires some form of supplemental heat. The amount of heat needed will depend on the prevailing climate. An existing home-heating system cannot provide adequate heat.

2 Consider supplemental heating systems fuelled by gas, oil or electricity. The local climate, as well as price and availability of fuels in your area, will determine the actual choice of system.

3 Air movement in a greenhouse is essential to healthy plants. During the winter, moving warm air helps maintain an even temperature throughout the greenhouse, while in the heat of the summer, air helps to cool them.

4 Fans integrated with the heating system may be sufficient to provide necessary air movement in the winter months, but supplemental fans are probably a requirement for the hot summer months.

Things You'll Need

- ❏ Shovels and concrete
- ❏ Tools such as hammers, saws, nails, screws, utility knife
- ❏ Framing materials such as wood and metal
- ❏ Concrete pavers
- ❏ Supplemental heating system
- ❏ Small aggregate gravel
- ❏ Supplemental fans
- ❏ Greenhouse plans
- ❏ Greenhouse covering

---

579 Build a Treehouse

There is much to consider when building a quality treehouse. Location, support, design and safety are all important.

⊙ Steps

1 Choose a tree. Consider the height and branch thickness before building your treehouse. You don't want it too high, especially for children. The branches holding the points where you place the supports must be able to bear the weight of each part of the treehouse it is supporting.

✱ Tips

Use bolts not nails for supports.

Be simplistic in your design. Too many joints aren't good for the tree.

2   Plan your treehouse. Be sure to consider practical and legal planning
    issues. The practical planning is about the design of your treehouse.
    The legal planning concerns the laws that you may need to abide by.

3   Develop your framing plan. Rigid framed supports are the easiest, since
    movement dilemmas are non-existent. You might try this design for small
    trees or at the top of trees. Careful attention must be paid to limiting
    movement in the branches. Triangles are the strongest building shapes,
    so incorporate them into your design. Give the platform a test run by
    placing sandbags that will be heavier than your expected final load on
    to the platform for a couple of days to be sure your design is safe.

4   Decide which type of support you will need to keep your floor safely
    attached to your tree. Depending on your tree, you will either need fixed
    or flexible support. Fixed joints are used for connections between trees
    that don't move much and use bolts. Flexible joints are used for
    connections between trees that move around a lot.

5   Pick your attachment materials. Metal brackets are used for both fixed
    and flexible joints. Knee braces are frequently used in treehouses,
    especially for treehouses in single trees. They are strong and can hold
    heavy loads. Cables allow beams to be suspended to make floating
    attachments to the tree. They also give extra support to long spans.

⚠ Warning

You are responsible for keeping
the people safe who may visit the
treehouse. If at any time you are
unsure of what you are doing,
seek professional advice.

Build a Brick or Stone Retaining Wall

580

A retaining wall can be built out of anything – from stone to
wood to poured concrete – and it can significantly alter the
contours of your garden.

◎ Steps

1   Figure out where and why you want a wall: at the bottom of a gentle
    slope to create a new planting bed? Between two beds to provide
    contour and definition?

2   Decide on your building material – brick gives a formal elegance and
    stone a European air.

3   For reinforced walls you need the depth of footings and piers to equal the
    height of the wall. For example: for a 1-m (3-ft) wall, you need footing 0.3 m
    (1 ft) deep and wide to go the entire distance of the wall. The footing will
    make an L shape, having the extra surface footing behind your wall.

4   Lay the rebar flat in the bed of footings 5 cm (2 in) above the soil so the
    concrete touches the soil, but the rebar does not touch the soil.

5   Piers are 0.6 m (2 ft) deep every 1 m (3 ft) of wall and on every corner.
    Piers are set behind the wall below the bed of footing. Top the footing
    with cinderblocks that will be the same height as your wall.

6   The rebar will go through the centre of each cinder block. Fill each cinder
    block with concrete.

7   Reinforce each level of cinder block with rebar running horizontal and tied
    to the vertical rebar with tie wire. Once you create your cinderblock wall,
    you are ready to face it with whatever material you desire – brick, stone,
    stucco, etc.

✳ Tip

For reinforced walls you need the
depth of footings and piers to
equal the height of the wall.

⚠ Warning

A retaining wall is like a dam: the
higher the wall and the heavier
the soil behind it, the greater the
pressure on the wall.

581 | Put Up Fence Panels

A privacy fence not only adds value to the property, but it also affords privacy and keeps your dogs in the garden.

⊙Steps

1   Measure 20 cm (8 in) from the property line and mark the measurements with ground paint.

2   Measure and mark off the postholes. The average fence panel is 2.4 m (8 ft) wide, so the postholes need to be spaced apart slightly less than this, allowing around 5 cm (2 in) on each end to overlap the fence posts.

3   Dig out the corner holes to about 0.6 m (2 ft) deep. Sink a post into the hole. Add large rocks or broken cement blocks to help steady the posts. Fill the holes with concrete.

4   Tack a string to the top of one post and run it to the next post. This will be used to ensure the rest of the posts are the same height. Dig the rest of the postholes and add large rocks or broken cement.

5   Let the cement cure for at least 48 hours. Once it is cured, attach the fence panels. Nail or screw the fence panels to the posts.

6   Stain or paint both sides of the fence if you desire.

Things You'll Need

- ❑ Wood fence panels
- ❑ 4 x 4 in x 8-ft posts
- ❑ String
- ❑ Cement

582 | Maintain a Trellis

With a trellis, you can train climber plants such as clematis, bougainvillea, honeysuckle or a number of other plants to add beauty to your landscape.

⊙Steps

1   Choose a metal trellis if you want a low-maintenance garden ornament. Select a powder coating paint for your trellis, which will last longer. Allow the trellis to develop a natural patina or rust as it's exposed to the elements, or follow a rusting procedure. Combine one cup of hydrogen peroxide, one cup of vinegar and one teaspoon of salt. Put the mixture in a spray bottle. Put the trellis on a protective tarp in an open, safe area in your garden. Spray the trellis completely with the mixture. Let the mixture sit on the trellis for an hour or more, depending on how "aged" you want your trellis to be then rinse the mixture off with water.

2   For wood trellises select a high-quality wood, such as cedar or mahogany. Treat an unfinished wood trellis with a water-repellent/ fungicide sealant to guard against shrinking and warping, and resist mildew and moisture. Choose stain instead of paint if you want a little colour, as it will be difficult to repaint the arbour as plants begin to grow up the trellis. You can find latex or oil-based stain in a variety of colours.

3   Choose the site for installation carefully. It can be difficult to relocate a trellis once the climbing plants are established in your landscape. Make sure the trellis is anchored securely in the ground. Check periodically to see how the trellis is holding up under the weight of the vines, especially wisteria, which can be very heavy.

⚠ Warning

Keep the mixture away from your eyes.

Stain a Deck   583

Staining your deck will keep it looking good – it will restore its natural oils and protect it from ultraviolet rays and water damage.

⊙ Steps

1. Thoroughly clean the deck. Use deck cleaner or a pressure washer, which uses forcefully ejected water to clean surfaces, for this. Let the deck dry.

2. Fill a small bucket or rolling pan with the stain. Immerse a brush or long-handled roller into the stain. Absorb only enough stain for a few strokes.

3. Roll or brush-stain the deck. Make sure you apply the stain evenly.

4. Wipe excess stain or dark spots with rags. Let the stain set for 24 hours.

✹ Tip

Avoid staining the deck in extreme weather.

⚠ Warning

Use extreme care when using a pressure washer – the force of the water can cause injury to people and animals.

Clean a Fish Pond   584

Cleaning a fish pond is a dirty job, but it must be done if you want to keep your pond attractive and its residents healthy.

⊙ Steps

1. Remove the fish and other animals from the fish pond. Suction or bucket out the pond water, reserving some for the holding tank or wading pool. Fill the wading pool with about a half-and-half ratio of pond water and fresh, dechlorinated water.

2. Pull out pond plants carefully from ledges and place in a shady area in pots. Drain the remaining water out of the pond. Take out any large rocks or decorative pond items and spray clean with the water hose.

3. Scrub the lining of the pond gently with a brush, using fresh water. Vacuum the remaining debris using a wet-dry or shop vac. Spray down filters and pumps with a water hose.

4. Replace all plants, rocks and other decorations back to the fish pond. Return the fish and other pond life to their freshly cleaned habitat.

⚠ Warning

Always use extreme care when removing fish and other pond life, and make sure they are temporarily housed in an environment that suits their needs while you clean the pond.

Clean Swimming-Pool Sides   585

In order to remain usable, regular swimming-pool maintenance must be performed throughout the year.

⊙ Steps

1. Use a small damp sponge to wipe off as much of the calcium build-up as possible from the tiles on the sides of the pool.

2. Use a pumice stone on individual tiles to gently buff away any calcium build-up that is visible. Use a spray bottle with tap water to wash away the excess calcium. Wipe off the tile with a dry towel.

3. Use a clean, dry towel again to wipe off the tiles on the sides of the swimming pool.

✹ Tip

Make sure you purchase the correct type of pumice stone, made specifically for swimming pools, and not one that is used in the bath.

586 | Set Up Email in Outlook Express

Setting up your email in Outlook Express is fairly easy, but requires keen attention to detail.

Steps

1. Open Outlook Express. The Internet connection wizard will automatically open, too.

2. Enter the name you want to appear on your outgoing emails in the Display Name field. This name will appear on every mail you send. Click Next.

3. Type the email address given to you by your Internet provider into the Email Address field. Click Next.

4. Enter the type of server your Internet provider uses. In most cases, this will be the Pop3 server. Click Next.

5. Fill in your name and enter the name that you want to appear on your outgoing emails in the Internet mail login screen. If you want the computer to remember you when you sign on, enter your password and check the Remember Me box. Click Next and then Finish.

✳ Tip

Verify all your information with your Internet provider before setting up your email.

⚠ Warning

When entering the email address, password and incoming and outgoing mail server addresses, be exact. Your email will not work if there are any mistakes in this information.

587 | Create a Hotmail Email Account

Hotmail offers free email accounts that are easy to use.

Steps

1. Go to the Hotmail website and click on the Sign Up button.

2. Look for the option that is just for opening up a Hotmail account. Click the Get It button underneath that option.

3. Under Create a Windows Live ID, type in a unique email address. A combination of letters with numbers or symbols is more likely to be unique.

4. Next to where you typed in your proposed email address is a dropdown menu. Click on the arrow and select Hotmail.com.

5. Click the Check Availability button. If a message appears stating that this email address has already been taken, try other email addresses until Hotmail approves the one you have requested.

6. Under Choose Your Password, type in a password between seven and 16 characters. Retype the password in the field below.

7. Under Enter Password Reset Information, type in another email address where Hotmail can send you information about resetting your password.

8. Click on the dropdown menu to select a security question. Type in an answer that you will remember.

9. Fill in your personal information. Whatever name you fill in here will display on any email that you send from your Hotmail account.

10. Click on the Windows Live Service Agreement and the Privacy Statement. Then click I Accept to open your Hotmail account.

✳ Tip

Always make sure you write down your password so you don't forget it, but keep it in a secure place, away from prying eyes!

Use the Apple Mac Mail Program 588

Apple's email program, which ships free with every Mac, is one of the best email clients. The program is simply called Mail.

⊙ Steps

1 Get your email account information from your Internet service provider. You will need to know what type of account it is, your email address and password. You may also need the incoming and outgoing server names, and outgoing server password.

2 Open your Mac's Mail program by clicking on it in the dock. Click on the File menu, then Add Account.

3 Fill in your name, email address and password in the first window. Check the box next to Automatically Set Up Account and click Create. If you are using any one of the popular email services (Gmail, Yahoo! or AOL), the Mail program will be able to automatically fill in all the settings. If you are using a more obscure service, you may have to fill in that information manually.

4 Set up mailboxes, subscribe to RSS feeds, use Spotlight for searching, pick out e-stationary and make yourself reminder notes.

5 Use Mail with iPhoto to share pictures, iCal to keep appointments straight and keep track of your to-do items, and Safari to manage your blog subscriptions.

✳ Tip
You can set up Mail so that your emails can be divided into project folders and subfolders to keep you organised.

Create an Email Signature 589

An email signature is like a virtual business card. You can include all your major contact information, design elements, logo and other details to help you stand out among the many.

⊙ Steps

1 Open a new document in your favourite drawing or photo-manipulation software, such as Photoshop.

2 Set the new document to the width and height you want, 72 dpi and transparent background.

3 Create a new layer in your document. Fill the layer with a colour, texture and/or background image.

4 Select the Type tool and add text – your name, title, company, telephone number, fax number, street address, email address and website address.

5 Add a photo, logo or other graphic.

6 Save the project in a file format that will leave the layers intact, such as a PSD file.

7 Flatten the image and optimise for web.

8 Use the Save As command to save a copy of your project as a JPG file.

9 Attach the JPG file to all your outgoing emails.

⚠ Warning
Be careful about the amount of personal info you include in your signature and who you send it to.

590 | Send a Web Page as an Email Attachment

Have you ever been looking at a web page and thought you'd like to send it to one of your friends? This can be done straight from your browser.

⊙ Steps

Internet Explorer 5

1 Go to a web page.

2 Open the File menu and click Send.

3 Click Page by Email.

4 Type the recipient's email address in the To box.

5 Click Send.

Netscape Navigator

1 Go to a web page.

2 Open File and click Mail Document.

3 Type the recipient's email address in the To box.

4 Click Send.

✳ Tip

If you are using a different browser, search the File dropdown menu to find the correct way of sending pages.

591 | Set Up Email Filters

Email filters can block spam and other unwanted email messages by automatically deleting them.

⊙ Steps

1 Open your email program.

2 Locate the Filters section, usually found under Edit, Options or Tools on the menu bar.

3 Click New and type the name of the new filter. Make sure it's easy to remember, such as "Junk Email".

4 Enter the filter conditions, or "rules". Conditions are requirements the email must meet (for example, the sender is Joe Smith or the subject includes the words "Make Money Fast!") in order for the action to take place.

5 Select the action you want the program to perform with filtered email. You can delete the message, move it to another folder or request other actions, depending on the mail program.

6 Click OK or Save to save your new filter. Continue to add filters as necessary to ensure all your unwanted emails are dealt with.

✳ Tips

In Netscape Messenger, the filters are found under the Message Filters command in the Edit menu.

In Microsoft Outlook, open the Tools menu, select Message Rules and then Mail.

⚠ Warning

Avoid overly general email filters. Filtering email from "Joe A. Smith" is fine, but filtering email from "Smith" means you might miss emails from other Smiths.

Avoid Getting Spam and Junk Email   **592**

Spam is the scourge of the Information Age. Just as telemarketers invade your phone line, electronic advertisers get to you through email.

⊙ Steps

1. Read the privacy policy of your email provider. Make sure that your email address isn't being leaked from the source.

2. Use the spam and junk mail filters of your email service. These services are included in the price of your email, so you might as well get your money's worth.

3. Mark or check spam that slips through the filter. Some email providers have their own spam filter that uses your input to become better at intercepting junk email.

4. Double-check online forms. If your email information is not required, don't give it out.

5. Get more than one email address. Have distinct addresses for personal, business, shopping and networking. This keeps the important addresses free of spam and junk email.

6. Purchase and use anti-spam software. This usually comes bundled with virus protection and privacy software.

❋ Tips

Scan electronic forms carefully. Some forms have check boxes that give you the option to not have your information permanently stored by the site. Use this tool to keep your inbox free of junk email.

Yahoo, Google and some other companies offer free email service. Create a unique email address at each service and strictly use that email account for one task.

⚠ Warning

Do not put your email address out in public areas of websites. Anybody who can access the site can use your address.

Block a Sender by Email Address in Hotmail   **593**

Spam is part of the email world, just like junk mail is in the real world. However, there are ways of blocking spammers with your Hotmail email account.

⊙ Steps

1. Open your Hotmail email account. Click on Options.

2. Read the list of available options. Select Safe and Blocked Senders. Then choose Blocked Senders. A column appears, along with an information box.

3. Choose the information box, and type the email address that you wish to block.

4. Select the box that says Add. The email address will be moved to the column that says Blocked Users.

5. Repeat Steps 3 and 4 until all the email addresses are in your blocked email list.

6. Reverse your decision by opening the Options menu in Hotmail and choosing Block Email Users. This time when the column opens, choose from the Blocked Users side. Highlight the address or addresses you want to unblock. Click on the arrow that says Remove.

❋ Tip

Most other email account providers offer spam-blocking functions, too.

594 | Avoid Email Scams to Prevent Identity Theft

One of the fastest, and sometimes easiest, ways for people to steal your information is through your email. A way to prevent identity theft is to avoid the email scams.

Steps

1 Be cautious of any email asking for your details such as your National Insurance number, email user name or password, birth date or any other type of personal information.

2 If an email is from an unfamiliar email address and you choose to read it, do so with caution. Read it carefully for typos, grammatical errors or poor phrasing. Many identity theft rings include people for whom English is not their first language.

3 Always protect your computer and email passwords. Whenever you make a password, especially for bank accounts, make sure you create a strong password. Usually, this means including letters, numbers and characters.

4 If you think someone has tried to access your email account, contact your email provider. You should immediately change your password. If you have the software, run a virus check on your computer.

5 Do not reply to a suspicious email. Some email providers, such as Hotmail, have a section to report suspicious emails or a phishing scam. Take an active role in preventing identity theft.

6 Never reply to a request for money.

✱ Tip

Never follow links set within emails asking you to change your account information.

595 | Write a Business Email

Writing an effective business email is important in an era when the majority of business communication uses this medium.

Steps

1 Get to the point immediately. Don't use the first few paragraphs for justification and then make the request in the last paragraph. Your readers may have deleted the email after the second paragraph.

2 Don't include humour or personal information. Your email may be forwarded to others.

3 Don't include sensitive information, for example, bank-account numbers, passwords or credit-card numbers. Unless the email is encrypted, it is not secure.

4 Use proper grammar. Avoid common expressions such as "like this", "oh my god", and so on. People judge you by the way you express yourself.

5 Use an email list if your email is going to many recipients, especially if it is your client list. Most people don't want their email address exposed, and you don't want to advertise your client list.

6 Proofread and spell check.

✱ Tip

The way you write business emails should be entirely different from personal emails. Don't get too chummy in your business emails.

Master Common Email Slang   596

Now that you're on the Internet, you'll want to impress people with your email lingo. These common terms will also help you keep your message concise and to the point.

⊚ Steps

1   Familiarise yourself with the following common email terms:

• Newbie: a person who is new to the Internet. This term usually carries the connotation of inexperience and naiveté.

• Netiquette: etiquette practised on the Internet. Netiquette is often dynamic and hard to define, but the netiquette of the specific forum you're using will become apparent after you use the forum for a while.

• Flame: a public berating of one person by another on an Internet forum. Flames are usually provoked and are often the result of the flame victim transgressing a rule of the forum or violating netiquette.

• Spam: unsolicited mass email. Think of it as junk email.

• Sig file: truncated term for signature file, a short message that automatically attaches itself to outgoing email messages. Consult your specific software for information about creating and maintaining sig files.

• Sig quote: a (usually famous) quotation used in a sig file.

2   Familiarise yourself with the following common abbreviations:

• LOL: laughing out loud.

• ROFL: rolling on floor laughing.

• IMO: in my opinion.

• IMHO: in my humble opinion.

• BTW: by the way.

• TTFN: ta ta for now.

• TTYL: talk to you later.

• FAQ: frequently asked questions.

✳ Tip

Familiarise yourself with slang by visiting one of the many web pages that list web slang terms.

Teach Your Child About Internet Safety   597

The World Wide Web is a wonderful tool; with a little bit of education and caution, surfing the Internet can be a great experience for your kids.

⊚ Steps

1   Help your child pick out a screen name or username. Avoid names that include a name and/or an age.

2   Surf the Internet with your child, letting him or her lead your exploration together (if your child is experienced enough).

3   Visit some sites for children together.

✳ Tips

You can choose an online service that has parental control features, or buy blocking software to design your own control system.

Monitor your child when he or she is online.

4   Teach your child that other people are using the Internet just as you are, and explain that it can be hard to tell whether or not they're telling the truth about themselves.

5   Discuss with your child the potentially harmful topics that could show up on the Internet, such as violence, hate material and pornography.

6   Warn your child not to give out personal information over the Internet, send pictures of himself or herself, or meet someone in person without your permission.

7   Warn your child not to join any mailing lists without your permission.

8   Encourage your child not to visit sites or respond to messages that seem strange or scary.

9   Encourage your child to speak to you or a teacher whenever he or she encounters anything that makes him or her uncomfortable.

If your child receives offensive material over the Internet, save it and contact your Internet service provider and the police immediately.

598 | Protect Your Data from Attack While Online

If file-sharing is enabled on your computer, your hard disk is available to anyone on your network. These instructions explain how to disable file sharing.

⊙ Steps

Windows 95/98

1   Click Start.

2   Click Settings.

3   Click Control Panel.

4   Double-click Network.

5   Click the Configuration tab.

6   Click the File and Print Sharing button.

7   Make sure the box to the left of "I want to be able to give others access to my files" is blank.

8   Click OK twice.

Mac Operating System

1   Select Control Panels from under the Apple menu.

2   Select the Sharing Setup or File Sharing control panel.

3   Look for a Start button and "File sharing is off" in the Status window. If you see a Stop button, proceed to the next step. If you see a Start button, file sharing is already off.

4   Click Stop.

5   Type 10 in the box under "How many minutes until file sharing is disabled?"

6   Click OK.

7   Close the window when the control panel indicates that file sharing is off.

 ✳ Tip

If you want to share files with others on a local network and still be safe, then you can set access privileges to only share files with specified users.

Use RoboForm to Remember Your Passwords `599`

RoboForm can remember your passwords and can log you into a protected Internet site with just one click.

⊙ Steps

1   Download RoboForm free at www.roboform.com. Follow the on-screen directions to install. The finished installation will include the RoboForm toolbar, which you can have at the top or bottom of your browser window. You can also choose not to have the toolbar display by editing your Toolbar selections.

2   Go to a username and password-protected website. Enter your username and password and click to enter the secured area. RoboForm will prompt you to save the settings as a passcode. Click the RoboForm Save option, and the URL, username and password will be saved.

3   To return to a site, click on the Logins button on the RoboForm toolbar and then on the site you want to visit. The website will launch, and your username and password will fill in automatically.

✴ Tips

Check your forms to make sure that all the right information is in the right places.

Your information is stored on your computer, not online.

⚠ Warning

Never give out your passwords.

Hide an IP Address `600`

With Internet privacy becoming a thing of the past, hiding the IP (Internet protocol) address is a good way to make sure that Internet sites are not tracking your activities.

⊙ Steps

1   Decide if the need for hiding the IP address is worth a fee. Many software options allow a user to hide their IP address by installing software that masks the native IP address. These applications are thorough but there are free options available.

2   Try out the pay software before buying it. Often software downloads allow the user a trial period to use and evaluate its effectiveness. Understand that free trial-period programs sometimes have limited capabilities, though, to encourage you to buy the full product.

3   Locate a free web-proxy service. While not as secure as some options, free proxy can provide a passable level of anonymity on the Internet. Be aware that most company web filters block access to most proxy servers on the Internet.

4   Download and install the free software that hides an IP address. These software platforms are not as powerful as the pay options but offer a serviceable option. Some of the downloads come with adware and spyware that compromise a computer user's privacy, so using shareware can be counterproductive to your Internet privacy.

⚠ Warning

Not all websites will accept visitors with unclear or unintelligible IP addresses. You may have to use a traditional method of access to use some websites.

601 Remove Spyware from Your Computer

Are you having trouble with your computer? Do you think the issue might be caused by a virus? This tutorial will make quick work of your computer's problems!

⊙ Steps

1 Understand that keeping current with the latest computer security programs is vital for your computer's health.

2 Go to www.download.com, search for Malware Bytes and download it.

3 Install and run the program according to the onscreen instructions.

4 Alternatively, try Spybot Search and Destroy. Also, Google search the latest trends with security, and your problems will be easier to handle in the future.

✳ Tips

Installing reputable anti-virus programs, personal firewall programs and pop-up blocker programs can help to avoid having spyware installed on a computer.

Disabling third-party cookies can also help stop spyware. Websites use cookies stored on a computer to track where a user has been.

602 Protect Against Screamers

A screamer starts out as a seemingly innocuous image or video. Towards the end, a scary image pops out and screams at the viewer.

⊙ Steps

1 Beware of any email that tells you to stare intently at an image on the screen, or to watch a video very closely. They may also prompt you during the video to "look closer".

2 Protect yourself if you suspect an image you're viewing might be a screamer by sitting back a little from your computer screen, and not giving it your undivided attention. This might lessen the jolt just a little if it does turn out to be a screamer.

3 Be wary of an email that tells you to turn your computer's speakers up before viewing the image.

4 Use caution if you're watching a video that seems harmless enough, but suddenly the audio drops so low that you're tempted turn up your speakers.

✳ Tip

Never forward an email with a link to a screamer. You might think they're harmless fun, but they can be a real shock to some people.

603 Determine if You Really Are on Your Bank's Website

While spoofed emails are rarely a problem with local banks, national banks have to deal with deflecting phishers targeting their customers.

⊙ Steps

1 Do not use links from emails, but type in your bank's address instead.

⚠ Warnings

Never give out personal information over email.

2 Sign in (if you use Internet Explorer) and look for a closed lock on the bottom right of your screen.

3 Double-click on the lock icon to bring up a security certificate. The name on the certificate should be your bank's.

4 Call your bank to ask for help if you are still concerned.

Never use email links to get to important websites.

Don't rely on reading the link or address bar. There are ways to change these displays to fool you and your computer.

Set Language Preferences in Google   604

You can use Google search to find results in a particular language or even to translate a whole web page. The default language is English.

⊙ Steps

1 Go to the Google search homepage, www.google.com.

2 Click on the Advanced Search link beside the search box. Specify the language of your choice in the Language section. This is recommended if it is a one-off search in that language. If you need to make the language selection permanent, follow Steps 3 and 4 below.

3 Click on the Preferences link beside the search box. Select from the list of languages given in the Search Language section and save the preferences. This is recommended if you frequently search for pages in a particular language.

4 Set Google to display its tips and messages in any language. This can be done by clicking on the Preferences link and selecting an Interface Language from the dropdown menu.

✳ Tip

Copy a web address and paste it into the "Translate a Web Page" field to read foreign language pages in English.

Find a Definition Using Google   605

Google search offers you the function of finding definitions for a keyword from online sources. Here's how to do it.

⊙ Steps

1 Go to the Google search homepage, www.google.com.

2 Enter the word "define" followed by a space and the keyword that you want defined. This will find the pages where Google could source the definitions.

3 Alternatively, you can enter the word define followed by a colon, followed by the keyword without any spaces. This will display a list of definitions from multiple online sources.

✳ Tip

Simply typing the word and "definition" will yield the same results, as Google automatically reformats the search term.

606 | Use Google Maps

Are you trying to find directions to a certain location? Are you just bored and want to learn something knew? Google Maps can be a fun and useful tool.

⊙ Steps

1 Go to Google's home page and click on the Maps option.

2 You will be redirected to Google Maps. Here you will be allowed to search like a normal search engine.

3 If you are looking for directions to a specific place, click the Get Directions link. You will be allowed to type in two addresses, one for point A (where you are coming from), and one for point B (where you are going).

4 After searching or typing in an address, the map will change and you"ll be able to see what you're looking for. Right click once on the map for different options, or double right click to zoom out. You can also double left click to zoom in.

5 The map you are looking at is the Street Map. This image shows you all the street information as any other map would. Towards the top right, click on Satellite. You will see a satellite image of the world and you will be zoomed in to the place you have searched for.

6 The Terrain option shows you the landscape around the place you are viewing. Depending on how far you are zoomed in or out, you may or may not see the individual cities or streets. Towards the left of the map there is a scroll that increases or decreases the zoom.

7 You can also create Personalised Maps, create locations and draw lines to your favourite spots.

✳ **Tips**

Try looking for your house with your car outside.

Google maps is free.

607 | Use America Online Keywords

AOL keywords act as shortcuts to associated content areas within AOL. Type in a keyword to go to the appropriate area.

⊙ Steps

1 Sign on to AOL.

2 Type in a keyword in the address bar on the AOL taskbar.

3 Click on Go to the right of the bar.

4 If you don't know what word to type in, click on Keyword to the right of the address bar, then click on Keyword List.

5 Click on the List Most Popular tab, the List Alphabetically tab or the List By Channel tab.

6 Click on the keyword you want and it will take you to the associated AOL content area.

✳ **Tip**

To find most searched keywords check out AOL Hot Searches for daily top searched keywords.

Conduct an Advanced Internet Search **608**

To conduct an advanced search on the Internet, use Boolean operators, such as "and" and "or", to make your search as specific as possible.

⊙ Steps

1 Go to a search engine.

2 To find documents containing an exact phrase, type the phrase, surrounded by quotation marks, into the search field.

3 To find documents containing a pair of words, but not necessarily together, type the words separated by the word AND in all caps. For example, typing "fish AND fingers" (without the quotation marks) will return pages that contain "fish", "fingers" and "fish fingers".

4 To find documents containing either one word or the other, type the words separated by the word OR in all caps. For example, typing "fish OR fingers" (without the quotation marks) will return documents that contain "fish" or "fingers" or both.

5 To exclude a word from your search, type the word you wish to exclude into the search field, preceded by the word NOT in all caps. For example, typing "fish NOT salmon" (without the quotation marks) will return only documents that do contain the word "fish" and do not contain the word "salmon".

6 To find documents that contain two words separated by 10 to 25 words, type the two words separated by the word NEAR in all caps, into the search field. If your search expression is lengthy or complicated, use parentheses to separate the different parts. For example, typing "fish OR fingers NOT (salmon OR trout)" will get you entries that have the words "fish" or "fingers" or both, but do not have the words "salmon" or "trout".

✳ Tips

Check the directions for the search engine you're using. Some require very specific syntax.

Some search engines allow the following symbolic substitutions for Boolean words: & for AND, | for OR, ! for NOT, and ~ for NEAR. But not all searches allow this, so if your query comes up blank, try using words instead.

Some search engines don't support the Boolean words "NEAR" or "NOT".

Use the Parental Controls on Internet Explorer **609**

Internet Explorer has parental controls that you can adjust according to a child's age and your own values.

⊙ Steps

1 Go to Internet Explorer on your computer. Click on Tools from the toolbar in the upper right-hand corner of the browser.

2 Select the Content tab.

3 Find the Content Advisor heading and click on the button labelled Enable.

4 Choose a category from the list. This list will present you with a variety of content categories that you may not want your children to see, such as sites depicting drug or alcohol use, violent images, nudity or bad language.

✳ Tip

If you need further assistance with how to use the parental controls on Internet Explorer, head to its extensive FAQs page.

⚠ Warning

These instructions are meant to be used with Internet Explorer 7.0. Other versions of Internet Explorer may not be compatible with these steps.

5   Click on the category you want to control. Then use your mouse to move the slider below the list to set the degree of restriction you want on that type of site. The degree of restriction can range from no restriction at all to the complete blocking of those sorts of sites.

6   Click OK.

7   Set a password. You will be prompted to do so at this point. Setting a password will ensure that no one but you is able to adjust the parental control settings.

610 Bookmark a Web Page

Have you ever gone to a site and liked it so much you wanted to keep going back? You can bookmark it so next time all you have to do is choose it from a menu.

⊙ **Steps**

1   Find a web page you want to save.

2   While you're viewing it, open the Bookmarks menu if you're using Netscape Navigator, or the Favourites menu if you're using Internet Explorer.

3   Click Add Bookmarks in Netscape Navigator, or Add to Favourites in Internet Explorer.

✱ Tips

You can create folders for different categories and put your favourites in them so the list doesn't get too long.

You can rename or delete your favourites at any time.

611 Go Back to a Recently Viewed Web Page

Want to go back to a web page you visited, but you don't remember the address? Here are a few ways of returning to recently viewed pages.

⊙ **Steps**

1   Click the Back button on your browser. This takes you back to the most recently viewed page. You can click Back again to go back further. Click Forward to go through the pages in the same order you viewed them.

2   In Internet Explorer 5, you can use the Go To command in the View menu to display a list of the pages you've visited. Click a page to go to it. In Netscape Navigator, use the Go menu instead.

3   Click the down arrow to the right of the address in your browser. The menu that appears contains web pages for which you've actually typed in the address (you haven't followed a link or bookmark to get there). Click on the address of the site you want to go back to from the menu that comes down.

4   Use the History feature. This shows all the pages you've visited during the past day, week and month. Click History on the toolbar. In the list that appears on the left of your browser, either click on a site in the list or click a folder (such as Two Weeks Ago) to see the sites listed there.

✱ Tip

To close History, click X in the the corner.

⚠ Warning

Browsers automatically suggest the completed URL as you begin to type in a website name. Deleting web pages from your history temporarily eliminates this function.

Delete Your Browser's History

612

Want to make sure nobody can snoop and see where you've been on the Internet? Sometimes being able to erase browser history can come in handy, especially on shared computers.

Steps

1 Click Start on the desktop.

2 Go to Settings.

3 Click Control Panel.

4 Double-click Internet Options.

5 Make sure the General tab is selected.

6 Click Clear History in the History box.

7 Click OK when it asks if you want to delete all the items in your history folder.

8 Click OK at the bottom of the General box to exit.

❋ Tip

On a Mac, look for command names like Preferences, Internet Options or Settings, and options like Clear or Delete History.

Change Your Browser's Home Page

613

You can have your browser start up with any page you want, be it a search engine or your home page.

Steps

Internet Explorer 5.0

1 Open the Tools menu and choose Internet Options.

2 Make sure the General tab is selected.

3 Click Use Current in the Home Page area if you're viewing the web page you want to select.

4 Type in the URL of the web page you want if you aren't viewing it.

5 Click OK.

Netscape Navigator

1 Open the Options menu and choose General Preferences.

2 Make sure the Appearance tab is selected.

3 Type in the address of the web page you want in the Startup box.

4 Click OK.

❋ Tip

When choosing a home page, it is a good idea to select a page that does not contain many pictures and advertisements. Plain and simple pages load much quicker and are easier to navigate.

614 Enable Cookies

When you visit a website, the server may place a cookie on your hard drive. These very small files contain information unique to you, which the web server will "read" to recognise you when you revisit the site.

⊙ Steps

Internet Explorer 6.0

1 Click Internet Options on the Tools menu.

2 Select the Privacy tab.

3 Make sure the privacy level is no higher than Medium High.

4 Click the OK button.

FireFox 1.5

1 Select Options on the Tools menu.

2 Click on the Cookies tab.

3 Make sure the box Allow Sites to Accept Cookies is checked.

4 Click OK.

Netscape Versions 6 and 7.1

1 Select Preferences on the Edit menu.

2 Click the Privacy and Security tab. Then click Cookies.

3 Click on the box to Enable All Cookies.

4 Click OK.

✳ Tips

Periodically delete old cookies from your hard drive. Click Start, select Search, and then click on All Files and Folders. Type in cookie for all or part of the file name, and then click Search. This will show you the location of the cookies on your hard drive.

If you've enabled cookies for certain websites and they are not being saved, you might want to check your computer's firewall and anti-spyware programs. Depending on these software settings, the cookies might be removed before being stored on your computer, or they may only be stored until you close the web browser. Refer to your software manual for detailed instructions.

615 Create a Podcast

A podcast is simply a series of audio files that you make available for others to hear. It is called a podcast because it is usually broadcast on a daily or weekly basis.

⊙ Steps

1 Choose a topic for your podcast.

2 Decide on the frequency you would like to publish your podcast. A news-based podcast is more effective when published daily, while a story-based podcast could be published weekly.

3 Write a script for your podcast. Sometimes it is valuable to write out what you want to say in your podcast. This helps make your podcast sound more professional and eliminate ums and ers and uncomfortable pauses.

4 Record your audio file. Work with audio-recording software that is easy for you to understand and use. Complicated software will do nothing

✳ Tip

Remember that listeners can only hear your voice, not see you, in an audio podcast. Your topic or theme should be something about which you are truly passionate, which listeners will sense in your voice.

⚠ Warnings

Some audio-editing and recording software will require that you install an MP3 encoder to convert or export your audio file to more than waste time as you try to figure out the features. Audacity is an easy and free tool to use.

5 Convert your audio file to MP3 format. Your audio-recording software will probably save your audio recording in its own format, so you will need to Save As or Export to MP3 format so your listeners can open and hear the file.

6 Upload your MP3 file to your web server.

7 Create an article or blog post introducing your podcast and describing what you are discussing in the podcast.

8 Link your MP3 file to your new article or blog post. Your link will look similar to this:
< a href="http://yourwebserver.com/mypodcast.mp3">Click Here to Listen.

MP3 format. Check the user manual to see which converters your audio software requires or recommends.

When uploading your podcast to your web server, be sure to upload it in binary format. In any other format, you will risk corrupting your file.

Always test your MP3 file link to make sure it is pointing to the correct file and that the MP3 opens.

Start a Blog   616

Today on the Internet, anyone can start a successful blog. All blog-related tools have been simplified so that even the most inexperienced Internet users can learn what to do without much of a learning curve.

◉ Steps

1 Decide what you are going to write about. Popular topics include celebrity gossip, sports, website and product reviews, and film reviews, but you can write about anything as long as it interests you.

2 Decide which blog-hosting site you would like to use. Some of the most popular ones are blogger.com and wordpress.com. Both of these sites are very user friendly and make setting up a blog easy.

3 Your blog must provide readers with worthwhile information that is updated frequently. Keeping your blog's content fresh and unique is very important. Try to avoid using a lot of dated information as it becomes antiquated and is no longer relevant. Writing about topics that will be useful for years to come.

4 No blog can be successful without readers. Register your site with Google so it can be searched for information and then added to their search engine. Add your blogs to directories like Technorati so they can be recognised by fellow bloggers. Read other blogs that are about similar topics as yours and comment on the writer's content.

5 If you want to monetise your blog you must learn about SEO (Search Engine Optimisation), SEM (Search Engine Marketing), and link exchanges. It is also a good idea to participate in affiliate marketing programs and advertising as a way to generate revenue.

✳ Tips

Add photos when possible to your blog posts.

Blogging can be a good way to meet people, share your thougts, or even make money.

617 Set Up a PayPal Account

PayPal is a secure way of paying for goods and services over the Internet. Popular websites such as eBay usually offer the buyer the opportunity pay via PayPal.

⊙ Steps

1 Go to PayPal.com and fill in your personal information. Untick the Link Account to Credit Card option.

2 When you've submitted the page, it will provide an option for linking, once again, to your credit card or your bank account. Choose Bank Account. Inside, type in your bank name, account type, account number, and sort code.

3 PayPal will verify your account, and confirm that you are the owner of the account. To do this, it will make two very small deposits into your bank account, which you need to verify.

4 Once verified, Paypal will instantly be connected to your bank account.

✴ Tip

It's never a bad idea to open up a second bank account for Paypal.

618 Make a YouTube Video

Want to get into the world of video podcasting? Have some home videos that you want the world to see? Want to market a product? YouTube is the place.

⊙ Steps

1 Make a video using a digital camera, web cam or mobile phone. You can upload a YouTube video directly from a phone if you set up a Mobile Profile in YouTube. With a high-speed connection, it should generally take a few minutes.

2 Edit your movie. Programs such as Mac's iMovie or Windows' MovieMaker are both good. Add titles, effects and edit it to cut out a bad take, for example.

3 Resize the video so it looks best in YouTube. The site accepts QuickTime .MOV, Windows .AVI, or .MPG files at 340 x 240 resolution. There's a 100 MB size and 10-minute length limit.

4 Create a YouTube account. Click on Upload Videos in the upper right corner of the home page.

5 Create a title, description, tags, category and set language. The more information the better to help people find the video.

✴ Tips

You can also use the Quick Capture feature to upload to YouTube straight from a web cam. No uploading needed.

Once you've got a video ready, upload it to other sites, such as Google Video.

Market the video: post it on blogs, message boards, social-networking sites, and email it.

⚠ Warning

Don't post anything that's copyrighted or libellous. Check the Terms of Service.

Use an iTunes Gift Card 619

There's nothing like the gift of music, and as more and more people download music rather than buying it in shops, iTunes gift cards are the ideal present.

Steps

1 Launch iTunes.

2 On the left side of the iTunes application, click on the option for iTunes Store.

3 Once the store opens, click on Redeem under Quick Links on the right.

4 Enter the code that appears under the scratch-off area (16 characters, alphanumeric). The code usually begins with an X.

5 You will now see your gift-card amount in the upper right part of the iTunes store screen.

6 Browse and find the music you wish to purchase. When checking out, you have the option to enter payment information. This is optional as long as your purchase is less than your balance amount. If you are trying to check out and owe more than your gift-card amount, you will have to enter payment information.

✻ Tip

The card will not add to your account if it has not been activated.

⚠ Warning

Do not try to enter the code twice. Once entered, the code becomes invalid.

Set Up a Facebook Account 620

It takes just a few minutes to set up a Facebook account, after which you could be chatting with old friends from school or college in no time.

Steps

1 Go to Facebook.com and click on Sign Up, which takes you to a web form.

2 Fill out the form that asks for your full name, your current status, email address, a password and your birthday. You'll also have to type in a series of letters and numbers for a security check as well as check a box saying that you understand and agree to the terms of use and privacy policy. Click the Sign up Now! button when you have completed the form.

3 Wait for your confirmation email then click on the link in the email to confirm that you have registered for a Facebook account. You will then be logged into Facebook.

4 When you first set up a Facebook account, you have the opportunity to search your email address book for possible friends and contacts. Type in your email address and password to do a search, or try searching by school or company.

✻ Tip

Make the most of your new Facebook account by uploading a few pictures and filling out your profile.

621 | Make Facebook Private

Identity-theft prevention and protecting your privacy are very important online. To set your Facebook profile to private, follow the simple steps below.

⊙ Steps

1 Log in to your Facebook account at www.facebook.com.

2 Click Settings near the upper right-hand corner of your profile page.

3 On the next page, click Manage to the right of Privacy, and then click Profile.

4 Under the Basic tab, select Only Friends next to each option, and click the Save Changes button. Under the Contact Information tab, also select Only Friends next to each option, and save the changes. This will ensure that only the friends you approve can view your profile information.

5 Click on the Privacy link again, and proceed as directed to change your settings related to people searching for you, what gets posted about you on Facebook, and what information is disclosed about you when you use the Applications feature.

✱ Tip

Facebook may seem overwhelming, but it is relatively simple and easy to get to know.

⚠ Warning

Internet stalking is as illegal as physical stalking. Police can trace IP addresses to the computer that sends the menacing messages.

622 | Create an Event on Facebook

From private parties to organised trips over school holidays, you can organise and publicise any event using Facebook.

⊙ Steps

1 Log in to your Facebook account.

2 Select My Events from the navigation menu. You will be taken to a page with all the events you are currently planning to attend.

3 Hit the Create Event button.

4 Fill in all the details about your event, including the time and place. You can always edit these later, but try to get as much detail in as you can initially.

5 Choose the level of access to your event. If the event is open, anyone can see the details and add himself or herself to the guest list. If the event is closed, only the time and description is shown to uninvited guests. Facebook users can request to be added to the guest list for complete event info. A secret event will not appear in search results and will only be seen by those people you invite.

6 Click Create Event to complete your event details.

7 Upload a photo that represents the event. Use the Browse feature to find a photo on your hard drive to upload.

8 Invite guests. Select your friends on Facebook and other users to attend your event. You can even send emails to people not on Facebook.

✱ Tips

Import your address book from your free email provider or mail software to easily send invites to everyone you know.

Go to My Events at any time to see the status of your party. Check on who has replied and who isn't attending.

Facebook is a great way to spread the word about a worthy cause. Create a group for your special cause and have your group host a fundraising event.

⚠ Warning

If you are creating an open event, do not put your home address as the location. With open events, anyone can see the details, including location of the event. Personal data like phone numbers and addresses should be kept private.

Use Twitter `623`

Twitter is a social-networking service that provides you with an opportunity to send and read short posts. Each "tweet" is limited to 140 characters and usually answers the question, "What are you doing?"

⊙ Steps

1 Set up a free Twitter account. You can either set up one account for your personal use or you can create one account for yourself, under your own name, and another account for your business or organisation. Businesses can even create an account for each of their employees with different names, but a common theme.

2 Begin building your network. Start by following people that share common interests or affiliations. You can find them by using TweetScan to search for recent tweets. If you have a list of contacts in your email client or on other social networks, you can scan for them on Twitter. You might also contact them directly to let them know that you're now on Twitter. You can also add a link to your Twitter profile with your email so people know they can follow you there. If a person decides to follow you, follow them back. This is common courtesy and a great way to build your network.

3 Start tweeting. Introduce yourself with an initial tweet that explains your purpose for being on Twitter. Tweet regularly, but don't over-tweet. If you post too often, followers might begin to think your posts are annoying and stop following you. Try to post at least one or two tweets per day, but no more than five.

✳ Tips

You don't need to log in to Twitter to use their service. You can send and receive updates using your mobile phone, RSS feeds or by email.

Most social networks provide an application that will post your updates automatically on Twitter. Facebook has an application called Twitterific.

Create a Profile on MySpace `624`

As a worldwide social-networking website, MySpace allows you to create a profile and link up with your friends online.

⊙ Steps

1 Head to the MySpace home page and click Sign Up!

2 Fill in your email address, name and password. Be sure to choose a password that is easy for you to remember, but not so easy that others can figure it out.

3 Choose the language and country of your choice by picking from the dropdown list. MySpace has sites focused towards several countries.

4 Upload a personal photo. This photo will be your initial image on your profile. You may choose to upload a photo later by selecting Skip for Now.

5 Share your new profile. Invite your friends to create a profile on MySpace by entering their email addresses separated by a comma. You can also Skip for Now to complete your registration without inviting your friends.

6 Personalise your profile by clicking on Edit Profile. From a short bio in the About Me section to your favourite books and films, fill in the appropriate boxes with your interests.

✳ Tip

You must verify your email address after you complete registration to unlock the full potential of your profile. If you don't receive the initial verification email, click on the link under Verify Your Email Address to resend it.

⚠ Warning

Unless the birthday you enter makes you under 13, your profile will be public initially. To change your privacy settings click on Account Settings and Change Settings for privacy.

7   Add more photos. Click on Add/Edit Photos to upload additional photos. Photos must be under 600k in a GIF or JPG format.

8   Customise your profile further by adding a video. Click on Add/Change Videos to choose a video for your page. You can upload your own or select from a public video.

9   Personalise your URL by picking your MySpace Name/URL. This gives your MySpace profile a URL that can easily be remembered and typed into the address bar.

625 | Succeed Selling on eBay

Whether you have on online shop or just want to sell a few personal items that aren't of value to you any more, selling on eBay can be the key to a lucrative income or some extra cash.

⊙ Steps

1   Picture it. People like to see the items they are interested in buying. Investing in quality photographs to illustrate your products will get you more bids and higher selling prices.

2   Do your homework. Before listing a certain item, browse eBay to learn the prices of similar items you plan on listing. You can also pick up on key details about the product that are important to include when landing a sale.

3   Know shipping costs. The best method and type of shipping depends on the item you are selling. The best sellers know the ideal way to ship each item, and they have accurate shipping rates posted within the item's description.

4   Craft the content of your listing. Research to learn about writing listings that include the power of search-engine keywords. Take the time to create a well-written ad that will answer all important questions about the product while marketing it at the same time.

5   Accept a variety of payment options. The more choices potential buyers have when it comes to purchasing your item, the higher the number of bidders you will see.

6   Focus on positive feedback. Feedback is an important aspect of eBay. It tells others you are a reliable buyer and seller, makes you more attractive to do business with, and inclines others to bid higher for the sake of that trust.

7   Act professionally. Treat customers just as you would if you were running a traditional business and facing customers in person.

✱ Tips

Research thoroughly before you jump into it.

Make sure you can sell the item you have in mind.

Have a PayPal account for faster and more secure payments

Buy a Car on eBay Motors

Using eBay Motors is a quick and convenient way to buy your next car. You can search for the type of car you want from the comfort of your own home, without having to spend long hours trekking through used car dealers.

⊙ Steps

1   Visit eBay and sign in.

2   Click on eBay Motors.

3   Use the dropdown menus to locate the kind of car you want. You can search by make, model or both.

4   Click Search when you have selected the make and model you require.

5   View the list of cars that match your search specifications.

6   Select a car that interests you by clicking on it.

7   Read the description of the car, look at the pictures and review the shipping and payment policy of the seller.

8   Click on the Place Bid button.

9   Enter your bid amount. If you are the first bidder, you must enter at least the minimum bid required by the seller. If there are already other bids, you must bid higher than the highest bid already in place.

10 Click Continue.

11 Inspect your bid for accuracy to make sure you've entered all the right information. If everything is in order, click Confirm Bid.

12 Sit back and wait to see if you win. Other bidders may bid higher than you on this car. If this happens, you will have to make a higher bid in order to win. eBay will inform you via email when you have been outbid on any item.

13 Bask in the winning glow. If you win the car, eBay will send you an email letting you know. At that point, you should make payment according to the seller's instructions in the listing.

14 Pick up your car or arrange with the seller to have it shipped to you. The seller will be contacting you via email after you win the auction, so you can make shipping arrangements at that time.

✱ Tip

For additional information about buying or selling a car on eBay Motors, visit the Help page at eBay.

⚠ Warning

Help eBay to help you. Keep your login information secure and change it often. This helps reduce the chance of hackers or identity thieves accessing the personal information you store on eBay.

627 Contribute to Wikipedia

Wikipedia is the most democratic website of the information age, allowing all members of the online community to contribute. Thousands of people from around the globe are constantly adding information on thousands of subjects. Here's how.

Create an Account

- Go to the Wikipedia home page and choose your language.

- Select Sign In/Create Account.

- Create a username and password.

- Enter any other information requested by Wikipedia. Click Create Account.

- You will receive a confirmation email from Wikipedia. Read the email, then click on the link to confirm your login information.

- Review the information on the Wikipedia page. It should say that you have suc- cessfully confirmed your login information and created your Wikipedia account.

- Edit your preferences. This personalises your experience at Wikipedia and ensures your security.

Learn About Wikipedia

- Click Editing Wikipedia and Creating Pages – How To. Then click Start a New Page.

- Click Develop the Article for detailed information on the stages an article goes through. Follow the Editing Help link to get information on how to format your article.

- Determine if your idea is suitable for Wikipedia. Follow the link on the Article Development page to Belong in Wikipedia to understand Wikipedia's guidelines.

- Research current Wikipedia content for related material.

- Check out the editing tutorial on Wikipedia for information on how to edit and submit an article.

- Experiment in the Sandbox before you submit your first article.

Plan for Success

- Read the guidelines for choosing a page name. From the Wikipedia Main Page click Help, followed by Editing Wikipedia. Choose Name a Page under the Creating Pages – How To section.

- Learn to translate articles. Select Help on the Main Page, and then click on Editing Wikipedia. Choose Translate Articles under the Article Maintenance – How To heading.

- Learn to make links and cite references. Click Help then Links and References.

- Follow the guidelines to add images.

- Monitor changes for enhancement and vandalism. Select Help, then Keeping Track of Changes, followed by Recent Changes.

- Learn to revert a page to undo vandalism.

Submit an Article

- Go to the Help page, and then click Editing Wikipedia. Under Creating Pages – How To, click Start a New Page. Select Starting a Page From a Link, or After a Search from the Contents box.

- Select Starting a Page Through the URL from the Contents box for an alternative method of starting a page. You can also choose Creating an Empty Page from the Contents box or Creating Using a Redirect to a Sub or Supra Topic Page from the Contents box.

- Write and submit an article or article stub.

- When adding content or comments to Wikipedia pages, never include your con- tact information, such as phone numbers or email addresses.

reference

Correct an Existing Article in Wikipedia 628

As well as allowing you to contribute articles, Wikipedia also lets you edit and make corrections to existing articles.

⊙ Steps

1 Go to the Wikipedia home page.

2 Write the name of the subject in the search box and click on Go or press Enter.

3 Click on Edit This Page or Edit on each section of the page. This will take you to the Edit Page.

4 Make the necessary corrections in the edit page using the Wikipedia Manual of Style.

5 Sign your corrections and timestamp them. For example, use four tildes "~" to timestamp any edit.

6 Provide at least one reason for making the correction in the Edit Summary box.

7 See changes in the article by clicking the Show Preview button.

8 Save the page and submit to Wikipedia for approval.

✳ Tip

Be precise in making the corrections. You may receive feedback from the Talk page immediately from other users.

⚠ Warning

Do not make corrections if you are uncertain. You should have valid and genuine reason for making any correction.

Write an eHow Article 629

Do you know how to do something that other people don't? Want to teach them how to do it but don't know how? Follow these steps to create a useful eHow article.

⊙ Steps

1 Pick a topic. Be familiar with the topic because you want to share what you know. When coming up with the topic, think about your hobbies and interests; your best articles will come from there.

2 Register for an eHow account. Pick a username and build your profile so that others can get to know you and your background. It's always reassuring to know that the person you're getting How To info from has a personal interest in the topic, so remember to include your hobbies.

3 Click on the Write an Article tab at the top of your profile. This will take you to the eHow article template form to enter your article. It is organised with fields for a title, introduction, ingredients needed, steps-by-step directions, tips and warnings, and website resources.

4 Create and upload a video. Adding a video is optional, but you might find that visual directions are better at getting messages across than written words. Nevertheless, a video must accompany text, just in case the clip fails to play.

5 Add content. Starting with the title, try to use words that people will search for on the Internet. Those words will make it easier for people to find your article.

✳ Tips

Your eHow articles are available for you to edit, even after they have been published.

Remember to use the spell check. This is an educational site, so don't teach people to write poorly.

⚠ Warning

Profanity, indecent images and inappropriate content will be short-lived on the site. It's just not worth it to try.

6   The introduction should consist of information that states what people will get out of the article. This is a good place to include background information about the topic that just won't fit in the steps.

7   Include What You'll Need when necessary so that readers have a list of the materials needed to get through the steps.

8   Add the steps. They should be written in layman's terms so that anyone can follow them. Keep it simple – don't use 30 words when 10 will do, and avoid repeating yourself. Consider that you're contributing to a professional reference work and write accordingly.

9   Post pictures for visual aids. You can upload a primary image at the top of the article and include photos to go with each step. Remember, you must own the photo or have permission if it's a copyrighted photo to post it online. Click on the Add an Image button to upload.

10 Add any tips and warnings that will help people get through the step-by-step process. Then end each article with website links that can provide additional information or resources about the topic.

11 Always use spell check! You are the expert and experts don't make mistakes. Articles should be well-written and free of spelling, grammar and punctuation errors.

12 Categorise the article. Keep articles organised and searchable by filing the article under the best category options.

13 Save and preview the article when it's ready. If everything looks right, hit the Publish button and your article will automatically post on eHow.

630 Find Free Web Space

Every web page needs a home, and finding free web space for your home page is very easy.

⊙ Steps

1   Check with your Internet service provider (ISP). Most ISPs offer 2 to 10 MB of web space with your account.

2   Visit websites that offer directory listings of free web space. These sites typically allow you to select the options you need and display a list of providers meeting those needs.

3   Determine the amount of space you need. In Internet Explorer, find the file for one of the pages on your website; right-click on the file with your mouse and select Properties. Multiply this number by the number of web pages you plan to add.

4   Read the terms and conditions before agreeing to use its site. Some providers require banners or other ads on users' web pages.

5   Print out the instructions for uploading your site to the provider's site. Read the FAQ (frequently asked questions) or send an email message to technical support if you have any questions.

6   Upload the site following the printed instructions.

7   Type the address you were assigned into your web browser to view your uploaded web pages.

✳ Tips

You can also find free space by typing "free web space" into any search engine.

Some web providers offer "domain hosting", which means you get your own web domain name at a nominal charge.

Some free providers host personal pages, while others are geared towards business pages.

Choose a Web-Design Application 631

There are many web-design applications available to create web pages. In some of them, you don't have to know HTML to create a page.

⊙ **Steps**

1   Evaluate your design style. Visual designers may prefer WYSIWYG (What You See Is What You Get) applications, where you don't need to know HTML, while technical designers like standard text editors and others combine visual with technical.

2   Type "web authoring" or "web design tools" into a search engine. The search engine will display listings of several sites that offer retail, evaluation, shareware and freeware design applications.

3   Go to a shareware site to find a variety of web-design programs free to try (shareware) or free to use (freeware).

4   Retail sites like Adobe sometimes offer trial versions of their programs that you can download, so you can try them out before you make a decision. The trial versions usually work for a limited time or only include limited features.

5   Download a trial, shareware or freeware application and install it on your hard drive.

6   Use the application's tutorials and help files to familiarise yourself with how the program works. For standard text editors, use an HTML reference guide.

7   Open an existing page in the new program to see what the web page looks like in the program.

8   Create a sample website in your application. Open the new page in your browser to view it.

✱ Tip

The easiest way to familiarise yourself with a program is to look at existing web pages using the program. Are they easy to read? Are the tags well placed?

Format Web Text 632

If you remember only one thing about designing a web site, it should be this: content is king. Text that is written and formatted well is your most valuable asset.

⊙ **Steps**

1   Use the most common screen size. Not all monitors and screen resolutions are the same, so to ensure that your visitors can see all your text, either use the smallest common fixed width (750 pixel width is good, but a 600 pixel width is safer), or use 75–90 per cent width if possible. This leaves room along the sides, no matter how wide or narrow your visitor's screen is. The worst thing you can do is make your visitor scroll sideways!

2   Justify the screen alignment. Justify only the left side for clean, professional-looking text.

✱ Tip

Subtlety and legibility are always best.

3 Only use one font face for text consistency. If you feel that you absolutely must have two, use one for subtitles and one for regular text. Verdana
(a sans-serif font) and Georgia (a serif font) were created especially for
on-screen viewing. (Serifs are those little "ticks" or "feet" at the ends of
letters. Sans-serif fonts are generally easier to read on a monitor.) Other
monitor-friendly sans-serif fonts are Arial, Tahoma, Trebuchet MS, and
for a more jovial feel, Comic Sans MS. All have good italic and bold
versions, too.

4 Use moderate font sizes. Use a slightly larger size for subtitles, and possibly a larger size for your page title. The most common text size is 10 or
12 pt (point), depending on the initial size of the font. (i.e. Arial is much
narrower than Verdana). You could then make your subtitles 14 pt, and
perhaps your main title 18 pt. Experiment and see what looks good, but
not overbearing.

5 Use subtle colours. Black (or very dark) text on a white (or very light)
background is best. A subtle background is fine, but an odd combination
like dark green text on a pink background will send your visitors to the
eye doctor. Keep your colours simple to avoid eyestrain and frustration.

6 Go easy on the extra effects. Bold, italics and underline are the most
common formatting effects that will help make parts of your text stand
out. Most people consider them interchangeable, but they should not be
used on the same page if you can help it, and never on the same word.
One effect alone is enough to get your reader's attention. Try not to type
anything in all caps, unless you have no other choice. Just like in an
email, if your message is written in all caps, it looks like you're shouting
at your reader.

633 Add a Table to a Web Page with FrontPage

Use tables to organise data or to anchor components on a page
(using a table is one way to regulate spacing between objects).
This tutorial uses Microsoft FrontPage 2000.

⊙ **Steps**

1 Start the Front Page program and open an existing web.

2 Open the page to be edited and position the cursor where the table will
be placed.

3 Choose Insert Table from the Table menu.

4 Set the table properties (number of rows and columns, padding and so
on) using the Insert Table dialogue box and click OK.

5 Add background colours and make other changes to the table properties
by placing the cursor in the table and choosing Table Properties from the
Table menu.

6 Save the page when finished.

7 Preview the page in a web browser by choosing Preview in Browser from
the File menu. From the dialogue box, choose which browser to use and
what settings.

✳ **Tips**

Cell padding allows you to put
space between the border of the
cell and the content.

Use the Draw Table command to
draw your table by dragging from
corner to corner to make the outline, then dragging to draw in
rows and columns.

Add the Date and Time to a Web Page 634

Once you've mastered HTML and are ready to tackle the basics of JavaScript, adding this small code to your web page allows users to see the date and time!

⊙Steps

1   Learn HTML. Because HTML is the key to learning JavaScript, it is essential that you have the basics down.

2   Learn JavaScript. Most well-functioning date/time codes are written in JavaScript.

3   Visit sites that have the date and time on their page. You can select View Source from the View menu to look at the source code for the clock.

4   Go to websites that offer free scripts, such as HotStyle or Webmonkey. These sites offer step-by-step directions for using free scripts, as well as links to other free script sites.

5   Copy and paste the script to your web page. Test it in your browser before uploading to your web page.

✱ Tip

If you use a free script, add a courtesy button or reference to the provider on your page.

⚠ Warnings

You may need to get permission before using JavaScript from another website.

Not all browsers support scripts. Be sure to follow directions for providing alternatives to scripts on your web page.

Add a Decorative Border to a Web Page 635

Use a side border background to create contrast on your web page. The side border is a colour or pattern, while the rest of the page is white for easy readability.

⊙Steps

1   Open Paint Shop Pro. Click on the File menu and select New.

2   Set the image dimensions at 100 pixels high, 100 pixels wide, with a white background and 16.7 million colours for the image type.

3   Click on the Fill tool.

4   Click on the Foreground box. Choose the foreground colour and click OK.

5   Choose Solid Colour from the fill style on the Control toolbar. Set the Match Mode for RGB, make the tolerance 20 per cent and make the opacity 100 per cent.

6   Click on the image to fill it with the colour. Select Undo from the Edit menu and make changes if you aren't happy with it.

7   Select copy from the Edit menu to copy the filled image.

8   Click on the File menu and select New. Set the new image's dimensions at 100 pixels high, 1,000 pixels wide, with a white background and 16.7 million colours for the image type.

9   Click on the Edit menu and select Paste. Choose Paste as New Selection.

10   Use the cursor to move the image to the far left, aligning it with the top and edge of the blank image. Make sure no white space shows.

11   Choose Save As from the File menu and save the image.

✱ Tips

Like all backgrounds, a bordered background is simply an image tiling down the page. If there is white space anywhere but on the right side of the image, it will appear as spaces on the page.

You can make the coloured border larger by increasing the size of the first image.

636 Speed Up Download Time on a Web Page

Fast web pages are the key to keeping visitors interested. There are many ways to optimise a site for fast download.

⊙ Steps

1 Begin at the root of your page: keep the background graphic simple or use a colour for the background instead of a graphic.

2 Keep images small and use the HEIGHT and WIDTH hypertext tags to specify size. Visit a website, such as GifCruncher, that will automatically reduce your GIF pictures without sacrificing quality.

3 Always use the HEIGHT and WIIDTH tags for an image, even if you've already resized it in a paint program. Specifying the height and width allows the browser to finish the rest of the page while loading the image.

4 Reduce the number of images used in general. The best web pages are uncluttered, easy to read and fast.

5 Use the HR tag to insert a horizontal line instead of using a graphic line, which takes up space.

6 Create several small tables instead of one large table on the web page. Each table has to load separately before the viewer can see the contents – with smaller tables, the viewer will see content loading faster.

7 Limit the number of advertisement banners on a web page. Each advertisement banner must call up information from another site; if that site is slow, so is your page.

8 Keep the page short and simple. Create other pages for information that doesn't belong on the welcome page.

9 Use the same background, fonts and, if possible, images throughout your website. Once an image has been loaded, it usually remains in the viewer's cache file and does not have to be reloaded when a viewer visits another page with the same image.

10 Keep special effects, animations, scrolling text and other images to a minimum. These eye-catching effects can bog down a page.

✳ Tip

Try to keep each page below 25K, including graphics and special effects.

⚠ Warning

Do not save bandwidth by linking to an image on another website. Download the image to the hard drive and insert a link to the other website.

Protect Against Credit-Card Fraud 637

Keep your cards in a safe place and follow these steps to
protect against credit-card fraud.

⊙Steps

1 Memorise any pin numbers you obtain with your credit cards and
destroy letters containing pin numbers. Choose pin numbers you
can remember, but don't choose numbers related to your birth date,
National Insurance number or family names.

2 Throw away any credit cards you don't use. They could be stolen and
you wouldn't notice until you received the bill.

3 Sign your credit cards immediately after you receive them. Know when
your new credit cards or bills should arrive in the post. If they don't arrive
when expected, contact your card company.

4 Shield your hand and card when entering credit-card pin numbers into
an ATM. Enter the numbers quickly with multiple fingers.

5 Check the security of online websites before purchasing from them.
Don't give any personal information until you know it is secure.

6 Immediately report any lost or stolen credit cards to your card company.
Keep credit-card numbers and credit-card company telephone numbers
in a secure place.

⚠ Warning

Never give your credit-card
number to an unsolicited caller.

Avoid a False Positive on a Drug Test 638

The likelihood of failing a drug test when you haven't taken
any illegal drugs depends on numerous circumstances, but
the situation must be handled carefully.

⊙Steps

1 Research what medication you take can give you a false positive on your
drug test. Skip those drugs for at least 72 hours before your drug test.

2 Talk with your doctor before taking your drug test. Fill out a detailed
medication list of all over-the-counter and prescription medications to
give to your doctor before your test. This way your doctor should know
that your positive result is because of your medication and not due to
illegal drugs.

3 Watch what you eat. Certain foods can deliver a positive reading on your
drug test. If you eat anything with poppy seeds change your dietary
habits temporarily to get a more favourable test result.

4 Ask for a different type of drug test if you've had multiple false positive
results. Get tested through saliva, hair or sweat samples to see if the
results change in your favour.

5 Discuss your results with your doctor and look into why your test results
came back positive when you don't take drugs. Doctors use gas chro-
matography or mass spectrometry to get in-depth results of your sample
by breaking down its components differently.

✱ Tip

Take a home drug test as
practice to get an idea of what
a real drug test is like. Know
what to expect before getting
the official test done.

⚠ Warning

Don't try to pass off someone
else's drug test sample as your
own, regardless of your motives.

639 | Know Your Rights if Caught Shoplifting

Shoplifting costs retailers millions of pounds every year, but there are many cases of false arrests that violate the rights of the person accused of the crime.

⊙ Steps

Probable Cause for Shoplifting

1 A merchant must provide probable cause for shoplifting – which must satisfy certain criteria – before you can be detained.

2 A merchant must see you select the store merchandise. If an employee sees you after you have an item in your hand, there is doubt as to where the item came from and it may not stand up in court.

3 Someone must see you hide or carry away merchandise or see you emerge from a fitting room with fewer items than when you went in.

4 A witness must maintain visual surveillance of you throughout your stay in the shop to provide probable cause for detaining you.

5 You must have left the shop's premises before you can be approached for not paying for items.

Know Your Rights

1 If you are caught with merchandise, a merchant has the right to detain and question you, and have you arrested.

2 Other customers or employees who do not satisfy the requirements of probable cause for your arrest may be considered unreliable witnesses.

3 The use of excessive force in your detainment can be a violation of your rights.

4 If you are not allowed to leave a room, a chair or other confined space, or if security guards or shop employees are acting out of their jurisdiction of power, you may be entitled to claims of false imprisonment.

5 Co-operate with the police if you are caught. Attempting to fight or flee will only make matters worse and may result in a more severe sentence.

⚠ Warning

A shoplifting offence can remain on your permanent record for years. Multiple offences can result in steep fines and prison sentences.

640 | Pass a Parole Hearing

After serving part of a sentence, a prisoner can win parole – release from a correctional facility into a community where he or she will finish the sentence under close supervision.

⊙ Steps

1 Apply for parole. Prisoners must fill out a parole application and sign it to be considered.

2 Wait for notification from a parole officer, who will let you know when your parole hearing is scheduled.

⚠ Warning

Parole hearings can be nearly as psychologically gruelling as a jury trial. Be prepared to face your victims again. This is a good time to express remorse.

3   Expect an initial parole hearing within a few months after your prison sentence begins.

4   Know what to expect. Talk with your lawyer, a parole-board representative, experienced clergymen and social-service agency workers who can prepare you for the hearing.

5   Answer all questions directly and honestly.

6   The victims may be asked to testify at your parole hearing. Prepare yourself to face them, as well as any witnesses who may also be called to testify for or against you.

7   File an appeal. Should the parole commission rule against you, you have the right to file an appeal.

8   Seek the help of a support group after you pass your parole hearing. Many parole arrangements require parolees to attend regular support groups for alcohol or drug abuse, such as Alcoholics Anonymous.

File for a Restraining Order | 641

You can obtain a restraining order most quickly by calling the police. Family court personnel and shelter volunteers can also assist you in getting one.

⊚ Steps

1   Call 999 if you're in immediate danger. Call if you're being threatened, being abused, or if you've just been abused and the abuse has ended. Tell the police you want to press charges. The criminal court will issue a restraining order immediately if the case is prosecuted.

2   Get yourself and your children to safety. Find a local domestic-violence shelter and ask for help. The staff there may be able to get you to a safe house and help you file for a restraining order.

3   Go to the police station and ask how to press charges if you didn't call the police immediately after the abuse happened. Make sure you obtain any necessary papers.

4   Call your local family court and find out how to file for a restraining order in that court. Go to the court and get the papers you need.

5   Fill out all papers that are given to you. Include National Insurance numbers, birth dates, dates abuse occurred, names of witnesses, any photographs that were taken, and details about exactly how you were abused.

6   Protect your children from abuse by obtaining restraining orders for them as well. Your children may be entitled to restraining orders if they were physically abused, emotionally abused or witnesses to abuse that happened to you.

7   Know that you can request a restraining order during a divorce. You may do so when you file or at any time during the case.

✱ Tips

Hire a lawyer if you can afford to. This can be very helpful in family court.

You can get a restraining order if you're afraid you'll be harmed but nothing has actually happened yet.

⚠ Warnings

Get yourself out of the abusive situation. Your safety and that of your children is the priority.

Understand that in criminal court, you're not the one who has to prove the abuse happened.

642 | Testify in a Child Custody Case

Moat people are nervous when they testify in court. Answer questions completely, be honest and try to remain calm.

Steps

1 Speak to your lawyer before the court date and find out what questions they will be asking as well as what you can expect from the other lawyer.

2 Rehearse your testimony with your lawyer, but do not memorise lines or plan a performance.

3 Dress appropriately for court.

4 Sit on the witness stand when you are called. Swear the oath the judge asks you.

5 Refer to the judge as Your Honour, the lawyers as Mr or Ms, and do not speak to the other parent directly.

6 Keep your hands in your lap and try not to fidget. Request a glass of water if your mouth is dry.

7 Look at the person who is questioning you and listen carefully to the question.

8 Be quiet if there is an objection to a question being asked of you or if the judge speaks. Ask to have a question rephrased if you do not understand it.

9 Do not treat the opposing lawyer as an enemy. He or she is just doing a job. If you are treated unfairly, the judge or your lawyer will intervene.

10 Avoid evasions. The judge can tell if you are avoiding answering a question. This does not mean you have to offer information that is not requested.

11 Try not to become angry, upset or loud, which will prevent your story being heard. Ask for a break if you become overly emotional, begin to cry, need to go to the toilet or need some air.

12 Speak loudly and clearly. Do not use obscenities unless you are quoting what you heard someone say.

13 Remain quiet while others are testifying. If you need to tell your lawyer something, write it down or whisper it.

Tips

If your lawyer forgets to ask you about something important, or you think of something you would like the court to know, ask if you can speak privately with your lawyer.

Judges appreciate witnesses who are cooperative, calm and rational. They become annoyed with those that raise their voices, refuse to follow directions and make things difficult.

643 | Increase Your Child Support

Gather information that shows that your income does not cover expenses, and file papers in court requesting an increase in child support.

Steps

1 Learn what is necessary to prove the need for an increase in child support. Check laws on the Internet, in books or by hiring or talking to a lawyer.

Warning

Do not make any informal agreement with the other parent about child-support modification. It is important to have the court handle all modifications so that everything is enforceable.

2   Determine to which court you will need to bring your case. Check with the court that issued your current order or judgement. If this is not the correct place, the court staff will be able to tell you where to go.

3   Obtain the necessary forms. Ask the court staff for assistance in completing the forms if you don't understand everything.

4   Gather all the paperwork you can that shows why you need an increase in child support. Proof of tuition, clothing costs, housing costs, medical bills and any loss of income you have suffered are important. You want to show the court that the money coming in is not enough to cover your family's expenses.

5   Be prepared to testify if the case goes to trial. You will need to explain the meaning of all the documents you are presenting.

6   Remember that the court will only be interested in information that shows that the child is not being adequately supported. Your lack of money to buy cigarettes or new clothes for yourself is not considered important.

Get Custody of Your Pet in a Divorce   644

Animals are often treated like children in a family and it can be painful if you have to let go of one during a break-up. Here's how to get custody of this "child" when you face divorce.

⊚ Steps

1   Understand that no matter how much your pet may seem like a family member, to a court it is just another possession to be divided at divorce.

2   Know that if the animal was yours before the marriage or if you have been the primary caretaker of the animal during the marriage, you are more likely to be awarded possession.

3   Tell your lawyer how important your pet is to you and make sure he or she treats this as a priority.

4   Realise that if you have children, it makes the most sense for the pet to live where the children will live, since they have probably formed an attachment.

5   Try to talk to your spouse about the pet and see if you can work something out. You might be able to make visitation arrangements.

6   Avoid separating pets if you have two or more of the same species. This could cause depression or anxiety for the animals.

7   Recognise that if you have a valuable pet, such as a show dog or show cat, the animal will be carefully considered by the court as a valuable asset – and possibly as a business if, for example, you show the animal and/or collect stud fees.

8   Show the court that you are the person best able to care for the animal – you have time to play with it, exercise it and groom it. Show that you have space in your home for the animal. If necessary, ask your vet to testify about your ability to care for the animal.

✽ Tip

If you considered and treated your pet as a family member, you're likely to encounter some sadness. You can work through the adjustment by talking with another pet owner or someone else who can offer support.

645 | Feel Safe After a Robbery

Robbery means that the victim has witnessed the crime in progress, which can be traumatising. Victims of robberies often find it difficult to feel safe.

⊙ **Steps**

1 Install an alarm system in your home. Display the alarm company's logo prominently on your lawn or on your front door to warn would-be intruders.

2 Meet with a support group. You can find one in your area by searching the Internet.

3 Talk to a counsellor. This is a healthy way to get your feelings out in a safe, nurturing environment.

4 Learn self-defence. Even knowing a few moves can help you feel safer and give you confidence.

5 Get a guard dog. A dog's bark is often enough to discourage a break-in, and having a dog around can be very comforting – as well as being good company.

6 Remember that you have the right to remain anonymous to the offender during the identification process.

⚠ **Warning**

Don't expect to feel safe again overnight. The sense of intrusion and violation may take some time to subside. Seek whatever support you need.

646 | Prevent Sexual Harassment

When confronted with sexual-harassment charges, many defendants plead ignorance about its exact definition. Ignorance is no excuse, though, and your employees have the right to work in a harassment-free environment.

⊙ **Steps**

1 Put your company's sexual-harassment policy in writing and have every employee read it and sign it. The policy should be stated in clear, easy-to-understand language and every employee should be given the opportunity to ask pertinent questions afterwards.

2 Adopt a clear zero-tolerance policy towards sexual harassment to prevent its occurrence in your workplace. State in no uncertain terms that anyone found guilty of sexual harassment will have their employment terminated immediately, with no exceptions.

3 Explain to all employees that any claim of sexual harassment will be investigated thoroughly in a consistent and objective manner. In addition, all employees should be informed of the proper procedures involved when reporting an incidence of sexual harassment.

4 Review the company's sexual-harassment policy with all employees on an annual basis. This meeting should include a thorough explanation of what sexual harassment is and how it affects the company in a negative way. Remind your employees that they have a right to work in a company that is free from sexual harassment.

✳ **Tip**

A company that doesn't properly attend to a sexual-harassment problem will experience financial liabilities in the form of lawsuits, decreased productivity and poor employee morale.

5   Train the management of the company in identifying and preventing sexual harassment in the workplace by reviewing all reporting procedures and by insisting that every claim of sexual harassment is handled in the same way, with seriousness and objectivity. This training should be performed separately from the meeting held for other employees in order to be effective.

6   Talk to employees about conditions in the workplace. Ask them if they have seen instances of sexual harassment, and if those claims were handled properly. Keep the lines of communication open at all times to prevent sexual harassment from occurring.

7   Take all sexual harassment claims seriously. Don't try to comment on the claim or downplay the incident. Write down all the facts and follow company policy to the letter.

Fight Against Workplace Discrimination   647

In addition to being illegal, discrimination in the workplace can make for a very hostile work environment, not just for the person being discriminated against, but for all employees.

⊚ Steps

1   Speak up when something makes you uncomfortable. Many of us don't like to hear prejudicial jokes, but few of us actually let the speaker know that we are offended.

2   Perform above and beyond what is expected of you. The best way to fight any battle is to be prepared. Staying positive, professional and productive decreases your chances of being discriminated against if you are a member of a protected class. It's hard to legitimately deny a raise or promotion to an exemplary employee.

3   Check in with your supervisor if you think other, less-qualified co-workers are progressing up the career ladder before you. It may not be discrimination – there may be areas in which you need to improve your work. However, if the promotion is the result of discriminatory practices, your questions will alert your supervisor and encourage him or her to look into the situation.

4   Join or start a diversity mentoring and recruitment programme. Ask minority employees in higher positions for advice about how to progress in your career and pass that knowledge on to others when you do move up. Similarly, work with your employees or employer to create strategies to actively recruit candidates who can do the job well and add diversity to the workplace.

5   Fight the winning battles. If, despite your best efforts, you find that your workplace is rampant with discrimination, it may be a sign that you're not in the right place. That's not to say you shouldn't file a claim if you've been discriminated against, but you may want to consider whether you need to look for a more positive, diverse work environment.

✳ Tip

Set a good example. Employers in particular need to make sure they are living up to the same expectations they place on their employees.

648 | Be a Whistle-Blower

Blowing the whistle on an employer who is engaged in illegal, unethical or dangerous workplace activities is a risky business that requires organisation.

◎ Steps

1 Formulate a plan of action that includes the best time and place to blow the whistle. Learn about whistle-blowing laws through Internet research and consult a lawyer before reporting any wrongdoing.

2 Keep your plans to yourself. Other than consulting a lawyer, do not share your whistle-blowing plans. If you confide in a co-worker you increase the risk of management discovering your plan before it comes to fruition.

3 Discard your false illusions of workplace privacy. In today's high-tech workplace no email, phone conversation or instant message is irretrievable. If you communicate with anyone about your employer's activities, assume that your employer will be able to access this communication.

4 Increase your credibility by maintaining a detailed record of workplace activities. A dated account of wrongdoings will hold up much better in court than one person's foggy recollections. Keep this log at home.

5 Use precise wording when crafting a whistle-blower's report. A lawyer can help you draw up this document, so that the employer cannot argue that you were being vengeful.

6 Stick to the known facts when reporting any misconduct at your place of employment. Using only facts increases your credibility.

7 Focus on the future. Blowing the whistle on your employer can be all-consuming for a period of time, but you must think of the next step in your professional life. Before agreeing on a settlement or voluntarily leaving your company, consult with a lawyer to ensure that the whistle-blowing episode does not adversely affect your future career.

❋ Tip

Emotions run high in employees who believe their workplace is engaged in unethical activities. Stay calm and be prepared.

⚠ Warning

Don't fill any gaps in what you know with presumptions.

649 | Spot a Speed-Trap Location

To avoid a speeding ticket altogether you have to be able to recognise a speed-trap location before it's too late.

◎ Steps

1 The most common places for a speed-trap location are under bridges and on bends in the road. If you look ahead and see other people's brake lights going on suddenly, it's is a good indication that a speed trap is near.

2 Anywhere that the speed limit drops, particularly near the top or bottom of a hill, is a prime area for a speed trap. They are most commonly found on side streets.

3 Areas where a road turns into a small stretch of town and then back again is another situation where you might encounter a speed trap. This is particularly bad for people who are unfamiliar with the area.

❋ Tip

Keep your eye out for mobile cameras. These are often position on overpasses on motorways.

⚠ Warning

There's a reason there are speed limits, and they should be adhered to.

4   Purchasing a radar detector is without a doubt an excellent way to spot a speed-trap location. A radar detector can alert you to a possible speed trap miles ahead and is perfectly legal to own.

Spot a Fake ID   650

Thanks to technological advances, fake IDs are much harder to detect than in the past, and there are sites online where people can purchase a convincing driving licence.

⊙ Steps

1   Watch the person who has the ID for signs of nervousness. Nervous body language such as darting eyes or fidgeting can signify it is fake. Be wary if the person clearly looks young.

2   Compare the person to the picture. Keep in mind hairstyles and hair colours change, so you should be looking at facial features.

3   Look for signs of tampering. Fuzzy numbers or letters, red-eye in the photo or bumpy surfaces are good clues.

4   Check for an ID that is marked as a duplicate. This could indicate the original licence holder may have requested a second licence for some-one to use.

5   Ask the person for a second or even third form of ID if you are still unsure. In the case of a borrowed driving licence where the person looks similar to the original owner of the ID, it is unlikely there will be multiple cards with the same name as the ID. Ask for credit cards.

6   Talk to the person, and insert key questions that are not usually thought of when someone changes the dates on a licence. Ask for the person's zodiac sign or graduation year. When you believe it is a borrowed ID, ask what the middle initial stands for and see if there is a hesitation before the response.

✱ Tip

If you are not absolutely sure an ID is real, do not serve alcohol to the person.

Deal With a Hit and Run   651

A hit and run can be a scary experience, especially if you are the one who is hit. The impulse is to panic, but this is the worst response.

⊙ Steps

1   Stay calm. The more collected you are, the better you'll be able to handle whatever happens in the next few minutes.

2   Try to get the licence plate of the car that hit you. If you cannot, try to study the vehicle so you can give an accurate description to the police and to your insurance company.

3   Make sure that everyone in the car is OK, including yourself.

4   Call 999. If you do not have a phone, ask someone to call for you.

✱ Tip

Do not attempt to chase down the person who hit you. Your vehicle may be more damaged than you think, thus resulting in more costly repairs.

5   Ask witnesses to give a clear account to the police when the officers arrive on the scene.

6   Give the police a detailed account of the accident, especially if you are uable to give them the licence plate of the vehicle that hit you. A careful description of the car and exactly what occurred will be helpful for the police in tracking down the perpetrator.

7   Take pictures of your car and the scene of the hit and run as evidence to give to the police and the insurance company. These may also be useful should the incident come to court.

8   Ask a mechanic to give you an estimate on the repairs needed to make your car roadworthy again.

---

652 Learn the Highway Code

Learning the Highway Code is essential if you want to pass your test and drive safely.

⊙ Steps

1   Apply for your provisional driving licence – you'll need this to start driving.

2   Before you have any lessons, buy the Highway Code book.

3   Do not rush your learning because you will need all this knowledge to be able to drive properly. You may be eager to take your test, but if you rush it, you'll only end up having to retake it.

4   Try and break each section down and make sure that you learn it properly. You may want to get someone to keep testing you, and it is also a good idea to make notes.

5   When you learn each section of the Highway Code, try and apply some of it when you are learning to drive. Take a look at road signs and other things on the road in order to get an idea of your surroundings.

✳ Tip

Take your time learning the Highway Code – it is something that can help to keep you and others safe whilst you are out on the road.

---

653 License a Trademark

A trademark is a name, figure or design created by a company to distinguish its product or service. A registered trademark can be licensed to another firm in return for a royalty.

Steps

1   Get your trademark registered with the Patent and Trademark office to claim legal ownership over your trademark. Without the registration, the trademark is just another design or symbol.

2   Know your licensee well. Get information regarding their standing in the business, their product range, the scope for their products and the scale of production and distribution.

3   Know your rights fully before licensing your trademark. Trademarks may be territorial or limited to a certain product, so complete knowledge of the extent of trademark rights is very important before licensing.

✳ Tip

Before licensing, make sure your licensee will do justice to your trademark. Ally with the wrong firm and your standing could take a hit.

4   Decide on the terms and conditions of the royalty. You can opt for a flat fee or choose to go with a percentage of the sales, depending upon the mutual agreement.

5   Exercise a strict quality control on the products manufactured by the licensee, be it adhering to the quality standards or display of the trademark. You can pull up the licensee for failing to meet with the required quality standards.

6   Insist on a termination provision. If the licensee doesn't play fair or doesn't perform well, you can terminate the contract.

Market Your Patent   654

For inventors, marketing = manufacturing + distribution. Here's an overview of your options for getting your invention made and out the door.

⊙ Steps

1   Understand that there are many factors to consider when deciding whether an invention is marketable. These include its cost, size, effect on health and safety, time-saving aspects, ease of use, ease of production, durability, ease of repairs and reliability. You should also consider the potential market for your invention.

2   Begin the manufacturing and distribution process as soon after filing your patent application as possible – this can even be before the patent has been issued.

3   Create an actual working model of your invention for demonstration to potential customers, manufacturers or distributors. Working models are far more effective than specs on a piece of paper.

4   Decide how your invention is to be manufactured and distributed. Some options include the following: find someone else to manufacture and distribute it for you; use an invention broker to arrange the manufacturing and distribution on your behalf; manufacture and distribute it yourself; sell your invention to a manufacturing/distribution company outright.

5   Persevere. Successfully getting an invention to market is usually a difficult and time-consuming process.

✱ Tips

If you want your invention to be successful, pursue commercial exploitation with all the energy that you can devote to it.

Use an "inventor's notebook" to carefully document your idea, detailing how and when you came up with it.

⚠ Warning

This information is not intended as a substitute for personalised advice from a lawyer.

Detect Acts of Plagiarism   655

Plagiarism is commonplace amongst the lazy. It is not easy to detect, but the Internet provides much more effective ways of discovery than ever before.

⊙ Steps

1   Open up your web browser and navigate to the Google search engine: http://www.google.com.

✱ Tip

Feed Google lines or carefully and intricately worded sections instead of paragraphs if a search for the latter proves to be futile.

2   Copy an entire line or paragraph from the work that is highly suspect and paste it into the search field in Google.

3   Enclose this selection with inverted commas. This specific action will force Google to search for the enclosed section in its entirety without any breaks, instead of piecemeal.

4   Should you be successful, Google will spit out the original published work and the sites it is on.

⚠ **Warning**

This act of detection is easily thwarted by a cunning act of lifting and pasting of text. As such, break down the suspected work into smaller chunks for more successful snares instead.

656 Get Permission to Use Copyrighted Material

Protect yourself as a writer and prevent getting smacked with a lawsuit for "borrowing" copyrighted materials.

◉ **Steps**

1   Determine if you need permission to quote a copyrighted source. One short sentence from certain print material, for instance, may not require written permission. Ask a professional – your editor, publisher, lawyer or public library reference librarian – if you need permission to quote the particular source.

2   Contact the publisher of the material you wish to use. Ask for the address or phone number of the publisher's Permissions Department. Some publishers will send you a required permission form to fill out. Other publishing houses may ask for your request in a letter.

3   Start the process of securing permission long before your publication date. Some publishers take months to respond to permission requests.

4   Fill out the request form or write your request letter. Be clear, concise and thorough. Generally speaking, your permission request letter should include title, volume and issue number, author and/or editor, and edition of the proposed source; the exact material to be used, including page numbers, chapters, edition, copyright date, the number of copies to be made, the dates of usage; the form of distribution – i.e., classroom, newsletter, trade book, commercial or magazine article; and whether or not the material is to be sold.

5   Give the author and publisher credit in your book or article's source notes whenever possible, even if you don't need written permission.

6   If you need permission to quote a non-print source, such as a piece of art, contact the artist or art dealer, or the Estate in the case of an artist who is no longer living (information is usually available on the Internet). You need to show that you have made every effort to locate the copyright holder, so keep a track of everywhere you have tried.

7   If you need permission to quote a song lyric, find out who owns the rights to the song. Like publishing companies, most record companies have departments that deal exclusively in copyrights and permissions.

✳ **Tip**

Many larger publishers post their copyright permission request forms on their Internet home page.

⚠ **Warnings**

Don't be surprised if you are charged a hefty fee to use copyrighted material. While some people will let you quote their work free of charge, others are not as generous.

Don't assume that you can use the work of a lesser-known author or obscure or older works without permission. A copyright is a copyright.

Note that different laws apply to use of Internet sources.

Write a Living Will   **657**

An advance medical directive, or living will, spells out your
preferences regarding the use of medical treatment to delay
an inevitable death.

⊙ Steps

1   Discuss your beliefs and wishes with your partner or spouse, family
    members, friends, clergy and your doctor.

2   You can find living will forms on the Internet (at no cost), or you can
    simply write out your wishes as an advanced directive. A lawyer can
    help shape this.

3   Review the forms carefully. You may need the advice of your doctor
    when specifying which types of treatment you do not want. You can
    differentiate between life-prolonging procedures and those that
    alleviate pain. Detail specific wishes you have about your care that
    the form doesn't cover.

4   Sign the living will form and get it witnessed. An improperly signed or
    witnessed will may be ruled invalid.

5   Give copies to your family members, doctor and lawyer. Put a copy in
    your home medical file.

✱ Tip

You'll need to appoint someone
to speak on your behalf if you
cannot communicate. This person will ensure that informed
decisions are made.

Contest a Will   **658**

Wills can be contested in the event that family members do not
agree on how property and custody issues have been handled.

⊙ Steps

1   Talk with family members about the terms of the will. Find out if others
    in the family have the same questions or concerns and consult with a
    lawyer together.

2   Contact an estate planning lawyer to go over the will with you. It does
    not have to be the same lawyer that drafted the original document.

3   Determine with your lawyer on what grounds you are contesting.
    A person having a will drawn up must be of sound mind at the time.

4   Decide if you feel there was fraud involved in the will. If the will is very far
    from what you feel it should be, it is possible your loved one was misled.

5   Be sure the will that is being carried out is the most up to date
    will of your loved one. The most recent will is the only one that is
    legally binding.

6   Make a decision as to how much you will spend to contest the will.
    This process is long and detailed. You should decide if the outcome
    will be worth the fight.

✱ Tip

The best way to contest a will,
or begin the process, is through
a qualified estate planning lawyer.
This person will be able to give
you all the help you need right
from the start.

⚠ Warning

Understand the risks to family
relationships before contesting
a will. Families can be easily torn
apart when fighting over money
and property.

659 | Manage a Large Inheritance

If you've recently inherited large amounts of money or items, it is important to manage them correctly so that you make the best financial decisions possible.

⊙ Steps

1 Call a number of financial advisors to find the best professional with which to work. You should consider their price, personality, skill and availability. You want to make sure you're receving the best possible advice, as few people are equipped to deal with sudden changes in their personal financial circumstances.

2 Hire a lawyer who specialises in estates to make sure that you are legally protected.

3 Pay taxes on your inheritance.

4 Gather the paperwork for all the things you have inherited. Keep these items in a safe place.

5 Have items like jewellery and homes appraised so that you know their true values and can make sure the insurance you get is adequate to cover it all.

6 Make sure your financial advisor completely explains your options. Make sure you fully understand the choices you have to make before you make them.

7 Review your financial options monthly in order to make sure you are still doing the best things possible with your money and items.

❋ Tip

Wait a week or so after the funeral to read the will if possible so that people will be thinking more clearly and less emotionally.

660 | Serve on a Jury

Having to do jury duty might seem like a chore – taking you away from work and family – but it is everyone's responsibility to take their turn, and take it seriously.

⊙ Steps

1 Communicate with your employer. Sit down with human resources and find out about what compensation you're entitled to while you're away from the office.

2 Arrive for jury duty at the appointed time. Do your homework in advance by making sure you have the directions to the court house and parking instructions to avoid last-minute panic and stress.

3 Keep the chit-chat to a minimum. You're there to provide a public service, not to expand your social circle. Give your full attention to the testimonies and evidence presented.

4 Avoid discussions about the case. This means with everyone: family, friends, the lawyers, witnesses and other jurors. Stay away from any media coverage about the case by not reading the newspapers or watching the news.

❋ Tips

Bring something to read or puzzles to keep you occupied during times when you have nothing to do.

Make sure that you get a good night's sleep every evening before you have to serve on a jury. It will help make the long day more tolerable and keep your mind sharp.

5   Be prepared to take notes. You may become overwhelmed by the sheer number of witnesses testifying and by the whole trial process in general. Carry a small notebook and pen with you to court to jot down names and testimony details that you might forget during the period of deliberation. Just make sure you don't get so wrapped up in writing that you're not actually listening.

6   Know what to expect from the judge, lawyers and witnesses. You may have seen countless courtroom dramas on television, but in reality the players aren't as smooth and polished as actors.

7   Pay close attention to the judge's jury instructions. Once deliberations begin, you need to form your opinion based on the evidence presented, not your personal feelings or the feelings of the other jurors. However, go into the deliberation room with a clear head and be open to what the jurors say. You may have missed something that they picked up on during the trial.

Deal with a Stalker   661

Finding you have a stalker is one of the scariest situations you can find yourself in. Whether the stalking is physical or electronic, there are steps you can take to deal with it.

⊙ Steps

1   Seek help. This is a very serious matter. Avoid denying the problem or keeping it to yourself.

2   Remove yourself from the stalker's reach. This should be your first priority. Cut off all communication with the stalker. Avoid responding to telephone calls or text messages.

3   Get a new phone number and make sure it's unlisted. Keep the old phone number but leave that particular phone hooked up to an answering machine.

4   Block your address at official institutions such as the DVLA and your local electorate office. These are steps to cut off your contact with the stalker.

5   Have your post delivered to a private post-office box. Avoid accepting a package unless you have ordered it or expected it. Shred discarded papers and post.

6   Consider getting a dog if you don't already have one.

7   Get a mobile phone and keep it with you at all times, even inside your house.

8   Document everything. Keep answering-machine tapes, letters, gifts and logs of suspicious happenings.

9   Make several left- or right-hand turns in succession if you think you're being followed while in your car. If the other car continues to follow you, drive to the nearest police station – never home or to a friend's house. Sound your car horn to attract attention.

✳ Tips

Let someone down easy instead of giving a definitive "no". Using a nice rebuff on an obsessive suitor might help ward them off.

Take a self-defence class and learn security awareness.

Never give out personal details to someone online.

Choose a genderless name if you use online chat areas.

⚠ Warning

If you have any hesitations or suspicions, do not arrange to see anybody you've met online.

10 Consult the local police if you receive a threat. Do not hesitate. It's their job to protect you.

11 Get emotional support from the numerous Internet resources and from family and friends, neighbours, co-workers and victim-support groups. Take care of yourself as best you can.

12 Bear in mind that seeking a restraining order or protective order is often not advisable. This frequently provokes a stalker to react violently.

662 | Respond to False Accusations

Nothing is more frustrating than being accused of something you didn't do. Here are some tips on how to deal with false accusations and set the record straight.

⊙ Steps

1 Say nothing. If someone has accused you of something, they are probably already frustrated or angry. By telling them you are innocent you will probably only inflame the argument. If an accusation requires an immediate answer, suggest a change of setting. Calmly and rationally say to the person that you believe they are mistaken. This will diffuse the momentary tension. Again, do this immediately only if necessary.

2 Consider representation. Now that you've been accused of something, take a moment to seriously consider if you need council, legal or other-wise. If you are not sure, call a lawyer and speak to them. Usually there is no charge for an initial consultation. Certain matters seem small, but can quickly get out of control.

3 Gather evidence. Since you know you are innocent, now is the time to gather the evidence that supports your claim. Think about credit-card receipts, appointments, emails, bank records – anything in written form that can support your claim.

4 Prepare your argument. Take your evidence and organise it in a way that makes logical sense to support your claim. If you have been accused of cheating on a spouse, for example, start with where you were on the night in question, show receipts or emails to support your claim in chronological order. If someone accuses you of something in writing, respond to their claim in writing to create a paper trail that you can use as evidence.

5 Contact the person who made the accusation. If this is a matter that should be addressed face to face, schedule a time you can meet to share your side of the story. Remember, stay calm and respectful on the phone. Do not meet on their turf. Suggest somewhere neutral.

6 Explain your side. Remember to keep emotion out of the way. If you've done your homework properly and have evidence, it should be fairly easy to eradicate the claim. Lay your evidence out and give them a chance to respond. Do not expect an apology. Understand that sometimes people need to "agree to disagree".

✳ Tip

Make sure you have a piece of evidence to deny each point of your opponent's claim.

⚠ Warning

If the accusation is criminal, seek legal council immediately. This article is intended for issues that can be resolved without use of the law.

Write a Legal Memorandum 663

A legal memorandum is a document that lawyers use to analyse legal issues and evaluate the facts of a given case.

⊙ Steps

1 Write the "Issue". The first heading of the legal memo should be the "Issue" section. This is a description of the legal issue or legal question to be researched and it should be limited to one sentence. The issue may also be written in the form of a question.

2 Write a "Short Answer" section. Directly answer the legal issue and briefly describe the law upon which your answer is based. This section should be no longer than two or three sentences.

3 Write a brief "Statement of the Facts" section. This section should describe in a neutral, narrative form the facts that the client has provided. It should include only the facts that have a bearing on the issue and should be as brief as possible.

4 Write the "Analysis" section. This is the main body of a legal memo. It must clearly apply the case law you have researched to the facts. Include proper citations whenever you refer to a case law or other law, such as statutes and regulations. You should not include any secondary resources, such as legal encyclopedias.

5 Write a "Recommendations" section. If you must determine whether the client's case is viable, discuss in this section why the client will prevail or lose based upon your analysis. Base your recommendation solely on your analysis of the legal issue; the purpose of a legal memo is to neutrally evaluate a legal issue, not to advocate a position.

6 Every lawyer or firm has specific preferences for the format of internal legal memos. Seek out samples and conform your memo to match them. Once you have finished drafting the Analysis section, return to the Statement of the Facts and delete any facts there that you did not refer to in your Analysis section. Attach copies of all the cases and other sources you cited to your memo and highlight the portions to which you referred.

✳ Tip

Clerks or paralegals may also provide preliminary research legal memoranda.

664 | Plan Your Family

Like every other major life decision, the more thought and planning that go into addressing issues about raising children, the better off your entire family will be.

◎ Steps

1 Evaluate your and your partner's lifestyles for kid compatibility. Workaholics are an asset in the office, but a liability when it comes to spending time with your little one. Discuss values and expectations, as well as ways to adjust workloads and travel schedules to bring your focus and energy back home.

2 Try to consciously address feelings of ambivalence about parenthood before age 30. Women and men who start seriously trying in their late thirties have often waited too long.

3 Start saving money. That cute little bottom will completely change your bottom line. And it's not too early to think about how to finance private schools – or even college.

4 Make sure that your relationship is ready and that both of you want to start a family. Check out what each of you expects from the other after the baby comes. Does the working parent expect to pat the baby and have a glass of wine every night while the stay-at-home parent takes care of the child? Who will get up to do the feedings? How will you handle the stress and conflicts of two very different styles of jobs?

5 Cultivate a good support system and practise asking for help. Ideally, you'll want friends who are going through the same thing and whom you can rely on to answer questions and offer help.

6 Discuss what happens after the baby comes. How long a maternity leave will you plan for? Will one of you stay home full-time and care for the baby? How will you juggle work schedules if both of you return to work?

7 Start looking at childcare options if neither parent will be staying home. Many of the good nurseries have waiting lists.

❋ Tip

Fine-tune communication skills with your partner. Where you may have hours or days to discuss and resolve issues now, after the baby comes it'll be only a few moments here and there.

⚠ Warning

Understand that nothing will ever be the same again. Your relationship with your spouse, your free time, the way you view the world, your relationship to your work – all will be completely different.

665 | Increase Chances of Conception

If you are anxious to conceive, there are methods that you can use to increase your odds of conception.

◎ Steps

1 Figure out the best time to have sex with your partner. You want to try and conceive when ovulation occurs. Monitoring your basal body temperature helps you figure out this time. Ovulation ends when the temperature reaches its peak.

2 Buy an over-the-counter ovulation predictor. These kits let you know when you are ovulating by analysing your urine.

3 Have an orgasm. A woman's orgasm increases blood flow to the cervix. This helps the sperm to get sucked up into the cervix.

❋ Tip

Speak to a doctor to rule out any medical problems if you have been unable to conceive after trying for a year.

⚠ Warning

Fertility teas and herbs are available, but have not been proven to be effective.

4   Avoid stress. Stress can cause fertility problems. Sometimes a relaxing holiday can help a couple conceive.

5   Make lifestyle changes in order to increase chances of conception. Avoid caffeine, alcohol, cigarettes and certain medications. All these items can make getting pregnant more difficult.

Announce an Unplanned Pregnancy 666

If you are coping with the news of an unplanned pregnancy, you might be wondering how to share this unexpected revelation with others.

Steps

1   Seek the advice of a healthcare professional first. Obstetricians are used to providing care to women facing an unplanned pregnancy and can also help to get the pregnancy off to a healthy start.

2   Share the announcement with your partner next, if possible. The two most important people in planning the unborn child's future are the mother and the father. If the two of you present a united front, telling others is easier.

3   Decide with your partner what course of action you will take before telling others. If you have decided to announce the pregnancy, this probably means you are going through with it. This leaves you with two options. You can raise the child yourself or put it up for adoption.

4   Confide in a respected member of your faith if you have one. Religious leaders can be a source of tremendous comfort and support during times of emotional upheaval.

5   Make a list of the family members and friends you want to share your unplanned pregnancy with. Prioritise this list in order of the amount of unconditional love and support these individuals will provide. Tell the most supportive people first and the least supportive people last.

6   Rely on the grapevine to spread the news to people you may not wish to deal with initially. After you have come to terms with your unplanned pregnancy and you have strengthened your immediate support network, you can face these individuals.

✳ Tip

Keep in mind that holiday gatherings or times of stress are generally not the best time to break the news of an unplanned pregnancy.

Ask for Maternity Leave 667

Gearing up for maternity leave can be a tough business, especially if it's your first baby.

Steps

1   Pay attention to how other women at your company handle maternity leave; ask people you trust for strategic advice.

2   Read your company's personnel handbook for official company policies. Talk to a human-resources representative, if your company has one.

✳ Tip

If your company has more than a certain number of employees, you can't be fired for being pregnant – check out the law!

3   Think through your ideal: How long will your leave be? Do you want
     to come back part-time at first? Do you want to work from home?
     Or perhaps you would prefer to simply modify your job responsibilities
     or the number of hours you work.

4   Sickness, holiday and personal days, disability and paid and unpaid
     time can be part of your maternity leave; develop a clear and thorough
     proposal for your boss.

5   Wait to talk to your boss until your pregnancy is well-established –
     but tell before you're obviously showing.

6   Consider your boss's possible reaction and think through how to
     respond to any questions and concerns. Have suggested solutions
     ready for any problems or challenges your absence might cause.

7   Negotiate for the length and type of leave you want.

8   Give your boss and co-workers plenty of time to adjust to the idea of
     your absence.

668 | Understand the Results of Amniocentesis

Any testing to do with your unborn child can be nerve-wracking,
and your doctor will explain the results of the amniocentesis to
you, but here are a few guidelines.

⊙ Steps

1   Understand that normal amniotic fluid is clear. It may contain a few white
     flecks later on in the pregnancy. Blood in amniotic fluid usually belongs
     to the mother and is not generally something to worry about.

2   Understand that the presence of faeces in the amniotic fluid in the third
     trimester may mean foetal distress.

3   Understand that chromosomes from the amniotic fluid will be analysed
     for Down's syndrome and that levels of alpha-fetoprotein will be
     measured to check for spina bifida – amniocentesis is 100 per cent
     effective in detecting them.

4   Understand that chromosomal analysis will reveal the sex of the baby
     and help pinpoint any sex-related diseases such as haemophilia.

5   Understand that other genes will be analysed to detect substances that
     relate to developmental and metabolic disorders.

6   Be patient. The results from amniocentesis may take up to two weeks
     to be available. Your obstetrician will want to meet with you in person
     to discuss the results.

7   Understand that amniocentesis will not always be able to determine if
     your baby will be healthy. A normal amniocentesis does not guarantee
     a baby without problems.

✱ Tip

Consider Chorionic Villi Sampling
if you are concerned about a
possible genetic disorder or birth
defect. Similar to amniocentesis,
this can be performed earlier in
the pregnancy, and results are
available sooner.

⚠ Warning

If you have any questions or
concerns, contact a physician
or other healthcare professional
before engaging in any activity
related to health and diet. This
information is not intended as
a substitute for professional
medical advice or treatment.

Eat for Two 669

Eating for two doesn't just mean two scoops of ice cream. Here are a few tips on making sure you and your unborn baby are getting the proper nutrients.

⊙ Steps

1 Increase your daily caloric intake by about 300 calories.

2 Eat plenty of fibre and drink at least eight glasses of filtered water a day to keep things moving.

3 Cut back on caffeine and artificial sweeteners, especially during the first trimester.

4 Avoid smoking, alcohol and recreational drug use throughout pregnancy.

5 Do not try to lose weight while pregnant unless your doctor suggests you do.

6 Grab those chicken thighs and eat at least 10 g (0.4 oz) of protein a day.

7 Slurp at least 10 micrograms of vitamin D daily in your milkshakes, yoghurt or non-fat milk.

8 Be sure to get at least 1,200 mg of calcium and phosphorus daily.

9 Snack on two dried apricots to get your 400 micrograms of folic acid every day.

10 Don't let the sun go down without eating at least 30 mg of iron and 15 mg of zinc every day.

11 Guarantee the above intakes by taking a pre-natal vitamin. Discuss options with your healthcare provider.

✳ Tips

Continue to exercise normally unless your doctor recommends that you stop.

The food choices listed are only examples of how you can get the required amount of vitamins and minerals through your diet.

Choose organic produce and hormone-free meat and dairy products when possible.

Sleep Comfortably During Pregnancy 670

Should you lie on your left side or your right side? On your back? Follow these pregnancy sleep tips and you may be able to get a good night's sleep.

⊙ Steps

1 Wear comfortable clothing when going to sleep.

2 After you lie down, concentrate on sleep and listen to the signals your body gives. Does your back hurt? Does your abdomen feel pressure? Are any limbs falling asleep?

3 Find a position other than lying on your abdomen if your stomach feels too much pressure against it. Sleeping on your stomach will become increasingly difficult as the baby grows.

4 Roll to one side or the other if your arms or legs are falling asleep. Sleep on your left side to provide you and the baby with optimal blood flow.

5 Use pillows for props if you are experiencing back pain or extreme discomfort. Put pillows between your legs while lying on your side to help alleviate lower back pain.

✳ Tips

Lying in a semi-reclined position with plenty of pillows for support is helpful when any lying-down position causes discomfort.

Choose an airy, lightweight duvet to keep your body temperature comfortable.

Adjust your position frequently to avoid pain or soreness in any one area.

Invest in new full pillows. You deserve it.

6   Place a pillow directly under your growing abdomen if the weight of the baby begins pulling your middle spine.

7   Use a full, firm pillow under your head or a neck pillow under your neck to keep your neck aligned with your spine and provide support for your shoulders.

8   Wear a maternity belt – as well as using pillows – for added back support. A maternity belt or other abdominal support will help keep your back strong during the day, too.

⚠ **Warning**

Consult your doctor if you experience any severe light-headedness, dizziness, or if you have very noticeable heart palpitations or trouble breathing.

671 | Prepare for a Caesarean Section

If you're scheduled for a caesarean section, you'll want to plan ahead to make the day go smoothly.

⊙ **Steps**

1   Take a special C-section antenatal class, if you're not too far along when you learn how you'll be giving birth.

2   Expect a longer hospital stay. Have someone lined up to care for older children, pets and your house.

3   Follow your doctor's advice about what to eat before surgery. Because of the anaesthestic you will need, doctors generally recommend no food or water for 12 hours prior to surgery.

4   Go out and have a nice dinner the night before – you won't be eating solid food again for up to 48 hours.

5   Take a long bath – it will be a while before you'll have that luxury again.

6   Ask for a local anaesthetic if you want to be awake for the arrival of your baby.

7   Ask whether your partner can be with you in the operating room, if that makes you (and your partner) more comfortable.

8   Ask to hold the baby straight after delivery.

9   Tell your doctor you want to breast-feed immediately, if you feel up to it.

✱ **Tips**

Ask questions throughout the operation so that you can understand and be comfortable with each step of the procedure.

If you let labour progress a bit before the C-section, your baby will have the advantage of uterine contractions to stimulate breathing after birth.

672 | Be an Involved Father During Pregnancy

Being an involved father during your partner's pregnancy is one of the most important things you can do. Staying involved allows your partner to feel safe, loved and cared about.

⊙ **Steps**

1   Be open about your feelings and concerns with your partner. Your partner isn't the only one allowed to say how she feels.

2   Talk to your partner honestly about sex. Find out if there are any positions that are extremely uncomfortable. Pregnancy alters hormones and can also put a lot of pressure on her cervix.

✱ **Tips**

Be kind, gentle and compassionate with your partner.

Expect mood swings as the hormones balance in her pregnancy.

Be involved and aware of what is going on with her and the baby.

How to Do More of *(Just About)* **Everything**

3   Massage your partner's belly. Using light touch over her skin, called "effleurage", will probably encourage the baby to shift around and roll beneath your fingers.

4   Talk to and play with your baby. Babies love to hear voices and the amniotic fluid acts as a conductor for sound. Your baby will not only recognise your voice, but will respond to it after it is born.

5   Go with your partner to her doctor visits and scan appointments.

6   Attend antenatal classes together. No matter which type of class you attend, you will learn about different positions, coping techniques, medicinal varieties and newborn care.

7   Plan to do a bellycast one evening. Bellycasts are a great way for you and your partner to bond with the baby while creating a lifetime memory of how her belly looked with the baby inside.

8   Read and share books about pregnancy and parenting. Sharing the books will ensure that you are able to discuss with her different styles and ideas. She will appreciate the fact that you are learning with her.

9   Create a birth plan together. Birth plans are a unique way to figure out what you would like to do during the labour and delivery if no complications arise.

10 Talk to other fathers. There are lots of new fathers who are looking for companion dads. It is a good idea to share male-bonding time, and you may even be able to learn or teach something new.

Deliver a Baby   673

The contractions are coming faster and the baby's not waiting. Whether you're the father, a friend or just an innocent bystander, you need to know that there's more to do than boil water and get towels.

⊚ Steps

1   Call 999. Rally passers-by to help. Even if help is far away and you'll be on your own during the birth, you will want someone to walk you through it.

2   Do not freak out. Childbirth is designed to be noisy, messy and scary as a deterrent to the less committed. Your role is to be comforting and reassuring no matter how awful you feel.

3   Ask the woman if there are any problems you should be aware of in order to tell emergency personnel. Is she having twins? If the baby is oriented with its head up (a breech delivery), renew your efforts to get help quickly. In the meantime, wash your hands.

4   Talk to the woman. Tell her to breathe. If she feels like pushing, encourage her to pant instead. Wait until the contractions are strong and the baby is emerging (crowning). Have her push when contractions are strong and rest at other times.

5   Spread out a shower curtain, clean towels or newspaper. Help the woman sit at the edge of a bed or table with her hips hanging off and knees apart. If labour is too far along or it's too painful to climb on a bed

✱ Tips

Many people choose to have a baby at home. Do plenty of research before you commit to this so you know both the risks and benefits, and the amount of work involved.

If you're in a car, have the woman lie down with one foot on the floor and the other on the seat.

Collect towels and blankets (or a shirt or jacket) to dry off the baby and keep everyone warm afterwards.

A woman's waters can break hours before birth actually occurs. However, if contractions are less than two minutes apart, get ready. Irregular contractions could mean she's in false labour, and she probably has time to wait for help.

or table, place a stack of newspapers or towels under her hips to raise them high enough to help deliver the baby's shoulders.

6 Cup the baby's head in your hands once it starts to come out and move it slightly downwards as the woman pushes. If the umbilical cord is wrapped around the head or neck, gently work it free and clear the baby's mouth of any obstructions. Help the shoulders to ease out one at a time. Once both shoulders are clear, the baby should slip right out – so hang on!

7 Wipe the baby's face with a towel and check that the nose and mouth are clear. Suction the mouth if you have a syringe.

8 Wrap the baby in a clean towel or shirt and gently lay it on the mother's abdomen or at her breast (depending on how long the cord is). Nobody slaps newborns any more.

9 Do not try to pull the placenta out. If it comes out on its own, wrap it in a newspaper or towel and keep it above the level of the baby's head until help arrives. Do not cut the cord.

10 Keep the mother and baby comfortable, warm and dry, and do nothing else if help is on the way. If help is not coming, get them to a hospital as soon as possible.

674 Trim a Baby's Nails

Baby nails seem to grow at a rapid rate – and almost constantly need to be trimmed. It can be daunting to trim those tiny nails.

⊙ Steps

1 Relax your baby. It is easiest to trim your baby's nails while they are in their most relaxed state. This may be during nursing or feeding from a bottle, during a nap or even after a bath.

2 Hold your baby's fingers or toes in one hand while holding the clippers in the other hand. Your grip should be firm but not so strong that you cause discomfort or pain.

3 Bring the clippers to the finger or toenail that you wish to cut, being careful not to nip a nearby finger or toe with the side of the clippers. The back edge of the clipper should be on the inside of the nail, behind the white exposed part of the nail.

4 Clip the nail gently while pushing down the pad of the finger or toe. You must not clip the nail too quickly in case the baby moves or you accidentally push the clippers too far down into the nail bed.

5 Smooth any rough edges of the nail with an emery board after clipping. This will prevent a sharp edge of a nail from scratching you or your baby.

6 Resist the urge to bite off your baby's fingernails to trim them out of fear of using nail clippers. Biting off nails increases the odds of introducing bacteria into any open wounds.

✻ Tips

Cut fingernails along the curve of the finger but cut toenails straight across to prevent ingrown toe nails.

If you are uncomfortable using nail clippers on your baby, use an emery board.

⚠ Warning

Stop trimming if you draw blood when trimming nails. Apply pressure to the wound to stop it from bleeding.

Interpret a Newborn's Expressions 675

For months you've been paying attention to the kicks and turns *in utero*. Now your baby is out and about, and you can see its little face. But what do those expressions mean?

◎ Steps

1 Know that a newborn has two principal means of communicating: smiling and crying. He or she will cry when in pain or discomfort and learn to smile when comfortable.

2 Notice that the first smiles will probably come fleetingly as your baby sleeps, in the first week of life.

3 Watch the smile change. In the second week the baby will probably smile with his or her eyes open, usually after feeding. They may have a glassy, faraway look.

4 In the third or fourth week, your baby will probably have mastered a social smile, responding to your voice and making eye contact.

5 Observe when your baby is alert and calm. He or she will look around, listen to sounds and appear wide-eyed and aware, with energies focused on taking in information.

6 Know that some babies will become quiet and alert after feeding; others will be attentive when they first wake up.

✳ Tip

Remember that children develop at different paces and often unevenly, with spurts and plateaus.

⚠ Warning

Consult with your paediatrician if you have any worries about your child's behaviour or development.

Find the Best Car Seat for Your Child 676

With so many car seats out there, it can be hard to figure out which one is the best one for your child.

◎ Steps

1 Know your child's information. The type of car seat will depend on your child's age, weight and height.

2 Determine whether you need a rear-facing, convertible (rear- or forward-facing) or forward-facing car seat. Rear-facing car seats are used for infants under one year. Some car seats go up to 16 kg (35 lb) in the rear-facing position. Convertible car seats can be turned from rear facing to front facing and will last for a long time. Some front-facing car seats become booster seats and are used until your child is large enough to sit in the seat by themselves.

3 Determine where you will install the car seat in your vehicle. Consult your vehicle owner's manual to determine the recommended installation locations. Some vehicles require that you install car seats only in the side positions and not in the middle.

4 Go to a comparison website to determine which models fit well into your vehicle.

5 Finally, purchase your desired car seat.

✳ Tip

If you are installing multiple car seats in your vehicle, consider the width of the seat you choose. Some models are designed to be narrower.

⚠ Warnings

Purchase your car seat from a reputable source. It is not recommended that you purchase a used car seat.

Your child should stay rear-facing for as long as possible. This is the safest position during a crash because the force of the impact is directed through larger parts of the body, instead of the head and neck.

677 | Know When to Call the Doctor for Your New Baby

Being new parents can be worrying, and it's tempting to call the doctor about everything. Here are a few occasions when it's right to do so.

Steps

1 If your child isn't eating. An infant can get dehydrated in just a few hours. If you are breastfeeding, look to see that your baby is making gulping sounds, and make sure your baby has wet nappies. At first, they should have three to four wet nappies a day, and build up to six to eight each day.

2 If your baby can't keep food down and has chronic vomiting. If your baby is constantly vomiting, they aren't getting the nutrition they need, and it could be anything from having intolerance to the formula you use to a neurological issue.

3 If your child feels too hot or too cold, you should take their temperature and if it is below 36°C (97°F), or above 38°C (100.4°F), you should call the doctor and have them seen straight away.

4 If your child looks yellow it's probably jaundice, which affects many newborns. It's usually harmless, but it does need to be treated. If it's a mild case, your doctor may tell you just to put your baby near a window for a little bit each day to get some UV rays, but don't put your newborn in direct sunlight.

5 If your baby has a cough that is persistent or mucusy, or they look like they are having trouble breathing, call your doctor. Most infants hiccup and sneeze often, but a cough is another story. They could have a respiratory infection, so don't hesitate to call your doctor.

✻ Tip

If your baby is ever acting lethargic, or different than you feel is normal, always call your doctor.

678 | Deal with Post-Natal Depression

If you or someone you know is suffering from post-natal depression, take it seriously and get help.

Steps

1 Treat yourself right. Know that you are not alone in this struggle. Being a mother, especially a first-time mother, is demanding. It takes a lot of personal sacrifice for the first three to six months, but it will get easier.

2 Sleep. Heed the old saying, "Sleep when your baby sleeps". Let the answering machine pick up the phone and ask your husband to return calls.

3 Ask for help. Let a neighbour make you dinner. Have your mother-in-law watch the baby while you sleep, shop, exercise or take a bath. Find a person you trust to watch the baby on days you just can't take it. If you know other people with young children, they will be more than happy to help.

4 Share your feelings with other women. Find someone you can talk to and let it all hang out. Cry, vent, complain – let them know how hard this is

✻ Tips

Make meals ahead of time and freeze them for the days you just can't get it together. You will have something to throw in the oven for dinner.

Do the laundry once a week. Don't clean if you don't feel up to it; it can wait. Put off thank-you cards until you feel like doing them. Pretend you're not home when unexpected visitors arrive, or politely ask them to come at another time.

How to Do More of *(Just About)* Everything

for you and that you appreciate them letting you get things off
your chest.

5   Join a support group. If you don't have anyone to talk to and can't find
a group on your own, call your local hospital. The maternity ward may be
able to point you in the right direction.

6   Exercise. Increased metabolism is a result of exercise and will significantly improve your frame of mind and health. Try walking for 10
minutes every morning and gradually work up to a speed and time
that fits your schedule.

7   Take time to look good. Put on some makeup if you usually wear it. Buy
a new outfit. Change your hairstyle. Have a facial or manicure. Spend
time on you.

8   Eat right. Eat breakfast every day – it's a good start. Stay away from
caffeine and sugar; they'll give you a quick boost, but you'll crash
after they wear off. Keep plenty of fresh fruit on hand. Fruit is a natural
energy booster.

9   Buy a book about post-natal depression and read it. There are many
women out there who suffer from this disease every day.

⚠ **Warning**

Seek professional help immediately if you have thoughts of
suicide or a desire to harm
your baby. If you actually do
harm your baby, call a crisis
line or your partner and ask for
help immediately.

Breast-Feed Twins   679

Is it possible to breast-feed twins? Absolutely! And it's important, because twins are often small or premature, and need all
the help they can get to grow healthy and strong.

◉ **Steps**

1   Before your babies arrive, line up as much household support as possible.
Try to arrange for help with your older children, housework and other
responsibilities so you can concentrate on your twins.

2   Hydrate – when your twins are born, get used to drinking lots of fluids
and eating frequent healthy snacks. You need extra calories to make
enough milk for two babies.

3   Nurse your babies simultaneously or separately – there are advantages
and disadvantages to each method. It may be easier to nurse them one
at a time, but it will take up more of your time each day. Nursing them
together increases your prolactin levels and can stimulate milk production;
it is also a time-saver!

4   Practise a number of nursing positions; many mothers of twins find that
one baby tucked under each arm is most successful. If this doesn't work
for you, try nursing in the crisscross position, with your babies facing
each other and the legs of one twin tucked behind the other twin. Try
the parallel position, with both babies facing the same way.

5   Try to breast-feed at least some of the time even if your babies receive
bottles. This will ensure that they get the antibodies and protective
properties of your breast milk, as well as nutrition from a combination
of breast milk and formula.

6   Alternate breasts rather than always nursing the baby on the same breast.

✳ **Tips**

If people offer to help out,
accept! Whether they bring
casseroles, do the washing up
or pick up your dry cleaning,
every little bit helps.

Try to get lots of rest. Your body
needs to recover from your pregnancy and birth experience, as
well as get used to the physical
demands of nursing twins,
especially during growth spurts.

If you are trying to breast-feed
exclusively without supplement-
ing, try to avoid dummies and
artificial nipples during the first
six weeks. This will give your milk
supply a chance to stabilise and
allow your babies to develop a
good latch.

⚠ **Warning**

Keep track of the wet and dirty
nappies that each baby produces
for the first couple of weeks.

680 | Wash Your Baby's Hair

While some babies enjoy bathtime and don't mind having their hair washed, others will scream blue murder through the process.

Steps

1 Consult your doctor or midwife about grooming products; they will be able to advise you, or possibly give you a few samples.

2 Ask the hospital or birthing centre to give you a demonstration on how to wash your child's hair.

3 Start off with sponge bathing. Babies don't need to be lathered up to get clean. Wet a flannel with warm water and gently rub your infant's hair until it is sufficiently clean. Be gentle, but don't avoid the soft spots; they are protected with a thick membrane.

4 Use mild, tear-free shampoos on older babies. Rinse the lather out thoroughly until none appears with gentle rubbing. To avoid drying out your baby's scalp, you will only need to shampoo two or three times a week.

5 Cradle your child's head in your hand if you are bathing in a big bath. Lather and rinse with one hand, while firmly supporting your child with the other.

❊ Tips

Have a toy ready to distract your baby because some children dislike having their hair washed.

Wash your child's hair last so that he or she does not have to sit in sudsy water, which can cause urinary tract infections.

Use a soft-bristled brush to brush your baby's hair after the bath.

⚠ Warning

Avoid using adult shampoo on your baby's soft hair and skin.

681 | Massage a Baby in Your Home

Setting up the home environment to be warm, quiet and comfortable is the first step towards a relaxing, loving experience as you give your baby a massage.

Steps

1 Select a room that is quiet and warm.

2 Find a position that is comfortable for both of you. Be careful of your back.

3 Either cradle the baby on a pillow on your lap or position your baby on a towel or blanket in front of you. When having their backs stroked, young babies love to be held against your chest.

4 Have massage oil handy.

5 Take off any jewellery that may scratch the baby's skin.

6 Undress the baby. Either leave on a babygrow or a nappy, or strip the baby down to his or her birthday suit. Be aware of room temperature.

7 Breathe deeply and relax. The baby will feel any tension in your body through your hands.

8 Swish the massage oil in your hands to give the baby a cue that you are ready to begin.

9 Talk to your baby while massaging. It is an interaction. Listen to your baby talk back to you.

❊ Tip

The best time to massage your baby is during their "quiet, alert" state when they are relaxed, have their eyes open and are looking straight at you.

⚠ Warning

Check with your baby's health-care provider before the first massage. Some babies may not enjoy it until they are a bit older.

Help a Teething Baby or Toddler · 682

Teething babies and toddlers can get really miserable, but there are a few simple things you can do to help relieve their pain and sadness.

☉ Steps

1. Watch for telltale signs of teething such as bright-red cheeks, low fever, unusual irritability and changes in nursing, feeding or sleeping patterns. Also look for inflamed gums, a mild rash around the mouth or an unexpected nappy rash.

2. Cuddle or nurse your baby even more than usual – he or she may be looking for extra comfort.

3. Massage their gums with your fingertips – many babies enjoy this, and it helps to ease the pain.

4. Dampen some flannels and freeze them, then offer them to your baby to chew on.

5. Get some teething toys that you can store in the fridge or freezer.

6. Provide cool, icy drinks to soothe your child's gums, if your child is old enough for drinks other than breast milk or formula.

7. Offer your child cool, smooth and comforting foods such as yoghurt, if they are old enough to eat them.

8. Clean the area around your child's mouth with a tissue or warm flannel if they are dribbling a lot.

9. Get some homeopathic teething tablets or liquid; many families find that these preparations help ease their children's discomfort.

10. Offer children's acetaminophen or another pain reliever approved by your doctor or pharmacist if your child is in severe pain.

✳ Tips

Store teething toys and frozen flannels in plastic resealable bags in the freezer – this helps to keep them from picking up scents and flavours from food stored nearby.

Try to distract your child from their discomfort by offering a change of scenery, a new toy or a fun activity – this will make it harder for them to concentrate on being miserable.

⚠ Warnings

Never give your child ice cubes to suck on.

Some teething babies occasionally go on "nursing strikes" during teething episodes, and refuse to nurse altogether. If this happens, consult your doctor.

Safely Prepare Baby Food · 683

It is important to handle food correctly to prevent your baby from contracting dangerous diseases like food poisoning, salmonella poisoning and E. coli.

☉ Steps

1. Always wash your hands before and after preparing food, and use clean utensils.

2. After using a chopping board for preparing poultry or raw meat, run the board through a dishwasher. If you don't have a dishwasher, wash with antibacterial soap and warm water.

3. Always wash cutting surfaces, knives and the sink with antibacterial soap and hot water after handling poultry.

4. Defrost food in the microwave or refrigerator, not on the kitchen counter.

⚠ Warnings

Never purchase food in tins with bulging tops or jars with broken seals. Also, if a tin hisses when you open it, throw away immediately – the food could be contaminated with botulism, a serious food poisoning.

Never give an infant foods on which they can choke, such as popcorn, nuts, grapes, firm vegetables or large chunks of meat.

5   Cook poultry, beef and pork until they are done in the middle: you should not be able to see any pink. Well done is best.

6   Do not allow uncooked poultry, meat or eggs to come into contact with cooked foods.

7   Cook eggs until the whites are firm and the yolks are thick.

Never refreeze frozen food that has thawed, with exception of bread.

Don't put leftover baby food back in the jar.

684 | Raise a Vegetarian Baby

Babies have a rather limited menu, with milk their main source of food for the first few months. But if you plan on raising your child as a vegetarian, then babyhood is the place to begin.

⊙ Steps

1   Deciding whether or not to breastfeed is a personal matter, but it is considered the best way to meet an infant's nutritional needs. It also helps boost the immune system.

2   Give soy-based formula if you decide not to breastfeed. Soy is less likely to cause allergies than cow's-milk-based formulas. Do not give regular soy milk to a baby less than a year old. It is not designed to meet a baby's special needs.

3   Avoid iron supplements during the baby's first three months, unless your paediatrician prescribes it. Babies are born with high iron stores and usually have enough to last about three months.

4   Introduce solid foods at about four to six months. This will vary from baby to baby.

5   Begin with rice cereal, which is easily digestible and the least likely to cause an allergic reaction.

6   Introduce other foods slowly. You can buy commercial baby foods or puree your own fruits and vegetables in a blender. If you buy prepared foods, buy ones that are free from added sugars, preservatives and any other additives that your baby does not need.

7   Feed your veggie baby the same as any other baby, except you won't be introducing animal products. You can follow the nutritional guidelines in any baby book and adapt them for a vegetarian diet.

8   Avoid letting other people convince you that it is necessary to start your baby on cow's milk. When your baby is old enough to come off formula, you can give him or her soy milk, juice, water, rice milk and any number of other nutritious beverages.

9   Make sure your baby is eating enough solids before weaning off formula or breastfeeding. You want to be sure that all nutritional bases are covered.

10 Find a doctor who will support you in your decision to raise a vegetarian child.

✽ Tip

As you would with any baby, you may want to give your vegetarian baby a multivitamin to ensure that he or she gets optimal nutrients.

⚠ Warning

If you have any questions or concerns, contact a physician or other healthcare professional.

Select the Right Baby Monitor 685

A baby monitor can help you get things done around the house while your baby naps in another room. And at night-time it can alert you when your baby is awake and needs attention.

Steps

1 Decide on a one-way or two-way system. A one-way monitor allows you to hear your child, while a two-way monitor allows your child to hear you as well.

2 A two-way monitor can be useful if you want to reassure your child as you head towards his or her room but shouldn't be used as a substitute for your presence.

3 Consider video. Video monitors make some parents feel more comfortable about being in a different room, as they can keep an eye on their babies. They are considerably more expensive than basic audio monitors, though.

4 Take the size of your home into account. Some baby monitors have more limited ranges than others, and some have trouble transmitting through thick concrete walls. In a small home, a simple monitor should be sufficient, but large homes on more than one level may require something more sophisticated.

5 Think portable. Many baby monitors have clips that allow you to attach the receiver to your belt or clothing.

6 Guard against interference. Many monitors are made less effective by mobile phones and cordless phones being used within a few streets of the neighbourhood. Some monitors are equipped with more than one channel to help deal with this problem.

7 Remember that a monitor is no substitute for supervision – always make sure that you can get to your baby within a few seconds if you have to.

✳ Tips

If your baby wakes up quietly, put a small toy or other safe object that jingles, rattles or rustles next to him or her – this way you will know as soon as he or she is awake.

Make sure the transmitter is close to your baby – within a few metres – so that it picks up even tiny sounds.

⚠ Warnings

Check batteries and adapter cords frequently to guard against malfunctions.

Avoid putting soft toys, thick blankets or quilts in your baby's cot. These could cause your baby to suffocate.

Teach Your Toddler Colours 686

Take advantage of every teachable moment by talking about and pointing out the colours in your life.

Steps

1 Read. Buy and read books that focus on colours. Your child should be able to recognise colour differences by the age of 18 months. The more you show your toddler colours, the faster your child will comprehend the differences in hues and recognise them as different colours.

2 Buy toys that have bright colours on them. Stick to the true reds, blues and yellows, and not pastel colours. Brightly coloured toys will have a greater contrast against the everyday objects in your home and will be easier for your toddler to distinguish.

⚠ Warnings

Your toddler is learning a new skill and will make mistakes, calling red blue and so forth. Don't criticise or reprimand your toddler for mistakes. He or she will learn eventually.

3   Talk to your child about colours. Say things like, "Are you going to wear a blue or red shirt today?" "Mummy has on green socks." "I love your orange ball." You will be teaching your child valuable language skills as well as colour differences.

4   Point out colours while you are out of the house. Show your child a red apple at the supermarket. Walk on the yellow or white lines in a car park. Slide down the big blue slide at the park.

5   Ask your child to choose what colour fruit or drink to have at lunch and dinner.

6   Buy your child his or her favourite colour clothes.

7   Play colour games. Put a drop of food colouring into your bubbles to make coloured bubbles. Let your child chase and pop them. Buy coloured blocks and build colour towers. Ask your toddler to get the colour you are building and add a block to the top of the tower. When you clean up, ask your toddler to pick up the red or blue or green blocks.

8   Paint. Colour. Glue. Cut. Art is the best way to teach your child about colour and reinforce creativity at the same time. Teach your child to use child-safe scissors and cut coloured paper. Put food colouring in glue and make coloured glue designs on white paper.

Colour blindness occurs in some children. At this age it is hard to tell, because your toddler is learning a new skill. If your child enters school and is still confusing colours, you should have him or her checked for colour blindness.

687 Teach Your Toddler Shapes

Start to prepare your toddler for school by reinforcing basic skills early on – shapes are everywhere.

◎ Steps

1   Read. Buy and read books that focus on shapes. Your child should be able to recognise shape differences by the age of 18 months.

2   Buy toys that are different shapes or that teach shapes. There are many shape-sorter toys available that will teach your child shapes as well as colours. Buy foam floor mats that promote shape learning.

3   Talk to your child about shapes. Say things like, "I see you have a square book." "You like eating that triangle sandwich, don't you?" "Do you want me to make triangles or squares for you to eat?"

4   Point out shapes while you are out of the house. Show your child the round fruits at the supermarket. Let your child hold the rectangular and circular money at the bank. Point out the circular tyres on cars. Look at the many shapes on your house and neighbours' houses.

5   Play shape games. Buy different-shaped blocks and build shape towers. Ask your toddler to get the shape you are building and add a block to the top of the tower. When you clean up, ask your toddler to pick up the square or triangle blocks.

6   Paint or colour shapes on paper while you are doing projects with your child. Cut out shapes, and glue them into objects or just make shape collages.

✳ Tips

Make shapes in the dirt or sand with sticks.

Draw shapes with chalk on your garden path.

How to Do More of *(Just About)* **Everything**

Sing with Toddlers **688**

Singing is a great way to interact and have fun with your child.

Steps

1 Listen to different kinds of music. Move to the music by dancing, marching or wiggling in silly ways. Get your child interested in music from the day you bring your baby home.

2 Play or sing the same songs over and over again. Repetition is the easiest and fastest way to teach your child a song.

3 Use songs to initiate transitions in your toddler's day. For breakfast sing, "If you're hungry and you know it clap your hands, sit at the table, give Mummy a kiss." Sing clean-up songs when you are picking up toys. Choose favourite songs to sing at bedtime.

4 Act out songs while you sing, such as "Itsy Bitsy Spider". Make up your own actions for songs such as "Twinkle Twinkle Little Star".

5 Buy a CD to listen to while in the car. Playing and singing children's music while travelling is also a good way to entertain bored children.

6 Include music in physical play. Move while the music is playing and freeze when the music stops. Teach rhythm by clapping and marching in time to music. Practise fast and slow by singing at different speeds.

❋ Tips

Collect different types of instruments for your child to play with.

Talk about different instruments you can hear when listening to music so your child learns about different aspects of music.

Teach Children to Blow Their Nose **689**

Blowing your nose may come naturally for you, but it's something small children must learn to do. Follow these steps to impart this simple skill.

Steps

1 Teach your child to blow through his or her mouth first. Birthday candles and bubbles are perfect items to help.

2 Show your child how to blow out a candle first. Then hold the candle a safe distance away from their face and tell your child to blow out the candle. Practice makes perfect.

3 Blow bubbles with your child. Again offer praise for successes.

4 Master the mouth-blowing techniques and then move on to the nose-blowing. Tell your child to watch you blow air through your nose. Hold a strip of tissue up to your nose and blow making the tissue move. Let your child try this.

5 Create games out of blowing through noses and mouths. Use a straw to blow small tissue balls across the kitchen table to score goals. Be very careful when using a straw in your child's nose. Hold it for them on the very outer edge of the nose.

6 Hold one nostril closed and make your child blow. Place a tissue strip under the open nostril and let them see the tissue moving.

7 Move on to a whole tissue under both nostrils as the last step. Tell your child to close their mouth and blow air through the nose into the tissue.

⚠ Warning

Make sure your child does not frequently blow hard through his or her nose. Some research suggests that mucus is actually pushed into the sinuses when a child blows his nose, thus making the congestion worse and the risk of ear infections greater.

690 | Cope with Bed Wetting

If you have a small child that involuntarily urinates during sleep more than once a month, here are some tips for coping.

⊙ Steps

1   Never blame your child for involuntary bed wetting. It is not his or her fault. Most of the time your child is ashamed or embarrassed about wetting the bed; you want to give support and encouragement not punishment and shame. In some cases your child may have a urinary tract infection or diabetes, but this is unlikely. Bed wetting is very common in children under the age of seven.

2   A good way to care for bed wetting is to buy disposable, absorbent underwear. Let your child wear them to bed. This will lessen their embarrassment.

3   Make sure your child urinates before getting into bed at night. Decrease his or her fluid intake for two hours before bedtime.

4   If your child has dribbling urine, weak urinary stream, painful urination, difficulty urinating, blood in the urine, or fever, call your doctor straight away. If your child does not show these symptoms and is over the age of eight, try disposable underwear. If your child experiences lower back pain or abdominal pain along with urination problems, call your doctor.

✱ Tip

Bedwetting is normal for younger children. Most doctors do not consider bedwetting to be a problem until the child is six or seven years old without staying dry overnight.

⚠ Warning

Never punish your child for bed-wetting. They cannot help that their body is not responding to the signals that the bladder is sending. Punishing your child for bedwetting will only exacerbate the problem.

691 | Quickly Babyproof a Hotel Room

Children need to stay safe, no matter where they are. Even hotel rooms can be easily babyproofed to make a holiday more relaxing for the whole family.

⊙ Steps

1   Let the hotel know you are travelling with a baby or toddler, and ask if they can make any arrangements to babyproof the room in advance – some hotels offer this service.

2   Pack safety items you may need, such as simple press-on outlet covers, twist ties to secure blind cords, or removable edge/corner guards for tables and low shelves.

3   Look under the bed. This is a great place for pens, paper clips, coins and other choking or injury hazards to hide.

4   Check wardrobes and drawers, and remove dangerous objects like pens, lighters and matches.

5   Close the bathroom door. A baby or toddler can drown in just a few centimetres of water.

6   Secure loose cords and wires. A crawling baby can easily bring down a heavy lamp, so push electrical appliances away from table edges and tuck wires out of reach.

7   Tie blind cords and curtain pulls up out of reach.

✱ Tips

With adhesive tape and twist ties, you can temporarily babyproof just about anything.

If your child will be sleeping in a big bed, bring a portable guard rail, or pull a couple of high-backed chairs next to the bed so that they can't fall out.

⚠ Warnings

Toddlers often lock themselves in bathrooms. Tape over the lock, or just keep the door closed and supervise at all times.

Close and lock all windows (even those with screens), especially those near a desk or table your child could climb on to.

Check the hot water temperature; it may be much hotter than your home tap water.

8   Crawl around the room. Spending a few minutes on your hands and knees will help you to identify possible hazards from your child's level.

9   Supervise your child. There's no substitute for adult attention and supervision.

Deal with Sibling Rivalry   692

Sibling rivalry may begin with fights and arguments, and end with long-lasting resentment. Here's how to nip it in the bud.

☉ Steps

1   Recognise the reasons for the sibling rivalry. Be brutally honest and ask yourself if your children are treated fairly. Take notice of their resentment and ask yourself if you are adding to the problem. Decide how to change what you are doing so all children feel special.

2   Treat your children as individuals. Do not compare your children or they begin to believe the other child is better than they are. Praise all your children for the good things they do.

3   Listen to both sides of every story. Discuss any issues with all the children present. Make them listen to their siblings' side of the story. Let them tell their side of the story as well. Never assume one child is lying or telling the truth.

4   Stop using negative nicknames. Nicknames such as Skinny, Chunk or Klutz lead to sibling resentment and poor self-esteem.

5   Recognise and cultivate talent in every child. All children deserve to hear that they have talent. Awareness of these strengths increases confidence and gives the children separate identities. Find ways to develop their talents so they all feel like they are special.

6   Spend one-on-one time with each child. Use the time to have fun and create a special bond with each child.

7   Reward your children when they work well together. This shows them that you recognise their positive behaviour. Children are more likely to repeat an action if they know you appreciate it.

✳ Tips

Always remain calm and do not let the children see that their fighting is getting to you. Avoid having shouting matches of your own.

Tell your children as often as possible that you love them and cherish them as individuals.

⚠ Warning

If a child is abused – emotionally, physically, mentally or sexually – you must always intervene.

Calm a Child's Irrational Fears   693

Some children are naturally more anxious than others, and can require a tremendous amount of understanding.

☉ Steps

1   Do not try to explain away the fears. No amount of logic will change another person's feelings. Trying to explain away the fears will only lead to arguments and will increase your frustration.

2   Give calm reassurances: "Mummy's not going to let that happen"; "I think the monsters took the night off tonight." If you can share a similar fear you experienced, this will reassure your child that you understand

✳ Tips

Encourage imaginative drawing or role-playing activities.

Try at all times to remain calm.

Try to limit your child's exposure to anxiety-provoking images on TV.

his or her fear. If possible, show how although you worried about it, everything turned out okay. In other words, the worst-case scenario never happened.

3   Make a "what if" book. Write the irrational fear or obsession at the top of the page. Have your child write in four or five things he is afraid will happen. Writing these fears down helps the child let go of them. If they are too young to write, have them draw pictures. If they bring the same fear up again, have them write more ideas underneath. If they can't think of any, have them write some silly and imaginative things. Remember, most irrational fears come from an overactive imagination! Try to reach the point where there is some humour in the situation.

4   If after using Step 3 some fears still persist, try positive redirection. Take the ideas they came up with and make up a story about that fear. Put the story in the third person, as if it is about another child's fears. Write one of the feared outcomes on each page. Then write a page asking "did any of these things happen?" Then write your own conclusion, explaining what actually happened. Add a happily ever after ending, and then encourage your child to illustrate the story. Save your completed story and read it with your child often!

694 | Prepare Your Child for Vaccinations

Preparing your child for a doctor's appointment or vaccination can be difficult. Here are a few things to help your child get ready for the appointment.

◎ Steps

1   Talk about the upcoming appointment positively. Tell your child what will happen (weighing, listening to their heart, checking their ears) and why it is so important.

2   When you talk about the vaccination, try to stay positive. Avoid saying that they don't hurt, as you don't want your child to think you lied to them. Instead focus on why they give immunisations. Explain how terrible diseases are often avoided because we get injections and how painful these illnesses are. If you feel you have to tell them, then say the injections do hurt sometimes, but not always.

3   Read children's books to your child about doctors' appointments. These books are fun and engaging. Your child will enjoy reading about other children seeing the doctor and how they might be scared, but it's not as scary as it seems. Some even discuss immunisations.

4   Give your child tylenol before the appointment. This will help to keep the pain of the injection site to a minimum.

5   Ask your child how they want you to be with them during the vaccinations. They might want to just hold your hand or sit on your lap.

6   Try to distract them. Ask them questions that require thought, such as the colour of the walls or what the pictures are. For more advanced kids, ask them to spell words or answer maths questions. Any distraction will keep them from concentrating on the immunisation, reducing the pain effect.

✳ **Tip**

Ask the doctor to explain the reason for the immunisation if you think it will help.

⚠ **Warning**

If your child is ill, avoid vaccinations until they are better.

Teach Your Child to Get Dressed

Some kids hate getting dressed and would stay in pyjamas all day, but when your children wear clothes that they like, dressing can be fun – as well as easier on you.

Steps

1 Let your child help in selecting their wardrobe, for the most part. Having likeable, comfortable clothes can make dressing on their own a lot less painful.

2 Allow your child to decorate hand-me-down clothes with their choice of patches to make them seem unique and almost new – and thus more fun to wear.

3 Decide what your child will wear to special or formal occasions. Explain that although they can choose their own everyday clothes, there are certain clothes that are more appropriate for certain events.

4 Tape on to each drawer a picture of the kinds of clothes it contains, such as trousers, socks or t-shirts. For younger children, review which articles of clothing go on which parts of the body.

5 Have your child decide the night before what they will wear the next day, and lay the items out over a chair; this will get them on the way to school much more quickly in the morning.

6 Turn the ordeal of dressing into a game. Perhaps you can have a race to see who can get dressed first.

7 Ask your child if they need help with any article of clothing before you jump in for the rescue. Whenever possible, show your child how to put something on instead of doing it for them.

❋ Tip

Clothes are psychologically important for children in terms of wanting to look like their peers. Unless completely inappropriate, consider giving in to your child's tastes, but do not be afraid to set wardrobe guidelines.

Teach a Child to Tie Shoelaces

Many children will get frustrated when trying to learn how to tie their shoelaces. While there's no miraculous solution other than patience and lots of practice, there are ways that you can help your child acquire this skill.

Steps

1 Wait until your child is ready. Most children develop the dexterity needed to tie shoelaces between the ages of four and six. Girls are often ready to learn slightly earlier than boys.

2 Make sure your child knows right from left before you try to teach them how to tie their shoes.

3 Choose one method of lace-tying, and teach it consistently. Make sure that everyone who may be trying to help your child learn this skill is offering the same method. Otherwise they may get confused.

4 Make up a game or poem to help your child remember the necessary steps for tying their laces.

❋ Tips

One easy method of shoe-tying is to have your child make two loops, then tie them together in a simple knot. This is easier than bow tying and just as effective.

If your child is left-handed and you aren't, try to find an adult "lefty" to help teach this skill.

5   Make sure that you and your child are side by side rather than opposite each other when you demonstrate. That way they'll be able to copy your movements rather than mirror them.

6   Give your child lots of praise when they get it right.

7   Make sure you teach your children how to do this, even though alternatives are available. Velcro shoes and elastic shoes without laces may be fun for the kids, but they'll have to learn how to tie their shoes eventually, and basic knot and bow tying is a good skill to learn young.

697 Bring Basic Sensory and Adaptive Skills into Everyday Play

These are very basic ways to bring learning skills into everyday play, including sensory activities, large motor skills, fine motor skills and language skills.

◉ Steps

1   Sensory activities are a great way to keep the hands busy. A simple way to let kids increase their sensory skills is to spray whipped cream on the table and let them create a masterpiece. Kids love to play with food. Ask them how it feels, smells and even tastes. With older kids you can use shaving cream, which moulds better, but you'll want to skip the taste part!

2   Large motor skills are easily used in active games. Burn off some off that energy before nap time by playing games that involve using large motor skills. Play a game of "Animals on the Farm". Have children pick an animal found on the farm and then act out that animal in both sound and motion. Have children try out different animals and then talk about which animal was their favourite to imitate.

3   Fine motor skills can be incorporated by playing sorting, stacking and building games. Have children build up those games by picking up small objects and sorting them into containers. Children can build up towers with blocks and then knock them down like a bulldozer or inclement weather i.e. "Oh no – along came the wind and knocked down my house."

4   Language skills are the simplest to add to everyday play. Interact with children while they are at play. Talk with them about what they are playing with, what size, shape and colour it is.

5   Name everyday objects as you do daily activities with kids, i.e. let's brush your "hair" with the "hairbrush", let's wash our "hands" in the "sink" with "soap" and "water". The more descriptive you are with your children about what they are doing, the quicker they will pick up on the importance of verbal skills and also the art of conversation.

✳ Tip

Simple interaction with your child is the best way to teach them. They learn from you.

Get Your Child to Wear Glasses 698

Sometimes it's difficult for children to understand why they have to wear glasses when most of their friends don't.

⊙ Steps

1 Do your best to help your child understand why they need to wear glasses; even some toddlers can understand when you explain that the glasses will help them see better.

2 Let your child help to choose their own frames by offering a selection of frames within your price range. Children won't wear glasses they hate.

3 Avoid buying glasses for your child to grow into – these will be uncomfortable, as well as less effective than glasses that fit properly.

4 Resort to bribery if necessary. Offer stickers as an incentive to wear glasses, or as a reward for keeping them on for a certain amount of time.

5 Make it clear to your child that certain activities require glasses: if your toddler brings you a book, insist that they put their glasses on before you read it.

6 Find some stories or picture books that show children wearing glasses or that deal with the issue of getting glasses.

7 Try to avoid conflicts and battles of will; if your toddler takes their glasses off after half an hour, wait before putting them back on.

8 Clean the lenses regularly – your child is more likely to keep them on if they can actually see through them. Show them how to clean them if they're old enough.

✳ Tips

If possible, get polycarbonate lenses; they are scratch-resistant and durable.

If you don't wear glasses, consider getting some empty frames to wear when with your child, just to show that you will willingly wear glasses too.

⚠ Warnings

If redness or sore patches appear on your child's nose or temples, take the glasses in for readjustment.

If you need to bribe your child to keep their glasses on, don't use food. This could lead to food-related emotional issues later in life.

Don't forget to check screws and other fittings regularly to make sure the glasses don't fall apart.

Assign Household Chores 699

Running a household efficiently is one of the most difficult tasks there is. Here are some ways to make it a little bit easier.

⊙ Steps

1 Teach younger children how to complete daily tasks: to make their beds and to take out only two or three toys at a time, putting them away before taking out more.

2 Ask older children and adults to take care of daily tasks as well: to wash and dry dishes as they use them; to keep bathrooms clean and dry; and to put clean clothing away in wardrobes or drawers and dirty clothes in the laundry basket.

3 Demonstrate to your children how to do a particular chore, and allow time and practice for them to do it right.

4 Make a chart of major chores, such as laundry, sweeping, shopping, cooking and taking out the rubbish, and rotate them every month.

5 Think of chores that the family can complete together. For instance, on a hot summer day, have everyone go outside and wash the car – and have a water fight while you're at it.

✳ Tip

For younger children, have them help create a daily schedule with their chores worked in. Routine is important for them.

⚠ Warning

Paying children to do basic chores might give them the idea that they should be rewarded for doing tasks that are part of their routine.

700 Take a Young Child Out in Public

While taking your child along on errands or social outings is sometimes a necessity, it also provides a good change of pace for the youngster. Follow these steps to ensure the outing is pleasant for all involved.

Steps

1   Call ahead of time and ask whether you can bring a baby or child along when meeting with a friend. Assure your friend that if the child starts to act up, you'll take him or her home.

2   Prepare your child for the outing. Make sure he or she is well rested to avoid crankiness and restlessness, and if he or she is old enough to understand, go over rules of proper behaviour before you leave the house.

3   Pack distractions like toys or food and distribute them as necessary.

4   Plan for your child's sleeping habits. Can you borrow a friend's bed? Will your child fall asleep in a pushchair?

5   Take your child to restaurants that cater to young children, if you can. Many restaurants supply highchairs along with paper, crayons and games to distract them.

6   Ask where you can go to change and feed your baby, whether you are in a public place or a friend's home.

7   When the day is done, praise your child for a successful outing.

✿ Tip

If you need to reprimand your child for improper behaviour, try to do so in private. Lower your voice and be calm but firm.

⚠ Warning

Sometimes, despite your foresight and efforts, your child will act up while in public. You may have no choice but to take him or her home.

701 Take a Road Trip with Kids

Just the thought of spending 12 to 14 hours or more in a car with children can cause many parents to have a panic attack. Here's how to do it painlessly.

Steps

1   Make sandwiches the night before leaving so your little riders will have a snack to eat along the way. Include a lot of non-messy snacks and drinks. Stay away from beverages that contain caffeine or lots of sugar. Don't forget to bring along a few bags to put rubbish in, otherwise you'll have some serious cleaning once you reach your destination.

2   Pack some fun things for younger kids to do along the way. Mad-Lib books, colouring books, coloured pencils (NOT crayons or markers – the heat will cause them to melt or explode), car games, cards and books (if you're travelling at night bring a torch or reading light) are all great for entertainment.

3   Surprises and new toys or books can take away the boredom. Purchase a few "surprises" for each child to do in the car. Don't let them have any of these items until you're on the road. Give the items out throughout your road trip.

✿ Tip

Remember to have patience, a sense of humour and let things roll.

⚠ Warning

Don't forget your child's comfort blanket or favourite toy.

4   Some parents swear by the DVD players in their cars. This is really great for young children. You can let them pick out a few new DVDs before leaving.

5   Bring headphones and iPods for each child so there is no arguing over music.

6   Bring a pillow and blanket for each child. It's also a good idea to cover the seats with an old blanket or sleeping bag in case of spills.

7   Make sure the kids dress comfortably. Tight pony tails, waistbands that fit too tightly, shirts that are too hot or dresses with itchy lace or fabric will make your child more irritable and miserable. Don't make them wear shoes in the car. Let them get comfy.

Communicate Effectively with a Teen   702

It sounds contradictory, but to communicate well with a teen you need to learn to listen.

☉ Steps

1   Practise the basics of overall good communication: empathy, flexibility and open-mindedness.

2   Make yourself available and accessible.

3   Remain consistent in your answers and reasoning during decision-making and disciplining.

4   Count to 10 before you speak, especially if you are agitated.

5   Give yourself 10 minutes to make a decision, even if you know what it will be. Your child will come to expect it and not blindside you with changes in plans.

6   Practise a controlled demeanour and calm tone, even when it's difficult. Avoid being sarcastic or raising your voice.

7   Learn to apologise.

8   Have dinner together as a family, every night if possible. Family time generates good feelings among family members, which enhances the likelihood of successfully communicating.

✳ Tips

If dialogue breaks down, consider writing notes to say what you need to.

Try to make it easy for your teen to come to you with deep emotions and problems. On these occasions, listen to everything your teenager has to say before jumping in with advice. Avoid being preachy.

Encourage Your Teenager to Avoid Drugs   703

Teaching your teenager to avoid drugs starts with straightforward discussion about the consequences of taking mind-altering substances.

☉ Steps

1   Talk about the immediate and long-term effects of consuming drugs, tobacco or alcohol: bad breath, stained teeth, increased risk of cancer and liver disease.

⚠ Warning

Don't start the conversation by being confrontational, even if you suspect (or have evidence) that your teenager is using drugs.

2 Discuss impaired judgment and related risks of mind-altering substances such as driving under the influence or finding yourself in dangerous sexual situations.

3 Mention the role of drugs in interfering with a student's future plans, such as going to college and eventually starting a family.

4 Point out the dangers of alcohol, tobacco and other drugs in relation to pregnancy, including birth defects in newborns.

5 Warn your teen about the hazards of combining drugs.

6 Discuss medical marijuana and the debate over the legalisation of marijuana. Be open-minded – they may have been educated about this at school and have formed their own opinion. Respect this.

7 Explain that the component of marijuana with medicinal value is delta-9-terhydrocannabinol (THC). It can be prescribed by doctors in pill form, which lacks the cancer-causing chemicals of smoked marijuana.

8 Praise and encourage your teen when he or she makes good decisions and achieves long-worked-for goals.

704 | Avoid Teen Pregnancy

Handling pregnancy and parenthood at an early age takes its toll on the emotional, physical and financial well-being of a teenager.

Steps

1 Start to speak to your child at an early age on a frequent basis about self-respect, love, sex and relationships. Choose conversations appropriate for their age and comfort level. Communicating about sex is an ongoing conversation throughout adolescence.

2 Try not to corner your child with one-sided questions, but make it a two-way conversation. Correct any misconceptions that he or she may have sensitively, without ridiculing. Discuss the effects of unplanned pregnancy and sexually transmitted diseases.

3 Be specific while talking about contraception and disease prevention. Asking a hormonally charged teenager not to have sex does not help. Be realistic and discuss everything from being ready emotionally to using effective contraception.

4 Use real-life stories to show the teenager why parenthood at an early age is difficult. Exercise practical drills for your teenager, like babysitting, to help them understand the responsibility.

5 Play an active role in knowing your teenager's friends and partners. Supervise his or her activities with rules, curfews and expectations.

6 Encourage your teenagers in healthy practices like reading and sports. Reward their achievements and help them plan a positive future with meaningful goals.

 ✻ Tip

Continue talking openly even if your teenager looks disinterested. Teenagers look for their parents' support and guidance even when they feel independent.

⚠ Warning

Discourage your child from dating older teens on a steady basis.

Reform a Teen Bully 705

When parents find out their teen is being bullied, their emotions fluctuate between anger and sadness. When parents find out their teen is doing the bullying, they find themselves not only angry and sad, but embarrassed too.

⊙ Steps

1 Emphasise the seriousness of the situation. You need to sit down with your teen and make sure he or she understands the gravity of the situation and that bullying behaviour is unacceptable. Follow up with consequences and discipline, and be consistent and firm.

2 Reach out to the teachers to let them know that you're aware of what's going on and that you're handling it at home. A consistent plan of action both at home and at school will reinforce acceptable behaviour.

3 The fact that your teen is bullying others should tell you that they lack empathy. It's crucial for your child's development to respect others and to have a sense of how their actions make others feel. Pose the question of how they would feel if someone were to bully them.

4 Know what your teen is doing and with whom. This will better enable you to guide him or her in making the right choices when they choose a peer group. If you don't feel that they're hanging out with good role models, put a stop to them socialising with bad influences.

5 Get them involved in outside activities. Very often, a bully doesn't have much else going on in their life. Encourage them to try a sport, hobby or community service. The more they fill spare time with enriching activities, the less they have to focus on others. They'll also make new friends and have a sense of accomplishment.

6 Make yourself their role model. A bully usually learns behaviour at home, and if you've been showing your anger in response to disappointing situations, then they'll eventually emulate you. Show your teen how to positively respond instead.

7 Offer up praise. When you spot reform in your teen, give them the good words. This will reinforce their efforts to change their negative behaviour and encourage them to continue acting positively towards their peers.

✳ Tips

Try to find mentors for your bullying teen. While you're the first person they look to for cues, having other people around to provide positive role models can only help.

Develop a dialogue with your teen. Rather than only laying down the punishment, try to get them to open up about why they are bullying.

⚠ Warning

Know when to get outside help. If your partnership with the school isn't working, it's time to take your teen to a professional, such as a psychiatrist, psychologist or counsellor.

Get Help for an Anorexic Teen 706

Anorexia is a serious and sometimes life-threatening eating disorder whose sufferers often starve themselves to lose excessive amounts of weight.

⊙ Steps

1 Spot the warning signs. Anorexic teens often skip meals, refuse to eat in front of others, obsess over food labels, weigh themselves constantly and exercise compulsively.

✳ Tip

In addition to developing odd behaviours about food, anorexic teens may withdraw from friends and family members. They may also lose interest in activities they previously enjoyed.

2 Address the problem as soon as you suspect your teen may have anorexia. The longer the illness goes untreated, the harder it is for your teen to recover.

3 Seek therapy or counselling. Family therapy is often a critical step on the pathway to recovery for anorexic teens. Parents play an important role in shaping teens' perceptions of their bodies.

4 Talk with your teen about unattainable images of physical perfection she may see in the media. Magazines, films and television shows promote unrealistic ideals of beauty, and it's essential that your teen realises that her self-worth is not tied to her weight or her outward appearance.

5 Research outpatient treatment options, which your local hospital probably offers. Outpatient treatment includes group counselling, where your teen can talk to other people who are suffering from anorexia, as well as sessions with professional counsellors or therapists.

6 Consider in-patient treatment, where your child stays in a facility for at least two weeks and undergoes intense treatment for anorexia. In these facilities, your teen's physical health is monitored on a daily basis, her eating and nutrition are scrutinised and she attends both private and group therapy sessions.

⚠ **Warnings**

It's common for teens to relapse following treatment, so closely monitor her behaviour. If you notice the warning signs of anorexia emerging again, immediately seek help for her.

Some teens require several in-patient stays before they recover. Be prepared for this.

---

707 | Prevent Truancy

Preventing truancy is about more than just forcing the child to attend school. You must identify and address the root cause.

◉ **Steps**

1 Insist on accurate record-keeping. If your child has truancy issues, the school's attendance policies may not be consistent or effective enough to track your child.

2 Ask the school to notify you when your child is absent. The school must notify you whether the absence is excused or unexcused to ensure the child is not forging their own excuses.

3 Investigate the safety of the child's school. An environment with gang or bullying issues encourages truancy.

4 Explore alternative schools in your district. Other truant students can negatively influence your child and you may need to switch schools for severe problems.

5 Escort your child to school, whether by walking or driving the child.

6 Work with your child on subjects with which they struggle. Children skip school to avoid facing embarrassment in the classroom when their academic performance is poor.

7 Make school a priority. Students must not miss school to help with the family business or to attend holidays that fall during the school year. Allowing students to miss school for reasons other than illness or family emergencies sends the message that school is not important.

⚠ **Warning**

In many cases of repeated truancy parents are held responsible by the authorities – always know where your child is.

Be a Good Parent 708

A big part of good parenting is establishing respect between parents and children. Your children need to know what you expect of them, and you in turn must learn to listen and wait. Patience is the key to being a good parent.

⊙ Steps

1   Slow down. Babies and children live in a different time frame from adults – usually a much slower one. Keep this in mind as you talk to your child, care for your children and go about your day together.

2   Observe your children. You'll be amazed at how well you'll get to know them by sitting back and simply watching. This focused awareness will help you better understand moods, abilities and temperament. Listening is important, too.

3   Stay optimistic. Optimism is contagious; so is negativity. Show your child through your behaviour how to overcome minor setbacks. Lead by example. Don't swear and get angry when you hit a setback. Focus on moving forward.

4   Accept and acknowledge your children's feelings and desires. Let them know it's OK if they feels sad, scared or angry.

5   Tell your children your expectations. Children won't always comply straight away, but they need to understand clearly what a parent expects: "I want you to put on your sweater. We're going outside." or "I want your feet to stay off the sofa!" Always explain why you are asking them to do something, though.

6   Set appropriate limits. Even when you acknowledge a feeling or desire, you must make children aware of appropriate behaviour and rules from an early age: "I can see you're angry at your friend because he took the toy from you, but I won't let you hit him. Hitting is not something we do in our family."

7   Wait. Let your children do as much as they can on their own – learn to walk, put on their socks, resolve conflicts with their friends. Anxiety or the desire to help often tempts parents to rush in and solve the problem for their children. A better response would be to wait and see what your children can manage on their own.

8   Behave genuinely. Just as you accept your children's moods, though not always their behaviour, it's OK to have a sad or angry thought yourself and express it appropriately: "I'm really tired at the moment but I'm listening to you." A parent's genuineness prepares a child for life.

9   Nurture yourself and your marriage. Make arrangements to have some guilt-free time to take care of your own needs. Plan a date with your partner and forget the kids for a while.

❋ Tips

Build more time into your schedule so you can slow down with your child and enjoy your time together. Continuous hurried behaviour creates stress for both you and your child.

Start a babysitting circle with neighbourhood parents so you can have a few hours to yourself or a date with your partner.

⚠ Warning

Monitor your children if they're having a dispute with a friend. Feelings can quickly escalate, and a parent may need to intervene. Safety should always be your priority.

709 | Become a Good Stepmother

If being a mother is the toughest job in the world, then being a stepmother comes a close second. It's never easy to step in and fill a mother's role. Becoming a good stepmother takes patience and practice.

Steps

1 Get to know your stepchildren before marrying their father. This can make the transition from "dad's girlfriend" to stepmother much easier. Don't attempt to take over the mother's role.

2 Remember that you are not equal to your stepchildren's father. Always communicate with him when it comes to punishments, rules and other aspects of the children's upbringing.

3 Interact with your stepchildren. Show interest in their schoolwork, their friends, their hobbies and extracurricular activities. Be available for them.

4 Show respect for your stepchildren's real mother. Never talk badly about her in front of them. If she's alive, be friendly with her.

5 Develop a relationship with your stepchildren based on who you are. Establish your own place in their lives and develop your own bond.

6 Prepare for the inevitable test of wills. Your stepchildren may push your boundaries. Show them respect but ask for it too.

7 Don't force your stepchildren to call you "mum" if they are uncomfortable doing so. This just builds resentment.

8 Build their trust. Have an understanding ear when they need to talk.

✱ Tip

Always put yourself in his child's shoes before responding.

⚠ Warning

There are going to be times when your partner sides with his child over you. It will happen. Be prepared.

---

710 | Choose a Good Babysitter

A good babysitter can restore a measure of sanity to the lives of even the most harried parents.

Steps

1 Talk to trusted friends and relatives. The best person to look after your child is someone with experience and good references.

2 Look in your neighbourhood and approach someone suitable.

3 Choose someone old enough. A sitter who is 11 or older should be qualified to look after older children. An infant requires an older caretaker.

4 Ask lots of questions. Have a checklist handy when interviewing potential sitters. Include questions about experience, first aid or CPR training, transportation and payment.

5 Watch the potential sitter interact with your child. Watch or listen closely for discipline strategies and ability to guide or redirect play.

6 If your sitter is an adolescent, meet his or her parents. Make sure the parents will be available for any problems or emergencies that arise.

✱ Tip

Lay down the rules of your house the very first time the sitter works for you. Include discipline approaches, feeding and bed-times, and do's and don'ts for the sitter to adhere to.

⚠ Warning

When your children are old enough to understand, talk to them about different types of abuse. Make it very clear that you want to know if something or someone hurts them or makes them feel uncomfortable.

✓ 711 Find a Nanny

The safety and well-being of their children is of utmost importance to parents – especially when it's time to go back to work and leave them in the hands of someone else. Finding a nanny can be a very stressful process for many parents. Here are some of the key questions to ask both yourself and your prospective nanny.

❑ **What kind of nanny do you need?**

A live-out nanny is one that comes to your home when scheduled to watch your child and leaves when you return home. Often these nannies will help with housekeeping and transportation for the children, but they do not stay overnight. In contrast, a live-in nanny resides with the family and is on call almost all the time.

❑ **How much do you want to spend?**

Research what experienced nannies who offer what you are looking for are charging. Often a care provider will have a set rate, but there is also room for negotiation, so set a range you are willing to work with. Whether you pay per hour or as a flat-rate salary is an important distinction to make.

❑ **What do you want your nanny to do?**

Now that you know what you are looking for, write up a job description that includes the duties of the job, the expectations, the pay rate, and when you would like the nanny to begin. At this point, it could be a good idea to get the children involved and ask them what they would like in a nanny. Obviously, some of these suggestions should be taken with a pinch of salt, but you may find out some interesting things about what your children prefer in discipline styles and personalities. Ultimately, you want to make sure that not only do you like the new nanny, but the children do as well.

❑ **Where can you find a nanny?**

Using an agency can cost some money, but usually they do background screening and reference checks for you. You can also look online for care-provider sites or you can place an ad in the newspaper. Always pay for a criminal background check, though.

Once you have selected some prospective candidates, you'll want to meet them and interview them. First see how well they interact with your children – if your kids don't like them, don't employ them. They're the ones who will have to spend most time with them, after all. When you finally sit down to the interview, consider the following questions.

❑ What is your background and experience in nannying?

❑ What is your discipline style?

❑ How many children have you worked with at a time?

❑ Do you have any children of your own, and would you be bringing them along?

❑ What is your usual pay rate?

❑ What additional duties are you willing to perform?

❑ What are your interests/hobbies?

❑ How will you keep the children occupied during their time with you?

When you find a nanny that meets your qualifications and that you feel comfortable hiring, it is time to work out an agreement, get it in writing and decide on details. Make sure that both parties understand the agreement and what is expected of each party. Once this is finalised, you can begin to enjoy the benefits of this new addition to your family.

712 | Say Goodbye to Your Child at Daycare

Saying goodbye can be just as hard for parents as it is for their children. Goodbyes are a very important part of the process to help children feel safe and confident in the daycare setting.

⊙ **Steps**

1   Say goodbye to your child every time you leave, even if your child is busy playing.

2   Keep it short and sweet – long-drawn-out goodbyes are hard on everyone.

3   Tell your child (no matter how old) that you are leaving, who will be caring for them and that you will see them later. Inform your child who will be picking them up.

4   Establish a goodbye routine, such as reading one last book or giving a final wave goodbye from a window.

5   Enlist the support of your child's primary caregiver in the daycare setting if your child is having a hard time separating.

6   Encourage your child to bring something special to the childcare setting, such as a blanket or soft toy, to help when they need to be comforted.

7   Provide photographs of mum, dad and other special people for your child to look at when they are missing you.

8   Encourage your child to talk about their feelings when you pick them up. Remind them that you always come back.

✳ **Tip**

Some parents recommend reading a book to a child about another child going to daycare to help master any feelings of anxiety about separating.

713 | Cope with Empty Nest Syndrome

The time after a child leaves home can be difficult for a parent, but it can also be an opportunity for exciting changes.

⊙ **Steps**

1   Don't be alarmed if you experience feelings of sadness and loss of purpose when your last child leaves home. These are normal reactions.

2   Find someone to talk to, such as your spouse or a friend. If you don't feel better, consult a counsellor or therapist trained in the field.

3   Consider a support group. Even if you're not a joiner, a group with similar experiences can offer information, new friends and a sympathetic ear.

4   Find information about empty nest syndrome.

5   Become involved. Take up a new hobby, sport or volunteer effort to regain your sense of purpose and fill those lonely hours.

6   Find something to look forward to. Whether it's visiting your children or taking a holiday – by yourself, with your spouse or with friends – it will keep your mind on something positive.

7   Find a way to communicate regularly with the kids by phone, email or letters.

✳ **Tips**

Consider "adopting" a friend's toddler or a guide dog, or taking on a babysitting job. Lots of volunteer opportunities exist that will fulfil you and make the time fly by.

If you're married, consider this a time to become reacquainted with your spouse. Quiet evenings, long walks, impulsive trips and dinners out are all possible now that the kids aren't around.

If you've wanted a pet but felt you didn't have time, now's your chance.

Be a Good Grandparent   714

Being a good grandparent sounds easy, but there's a fine line to walk if you are to succeed in this role.

Steps

1   Start with the new parents. Your child and their spouse are the link between you and your new grandchild.

2   Offer your help in the first few weeks. Remember to ask what they need you to do, and realise that this isn't the time for you and your grandchild to bond. You're there to give some much-needed support and relief to the parents so that they can bond with their child.

3   Respect the new parents. Instead of criticising or correcting decisions and lifestyles, give your advice only when asked.

4   Give the gift of time. Whether you live far away or next door, your time will be the most important gift you can impart to your grandchild. With the new parents, set up times to visit or to take your grandchild overnight or for the weekend.

5   Remember birthdays and holidays. Send a card or email, or make a phone call on special occasions – or just for the fun of it. Show an interest in their interests. All it takes is asking what new song your grand-daughter learned in her piano lesson or who won your grandson's football match to start a dialogue and show how much you care.

6   Share your history with your grandchildren. Don't wait until they're old enough to listen to your stories of primary school or the snowstorms you had to walk through to get there. Start a journal and write it all down, including the names of all of your relatives that you can remember, important dates and funny stories.

✳ Tips

It's okay to spend a little one-on-one time with each grandchild without the fear of appearing to choose favourites. As long as each child gets their own "Granny Time" they will all benefit from these experiences.

Enjoy the simple things in life. Spending time with your grand-children doesn't have to mean an expensive outing to the shops, the cinema or an amusement park. Invite them over to bake, play games, rent DVDs or read stories.

Enjoy your role as grandparent. If you're not babysitting but simply visiting your grandchildren and their parents, don't discipline the children. That's for their parents to do, and you can sit back and finally be the fun one, not the "no" person.

Be a Good Godparent   715

Godparenting is a task that should not be entered into lightly. Make sure that you are able to fulfil all the obligations of a godparent before you agree to this rewarding responsibility.

Steps

1   Attend the baptism of the godchild. This service will solidify the child's relationship with the Church, as well as your relationship as a godparent.

2   Develop and nurture a caring relationship with your godchild. Send birthday cards every year, write letters, and keep in touch via phone, email or face-to-face meetings.

3   Take the time to discuss matters of religion or spirituality with your godchild once he or she is old enough.

4   Serve as a sponsor for the child's confirmation, if applicable.

5   Encourage the godchild to follow the faith of the chosen religion, and to attend mass regularly, if applicable.

✳ Tip

Godparents are conventionally obligated to act as legal custodians to their godchildren if anything happens to the parents. Many parents, though, do name a legal guardian in addition to the godparents. Make sure that your guardianship obligations are discussed in detail before you agree to accept the role.

716 Host a Harry Potter Party

Whether Harry Potter is your secret idol or the bane of your existence, the fact remains that kids love him! What better way to celebrate any occasion than letting Harry host your party?

⊙ Steps

1 Make your guest list and create invitations. Shop-bought Harry Potter cards are readily available, but if you're of a creative turn of mind you can make your own. Simple and familiar symbols to Harry Potter fans include lightning bolts, dragons, lions and broomsticks.

2 Decorate the party area with magical-themed items. Cut stars from cardboard and cover them with aluminium foil, hanging them from the ceiling to create Hogwarts' magical roof. Include a few atmospheric touches – a roaring fire, a handful of broomsticks in the corner, empty picture frames – whatever you have on hand can be transformed into a magical item! Don't forget to set up tables for food.

3 Divide your guest list into four teams, naming each team after a Hogwart's house (Ravenclaw, Gryffindor, Slytherin and Hufflepuff). When your guests arrive, assemble them for the sorting. As each child tries on the sorting hat, it shouts the name of the house that child belongs to. This can be done very simply by having the host "interpret" for the hat. For a more impressive effect, hide a walkie-talkie or open mobile phone somewhere in the hat's fabric and have an accomplice stand around the corner. The announcement will sound like it originates from the hat!

4 Give each child a piece of wood doweling and invite them to make their own magic wands. Provide art supplies for this activity (markers, paint, glue, glitter and anything else you can think of). As the children decorate, tell them that during the party the four houses will compete for the house cup by earning points. Any adult can award points for such things as helpfulness and manners. Points can also be earned by winning games.

5 Play Harry Potter-themed games, keeping track of the points each house wins. Some examples include pin-the-glasses-on-Harry's-face (easily constructed from poster board and markers) and making magical potions (combining different types of fizzy drinks and juice).

6 Award prizes to all children. Small magic tricks are often available as party prizes and make an excellent complement to a Harry Potter party. Have a small extra prize on hand for the house with the most points (stickers, small treats and card games all work well).

※ Tips

You can buy wood doweling cheaply at any hardware or craft shop, especially if you are willing to buy longer pieces and cut them yourself.

If your group is too small for four teams, simply divide them into Gryffindor and Slytherin.

717 Throw a Pirate-Themed Birthday Party

If your young swashbuckler wants a pirate-themed birthday party then get ready for a fun-filled celebration.

⊙ Steps

1 Make parchment invitations by soaking white paper in coffee until it turns brown, and set on a surface to dry. Gently burn the outer edges of each sheet so that it resembles a worn piece of parchment. Write in the party

※ Tip

A variation of this is to throw a *Pirates of the Caribbean* party, and have children dress as Captain Jack Sparrow.

details and work in phrases such as "Ahoy there, Matey" and refer to the party as "swashbuckling fun".

2   Fill a treasure chest and set it by the front door with a sign that says "Beware, Pirates Ahead". Place the chest on top of a sand-coloured tablecloth to resemble the beach, or if you do it outside you can use real sand. For the pirate booty, use plastic jewel beads, chocolate coins and plastic bowls or cups spray-painted gold.

3   Tape strips of red and black crêpe streamers to the ceiling along a wall to form a curtain. Then tape paper pirate hats, skeletons and parrots to the curtain for an awesome scene-setting display.

4   Cover tables in black and red cloth and decorate with pirate flag centre-pieces. To make the centrepiece, cover flower pots with black foil wrapping and place a chunk of polystyrene in each pot. Find pirate flag clip art and print it on your computer. Then cut out the flags and attach them to wooden skewers and insert in the polystyrene.

5   Serve dry snacks like crisps in miniature treasure chests or upside-down black tri-corner hats. Give your other snacks and drinks pirate names to add to the fun. Serve punch but refer to it as "grog". Make hidden treasure fairy cakes by inserting a jellybean inside the cake after it has cooled.

6   Have the party guests sit in a circle and place two chairs in the middle. Let the guest of honour sit in one seat and choose a birthday present to open. Have the gift-giver join them in the centre of the circle while they're opening the present. When they're done, give the guest a bag full of pirate-themed goodies like an eye patch, gold foil-covered chocolates, temporary tattoos and beads.

Select Children's Party Games   **718**

Planning a kid's party means more than cake and balloons. Keeping the kids entertained is also a big part of a successful children's party.

◉ Steps

1   Fill a piñata full of sweets and other prizes and have the children take turns wearing a blindfold. Each one can try to burst it open with a bat or stick.

2   Plan a treasure hunt or scavenger hunt for your next children's party. In this game, the object can be to either collect a specific item or several. Create a map to the hidden treasure or a list of items to find in a scavenger hunt and hand them out at the beginning of the party. Keep the game simple – remember the ultimate objective is to have fun!

3   Get older kids talking with 20 Questions. One player thinks of an object or person and the rest of the party has 20 questions to guess what that object is. The winner then becomes the next person to think of something and answer questions. Whoever can stump the whole party can be awarded a prize.

4   Have a craft-themed party and let the kids be creative. You can find beads and other craft projects at your local craft shop. If your party has a theme, such as princesses or pirates, you can create craft projects that will complement it.

✳ Tip

To keep party games fun and within budget, choose those that don't require added props or special equipment. Guessing games such as 20 Questions are inexpensive and entertaining for school-age children.

719 | Make Balloon Animals

Making balloon animals is a classic amusement at kids' parties and with a little patience and practice you can make balloon animals to entertain children of all ages.

⊙ Steps

1 Stretch a pencil balloon a few times. Place the balloon opening over the end of the pump so that it fits snugly. Hold the balloon in place with your non-dominant hand. Inflate the balloon slowly and steadily with the pump until there's about 15 cm (6 in) of uninflated balloon left.

2 Release a tiny bit of air so that there is enough balloon material left to tie a knot at the end.

3 Measure about 15 cm (6 in) from the knotted end of the balloon and bend until the balloon lies flat against itself. Grasp the balloon about 5 cm (2 in) from the bend you made.

4 Squeeze both sections of the balloon together at this 5 cm (2 in) mark and twist three times. The short section with the knot will be the balloon animal's nose and the loop will become the animal's ears.

5 Move your fingers about 2.5 cm (1 in) down the balloon and pinch; this will be the starting point for the front legs.

6 Measure about 15 cm (6 in) again and bend that section in half.

7 Twist the balloon together three times where the front legs begin and the bent end comes back to meet this point. Angle this newly made section downwards to be the legs.

8 Measure about 5 cm (2 in) and pinch the balloon. The section you pinched off will be the body and the point that is pinched will be the beginning of the back legs.

9 Repeat Steps 5 and 6, but realise that this time you are making the back legs. You should have a small bit of balloon left. That will be the tail.

10 Adjust the angles of the nose, ears, legs and tail as needed.

✱ Tips

By varying the lengths you can create different four-legged animals.

Be creative and try other balloon-twisting animals.

At a children's party, be sure to include everyone in the fun.

⚠ Warnings

Balloons are choking hazards. Keep balloons and balloon pieces away from young children and animals.

Balloons often pop. Warn children that this may happen.

720 | Make a Lollipop Tree

If you are looking for a unique centrepiece for a party, or something different for a table in your home, try lollipop trees.

⊙ Steps

1 Divide a bag of lollipops into three groups. One group will be used for the bottom of the tree, the second group will be for the middle and the third group will be for the top.

2 Trim the sticks of the middle group of lollipops to medium length and trim the sticks short for the group that will be on the top of the tree.

3 Buy or paint a polystyrene cone brown to look like the trunk of a tree.

✱ Tip

If you are going to allow guests to partake in the lollipops, buy some sugar-free ones and put them on the tree. Distinguish them by making sure they are of one colour.

4 Start with the bottom of the tree and take that group of lollipops to work with first. Poke the lollipops into the polystyrene cone to make the bottom of the tree.

5 Continue poking the lollipops into the cone, going from the bottom to the top.

Plan a Stag-Party Weekend

721

Although there is no set guide on when to begin planning a stag-party weekend, a good rule of thumb is to start planning at least two months before the intended date.

⊙ Steps

1 Pick the date. You should try to make the date at least two weeks before the wedding to allow time for recovery and for the groom to focus on last-minute wedding details. Don't set this date in stone until you hear back from all invited guests. You might need to make changes to fit everyone's schedule.

2 Send out invitations with a specific RSVP date. Knowing how many men will attend will allow you to decide what activities will work out best for the group.

3 Decide on a budget and stick to it. Depending on the events, the weekend might just be too expensive for some to attend. Consider everyone's finances when planning the events.

4 Assign a treasurer. Someone is going to have to collect all the money and pay for the expenses. Pick your treasurer based on responsibility and trust. The amount collected for the party may be small, but it could also be a large sum and you want to know that the treasurer is trustworthy enough to handle large sums and responsible enough to pay deposits on time.

5 Consider setting up temporary email accounts for those involved. Spouses and partners often share email accounts and the first rule of any stag party is secrecy.

6 After collecting RSVPs and calculating the budget, decide on the location. Stag-party weekends can be held locally or in a remote place halfway around the world. Be creative, just stay within the budget.

7 Plan for the stripper to appear on Saturday night. You want this last full night to be one to remember!

8 Create a nightclub, gentleman's club or bar itinerary and call to make sure the location is able to handle your numbers and that they are willing to deal with possible rowdiness.

9 Set up a kitty at the start of the party. Trying to collect funds on the Sunday morning after a hard few days of celebrations could be quite difficult. Having a kitty will also help keep the group together through most of the festivities.

10 Plan the stag prank. No stag party should be without at least one good prank on the groom. Try to meet with several of the invitees to plan this important aspect of the stag-party weekend.

✱ Tips

Consider that not all the guests are going to know each other. The daytime events should help break the ice and bring the group together so the evenings are more fun – and without incident.

Consider a belly dancer if the groom doesn't want a stripper. They can add a nice erotic flair to your weekend.

Hire a professional party company to work out all the details and make the reservations for you if planning a stag party weekend seems more than you can handle.

722 Plan a Hen-Party Weekend

A hen-party weekend is one of the most fun ways to celebrate a bride's last days of being single before her wedding day.

Steps

1 Decide on a guest list in collaboration with the bride-to-be. Make sure you include the bridal party and any other friends or family she would like to join in. Always ask the bride about preferences her guests might have about food, games and alcohol.

2 Determine the activities that the bride-to-be would like to enjoy on the hen-party weekend. Again, make sure these activities are things the group you are inviting will enjoy.

3 Contact venues that offer the activities that your group wants to participate in. A relaxing pampering weekend would require a spa setting where everyone could have treatments. If you are all about having a party weekend then make sure you book a place that offers nightclub activities. Book the weekend well in advance of the date that you have chosen to be certain of getting into your chosen activities.

4 Post invitations to everyone in the group who will participate in the hen-party weekend. Ask for responses to come in a timely manner – give a date to respond by. Another option for invitations that would avoid delays caused by conventional post is to send e-vites via email; the responses should come in more quickly.

5 Pack your bags and have fun with your hen-party group. Make a check-list of items to take so you can make sure you have everything you need for all the activities. Don't forget to have some fun items packed for the bride-to-be, such as a glitzy veil, a t-shirt proclaiming that she is the bride and perhaps a "bouquet" made from ribbons and bows.

* Tip

Choose a date that is most convenient for the bride-to-be for the hen-party weekend. You will not be able to accommodate everyone's schedule so you need to pick a date and stick with it.

⚠ Warning

Be specific regarding the cost of the hen-party weekend for all participants. This will avoid potentially uncomfortable situations when it is time to settle the bill.

723 Host a Baby Shower

When celebrating an event as joyous as a baby's imminent arrival, you can be as silly – or as traditional or creative – as you want to be.

Steps

1 Give yourself plenty of time to plan. Baby showers usually take place in the seventh or eighth month of pregnancy.

2 Decide whether the shower is for women only. Traditionally, you throw a baby shower for the mother-to-be, with only female friends and relatives as guests. But today, showers that include men – with both expectant parents as guests of honour – have become increasingly popular.

3 Determine the time of day and location – making sure above all that it's convenient for the guest(s) of honour – and approximately how many guests you'd like to invite.

4 Decide whether to make the shower a surprise. Keep your honourees' personalities in mind – remember that not everyone likes surprises.

* Tip

Baby-shower games could include guessing the names of celebrity babies, or a memory game where you put several baby-related products on a tray for everyone to memorise, then secretly remove one item and see who can correctly identify what's missing.

5   Think about possible shower themes, such as teddy bears, bottles or balloons. Or pick a gift theme like "Around the House", assigning each guest to bring a baby gift for use in a different room – the kitchen, the bedroom, the bathroom and so forth.

6   Create a guest list. If the shower is not a surprise, consult the guests of honour about who they'd like to invite; if it is a surprise, consult a close friend or relative to make sure you don't leave anyone out.

7   Send out invitations at least three weeks in advance. Include directions, surprise-party instructions if applicable, and the theme if you've chosen one. If possible, mention the colour scheme and theme of the baby's room as well.

8   Find out if the parents-to-be are registered for gifts at a particular shop. Have this information ready in case any of the guests ask.

9   Make a table centrepiece composed of flowers, a basket and candles, bouquets of baby socks or a doll. Coordinate the centrepiece and decorations with your theme if you've chosen one.

10 Decide if you want guests to play any games. If so, buy small gifts for the winners – some possible prizes could be chocolates, plants, notebooks, candles and bookmarks.

11 Make food, buy takeaway or hire a caterer. Don't forget supplies – cups, plates, napkins and utensils.

12 At the shower, keep track of presents as the guests of honour open them – this will help them when they're writing thank-you notes.

Throw a Housewarming   724

It's traditional to invite guests to celebrate your new home, and will a little planning you can have a housewarming to remember.

⊙ **Steps**

1   Keep the checklist you made when planning the party at hand as the party approaches.

2   Clean your house the day before the party. Remember that guests at a housewarming will expect a tour of your new home.

3   Prepare the food the day of the party. Make sure the bar is stocked and that you have enough ice. Organise serving pieces and platters as necessary.

4   Do last-minute things such as light candles, turn on music or set out appetisers just before guests arrive.

5   Give each guest a name tag if people at the party don't know each other. Make sure that everyone is introduced, with a brief explanation of his or her relationship to you.

6   Pour wine, make drinks or offer other beverages while guests are eating the appetisers or snack foods (depending on the kind of party you are hosting).

7   Offer informal tours of your new house. Show people around yourself, or, if you are too busy to do so, invite people to explore the home on

✳ **Tips**

You can specify "no gifts" on the invitation if you don't want people to bring presents.

Make sure you have mineral water or soft drinks for people who don't drink alcohol.

⚠ **Warning**

Unless everyone has brought a gift, open presents after the guests have departed. Make sure you send a thank-you note to each person who brought a gift.

their own. Try to be available to answer questions from guests about the house or your new neighbourhood.

8 Serve the main meal – if you are having one – or make sure that finger foods are replenished as needed throughout the party. When preparing, it's always best to buy a little more food than you think you'll need. There's nothing worse than running out of food (or drink) halfway through a party.

9 Express thanks to the guests for coming, and let them know you appreciate their relationship with you and your family.

725 | Host a Cocktail Party

Subtly sophisticated, short and sweet, cocktail parties are a great way to entertain your friends with minimum hassle.

⦿ Steps

1 Send out written invitations for large and formal affairs, telephone or email for smaller ones. Include the nature of the party (cocktails), the occasion, if any, the date, and the beginning and ending times of the party – cocktail parties are generally held between 6 and 8 p.m.

2 Make arrangements for a caterer and bartender if your party will be large (more than 25 people), and your budget permits. Otherwise, prepare a cocktail menu and plan out how you will prepare everything ahead of time.

3 For drinks, plan to have wine and beer, as well as supplies for several kinds of cocktails. Have non-alcoholic alternatives on hand as well, and make sure you have enough ice.

4 Remove large pieces of furniture or clutter from the room you plan to hold the party in. Set up two large tables – one for drinks, the other for hors d'oeuvres – a good distance from each other or at opposite ends of the room, to cut down on traffic around them.

5 Set up chairs and smaller tables around the room. Comfortable folding chairs and tables are adequate and easy to move around.

6 Decorate with table linen, candles and simple floral arrangements. The complexity of the arrangements and quality of the linen should reflect the formality of the event.

7 Ask your guests for their coats as soon as they enter, and hang the coats on a coat rack, in a wardrobe, or lie the coats neatly across a bed in an unused bedroom.

8 Tell your guests to help themselves to hors d'oeuvres. If there is no bartender, ask your guests what they would like to drink and serve them yourself.

9 Have a few party games up your sleeve to break the ice and encourage your guests to mingle.

✱ Tips

Indoors, scented candles are good for clearing the air of stuffiness and odours.

Be prepared to serve each guest 10–12 snacks and 3–4 drinks.

Things You'll Need

❑ Invitations
❑ Floral arrangements
❑ Scented candles
❑ Ice
❑ Alcohol
❑ Non-alcoholic drinks
❑ Cocktail glasses
❑ Cocktail shaker
❑ Table linen
❑ Folding chairs

Throw a Wine-Tasting Party 726

This particular party is helpful for practising the art of pairing wines with food. It is fun – and you don't have to be a wine expert to enjoy it.

⊙ Steps

1   Choose between two and five simple foods. These could be different types of cheese, prawns, chicken skewers, paté and olives. Try to have a balance between salty foods, rich foods, delicate foods, and so on.

2   Prepare a list of wines that are good matches, average matches and poor matches for each of the foods you have selected.

3   Have everybody attending the tasting bring a bottle of wine from the list.

4   Set up three glasses for each taster (glasses can be hired from some supermarkets if you don't have enough). Be sure to have good lighting and a white tablecloth.

5   Pour the good, average and poor matching wines that correspond to one of the food items.

6   Begin with a "starter taste" of wine individually, before tasting with the food. Encourage group discussions.

7   Serve the appropriate food item and then taste the poorly matching wine.

8   Sample the food with the average-matching wine.

9   Finally, sample the food with the good-matching wine.

10   Discuss your opinions.

11   Rinse the glasses with water and move on to the next food item and matching wines. You might cleanse your palate with dry crackers in between.

❋ Tip

If you plan to pour different types of wine, begin with light white wines and move towards the heartier ones in order to preserve your palate.

△ Warning

If any guests have had too much to drink, arrange for someone to give them a lift home or invite them to stay the night.

Host a Pool Party 727

Pool parties offer a sociable way to cool down and have some fun. Here are some steps to help you jump right in.

⊙ Steps

1   Remind guests to bring along their bathing suits, and their own towels if you won't have enough.

2   Plan a menu and purchase the food and drinks. Keep the food light – salads, fruit, vegetables and dip – since your guests will be swimming. Avoid alcohol for swimmers: serve fizzy drinks, teas and juices instead.

3   Clean the pool.

4   Provide a room for people to change into or out of bathing suits, if they need to. Have some extra sunscreen on hand and tell people to use it.

5   Set up a number of patio chairs and tables around the pool area for your guests.

❋ Tips

Inflatable beach balls and lilos help set the mood and provide entertainment for the guests.

Prepare a few indoor activities in case the weather is bad or changes unexpectedly.

6   Set up two additional large tables – one to hold the snacks, the other for the drinks.

7   Arrange an ample supply of plates, cups, napkins and utensils on the serving tables.

8   Set up a stereo and speaker system near the pool for some background music. Surf music is always good for a pool party.

9   Be creative when decorating. Arrange sand and seashells in kiddie pools or sandpits around the pool area to give the look of a seaside escape.

10 As the evening wears on, light the pool area with candles in lanterns, Christmas lights strung from trees or floating candles in the pool (as long as no one is swimming).

⚠ **Warnings**

Make sure you have someone keeping an eye on the pool at all times, especially when children are swimming.

Avoid alcohol when swimming.

---

728 | Throw an Oscar Party

What better way to celebrate the Oscars than with a party? Recreate the glitz, glamour and excitement of the Academy Awards in your own home.

◉ **Steps**

1   Make sure that you have plenty of comfortable seating and that everyone will have a clear view of the television.

2   Make a 90-minute compilation CD of recognisable movie themes to play in the background before and after the ceremony.

3   Dress for the Oscars. Wear dinner jackets and evening gowns with rhinestone necklaces.

4   Announce guests over a microphone as they arrive. For example, "And now please welcome last year's winner of the best supporting soccer coach, Stan Murphy."

5   Provide appetisers and both alcoholic and non-alcoholic drinks.

6   Pass out pens and ballots listing all the nominees and have everyone vote on who they think is going to win before the ceremony starts.

7   Tally the results after the ceremony ends.

8   Present a fake plastic Oscar to the person who gets the most right. Encourage the winner to make an acceptance speech.

✳ **Tips**

If you don't have a large TV, borrow one from a friend.

If you don't have the time or inclination to make a compilation CD, buy a CD of film tunes.

Make sure you have low lighting arranged for the ceremony – dark enough to watch the show, but not so dark that people can't easily get up to get a drink or go to the toilet.

⚠ **Warning**

As a responsible party host, see to it that your guests return home safely. If any guests have had too much to drink, call them a taxi or invite them to stay.

---

729 | Throw a Sixties-Themed Party

The Sixties were a party in themselves – a magical time – and recreating them for a memorable bash is relatively simple.

◉ **Steps**

1   Plan a couple of Sixties-themed activities like tie-dying t-shirts and stringing love beads; soon flower power will be the order of the day.

2   Get out your records. The Sixties were probably the richest, most varied time for popular music. Look for bands such as the Beatles, the Rolling Stones, Jimi Hendrix, Janis Joplin, Jefferson Airplane and Simon & Garfunkel. You'll need a record player – if you don't know what that is, ask your parents if you can borrow theirs.

3   Decorate with flower power. Cut big colourful flowers out of construction paper and tape them to walls, trees and anywhere else you want to make a splash. Sixties graphics were known for their day-glo colours and psychedelic imagery. If you have a lava lamp or two, be sure to add them to the mix.

4   Serve Sixties food. The Sixties were a time of experimentation and the foods eaten were no exception. A couple of bowls filled with brightly coloured punch is a lovely idea. If the party is for adults, go ahead and spike the punch with good vodka to really get the festivities going.

5   Wear Sixties clothes. Visit charity shops to find flares, fringed vests and long swirly skirts. T-shirts with slogans like "Make Love Not War" can still be found, or you can make your own with light-coloured shirts and permanent markers.

Plan a Formal Dinner Party   730

Treating your friends to an evening of good conversation, fine wine and a well-prepared meal is a wonderful gesture.

◉ Steps

1   Organise a budget for your dinner party. You should keep in mind money that will be spent on food and drinks such as wine or beer, as well as any entertainment or party supplies that you may require.

2   Determine how many people you would like to invite based on your budget and the amount of space you have available. Even the smallest dinner parties can be elegant affairs if the right amount of care and attention is paid during the planning stages.

3   Invite guests to your home with a written invitation at least two weeks in advance of your dinner party. If this is a very formal dinner party, you may wish to have invitations printed or engraved. Be sure to include a method for your guests to respond to your invitation. Only the most formal of invitations should include a reply card.

4   Plan your menu with the comfort of your guests – as well as your cooking skills – in mind. If you are hosting a party that will include vegetarian friends, make sure you cater for them, too. If someone is bringing a new partner you are unfamiliar with, ask about their dietary needs.

5   Remember that a formal dinner party is not the time to try out a new or challenging recipe. If you would like to feature a more gourmet dinner, consider hiring a private chef or caterer for the evening.

6   Set your dining table with your best linen, china and silverware. Formal dinner parties are among the few opportunities available to treat yourself and your guests to a complete dining experience, including a nicely dressed table.

✱ Tip

Remember that good manners are all about making those around you feel comfortable. Don't get hung up on etiquette at the risk of alienating or making your guests feel unwelcome.

731 | Pull Off a Last-Minute Party

Friends have called to say they're in town ... you just landed
a promotion ... the film you were going to see was sold out...
Whatever the reason, here's how to celebrate on the spur of
the moment.

⊚ Steps

1 Stock a range of party staples that can become an instant feast. Pasta is
easy and quick – and almost everyone has an extra packet in the cupboard. Other basics include balsamic vinegar and olive oil, Parmesan
cheese, tinned whole tomatoes, jars of pesto, sun-dried tomatoes,
crackers, crisps and jars of salsa, soy sauce and rice wine vinegar (for
easy dipping sauces), boxed cake mixes and ice cream.

2 Stock extra wine, champagne and beer, spirits and mixers. You can
blend margarita mix and tequila with ice in seconds.

3 Give them something to snack on. Always have nuts and olives at the
ready; put out crackers, crisps and salsa, raw vegetables and mayonnaise, or quesadillas cut into thin strips.

4 Fire up the grill. People can catch up outside while you make appetisers
(grilled bread with mozzarella and fresh basil), dinner (salmon, kebabs,
portobello-mushroom burgers) and even dessert (grilled peaches with
vanilla ice cream).

5 Let your guests assemble and serve their own meals from food bars,
with mashed potato fixings and chilli, build-your-own burritos or ice-
cream sundae ingredients.

6 Buy a roasted chicken for an impromptu dinner party and pull together
easy side dishes: smashed boiled red potatoes (skins on) with herbed
goat cheese mixed in, a green salad and the frozen green vegetables of
your choice cooked with a little butter and salt.

✳ Tips

Create mood lighting; glaring
bright lights can kill any party.
Turn off overhead lights, light
some candles and turn on low
table lamps.

If you're serving takeaway and
passing it off as home-made,
saute an onion and a few garlic
cloves on the stove over low
heat. The whole house will smell
like some serious home cooking.

732 | Select Adult Party Games

Planning party games for an event can help break the ice
among new acquaintances, create new and funny memories
among old friends – and might even start a romance or two.

⊚ Steps

1 Play a game of Autographs to help break the ice among new friends.
Each player is given a sheet of paper and a pen. Instruct them to
make their mark by drawing a picture, making a squiggle and tracing
their hand, then hand the piece of paper back to you. You then select
two detectives, who must try to determine which autograph belongs
to whom. The winner can be awarded a prize for identifying the most
correct autographs.

2 Gather friends together for a game of Charades. Here the party will
divide into two groups or teams. Suggested film or book titles or phrases
should be written ahead of time and placed in a bowl or basket. One
member from each team draws a slip of paper. The object of the game

✳ Tip

Keep games simple and easy
to play – your guests will enjoy
them more without having to
worry about complicated rules.

Things You'll Need

❑ Deck of cards

❑ Prizes

❑ Paper and pens

❑ Host a Murder Mystery kit

is to have your team members figure out your film, book or phrase within a certain amount of time. The teams can play for points or prizes – or just for fun.

3 See who gets the most kisses when you play Most Popular at your next party. This game is a perfect way to wile away the hours before midnight on New Year's Eve in particular. Each player must try to collect as many kisses (evidenced by lipstick marks on the face, hands and body) from the other guests before midnight.

4 Play dead and host a murder-mystery party. Select yourself or one of your party guests as the "body" and ask your guests to work together or separately to track down and identify the killer. To make the most of the evening, plan your menu around the theme and mix up some "killer" cocktails.

5 Play card games such as strip poker with your adult party guests. With each hand, the players should bet a piece of their clothing to remove if they lose. You can even alter traditional children's card games to adapt to a more adult theme.

Conduct Yourself at an Office Party 733

Office parties are a strange mix of Christmas cheer and office politics. If you take it easy on the booze, you may be able to avoid the most common office-party *faux pas*.

☉ Steps

1 Plan to go to the party. Even if office parties are not your cup of tea, you're part of the group and need to make an appearance.

2 Find out before the party what most people are wearing. You don't want to show up in a casual outfit if everyone else is going to be dressed to the nines.

3 Be conservative in your dress if you are a woman. Shockingly short dresses or plunging necklines are not appropriate for this type of business occasion.

4 Get to the party on time, or shortly after it starts. Even if you only stay for a short time, this is better than "popping in" at the end of the evening, which suggests you can't really be bothered.

5 Be sure to acknowledge all your co-workers, bosses and associates. Introduce your spouse or date, and include the spouses or dates of others in your conversations.

6 Avoid drinking too much. Overindulging may be the number-one cause of inappropriate remarks and behaviour at office parties.

7 Avoid pigging out. Loading up your plate or grabbing handfuls of hors d'oeuvres does not present a flattering image.

8 Go along with games or other arranged activities.

✱ Tips

If you know you will be drinking alcohol, eat a little something before you go to the party.

Make sure you thank the host or hostess before you leave the party. If the company paid for the party, thank your boss or the person in the office who arranged the party.

Before you bring your spouse or a date to the party, make sure he or she is invited.

734 Plan the Perfect Picnic

Planning a great picnic is not so much about flawless food and drink and wonderful weather. A happy picnic is about comfort, ease and good company.

⊙ Steps

1 Carry a cooler or food hamper that is appropriate in size for the number of people that you are inviting. If it is a picnic for two do not carry a large food hamper. If it is a large group do not try to stuff all the picnic items into one small cooler.

2 Choose a sheltered picnic area with chairs and tables. Your guests will thank you, especially if there is drizzle.

3 Take paper plates and cups instead of cumbersome ceramic dishes and heavy cutlery. This will prevent broken cutlery and dishwashing.

4 Buy finger foods from a deli that will make you and your guests happy. Try cherry tomatoes, cold roast chicken that you can tear off the bone, boiled eggs, organic chocolate bars. Think simple.

5 Make an easy to put together drink. Sweet tea is easy to mix and can be carried easily in a big plastic bottle.

6 Bring a large bottle of insect repellent for everyone to share.

7 Take a bottle of sunscreen for everyone to slather on.

✳ Tips

A small, light CD player with soothing music makes your food digest nicely.

Invest in a pre-packed picnic basket that holds everything but the kitchen sink.

735 Plan a Brunch

Planning a brunch with friends and family is easy, fun and provides a great opportunity to slow down and enjoy life with the people you love.

⊙ Steps

1 Pick a date and time. Sundays are usually the best brunch days, but any day is appropriate.

2 Invite some friends and/or family members. A phone call or email is sufficient for a casual brunch; send written invitations if the meal is celebrating something special.

3 Plan a menu that you'll enjoy preparing, with dishes that are easy for you to make. Pancakes and fruit bowls with pastries, hash browns and quiches are good choices for larger groups of people. Eggs, bacon, omelettes and sausages are easily prepared for smaller numbers.

4 Shop the day before and prepare as much as possible ahead of time. Clean your house in advance as well.

5 Wake up early and prepare yourself for the arrival of your guests. If you can prepare certain dishes at this time (pastries, for example), do so.

6 Set the table, and decorate it with fresh flowers.

7 Have coffee, soothing music and sunshine (if possible) ready.

✳ Tip

Serve mimosas if you know your guests will drink them.

Things You'll Need

❏ Fine china

❏ Champagne flutes

❏ Flowers

❏ Breakfast sets

❏ Silverware

❏ Relaxing CDs

❏ Champagne

8   Greet each guest with enthusiasm and a welcoming smile. In your spare time, whip up the remaining dishes.

9   Serve your guests, then yourself. Then sit down and relax with your friends and family.

Cook a Romantic Dinner for Two   736

A great way to spend Valentine's Day or any special occasion with your partner is to plan a romantic dinner.

⦿ Steps

1   Clean your flat or house. Clutter may be fine when you are by yourself, but it quickly cuts into the romance factor when you are trying to impress others.

2   Know your partner's likes and dislikes. Carnivore or vegetarian? Food allergies? These are important considerations as you plan your menu.

3   Find recipes online or in cookbooks. When you know what is on the menu, make a list of all the ingredients you'll need to make it. Also, check your cooking equipment – do you have the right materials?

4   Do your food shopping for all those ingredients you do not have on hand. Make sure you bring your shopping list! Adding a few candles and flowers to the list will help your romantic setting.

5   Organise your ingredients and cooking materials. When you have finished preparing something, get the mixing bowl or pot or pan out of the way to avoid a cluttered workspace.

6   Closely follow the recipes you chose. This is not the time to improvise.

7   As your dinner is cooking, set the table and arrange your dining space for maximum romantic effect.

8   Change into your romantic dinner outfit, and have a great evening!

✳ Tips

Romantic meals are all about presentation. Adjust the lighting to dim (candles help), choose music in advance and look your sexiest.

When planning the dinner, make notes on cooking times to know in advance the time the food will be on the table.

Ask a wine seller to suggest the perfect wine to accompany your meal.

⚠ Warnings

Don't overdo it. If you have limited cooking experience, make something simple or buy food that you can reheat.

Multi-course meals require multi-trips to the kitchen, which means loss of romance time.

Find and Hire a Caterer   737

Save yourself time, worry and hassle. Hire a caterer to do everything for you, right down to the clearing up.

⦿ Steps

1   Look through the Yellow Pages. It's a great resource for food and drink services.

2   Look for catering referral services, both local and national. You can find them online by using a major search engine like Google or Yahoo.

3   Ask your friends and relatives for recommendations.

4   Call cooking schools for their advice and referrals.

5   Prepare a list of questions to ask before calling caterers. Determine your budget and a have basic idea of what kind of food you want to serve before meeting with the caterer.

✳ Tips

Some questions to ask caterers: Do you add a gratuity to your price? Can you accommodate food preferences and special diets? How many electrical outlets do you need? What can you supply (such as dishes, utensils, valet parking, bartenders, table decorations, linens and coffee) and how much extra is each?

6   Set up an initial meeting to discuss the menu and the services you desire. Sample the caterer's food before you agree to hire them.

7   Agree on payment before the caterer arrives at the party. Lay down the law. Let the caterer know what expectations you have before the party starts. Ask the caterer what expectations and/or questions he or she might have.

Prepare yourself for the expense of hiring a caterer. Most caterers will require two payments: one before the event and one immediately following the event.

738 Plan Dinner-Party Seating

Diplomatic careers have advanced and derailed over a simple thing like dinner seating. Think of yourself as the ambassador of the table and set up seating to maximise your guests' enjoyment.

⊙ Steps

1   Write your guests' names on place cards.

2   Put yourself in the seat closest to the kitchen for quick getaways. Move clockwise around the table to map out the rest of the guests. Don't sit the hosts next to each other – spread them out to better cover the dinner-table territory.

3   Consider conflicting political affiliations, career connections, activities and sports pursuits or travel interests when seating guests. Spark the conversation with introductions such as "John, have you met Sally? She just got back from the same area of Thailand you visited last year."

4   Rotate. Have two people from each table move to another table for dessert and coffee. If you have one long table, ask every third person to take his or her wine glass and cutlery, and rotate between courses (when plates are cleared anyway).

5   Set up a buffet and let your guests sit wherever they want.

6   Manage troublesome, loud or contentious guests by giving them a job to do: mix drinks, help in the kitchen or serve appetisers.

✳ Tips

Place low-maintenance guests to your right and left. You'll be away from the table from time to time and need to make sure your companions will be comfortable without you there.

Seating charts can be done a day or two in advance or as soon as you have your RSVPs. You don't want to be playing musical chairs on the night of your dinner party.

It's a time-honoured custom to separate couples so that they mingle with other guests.

739 Fold a Napkin

For formal dinners, the dinner napkin should match the tablecloth. And forget about folding napkins into swans or boats – you're better off with a classic fold.

⊙ Steps

1   Take a 60-cm (24-in) square dinner napkin. Fold it in half once.

2   Fold the rectangle in half lengthwise (bringing the two short ends together) to make another square. Fold the square in half again. You now have a smaller rectangle.

3   Fold the two short ends of the smaller rectangle under each other to form a loose, partially rolled rectangle. Do not flatten the napkin completely.

✳ Tip

Smaller napkins can still be folded in the same way, but begin by making only two folds to form the smaller rectangle.

4   Make sure that if there is a monogram on the napkin, it shows at the lower left-hand corner of the rectangle. If the monogram is located at the centre of one side of the napkin, it should show in the middle third of the partially rolled rectangle.

5   Place the folded napkins in the centre of the service plates with the monograms facing the diner. Place the napkins on the side of the plate only if you put the first course on the table before the guests have been seated.

Say an Informal Grace   740

Saying grace doesn't have to be a sombre, God-fearing experience. Have fun. Be creative. Appreciate the meal.

☉ Steps

1   Figure out how you want to say grace. Do you want to sit individually and bow your head, stand up behind your chairs and hold hands, or stay seated and hold hands? Consider that since you will be giving an informal grace, you may simply want to stay seated, not hold hands and not bow your head, as this is usually done in deference to a higher being.

2   Decide who will lead the family and any guests in saying grace. Traditionally the head of the family takes the lead, but it is often a nice touch to have a child say grace.

3   Consider how lengthy the grace should be. Are there a lot of children present? They may fidget during a very long grace.

4   Think about how informal you want to be. Coarse language should generally be avoided. Humour, though, can lighten the mood.

5   Think about the ideas and events you want to address in your grace. Have family members travelled a long way to be at the meal? Have obstacles been overcome in the past year? Have joyous occasions marked the year? Consider quoting a favourite author or poet.

6   Once you've thought about what you want to say, practise to make it polished and succinct. Or simply revert back to your school days and throw off the classic: "Through the lips and over the gums, look out stomach, here it comes."

⚠ Warning

Remember that not everyone is of a religious turn of mind, so avoid lengthy and serious prayer so they don't feel uncomfortable.

Order Well at Restaurants   741

A restaurant menu tells you a story about the chef and his or her approach to food. Read it – not just to satisfy your cravings, but to discover this perspective.

☉ Steps

1   Choose restaurants wisely. Spend your money on quality not to quantity.

2   Research the restaurant you are dining in. Read reviews on the Internet, in books of reviews or in newspapers. Find out what the chef's strengths are.

❉ Tips

You will improve your palate for both food and wine by ordering carefully and intentionally.

Don't expect French food at an Italian restaurant. Know what to expect before you get there.

3 Approach the chef as an artist. Use the menu as a way to tap into this artistry.

4 Gauge the menu. Look over it thoroughly and carefully. See if you can discern themes – what the chef seems to like doing.

5 Based on your reading of reviews and the menu, order in the vein of what the chef likes to cook. Don't let the waiter rush you.

6 Order seasonally. Order lighter fare when the weather is hotter, and keep in mind what ingredients are in season at local markets.

7 Ask questions. Let the waiting staff advise you if they can discuss the menu without reading off a notepad. If you're interested in a particular entrée but not sure of a starter, for example, ask the waiting staff what's best with your entrée choice.

8 Consider, but don't limit yourself to, the specials; they should reflect seasonal availability.

Put yourself in the hands of the waiting staff. They are often food lovers and can offer valuable insight. In better restaurants, this is what they are there for.

742 Be the Life of the Party

You've seen those people who seem to be comfortable in any social situation. What's their secret?

Steps

1 Dress to kill. Wear something either very fashionable or very flashy (but tasteful), depending on your intent. Well-tailored clothes imply class; bold outfits are hard to forget.

2 Make a grand entrance – carry a kazoo and announce your arrival. Better yet, provide your friends with kazoos and let them do it for you.

3 Stand up straight and look people directly in the eye. Self-assurance is very attractive. If you have to fake it, then fake it. It gets easier the more you practise.

4 Smile and make eye contact with every person you speak with. But don't stare. Flirt a little. As the party progresses, flirt a lot. Don't end up alone in a room with someone, though. You'll miss the party and your chance to shine.

5 Compliment each person you talk to and find out something interesting about them. People are most interested in themselves.

6 Circulate! Don't get trapped with the same people all evening. Break away within five minutes of meeting someone and move on. You can always come back.

7 Be aware of current events and films, and have a couple of tasteful, funny jokes on hand. Avoid discussing money, politics, religion or yourself.

8 Introduce people you meet to each other. This gives you the appearance of being popular and helps you to remember names and faces.

9 Avoid anyone lurking by the food or doors. They are not likely to be interested in conversation.

Tips

It may help to keep an index card handy at first while you practise this. Slip away and make notes to yourself if you have a bad memory for names.

Don't drink so much you lose control. The life of the party isn't really the guy with the lampshade on his head.

Pour Beer

Pouring beer may sound like a very simple task, but there are tricks that will prevent too much foam in the middle of the glass instead of just at the top.

⊙ Steps

1 Choose the beer and glass type you will be using. You can research what types of beers go best with which types of glasses.

2 Open the beer and get a clean glass. A glass that has been chilled a few hours in the freezer first is best in order to keep the beer cold.

3 Angle the glass to 45° and begin to pour the beer. When pouring from a bar tap, placement should be in the middle of the glass, filling it about halfway into the glass.

4 Change to a 90° angle once the glass is a little more than halfway full and continue pouring the beer.

5 Complete the pour by leaving about 2.5 cm (1 in) of head at the top of the glass. The head releases the aroma of the beer and makes for a better presentation.

✳ Tips

Freeze glassware ahead of time for the best results.

When serving beer at a party or event, make sure you have a variety to meet the preferences of all your guests.

⚠ Warning

You are not doing the person consuming the beer a favour by providing them with more to drink by not leaving a head on it. The head helps improve the beer-drinking experience.

Behave During a Limousine Ride

Here is how to keep your limo ride stress free for you, the other passengers – and the driver.

⊙ Steps

1 Be where you are supposed to be. Technically, a botched pickup is no big deal to the limo company. After all, you're going to be billed for the ride, whether you and your friends are waiting in the right place or not. However, your guests may not appreciate cooling their heels for hours at a bus station in town when you actually told the limo driver to pick you up at your house.

2 Let the driver open the doors. Yes, you may be eager to impress your girlfriend, but you'll have to settle for her wonderment about the magnificent transportation you've arranged.

3 Don't play "pack the limo". The reason a limo company asks how many guests you'll be bringing is so it can dispatch a vehicle of the right size. Suddenly doubling your guest count will necessitate a long wait as the driver radios for a bigger limo.

4 Keep the drinking to a minimum. Part of the fun of riding a limo is having sufficient room (and sufficiently robust shock absorbers) to pour out a champagne toast. But if it's a two-hour ride to your destination, getting smashed will only annoy your driver and incur additional expenses.

5 Be nice to the driver. It's usually in your driver's interest to convey you quickly and safely to your destination, but if you insult him needlessly, he may just as well let you off at an abandoned coal mine on the outskirts of town.

✳ Tip

Always treat your driver with respect – he or she is not your servant, but a professional carrying out a job.

745 | Keep Financial Records Organised

It never seems important to keep financial papers organised –
that is, until you need to file your tax return. Save yourself the
panic by getting the job done now.

Steps

1 Buy a filing cabinet and sturdy hanging folders.

2 Buy manila folders to go inside the hanging folders.

3 Sort all your financial papers into piles and stack them chronologically.

4 Put your bank statements, credit-card information, cheque stubs,
receipts, tax information, mortgage papers, investment papers, insurance
policies and statements, loan agreements and any other financial papers
in separate hanging folders.

5 Further divide your tax information by year. Include tax returns, receipts,
National Insurance contribution information, copies of old tax returns and
other pertinent tax information.

6 Divide the bill stubs by the companies they represent.

7 Divide property papers by mortgage documents, home-improvement
receipts, second mortgages and so forth.

8 Put passbooks, car titles, stock certificates and yearly Individual
Retirement Account, pension and profit-sharing statements in a safety-
deposit box.

9 Keep your incoming papers, such as bills to be paid, in a separate place
where they are easily accessible.

Tips

Consult an accountant when
necessary.

Buy a locked filing cabinet for
extra security.

If you opt for a home safe
instead of a safety-deposit box,
make sure it's fireproof. Store it
out of plain view.

Keep tax information for at least
seven years and other financial
papers for at least three.

Consider buying financial planning software. Some programs
include online banking capabilities. Back up important software.

Warning

Keep up with your filing system,
or you'll have to organise it all
again next year!

746 | Set Up a Family Budget

A budget allows you to control your family's spending so that
you have enough money to pay your bills while also saving for
holidays, retirement and your children's education.

Steps

1 Get out three months of payslips and determine your average
monthly income.

2 Gather three months of bills, add them up and divide by three to
calculate your monthly fixed expenses such as rent or mortgage,
utilities and phone, car payments, insurance and student-loan payments.

3 Add together three months of other monthly expenses, including
food, clothing, credit-card expenses and cash outlays. Divide by
three and add the result to your monthly expense total.

4 Evaluate your expenses; look for opportunities to economise, and
develop a plan to cut back on spending in specific areas.

5 Develop a monthly budget and stick to it.

Tips

Commissions or other variable
income may have to be averaged
over six to 12 months.

Divide annual payments such
as taxes or life insurance by
12 and add them to your monthly
expenses.

Utility companies often average
annual bills into 12 monthly
payments so that customers
aren't faced with higher costs
during the winter months.

6   Set up a savings plan such as a savings account, pension scheme, ISA or other deposit account, and begin making regular deposits every month if you can.

7   Track your income and expenses monthly to evaluate how the plan is working, then fine-tune to produce the desired results. Use personal-finance software to gain an accurate overview of your spending and locate problematic habits.

Survive a Recession 747

It can be worrying when a recession hits, but there are simple ways to relieve stress and boost your income during this time.

⊙ Steps

1   Every Sunday buy the newspaper. Search for sale items you need and vouchers that you can use. Shop in sales and stockpile food, necessities and bottled water. This will help you to feel secure in case of any kind of emergency.

2   Every month when you begin the process of paying your bills, take one bill and reduce it. It is also helpful to make a list of your bills and figure out which ones you can reduce. Try to have some cash on hand, and some saved for emergencies.

3   Make a list of where your money goes. Keep a small notebook or file for this purpose. By writing down what you spend money on, you will be better able to see where you can reduce unnecessary spending. During these difficult economic times, reducing spending on unnecessary items is essential for living comfortably.

4   Shop for groceries in bulk, and eat at home more often. Buy staples such as cheese, pasta, beans, rice and meat. These items will last a long time. Meats can be frozen and used any time. Items such as bread and dairy can be bought as you need them. Think of meals you can make and freeze. Not only will you save money, but also a lot of time that you can use for other more important things. You can still eat out occasionally, or order takeaway, just don't do it all the time.

5   Put together a journal. In it write down ways that you can make extra money and add to your income. This would be a perfect time to start a business. Is there something you have always wanted to do – a hobby you are great at? There is no better time than the present. A recession is a good time to create something good out of something unpleasant.

6   Update your CV during this downtime. Consider a new line of work or something you have always wanted to do. If you have lost your job, now would be a great time to think about a new career.

7   Remember that recession is only temporary, and try not to feel depressed about the situation. This can be difficult if you have lost your job and are struggling financially, but be positive. The world has experienced recession before – and it will again. This will pass, and good things lie ahead!

✳ Tips

If you can't afford to pay cash for an item, you can't afford it.

Know what you are spending and what you are saving.

748 Keep Vehicle Mileage Tax Information

Tax law requires adequate records when deducting business use of your vehicle. Logging mileage and expenses contemporaneously will save you money and headaches.

⊙ Steps

Recording Mileage and Expenses

1   Write down the date, the number of miles driven and the business purpose for each business errand or trip, in one section of a notebook, and add each trip to the list.

2   Write down all expenses paid for operating and maintaining the vehicle in another section of the notebook.

3   List the date, the amount paid and the type of expense such as petrol, oil change, car insurance, car wash, repairs and breakdown membership. This is optional, but you may be able to claim actual expenses if the deduction is greater than the standard mileage rate.

4   Save your receipts in a file folder.

5   Log parking fees incurred for business purposes and the dates paid, in a third section. Save parking receipts in the file folder.

6   Log separately the dates, names of work-related courses taken and the miles driven directly from your work location to the course. If you attend a course on a non-workday, log the mileage to and from the course.

7   Note the round-trip commuting distance you travel from home to your place of business, if you are an employee or if you have a fixed work location away from your residence.

8   Keep records of any mileage or vehicle-expense reimbursements you may receive from your employer or clients.

Totalling Mileage and Expenses

1   Subtract the beginning odometer reading from the ending odometer reading to obtain your total mileage for the year.

2   Add up the business miles driven during the year.

3   Add up the miles driven to courses.

4   Add up the vehicle expenses paid during the year.

5   Add up any parking fees paid.

6   Calculate the number of days worked during the year and multiply that number by the round-trip distance to and from work.

7   Add up reimbursements for mileage and vehicle expenses received during the year.

8   Use these totals when preparing your income-tax return, or give the figures to your accountant.

⁂ Tips

If your employer has a policy of reimbursing you for mileage and you do not ask him or her to do so, you cannot deduct these miles on your tax return.

If your employer pays you less than the standard mileage rate, you may claim the difference.

Save Money for a Major Purchase 749

A major purchase such as a house, car or household appliance can be a distressing hit to your bank balance. Budgeting and saving for the purchase can often ease the pain.

Steps

1 Identify the purchase you want to make.

2 Estimate what it may cost by looking at similar products.

3 Determine when you want to make the purchase.

4 Determine how much money you want to pay at the time of the purchase and how much you want to finance, either on your credit card or through the seller.

5 Commit yourself to saving a set amount of money each month, either in a savings account or some other safe account, so that you will have enough money to make the purchase at the predetermined time.

6 Be diligent and patient – your savings will accumulate.

✳ Tip

It is safer to save more than you need rather than less.

⚠ Warnings

Avoid putting your savings into risky investments – you could make a lot of money, but you could lose a lot as well.

Watch the price of the item you wish to purchase. If it changes, you'll have to readjust your savings rate.

Take Inventory of Your Possessions 750

Making a permanent record of your possessions for insurance purposes, in case of theft or loss due to a natural disaster, can be a big help if disaster strikes.

Steps

1 Divide possessions into two categories: "theft-prone" items and "other" items.

2 Make a list of theft-prone items and record serial numbers.

3 Mark theft-prone items with your National Insurance number or other identifying mark, using an engraving tool.

4 List all other items and include brief descriptions.

5 Take photographs of items.

6 Include mundane possessions such as linen, clothing, kitchen utensils and decorations when taking photographs. The cost of replacing these items can add up to a significant amount if they are not insured.

7 Invest in adequate contents insurance.

8 Put the completed inventory in a safe place outside your home, such as a safety-deposit box.

✳ Tips

Most insurance companies have specific inventory formats to simplify the processing of claims.

Update the inventory regularly to include new acquisitions.

Talk to your insurance company about coverage of valuables that may require extra policy riders.

751 Safely Use an ATM Machine

To most of us, the ATM machine represents a quick stop for cash. Although this is normally a safe and secure process, Visa offers these safety tips for using the ATM.

Steps

1 Use caution when approaching an ATM machine at night, especially if the area is poorly lit or hidden behind trees or buildings. Take someone with you if possible, or choose another machine in a safer area.

2 Have your card ready before approaching the machine. Don't take time fumbling around in your purse or wallet.

3 Make sure no one can see you punch in your PIN number. Shield the keypad with your body.

4 Cancel your transaction and leave the location if you see any suspicious activity in the vicinity.

5 Don't count your cash while standing at the ATM. Immediately put it in your pocket or fold it in your hand and walk away.

6 At drive-up ATM machines, keep all your doors locked and passenger windows rolled up.

7 Always take the receipts with you. Compare your ATM receipts against your monthly bank statement. If you find any discrepancies, call the bank and ask them to clarify the charge.

8 If you lose your ATM card, contact the financial institution that issued your card immediately.

✳ Tips

In general, protect your ATM card from damage by keeping it in a safe place – don't allow it to bend or be scratched.

Memorise your PIN. If you must write it down, don't keep it in your wallet or purse or write it on the card itself.

When selecting a PIN, avoid numbers and letters that can be easily identified or associated with you. Do not use your initials, birth date or telephone number.

⚠ Warning

If you are using an indoor ATM that requires your card to open the door, avoid letting anyone you don't know come in with you.

752 Transfer a Credit-Card Balance

One of the best ways to begin eliminating your credit-card debt is to transfer the balance to a new card with a lower – sometimes even zero – interest rate.

Steps

1 Read the information about your new credit card thoroughly, paying particular attention to whether there are transfer fees associated with a balance transfer.

2 If you must use a company that charges a transfer fee, look for a financial institution that has a cap on the amount instead of a limitless fee based on a percentage of the money you're transferring,

3 Compare the details of the new credit card to your old one. Take a close look at the APR, grace period and any annual fees. Find out what will happen when the introductory rate on the new card expires – often this is when you take a hit, and it may not be worth it.

4 Speak with a representative of the new company and ask lots of questions. You should know whether there's a minimum amount you have to transfer and whether being late on a payment voids the transfer

✳ Tips

Keep making payments to your old company even after you transfer the balance, since you will need to continue making minimum payments on the balance until the transfer is complete.

If the introductory rate doesn't apply to new purchases, find out what the interest rate will be. If it's high, you may not want to use that card for anything other than your transferred balance.

agreement. Ask if the introductory rate applies to new purchases or only to transferred balances.

5   Perform some information-gathering about your old credit card. Find a copy of your most recent bill and the credit-card agreement, if you still have it. Have the customer-service number readily available, as well as your account number and current balance.

6   Call your old credit-card company and ask about any applicable account closure procedures.

7   Open the new credit-card account and complete a balance-transfer form with the most up-to-date information you have about your current balance.

8   Wait for a notice from your new credit-card company that the balance transfer has been completed, and verify this with your old company by making a quick phone call.

9   Ask your old credit-card company to generate a billing statement with a zero balance. When you receive the bill, call or write to close the account. Ensure that the company lets credit bureaus know that your account was closed at your request.

Dispute a Credit-Card Charge   753

An unrecognised or incorrect charge on your credit card statement can be alarming, but it is often a simple mistake. Here's how to find out, and what to do.

⊚ Steps

1   Identify any incorrect charges.

2   Contact the merchant directly if the charge amount is incorrect. Explain the situation and ask the merchant to correct it.

3   Contact your credit-card company if the merchant is unable or unwilling to assist you. Tell the credit-card company you would like to dispute a charge on your account.

4   Give your information to the credit-card company over the phone. Some companies will send you a form to complete, sign and return. These forms often require an explanation of the situation, as well as copies of any receipts.

5   Wait to hear the resolution. Your credit-card company is obligated to respond to you within 30 days of receiving your completed form.

6   If your dispute is denied, don't give up. Determine if there is additional information you can provide. Ask your credit-card company about your options.

✳ Tips

Try to gather any relevant receipts before engaging in a dispute. These can often speed up resolution.

Try to resolve the disputed charge with the merchant first. The merchant's phone number is sometimes listed on your credit-card statement next to the charge.

⚠ Warning

If there are multiple unrecognised charges on your bill, someone may have access to your account number, in which case you are the victim of fraud. Report this to your credit-card company as soon as possible.

754 | Eat Cheap When Eating Out

Eating out has become more expensive these days, and many people are cutting back, but this does not mean that you have to stop eating at restaurants altogether.

Steps

1 Choose the restaurant carefully. To still be able to eat out you will have o choose a restaurant with cheaper price tags. This does not mean you are limited to McDonalds, just don't select somewhere that the meal will come to £100 a head.

2 Drink water. By cutting out the alcohol you will automatically cut down on the final bill. If water is not your favourite beverage, try adding a sweetener to it and ask your waiter or waitress for extra lemon. You will be able to make your own lemonade right at the table for no cost. Many restaurants will not charge for water or lemons.

3 Share meals. Restaurants typically provide very large portions. You can share one entrée and just add a side salad to it for each person. This is a great idea for children as well.

4 Order a la cart. If you order from the menu you are probably ordering things you will not eat. If you order only the items you are craving you may be able to cut the cost.

5 Don't have three courses. Cut out the starters or desserts. If you really have to have them, try having them as your meal and just adding a side salad.

6 Look for vouchers. There are loads of places that offer two-for-one meal deals or a percentage off your bill. Search online.

7 Tip well. Be sure to still give a good tip, especially when using the water trick or when sharing meals. The waiting staff is still working hard to serve you so your normal tips would be appreciated rather than a percentage of the bill.

Tip

Watch for deals in your local newspaper – they often have vouchers that can be used for money off in restaurants.

755 | Get a Debt-Consolidation Loan

A debt-consolidation loan creates a new loan, often secured by your property, and pays off most or all of your debts – saving you money and saving your credit.

Steps

1 Add up all your debts. Include all credit cards and loans.

2 Check the interest rates you are paying on all the credit-card accounts and loans. Interest rates on credit cards will generally run from 20 to 30 per cent.

3 Find a lender. Contact several lenders and compare their loan products. Look in the Yellow Pages, ask a local estate agent for a referral or check the Internet.

4 Determine which lender has the best debt-consolidation loan for you.

Tip

A debt-consolidation loan should reduce the overall amount of monthly payments and interest you pay.

Warning

Interest paid on credit-card debt or personal loans is not tax-deductible.

Loans will vary in length, interest rate, amount loaned and type of interest rate (fixed or variable). The interest rate and loan programme you qualify for will depend on your credit, income and equity.

5   Complete a loan application and supply all requested documentation.

6   Submit copies of all credit-card and loan statements that will be paid off to the lender.

7   Complete the loan process. This typically takes three to four weeks.

Wire Money   756

Wire transfers are used to make business transactions, purchase homes and pay off debts.

⊚ Steps

1   Decide the amount of money that is to be wired or transferred.

2   Gather all the information regarding where the money will be transferred. This information needs to include the name of the bank or financial institution, the name of the account holder, the account number and sort code.

3   Go to the bank or financial institution from where the money will be wired. You will probably be asked to fill out a wire-transfer form. This form will authorise the wire transfer and give all the necessary information to your bank.

4   Ask what the fee will be for handling a wire transfer. This fee can be added to the money you are wiring or it can be deducted from your account depending on the policies of your bank or financial institution.

5   Contact the person or business on the receiving end of the wire transfer to let them know that the money has been wired, so that they can verify that it arrives in the appropriate account as anticipated.

 Tip

Most banks have cut-off times each day for wiring money. If you need the money transferred within the same day, you should conduct your wire transfer as early in the day as possible or make prior arrangements with your bank.

Open a Swiss Bank Account   757

Not many things are cooler than being able to say, "OK. I'll get you the money once I transfer it from my Swiss bank account."

⊚ Steps

1   Pick your bank. Out of the hundreds of Swiss banks, the two biggest are UBS and Credit Suisse. These two goliaths have the most extensive international networks and solid reputations.

2   Contact the bank you want to do business with. The bank will tell you the terms and conditions of doing business. Despite the famous secrecy of Swiss bank accounts, many bankers will want to get to know the person with whom they'll be doing business.

3   Make an initial deposit. Most banks require at least £1,000.

4   Brag. You now officially have a Swiss bank account and can legitimately act like a spy and/or criminal.

 Tip

Swiss law provides some of the stiffest regulations in the world as far as who can access your account. If protecting your assets from investigators is a priority, a Swiss account is the place.

758 | Decide When to Sell Stock

Evaluate a number of factors before you decide it's time to get out of a stock.

⊙ Steps

1 Consider selling if the price has dropped substantially or been stagnant.

2 Think about selling if the price has risen to or beyond a target that you established when you bought the stock.

3 Note whether the company's fundamentals remain strong.

4 Evaluate earnings trends, management changes, revenue growth and other basics to determine whether fundamentals are sound. Even if the stock price is sluggish or, for that matter, has hit new highs, you might want to hang on to the stock if fundamentals remain sound and growth prospects look good.

5 Visit your public library's business reference section and review reports by experts. Do they project no price appreciation for the stock?

6 Consider changes in the competition. If an effective new player or several hot new players have entered the market, your stock's growth prospects could be in jeopardy.

7 Think about the company's product line. If the company depends on one product alone and has no plans for broadening its base, perhaps you should think about selling.

✳ Tip

Consider the tax consequences of selling stock. If you have taxable capital gains, you might want to take some losses to reduce your taxes.

759 | Identify Money Scams

Money scams have been around for years, but the Internet has helped expand and make the scams much more popular and easier to disperse.

⊙ Steps

1 Be wary of any offer that promises overnight riches. There is no such thing as quick money, no matter what the advertising would want you to believe. Most of these schemes rely on information that is either next to impossible to find or extremely hard to follow through.

2 Avoid paying for information. Companies that require a sign-up fee are usually scams. You shouldn't have to pay to get accepted, since an authentic company should be making money from your work, in the form of percentages or by profiting from your final product.

3 Beware of anything that you receive via email. Legitimate companies don't search for workers by sending mass emails to anonymous people. Never follow a link inside an email from somebody you don't know.

4 Don't pay to receive a prize. If you have truly won a contest, you won't have to pay anything, not even shipping prizes or "access" fees to get the prize to your door. Companies that ask you to call a number to confirm your identity before you can receive your prize are most likely scams.

⚠ Warning

Never write back to someone you don't know with personal information, no matter how tempting the offer.

Find a Great Accountant 760

Whether you are overseeing a corporation or running a small business from home, you will at some time in your career need to engage the services of a good accountant.

⊙ Steps

1 Identify your needs. Do you need a bookkeeper to balance the cheque-book or someone to prepare financial statements and/or tax documents?

2 Determine the type of accountant needed, based on your needs. Many accountants can provide all the services you require or are part of an accounting company that can cover your needs.

3 Ask others, especially those in the same line of business as you, for their recommendations.

4 Look in the Yellow Pages or contact other companies for referrals.

5 Look beyond fees when evaluating accountants, and ensure you feel comfortable with your prospective accountant and his or her ability to quickly respond to and understand the changing needs of your business.

✳ Tips

Accountants may have office staff or junior accountants who are qualified to work at a lower pay rate.

Most accountants will give a free half-hour consultation. Ask – don't assume.

⚠ Warnings

When hiring friends or family, understand that you will lose all privacy with your finances.

If you feel uneasy with an accountant, don't hire him or her in spite of good credentials.

Teach Your Child About Financial Responsibility 761

From piggy banks to credit cards, there's plenty you can teach your child about money matters at any age.

⊙ Steps

1 Start talking about money with your children as early as age three. Take them to the shops and explain that you earn money so that you can buy things you need.

2 Give your children a small amount of money and let them buy something on their own.

3 Begin giving your children a small weekly allowance when they are six or seven years old, and set guidelines about how they can use the money.

4 Pick a date, such as a birthday, on which to give your children an annual raise. Increase their responsibilities as you increase their allowance.

5 Avoid withholding allowance if your child doesn't fulfil a responsibility; choose another form of discipline instead. It's hard for a child to learn budgeting skills if they don't know how much money will be coming in each week.

6 Start talking about long-term goals, such as saving for college or a car, when your children are between 11 and 14. Encourage them to earn extra money by mowing the neighbour's lawn, for example.

7 Consider opening a bank account in your child's name as an aid to saving and spending their earnings.

8 Consider encouraging your children to find a part-time job when they are 16 to 18 years old.

✳ Tips

When deciding on an allowance amount, consider the child's age, needs and your family's financial situation. Talk to other parents if you'd like to get an idea of typical allowances in your area.

Encourage your older child to work and save by offering to match each deposit they make in a savings account.

⚠ Warning

Keep your college-age child's credit-card use under careful supervision, providing guidelines as well as clearly stating the consequences of misuse.

9   Consider giving your children a credit card when they enter college, and discuss how to use it responsibly. Determine together what expenses you will pay for and what they must pay for. If the card is to be used only in emergencies, make that clear.

10 Teach your children about social responsibility as you teach them about money – for example, you could all donate money to a charity or volunteer your time at a shelter.

762 | Organise an Investment Club

If you're interested in investing in the stock market but don't know where to begin, start with an investment club.

⊙ Steps

1   Find and organise your members. Start a club that meets in person or one that convenes online. Having something in common is an important factor to consider – draw from family, friends, co-workers and fellow students. Limit the membership to 12 to 15.

2   Set a minimum monthly fee that each member is expected to contribute – for instance, £20 to £50. Some clubs set an initial contribution a bit higher to cement each member's commitment to the club. Each member's return is determined by his or her contributions to the club.

3   Make sure all members understand and agree on investment strategies before you even begin. Your club must have a unified purpose; it will not be successful if some members prefer short-term strategies while others want to buy and hold stocks.

4   Create the club's bylaws or rules. Select club officers and set committees to oversee club activities, serve as a co-signatory, to collect dues and maintain all the financials and tax forms.

5   Determine whether your club wants to work with a stockbroker or go it alone. If you go it alone, check out discount online brokerage houses. If you work with a broker, designate one member to deal with him or her in executing buy and sell orders. Someone needs to take care of the bookkeeping.

6   Look for a brokerage house with a good reputation and low trading costs. If all members are investment novices, consider using a broker for the first year or two until you get your sea legs, then switch to a discount broker to go it alone.

7   Conduct and use good research. Use online services, such as Yahoo Finance, Motley Fool and Morningstar. Follow the progress of a particular stock or family of stocks that the club is considering for purchase. Get as much information about the stocks as you can and make sure all members share this information.

8   Use your computer. Accounting software is available online for clubs that simplifies record-keeping, as well as investment software that makes it easier to find hidden gems. Find other ideas online. Email and chat rooms are great ways of communicating with each other, especially if you are part of an online club.

✱ Tips

If the group is small, make sure each member reviews a different magazine, website or newspaper for investment ideas.

Agree on a selling price for an investment and enter the order online or with your broker to avoid missing a selling opportunity between meetings.

Arrange expert presentations to educate members. Choose a stock expert one week and a bond expert the next.

⚠ Warnings

Some professional investment guides are expensive and may not be financially prudent for your club.

Make sure you understand how online investments work. If a stock price surges during the day and then falls, make sure the programme allows you to sell during the day, or you may be stuck with the closing price.

Only invest what you can afford to lose.

9 Be patient. It will take a couple of years, based on the ups and downs of the stock market and the economy, to see your investments grow. Members should consider both the club and its investments a long-term commitment, and the club's contract should include some sort of clause and even a small penalty that addresses what happens when someone withdraws funds early.

Set up a Trust 763

A trust is a good way to protect your assets during your life and after you pass away. It can provide financial security for your children and your spouse.

⊙ Steps

1 Investigate types of trusts. A "living trust" is one in which assets are used and controlled by you during your lifetime and are distributed when you die as directed by the trust. The probate process is avoided for assets put into the trust.

2 Unlike a living trust, a "testamentary trust" takes effect when you die. It is usually tied to a will and can help eliminate or reduce estate taxes for your beneficiaries. A testamentary trust does not avoid probate.

3 Set up the trust once you have determined the type you need. Determine who you want as your trustee (the person responsible for ensuring that the terms of the trust agreement are carried out).

4 Consult with your bank, lawyer or certified financial adviser.

5 Obtain the appropriate documents from your adviser (or purchase a software program to assist you) and complete them to set up the trust.

6 Fund a living trust. Identify which assets to include in your living trust. These are the assets over which you have control and wish to control during your lifetime.

7 Change the titles of these assets; put them in the name of your trust.

✳ Tips

You can take steps so that your trustee will administer the assets in your living trust if you become incapacitated for any reason.

Trusts are not public documents; your affairs remain private.

Even if an asset is mentioned in your living-trust documents, it is not a trust property unless ownership has been transferred to the trust.

⚠ Warning

Probate is the legal proceeding designed to validate a person's will and designate the person or persons who receive the assets. The process can take between nine and 12 months, and the total fees may equal five or six per cent of the total asset value.

Invest in Premium Bonds 764

Premium Bonds are government-issued debt securities. Instead of earning interest on these investments, participants are entered into a monthly draw for tax-free cash prizes.

⊙ Steps

1 Buy Premium Bonds directly from any bank or financial institution. You can purchase them in increments of £100, with a maximum holding amount of any one individual of £30,000. Each £100 investment gives you 100 numbers that are entered into a monthly draw, which means you have 100 chances to win.

2 Purchase your Premium Bonds from your nearest Post Office. This is where you can purchase all products and services from National Savings and Investments (NS&I).

✳ Tips

You must be age 16 or over in order to buy premium Bonds in your name. Purchasing Premium Bonds as a gift for a child must be done in an adult's name.

You can lower the minimum investment to £50 if you apply to make a monthly standing order of Premium Bonds.

3   Visit the official website of the NS&I, where you can purchase Premium
    Bonds directly over the Internet via a secure form. This is quickly
    becoming the easiest and most popular way for participants to
    purchase Premium Bonds, and to keep track of the winning ticket
    numbers in the monthly draws.

4   Get Premium Bonds over the telephone, or by sending a cheque by post
    to the NS&I. The contact information is available on the NS&I website.

5   Keep track of the monthly draws to see if you have won. Two grand
    prizes of £1 million pounds are awarded each month, with the rest of
    the prizes dependent upon how much was invested in any given month.
    Winnings are completely tax-free.

6   Cash in either the partial or whole amount of your bond investment at
    any time by downloading the form available online, or at any Post Office.
    You can then post the form to the NS&I headquarters in Blackpool, and
    the amount will either be deposited into your bank account, or a cheque
    will be issued within eight days.

765 Select a Good Mutual Fund

Sometimes it seems there are as many mutual funds as there
are people, but it's important to take the time to choose the
ones that furthers your investment goals.

Steps

1   Decide what percentage of your money you will allocate to mutual funds.
    If you'll be investing less than £15,000 to £20,000 overall, many investors
    advise that all your investments should be in mutual funds.

2   Determine how many mutual funds you will invest in. Three to five funds
    is generally considered an adequate amount of diversification.

3   Decide whether you'll deal directly with the fund manager or use a broker.

4   Diversify the funds you buy in terms of the size of the companies in their
    portfolios and the businesses that those companies are in.

5   Choose high-performance funds by using Internet resources and news-
    papers to pick those funds that have had the best performance over at
    least the last three years.

✳ Tip

Using a discount broker who
sells no-load funds without
taking a commission makes it
easy to switch from one fund
to another.

⚠ Warning

A large group of mutual funds
does not necessarily provide
diversification, because the
companies whose stocks they
hold will overlap.

766 Use a Stockbroker

Many savvy investors claim that the three main things you need
to play the market are money (to start out), time (to research
stocks) and a good stockbroker to help you make informed
decisions in a timely manner.

Steps

1   Research various brokers, familiarising yourself with the difference
    between full-service brokerages and discount brokerages.

✳ Tips

Go online. Many discount
brokers will let you set up
an account and execute your
trades over the Internet.

2   Evaluate the brokers' fee schedules, services and procedures, selecting a brokerage that meets your needs.

3   Read the small print in the brokerage agreement and ask questions.

4   Establish a cash account with the brokerage of your choice.

5   Research stocks and follow market news. When you decide to buy or sell, know what price you are willing to pay or what price you want to get for the stock.

6   Call the broker and ask for a quote on the stock you have decided to buy or sell. The quote tells you the highest price that anyone is willing to pay for the stock and the lowest price at which anyone is willing to sell it.

7   Decide what kind of order to place. You can place a market order, asking your broker to get the best price available at that moment, or you can place a limit order, asking the broker to buy or sell only when the stock reaches an agreed-upon price.

8   Place the order.

9   Get confirmation. The exchange on which the stock is traded will send the broker an electronic confirmation of the trade. You will receive written confirmation – and the bill – by post.

10   Make sure the broker has complied with your order.

Ask for help. If you feel uneasy about using a discount broker, ask someone who has done it before to assist you.

⚠ **Warning**

Investing in the stock market can be a rewarding and lucrative way to make your money work for you, but make sure you know what you are doing. Ignorance can cost you thousands of pounds. Don't be afraid to ask for advice.

Calculate a Return on an Investment   **767**

A Return on Investment (ROI) is calculated to measure the performance of one investment in relation to another. ROI is expressed as a percentage and is based on returns over an associated time period, usually one year. For example, a 25 per cent annual ROI means that a £100 investment would return £25 in one year. Thus, after one year, the total investment becomes £125.

✳ Tip

Calculators and computer spreadsheet programs can be very useful in calculating ROI. Refer to their instruction manuals for more information.

⊙ **Steps**

1   Write down the amount of your total investment, including fees and expenses, if any. For example, if you bought £950 worth of stock and your fees were £50, then your total investment is £950 + £50, or £1,000.

2   Write down the amount of profit or loss associated with your investment. If your £1,000 investment in stocks is worth £1,200 one year later, then your profit is £1,200 - £1,000, or £200.

3   Calculate the ROI by dividing the profit by the total investment: £200/£1000 = 0.20, or a 20 per cent annual ROI.

⚠ **Warning**

When comparing ROI for different investment opportunities, be sure all fees and expenses have been included to ensure a fair comparison. Some ROI quotes do not include fees and expenses, and can therefore be misleading.

768 | Get Life Insurance if You Have Medical Problems

Even if you're not in the best of health, life-insurance coverage at a reasonable cost is possible.

⊙ Steps

Getting Ready to Apply

1 Write down the names, addresses and phone numbers of all the medical professionals, agencies, clinics and hospitals you have used in the last 10 years.

2 Make a list of the medications you currently take. Be specific about the exact amount and frequency of dosage.

3 Recall the approximate dates of any major adult life events affecting your health and write them down, earliest first.

4 Disregard accidents from which you have fully recovered; they are not considered in underwriting.

5 Summarise all positive aspects about your health condition, such as "never smoked", "quit smoking in 1974", "take walks three times a week" etc.

6 Organise all this information in a folder and make at least one photocopy.

Applying for Coverage

1 Use your own insurance agent, or seek an insurance professional with experience in placing "impaired-risk" cases.

2 Make at least two formal applications for insurance to companies that are known to be aggressive underwriters.

3 Apply for the amount of death benefit that your beneficiaries actually need, according to your calculations and the advice you have received from trusted financial professionals.

4 Agree to take whatever medical tests and exams are required (they will be paid for by the insurance company) as soon as possible after you finish filling out the application forms.

Considering the Offers

1 Direct your agent to provide written documentation of any and all coverage offers that result from your applications.

2 Request a letter of explanation from any company that rates or declines you.

3 Choose the offer that gives you the most insurance coverage and policy guarantees for the least cost.

4 Regardless of the offers, have the insurance company send the results of all exams, tests and lab work to your doctor for your files.

❋ Tips

All offers, even declines, may be negotiable, especially if large sums of money are involved.

If appropriate to your situation, two people can be insured under the same policy if one of those persons is uninsurable.

Single-premium life policies require less-demanding medical qualification.

Although its insurance features are very limited, an annuity might provide some protection of assets if you can't medically qualify for a life policy.

⚠ Warnings

Avoid offers from very poorly rated insurance companies unless you are desperate for the coverage and they are the only ones that will issue a policy.

Underwriting impaired-risk cases takes longer than other types of applications.

You may be asked to take additional medical tests or have more tests done before a company will make an offer.

You have the right to full disclosure from the insurance company for the reasons they rated or declined your application for insurance.

Insure Jewellery

It may be worth insuring your jewellery separately from your contents insurance if the value exceeds that covered on your other policies.

⊙Steps

1   Have all your fine jewellery valued by an independent appraiser. Make sure each item is listed, described and valued on paper.

2   Read your home-owner's insurance policy to find out the amount of coverage it provides for items such as jewellery. The best insurance will cover loss, theft and damage.

3   Keep in mind that you can select coverage with or without a deductible.

4   Speak to your insurance agent about adding a rider to your home-owner's policy to cover jewellery that goes beyond the value of personal property covered in the basic policy.

5   Compare all insurance plans, as well as the reputation of each company, and choose the one that gives you the most coverage for your money and the most flexibility if you have to replace jewellery.

✱ Tips

Beyond having insurance, to keep your jewellery safe you should store it in a personal safe or in a safety-deposit box.

Having photos of jewellery items is important, as lost or stolen pieces can sometimes be recreated on the basis of a photograph.

⚠ Warning

All jewellery should be inspected on a regular basis for reassessment of value. If your jewellery is not valued appropriately, you will not be able to recover what you need to replace it if it is lost, damaged or stolen.

Buy Pet Health Insurance

Pet health insurance is becoming more popular for pampered pets and their owners, who like to be prepared when it comes to healthcare costs for their animals.

⊙Steps

1   Learn how pet health insurance works. Most pet plans allow you to use any vet or animal health clinic in the country.

2   Find out about the co-pay or what percentage of costs the pet health insurance plan will cover. Most plans pay a specified maximum amount per pet per year.

3   Determine your needs. How many dogs and cats do you have that you'll want to cover under a pet health insurance plan? How old are your animals, how healthy and what pre-existing conditions exist?

4   Compare plans. Look at each plan's co-pays, deductible and yearly cap. Get quotes from several different companies.

5   Evaluate the pet health insurance provider. Find out how long they have been in business and·look for reviews and ratings from their customers.

6   Purchase the pet health insurance plan you've chosen for your animals. Keep excellent records of all costs associated with your pet's health.

7   Submit vets bills to your health-insurance provider, keeping copies of everything for your records in case there is a mistake. Make timely claims to ensure you receive payments.

✱ Tip

With pet health insurance, you still pay your vet directly and receive partial or full reimbursements from the insurance company.

771 Manage Life-Insurance Payouts

The death benefit of a life-insurance policy may have brought you a significant amount of tax-free cash, but you'll fritter it away unless you manage it properly.

Steps

1 Send the life-insurance company a certified death certificate (not a photocopy) to receive the death benefit of the life-insurance policy on the deceased.

2 Carefully study the options for payout presented to you by the insurance company.

3 Call the policyholder-services department of the insurance company and discuss any questions you have with a trained counsellor.

4 After you have received the payout, first settle all final expenses and pay off all medical, hospital and terminal-care costs of the deceased that are not covered by insurance.

5 If the amount left over is significant, consult with a financial professional regarding appropriate options for using, saving and investing the money. They will know how best to invest your money.

6 If the amount left over is relatively small, consider placing the money in a money-market account with instant access.

7 Pay off all consumer debt.

8 Consider paying off any equity loans or your mortgage, but discuss these options with a financial advisor first – if you have good rates of interest on these loans, paying them off might not be the most sensible use of your money.

9 Before making any major purchases (car, furniture, travel, etc.), make sure that such expenditures will not adversely effect your long-term financial plans.

10 Invest with care and live prudently so that this amount of money will provide you with a long period of financial security and comfort.

11 Bear in mind that a sizeable death-benfit payment may catapult you into a higher tax bracket, so don't scrimp on paying for sound tax advice from a qualified accountant.

✳ Tips

Virtually all life-insurance companies provide considerate and sensitive assistance in helping you decide how to receive the death benefit of one of their policies.

Diversify your investments; well-managed mutual funds are a good way to do that.

Think of the principle as your "income generator", and withdraw interest or gains only if you need the money.

⚠ Warnings

Legal advice and assistance may also be necessary following the death of a spouse or close relative, but be prudent and don't pay for more legal time than is necessary.

Scam artists scour obituaries for new targets; beware of deals that sound too good to be true – they almost always are.

Close family members and relatives can be a great comfort during bereavement, but they don't always make the best financial advisers.

772 Calculate Mortgage Rates

When it comes to mortgage rates, there are many variables. Here are some handy tools for you to use when you need to perform mortgage rate-based calculations.

Steps

1 Mortgages have several moving parts: amount financed, interest rate and loan term. All this information together will be calculated to determine your monthly payment.

✳ Tip

Some websites that have mortgage calculators will even calculate in taxes and insurance.

2   How much does the home you want to purchase cost? Subtract your down payment (if any) from the purchase price and this is the amount you want to finance.

3   Take the amount you want to finance and plug it into an online mortgage calculator.

4   How long do you want to finance your home for? You'll want to plug this information into the calculator as well.

5   Research interest rates in your area. This can easily be done through looking at the property section of your local newspaper or through property websites.

6   Plug in the appropriate interest rate into the calculator. Hit Calculate.

7   You've just calculated your mortgage! Try changing some of the variables to see how it impacts your monthly payment and time required to pay off your mortgage.

Estimate Moving Costs   773

Moving all your worldly possessions from point A to point B is often more costly than you think. Here's how to estimate those costs more accurately.

⊙ Steps

1   Ask a representative of your chosen moving company to give you an estimate. Note what this estimate does or does not include.

2   Estimate the size of the van or lorry you will need if you are moving yourself. Make a list of any extra equipment you'll need: dollies, furniture pads, tow bars, rental cars and packing materials. Call a van rental company and ask for prices.

3   Add in the cost of labour to help you pack and load if you don't do it yourself.

4   Include the costs of moving your family members by air, train, bus or car – these all add up.

5   Remember to factor in accommodation and petrol costs if you will be travelling for more than a day.

6   Add in the cost of food for the trip, as well as entertainment costs if you plan to sightsee while you travel.

7   Include the cost of keeping things in temporary storage, if necessary.

8   Add in costs for temporary accommodation (such as a corporate apartment) if your new home is not immediately available.

9   Add in the costs to transport pets, and delicate or special items. There may also be fees to disconnect or connect utilities and insurance costs.

✱ Tips

When you get an estimate from a removal company, find out whether it is a binding (final price) or non-binding (other charges possible) estimate and exactly what services will be performed for that price.

Your current or new employer may cover or help with moving costs. Ask.

⚠ Warnings

If you use inferior materials/equipment in your move, broken objects may end up costing you more than the movers would have.

Shop around carefully before choosing removal companies and equipment. Be wary of fly-by-night operations.

774 Pay Rent Late

Tight on cash? Paying one month's rent a little late shouldn't cost you your flat or house. With some luck and tact, you can work out an agreement with your landlord.

Steps

1   Review your lease or rental agreement for clauses about late fees. Find out exactly what action your landlord may take under the terms of your contract.

2   Resolve to pay a late fee if your contract explicitly states that your landlord may impose them. Otherwise, your landlord cannot legally require you to pay a late fee.

3   Write a letter to your landlord explaining your situation and asking for some extra time. If possible, try not to ask for more than a few days.

4   Emphasise that your problems are temporary and reassure the landlord that in the future you'll be able to pay the rent on time.

5   Agree to pay a portion of the rent immediately, if possible, and promise to pay the balance by a specific date.

⚠ Warnings

Even if your contract doesn't mention late fees, it may be better to pay a small fee to avoid problems in the future. Chances are that if you refuse to pay £10 extra for handing in the rent a week late, the landlord will evict you at the next legal opportunity.

Tell the landlord you can't pay on time before you send in a late cheque. A landlord may be able to file for eviction if the rent is even one day late.

Don't write the landlord a cheque that will bounce.

775 Get Back a Rent Deposit

Remember that extra cash you put up at the beginning of your lease? If you want to see that rental deposit again, make sure you leave your place in tip-top condition when you move out.

Steps

1   Clean your apartment thoroughly, including the refrigerator, oven and bathroom.

2   Document your cleaning work with pictures and witnesses.

3   Arrange to meet with your landlord or manager and tour the cleaned accommodation.

4   Check the condition of the accommodation against what it was like when you moved in (you should have a list documenting existing damage).

5   Work out any disputes on the spot, if possible.

6   Ask for the security deposit before you leave.

7   Write a formal letter demanding your deposit if you do not receive the deposit within a few weeks.

✳ Tips

If the landlord cannot tour the apartment with you, bring a witness in his place, take some photos and keep all receipts for cleaning materials in case you need to sue in the small-claims court.

If your landlord deliberately holds back your deposit and the formal letter of demand is unsuccessful, you may consider mediation or suing your landlord for the deposit.

Name Your Dog 776

Others will see your dog's name as a reflection of the dog's personality or even your own. Choose wisely, but have fun, too.

Steps

1. Keep the name short, preferably one or two syllables. This will be easier for your dog to learn and remember.

2. Choose from a plethora of the usual dog names: Spot, Patch, Poochie, Rover ... or, for the ultimate in typical canine titles, Dog – pronounced "Dawg".

3. Match the name to your dog's personality. A noble hound may be fit to be King; a timid pooch may solicit the name Fluffy.

4. Bestow upon your dog the honour of being named after your favourite food: Biscuit, Sugar or Cream Puff.

5. Express your sense of humour. Christen your happy Lab Spike, your perpetually growling bulldog Cuddles, or your great dane Tim (as in Tiny Tim).

6. Go the creative route. Take your canine companion's name from the title of your favourite book, your current or a past lover, the name of your favourite actor, a line from your favourite song or the street where you grew up.

⚠ Warning

Be sure the name is distinct from any command words you'll be teaching your dog. For instance, if you name your dog Noah, you'll have to find creative ways of using the word "no".

Train Your Dog to Sit 777

Use patience, encouragement and treats to teach your dog one of the most basic of all commands – "Sit".

Steps

1. Stand in front of your dog.

2. Hold a treat right near your pet's nose, just out of his or her reach.

3. Slowly move the treat over your pup's head and towards his or her tail.

4. Say your dog's name, and give the command "Sit" .

5. Keep the treat at nose level. If the treat is held too high, the dog will jump to reach it.

6. Say the word "Good" at the exact second the dog sits.

7. Praise abundantly and give your pet a treat for any movement that resembles the sit position.

8. Release your pet from the sit position with the "Release" or "Free" command.

9. Repeat for five minutes.

✱ Tip

Get your pup familiarised with his or her name as soon as possible. In a pleased and happy voice, say the name. When the dog looks at you, give praise and treats. Repeat for several days.

778 | Train Your Dog to Heel

Using a lead and jerking your dog's neck is not necessary to train him to heel. Tasty treats and an abundance of praise will usually do the trick.

⊙ **Steps**

1 Have your dog on your left side, facing the same direction as you.

2 In your left hand hold food in front of your dog's nose.

3 Give the command "Heel" and begin taking steps while keeping the treat in front of your left hip.

4 Note that it may take several attempts to keep your dog focused on the food.

5 Say the word "Good" at the exact moment your dog walks as you walk.

6 Give your dog the food, along with an abundance of praise for even the slightest show of understanding.

7 Train in short, five-minute intervals throughout the day.

8 Be very patient and positive, and have fun.

✱ Tip

Try enrolling in an obedience class with your dog. These are a good way to make sure your dog is learning commands properly.

779 | Train Your Dog to Stay

Teaching your dog to stay involves the same positive reinforcement techniques necessary for all training.

⊙ **Steps**

1 Be sure your dog understands a release command, such as "Free" or "Okay" before teaching this command.

2 Have your dog sit or lie down in front of you.

3 Place your hand, palm open, in front of your dog's nose and give the command "Stay".

4 Say "Good" at the exact moment your dog exhibits the behaviour you want.

5 Give the release command immediately after (within one to two seconds), followed by treats and unlimited praise.

6 Reward your pet even if he or she only stayed for one second; and always offer rewards for even slight indications of understanding.

7 Lengthen the amount of time your pet remains in the stay position very gradually and slowly move further away.

8 Remember to give the release command after every successful "stay" as you increase the length of time your dog must remain in the position.

9 Avoid going into another room until your dog fully understands the command.

10 Train in five-minute sessions.

✱ Tip

Give the release command for a sit/stay after one minute maximum. You may have the dog in a down/stay for longer periods of time.

Teach a Dog to Pick Up Items Off the Floor · 780

It doesn't matter how old you are – having a dog that can pick things up for you can be a huge help!

⊙ Steps

1 Understand that most dogs will want to get something in return for doing a trick – whether they get a dog treat or a hug and a pat on the head. Have a few small dog treats on hand for the first few times you teach your dog to do this trick.

2 Drop something on the floor that you don't care about, such as a small plastic cup. Accidentally knock it off of the table when the dog is in the room, for example. Don't throw it to the ground like you would do their dog toy.

3 Call the dog over by name. When the dog is standing right over the item, bend down, pick it up and touch it to their mouth and say "(dog's name) pick it up" Then put the item back on the ground.

4 Keep saying "(dog's name) pick it up" and putting the item from the floor to the dog's mouth a couple of times. The dog will probably try to grab it in his or her mouth – that's okay. Let them do it but take it out of their mouth and put it back on the floor. Finally, put the item back on the floor, point at the item and say "pick it up". If the dog picks it up, praise him.

5 Call the dog over to you while he or she still has the item in their mouth. Again, give lots of praise but this time give them a dog treat. If it doesn't work straight away, don't lose patience; just keep at it.

6 Each time the dog picks up the item that you ask them to and brings it over to you, give them a dog treat and move further away from where you dropped the item. Stay in the same room, though. Straight after you point to the item and tell the dog to pick it up, move to a further location but keep saying "(dog's name) pick it up". This will teach the dog that even if you aren't in the area, it's okay to pick the item up off the floor.

7 Move on to another item. Pretty soon the dog will get the sense that when an item falls to the floor they are to pick it up without being told.

⚠ Warning

Never let the dog see you throw an item on the floor and then ask them to pick it up. "Accidentally" drop it. If the dog sees you drop it, he or she will consider it to be a game.

Muzzle a Dog · 781

Despite the look, a muzzle is not cruel when used on an injured, frightened or upset animal. Dogs that are hurt or upset can bite, making the use of a muzzle necessary.

⊙ Steps

1 Use nylon tights or a long strip of material.

2 Place the strip of material on top of the dog's nose.

3 Loop the material under the dog's chin and tie it into a knot or bow.

4 Bring the ends of the material back behind the dog's ears, and tie into a knot or bow.

✳ Tip

Avoid using masking tape or electrical tape to muzzle your pet. Removal could upset your dog even more.

5 Avoid tying the knot or bow too tightly.

6 Use a muzzle only for a few minutes at a time; never leave it on for an extended period.

7 Consult your vet about whether it's appropriate to buy your dog a commercial muzzle, such as a basket muzzle. Ask what type of muzzle is recommended for your pet.

⚠ **Warning**

Never exercise your dog with a muzzle. A dog sweats by panting and can quickly overheat if its mouth is clamped shut.

782 Retrain an Aggressive Dog

Dogs that express displeasure by showing their teeth or biting are often the ones who don't understand the family-pack order or those who, for lack of a better leader, have taken up the alpha role themselves.

⚠ **Warning**

Remember that it is not always possible to retrain an agressive dog. If your dog continues to show signs of aggression after several months, it may need to be destroyed.

◉ **Steps**

1 Have your dog spayed or neutered if you haven't already done so. This won't make much difference in the personality of a male over 18 months old; but do it anyway because breeding an aggressive dog is irresponsible.

2 Establish yourself as the pack leader and put the dog at the bottom of the pecking order, below all other family members. Control everything about the dog's life: when and where he eats, what toys he can have, where he sleeps, when he gets to go outside. Crate the dog when you can't keep an eye on him.

3 Use a prong collar or a remote collar to correct your dog when he misbehaves. Because dogs don't have our language ability, you can't correct a dog by explaining to him why you don't want him to chew the furniture. Dogs learn best by a combination of positive and negative reinforcement: praise when he's good, appropriate correction when he's bad.

4 Socialise your dog. Once you've established that you're the pack leader, your dog will look to you for instruction on how to behave in new situations. Don't inadvertently praise your dog when he's afraid by petting him or speaking in gentle tones. This doesn't calm your dog; it says to him that he's reacting correctly.

5 Practise submission exercises and taking the dog's food or toys away while he's eating or playing.

6 Contact a professional trainer if at any time you become afraid of your dog, or you think he might hurt someone. A professional can decide whether your dog can be rehabilitated.

Dye a Poodle 783

A poodle's fur can be dyed easily with non-toxic ingredients that wash out over time.

☉ Steps

1. Fill a large bowl with lukewarm water. If you are using many colours, fill up a few different bowls so each colour has its own bowl.

2. Drop three to five drops of food colouring into the bowl of water. Mix it with a spoon and see if it's the colour you desire. If you want the colour to be darker or more vibrant, add more food colouring. Only add one or two drops at a time, because the colour can change quickly.

3. Brush your poodle's fur and get out all the knots. If you have time, have your poodle groomed so its fur is the right length and shape.

4. Dab the sponge in the coloured water and pat it on to the fur that you wish to dye. Continue sponging until the area is thoroughly dyed. If you are using different colours, you should use a new space for each colour.

5. Blow-dry the poodle's fur so that the colour can set. You don't want the dog walking around the house with wet food colouring, because it can get on your furniture and carpet.

✳ Tip

Mix the food colourings to get different shades and colours.

⚠ Warning

Avoid your dog's eyes when sponging on the water.

Care for a Found Dog 784

Care for a stray dog so that he can either be returned to his proper owner or taken to the appropriate shelter.

☉ Steps

1. Check for dog tags.

2. Ask around the immediate area in case the dog lives nearby.

3. Leave the dog in the area and call a local animal shelter if you're uncomfortable taking him home.

4. Call the animal shelter and humane society to report a found dog even if you do take the dog home.

5. Give the dog food, water and a place to rest.

6. Check the newspaper for any lost dog reports. Check frequently.

7. Keep the dog until the owner is found or take the dog to the appropriate agency after 24 hours.

8. Stay in contact with agencies, hang flyers and place ads in local newspapers if you decide to keep the dog in your home.

⚠ Warning

Avoid approaching a dog that exhibits aggressive behaviour.

785 | Care for an Ageing Dog

Dogs begin to show signs of ageing anywhere between six and 13 years. An older dog needs special care and attention to keep them comfortable and feeling loved in their old age.

⊙ Steps

1   Exercise your older dog moderately every day. Try not to overdo it. Watch for excess panting and drooping tail – these are signs that the exercise has become too much for your dog.

2   Feed him high-quality dog food that is specific to his dietary needs. Older dogs require different nutrients from young ones to keep them healthy.

3   Be consistent with his schedule and minimise household disruption.

4   Pet and cuddle your dog frequently to reassure him that he is still your puppy.

5   Groom him regularly, checking for lumps and bumps.

6   Take him to the vet at least once a year. Your vet will screen your dog for kidney, liver, pancreatic and heart disease.

⚠ **Warning**

If your dog has poor sight, avoid rearranging the furniture.

786 | Make Home-Made Dog Food

Despite the huge variety of shop-bought dog foods available, nothing beats creating a tasty treat at home, especially for your dog.

⊙ Steps

1   Know that it is wise to check with your vet before switching to home-made dog food.

2   Understand that dogs need a diet that consists of 40 per cent meat, 30 per cent vegetables and 30 per cent starch. Follow this formula to ensure that your dog has a well-balanced diet.

3   Cook meat before feeding it to your dog.

4   Consider the fact that many experts believe commercial dog food is actually unhealthy for dogs. Often the meat that is used in dog food is of a quality considered unfit for humans.

5   Try making a mixture of ground turkey, rice and carrot for your own dog food. Meals made of minced beef, brown rice, brewer's yeast and carrots are also popular.

6   Rotate the foods you feed your dog so that the dog gets a variety of foods.

7   Use oatmeal, pasta, rice or potatoes to fulfil your dog's starch requirement.

8   Keep cooked dog food in the refrigerator no longer than three days.

❋ Tip

When you first switch to home-made dog food, try mixing commercial dog food with the food you have prepared to help your dog make the transition.

⚠ **Warning**

Do not feed your dog chocolate.

Get a Cat to Play with You 787

Cats all have unique personalities, so it takes some time to figure out what makes an individual cat playful.

☉ Steps

1 Start with affection. If a cat is reluctant to play with you, the chances are that he or she doesn't feel comfortable around you yet. Think about when you were a kid: would you want to play with a stranger? Let the cat come to you and gradually get used to your companionship.

2 Don't force it. Cats have their own agendas; if they don't want to play then trying to do so will only irritate them.

3 Try a variety of toys. Like people, cats have their favourite toys. Don't assume that every cat toy you bring home will be an instant success. After a while you'll learn what the cat likes or dislikes (i.e. feathers, sparkly toys, toys that make noise, etc.).

4 Remember to mimic nature. Don't assume that just dangling a toy in front of your cat will make him or her want to frolic. When kittens play, they are practising their natural hunting skills, so try to create a play environment similar to that they would find in the wild. Cats want an opportunity to stalk and pounce on the toy, and they can't do this if you're sticking the toy right in front of them.

5 Keep the cat's age in mind. Young cats are more playful than adults, it's that simple. An older cat may not want to play as much, so don't further dissuade the cat from playing by being overly zealous. If the cat isn't frisky, don't think you can make him or her play with you. Elderly cats still play, just not as often, so give it time and be patient.

✳ Tip

Be patient – cats are more independent than dogs and can be more aloof.

Keep a Cat Off the Furniture 788

Cats may be more difficult to train than dogs because of their personalities, but here are some helpful tips on training your cat not to get on things he shouldn't.

☉ Steps

1 Prepare yourself to train your cat using positive reinforcement and praise. That means training without the use of punishment or reprimands. A reward system is one of the most successful ways to train your cat.

2 Introduce a mechanical clicker, and follow the sound by a small treat. Give these for no reason or expected behaviour at first. You are associating the sound to the tasty treat, and your cat will begin to react with anticipation to the sound.

3 If you want your cat to stay off the furniture, associate a command word such as "off" with the clicker.

4 Show your cat the treat hidden in your hand, and motion your hand down while stating firmly "off". Reward this behaviour with the treat. This may come in stages so reward each effort or motion to come off the sofa.

✳ Tips

Get off to a good start by planning on at least 15 minutes of quiet time with just you and your cat to introduce the clicker and treat.

There are several products on the market that serve as repellants. Read the instructions and manuals before deciding if one of these tools is right for you.

⚠ Warning

Don't get frustrated. Reprimands and punishment will not help.

5   Create successful situations for your cat so you may reward him or her
     for behaviour you want.

6   Make sure your cat has other outlets for its behaviour. Scratching the
     claws is part of a cat's nature, so provide a scratching post.

7   Do not prepare your cat's food on the kitchen surface if that is an area
     forbidden to the cat. Sheets of aluminium foil laid along the surface may
     serve as a temporary deterrent.

789 Get a Cat Out of a Tree

It is important to remain calm if your kitten or cat gets caught
in a tree. It is probably very scared, and by remaining calm
yourself, you will keep the cat calm too.

Steps

1   Avoid mass panic. Given time and privacy, the cat will probably find a
     way down on its own.

2   If several hours have passed, try to lure the cat down by opening a tin
     of its favourite food underneath the tree. Call out its name in a calm,
     reassuring voice.

3   Lean a wooden ladder up against the tree near the cat so it can climb
     down. Leave it alone with the ladder for at least 15 minutes so it can
     climb down on its own.

4   If the cat is too freaked out to use the ladder, put on work gloves and a
     thick coat to protect yourself and climb up the ladder to retrieve it.

5   Grab the cat by the nape of the neck to reduce your chances of getting
     scratched and to induce calmness in the cat.

6   If your efforts only send the cat further up the tree, call an animal shelter
     or a local humane society. A professional animal handler can rescue the
     cat quite quickly.

✳ Tips

Do not leave the cat stuck in the
tree overnight. It will be terrified
and might fall victim to a night
predator such as an owl.

If a dog has chased the cat
up the tree, make sure the dog
is removed from the premises
so the cat feels secure enough
to climb down.

790 Use a Litter Box

Cats have a natural instinct to defecate on dirt or sand, but you
may have to experiment with different boxes and litter material
to find the best match for your cat.

Steps

1   Provide a litter box large enough for an adult cat to stand and turn
     around in.

2   Get a box that is low enough for an ageing cat or tiny kitten to climb
     into, such as a shallow rectangular baking tin.

3   Try both covered and uncovered litter boxes. Some cats don't like
     covered boxes.

4   Place litter boxes in quiet areas.

✳ Tips

Place carpet in litter boxes
instead of litter material for cats
that soil the carpet. Gradually
add litter into the box and get
rid of the carpet.

Your cat may change litter habits
because of stress.

5   Provide a litter box for each cat in your household and place them in different areas. Be sure to keep the litter box away from food and water.

6   Use fine litter that clumps, or try litter material such as wood shavings or newspaper until you find a material your cat likes.

7   Avoid changing the type of litter material if your cat likes it. If you must make a change, set out a new box containing the new litter material in addition to the old, or gradually mix the new litter in with the old.

8   Remove waste from litter boxes daily, and remove and replenish litter material weekly.

9   Have extra litter boxes available for your cat's use if you're unable to change litter material regularly.

If only one of several boxes is being used, it may be because it has a better location or because the others are dirty.

⚠ **Warning**

Consult a pet behaviourist or vet if your cat keeps urinating or defecating outside the box.

Prevent Hairballs in Cats 791

Hairballs can cause vomiting, loss of appetite and constipation in your cat. In rare cases, removal may require surgery.

⊙ **Steps**

1   Brush your cat daily, especially while it's shedding, to help prevent hairballs from forming in the stomach.

2   Use a bristle or rubber brush for short-haired cats.

3   Brush long-haired cats with a wide-toothed comb or wire slicker brush.

4   Feed your cat a "hairball control" cat food high in vegetable fibre, or administer a commercial hairball prevention preparation available from your vet or at pet shops.

5   Alternatively, mix one teaspoon of mineral oil or petroleum jelly into your cat's food, as a home remedy.

6   Understand that feeding other oils, such as vegetable oil, to your cat will be ineffective, because they will be digested and absorbed.

❋ Tip

Groom long-haired cats more frequently than short-haired varieties.

Determine if a Cat Has Ringworm 792

Cats can become infected with ringworm by digging in infected soil, from infected rodents or their dens, or from other infected cats, dogs or humans.

⊙ **Steps**

1   Watch your cat for symptoms if you know that it has been exposed to another infected animal or human. Ringworm is contagious and it is not uncommon for it to be spread between household members when one catches it.

2   Look for circular patches of hair loss on your cat, especially on the head and limbs. This is the most recognised symptom of ringworm. You may see red spots or bumps that gradually spread into a circle or oval.

❋ Tip

Your vet will be able to offer good advice on the prevention and treatment of ringworm.

3   Examine your cat for patchy areas of baldness, skin that is dry, flaky or itchy, or signs that the claw or claw bed have become infected. These can all be signs of ringworm. Bear in mind, however, that they may indicate other issues as well.

4   Use an ultraviolet lamp on your cat. Around 50 per cent of ringworm strains will glow a fluorescent green under the light of one of these lamps. Bear in mind, though, that as all strains will not appear, this is not a foolproof test for ringworm.

5   Have your vet do a culture from your cat's hair. The lab will be able to determine the exact species of fungus present, which may help treat persistent cases.

6   Treat all cats within a household as soon as one of them has been diagnosed with ringworm. Some cats may not show symptoms of the disease, but will continue to carry the infection and potentially spread or re-infect other cats.

793 Medicate Your Cat with a Pill

Most cat owners cringe when the vet says Tabby will have to take a pill. Follow the steps below to make this task less stressful for you and your pet.

◉ Steps

1   Check the label to make sure the medication is for your cat, and for the specific medical condition it's being treated for. Make sure the medicine is not out of date.

2   Place the cat where it's comfortable – on your lap or a textured surface such as the carpet, a sofa or a bed.

3   Kneel or sit beside your cat with the pill or capsule in your right hand, between your thumb and index finger.

4   Place your left hand on your cat's head. Put your thumb behind its right canine tooth and your left index finger behind its left canine tooth.

5   Lift its lips gently – don't pinch – and place the middle finger of your right hand on the incisor teeth of its lower jaw.

6   Open your cat's mouth by pushing down on its lower jaw with the middle finger of your right hand while tilting its nose upwards with your left hand.

7   Deposit or drop the pill or capsule in the back of your cat's mouth, behind its tongue.

8   Close its mouth and quickly point its nose down at a sharp angle. This will cause your cat to swallow automatically.

9   Do not attempt to conceal the medication in your cat's food or water. If your cat refuses to eat or drink, its will not get the proper dose of medication and will become dehydrated, which could worsen its condition.

✳ Tips

Remain calm and relaxed. Your cat will sense if you are anxious and react accordingly.

Trim your cat's nails to avoid being scratched.

Call your vet and ask for a demonstration or a different form of medication if you are unable to give it as prescribed.

⚠ Warnings

Use caution if your cat has a history of biting or scratching.

Check with your vet to be certain it's safe to handle the medication if you are pregnant.

Care for an Ageing Cat   794

It is not uncommon for a cat to reach 18 to 20 years of age, and they are considered middle-aged by their eighth birthday.

Steps

1   Maintain a close relationship with your vet. Be certain he is aware of the rapid advances in this expanding area of veterinary medical knowledge.

2   Visit your vet at least once a year for recommended vaccinations and a complete physical examination.

3   Allow preventive health maintenance procedures to be performed.

4   Recognise the importance of clean teeth and healthy gums. Preventative dental healthcare has been a key contributor to the increase in quality and length of life in cats.

5   Be absolutely certain that your cat is parasite free – no fleas or worms.

6   Provide a diet formulated to meet the requirements of older cats. Nutritional requirements begin to change when your cat reaches about eight years old.

7   Add extra fibre to its diet each day, helping to prevent hairballs and improve overall digestive function.

8   Recognise that older cats love to be warm and comfy. Provide your cat with a heat source, like a heating pad set on low, throughout the year, not just when you think it's cold.

9   Realise cats, especially old cats, like their privacy. Provide them with a place to take an uninterrupted catnap away from the kids and other pets.

10 Groom your cat daily to keep its coat shiny and prevent it from ingesting hair when it grooms itself.

11 Continue to play with and hold your cat each day. Cats love attention and your touch will let it know you that you still love and care for it.

✴ Tips

Expect your cat to live a long time. The personality of an older cat is very rewarding.

Think about adopting a kitten when your cat is 10 or 12 years old. This gives it time to adjust to the new addition while it is young enough to defend itself and old enough to teach the kitten something about life.

Make Home-Made Cat Food   795

Believe it or not, cat food can be made at home using ground meats and flavourings.

Steps

1   Understand that there are certain foods that should be avoided when you make your own cat food. Never feed your cat chocolate, onions, pork (including bacon), raw fish, raw eggs, milk or bones. Each of these has its own ill-effects on cats.

2   Realise that you should not feed your cat dog food. Cats require five times more protein than dogs do, so dog food will not meet cats' nutritional needs. Avoid feeding your cat a vegetarian diet for the same reason.

✴ Tips

Consult your vet about giving your cat vitamin and mineral supplements.

Keep cooked cat food in the refrigerator for no more than three days.

3 Limit the amount and use of tuna because of the risks associated with the mercury levels in it.

4 Feed liver in moderation and not at all if you're giving your cat vitamin A supplements. Overdoses of vitamin A can be toxic.

5 Know that many cat-food recipes are available on the Internet and in books.

6 Look for recipes that are high in protein content.

7 Include some small amounts of vegetables in your cat's food.

8 Opt for another tasty treat. Cook together 100 g (4 oz) meat, two whole eggs (cats can only eat cooked eggs), one tablespoon of carrot, one tablespoon of cottage cheese and one of sunflower oil. Recognise that you should cook meat before feeding it to your cat.

9 Add flavourings such as kelp powder to the food you cook for your cat. Small amounts of dairy products are acceptable, but cats should not drink a lot of milk. Use lactose-free milk instead.

10 Combine some dry, commercial cat food with meat, eggs, lactose-free milk and flavourings to get your cat used to eating homemade cat food.

796 | Pick a Healthy Hamster

Hamsters are adorable pets, loved by children and adults. They are relatively easy to care for. To fully enjoy your hamster, though, it is important to pick a healthy one.

⊙ Steps

1 Visit the pet shop in the evening when hamsters are likely to be more active and energetic, since they are nocturnal animals.

2 Observe their general behaviour and overall condition.

3 Look for a hamster that is active, alert, energetic and playful.

4 Tap lightly on the cage and see if it responds.

5 Check the coat and make sure that is nice and smooth, not dull.

6 Look at its eyes. They should be bright and clear, not watery.

7 Check its breathing. A healthy hamster's breathing is clear and there should be no discharge from its nose. The area around the nostrils should be dry and not have a crusty look.

8 Check its behind. Make sure it is clean. If it appears wet or dirty, the hamster may have diarrhoea, which is a symptom of wet tail. This is very difficult to cure. Bring this to the attention of the pet attendant immediately, as it is contagious and the other hamsters in the cage may become infected.

9 Pick a hamster with a broad, round body. This indicates that it is eating well. Avoid hamsters that have lumps or bumps on their body.

✳ Tips

Observe how the hamster interacts with other hamsters. This will tell you something about its personality.

Ask the pet attendant if you may handle the hamster you are considering selecting.

Groom Your Rabbit 797

To help keep your rabbit healthy, follow a good grooming programme.

Steps

1 Cut your rabbit's nails every three or four months.

2 Clip only the tip of the nail, being careful not to cut into the quick.

3 Have a bottle of "stop bleed" on hand in case you cause the nail to bleed. This will help clot the cut.

4 Brush your rabbit twice a week to remove dead hair. Use a cat brush.

5 Wash a rabbit only if you have to. Then wash only the soiled area – not the whole rabbit. Don't get water in its ears or up his nose.

6 Keep the cage clean to prevent having to wash your rabbit.

✳ **Tip**

Only use special pet nail clippers when trimming your rabbit's nails (or those of any animal).

House a Guinea Pig 798

Guinea pigs are great pets for older children. They enjoy people and may even curl up and go to sleep on the laps of calm children.

Steps

1 Pick a well-ventilated cage with a solid bottom as housing for your guinea pig. Guinea pigs housed in cages with mesh bottoms often break their legs, toenails and develop sores on their feet.

2 Make sure your guinea pig's cage is big enough for them. You need at least 645 sq cm (100 sq in) of flooring per adult, and many experts recommend 0.7 sq m (7.5 sq ft) of cage for one guinea pig and more for a pair. Guinea pigs that are housed in small cages often fight.

3 Consider purchasing a multi-level cage to increase the floor space of the cage without increasing the space you'll need for the cage.

4 Decide where you'll put your guinea pig's housing before purchasing it. Cages should be in a place where they can interact with the family, but not in high-traffic areas since guinea pigs do need peace and quiet. Cages should be placed away from direct sunlight and drafts, and many experts do not recommend guinea pigs be housed in a child's bedroom.

✳ **Tip**

Put a hidey house in your guinea pig's cage, especially if you have multiple guinea pigs.

⚠ **Warning**

Avoid a wooden cage as guinea pigs can chew holes in these. Wooden cages are also perfect breeding grounds for fungus and bacteria, and can be difficult to keep clean.

Clean Out a Rat Cage 799

Maintaining a clean habitat for your pet rat is important to keep the rat both happy and healthy.

Steps

1 Remove your rat from its cage and place in a safe, confined area, such as another cage or enclosed space.

2   Discard any litter, shavings, old food or other waste material.

3   Remove the food dish, water dish and accessories from the cage. Soak dishes and water-safe accessories in hot, soapy water using a household dish soap.

4   Scrub the cage using hot, soapy water and a scrub brush. Make sure you remove all debris from the cage bottom and walls. Scrub the cage accessories as well.

5   Rinse the cage and accessories thoroughly with hot water.

6   Disinfect the cage and all accessories with a sanitising solution. Spray for at least two minutes and then wipe clean.

7   Allow the cage and accessories to air dry, if possible, or dry with paper towels.

8   Return the cage accessories to the cage. Fill the food and water dishes. Provide fresh shavings and litter as appropriate.

9   Return your rat to a clean home.

 Tips

Keep a number of cloth accessories on hand. Rotate them weekly, washing those not in use in your washing machine.

Glass aquarium cages may require cleaning twice a week depending on the number of rats, as urine causes build-up of the chemical ammonia, which is harmful to both rodent and human respiratory systems.

⚠ **Warnings**

Do not use scented (perfumed) cleaners or detergents.

Clean your rat's cage in a well-ventilated area.

---

800   Feed your Ferret

Ferrets are obligate carnivores, which means they require a diet that's very high in meat-based protein and fat.

◎ **Steps**

1   Purchase a high-quality ferret food, a high-quality kitten food or a natural meat diet.

2   Choose a food that contains a minimum protein level of 34 per cent and a minimum fat level of 19 per cent. Younger ferrets (under one year of age) require a food with a higher fat content of 20 to 22 per cent.

3   Review the ingredient list carefully. The first ingredient must be a meat source – for example, chicken, chicken meal, lamb or beef. Avoid corn because it is very difficult for a ferret to digest and can cause health problems such as urinary tract infections.

4   Read the ingredient list to make sure that taurine is included. Taurine is an essential ingredient for a ferret's diet.

5   Try to introduce a wide variety of foods during the first six months of your ferret's life. Ferrets imprint on foods when they're young, so this will make things easier if you need to change your ferret's food later on.

6   Consider feeding your ferret a mixture of at least two high-quality foods because ferrets can be very picky eaters.

7   Place the food and water bowls away from the litter pan, preferably on another level of the cage.

8   Keep a full bowl of food available at all times; a ferret's digestive system takes only about three to four hours from intake to output.

9   Be sure to keep water available at all times as well, in either a bottle, a bowl or both. Change the water daily for freshness.

 Tips

Because some ferrets like to dig in their food and water or spill their dishes, a crock-lock dish that attaches to the side of the cage is recommended.

Ferrets like to play in their water bowls and make a mess. To prevent this, attach the water bowl higher up the side of the cage, or give your ferret a separate water dish just for playing in. Put a dish of water inside a bigger dishpan so that the ferret can play in the water without soaking the floor.

⚠ **Warning**

Dog food does not contain taurine and is not an appropriate diet for a ferret.

Play with a Pet Iguana | 801

Pet iguanas can engage in two types of play: individual and partner play with a human or another animal. Encourage play by paying attention to what your pet iguana likes to do.

⊙ Steps

1 Hang securely mounted ropes or fabric that your pet iguana can swing from. Play with the ropes yourself, swinging them back and forth and pretending that they are yours, to encourage your pet to play with them.

2 Let your iguana climb over your arms or legs, and move it around from spot to spot. Pay attention to your iguana and whether it likes this type of play. Be aware that your pet will be more receptive during some periods than others.

3 Spend time with your iguana. You can pet or feed it during this time, but the time itself will be a change of pace and activity for your pet.

4 Hold your pet iguana and take a walk outside. You can pick edible flowers or plants for it while you're out.

5 Create targets for your iguana to leap at. Jumping and leaping is natural behaviour for iguanas and many like to jump towards "green" things, as they would to plants in the wild. Entice your pet iguana with pillows, hammocks made for pets or a mound of spare blankets.

6 Provide a tub of water if your iguana likes to dive in, but make sure that it is big and deep enough that your iguana isn't injured when it jumps in.

⚠ Warnings

Fake plants should not be used for play as the wire that supports them is often thinly wrapped and it can poke out.

Never leave a pet iguana to play unsupervised with another family pet. While they generally get on well, injuries can happen.

Breed Frogs | 802

Breeding frogs can be a tricky process, as it involves convincing the frogs that they want to mate!

⊙ Steps

1 Understand that you cannot force your frogs to breed. You can, however, create conditions that will make them more likely to breed.

2 Make sure you have a male and a female frog. It can be difficult to identify the sexes, but some females have a triangle-like protrusion between their rear legs. The best way to be sure you have both sexes is to ask before buying.

3 Learn about the type of climate your type of frog naturally lives in. You need to replicate spring in that climate to make your frogs think it is time to breed.

4 Be sure to provide plants for the frogs to hibernate under or climb on (if you have a tree frog).

5 Understand that the length of the cold or dry spell will vary with the type of frog.

✳ Tips

Do not release your tadpoles into the wild unless they are a local species of frog.

Once your tadpoles hatch, separate them into individual containers or provide them with lots of floating plant life to hide in. Tadpoles will eat each other.

6   Provide your frogs with fresh water at all times, even if you are simulating a dry spell.

7   Watch for your frogs to mate. The male will climb on top of the female and fertilise her eggs as they are laid.

8   Separate your frogs from their eggs so they do not attempt to eat them.

9   Expect your eggs to hatch into tadpoles in six to 21 days, depending on your type of frog.

803 Charm a Snake

Charming a snake takes skill. Here's how to do it like all those snake charmers you've seen in films.

Steps

1   Take the cobra and place it in the Indian basket with a lid over the top.

2   Draw a crowd by explaining how you have just returned from India and learned the magic talent of snake-charming. Wait until you have a nice large crowd gathered in a semicircle around you, ready to watch you perform your trick.

3   Act it up. Trance and fixate your energies to make enough power to charm the snake. Ask for a moment or two of silence while your get your mystic powers in full force. You want complete control over the very dangerous cobra.

4   Set the basket in front of you as you sit down, cross-legged in a trance.

5   Pick up your flute, take off the lid and begin to play music and sway the flute. You can chant while swaying if you don't have a flute.

6   Watch as the cobra lifts its head out of the basket and forms its hood, and sways gradually to and fro. Keep playing the music.

7   Play the music for a while. Then, take the lid, slowly close the cobra into the basket and ask for rupees.

✹ Tips

Snakes are deaf and the music is just for show.

Cobras naturally come out of dark baskets into the light.

Cobras have a tendency to naturally sway.

804 Care for Your Fish

Fish need an optimal environment. These general guidelines apply to most freshwater fish in pet shops. Saltwater or tropical fish have different requirements.

Steps

1   Start off with healthy fish. View every fish in that tank before you purchase one. They should move about the tank with purpose and not display any signs of sickness, such as cloudy eyes or slimy-looking bodies.

2   Keep new fish in a quarantine tank with the same water quality as the main tank. They should stay there for at least two weeks (preferably

✹ Tip

Make sure your tank is large enough – about 200 sq cm (30 sq in) of surface area per fish. Increase the size of the tank by 50 to 100 per cent before adding more fish.

three) before you introduce them to the new tank. When you start getting impatient, think about how much trouble it would be to treat the entire population for infection instead of just one fish.

3   Place the tank against an inside wall, away from windows, doors and heating systems, to prevent drafts and sudden temperature changes in the water.

4   Maintain the water quality. Test the ammonia, nitrite and pH levels regularly with a special kit. Chemical imbalances are a leading cause of sickness in fish. Once the water quality is acceptable, use a special filtered siphon to change 20 per cent of the water every 10 days. A pet shop that sells fish should also sell test kits and siphons.

5   Provide your fish with a diet of commercially prepared fish food. Store it in a cool, dry place for no more than a few months.

6   Remove waste and uneaten food with a net every other day. Rinse the net thoroughly before and after use to avoid the potential spread of infection.

7   Keep a canopy or hood over the tank at all times. Some fish are jumpers.

8   Don't let your fish get stressed by poor water conditions, drastic lighting changes or constant activity outside the tank. These things will lower their resistance to disease.

⚠ **Warnings**

Mixing faster and stronger fish with slower, weaker ones is a bad idea. The slower fish will not get enough to eat, and the others will be overfed.

Discuss what types of fish are compatible in a tank and which to keep separate – some species can be very territorial and will kill other fish.

Tell if a Goldfish is Pregnant | 805

Every now and then a goldfish bought at a pet shop will arrive pregnant. However, it can be hard to tell whether the goldfish is ready to lay eggs.

◎ **Steps**

1   Determine the sex of your goldfish. Some varieties of goldfish are naturally fatter in the middle than others. Male goldfish will often have white tubercles on their gills. Females will often be slightly larger in size than males.

2   Prepare the tank for ideal egg-laying conditions. If you suspect your goldfish is pregnant you should be ready to care for the eggs. Use a large tank and plant it with live foxtail and hornwort plants. Keep the water temperature around 21°C (70°F).

3   Keep watch over the next few weeks to see if the goldfish gets any bigger. If she does, she probably is carrying eggs. Make sure she is the only goldfish in the tank.

4   After a few weeks, the goldfish should lay her eggs.

5   Separate the goldfish from the eggs. Place her in another tank. Wait for the goldfish eggs to hatch. When they do, leave them in a spawning tank for several weeks as they grow stronger. Once the eggs hatch, turn the water temperature down so the water is a little cooler.

✳ Tip

If male and female goldfish are kept separate in different spawning tanks, they will probably be ready to mate after a few weeks. Place the fish together overnight and see what happens!

⚠ **Warning**

It is easy to kill goldfish when they are pregnant. Make sure you treat them very gently.

806 | Dispose of a Dead Goldfish

When your beloved pet goldfish turns belly-up take these precautions as you escort him to the great beyond.

Steps

1 Use a mesh net to remove the dead goldfish from its tank.

2 Place the goldfish in a small box and bury it outdoors if you prefer. Make sure you make a deep hole so neighbourhood pets won't get curious and start digging.

3 Place your goldfish on a saucer or wrap it up in tissue if you'd like to dispose of it the other way…

4 Go into the bathroom. Slide the dead fish off the saucer into the toilet bowl, or throw the tissue-wrapped fish in the toilet.

5 Say a few words of respect to the dearly departed, if you wish.

6 Flush.

7 Wash your hands and the saucer (if you used one) thoroughly with soap and hot water.

8 Consider changing the tank water and cleaning the net and tank thoroughly if you have other fish or want to get a new one, in case your pet died of disease.

⚠ Warning

Soap and cleaning detergents are hazardous to fish. Avoid using these products unless you're dying to officiate another fish funeral.

807 | Mount a Horse

There's a lot more to mounting a horse than simply jumping on. A proper mount goes a long way towards establishing trust between the horse and the rider.

Steps

1 Take the reins in your left hand (drape the slack over the horse's right side). Grasp hold of the base of the horse's mane with your left hand as well.

2 Use your right hand to turn the left stirrup iron towards you. Put your left foot in the stirrup, parallel to the horse's side.

3 Grab the back of the saddle, or cantle, with your right hand.

4 Bounce on the ball of your right foot.

5 Push off with your right foot and put your weight on your left foot (in the stirrup), while simultaneously pulling on the saddle and the horse's neck.

6 Balance on your hands and left foot in a standing position, then swing your right foot over the horse as you release your right hand from the saddle.

7 Lower yourself gently into the saddle.

8 Put your right foot in the stirrup and take up the slack in the reins.

✳ Tips

Keep the reins in your hands at all times.

Try using a block for mounting, or have someone boost you on to the horse if you are having difficulty.

⚠ Warnings

Always wear a hard hat and proper riding boots when you go riding.

Horse riding is an inherently dangerous activity that can result in serious injury or death. We recommend that you seek proper training and equipment before attempting this activity.

Walk a Horse | 808

Going for a walk on horseback is easy – as long as you remember to take it easy!

Steps

1 Gently gather the reins towards you, taking up the slack.

2 Squeeze both legs against the sides of the horse, behind the girth, and push your hips forward at the same time.

3 Relax the pressure of your legs when the horse responds, and move your hands forward slightly to prevent jerking on the horse's mouth.

4 Relax and follow the movement of the horse as you sit tall in the saddle.

5 Keep your heels down and your arms, wrists and fingers relaxed.

✳ Tips

Keep your legs under you, not too far forward or back, and your feet parallel to the horse's sides. Do not stick out your toes.

Always wear a hard hat and proper riding boots when you ride.

Avoid riding alone.

Trot | 809

Rather than looking like a large horseback bobble-head, follow these instructions for a smooth ride through the countryside.

Steps

1 Shorten your reins; take up the slack, but don't hold too tight.

2 Squeeze your calves against the horse's sides and/or tap lightly with your heels.

3 Simultaneously push your hips forwards.

4 Keep your hands steady and bring them back to their normal position after the horse begins trotting.

5 Sit tall and relaxed, and follow the motion of the horse with your hips.

6 Glance down at the outside shoulder of the horse to post. As it moves forwards, rise out of the saddle.

7 Simultaneously tighten your knees and put more weight in your stirrups, down towards your heels, as you rise.

8 Sit gently back down as the horse's shoulder moves back, rolling back on your thighs.

✳ Tips

Posting allows you to trot on a horse comfortably without bouncing about.

Keep your arms and hands still, and your elbows and knees in.

Keep your legs under your body for balance.

Keep your back straight and your shoulders back.

⚠ Warning

To learn how to ride properly and safely, take lessons from a qualified instructor.

Canter | 810

Non-verbal communication is key when directing a horse. Here's how to be convincing while in the saddle.

Steps

1 Gather up the reins while walking the horse in a fenced area.

2 Turn the horse's head slightly towards the fence, and use your outside leg to push its rear away from the fence.

✳ Tips

Bank on turns.

Try making a kissing noise as you signal the horse to canter.

3 Shift your weight forwards and to the inside, keeping your inside leg close to the horse's side.

4 Move your outside leg behind the girth, squeeze or give a light kick, and loosen the reins slightly so you don't jerk the horse's mouth.

5 Follow the motion of the horse with your hips.

6 Trot the horse slowly. Make sure you shorten your reins before going into a canter.

7 Squeeze your outside leg behind the horse's girth, keeping your inside leg passive but close to the horse's side.

8 Keep your heels down and lean back slightly, following the motion of the horse with your hips.

9 If the horse does not break into a canter, slow it down and try again.

811 | Groom a Horse

Grooming a horse not only helps to keep him clean, but is a good time to bond, as well as to do a quick check-up on your animal.

Steps

1 Use a halter and lead rope to bring your horse in from the pasture or out of the stall.

2 Tie your horse loosely to a railing to prevent your horse from wandering off when your back is turned.

3 Use a soft-bristled brush and start with your horse's face. Brush the forelock and face, being careful to stay away from the eyes.

4 Look for any drainage from the eyes and make sure your horse's ears don't have anything in them.

5 Use a medium-bristled brush for your horse's body. Start at the neck and work your way down.

6 Look for any cuts or bumps that need treatment.

7 Brush the entire body, including the stomach and legs.

8 Run your hands down the horse's legs to feel for any swelling.

9 Spray conditioner or detangler in mane and tail to make brushing easier.

10 Use a stiff-bristled brush for the mane and tail.

11 Use a hoof pick on each hoof.

12 Check for abscesses or other hoof abnormalities.

13 Notice any changes in your horse. Is there discharge from the horse's nose? Are the gums pink? Does your horse seem alert?

14 Spray fly repellant over your horse's body. Be careful not to get fly spray in the horse's eyes.

Tips

If your horse is kept in a stall and the stall hasn't been cleaned, make sure there are plenty of piles of manure. A well-functioning digestive system is extremely important in a horse.

If your horse drinks from a bucket and it hasn't been refilled yet, look to see how much water the horse has drunk.

Feed a Horse Carrots 812

Horses have always loved to eat carrots, and people have always loved to feed carrots to them. However, you should always be careful when feeding animals.

⊙ Steps

1. Slice several carrots lengthwise, into "fingers". Carrots should never be fed in chunks because they can lodge in a horse's throat and cause suffocation.

2. Insist that the horse displays good manners. It should not rush you or crowd you when it sees that you have carrots in your hand or pocket.

3. Spread your hand out flat, palm up. Be careful not to let your fingertips roll up. It is best if you arch your palm slightly backwards, with your fingertips bent towards the ground.

4. Place one carrot finger in your palm.

5. Put your hand a few feet away from the horse's mouth. The horse should extend its neck to get to your palm. Never let the horse overpower you with its head, shoulders and body when it eats the carrot.

6. Let the horse finish the carrot. Don't put another carrot on the palm of your hand until it has chewed the first piece.

✱ Tip

Letting small children feed carrots to a horse is acceptable, but caution must be exercised. Let the child place a flattened hand, palm up against your own. Lay the carrot on the child's palm and invite the horse to eat.

⚠ Warning

Horses' jaws are powerful, and their teeth are enormous. In a split second, a horse can bite through a finger, bone and all. Don't feed carrots to strange, irritable or wild horses.

Determine if a Horse is Ill 813

Become accustomed to your horse's moods and physical condition. The more you understand what's normal for your horse, the more you'll be able to detect what's abnormal.

⊙ Steps

1. Give your horse a brief visual exam every time you see it.

2. Learn how to take its temperature, heart rate and respiratory rate.

3. Perform a physical exam if a horse that's usually bright, alert and responsive is acting dull, slow and depressed.

4. Notice if the horse is exhibiting a decrease in appetite. Be especially concerned if your horse has stopped eating or drinking.

5. Notice signs of pain or discomfort such as pawing, looking or biting at a flank, getting up and down frequently, favouring a leg and rolling. Be sure to distinguish between your horse's normal and abnormal rolling habits.

6. Take your horse's temperature using a rectal thermometer. It's impossible to tell if a horse has a fever by visual inspection alone. A horse's normal temperature is between 37°C and 38°C (99°F and 101°F).

7. Call the vet immediately if you determine that your horse is not feeling well.

✱ Tip

When in doubt, call your vet. It is better to be overly cautious.

⚠ Warning

Do not take a "wait and see" approach. A horse declines rapidly upon the onset of symptoms.

814 | Deliver a Foal

After waiting 11+ months, it is time for your foal's arrival.
Once the mare starts showing signs that foaling is imminent,
she should not be left unattended.

⊙ Steps

1 Common signs that a mare is getting ready to foal are pawing, sweating, rolling, looking or kicking at her belly.

2 Be very quiet during foaling. Mares will interrupt labour if disturbed.

3 Before delivery, wrap the mare's tail with a gauze wrap, wash the perineum and udder with providine soap scrub or a mild liquid soap.

4 Avoid Step 3 if the mare is stressed, nervous or if it is a maiden mare. In these cases, leave her alone.

5 Understand that this stage can last from five minutes to an hour and begins with the mare's water breaking. She will expel a large amount of a clear to cloudy yellowish liquid. The mare will then usually stand for several minutes, walk around and lick the fluid off bedding until delivery.

6 Record the time at which fluid is expelled. This is very important.

7 Within five to 10 minutes of loss of fluid, look for the appearance of an opaque, white amniotic membrane at the vulva.

8 Observe whether, as more membrane becomes exposed, you can see more of the foal's feet. They should be staggered with one foot several centimetres in front of the other so that shoulders are aligned properly, followed closely by the muzzle.

9 Observe whether the nose of the foal and both front fetlocks are out and clear of the vulva. If the nose is not visible, call the vet immediately.

10 Look for fast, forceful and obvious abdominal contractions. With each contraction you should see more of the foal.

✱ Tips

As membrane becomes exposed the mare will lie down but may get up again.

The entire delivery stage should not exceed 30–40 minutes.

Call the vet immediately if you cannot see membrane after 10 minutes of loss of fluid. This could indicate an abnormal foal position.

⚠ Warnings

Retention of the head or one foreleg could lead to fatal consequences for both mare and foal.

Call the vet immediately if contractions are forceful but are not causing noticeable progress.

815 | Milk a Cow

A pail, short stool, two hands and a very gentle milk cow are all
you need to enjoy fresh milk every day.

⊙ Steps

1 Milk at the same time daily.

2 Sit on the same side of the cow each day. This will help your cow feel more comfortable – cows like routine.

3 Place the cow in a stanchion if this makes you feel more at ease. If your cow is an old hand at being milked, this probably won't be necessary. Ask the farmer you purchased her from what her routine was with the farmer.

4 Place the stool at a right angle to the cow and sit with your head resting on her flank.

✱ Tip

If you milk your cow regularly and maintain a good feeding programme, your cow can give you milk for up to 10 months.

⚠ Warning

Remember that even the nicest cow can kick, so always be aware of this. If you are nervous or too rough with her, this will cause problems.

5 Wash her udder with warm water and a clean cloth.

6 Place a pail under the teats and take a teat into the palm of your hand.

7 Squeeze the teat at the top with your thumb and forefinger. Continue squeezing each finger around the teat, forcing the milk in a stream until all your fingers are around the teat. Release the teat.

8 Repeat until only a small amount of milk comes out and the udder is soft to the touch.

Shear Sheep   816

Shearing a sheep is like having a hair cut. Some sheep farmers shear their own sheep, while others hire professional shearers to do it for them.

☉ Steps

1 Hold the sheep in a clean area or pen while waiting to be sheared to keep the wool clean.

2 Find a clean rug for the sheep to stand on while being sheared. Shear sheep away from their pen or sleeping area.

3 Get rid of any faeces or other debris that might be present in the coat before shearing.

4 Shear sheep in warm weather to bring out the oils in the coat. This will help keep the blades lubricated to produce a more even coat.

5 Cut close to the body of the sheep.

6 Keep the coat all in one piece as you shear. Do not go back and shear a second time.

✳ Tips

Don't shear sheep too late in the season, as some natural shedding will occur and reduce the overall weight of the wool. This decreases the value of the wool at market.

Store wool in a clean dry place before taking to market. Tie the fleece with paper twine so that the most valuable part of the wool is towards the outside.

Care for Your Goat   817

Good herd management will provide years of companionship, dairy products and meat. Goats also make good pets and show animals for smaller children.

☉ Steps

1 Provide a dry shelter for goats. A good shelter for most climates is a three-sided barn with a pitched roof. Place straw or dry bedding in a barn.

2 Feed goats in a clean feeder that they cannot stand in and soil the feed.

3 Check your goats' hooves every month and trim as needed. Clean and medicate any hoof-rot areas.

4 Worm your goats twice a year with a paste wormer.

5 Watch for lice and dust when needed.

6 Check with a local vet about any vaccinations your goat may need if you plan to drink the milk.

7 Shave goats in the summer months if you live in a hot area.

⚠ Warning

Always read warning labels about meat or dairy consumption on any medications you use on your animal.

818 Keep a Pet Chicken

You probably think of chickens only as food sources or dancing TV characters, but there are many people who keep these birds as pets – you can adopt a chicken as part of your family.

⊙ Steps

1   Choose the right chicken food. Buy layer feed for egg-laying chickens and starter feed for younger chickens. Buy a feeder that either hangs or stands off the ground so that your pet doesn't contaminate her own food.

2   Change the water daily. Chickens don't like dirty water and won't drink if the water isn't relatively fresh. They can quickly become dehydrated.

3   Throw scratch around. This is the equivalent of catnip for chickens, so give it only as a treat.

4   Aid digestion with grit. Chickens don't have teeth, so you need to provide poultry grit in containers or add it to their feed. The small rocks help break down the feed before it passes on to the stomach.

5   Make a comfortable bed. One of your options is pinewood shavings, which provide maximum absorbency for droppings.

6   Allow the chicken to get as dirty as she likes. Dust baths are an essential part of the chicken's routine, as they prevent lice and mites from nesting in feathers.

7   Provide a safe home. If you decide to keep your pet chicken in a coop, close the door to it every night before you retire. If your chickens are free-range, provide shelter from predators.

✱ Tips

If you're going out of town for a few days, you can leave chickens unattended as long as you leave them enough food and water.

Change the bedding monthly for maximum sanitation.

Give your coop a thorough scrub-down twice a year, including all feeders.

⚠ Warnings

Don't feed your chickens any bones, citrus fruits or peels, garlic, onion or large servings of meat.

Resist the temptation to bring your coop indoors or heat it during the winter months so that your chicken can adapt to cold temperatures.

819 Choose an Exotic Pet

Some people are cat people. Some are strictly dog people. Others want something different and opt for an exotic pet.

⊙ Steps

1   Check the law. Some animals are strictly forbidden. The last thing you want is to be saddled with a fine and other legal troubles. Be informed before you buy.

2   Consider your pet's needs. You need to determine what kind of space it will require, what food will cost and its social needs. Some animals need other animals nearby, while others prefer to be left alone.

3   Look at your lifestyle. While friends and family might be happy to feed your dog while you are on holiday, they might be more hesitant to feed your skunk. If you travel often, an exotic pet may not be for you.

4   Find a vet in your area that will treat the kind of animal you are considering. It can sometimes be difficult to find a veterinarian that treats these unusual animals.

5   Research the animal and find out its temperament. It will be important to know whether the new pet will be safe to have around your children and your other pets.

⚠ Warning

Think carefully before choosing an exotic pet – they require much more care and attention than a domestic animal.

Feed a Pet Wolf 820

Having a wolf or any exotic creature for a pet can be a fun experience, but it can also present challenges different from the basic responsibilities of owning a domesticated dog or cat.

Steps

1 Provide plenty of water. Since your wolf needs a large amount of space to live, consider having more than one water source available for it. If the land you live on has a natural body of water, such as a stream that is clean and accessible, this will work fine. If not, place large bowls or troughs of water around the animal's living area and make sure that the water is always fresh and clean.

2 Avoid "people food". A wolf's digestive system is not equipped to digest preservatives, nitrates and other ingredients in man-made food products not found in the wild.

3 Find the right food. There is animal feed made specifically to meet the unique dietary needs of exotic animals. These kinds of feed can help maintain your pet wolf's nutrient and vitamin intake to keep its diet healthy and well-balanced.

4 Supplement with fresh food. Giving your pet wolf fresh meat in addition to its regular food is not only a good source of iron and protein, but also meets the wild instinct to eat freshly killed game.

5 Understand eating habits. Your wolf may be a pet, but it still has eating habits as though it were living in the wild. It is customary for a wolf to kill an animal and eat, then go without food for a day or two before returning to the kill and eating more. Your pet wolf may not eat on a regular basis like a domesticated dog. This is not necessarily a sign of illness or poor health, but if you notice that your wolf is going a long time without eating and is becoming listless or emaciated, contact your vet.

⚠ Warning

Your wolf isn't a dog so don't treat it like one. Trying to train a wolf to fetch sticks and play dead will only lead to disappointment.

Groom a Pet Tiger 821

A pet tiger needs a proper grooming every few months, so follow these steps to get it done safely and quickly.

Steps

1 Hire a professional. Even if you're the best tiger nail-clipper in the world, you need to hire a professional to oversee the process.

2 Sedate the animal. The handler or vet must sedate your pet tiger before you can start grooming it. Skipping the sedation step can lead to injury to both you and your tiger.

3 Trim the tiger's claws. Trimming the tiger's claws will make the cat safer. A vet has tools made specially to trim thick claws, so let the expert do the work here.

4 Check for and remove parasites. Think of the grooming as a medical opportunity in addition to a cleaning. Look for parasites like ticks and fleas that you can remove from the animal while it's sedated.

⚠ Warning

Never forget that your tiger isn't a fluffy kitten. One swipe of its claws and you're in serious trouble. Proceed with caution.

5   Clean where the tiger can't. There are places where a tiger can't reach with its tongue (though, rest assured, it does have a method for getting to those places). Pay special attention to the paw pads, between the toes and the animal's head. Clean the tiger and give it a once-over to look for any sores and tender spots that the animal might have.

822 Approach a Potbellied Pig

Like any pet, pigs don't respond positively if startled or rushed upon, whether by a familiar face or a stranger. For a warm, inviting encounter, consider the following approach.

⊙ Steps

1   Ensure that your pet pig has a safe, comforting and quiet place to rest, especially during the first week or so of getting to know you.

2   Stand back and away from your pig so he can see you clearly. Potbellied pigs have a different field of vision from humans.

3   Allow your pet to approach you on his own terms. Don't force the interaction – let your pig dictate all socialising at the speed he's comfortable with.

4   Talk softly and let him smell you.

5   Avoid startling the pig with sudden movements and noises. If startled, a potbellied pig could bite you.

6   Rub your pet's belly and the area behind his ears.

7   Avoid extending your fingers out for the pig to sniff. Because of poor eyesight, pigs will sometimes mistake fingers for food and bite them.

8   Refrain from picking up your pet potbellied pig. Besides being heavy, pigs just don't like being lifted or restrained.

9   Look for signs of aggression, demonstrated through posturing or chomping or snapping of the mouth.

10 Introduce your pet pig to strangers and small groups gradually. Once he's used to meeting new faces, you can consider having larger groups around without startling him.

⚠ Warning

If your pig shows signs of anger don't try to calm him – just get out of his way!

Dress for a First Date – Women 823

If you're a woman dressing for a first date, confidence is the name of the game.

⊙ Steps

1   Ask your date about the event: will you need park clothes, beachwear, an urban dinner outfit or rock-climbing gear?

2   Aim for the middle ground on date one. Neutral colours, classic styles and great accessories are always comfortable, especially if you don't know your destination.

3   Assess your position. Will you convey "career", "artistic", "dynamite" or "easy confidence"?

4   Decide what makes you feel pretty, sexy, confident or comfortable. Do you want to be more sexy than sedate, or look sophisticated?

5   Choose your colours. That little black dress, silver jewellery and an exotic shawl could be stylish and sophisticated. Pastels, gingham or flowing lines suggest softness. Tie-dye can be fun or whimsical.

6   Be yourself. If you're at ease with lower necklines and revealing clothes, go for it if it feels appropriate.

7   Think comfort. Stiletto heels, new styles or a skimpy skirt may make you uncomfortable and distract you from your date.

8   Dress it up or down. Classic separates can be easily paired with one extra-special piece for a boost.

❉ Tip

Remember – you only get one chance to make a first impression.

Dress for a First Date – Men 824

If clothes make the man, this your main opportunity to be the man you always wanted.

⊙ Steps

1   Decide with your date what tone you want to set for the event, and whether it is a formal, casual or specific event.

2   Make an honest impression and a statement about your style and attitude at a casual dinner or first date.

3   Pick from the classic basics unless you have a specific side of yourself to express. For most guys, that means combats, jeans or casual trousers.

4   Choose button-down shirts in blue, white or patterns. They pair up well with most trousers and are attractive without being fussy. They layer well over a t-shirt and under a sweater, too.

5   Show off those pecs in a knit shirt or t-shirt for comfort and versatility.

6   Wear a dress shirt and tie, with or without a blazer to convey your attention to detail and your civility while still being casual.

❉ Tips

That mesh tank or talking t-shirt will not go unnoticed. Everything you choose to wear on a first date gets a lot of attention.

Ask your date if the event will require a suit or dressy outfit. Nothing is more dampening than the wrong clothes.

⚠ Warning

A first date is probably not the time to experiment with bow ties, hair dyes or a new style such as a kilt, unless you'll feel comfortable with the results.

7 Decide on your footwear. Trainers are accepted in most places but generally lace-ups, boots or loafers look better for a date. Sandals can be clean-cut, counterculture or sporty.

8 Wear neutral colours if you want your conversation to do the talking.

9 Remember that personal grooming says more about you than your choice of clothes.

825 Choose a Restaurant for a Date

Choosing a restaurant for a date can be an adventure. Remember, a place to eat isn't just about the food – it should also allow for pleasant interaction.

⊙ Steps

1 Turn down the volume – the place should let you and your date get to know one another without needing to shout.

2 Remember the importance of service – you and your date need time and privacy; you don't need attitude or neglect.

3 Think about the lighting. Make sure you can see each other, but you might want to avoid the tell-all threat of cafeteria lighting.

4 Consider the cost. Try to pick a restaurant you can afford, whether or not you're picking up the bill.

5 Opt for a place you're familiar with. However, don't go to a place where everyone knows you on a first-name basis – your date might feel uncomfortable.

6 Pick a place where both you and your date can eat. Ask your date ahead of time about any special food preferences or dislikes.

✳ Tips

A coffee shop can be a quiet, well-lit and casual place for a first date.

Theme restaurants or ethnic cuisine can make for an enjoyable time and interesting conversation.

On a first date, pick a restaurant that's easy to find – getting lost may lead to unwanted tension.

Who pays at the restaurant depends on who asks whom. The person who asked should pay on a first date.

826 Impress a Man

Men are easier to impress than women, right? Sometimes...

⊙ Steps

1 Remember that men like women with confidence. If you like who you are, they'll like who you are.

2 Practise being independent. It takes a lot of the pressure off men to know they don't have to take care of you.

3 Don't play dumb. If that's what it takes to impress a certain man, do you really want him?

4 Dress well. Wear whatever you have on with your own style. Guys like those black-seamed stockings and flashy high heels, sure, but you'll be more fun if you're comfortable.

5 Don't worry if you don't look like a supermodel. After all, you don't demand that the men in your life all look like film stars, right? There are more important things. Give men credit for knowing that.

✳ Tip

While you're busy impressing your man, don't forget to take the time to make sure he's worth impressing. It's a two-way street – you should impress each other.

6   Be engaging. A woman who is sitting with a bunch of men is intriguing. Those guys are sitting with her for a reason. Other men will want to know what it is.

7   Notice what a man is wearing and compliment him. Men often go to a lot of trouble to look good, but rarely get as many compliments as women do.

8   Don't drink too much. Your inhibitions will be lowered and you might say or do things you wouldn't normally do.

9   Be appreciative. Say thanks when it's appropriate. Smile when you say it. It means a lot.

10 Ask the man about his work, his hobbies, his interests. Listen carefully and ask questions. Find out what he's interested in. If you can hold your own in a discussion on football, Formula One or fishing, you're in.

11 Be relaxed and easy to get along with. The more comfortable you are, the more comfortable the people around you are. You might not be the only one who's nervous.

Impress a Woman   827

Since the dawn of time, men have been asking the same question – what do women really want? Here are some ideas on how to impress a woman.

⊙ Steps

1   Ask her about herself, her ambitions, her life. Be interested. It's a rare woman who wants to sit around all night listening to a man talk about himself.

2   Be presentable. Women are notorious accessorisers, and whether she'll admit it to you or not, you are an accessory. Other women will judge her on her choice. A clean, nice-smelling man with well-fitting clothes is a real prize.

3   Make eye contact. A lot. And smile – in a friendly way. Don't leer.

4   Be a gentleman. It's a myth that chivalry is dead, right? There are just a few women out there messing it up for everyone else. Most women really do like to have doors held open for them.

5   Learn to dance. Women will flock to you – all of them will be impressed.

6   Be funny without being crude. It's an art.

7   Compliment her. Notice her shoes or her watch – something that shows you're paying attention. Women change their clothes six times before they leave the house; it's nice to find someone who appreciates the final choice.

8   It's hard for a woman not to be impressed with a man who is impressed with her. If you really like her, tell her so. You don't have to make a big deal about it, just let her know you admire her.

✱ Tips

Don't stare at her – or other women!

Don't guide her around a room. The hand-on-the-elbow steering technique is very annoying. The hand-on-the-small-of-the-back technique is usually too intimate.

828 | Impress a Girl With a Skateboard

When trying to impress a girl that you have a crush on, ride your skateboard and show off your skateboarding skills.

Steps

1 Casually ride your skateboard in front of the girl who you have a crush on. Make sure that you don't try to act too cool and begin to try to impress with tricks that you don't know how to do. You'll end up being embarrassed.

2 Make eye contact and smile at the girl when you are riding on your skateboard. Wave every now and then so that the girl knows you are interested in her.

3 Bring your radio with you and play some music in the background while you're skateboarding. If you know what kind of music is your girl's favourite, play it just to impress her even more.

4 Perform some tricks that you know how to do – and land them. If you have a ramp, use it to show off your skateboarding talent.

5 Ask the girl if she would like to try to ride on your skateboard. This would be a great way to get close to her. Tell her that you could hold her hand or her waist while she has a go.

⚠ Warning
Don't try to be too clever – you won't look very impressive if you fall on your face!

829 | Know It's the Right Time to Have Sex

Sex is important in any relationship. To avoid headache and heartache afterwards, take the steps to know if it's the right time.

Steps

1 Think about sex with your partner. Be clear on your position in the relationship before doing anything.

2 Talk about sex with your partner. Find out what your partner thinks and state your position. If this seems uncomfortable, then sex will too.

3 Think about how well you really know your partner. Sex is all about trust and intimacy; make sure you have that with each other beforehand.

4 Ask yourself if you are passionate about your partner. If sex is just something to do, you might be making a mistake.

5 See each other more than once a week.

6 Date for a while. Be comfortable with one another.

7 Ask yourself if you enjoy making contact with the other person. Little things like hugs and kisses are good indicators that sex is an appropriate step.

8 Be prepared for safe sex. Take the necessary precautions so that sex can be enjoyable, both during and afterwards.

9 Have fun. Try not to anticipate the best sex of your life. Relax and go through the steps in determining if the right time to have sex is now.

⚠ Warning
Sex is a serious step in any relationship and may result in pregnancy.

Remain Sane and Safe While Dating Online

830

While Internet dating is all the rage, it can be a rude awakening for those who are unprepared for its drawbacks.

⊙ Steps

1 Pick a dating service. Some have special offers such as six months free if you don't meet someone you like in the first six months.

2 Remember that people have many motives for join dating services – they might just be looking for friendship rather than a relationship.

3 Write your profile. Be honest. If you're looking for marriage, say so. This will weed out a lot of people that would waste your time. Be upbeat and use humour in your profile. Don't lie about your age. Don't lie about your interests.

4 If you're a woman, do the picking, the winking etc. Choose men that live within 10 to 15 minutes from your house. If you want to date with any frequency, living far from each other makes it very difficult.

5 Read the profiles. Don't even look at the men or women who have a profile that is sparse. This shows that they either don't care enough to write anything or that they're hiding something.

6 You have found a profile that sounds interesting. The person is reason-ably attractive in the picture. If it's not a professional photo, most people look much better in person than in the photos. Email them and see what happens.

7 If they're interested, talk to them on the phone at least three times before meeting them. These phone conversations can reveal a lot about a person. If the conversations go well, it will make meeting face to face a lot more comfortable.

8 Meet them during the day, in a public place, when you meet for the first time.

⚠ Warning

Dating online can be a great way to meet new people, but be careful of your personal safety at all times.

Protect Yourself from Date Rape

831

It's an oft-cited fact that women are more likely to be raped by someone they know than by a stranger.

⊙ Steps

1 Realise that date rape typically occurs when the couple is alone. Go out in a group with new dates.

2 Avoid drinking or doing drugs, which could affect your judgement and make it easier for someone to take advantage of you.

3 Be aware of your date intruding on your personal space. This is a sign that he may not respect your boundaries.

4 Be clear with the signals you send out so a man doesn't have to guess what you mean. Speak up if you feel things are getting out of hand.

5 Set sexual limits. It's okay to stop sexual activity when you've had enough.

✱ Tip

Remember that there is no excuse for rape. Try to be aware and minimise your risks as much as you can.

6   Examine unconscious messages you may be sending out that could be putting you at risk. For instance, consider the way you dress, walk, gesture and talk.

7   Pay your own way to retain your independence and avoid a man feeling you "owe him something" in return for your meal.

8   Trust your instincts. If you feel uncomfortable, remove yourself from the situation immediately, even if you think you're being rude.

9   Always carry a taxi fare so you can get yourself home if you need to.

10 Avoid going to a man's home or inviting him to yours until you know him very well.

---

832 | Make Him Feel Special

Sometimes every man needs a boost. Here are some simple steps to remind him how special he is and to boost his ego.

⊙ Steps

1   Always be interested in his job, and point out what you love about what he does. If he's really great at negotiating, or speaking in public, or building websites, tell him. It is always good for him to know that you find this part of his life exciting as well. Ask for his advice with your own job, when you feel his expertise could help you.

2   Flirt with him when he is not expecting you to, like in very crowded places or during those awkward family gatherings.

3   Make compliments that are unique to him, such as telling him you love how he smiles in a certain way or you love how he walks.

4   Sometimes it's nice to act jealous. But do it in a nice way – when you see a girl checking him out, give him a kiss that'll leave him breathless, and whisper in his ear that he is all yours. This is only to be done sparingly.

5   Tell him that he is handsome. Tell him that you love him. Sometimes we forget saying these things to our significant others with the stress of routine. This doesn't mean hearing it becomes any less important.

❋ Tip

It takes very little to make a man feel special – and it's the small things that count.

---

833 | Handle a Cheating Girlfriend

If her cheatin' heart is more than you can stand, it's time for you to change your tune or face the music.

⊙ Steps

1   Think about the source of your suspicion. If you heard it from a friend who heard it from a friend who heard it from another, look for more reliable information.

2   Make sure that jealousy and insecurity are not making you falsely accuse someone you care about.

❋ Tips

This does not have to get ugly. Wait until you are able to address the issue as rationally as possible. Regardless of her cheating, remember that you cared about her once, and you still may.

---

3 Trust your instincts. If you think that your girlfriend is cheating on you, then ask her. If she denies it but you don't believe her, make sure your mistrust is based on something you witness or experience.

4 Noticing a change in your relationship or her behaviour would make your suspicion reasonable. Seeing her with someone else who looks clearly to be more than a friend, is pretty solid evidence.

5 Consider your physical health and emotional wellbeing. Could she be putting you at risk of sexually transmitted diseases? Can you deal with being one of many?

6 Think about what you would tell a sibling or a best friend to do in your situation. Is fear keeping you from following your own advice?

7 Discuss your feelings with your girlfriend. Tell her how her cheating is affecting you. Explain what you're looking for in this relationship.

8 Listen to what she has to say. Her response to your concerns should give you the information you need to do what is right for you.

9 Inform your girlfriend of your decision, whether it is to forgive her and start over, have a brief separation while you figure out what to do, or part ways.

You don't need to console her, but you will feel better about yourself if you take the high road.

⚠ **Warning**

If she cheats on you once, shame on her! If she cheats on you twice or more, well, you know the rest...

Find Your Secret Admirer

834

Find your secret admirer by putting on your detective's hat and following clues that can lead you to his or her identity.

◉ Steps

1 If you receive a handwritten note from your secret admirer, analyse the handwriting to see if the penmanship is familiar to you. Compare the handwriting to other notes or signatures from people you know.

2 If you receive flowers or other gifts from your secret admirer, call or visit the shop or supplier of the gift to enquire about the sender. Ask sales representatives to trace the sales transaction and provide you with the sender's name on the basis of the payment method, such as a cheque or credit card. Ask for a physical description of the sender if the transaction was a cash sale.

3 If a package mysteriously appears on your doorstep, ask neighbours if they noticed who delivered the package. Ask if they can provide a physical description of the person who delivered the item.

4 If you receive an anonymous message from a secret admirer email service, check the database of the email service and see if you can spot a familiar name.

5 Consider individuals who have been flirting with you or paying more attention to you than normal as possible candidates for being your secret admirer.

6 Enlist the help of your friends. Ask if they've noticed anyone displaying special interest in you.

✳ **Tip**

It's more than likely that your secret admirer wants you to discover his or her identity. Look carefully for any clues that might lead you to discover who they are.

835 Break an Engagement

Ending an engagement when you know a relationship isn't right can save you the greater pain of a divorce.

⊙ Steps

1 Follow the law regarding the ring. Etiquette requires that it always be returned no matter who calls off the marriage. If the man breaks off the engagement, the woman may feel justified in keeping the ring as a form of compensation for the heartache, but it will only be a painful reminder of your relationship. Whatever the circumstances, it's best to return the ring and allow both parties to gain closure.

2 Keep the conversation polite. Be honest, but not harsh. The person may learn lessons he or she can apply to future relationships.

3 Choose the right place to end the relationship. Never do it over the phone or in a place that is too public. Pick a place where you can both leave once the discussion is over. If you live together, make arrangements to stay with someone until you both figure out who will move out.

4 Time it right. Do not choose holidays or other special times to end the engagement. Do it in the middle of the week if possible. Work can take the other person's mind off the relationship, at least temporarily.

5 Plan what you're going to say so you effectively communicate your decision. Try not to let tears get in the way and do not show that you are relieved. Remain as neutral as possible.

6 Wait to discuss any details about cancelling the wedding until later. If you're early in your engagement and no formal wedding invitations have been sent, make a list of people you've told about your engagement.

7 Call or email the people you told about the engagement. Do not send a broadcast email. Let the other person take care of notifying his or her friends and family of the break-up.

✳ Tip

Make sure you're both sober for the discussion. Drinking will only make you overly emotional.

836 Ask Your Girlfriend's Father for Her Hand in Marriage

Have you found the girl of your dreams? Be traditional and approach her father to ask for her hand in marriage.

⊙ Steps

1 Be prepared. Think about what you'll say to your girlfriend's father before you arrange to talk with him.

2 Ask for a few minutes to speak to him in private or in the presence of your girlfriend. Unless distance prohibits a personal meeting, arrange to discuss the matter with him face to face.

3 Present yourself in a positive light to make a good impression, show your respect for him and reflect on the seriousness of the issue.

4 Explain the depth of your feelings for his daughter and inform him that she is the most important person in the world to you.

✳ Tip

You'll probably earn points with your girlfriend's father by the mere act of asking for her hand in marriage. Asking his permission to marry his daughter demonstrates your respect for her family and their feelings.

5   Put yourself in his place. How would you feel about entrusting your little girl's heart to another man? Tell him about the plans you've made for a future with his daughter. Assure him that you will do everything you can to make her happy for the rest of your lives.

6   Assure him that you realise marriage is a serious issue with serious responsibilities, and that you have given appropriate consideration to the matter of marrying his daughter.

7   Respectfully ask for your girlfriend's hand in marriage.

Be the Perfect Husband   837

You swept her off of her feet, walked down the aisle and dreamed dreams of forever together. Your dreams can be reality, but marriage takes work.

⊙ Steps

1   Listen to her. Women want and need their husbands to listen, whereas men hear a problem or concern and immediately think of how it can be fixed. Often a little time to work things through is all she needs.

2   Show her that you love her. The smallest things can be the most meaningful. Leave her a note. Tell her how much you care. Surprise her with dinner or flowers.

3   Compliment her. Positive confirmations will make her feel better about herself, which will only strengthen your connection.

4   Tell her you love her – and why.

5   Show interest in things and people that make her happy. She'll value your thoughtfulness.

✳ Tip

No relationship is perfect. Observation, compassion and communication can always be improved when it comes to your significant other. Learn from each other, and your marriage will continue to grow.

Be the Perfect Wife   838

In the twenty-first century, the role of a wife has completely changed from the 1950s. Can there be a perfect wife?

⊙ Steps

1   Believe in him. Your husband needs to know that if he fails to succeed at something or makes a mistake, you'll still be there for him. Your emotional support gives him confidence.

2   Accept who he is. No one is flawless, and though there may be some things you'd like to change about him, he is who he is. He needs to feel loved by you for who and what he is, not what he could be changed into.

3   Give him guy time. Just as women like to bond by shopping, phone conversations or other quality time, men need time to communicate and spend time with male friends. It can be a stress reliever and a time for them to kick back and relax.

4   Communicate gently. This doesn't mean you have to be subtle or indirect when talking with your husband, just be aware of your tone

✳ Tip

Remember – you don't have to be perfect all the time. Your husband may find the fact that you are hopeless at cooking endearing, for example.

in an argumentive state that could be described by him as nagging.

5   Encourage him. If your husband has a dream or something you know he would absolutely love to do but needs a little nudge, give him a push and boost of confidence. He'll see your support but also take your encouragement as reinforcement of your desire for him to be happy.

6   Be direct and to the point. Men can sometimes get lost in too much detail, and aren't the best at mind-reading. If you want or need something, tell him – don't expect him to know what's on your mind.

839   Revitalise Your Marriage

There are many different ways to put the spark back into your marriage and, if successful, restore your relationship.

⊙ Steps

1   Make your relationship a priority and start making time for each other. First and foremost, you must put your relationship ahead of anything that may be standing in your way.

2   Change your routine. Do something different each day for each other to show that you care.

3   Thank your spouse. In long-term marriages, sometimes people forget to thank one another for the simple chores they perform each day.

4   Compliment your spouse. Sometimes a little effort goes a long way, and compliments tend to give your significant other just the boost they need.

5   Try something spontaneous. Maybe go away for a weekend, or stay in bed and have breakfast together. Take time with your spouse to learn more about each other and rediscover your love.

6   Communicate. Most women tend to talk more than the men in relationships, but be sure to open up communication with your significant other.

7   Make a list. Each partner should put together a list of things they've always wanted to see, do or try. Then the two of you can go together and experience new things and discover more about pastimes that really interest the other person.

8   Plan a romantic getaway. Some couples need time away with one another. Plan a romantic dinner, or go to a fantasy hotel room and give yourselves space to redefine and explore your physical relationship with one another.

✳ Tips

Changing your routine could mean anything from surprising your spouse with an unplanned lunch or taking a late-night walk together. Most surprises will rekindle the romance.

Through all this, you should be focused on your partner, learning more about who they are.

⚠ Warning

This may require more time than previously allotted, so be sure to not get back into the habit of placing your relationship on the back burner.

840   Date Your Spouse

Even after years of marriage, you can keep the spark alive in your relationship by setting aside time to go on dates.

⊙ Steps

1   Make a list of things you and your spouse like to do together.

✳ Tips

Call your spouse and ask for a date.

2   Include at least 10 things on your list. The things you choose can cost money – going to the cinema or the theatre – or be free – taking a walk on the beach or having a candlelit dinner on the living-room floor.

3   Check your schedules. Set aside at least one day per month for you and your partner to make a date.

4   Take time to prepare for your date. Act like you did when you and your partner first started dating, taking extra time to feel and look your best.

5   Hold hands, open doors for each other and lock arms. Be excited and enthusiastic about your date.

6   Arrange for your children to stay with relatives so you can plan weekends alone with your spouse.

When your date is supposed to start, pretend you are picking your spouse up by knocking on the door.

Bring flowers or chocolates. Play it up as much as possible. Have fun.

Find a reliable babysitter and book him or her in advance for your dates.

Pamper a Spouse   841

It's important to show your spouse how grateful you are that he or she is in your life. That means doing things to make the other person feel extra special.

⦿ Steps

✳ Tip

Small things can make a big difference, and keep your partner feeling special.

1   Get up early while she is still asleep. Fix a breakfast fit for royalty. Serve freshly ground coffee or a pot of brewed tea. Place fresh flowers or a single rose in a vase on the bedside table. Wake up your spouse with a bright smile and breakfast in bed.

2   Prepare an invigorating blend of aromatherapy oils and get them nice and warm. Pamper your spouse with a morning massage to stimulate the blood flow and get those muscles moving. Peppermint oil is a good choice to help him wake up and feel refreshed.

3   Run the shower water ahead of time to get it ready. Set out the towels and flannels. Leave a new bar of natural soap and other essentials in the bathroom.

4   Buy a relaxing spa treatment to surprise your spouse. Manicure, pedicure, facial or body wraps are all terrific choices.

5   Spoil your spouse with a mini shopping spree. Take her to her favourite shop and let her pick out any item within a certain price range. Or buy a gift certificate and hand it to him in the morning before you leave.

6   Coddle your spouse with a gourmet picnic lunch. Drive to a scenic place, pull out the blanket and set up lunch for two. If the weather isn't co-operating, plan lunch or dinner at a romantic restaurant instead. Speak to the waiter ahead of time and ask him to bring out dessert with a candle on it – no singing, please.

7   Please your spouse with a card at the end of the day. Let your spouse know how grateful you are to share your life with them. Serve a drink and some fine chocolates and re-cap the day together.

842 | Live with an Alcoholic

Alcoholism is called a "family disease" because it affects the drinker and everyone around them. Living with an alcoholic is tumultuous and tiring.

⊙ Steps

1 Take care of yourself. Do what you need to do to make sure that you are okay. You can't help your loved one with alcoholism if you aren't operating at 100 per cent.

2 Accept that it's not your fault. You cannot control anyone else's behaviour and this is especially true of alcoholics. You can't make a person stop drinking. You can't force a person into recovery.

3 Learn about the disease. Understanding the nature of alcoholism will help you cope with the effects of your loved one's problem. Read literature to learn the ideal role for you to play in that person's potential recovery.

4 Seek help. There are support groups available for people in your position. Speak with a counsellor. You don't have do it alone.

5 Allow the disease to run its course. This is probably the most difficult step, but you have to stop enabling your alcoholic. Don't police your loved one's drinking. Take a non-judgemental but firm stance. An alcoholic needs to hit rock bottom in order to desire change.

6 Be patient. It is difficult to watch your loved one's life be destroyed, but resist the urge to step in. Be there when your alcoholic is ready to recover, but don't allow the disease to consume you too.

☀ Tip

Try to stay positive with the alcoholic about his or her chances for beating the disease.

⚠ Warning

Alcoholism can lead to death, so consider this a serious problem.

843 | Catch a Cheating Spouse

If you think your spouse might be cheating, there are some subtle ways to find out.

⊙ Steps

1 Prepare yourself for what the results of your findings will be. If your spouse is cheating, think about what you will do. Examine options like trying to work things out with your spouse and seeing a counsellor or, at the other end of the spectrum, divorce. You may want to speak to a lawyer before you confront your spouse.

2 Look for unusual changes in behaviour. Sometimes at the beginning of an affair, the cheating spouse will become overly loving to compensate for their feelings of guilt. They may buy presents or do other things that they would not normally do without a reason.

3 Take a look at their recent schedule. If they've begun excessively working late, going on unusual company trips or having unexpected work meetings, they may be up to something else. Cheating spouses exhibit a desire to be alone more often than usual.

4 Examine their phone bill. It will list every call made and received from his or her phone and will show you any suspicious numbers. Look first for

☀ Tip

A cheating spouse is something you never want to discover, but if the signs are there then you must deal with the situation.

calls made in the morning just after they have left the house or calls made on their drive home.

5   Check to see if your spouse has taken a newfound interest in his or her appearance. If they're doing things like buying a lot of new clothes and underwear, aftershave or perfume and updating their appearance in other ways, that may be a telltale sign that they're doing it for someone other than you.

6   Examine their spending habits. Watch out for odd purchases and large withdrawals of cash from your bank account. Check for receipts in their wallet. Also make sure the times stamped on the receipts match up with the story they tell you.

7   Track the mileage on their car. Some experts recommend jotting down a log of their mileage and arrival times each day. If your spouse is driving many more miles than they normally would or filling up their tank more often, that will indicate they're going somewhere that they didn't used to frequent.

8   Do their laundry. It's almost a cliché, but lipstick on the collar is a dead giveaway. If your spouse's clothes smell like someone else's perfume or aftershave, you have to wonder how it got there.

9   Take a look at your spouse's credit-card bill and see if there are expenditures that might indicate a romantic rendezvous, such as restaurant charges for dinners you didn't attend.

10 Ask! Many cheating spouses are eager to confess.

11 Hire a private investigator. A PI can be expensive, but a professional can gather evidence more quickly than you.

Tell Your Wife You'd Had an Affair   **844**

An affair can blight the trust that you and your wife have developed over the years, but so do secrets and lies, so come clean.

⊙ **Steps**

1   End the affair. Your spouse is your life partner, and the affair was just a spontaneous fling. You can't throw away years of love for a one-night stand.

2   Let her know that you had an affair. Tell your wife that the affair is over, and that you regret it.

3   Say you are sorry, and mean it. You have to truly show remorse about what you have done.

4   Answer any questions she might have, even if they involve details. Sometimes knowing exactly what went on helps your spouse come to terms with your affair.

5   Be prepared to answer why the affair happened. If your affair came about as a result of some of your needs not being met, say so, but be as tactful as possible about it.

6   Let her know, beyond a shadow of a doubt, that you are willing to work through this. Prove it with actions, not just words.

✱ **Tips**

If you don't feel remorse about your affair, maybe your relationship with your wife needs to end.

It's natural for you to shy away from the details of an affair; it is just as natural for your wife to get at those details. She is trying to find out why this happened.

⚠ **Warnings**

Don't give gifts to apologise. The next time you give your wife a gift, she will be thinking "Now what did you do?"

Before you tell your wife, take some time to determine why the affair happened.

845 | Survive a Separation

A separation is a time to reflect on your relationship, your partner and yourself. However, it can seem more permanent than it should if you carry it out unprepared.

◎ Steps

1   Set some rules about how you're going to carry out your separation. Stay away from each other for at least three months with the option to extend it.

2   Decide where you and your spouse are going to live. Set up a visitation schedule with your children so that they don't feel like they're losing a parent already.

3   Get together to tell your children. It'll be hard for them to understand this isn't a permanent separation, but your positive attitude will help.

4   Figure out when your marriage started going wrong. Be fair but truthful. Practise empathy in assessing how your spouse feels about whatever is disturbing your marriage.

5   Assess your needs. They have probably changed since you first got married. A separation is the perfect time to figure out how you want to grow and whether you and your spouse can support each other's growth.

6   Attend counselling individually and as a couple. A professional helps distance you from the emotional dilemmas in your marriage.

7   Practise your listening skills when you talk to your spouse about your marriage. Withhold judgement, no matter what your problems are. Concentrate on finding solutions.

✳ Tip

Keep a journal detailing the story of your marriage. Writing things down will help you think clearly.

⚠ Warnings

Don't date others under any circumstances. This detracts from the self-reflective purpose of the separation.

Avoid promising your kids you'll get back together, even if you're pretty sure you will.

846 | Marry a Millionaire

It's just as easy to love a rich man as a poor man. In some ways it may be easier....

◎ Steps

1   Get an education. The wealthy have always valued education. If you want to make one fall in love with you it will help if you can talk intelligently about literature, music and art.

2   Learn about business. Of course the rich are interested in money – that's how they got rich. If you can talk about business and money management sensibly, you can captivate him with your grasp of finances.

3   Develop an interest in politics – that's where the money is. Whatever position you choose to fill, volunteer in a political office and you might be on your way to true love.

4   Visit the best salon in town. You have to look your best, and a good haircut and manicure are the best investment if you want to snag a millionaire.

5   Exercise and lose weight if you need to. A fit body is a beautiful body regardless of the clothes you wear. Stay fit to keep his attention.

✳ Tip

Make him wait for sex. Your mother was right. He won't marry the cow if he can get the milk for free. Besides, you're much more mysterious if you play hard to get.

6   Shop carefully. Buy the best clothes you can afford, but don't let the labels show. A millionaire will recognise the quality and know that you're a class act.

7   Move. You need to live in the right neighbourhood if you want to meet the right people. Even if you can only afford a sad little run-down shack, you'll be walking the right streets.

8   Eat out and eat early. The wealthy often eat lunch early to beat the crowds. Maybe you'll meet the millionaire of your dreams over a fabulous Greek salad.

9   Party, party, party. If you wait until after 10 p.m., you can hit up the best parties at the best hotels and meet the millionaire of your dreams.

Be a Trophy Wife
847

Sure, being a trophy wife may seem like a day at the spa, but the shoes of a trophy wife, albeit stylish and to die for, aren't easy to fill.

⊙ **Steps**

1   Turn heads, especially his boss's, his father's and all his colleagues'. When you show up on your man's arm, onlookers should lose their train of thought, nervously clear their throats and instinctively hide their wedding bands.

2   Network, even when you're off the clock. A company cocktail hour here and a golf fundraiser there would be a piece of cake – fat free, at that – but the real work starts when he's not looking. You should be networking at the salon, the country club, the gym and anywhere else where his name needs to be dropped.

3   Nail the gardener. Or the pool boy. Or the handyman. Take your pick. You work hard for your man and he has no responsibility to thank you for it, so find someone else to thank you for your services. Just make sure he's more ripped, has more hair and looks hot when sweaty.

4   Organise parties, fundraisers and dinners, even when you haven't seen your man in person since last week. He needs your assistance even when he's invisible.

5   Mind the three B's: Blonde, Boobs, BMW. Keep them well-maintained and up-to-date.

6   Look good in Lycra. Have your man arrange for a gym membership and use it regularly, if only to make an appearance. Order salads when in public, but don't eat them. Overindulge on wine and champagne. Drink coffee, coffee drinks and anything else, as long as it's in a coffee cup. Your meals should really only consist of drinking.

✳ Tip

It might sound like the role of your dreams, but being a trophy wife can be hard work!

848 Help Your Child Understand Divorce

By being honest, loving and supportive, hopefully you can help your child comprehend and eventually accept your divorce.

⦿ Steps

1 It is best if both parents can talk to the child together. Choose a time and place that is relaxed, safe and comfortable.

2 Explain that mum and dad have decided not to live together any more and not to be married any longer. Explain that this is what divorce means. However, be sure to reiterate that no matter what, you will always continue to be parents together.

3 Give details about who will be living where, and when the child will see the other parent. If those details are not finalised and the child is capable of expressing their opinion about what they would like to have happen, try considering their desires. When parents divorce, even something as simple as whether the child gets to stay in the same school is a major concern for him/her.

4 Reassure your child that you both love him or her very much and always will. Explain that parents can stop loving each other but that parents never stop loving their children.

5 Tell your child that this is not his or her fault. Repeat this over and over until it is understood. However, don't expect your child to simply accept this statement as fact. Children are incredibly sensitive and can easily blame themselves if problems arise between their parents.

6 Do not give your child details about why you are divorcing. It's okay to explain that you don't want to argue any more or that you aren't happy living together, but your child does not need to know everything that led up to this.

7 While it's important not to talk badly about your soon-to-be ex, it can still be useful to express your emotions to your child about the changes occurring in your lives. Be open about how sad, hurt or upset you are. Encourage your child to be open about his or her emotions as well. Explain that it is good to be honest with one another about how you feel.

8 Avoid arguing with your spouse in front of your child. This is extremely difficult to do, especially in divorce situations, when egos and tempers often flare.

9 Have your child ask questions. Answer all of them as honestly and completely as you can.

10 Expect your child to spend a long time adjusting to the new situation.

11 Make sure that no matter what the custody arrangement ends up being, the child spends time with both parents. Having positive influences from both the mother and father is extremely important to a child's emotional and psychological development.

✳ Tips

If your child is having difficulty accepting the divorce, take him or her to a counsellor.

If you are having difficulty managing as a single parent or feel very depressed, see a counsellor or therapist.

Be patient with your child. Questions and issues will come up over time as your child deals with the divorce. Try to answer these questions and deal with these issues as best you can.

⚠ Warnings

If you and your spouse cannot be together without tension, then talk to your child separately about the divorce.

If you or your child is in physical danger from your spouse, go to a safe house with your child, contact the police, and do everything necessary to protect yourselves. Worry about explaining things to your child later.

Protect Your Assets During a Divorce
849

During a divorce you should gather all the information you can about your assets and move those that you feel are in danger.

⊚ Steps

1. Meet with a lawyer and ask him or her about property division and what the law dictates. Get specific advice for how to handle your particular unique situation.

2. Gather all the records you can find that detail bank accounts, pensions, investments, expensive items and the value of your home and vehicles and any other large, important things you own. Make a list of other assets that exist and describe them. This will be proof for the court of what the marital assets are.

3. Secure items such as deeds, vehicle titles, jewellery and expensive collections in a safety-deposit box.

4. Find out if your spouse has taken anything that you believe belongs to you and make a list of what is missing.

5. Have valuations performed on expensive items such as houses, antiques and jewellery. This will provide you with proof of the fair market value of the items.

6. Remove any powers of attorney you have given your spouse to assets that are in your name alone. Destroy any general powers of attorney you may have signed, giving your spouse the right to act on your behalf in legal and financial matters.

7. Cancel any joint credit cards. You are liable to the company for any amounts charged on the card whether or not you made the purchase.

8. Consider closing all joint bank accounts and investments. Talk to a lawyer about the law regarding this. If you believe your spouse may take those assets and spend or hide them, then you are probably safe in removing them with an intent to preserve them. It is always legal for you and your spouse to close such accounts together and divide them between yourselves.

9. Obtain a restraining order preventing your spouse from taking or spending marital assets. You will probably need a lawyer to do so.

✳ Tips

Try not to become obsessed with material goods and money. People often focus on getting every penny they can in a divorce. In the long run, it may be best to think about your children and your emotional health.

If your divorce case has already been filed, remember that all your assets are under the control and scrutiny of the court.

Get Alimony
850

Alimony goes a long way towards easing the transition from being married to being divorced.

⊚ Steps

1. Prove the standard of living to which you've become accustomed. For example, if you routinely get a weekly massage, or you have a weekly cleaner and have for years, it is reasonable to ask that your spouse continues paying for the expenses.

✳ Tip

Alimony must be provided for in the divorce agreement. Any other sort of arrangement is not "alimony" per its legal definition.

2   Demonstrate your contribution, if not monetary, as a homemaker or parent. Your role in the marriage has value. Note any contributions you have made to the career or education of your spouse.

3   Provide information about earning capacity, other income, such as interest, dividends and capital gains of your spouse. Bank records and income-tax records are the best proof of income earned.

4   Negotiate with your partner first to determine the amount of support and length of alimony payments. Depending on many factors, alimony might be paid for a year or two, or "for life" unless the recipient remarries or cohabitates with a new partner.

5   Involve the judge to review the situation if you and your partner cannot come to terms. A judge will consider any factor presented by either side when determining the amount of alimony and length of time of alimony payments.

6   Consider taking a life and disability insurance policy on your ex-spouse. As an "interested party" you are allowed to do this. In the event the person paying is disabled or dies, the policy would cover the terms of the maintenance income you've been awarded.

851 | Deal with Divorced Parents

No matter how old you are, if your parents divorce you feel it. Even if you knew their relationship was doomed or you wanted it to end, at some point you have to deal with the pain of watching your parents divorce.

Steps

1   Stay involved with your parents. Just because your family dynamics change, it doesn't mean you lose a parent. The trick is not to let your parents put you in the middle of their problems. It is not appropriate for a parent to vent about your other parent, ask you to take sides or ask you to deliver a message from them.

2   Express your feelings. Tell your parents, friends, therapist, diary or family pet how you feel. It's important to get your emotions out. If it's not too uncomfortable, speak directly with your parents about how the divorce and their actions are impacting your life. The sooner you begin a conversation about how the changes affect you, the better.

3   Be patient with the changes. If you're still living at home, you may have to deal with moving, split custody, step parents or new financial challenges. Create a daily routine that works for you. Incorporate the changes into your life. Talk with your parents about any issues or concerns you have with the changes.

4   Help your siblings. If anyone understands what you're going through, it's your brothers or sisters. Work as a team to remain positive. Talk about your future and laugh together.

✱ Tip

You are not to blame. It is not your fault that your parents divorced. Say this until you believe it.

⚠ Warning

Do not pick sides. As hard as it may be, keep an open mind and give both parents a chance to be a part of your life.

Be a Good Son 852

You love your parents with all your heart and you want to be the best son you can be, but it's not always easy. Here are some ideas for showing your parents how much you love them.

◉ Steps

1 Visit your parents. Nothing says "I love you" more than spending time with someone. Parents spend their lives giving you their time. Be a good son and give some time back to them.

2 Help with house repairs and gardening. Your parents will be grateful when you offer to share in the hard work around the house.

3 Help with car repairs. Everyone appreciates a son who can fix a car. Change their oil, fill up the wiper fluid and wash the car.

4 Get a good education. Make your parents proud by educating yourself. Most parents dream of their child going out into the world with an education that can help them start a career.

5 Get a good job. Show your parents that you can support yourself. A good son can take care of himself and those he loves. Let your parents see the time and effort they spent raising you helped create a good person who can live independently.

6 Be kind to your siblings. Help them in any way you can. Parents want their children to get along. It's comforting for them to know you will have each other after they are gone.

7 Remember anniversaries and birthdays. Call your parents on special days and visit when you can. Bring your children if you have any. Your parents will love having you and your family around.

8 Thank your parents for all they have done for you. Tell them how you feel and how much they mean to you. People often forget to say, "I love you and you're important to me." Tell your parents you care – and tell them often.

✳ Tip

Be a kind and caring person. Help people. Be considerate. Any parent would be proud of a son who has a good heart. Be that son.

Begin a Family Tree 853

Exploring your family history and creating a family tree can be a fun and fascinating activity for everyone in the family.

◉ Steps

1 Start with what you know. Using first an ancestral chart, fill in everything you know, starting with you. Search online for ancestral chart to find examples. Do the same with family group sheets, one sheet for each couple on your ancestral chart. Gather any photos you have of the people on your chart or any photos where you're unsure of who they are.

2 Find out what your family knows. Take your charts and photos and talk to your siblings, parents, uncles and aunts, grandparents, cousins, etc. Use the charts and photos to help jog people's memories. Ask to make copies of any documents, family Bibles or photos they may have. Make notes on what everyone says and add the information to your charts.

✳ Tips

Sometimes you'll get conflicting information. Write it all down and do what you can later to verify it.

Use a tape recorder so you get all the details of any family story you might hear.

Write down your source when you write down information, whether it's a person or a book or newspaper. If you get conflicting information later you'll want

3 Visit libraries, especially those in areas that you know your family lived in. Libraries have many resources such as school yearbooks, cemetery records and other family histories that may include your ancestors. Ask the librarian if they have a genealogist on staff who could help you locate records. Some libraries specialise in genealogy, so make a few calls to find the one nearest you for searching census or newspaper records.

4 Visit government buildings that house records in areas where your family lived. Get copies of records, such as birth certificates, marriage licences, death certificates. These often have maiden names, parents' names and other information that you may be looking for or need to verify. Many of these can be ordered online from the National Archives.

5 Go online. There are a number of free family search sites, such as Rootsweb, where you can search other family trees to find other people who are researching your family name. There are passenger lists you can find. Even simply searching for a person's name often reveals sources of information.

6 Subscribe to online search sites. To go even further you can subscribe to a site like Ancestry, where you have access to thousands of records, including census and military records. These are easily searchable and will save you a lot of time if you're serious about your search. If going this route.

to gauge which source is more reliable. You may want to look up the source later to verify or check your facts. It's easier when you have that information at your fingertips.

⚠ Warning

Don't expect to be able to find every ancestor. Certain families are easy to find records for, but others just seem to disappear and all you can do is keep digging.

854 | Make a Family Time Capsule

A time capsule can be a great family project to commemorate a special occasion. Fill it with photographs and mementos, and put it away for as long as you like.

⊙ Steps

1 Determine how long you want to put your time capsule away. Is it something you want to look at in five years? 10? 20? Will you take it out for a special occasion, such as an anniversary or a 21st birthday? Or do you want to hide it away for the next generation to find?

2 Decide where to put it. Keep in mind that you may move before the appointed time, so think about putting it where you can easily find it.

3 Decide what container to use. You can buy containers designed for time capsules, or use any waterproof, airtight and preferably fireproof vessel.

4 Ask everyone in the family to contribute an item – clippings, photographs, letters, arts and crafts, toys or just about anything else that fits into the capsule.

5 Protect the contents from decay. Put them into individual, airtight plastic bags and store them in a cool, dry location. For extra protection, consider copying them on to acid-free paper first.

6 Store photographs correctly – ask at a photography or craft shop if you aren't sure how to treat your photos.

7 Leave out any substance that could decay and damage the other contents of the box. This includes rubber, wool, wood, PVC, and

✳ Tips

Black-and-white photos last longer than colour photos and will not fade as much – use them whenever possible.

Have each family member include a letter to the older version of himself or herself, or to future generations, if the capsule will be stored that long. Mention favourite foods, music, books, films and hobbies.

If you plan to seal the time capsule away for more than a generation, include instructions for using any equipment or recordings you include. Your CDs and DVDs may well be obsolete 100 years from now.

any perishable or edible item. If you must include any of these, put them in an airtight plastic bag.

8   Mark everything clearly so you or others will know where each item came from and who included it when the time comes to open the capsule. Don't assume you will remember all the details. You may also want to include a detailed inventory of all the items.

9   Fill the capsule and seal it, then put it out of sight and out of mind. Make sure you store your capsule in a place where your kids won't get impatient, wanting to look at it every day.

10   Leave yourself a reminder about the time capsule in a place where you are likely to find it if you move or if your home suffers any damage.

Visit a New Mother and Child   **855**

The birth of a new child is a joyous occasion for a family. Be among the first to congratulate them on – and help them ease into – this momentous time.

⊙ Steps

1   Wait until the mother and child have been home from the hospital for a few days before planning to visit.

2   Call first to find out the most convenient time for the mother to receive visitors.

3   Consider bringing a gift of food to fill their fridge, or order out for them.

4   Consider baby clothes, toys or books for the newborn. Or, if the mother has already had a baby shower, bring nursery decorations such as pictures or picture frames.

5   Show sensitivity by bringing a little something for any older siblings as well – they may be feeling neglected.

6   Try not to visit for too long, and maintain a positive attitude throughout. This is sure to be appreciated by the mother, who may still be regaining her physical and emotional strength.

✳ Tip

Sometimes your attention can be the best present for an older sibling. Spend part of the day with the baby's brothers or sisters to demonstrate that they are important, too.

Support Someone Who Has Had a Miscarriage or Stillbirth   **856**

It's hard to know how to help someone who has recently lost a baby to miscarriage or a stillbirth. Although you can't make the pain go away, there are many ways that you can support the parents and help them deal with their grief.

✳ Tip

Refer to the baby by name, if they have chosen and announced a name. Many grieving parents are comforted by this acknowledgement that their baby existed.

⊙ Steps

1   Be there for them. Many grieving parents retreat from the world for a while, so make an effort to keep calling, visiting and just letting them know that you are there if they need you.

2   Acknowledge their loss, don't pretend it never happened. Even an early miscarriage can cause significant and lasting grief to a couple, and should not be ignored or minimised.

3   Listen to them. They may need to talk about the loss of their baby; some parents even keep photographs of a stillborn baby that they like to show to their friends. Just follow their lead, and talk when they need to talk.

4   Offer to help them commemorate their baby. Some parents choose to hold funeral or memorial services to give them closure, while others choose to fill a grief journal or special box with thoughts and mementos of their lost baby. Ask if you can help them with any preparations they need to make.

5   Help out by offering to field calls or answer letters and cards until they feel up to it.

6   Remember that grandparents and siblings also grieve; although their loss may not be as immediate or intense as that of the baby's parents, they may still need some help getting through the next few weeks and months.

7   Take care of the parents as much as possible – bring casseroles or groceries, offer to help with cleaning and laundry, or just ask them what they would like you to do.

⚠ **Warnings**

Avoid saying anything that might make them feel guilty. Although they may express feelings of guilt themselves, just keep reassuring them that there was nothing they could have done.

Avoid saying "it was for the best" or "you can always have another baby". Many people use statements like this in an effort to be helpful, but this is not what grieving parents need to hear.

857   Support a Handicapped Family Member

The type of support you can give to a mentally disabled family member depends on your financial situation and how close by you live, but any effort will be appreciated.

◉ Steps

1   Provide financial support to your disabled family member or the person providing for them. Parents of handicapped persons are often blindsided by he cost of providing round-the-clock care. Financial support is sometimes the best way to help.

2   Attend school or organised functions. If your family member is in the Special Olympics, take the time to go and support their efforts.

3   Visit your disabled family member at their home. They may not notice your efforts, depending on their severity, but the parents or the person providing their care appreciates it more than you know.

4   Include your disabled family member in conversations, if possible. They are not second-class citizens, so make sure their opinion is taken into consideration and ensure that they feel like part of the family.

5   Celebrate their accomplishments. They may never graduate from college, but when they learn to read or ride a bike, it should be a huge deal.

✳ **Tips**

People don't always want to accept financial help, so you may consider anonymously giving. Being recognised for your good deeds is less important than doing good deeds.

If you live near your disabled family member, volunteer with their school functions or even at their Special Olympic events.

⚠ **Warning**

Don't be discouraged. A mentally disabled person may or may not appreciate your support. Keep supporting your family member, no matter what.

Help a Victim of Spousal Abuse   858

Although most victims of spousal abuse are women, there are some men who are abused by their wives. It is important to remember that whether the abused person is a man or a woman, they are living a life of fear and often will need help to get themselves away from the abuser.

Steps

1   Validate the person's fear. Spousal abuse is a very frightening thing to live with and it is often very hard for the abused person to talk about the abuse. Let him or her know that fear is a very normal response and it is okay for them to be afraid.

2   Try not to let the abuser keep you away from the victim. Most abusers will isolate their victim from friends, family and any other support network they might have. It is important that you not allow this to happen to you. Even if it means you have to sneak to see the abused person behind the abuser's back.

3   Be a good listener. When the victim is ready to talk about the abuse, it is important that he or she has someone who is willing to listen.

4   Provide information about restraining orders, local shelters and support groups in the area.

5   Support their needs even if they are not ready to leave the abuser yet. Understand that leaving is often hard and it might take time before they are ready to get themselves out of the relationship. It is also possible that they might leave and then return to the abuser again. This can be very frustrating for the person trying to help, but it is important to stay supportive.

6   Help the victim to build self-esteem. A trip to the beauty salon for a new hairstyle or a day spent shopping for some new clothes can be great self-esteem builders.

7   Recommend that when they are ready to leave that they get as far away as possible. If they have relatives in another county that would be a good place to go. If they are going to a shelter, they should go to one in a different county. Usually the abuser will try to get the victim back. The further away they are the more difficult this will be for the person who has been abusing them.

✳ Tips

Understand that nobody deserves to be abused. If you suspect someone is being abused, take action immediately.

It is important to be patient when helping a victim of spousal abuse. Healing, both physical and emotional, takes time. Do not give up on the person.

859 Prevent Child Abuse

Teach your children the difference between acceptable and unacceptable touching, and to trust their instincts about people. Educate yourself about the signs of abuse so you'll be able to detect it.

Educate

- Explain that no one has the right to hurt your child or touch him or her in private areas or touch in any way that makes him or her feel uncomfortable.

- Tell your children that the words they need to remember are No, Go, Yell, Tell. If anyone touches them in a way they don't like or tries to get them to go with a stranger or person they don't feel comfortable with they should always say "No!" and ...

- Go away from the person or situation as quickly as possible.

- Use their danger voice to yell. A danger voice is a very loud, low-pitched yell, that gets attention immediately. It is not a high-pitched screech. It should never be used in any other situation.

- Tell a parent, teacher or other caregiver immediately about what happened.

- Help your children understand that they need to be wary not just of the traditional idea of "strangers" but of anyone who makes them feel uncomfortable, even if it is someone they know – like the next-door neighbour.

- Talk to your children about situations they must avoid, like taking any food or medicine from a person who is not a parent, teacher, caregiver or close friend. Help them understand how to identify a police officer. Take them to the local police station and let them see what a uniform looks like and what a badge looks like.

- Show your children how to make a call from a phone box and how to call 999. If they have a mobile phone, make sure their home number is on speed-dial.

React

- Understand that "child abuse" means any kind of harm done to a child and does not just mean sexual abuse

- Learn what the signs of abuse are so that you will notice if something is going on with your child. Look for bruises, burns, bloody or missing underwear, difficulty with bowel movements or urination, problems with walking or sitting, behaviour problems, inappropriate sexual behaviour, sore genitals or anything that just makes you feel there is something amiss.

- Trust your instincts – you know your child better than anyone and if you sense that something is wrong, you're likely to be right.

- Don't stick your head in the sand if you suspect a partner or anyone else is abusing your child. Every second you delay in dealing with it causes more mental and emotional damage to the child.

- Get help from the police, social services or from a child-abuse hotline if you suspect there is a problem.

- If you suspect someone else's child is being abused, look for any of the above signs. You should also notice if the child is hungry all the time, very thin, dirty, wears unwashed clothes, has fading bruises, is depressed or withdrawn or shrinks away from adults.

- If you suspect it, report it. It is better to make a mistake than to allow a child to be harmed or even killed.

- Do not try to handle the situation on your own if you suspect child abuse. Get the authorities and trained professionals involved immediately.

reference

Cope with Elderly Parents Moving In 860

There may come a time when you invite your ageing parents or in-laws to move in with you. Although this arrangement can work very well, it can also be stressful for everyone involved.

◎ Steps

1 Discuss everything in advance. Your parents are probably used to living independently in their own home, and it may be difficult for them to adjust to living under someone else's roof, with someone else's routines and expectations.

2 Talk about all the issues you can think of before they move in, create an atmosphere of mutual respect, and try to come to some compromises that will work for everyone in the family.

3 Clearly establish the "house rules" as tactfully as possible, and agree on each person's responsibilities and limits within the home. Each family has its own identity, and the addition of elderly parents to the formula can often disrupt family harmony for a while, even when it's handled with great care and sensitivity.

4 Consider your children, if they still live at home. When Grandma and Grandpa move in, it can be a difficult adjustment for kids and teens, so set some boundaries that everyone can live with. Your children need to be considerate of their grandparents, but the grandparents also need to step back and let you discipline your own children when necessary.

5 Make sure everyone has some privacy. This may mean adding a separate suite to your home, installing an extra bathroom or even just rearranging your home slightly. Even though your parents no longer live in their own home, they'll still want some space of their own and some private time to themselves.

6 Figure out what goes where. This may sound obvious, but it can be tricky. Your parents have been surrounded by their own furniture and possessions for many years, but your house is almost certainly not big enough for two sets of furnishings. Perhaps some things can be sold, given to relatives or put into storage.

7 Work out a budget. Will your parents be contributing some of their pension money to cover household expenses, or will you be paying for everything? Never make assumptions, especially when it comes to finances. Discuss the situation ahead of time.

8 Let your parents help around the house if they want to and are physically able to. Many seniors connect their sense of self-worth with their "use-fulness" and it can be difficult emotionally if most or all of their daily tasks are taken over by someone else.

9 Encourage your parents to maintain their independence and to stay active. This will benefit their physical and emotional health.

10 Be patient – it can take a while for the rhythms of the household to re-establish themselves after such a big change.

✳ Tip

Try to hold regular family confer-ences so that everyone can talk about issues or problems that may come up. It's often much easier to discuss awkward subjects when everyone is together and in the mood to talk.

⚠ Warning

Consider safety issues for children and seniors living in the same house. Make sure your parents don't leave medications or non-childproof bottles within reach of little ones, and make sure your kids don't leave toys on the stairs or puddles of water on the floor.

861 | Survive the Loss of a Spouse

The death of a spouse is one of the most traumatic experiences one can face, even if the death was expected.

Steps

1   Acknowledge the pain and allow yourself a grieving period. Give yourself permission to mourn.

2   Understand that you will experience a range of emotions, often unpredictable at times. There is no specific pattern to grief that you can expect, but feeling angry, sad and confused at times are steps along the path to feeling better.

3   Know that you have the strength and ability to cope. A time will come when you have to make the decision to work on moving forward. Talk to friends and family, join a support group and write down your thoughts and feelings to help with healing.

4   Realise that you may continue to have unexpected times of grief when anniversaries, birthdays, Christmas and other special occasions arise in the future.

5   Take care of yourself. Go to scheduled medical check-ups, exercise regularly and maintain relationships with family and friends.

6   Contact a grief counsellor if you feel your loss is unbearable, and are concerned about your health and well-being.

✳ Tip

It's a cliché, but time is a great healer. You will never forget your spouse, but in time the pain will fade and you'll be able to remember them with joy.

862 | Repair a Friendship

Realise that a little tiff is no reason to throw years of companionship down the proverbial drain. Here are some quick tips to repair a friendship and get back your best pal.

Steps

1   Open the lines of communication. Nothing will happen unless you can communicate with your friend, so do what you can to start the discussion. Use whatever medium you can: instant messages, texting, email, phone or (if possible) face-to-face conversation.

2   Tell them how you feel and ask how they feel. Always do so in a calm, courteous way, repeatedly emphasising that you want to be friends again.

3   Give them some space. If communication doesn't work, one or both of you are too emotionally charged to set things right at this point. Let things cool down before you try anything else. Plus, sometimes absence makes the heart grow fonder!

4   Swallow your pride. If things still aren't working out, honestly assess whether it is you who is in the wrong. Try seeing things from your friend's perspective. How would you act in their position?

5   Apologise when you're wrong. You might be thinking that you, too, were wronged, but that doesn't mean you can't apologise for wronging your friend.

✳ Tips

Don't force a friendship just because you think you ought to be friends with them. Know when it's right to end things.

Be willing to admit you're wrong and move past the incident.

6 Talk to your other friends. They may help you think of a way to fix the friendship. If nothing else, you'll be in friendly company.

7 Accept that friendships change. If none of these tactics work, it may be time to accept that sometimes the best thing is for two formerly close people to go their separate ways.

Resolve a Dispute with a Neighbour 863

Your neighbours can be a blessing or a curse. One thing they will always be is right next door, so strive for cooperation rather than conflict.

⊙ Steps

1 Find out the facts. Determine whether this disturbance is a one-off problem or a constant occurrence.

2 Vent your feelings before you approach your neighbour: talk to a friend or spouse, whack your bed with a tennis raqcet or roll up the windows in your car and scream.

3 Write it out. Get clear in your head about what is bothering you and what you want done about it.

4 Figure out who is responsible for the disturbance. You want to negotiate with the proper party.

5 Talk to your other neighbours and find out whether they share your concern. This is simply for your information; try not to aggravate the situation by building an angry alliance.

6 Arrange a time to meet with your neighbour and choose a neutral location.

7 Ease into it. Start off with pleasant banter.

8 Create a cooperative atmosphere. Rather than attacking your neighbour, ask for assistance in finding a solution.

9 Find common ground and focus on what you do agree on.

10 Search for a solution that satisfies both parties' needs.

✳ Tips

Keep a record of all your interactions with your neighbour.

Be neighbourly, keep an open mind and be willing to compromise.

Write a letter presenting your concern if you are uncomfortable meeting in person.

⚠ Warning

Stop negotiating if your neighbour behaves unreasonable and the situation worsens; enlist a neutral party to assist you.

Get Along with a Housemate 864

If you live with a housemate, establish some ground rules up front and learn to approach problems in a diplomatic manner if you want your household to be a peaceful one.

⊙ Steps

1 Approach your housemate about your concerns and gripes in a calm, tactful manner. Don't let tensions build to the point of boiling tempers.

2 Respect your housemate's privacy and opinions. Try to compromise on sensitive issues.

✳ Tips

In a disagreement, begin your statements with "I" as in "I get annoyed when you leave your dishes in the sink" instead of "You're such a pig!"

3   Work together to determine shared responsibilities, such as cleaning and cooking, and establish a set of household rules.

4   Set up rules about food, company, chores, noise, tobacco and alcohol use and parking. Make sure each person's expectations and responsibilities are clear.

5   Establish and adhere to financial arrangements for sharing the costs of rent, utilities, food, repairs and furnishings.

6   Ask your housemate to work with you on creating a housemate agreement that outlines the shared responsibilities and spells out methods of resolving disagreements.

7   Put your housemate agreement in writing. Sign and date the agreement.

8   Be considerate about phone use. Don't tie up the only phone line – consider getting separate lines. Jot down legible messages when taking calls for your housemate.

Ask an impartial third party, such as a mutual acquaintance, to serve as a mediator for major disagreements.

⚠ **Warning**

Re-evaluate your compatibility with your housemate if recurring disputes cannot be settled to your satisfaction.

---

865 | Comfort a Friend After a Break-Up

Sometimes the steadiness of friendship is the best remedy for the ups and downs of the romance rollercoaster. Here are some tips for helping out a friend in need.

◉ **Steps**

1   Spend time with your friend, ideally in person.

2   Let your friend talk. If he or she is not talking, encourage it. Keep lots of tissues handy.

3   Try distractions. Films, sightseeing, outdoor activities and games are good ideas.

4   Indulge your friend with chocolates, massages, facials, shopping sprees – whatever lets him or her concentrate on pleasure instead of pain.

5   Send a card to lift your friend's spirits if you can't be there in person.

6   Be patient. Some things take a long time to get over.

✳ **Tips**

Even if you think the break-up was your friend's fault, now is not the time to say so.

Avoid such phrases as "There are other fish in the sea". These comments won't be helpful.

Be careful not to bash the ex too much. That kind of talk may make your friend distrust his or her own judgement, or distrust yours.

---

866 | Reach Out to the Elderly in Your Community

If you have a little time to spare, consider spending some of it with senior citizens in your community. You may be able to make a big difference in someone's life just by giving an hour or so each week.

✳ **Tip**

Look online for vacancies for volunteers at local retirement homes.

◉ **Steps**

1   Volunteer to read out loud, play board games or play the piano and sing at a local nursing home or extended-care facility. Many seniors love to have visitors, especially if their family lives in a different city.

2   Visit your local retirement home or community centre, and ask about volunteer opportunities. There may be a whole list of possibilities!

3   Offer to go shopping or run errands for someone at a local semi-independent senior community.

4   Give a few hours a week to Meals on Wheels, dropping off dinners to elderly residents in your area.

5   Give regular lifts to someone who no longer drives; ask your local community volunteer coordinators if they know of anyone, or ask at a nearby nursing home.

6   Join a "Rent-a-Grandma" programme. Many senior centres and care facilities invite parents and children to visit so that elderly residents can spend some time with babies, toddlers and even school-age kids.

7   Ask at a nursing home if you and your pet can visit. Some facilities like to have people with well-behaved dogs, cats and other small animals visit the residents.

8   If you are involved with sports and fitness, volunteer to help with physical activities at a local senior centre or home.

9   At holiday times, offer to participate in seasonal or spiritual celebrations at a local nursing home or care facility, or invite a senior to share in a holiday dinner at your home.

Respond to a Homophobic Comment 867

Whether they come from a co-worker, a family member or someone else, homophobic comments can hurt.

⊙ Steps

1   Consider the source. If the person is known to often make off-colour remarks, it's unlikely that anything you say will change him.

2   Consider the source again. If the person is in a position of power over you, tread carefully.

3   Find a way to make a constructive comment. For example, if someone uses an outdated or inappropriate term to refer to a gay or lesbian person, gently explain what term is now considered appropriate.

4   Attempt to treat everyone with respect, even if they don't respect you. They'll be more likely to listen to you and you'll be less likely to get upset.

5   Decide if you want to confront the person the moment the incident occurs or wait until later. If you wait, your comments may be taken more seriously rather than seeming like an off-the-cuff remark.

6   Try not to embarrass the person in front of others. Take him aside or wait to speak with him when he returns to his office or goes to a different room.

7   Use a calm tone and explain what you objected to and why.

8   Watch for signs that the person really understands you. Give up if he doesn't, and perhaps try again later, but follow up with appropriate materials and information if he seems genuinely open to learning about gays and lesbians.

✳ Tip

Expect to be treated well by everyone, including your family. While it's sometimes okay to give family a little more leeway, family members should still respect you and your sexual orientation.

⚠ Warning

Avoid physically and emotionally abusive situations at all costs. Walk away from a situation if the tension escalates.

9   Make friends with the person, even if he doesn't seem to be opening up to gays and lesbians. The best way for people to gain information about the gay community is to get to know gay people.

868   Say No Without Feeling Guilty

Are you chronically over-committed? Rushing from one task to another, with no time for yourself? The key is to have a strong vision of what you want to say yes to. Then you'll feel far more confident saying no.

⊙ Steps

1   Decide which activities you truly love. If you stay focused on those things, then the next time you are asked to volunteer or get involved in a time-consuming activity, just check in. If the request takes you too far from what you are already dedicating yourself to, it's easier to say no.

2   Get over the need to be nice. Stop being afraid to disappoint people, and let go of the sense of importance you get from feeling like you're indispensable.

3   Be clear when you say no. Ambiguities like "Maybe after the first of the year" or "Let me get back to you" leave the other person thinking you're actually interested, when you're not.

4   Practise saying no in non-threatening situations, when you have little at stake and success is almost assured. Then you'll work up to resigning from the board of directors and stop signing up for committee work. Learn that carving out time for yourself and your family requires no reason and no apology.

5   Say no to requests for money in simple language and give no explanation. Contribute to the causes that excite you and complement your values. Then you'll feel confident saying, "My contributions have already been allocated this year".

6   Re-evaluate your current commitments. You may have agreed to a long-term commitment months ago, but now see that it's not working for you. Talk with the people involved and come up with an arrangement that works for everyone.

✳ Tip

Keep it simple. The most effective nos are the least complicated. The more details you supply, the more likely it is that the other person will challenge you or try to change your mind.

869   Just Get Over It

We all make mistakes, right? What's done is done, and you'll have to live with it for the rest of your life – but that doesn't mean you have to carry around an additional, useless burden of guilt and remorse.

⊙ Steps

1   Don't dwell on it. Sure, you could have done things a different way, or been more considerate of other peoples' feelings, but replaying it in your head, over and over, is a one-way ticket to the loony bin.

✳ Tips

Remember, there's nothing more boring than someone who goes on and on about their own failings in an effort to get affirmation that they've done no wrong.

2   Don't be too hard on yourself. Think about it: if another person (let's just say, for example's sake, the Pope) had been in the exact same circumstances, do you think he would have done things any differently? Probably not, right? So what's the use of holding yourself to a higher standard than any other person in the entire world, especially one with such a fancy hat?

3   Put things in perspective. It's not like you fell asleep at a nuclear weapons plant and allowed al-Qaeda operatives to steal weapons-grade plutonium. It was just a simple mistake – nothing crucial in the larger scheme of things, and certainly nothing no one else but you will remember five or 10 years from now.

4   Resolve not to make the same mistake twice. Considering how awful you feel right now, the odds of doing whatever it was you did all over again must seem pretty low. However, history has a way of repeating itself, so don't lapse into complacency and wind up doing that thing you did a second time. Remember, even the Pope does careless things occasionally, but he didn't get elected Pope by doing them twice, did he?

5   Don't get all drama-queeny. The fact is, most people are preoccupied with their own list of things that they've come to regret, so the last thing they want is to listen to your self-important litany of woe. These are the same folks who are most likely to grab you by the shoulders, give you a good shake and yell "Just get over it!"

870 Save a Penalty Kick

Nobody expects the goalie to save a penalty kick, so relax and commit yourself to one side or the other.

⊙ Steps

1 Stay loose and limber as your team mates argue the call and the referees get into position.

2 Watch the shooter to see if he seems to be looking towards a particular corner – that might be a hint.

3 Determine which foot the shooter kicks with.

4 Decide which corner you're going to dive towards before the shooter approaches the ball.

5 Align yourself in the centre of the goal on the goal line.

6 Wait for the whistle signalling the start of play.

7 Dive to your chosen corner with your arms completely extended the moment the shooter touches the ball.

8 Knock the ball away from the goal.

9 Get to your feet immediately after you save the ball because the game is live once you touch it.

✱ Tips

The rules state that the goalie must wait until the ball is kicked before moving, but most goalies will move before. As long as it's not blatantly obvious, referees usually allow a quick step.

Commit yourself to the dive. As a goalie, you can't be afraid to throw your body around.

⚠ Warning

If you have any condition that would impair or limit your ability to engage in physical activity, please consult a physician before attempting this activity.

871 Set Up a Goal Kick

Goal kicks are awarded when an offensive player knocks the ball past the goal line and out of bounds. The defence then takes control of the ball, and tries to get it as far away from the goal as possible.

⊙ Steps

1 Place the ball within the goal area, where a member of the defensive team will conduct the goal kick.

2 Remain outside the penalty area, if you're on the opposing team, until the ball is kicked into play.

3 Kick the ball from the selected point.

4 Keep in mind that the ball is in play when it's kicked directly beyond the penalty area. If the ball isn't kicked directly beyond the penalty area, the kicker takes the kick again.

5 Avoid touching the ball a second time, if you're the kicker, until the ball has been touched by another player.

⚠ Warnings

If the kicker touches the ball a second time (except with his or her hands), an indirect free kick is awarded to the opposing team at the spot of the infraction.

If the kicker touches the ball with his or her hands before another player touches the goal kick, a direct free kick is awarded to the opposing team at the point of the infraction. A penalty kick is awarded if the infraction occurred in the penalty area.

Chip a Football | 872

The shortest distance between you and your team mate may be a straight line, but defenders sometimes don't cooperate. So, send a flying ball that's easy for your team mate to get hold of.

⊙ **Steps**

1 Understand that a "chip" is when the ball travels in a tall arc. Usually a quick kick is used to send the ball up and over a short distance, rather than in a long, soaring flight.

2 Approach the ball at a slight angle.

3 Place your non-kicking foot approximately 15 cm (6 in) to the side of the ball and slightly behind it.

4 Take a back swing with your kicking leg, keeping in mind that a shorter back swing will allow you more control and better placement.

5 Angle your toe down – imagine your foot to be wedgelike – as you make contact with the ball below its centre.

6 Lean your body back as you kick to increase the lift of the ball. The further you lean back, the greater the ball's arc.

7 A proper chip should have backspin, which makes it easy for your team mate to control. A ball spinning backwards is less likely to run away from the receiver once contact is made.

8 Use a chip as a goal shot if you wish. If the goalkeeper has come out to cut down the angle of your shot, chipping the ball over his head is a good technique for scoring a goal.

✳ Tip

Be comfortable chipping with both feet, and chipping dead balls as well as moving ones.

Trap a Football with Your Thigh | 873

A thigh trap is most useful when the ball is dropping towards you and is already below your waist.

⊙ **Steps**

1 Raise your thigh to meet the ball.

2 Allow your thigh to move in the direction of the ball as you make contact.

3 Absorb the ball's momentum.

4 Allow the ball to drop to your feet.

✳ Tips

The object of trapping the ball is to slow its momentum and change its direction.

You want to provide a pliant surface rather than a rigid one.

874 | Do a Two-Handed Pass in Rugby

The two-handed pass in rugby is used primarily to pass the ball to another player when you are in danger of being tackled.

⊚ Steps

1   Grasp the ball firmly with both hands. This will give you the most effective ball control.

2   Keep the ball away from your opponent. Your opponent will usually try to tackle you around waist level or lower. Keep the ball above your opponent if this is the case.

3   Pick a supporting team member to pass the ball to. The supporting team member should be clear of any potential tackles.

4   Make eye contact with the supporting team member that you want to pass the ball to. This is a good non-verbal way to let them know the ball is coming their way.

5   Hold the ball so that it is almost perpendicular to the ground. Slightly tilt the forward tip of the ball towards the ground.

6   Pass the ball with a firm, swift motion using both hands to propel the ball. This will give you good ball control. Pass the ball over the opponent who is tackling you.

✳ Tip

Make sure that you check for opponents who can intercept the ball when you are looking for a supporting team member to pass the ball to.

875 | Do a Drop Kick in Rugby

In rugby, ball control is essential. The drop kick is a rugby skill that allows you to place the ball in the location of your choice. With a little practice and the right technique, you'll have a great time playing rugby with more enthusiasm and skill than ever.

⊚ Steps

1   Grab the ball so that one point is pointed over the shoulder of your dominant foot. This way, the ball will bounce towards you when you drop it.

2   Stand with your weight on your dominant foot. As you drop the ball, take a step forwards and place your weight on your non-dominant foot. This frees your dominant foot to make the kick.

3   Drop the ball so it falls down without moving sideways from where you were holding it. This will cause it to bounce directly back towards you, allowing you to kick it with more force.

4   Kick the ball as it comes back off the ground using the top of your foot. Use your toes to propel the ball forwards.

5   When you begin to use the rugby drop kick, the ball is likely to spiral off in many directions. As you begin to understand the way the ball moves, you'll adjust your drop and your foot placement.

✳ Tip

Ask a friend to tape you as you perform the drop kick. Perform multiple kicks during this session so you can see the differences in your posture and position.

Play Bind in Rugby 876

Binding in rugby is an offensive move to protect a grounded ball while driving the defence back long enough to allow a team mate to take the ball and advance it around or behind the bind. It's an effective open-field tactic when the binders work together.

⊙ **Steps**

1   Join the bind from the back. This is the only legal way to come into a bind.

2   Come in low to the ground with your buttocks down and your head up. Throw your inside arm low across the back of your team mate, and bring your inside shoulder in against the backside of the player you're binding to.

3   Allow your third team mate on the opposite side of the ball holder to throw their arm over yours to lock together, forming a strong support across the backside of the player on the ball. The three of you are now joined in a bind to push the defence back away from the ball.

4   Drive together with your legs to push into the defence and force them back away from to ball. Keep low to push into the defensive players at about waist level. Continue driving the defence back with your legs churning to about one yard past the ball to allow a team mate behind, usually the scrum half, to take it and follow or move around the bind to advance the ball.

✱ Tip

Rugby often looks chaotic to the uninitiated, but it's actually a very controlled and strategic game. Watch closely and you'll see that all 15 players on a team have specific roles to play in gaining control of the ball and moving it forwards to score.

Condition for Rugby 877

Rugby is a very physical sport that requires intense conditioning. Strength training, cardiovascular training, endurance training and specific skill training all prepare athletes to be in peak condition for the rugby season.

⊙ **Steps·**

1   Eat a proper diet even during the off-season to keep your body at a healthy weight. This is important to remember when you participate in rugby – or indeed any sport.

2   Rehabilitate old injuries. Ask your coach or trainer for a physiotherapy programme to help strengthen the areas affected by old injuries.

3   Stretch often. Stretching keeps muscles limber, which helps prevent injuries caused by muscle fatigue.

4   Lift weights. Strength conditioning is important because of the intense physical performance required during a rugby match.

5   Do cardiovascular conditioning. Running is a good choice because it mimics the movement up and down the pitch.

✱ Tips

Remember to drink plenty of water when you are participating in any sports or fitness programme.

Get a thorough check-up with your doctor before you begin playing any sport or start a serious conditioning programme.

⚠ Warning

Stop any activity immediately if you feel any pain or if you begin to feel dizzy.

6   Perform speed and skill drills as often as possible. This will help to keep your body and mind ready for anything during a rugby match.

7   Practise often by participating in informal matches. The more you practise in a match setting, the better condition you will be for the actual rugby season.

878   Tee Up a Golf Ball

Teeing up a golf ball makes it easier to hit a ball into the air and usually prevents damage to the tee box.

⊙ Steps

1 . Push the golf tee into the ground.

2   Place the golf ball on top of the tee.

3   Adjust the tee so that when the golf ball is on it, half the ball is above the club when the club is behind the ball.

4   Hit the golf ball and pick up the tee to use on the next hole.

✱ Tips

Place tape around the shaft of the golf tee to allow you to tee the ball at the same height for each tee shot.

For different golf clubs, tee up the golf ball at different heights. A pitching wedge should be teed lower than a driver.

879   Hit a Straight Drive in Golf

In golf, the drive sets the tone for the rest of the hole. If you hit a solid drive down the middle of the fairway, you're putting yourself in a great position for future shots.

⊙ Steps

1   First, address the ball properly. You should have your legs about a shoulder width apart and the line of your stance should be parallel to the direction you intend to hit the ball. The ball should be teed up in the middle of your stance or a little forward from the middle.

2   Bend your legs a little bit and shake out any tension. Different players have different routines, but the point is to get yourself prepared to hit a nice, clean shot.

3   Keeping your eyes on the ball, bring the club back. Your should allow your torso to rotate as you bring the club back, but keep your head down. At the height of your backswing the club should be parallel to the ground.

4   Start your forward motion by rotating your hips, allowing your torso and arms to follow. The movement should feel smooth, with all the parts of your body working together.

5   Keep your head down as you swing through the ball.

6   Make sure you stay in form as you follow through. You should think of the beginning of your swing, contact and follow-through as one action rather than trying to "hit" the ball. The best way to understand this concept is to go to the driving range and take note of how your swing feels when you hit a great drive.

✱ Tip

Try to keep your body as upright as possible and stay loose, with your shoulders, hands and chest facing square forward.

Hit a Draw Shot in Golf   **880**

A draw, or hook, shot starts right and then curves left. Use it when a direct shot at your target is blocked.

⊙ Steps

1   Set up your golf shot with your usual alignment and grip.

2   Adjust your feet to aim to the right of your target. The angle of your feet depends on your individual swing and desired results, and can range from 5–45°. Try 10–15° to the right to start.

3   Aim the club face directly at your target and use your normal grip.

4   Swing normally.

5   Resist the temptation to turn too soon and watch the ball's flight.

6   Consider external factors, such as wind direction and strength, slope, how the ball sits on the ground, obstacles, hazards and margin of error, when choosing your club and execution.

7   Try not to change your normal swing. Make the changes to your grip and alignment, and trust your normal swing to do the work for you.

✳ Tips

Note that these instructions are intended for right-handed players. Reverse them if you are left-handed.

Test the intentional hook shot with all your clubs and note the different results with each one.

⚠ Warning

Do not try severe hooks straight away. Start with mild hooks and gradually work your way into the more dramatic ones.

Clean Golf Clubs   **881**

Clean golf club heads and grips are key to making effective contact with a golf ball; sand, grass, dirt and other materials accumulate where they should not, interfering with the job your clubs are designed to perform.

⊙ Steps

1   Clean golf club grips using warm water, liquid soap and a scrubbing brush. Scrub the grip until all its pores are unclogged.

2   Soak your golf-club heads for 10 minutes, or longer if you think necessary, in a bucket filled with warm water and liquid soap. This will loosen debris trapped in the grooves.

3   Dry the club heads using a flannel, pulling out any loosened debris.

4   Use a rotating brass brush at a low speed, focusing on any dirty groove areas.

5   Polish the club heads with a polishing cloth (those designed for cleaning jewellery work well) or a rotating polish brush.

✳ Tips

If your grips become too smooth, try rubbing them with a wire brush or fine sandpaper.

Use covers for club heads to keep them clean and prevent scratches and chipping.

⚠ Warning

Using steel wool on any non-rusted part of your club can cause permanent damage, and you should use it gently on rusted areas.

✓ 882 Understand the Rules of Cricket

Cricket is a hugely popular sport played throughout the world, yet there are still areas where the game has not been widely received or understood. This chart explains the rules of this sometimes-complicated game.

chart

THE BASICS	SCORING	PLAYING
Each team has 11 players. The field size on which the game is played can vary, but it will be oval, around 168 m (550 ft) in diameter. The pitch is a strip of earth in the middle of the field around 17 m (55 ft) long. At each end of the pitch is a wicket – three wooden poles called stumps topped with three pieces of wood, called bails. There will be two umpires (referees) on the field. The batting team provides two batsmen who stand at either end of the pitch. The fielding team stands within the wider field. One member of the fielding team is the bowler. The bowler will run or walk towards the pitch and bowl the ball over-arm to the wicket at the other end of the pitch. The bowler's objective is to get the batsmen out. The batsmen are trying to score as many points as possible. The game is over when all 10 batsmen are out or the allotted time limit or bowls have been reached; this is classed as the end of the inning.	One point is gained each time the batsmen run to the opposite end of the pitch after the ball has been hit. Four points are scored if the batsman hits the ball over the boundary – the limits of the field. Six points are scored if the ball does not hit the ground before going over the boundary. One point is scored for the batting team if the bowler bowls a "no-ball" by overstepping the mark on the pitch where the ball was released or by bending his arm during the bowl. It's a rule of the game that the bowler must have a straight arm when he bowls the ball. One point is given to the batting team for a "wide" – when the bowl goes too wide from the batter, giving them no opportunity to hit it. The fielding team has to try and stump out the batsmen by hitting off the bails before the running batsmen get safely back to the wicket. Longer Test matches can end in a tie because the game is time capped. This happens when both teams still have batsmen in at the end of the time.	The fielding team can get the batting team out in numerous ways: Fielders can hit the stumps while the batters are still running between the wickets. Fielders can catch a ball that the batsman has hit before it touches the ground. They can bowl him out by the ball knocking off the bails directly from the bowl. The most subjective way of the batter getting out is LBW – leg before wicket. This happens when the batter puts his leg in the way of a ball that is going to hit the stumps to prevent the bails being knocked off. This only applies if the batter did not make contact with the ball with his bat before it touches his leg. The winner is declared once all the innings and overs (the name for six consecutive bowls by one bowler) have been played. The team with the most points wins.

Reverse Swing a Cricket Ball — 883

In the game of cricket, once a ball gets older and worn out, it will get heavier on one side than the other due to wear and tear from hitting the ball. This imbalance of weight will cause the ball to turn in the opposite direction that it typically would on a swing in the air, throwing off the batsman.

Steps

1   Locate a cricket ball that has one dull side and one shiny side in order to make this swing work correctly.

2   Hold the cricket ball with your fingers at the seam of the ball. Keep the shiny side on the right if you want the ball to move away from a right-handed baseman, and the shiny side on the left if you want to move the ball in. Keep the seam as vertical and straight as you can.

3   Bend the wrist while holding the cricket ball downwards so that the part of the ball that is closest to your body is positioned facing approximately 30° downwards.

4   Keep your head and hand at the shoulder at roughly a 50–60° angle. Your bowling hand should remain angled as you bowl, and you should keep your hand as far away from your head as you can.

5   Pitch the ball up high and as fast as you can. The ball needs to be thrown at 130 km/h (80 mph) or so to make this swing work.

6   Follow through with the ball. Make sure that the ball goes between your body and the stumps (the vertical posts) when you follow through on this swing.

☀ Tips

While playing the game, try to wear your ball on one side more than the other and keep the shiny side as shiny as possible, to create a ball that will work with this swing.

Test the ball to see if you can use it for a reverse swing by throwing it straight. If it swings a bit towards the shiny side you can use it for this swing.

⚠ Warning

Let the ball wear naturally. Don't tamper with the ball with knives and other things to speed the process. Ball tampering is illegal in the game and could get you banned.

Make a Layup in Basketball — 884

Making a layup (a close-range shot on the run) is one of the easiest ways to score points in basketball. These instructions describe a right-handed layup; reverse them if you're a lefty.

Steps

1   Stand at the far right-hand edge of the free-throw line.

2   Dribble the ball with your right hand.

3   Concentrate on the shooting square painted on the backboard. The upper right-hand hand corner is the most important.

4   Approach the basket slowly, dribbling the ball. Stop dribbling when you're 1.5–2.5 m (5–8 ft) from the basket.

5   Pick up the ball while you're stepping with your right foot. Take another step and plant your left foot, then jump off it.

6   Bring your right knee up towards your chest as you jump. Aim for the upper right-hand corner of the box on the backboard.

7   Shoot the ball with your right hand.

☀ Tips

Smoothness is the key. Pick up the ball, take your step, jump and shoot in one fluid motion.

Practise both left- and right-handed layups. It will be more difficult with your weaker hand, but worth the effort.

⚠ Warning

If you have any condition that would impair or limit your ability to engage in physical activity, please consult a physician before attempting this activity.

885 | Crossover Dribble in Basketball

This move is so simple, yet it makes you look so good – and your opponent so bad.

⊙ Steps

1 Dribble the ball in your dominant hand (let's pretend you're right-handed for the purpose of this example).

2 Use your body as a slight barrier between the ball and your defender, but still face your defender.

3 Take a step with your left foot.

4 Follow that with a step with your right foot.

5 Let the defender move in the direction you appear to be heading.

6 Switch the ball to your left hand with a quick, low bounce directly in front of your defender.

7 Take a step with your left foot around the defender.

8 Drive to the basket.

❋ Tips

The crossover dribble is easier to pull off if you really act as if you're going to drive in the initial direction you're heading.

The faster you can go through these steps, the harder it is for the defender to keep up.

886 | Swing a Tennis Racquet

Tennis is a difficult sport to master, especially if you neglect the basics. The forehand is the foundation of your game, and to be a threat on the court you must be comfortable with this shot.

⊙ Steps

1 Get a grip! The standard grip for a simple forehand is the eastern grip. This is the most natural grip for beginners because it feels most like a handshake.

2 Prepare early. This is the key to a successful tennis swing, whether it's a backhand or a forehand. Even if you have sound mechanics, a hurried shot is likely to result in errors. Keep your feet moving as you prepare for your swing, which will enable you to make last-minute adjustments to accommodate the flight of the oncoming ball.

3 Keep your eye on the ball and your racquet back. Turn your shoulders to establish a sideways stance. Your racquet should be well behind you at around waist height and pointing away from the oncoming ball.

4 Aim for the optimum zone for hitting the ball: around waist height. If the ball coming towards you has a low bounce, bend your knees rather than standing upright and reaching down for the shot. This way you can still play the ball around waist height, even though your waist is closer to the ground.

5 Step into the shot, transferring your weight from your back foot to the front foot. Keep the racquet head at around the same height as your racquet hand, keep the wrist firm and swing the racquet towards the ball. With the racquet face square to the ball, make contact slightly in front of your body, around the point where your front foot is planted.

❋ Tip

When you move into the shot, keep the toes of your back foot on the ground. Your heel may be raised, but if your foot leaves the ground completely, you'll lose the stability and balance necessary for an accurate shot.

6 Follow through with the racquet to ensure a smooth and accurate shot. Your follow-through should follow the path that you want the ball to take, and the racquet head should end up high, somewhere around the opposite shoulder. Your follow-through should naturally help your shoulders turn into the shot, which is where much of the power for the shot comes from. Your torso should now be facing your intended target.

7 Get on to the balls of your feet at the end of your follow-through, and continue to move your feet so that you're ready and able to move into position for the next shot.

Hit a Drop Shot in Tennis   887

The drop shot is a surprise shot that can be very effective, especially when hit well and on soft courts.

⊙ Steps

1 Grip the racquet using the continental grip.

2 Turn your shoulders slightly while preparing the racquet, with a half to three-quarters backswing, depending on where you are on the court. The closer you are to the net, the less backswing you'll need.

3 Imagine "peeling" under the ball as you hit it, as if you're slicing the underside of an orange.

4 Extend your arms at all times.

5 Finish with the racquet up high.

6 Try not to bend your elbow during contact with the ball and while finishing the shot.

7 Hit this shot with a closed stance (crossing over with one foot) or an open stance (feet facing the net).

8 Practise a drop shot against a wall. Stand about 1.8–3.6 m (6–12 ft) from the wall. Think of bumping the ball, allowing it to bounce in front of you before hitting it. This exercise will develop your touch.

9 Practise a drop shot from the service line, slicing under the ball with the goal of having it bounce twice in the opposite service box.

✳ Tips

Consider a drop shot foremost when you are inside the baseline.

Note that a drop shot is more effective in singles tennis than in doubles.

⚠ Warning

Tennis is a physically demanding sport that can result in serious injury. We recommend that you seek the proper training before undertaking this activity.

Hit a Two-Handed Backhand Volley in Tennis   888

If you love the two-handed backhand ground stroke, chances are you'll comfortably adopt the two-handed backhand volley. Follow these steps and finish the point at the net.

⊙ Steps

1 Position yourself about 1 m (3 ft) from the net. Keep your feet spread about a shoulder-width apart.

2 Hold the racquet using a two-handed continental grip – use your non-dominant hand to support your dominant hand by overlapping or interlocking with it.

How to Do More of *(Just About)* **Everything**

3   Hold the racquet with the head vertical (strings perpendicular to the ground) and directly in front of you. The bottom of the handle should be even with your belly button.

4   Bend your knees slightly. You should be able to feel some strain on your quadriceps in your thighs.

5   Step towards the ball with your right foot (or left foot if you're left-handed). Turn your shoulders slightly to the left (or right) and keep both hands firm on the racquet.

6   Drive the racquet forwards in one smooth stroke as the ball draws even with your lead shoulder. The head should be pointing up and the ball should hit the middle of the racquet face evenly.

7   Continue to push the racquet forwards until the ball has been hit across the net. Concentrate on releasing the weak hand from the handle after the ball has made contact with the face.

8   Follow through on the ball with your swing, keeping a firm grip on the racquet so that it doesn't fly out of your hand.

889 Hit a Topspin Serve in Tennis

The topspin serve is a variation on the slice serve. It gives you another option to confuse your opponent.

⊙ Steps

1   Assume the normal service posture (feet sideways to the baseline, hands down and weight on the back foot).

2   Begin your serve as you would any other, by bringing your hands up together while simultaneously shifting your weight forwards.

3   Position the ball toss more directly in front of you or slightly over your head.

4   Attempt to catch the ball on its bottom centre.

5   Swing fast and aggressively, hitting up on the ball to enhance the spin. Racquet-head velocity is essential for good spin.

6   Follow through as you would with other serves.

✳ Tips

Be aware that the toss position is the main difference in any serve.

Attempt this serve (as well as the kick serve) only if you have no lower back problems.

890 Hit an Underhand Drop Shot in Badminton

Catch the shuttle late and low, barely hitting it so that it just clears the net – it should land too short for your opponent to get to.

⊙ Steps

1   Lunge forwards with your racquet foot to reach the shuttle. Reach it as soon as possible, before it falls too low. Net height is ideal.

2   Hold your racquet arm out with your racquet extended and level with the net.

✳ Tips

If you are further from the net, a slight wrist snap may be necessary to clear the net.

Try this shot either forehand or backhand.

3   Slide the racquet sideways as you make contact to give the shuttle some slice, causing it to tumble over the net. This shot is very hard to return.

4   Contact the shuttle with very little wrist action and no follow-through.

5   Keep your racquet face open, allowing the shuttle to simply bounce off your strings and barely clear the net.

6   Aim for the sideline furthest from your opponent's position.

7   Recover quickly to your ready position.

Backhand Swing in Badminton   891

Use the backhand swing for all badminton shots on the non-racquet side of your body. Practise hitting your backhand as well as your forehand for a balanced game.

⊙Steps

1   Notice the shuttlecock coming to your backhand side (your non-racquet side) from your ready position.

2   Pivot on your left foot and step your right foot around in front of your body, so your right shoulder is facing the net (left-handed players should reverse this step).

3   Bend your elbow to draw your right hand across your body, almost to your opposite shoulder, for your backswing. This motion will cause your body to coil up slightly.

4   Shift your weight to your back foot.

5   Uncoil your body and shift your weight to your forward foot.

6   Straighten your elbow as you swing.

7   Snap your wrist forwards as your racquet face connects with the shuttle, powering through the shot.

8   Follow through, allowing your wrist to relax and your palm to face upwards.

❋ Tips

Backhand shots are most often defensive shots, and should generally be hit high and deep.

Practise to make your backhand as strong as your forehand. Otherwise your opponents will capitalise on your weak side.

Assume a Basic Boxing Stance   892

"A novice boxer makes the mistake of standing like he's begging to be knocked out. The proper stance is like a posture that should be your starting point for every punch," says Joe Guson, pro-boxing trainer.

⊙Steps

1   Turn so that you're standing at a 45° angle to your opponent.

2   Keep your feet shoulder width apart or wider, with your front foot open and pointed towards your opponent and your back foot more perpendicular for support.

❋ Tip

"The most common errors in stance are low hands and standing too square to your opponent. Just turn sideways a bit, get the hands up and you'll be less of a target and better able to protect yourself," Guson says.

3   Hold your arms up high, with your elbows in tight to your body to protect your sides from body blows. Use your forearms and hands to ward off blows to your head.

4   Stand on the balls of your feet so you can react and move quickly.

---

893 | Throw a Hook in Boxing

"A great left hook consists of a bunch of precise separate movements that come together and appear as one smooth movement," says Joe Guson.

⚹ Tip

Do the opposite of these steps if you're left-handed.

⊙ Steps

1   Focus on your open target.

2   Come with your left from the side, assuming you're right-handed (reverse this if you're left-handed).

3   Bring your chin down into the inside of your left shoulder.

4   Pivot your toe, hips and hand in the direction of your punch.

5   Turn your hand over so that at the point of impact, your palm faces down.

6   Connect with your target with four flush knuckles.

---

894 | Lunge When Fencing

Because fencers typically stand too far apart to reach each other simply by extending the sword arm and weapon from the guard position, you must usually take a long step, or "lunge", to deliver a thrust or cut.

⚹ Tip

Although lunging involves several steps, the movement must be smooth, unbroken and accomplished in a single fluid motion.

⚠ Warning

Fencing is an inherently dangerous activity that can result in serious injury. We recommend that you seek proper training and equipment before attempting this activity.

⊙ Steps

1   Straighten the sword arm while simultaneously inclining the torso progressively forwards and bringing the hand to shoulder level.

2   Lift the leading foot slightly – toe first – only after you've completely straightened the sword arm.

3   Push hard with the left leg to propel the body rapidly forwards.

4   Carry the leading foot forwards swiftly, so that it just grazes the surface of the floor.

5   Wait until halfway through the lunge to vigorously throw the rear arm directly backwards until it forms a straight line parallel to the floor, palm upwards, fingers together, thumb out.

6   Land the foot heel first, so that the knee is positioned over the instep when the thigh becomes level with the floor. The rear arm should whip into full extension just as the leading foot hits the floor and the point arrives.

7   Keep your head and torso in line with the leading thigh.

8   Keep the sole of the rear foot flat on the floor and prevent it from sliding around.

9   At the conclusion of the lunge, both arms must be fully extended in a straight line level with the floor, shoulders relaxed, trunk profiled and inclined forwards, and head up, facing the adversary.

Enjoy Professional Wrestling   895

The scripted, over-the-top world of professional wrestling has made an indelible mark on pop culture. Those who know what to expect from this mix of sports and theatre cannot only enjoy it, but also feel like they're part of the show.

◎ Steps

1   Arrive early enough to see the dark matches. These are matches put on just for the live fans and are not televised.

2   Make a sign to hold up in the crowd. Writing it about a specific wrestler is good, but be creative.

3   Expect the unexpected. You never know when someone or something will interrupt a wrestling match or a wrestler's speech.

4   Taunt the heels, especially when they're in the ring with a microphone. Shouting "What?" after every phrase they say always works well.

5   Don't leave immediately after the last scheduled match is over. Often the wrestlers have something else planned for the live fans when the TV cameras go off.

6   Support your favourite wrestler by chanting his name during a match, especially if it looks like he's losing.

✹ Tip

Lose yourself in the performances. Professional wrestling is really no different from an action movie. The only difference is it's live.

⚠ Warning

Avoid checking the wrestling insider websites where the results of the matches may be hinted at or given away. It's more fun to watch the matches when you don't know what's going to happen.

Perform an Upper Block in Karate   896

An upper block (*jodan-uke*), also known as a rising block (*age-uke*), will ward off the attack, while setting you up for a counter-attack at the same time.

◎ Steps

1   Face forwards with one leg ahead of the other, keeping your legs shoulder width apart.

2   Turn your fist palm up on your forward arm, and extend it across your stomach, slightly below the waist.

3   Keep your other arm close to your body bent at a 90° angle, with your fist palm up. This position will guard your ribs against a side attack.

4   Raise your blocking arm up above your head in an arc, as if drawing a sword, until it is about a fist's distance above and forward of the top of your head.

✹ Tips

The arm should make an arc across the front of the body as it rises upwards.

Practise timing your blocks with a partner: as your partner swings a practice target downwards, lift and twist your arm to ward off the upper attack.

Practise blocks alternating your blocking arm to gain proficiency on either side.

5 Twist your wrist outwards and upwards at a 45° angle at the moment of impact. The blocking surface is the inside edge of the forearm.

6 Bring the other arm across the stomach during the block, and then withdraw quickly to the hip.

897 | Do Judo

The mental training in Judo teaches the student to back away from an opponent and let him beat himself. Unlike the brute force techniques used in other fighting sports, judo relies on leverage.

◉ Steps

1 Practise being aware of your opponent's strengths and weaknesses. You can continue this training all day as you go through your regular routines. It is a mindset that is taught in judo to be aware so you can take advantage of the knowledge that you gather when the time is right.

2 Obey the rules of the *dojo* and follow the commands of the master in charge, or sensei, when you sign up for classes. There is little or no tolerance for show-offs or people who will not follow the rules in judo class. Your behaviour is taken into consideration when you are vying for a belt in judo.

3 Cross train with other martial-arts techniques such as jui jitsu and kudo-ka to prepare yourself physically for judo practice. Especially if you plan to enter a mixed martial-arts competition, you will need to learn more offensive moves. Mixed martial-arts competitors are most frequently trained in a multitude of disciplines to get the best of each. Aerobic exercises can be very beneficial for athletes who spend a lot of time sparring, since the longer you can hold out, the better training session you can have.

4 Develop a spiritual practice that will make it easier to grasp the spiritual component of judo. Judo is a mind/body experience that relies on the judoka's ability to meditate as well as learn the techniques to throw, strike and take down an opponent. Judo teaches the student to find the *chi* or centre of his being and it is from there that guidance and wisdom come to make the judoka more able to protect himself from attackers.

✹ Tip

While Judo masters stress physical discipline and are as fit as any other athlete, they also demand an intellectual training period, backed up with spiritual practices to define the whole athlete.

⚠ Warning

The martial arts are physically demanding. Consult your physician for advice on whether or not you should pursue this activity.

898 Buy a Bicycle

There are so many different types of bicycles that making a decision can be difficult. The primary consideration is to get a bike that matches your needs and fits properly; after that, it's a matter of test-driving to see what you and your budget like.

Preparation

- Prepare to spend a reasonable amount of money at a good bike shop – this is not the time to be looking for cheap options.

- Test-ride before buying. Look for smooth shifting and good handling.

- Know what the bikes' components are: wheels, tyres, brakes, pedals, derailleurs, attachments etc.

- Understand what benefits are provided by different frame materials. Aluminium alloys are stiff and good for short rides, while chromoly and titanium frames absorb more vibration, making rides more comfortable.

- Choose pedals depending on your need. You can have a basic flat pedal, a basic pedal with a cage around it, and clipless pedals that require special shoes.

Road Bike

- Know that most road bikes are designed for lightweight and aerodynamic efficiency at the expense of comfort.

- Decide on your comfort needs. Don't get talked into a racing-style bike if you don't want one. Instead look for one with higher handlebars to take the strain off your back.

- Change the seat to suit your bottom line. Larger, well-cushioned seats are available.

- Examine wheel and tyre widths. Wider tyres are comfortable and more secure but slower. Racing bike tyres are fast but require more skill and concentration.

- Consider weight. A 15-kg (40-lb) bike is not as pleasant to ride as an 8-kg (22-lb) bike.

- Look for a frame length that allows you to move your hands to different positions.

Mountain Bike

- Mountain bikes are designed to tolerate rough treatment and abuse. They also give comfort and stability over rough terrain.

- Stand over the top tube of a prospective bike and make sure your feet touch the ground comfortably.

- Look for a frame that allows a comfortable, upright riding position. A cramped frame will not allow you to stand up and pedal.

- Decide if you want front suspension, full suspension or neither. Most mountain bikes include front suspension. Full suspension is fun for fast downhills but adds weight, cost and a decrease in pedalling efficiency.

- Do a subjective assessment of how the bike feels. How does the bike climb? Can you stand up and steer easily?

Top Tips

- The more you know about bicycle components, the more likely you will be to spot good deals. Expensive bikes have top-shelf component packages. Cheap bikes have cheap components, and mid-range bikes have a mixture.

- Unless you are a racer, extremely lightweight frames and wheels are not the best choice. They're designed to win races, not to provide stability and durability.

- There's no need to spend a lot on children's bicycles because they're quickly outgrown. Spend enough to get important safety features like good brakes.

- You can replace handlebars with a shape that suits your grip comfort needs and riding style.

reference

899 | Use Clipless Pedals

Clipless pedals allow you to get more power in every rotation. They may feel awkward at first, but they will make you a more efficient cyclist in the long run.

⊙ Steps

1. Put on your cleated shoes.

2. Spin one pedal to the bottom of the pedal rotation nearest the ground.

3. Slip the front of the shoe's cleat into the matching slot on the pedal.

4. Push down on the back of the pedal until the cleat snaps into place, which will be indicated by a loud click. This positioning can be tricky until you've had a certain amount of practice.

5. Push off and begin pedalling.

6. Push the other pedal to the bottom of the pedal stroke and repeat Steps 3 and 4 with your other foot when you have picked up enough speed to coast for a few yards.

7. Push one heel away from the bike and twist your foot out of the cleat to stop.

8. Some pedal clips can be adjusted using a screw in the back or middle of the pedal to change the amount of play your foot has to move laterally while still locked in the pedal. It also makes it easier to clip in when you're learning.

✳ Tip

Start learning in a big field or on a lawn if one's available to you – you and your bike will appreciate the soft landings.

⚠ Warning

It's almost a given that the first time you forget to twist your foot out of the pedal and fall over will be either at a busy crossroads or in front of a group of veteran cyclists. Try to ease the pain by realising just about everyone else has experienced it, too.

900 | Replace a Bike Chain

Attacked by a tree? Jumped by a rock? Or is that poor bike chain simply rusted and sad? There are plenty of ways a bike chain can jump off the pulley and keep you from using your bike.

⊙ Steps

Remove the Old Chain

1. Lean your bike on a wall or place in a repair stand.

2. Use a link-removal tool to place the chain in the channel section opposite the small crank.

3. Position the chain in the tool so that the tool's pin matches up with a pin in one of the chain's links.

4. Turn the tool's small screw crank so that it begins to push out the pin in the chain.

5. Push out the pin, unscrew the tool and take the chain out of the channel. The chain should separate.

6. Unthread the chain from the gears and set aside.

✳ Tips

Shifting into the smallest rear cog before starting gives you more slack chain to work with.

Some chains have "master" links that can be opened by hand without a link-removal tool.

If the chain slaps the frame while you're riding, or appears to sag, it's too long. Remove one link with the tool.

Dry lubricants, paraffin and some powdered chain treatments may have to be applied prior to installing the chain.

Install the New Chain

1. Thread the new chain through the gears. Be sure to run it the proper way through the derailleur, through the mechanism that shifts the front gears, around the rear of the bottom pulley and over the front of the top pulley.

2. Thread the other end of the chain through the front derailleur and over the front sprockets. (The front sprockets are the front gears, near the pedals.) The chain should pass through the "cage" of the front derailleur – the rectangular metal section that hangs over the front sprockets.

3. When the chain is threaded over the front and back gears, place the two ends together in the link-removal tool.

4. The new chain should have a pin already pushed partway out. If it does not, push one end of the new chain in the link tool and press the pin most of the way out.

5. Slip the links together, flip the tool over, and turn the tool's crank to press the pin back in. Turn eight to 10 times, or until the pin seals the links together and is flush on either side of the chain. The pin should not stick out on either side.

6. Lubricate the new chain.

Watch a Formula 1 Race   901

Formula 1 is truly a World Championship event, featuring races at 17 different circuits all over the globe. The season starts in Australia and ends in Abu Dhabi with stops in Bahrain, Monaco, Hungary, the UK and other locales in between.

⊙ Steps

✻ Tip
There's nothing like watching a Grand Prix live, but you can make an event of it from the comfort of your own living room.

The Race

1. Familiarise yourself with the schedule. Some races are broadcast live in the early morning hours because of time-zone differences. Many times, a race will be re-broadcast in the afternoon. Plan your race-day viewing ahead of time.

2. Don't just watch the race! Each race is preceded by a practice session and a qualifying session. Race position is determined during qualifying. Sometimes a pilot is penalised for making a mistake or for an unsanctioned modification to their car during qualifying, resulting in a starting position at the back of the grid.

3. Learn the circuit. Each race circuit presents its own challenges. Sometimes the challenge is racing on a city street! Sometimes a quick turn has to be taken at the start of the race or at the end of a long straight.

4. Check the weather. The temperature of the race track and the possibility of rain will affect the choice of tyre. Each team arrives with a hard and a soft compound set of tyres to run based on weather conditions.

5. Follow the race storylines. Televised races feature storylines about something relevant to the race. Will a certain pilot make a comeback? Will a particular car have a bad day? Will a team run two different strategies for each car?

6   Watch the celebration and press conference after the race. The press conference is an informative way to learn about the effort it took to win a race or to finish in the top three.

The Pilots

1   Know where a pilot stands in the points. A race winner is awarded 10 points. Second place is awarded 8 points. A pilot leading in the points might not race aggressively to reduce the chances of an accident. Some teams and pilots race all season in the hopes of scoring a point when winning isn't within reach.

2   Know something about the pilot's history. Jensen Button is considered a really great F1 pilot, but he did not win a race until after his 114th start. Knowing whether a pilot is defending a victory from the previous year lends to the excitement.

3   Watch for errors. If the pilot doesn't make any errors it doesn't mean the team or another pilot won't make one that could take the lead pilot out of the race.

4   Look for the pilots off-track. Mostly, these pilots are unknown outside the world of F1, but many of them have paid endorsements. Michael Schumacher was the world's highest-paid athlete for five years in a row prior to his retirement, earning more than well-known athletes like Tiger Woods.

The Cars

1   Turn up the volume! The start of an F1 race is unlike anything in the world. Twenty cars accelerating from 0 to 100 mph in three seconds is an incredible sight to see and even more thrilling to hear!

2   Know something about the technical sophistication of the cars. The cars are powered by V8 engines running special fuel to produce 750 horse-power. The combined weight of the car and pilot is less than 680 kg (1,500 lb). But there's more to it than just horsepower. Notice when a pilot has an accident, he removes the steering wheel – the steering wheel in an F1 car costs £75,000 and has more computing power than a desktop computer. It is the inspiration for normal cars that feature "pad-dle shifting" on the steering wheel.

3   Know where the manufacturer stands in the points total. F1 features two championships, one for the pilots and one for the manufacturers. The two teams with the best records each spend £300 million a year and these two teams aren't the sport's biggest spenders.

4   Watch the fans. Formula 1 fans are some of the most colourful in the world. The grandstands are usually a sea of Ferrari red. Other manufac-turer's have their fans, too, including those who root for the underdog.

5   Win the lottery and attend the historic F1 race at Monte Carlo in the Principality of Monaco. No race speaks more to the essence of the sport, which is sophisticated, high-tech glamour rather than rough-and-tumble racing.

Race an Indy Car 902

Indy cars require years of experience to fully master because of their potential for incredible speeds and relative lack of safety features.

✴ Tip

In order to participate in an Indy Car driving school, you will need to be at least 18 years of age and possess a valid driving licence.

◉ Steps

1 Consider gaining some racing experience with karts, midget racers or even stock cars before attempting to learn how to drive an Indy car. Most professional racers agree that this is an excellent way to familiarise yourself with how to manoeuvre a vehicle on a racetrack, learning how to interact with other drivers as well.

2 Take a ride in an Indy car to determine how comfortable you feel dealing with the pressure of the g-forces you will experience. Many driving and racing schools offer programmes in which you can ride as a passenger in specially modified cars used in the Indy 500 or Formula 1 racing.

3 Enrol in a driving school that will teach you how to race an Indy car. Many of these schools last just one day, allowing you to take several laps around a closed course after you have passed the course. In addition, many of these schools are owned or sponsored by professional drivers who will be able to give you tips and insight into how to become a better driver.

4 Visit a track on which Indy cars are raced, and observe as much as possible. Talk to the drivers about the steps they took to become professional racing drivers. Speak with crew members, as they can also give you plenty of insight into the world of Indy racing.

5 Decide whether you want to pursue a career in racing Indy cars. For many people, this path takes years of hard work and experience, especially considering the high cost of these cars. You will have to enrol in a driving school, and you may need to perform volunteer work in the racing field in order to develop the contacts you will need to become a professional Indy-car racer.

Teach a Child to Swim 903

A simple lesson plan, combined with patience and support, is the right approach to teaching a child how to swim.

◉ Steps

1 Hold the child beneath the armpits and walk them around in the water to develop a feeling of comfort in an aquatic environment. Smile and talk to demonstrate that this new place is fun and interesting.

2 Get the child to kick their legs. Have them hold on to the side of the pool so you can guide their legs. Then do it with your hands beneath their armpits to develop the feeling of motion.

3 Blow bubbles in the water with the child as they kick to get them used to putting their face in the water. Gradually begin dunking them down to practise holding their breath. Accompany the child underwater and play underwater games to get them to open their eyes.

✴ Tips

Take your time with each step. The first day, only do the first step. The second day, do the first step again and then add the second step. Start each new lesson with a review of the last lessons.

Play lots of games to make it fun. Take it slow. If a child learns to enjoy the water, swimming skills will develop naturally.

4 Support the child around their waist or chest and begin having them stroke with their arms. Demonstrate the motion yourself, and then guide the child's arms. Then let them do it on their own while you support them in the water. Have them keep kicking.

5 Have the child swim a short distance from the wall to you. Begin at a very short distance, so that they can almost jump the span at first. Gradually increase the distance.

6 Demonstrate to the child how to breathe by lifting or turning their head as the distance from you to them gets far enough to necessitate this.

7 Instruct the child to jump into the pool from the side with you there to catch them at first, and then increase the distance so that they must jump and swim.

⚠ Warning

Never leave a child unattended near or in a pool. Never take your eyes off a child near or in a pool. While confidence in a child is the best teacher, it can also be the biggest danger.

904 | Back Pike Dive from a Springboard

The back pike is an excellent first back dive for an intermediate springboard diver.

◉ Steps

1 Stand at attention at the starting position on the diving board, walk to the end and turn around, facing your back to the pool.

2 Extend your arms straight forwards from the shoulders, and stand on the balls of your feet on the end of the board with your heels hanging over. Attain this position by backing one foot over the edge, and then the other. Your feet should be parallel, and 2.5–5 cm (1–2 in) apart.

3 Lower your arms to your sides, take a moment to concentrate and prepare for your dive.

4 Raise your arms to a point slightly above your head while pushing down with your toes. This should slightly depress the springboard and give you a bit of upward lift.

5 Drop your arms suddenly back down to your sides while bending your knees. This action will give a deep bend to the springboard, preparing to propel you into the air.

6 Swing your arms suddenly upwards again and straighten your knees, jumping up and out. Swing your arms up in front of your face to give you the extra momentum backwards as they swing out over your head.

7 Lift your legs up into the air so that they point straight up, perpendicular to the water. Start doing this as soon as your feet leave the springboard.

8 Bend at the waist and reach with your arms to touch your toes with your fingertips. This is the pike position, inverted. Your rear end should be the lowest point of your body.

9 Keep your legs extended upwards and straighten your body out again, pointing your head down towards the water.

10 Bring your arms back to an extended position over your head by raising them to the sides, lateral to your body and not in front.

11 Enter the water with your body completely vertical and your hands touching the water first.

✳ Tips

Keep your arms and legs straight while in the pike position for the best-looking form.

Make sure you bring your arms up to the extended position in front of you on the way up, and to the sides on the way down. Bringing your arms up in front on the way down will cause your legs to drop and your lower back to arch. If this occurs you will not enter the water vertically.

If your legs are not coming into the pike position fast enough to give you the proper rotation at the peak of your dive, hold the pike position until your legs reach the proper vertical position, and then open.

⚠ Warnings

Make sure you project backwards as well as up when you leave the springboard, so that you don't crash into it on your way down.

Do not attempt backward dives unsupervised for the first time. Only attempt this dive with careful preparation and instruction.

Launch a Windsurf Board 905

This is the most basic technique you'll need to learn to begin windsurfing from the beach.

⊙ Steps

1 Bring your board and rig to the water's edge and prepare for action by attaching the mast to the board, inserting the dagger-board and putting on your life jacket.

2 Carry the board and rig into the water as a single unit. If you are absolutely unable to carry it by yourself, ask someone for help. If you are on soft sand, you can hold the nose of the board and the mast and drag the board into the water.

3 Enter the water knee deep with the board floating completely in the water and the sail on the leeward (downwind) side of the board.

4 Position yourself adjacent to the board on the windward (upwind) side and hoist the rig up by the up-haul line. Keep the clew facing leeward.

5 Grab the boom with both hands.

6 Place your back foot on to the windsurf board and follow it with your other foot.

7 Sheet in and you should sail immediately.

✽ Tip

Always handle your rig with the mast on the windward side.

⚠ Warnings

Always wear a life jacket when windsurfing.

Learn to windsurf when the conditions are mild.

Scull 906

Sculling is one of the most physically and mentally exhausting sports. Yet despite its incredibly taxing nature, there are very few sports that rival the rewards that sculling has to offer.

⊙ Steps

1 Extend your legs, lean back 10–20° and pull the oar handles towards your chest so that the handles are under your pectoral muscles and above your rib cage. Neither your hands nor the oar handles should really touch your body, since this can cause agitation and bruising. Not many people can configure the boat perfectly on their first row so keep practising. This position is technically called "the finish" because it is where you will finish your stroke. However, since rowing is a cyclical activity, it is also the beginning.

2 Feather the oar blade (if you haven't done so already). To feather a blade means to keep it parallel to the water.

3 Push your hands away from your body so that your arms are fully extended. This is the first step of "the recovery".

4 Lean your body forwards so that it is about 20–30° from being perpendicular with the water. This is the second step of "the recovery."

5 Slowly pull yourself up the slide by compressing your legs. This, along with the next step are the last parts of "the recovery".

✽ Tips

You can't row well until you can row well tired.

The boat will "set itself up", meaning that it will stay stable and won't rock too much if you make exactly the same motions with each oar at the same time. Speed and power also help to set the boat up.

⚠ Warning

Especially as a novice rower, it is incredibly important to row with a buddy. Capsizing can be very dangerous, but by having a buddy to help you out, you can improve safety immensely.

6   Square the blade (make it perpendicular to the water) just about when your hands pass over your knees. Squaring up early like this is a more advanced technique, but learning it early in your rowing career will give you a huge leg-up later. Used effectively it ensures maximum efficiency with every stroke by keeping the blade in the water longer during the drive.

7   Insert the blade into the water by lifting your hands. This is called "the catch".

8   Press first with your legs, then when your legs are fully extended, lean back to that starting position before pulling your hands to your chest again.

9   Repeat this motion over and over again to fly across the water.

---

907 | Ski Powder

Use the right technique and you'll be floating over the newly laid snow instead of sinking down to your ears in the stuff.

⊙ Steps

1   Start in a balanced stance – place your feet shoulder width apart while slightly flexing your ankles, knees and hips down towards the snow.

2   Keep your weight evenly distributed over the centre of both skis by leaning slightly forwards into your boots and placing your hips directly above the centre of your boots.

3   Initiate a turn by steering both feet in the direction you want to turn. Keep in mind that your lower body is flexing down towards the skis, weighting your skis down into the snow through the turn.

4   Plant your downhill pole in front of your body and down the hill. Your pole now becomes a target for you to turn around.

5   Keep your upper body facing downhill while skiing. Your upper body will remain stable while your lower body rotates independently with each turn.

6   Take weight off your skis at the end of the turn by pulling your ankles, knees and hips up. This movement will actually lift your skis to the top of the snow and make the next turn easier to perform.

7   Experiment with the length of turns – determine whether a long, medium or short turn performs best in the snow you're skiing.

8   String a number of turns together.

✳ Tips

Weighting and unweighting your skis is the key in powder. This is performed by flexing and extending your lower body, and is the movement that enables a skier to float through powder.

A common misconception is that you should lean back when skiing in powder. This will tire your legs especially quickly and will also make turning more difficult.

⚠ Warning

Skiing is a physically demanding sport that could result in serious injury. We recommend that you seek proper training and equipment before attempting this activity.

Snowboard a Halfpipe

Drop into the snowboard halfpipe for the first time to open up a whole new realm of snowboarding.

Steps

1 Learn to use both your edges effectively on the slopes. Learn 180s, 360s, jump airs and riding fakies. Until you have these skills down, you're not ready to ride the halfpipe.

2 Realise that you are not going to get your picture in the magazines on your first run. Concentrate only on the fundamentals on your first day of halfpipe riding. Don't worry about what you've seen and what everyone else is doing.

3 Wait for the halfpipe to be clear of other riders and for it to be your turn.

4 Side slide to the top of the halfpipe and look down. Plan your run, and do it realistically, thinking about turns and fakies.

5 Take a deep breath to calm yourself, and then enter the halfpipe, traversing across the flats towards the transition.

6 Ride a few feet up the transition, turn your head around to face the opposite direction and then ride down backwards. Absorb the transitions by flexing your knees.

7 Traverse the flats again, riding on your uphill rail and slightly downhill to keep up your speed.

8 Ride up the next wall fakie, and ride down forwards.

9 Approach the next transition. Roll from one edge to the other as you reach your high point on the wall. Do a small hop to take pressure off your board and to help you through the turn.

10 Continue down the halfpipe, doing fakies and turns.

Tips

Try to get higher and higher on the transition each turn.

If you fall, ride down the centre of the pipe to the end. Do not try to continue riding the halfpipe.

Don't let the other halfpipe riders intimidate you. Everyone was a beginner once, and you have just as much right to your turn as anyone else.

Warning

Make sure you're ready to snowboard in the halfpipe before you go there. Don't get overexcited by everything you see in magazines and videos. Learning the fundamentals will get you a lot further than big airs will.

Figure Skate

Figure skating is a fun way to stay in shape, especially during the winter. Here are some tips and techniques to help you learn to figure skate.

Steps

1 Warm up first. If you have never figure skated before, your muscles may not be prepared for the physical exertion that figure skating requires. Avoid injury by warming up your muscles first so that they are limber and ready to go. Do some toe touches, leg extensions and full body stretches to get you warmed up to figure skate.

2 Bend your knees. Trying to figure skate with your legs straight and rigid will make you feel stiff and off balance, which will be especially bad while you are still trying to get used to the extra weight of the skates on your feet. Keep your legs relaxed and bent slightly at the knees. This will give you more control over your feet and lower your centre of gravity closer to the ice.

Tip

Figure skates can be found at most sports shops, but you may get better deals and more choice using specialist stores online.

3   Push off and to the side. Once your legs are slightly bent, push off with your feet in a forward motion and glide your feet in an arc to the outside. This will allow your skate blade to stay completely on the ice and propel you forwards smoothly while balancing your weight on the length of the skate blade.

4   Use your toe picks. Toe picks are the metal teeth on the front end of a figure skate blade that are used for deceleration and braking. If you need to stop on your skates, move the front of your foot down until the picks grab the ice and slow you to a stop. Do not jam the picks down suddenly as your momentum could propel you over your feet and cause you to fall. If the skates you are wearing do not have toe picks on the front, they are actually ice-hockey skates instead of figure skates and require an entirely different way of stopping.

5   Get up and try again. If you're just learning to skate, you're probably going to fall a few times. Don't be discouraged by this. Learning to figure skate well takes time and practice, as well a few bumps and bruises, so you won't be a pro straight away. Remember that even Olympic champions have to start somewhere. So get up, dust yourself off and go for another lap around the rink.

910 | Kite Surf

Kite surfing, or kite boarding, is an exhilarating sport in which you can reach crazy speeds and insane heights.

◎ Steps

1   Newcomers to kite surfing should seek lessons before going out on their own. Kite surfing is a hazardous sport and requires a lot of specific knowledge and tactics. It's not a sport that you want to buy the equipment and try out on your own. Professional, hands-on instruction is the way to go.

2   If there are no kite-surfing schools or organisations in your area where you can learn, consider taking a holiday. Many beaches, lakes and reservoirs also offer kite surfing and lessons.

3   If you want to continue kite surfing after gaining some background and knowledge from your lesson(s) you will need equipment. Try contacting a local club. You should be able to meet up with some members and borrow equipment. You'll also be able to get some first-hand advice and discuss your interest in the sport with some dedicated enthusiasts. You can then determine if it's a sport that you'd like to invest in.

4   In general, you will need kites, a harness, bar to hold, lines and a board. Boards can include bindings to brace your feet, if you'd prefer to be strapped in. Determine the best type of kite and board for where you live. Although you'll want to get a number of kites for different wind conditions, it makes sense to start with the most commonly used size and type.

5   Your lesson and continued experience will give you a background in judging winds and using different types of kites, depending on wind speed and direction. When going out on your own, look for appropriate wind and weather conditions and be ready to get out there to take

⚠ Warnings

Pay careful attention to weather conditions both before going out and while kite surfing. Change in weather can be hazardous.

Be sure to have life jacket on at all times, in case you end up in the water far from land.

advantage. Listen closely to local weather forecasts and check out weather maps on the Internet.

6   Once you've had your lessons and acquired the right equipment, it's all about practice. Like any sport, kite surfing demands practice to become better. It's a good idea to go out with other kite surfers so you can practise together and get an idea of what you can do to improve. As you progress through the basics, you can begin to learn tricks and more advanced moves.

7   One great thing about kiting is that there are many ways to branch into new areas of the sport. With your knowledge of kites, you can try snow kiting (using a snowboard or skis), land-based kite boarding and even kite buggying.

Go Skydiving   911

You know what they say about skydivers, right? There are old skydivers and bold skydivers, but there are no old, bold skydivers. Picking a reliable instructor is therefore paramount.

⊙ **Steps**

 Tip

Ask about options for photographing or videotaping your jump. Some skydiving operations provide this service

1   Assemble a group to go with you. You will undoubtedly want witnesses to your bravery.

2   Call the skydiving operations in your area and interview them. You want to establish that they are certified by an independent oversight agency, that they will take the time to answer your questions and that they present a professional demeanour.

3   Verify their safety records. Ask if they have had any accidents. Call their certification agency to check.

4   Decide on a type of jump. Doing a jump by yourself (a solo jump) requires that you complete an instruction course, then jump using a static line. This line automatically opens your chute as you exit the plane, eliminating free fall. A tandem jump requires less instruction and allows you to experience a free fall since you are strapped to an instructor who does all the work, pulls the chute and controls the jump.

5   Make certain that you understand every element of the instruction. Do not allow yourself to be rushed through it. If the instructor is not answering your questions to a degree that makes you feel secure and confident, do not proceed.

6   Enrol in a certification course if you wish to pursue skydiving further. These instructor-led, multi-jump courses take several weeks or months and can be costly. But as a certified skydiver, you'll be allowed to perform jumps at will.

912 | Play Ultimate

The guidelines for this fast-paced combination of Frisbee, rugby and basketball have been adapted from the Ultimate Players Association's official rules.

Steps

1   Divide players into two teams of seven players each. Adjust the team size as needed or, for larger teams, substitute players during the game after a score.

2   Flip a disc (not a coin) to decide which team will begin as defence and which will begin as offence.

3   Line up on opposite sides of the field. The defence begins by throwing the disc to the offence.

4   Throw the disc (in any direction) to a team mate if you're on the offence, but know that it's illegal to run with it. When another player catches it, he or she must throw it to a team mate within 10 seconds.

5   Understand that one point is scored when an offensive player catches the disc in the end zone being guarded by the defence.

6   Give control of the disc to the defence if a thrower fails to complete a pass (waits more than 10 seconds, drops the disc, throws it out of bounds or throws an interception).

7   Keep in mind that ultimate is a non-contact sport. If contact occurs, a foul is called.

8   Understand that if the foul results in a turnover (change of disc possession from one team to another), play resumes as if the turnover hadn't taken place.

9   Repeat the play if the player who committed the foul (the person who initiated contact) disagrees with the call.

10 Know that the winning team is the one with the highest score at the end of two 24-minute halves. Games may also be played to a set number of points agreed on before the start of play.

✳ Tips

The 10-second countdown is given verbally by the defensive player guarding the thrower.

A regulation ultimate field is 70 x 40 yd, with a 25-yd end zone at either end (making the total playing area 120 x 40 yd).

913 | Street Luge

Street luges have been clocked moving faster than 130 km/h (80 mph), with the rider lying mere centimetres from the pavement.

Steps

1   Attend a street-luge event, such as the X Games, and see what it's all about. Talk with the riders and verify that they're not out of their minds.

2   Research what it takes to build a street luge, draw up your plan and gather your materials.

3   Build your custom street luge. Realise that this is a major aspect of the sport. The more research and knowledge you can pour into your custom luge, the better your luge experience will be.

✳ Tips

Men and women compete equally in the luge.

Safety should always come first – you really can die doing this.

Speed is the product of technical knowledge and fine-tuning your equipment.

How to Do More of *(Just About)* **Everything**

4 Gather your safety gear and bless it according to whatever religion you subscribe to.

5 Find other riders to take you out for your first runs, to show you the ropes and the courses to choose.

6 Practise regularly and keep your eyes open for events to enter.

7 Travel to and enter a competition. This is more fun if you do it with other riders.

8 Have fun meeting and riding with the other street-luge lunatics. Scout out other luges and riders, and learn from their equipment and experiences. Apply that knowledge to your luge and luge technique.

9 Be kind and helpful to new luge riders now that you are a ripper. Remember those guys who helped you get started.

⚠ **Warning**

Street luge is extrememly dangerous. Always wear proper protection when riding.

Survive When Competitive Eating   914

Competitive eating is not a sport for the faint of heart. It is physically taxing, yes, but also requires great mental focus, strategy and dexterity.

⊙ **Steps**

1 Focus your mind. This ability is a common attribute among the champions in competitive eating. You need to be completely in the moment and aware that you are asking your body to do something unusual in a very short amount of time.

2 Learn to suppress the gag reflex as you fill up. Your body will want you to quit and you will have to learn to overcome your body's natural signals.

3 Plan your strategy before the event. Know what bite sizes you can handle and how much soaking or smashing a food item might need before stuffing.

4 Burp to make more room, but be careful. You only want the air to come out, not the subject of the race.

5 Exercise regularly in between events. Taking in a large number of calories quickly does not change the fact that you have to burn more or an equal amount to what you consume. The most successful competitive eaters are not always the large ones. Some theorise that the more fat you have in the middle, the harder it is to put away large amounts of food in a short amount of time.

6 Limit the number of events to give yourself time to recover. Space out your participation in the events to allow the excess food to completely clear out. The salt alone in some of the food categories begs for much water and detoxification.

7 Explore different food type competitions as you build your stamina in the sport. This will give you a better idea of your capabilities and what makes sense for you to focus on.

⚠ **Warning**

Do not train at home. Sanctioned events with medical personnel on hand are the only way to go.

915 | Increase Stamina

Increasing your stamina is about more than just building muscle or increasing strength. It is about the energy produced from activity.

Steps

1 Set some goals for yourself. Do you want to increase your energy, build muscle or increase your strength and endurance?

2 Develop a training plan that is reasonable and achievable. To increase your stamina, you have to start small and gradually move up to the level you desire.

3 Begin your plan with walking. Walking can improve the efficiency of your heart and lungs, increase your energy level, strengthen the muscles in your legs and help promote a good night's rest.

4 Build on your walking by running if this is something you want to do. Some people can't tolerate running as it is harder on your knees and joints than walking.

5 Try riding a bicycle. It is important to find a form of exercise that you enjoy. If you enjoy what you are doing, you increase your chances of success and building on that success.

6 Give swimming a chance – it's great form of exercise that may surprise you. It is a low-impact form of exercise that tones your entire body and provides a great cardiovascular workout.

7 Push yourself past your limits. Once you begin an activity, you will begin to notice it becomes easier and you feel better both mentally and physically. This is an important step in increasing your stamina.

8 Walk longer distances, walk at a more brisk pace, run or ride your bike a mile further than last week, swim more laps or increase the weight and/or reps in a strength building workout. Whatever your task, continue to build on it. You will see and feel the results.

✳ Tips

Write down your goals and your plan. Then write down your improvements as you go along so you can visualise the changes you have made.

Share your plan with a partner that shares your goals. Having an accountability partner will give you both motivation, encouragement and support.

⚠ Warnings

You should be in overall good health when beginning an exercise routine or strength-building workout.

Sometimes things get worse before they get better, but push through this phase. If you are not used to activity, you may experience soreness and exhaustion as you condition your body.

916 | Weight Train at Home

One of the best things about weight training is that you really don't need an expensive gym membership or loads of fancy equipment to get results.

Steps

1 Clear out a workout space in your home. Pay special attention to relocating things you could stumble over.

2 Warm up with stretching and a brief cardiovascular workout of around five minutes.

3 Lie on your stomach on the floor. Place your hands a few centimetres wider than your shoulders. Perform a press-up using only one arm, even if you have to kneel to do so. Lifting your body with only one arm focuses the weight training on one muscle group.

✳ Tip

Perform your weight training slowly. Good form requires you to keep control of the weight on both the lift and the descent of each repetition.

⚠ Warning

Weight training using only resistance of your body will take longer to produce results.

4 Switch to the other arm and repeat the process. Add more reps (number of press-ups in one sitting) when you no longer reach muscle exhaustion.

5 Continue with that arm until you cannot push yourself up anymore.

6 Move on to lunges. Stand with one hand lightly resting on a chair for balance. Step forwards with one foot while slightly lowering your torso. Your forward knee should be above your foot. Your other knee should be at a 90° angle when performed correctly.

7 Continue your lunges by stepping forwards with the other foot. Keep going, alternating sides, until you have performed about 15 repetitions. You can also lunge walking forwards, rather than remaining in one place.

8 Work in some calf raises. Stand on the floor and hold a chair for balance if necessary. Slowly raise up on your toes. Then lower your heels back down almost to the floor. Remember to keep your calf taut through both the upwards and downwards motion. Repeat for 15 to 20 reps.

9 Train your thighs and firm your behind with squats. Stand with feet shoulder width apart. Keep your abdominal (stomach) muscles taut throughout. Slowly lower your torso as if you were sitting down, keeping your head up. Slowly return to almost standing and repeat.

Build Muscle 917

Whether you are already fit or if you are looking to start from scratch, weight training and healthy supplements can help you bulk up and build muscle.

⊙ **Steps**

1 Create a schedule that works for you. You have to keep to your weight-training schedule and be prudent in your food and supplement choices. When you become committed to bulking up, you have to take it seriously. If you train too much, you might burn yourself out and if you don't train enough, you might not get the results you are looking for.

2 Use a time limit. Many people think that if they work out for longer periods of time, they will be able to increase their muscle mass at a quicker rate. This is not true. Shorter training periods done effectively are much more beneficial in muscle-mass increase.

3 Use specific muscle exercises to increase muscle mass. Free weights are great for building muscle mass and can be effective because you use a variety of different angles.

4 Isolate muscle groups. Work on a specific area each time to prevent you from having any muscle injuries. It is good to write out a schedule of what muscles you will target each time you work out and keep to it.

5 Limit cardiovascular exercises. Cardio will keep burning off weight that you are trying to build. While cardio is good for the heart and blood flow, it doesn't really help if you want to bulk up and gain muscle.

6 Invest in muscle-building and weight-gain supplements. Creatine, whey, arginine and glutamine are just a few products you can use while building muscle mass.

⚠ Warning

Never take drugs such as steroids to help build muscle unless you have sought advice from a doctor.

918 Do a Proper Press-Up

Press-ups aren't just for army trainees; they are a great upper body, low-cost exercise. If you're just looking to tone up or gain strength but not too much mass, press-ups are a great exercise.

Steps

1   Lie chest-down with your hands at shoulder level, palms flat on the floor and slightly more than shoulder-width apart, your feet together and parallel to each other.

2   Look forwards rather than down at the floor. The first contact you make with the floor with any part of the face should be your chin, not your nose.

3   Keep your legs straight and your toes tucked under your feet.

4   Straighten your arms as you push your body up off the floor. Keep your palms fixed at the same position and keep your body straight. Try not to bend or arch your upper or lower back as you push up.

5   Exhale as your arms straighten out.

6   Pause for a moment.

7   Lower your body slowly towards the floor. Bend your arms and keep your palms in a fixed position. Keep your body straight and feet together.

8   Lower your body until your chest touches the floor. Try not to bend your back while lowering. Keep your knees off the floor, and inhale as you bend your arms.

9   Pause for a moment. Begin straightening your arms for a second push-up. Exhale as you raise your body.

10 For an easier exercise, lower your knees so that they rest on the floor. Keeping your back straight and your toes tucked under your feet, proceed with the exercise normally. This decreases the amount of pressure placed on your arms.

✻ Tip

For easier press-ups, have an exercise partner place a closed fist underneath your chest. As you lower your body, touch your chest to the fist, pause, then raise your body. This is a little easier than touching your chest to the floor.

919 Do Interval Training

To tap into a new, higher level of fitness and fat burning, try an interval workout. The combination of aerobic and anaerobic training will give a real boost to your health and make the rest of your workouts seem easier.

Steps

1   Begin with five to seven minutes of low-intensity work in your exercise mode. For example, walk or jog lightly to start.

2   Stretch the major muscle groups, paying particular attention to the lower body.

3   Exercise at a higher intensity for 10 minutes. Let your body continue to warm up and get ready for the workout to come.

✻ Tips

Always use the first 30 seconds of the aerobic portion to recover and literally catch your breath.

Think of the cycles as going up and down a mountain – as they ascend, it's hard and there's not much oxygen at the top, then the descent gets easier.

4 Start cycle one. Exercise for three minutes at a pace you could maintain for the entire workout. Then for one minute push yourself hard, with a short burst of activity that you couldn't do for longer than a minute.

5 Recover for 30 seconds or longer, but keep moving, and let your breath return to a normal workout level.

6 Understand that the cycle is three minutes aerobic/recovery and one minute anaerobic (3-to-1).

7 Complete eight cycles, the first four becoming progressively harder, with the hardest cycles being four and five, then decrease the intensity with cycles six, seven and eight.

8 Keep moving for another three to four minutes or until you feel your heart rate coming down.

9 Stretch the major muscles again, this time more deeply and for 20 to 30 seconds.

Notice that your heart rate is going way up and then way down; it should peak and valley quite a bit.

Plan to interval train only once or twice a week.

Allow for 48 hours of recovery between each session. It's okay to exercise during the 48 hours, but avoid strenuous exercise and anything high-impact.

Drink lots of water.

Get the Most Out of Your Spin Class   920

If you think biking indoors is boring, you haven't been to a good spin class. The instructor leads the exercises and keeps the focus, but you decide how hard to push.

⊙ Steps

1 Go regularly. Find a class that fits your schedule and be there once or twice every week. Don't let yourself off the hook just because the gym feels far away.

2 If you don't like one instructor, keep trying until you find one you do like.

3 Use your instructor as a resource. Tell her about your goals and don't be shy requesting workouts or even music.

4 Wear cycling shoes. Clipping into the pedals gives you more control, makes you more efficient, and works your hamstrings in addition to your quads. It will help your outdoor riding.

5 Stay hydrated. Spin classes tend to be intense so keep a water bottle within arms' reach and drink often.

6 Pace yourself. Spending all your juice on the first simulated hill climb means you'll struggle the rest of the class. A heart-rate monitor helps you keep your effort in the right range.

7 Imagine that you're really out there climbing that hill or sprinting to the finish. You'll feel more motivated and have more fun.

8 Adjust your bike's resistance knob slowly at first to feel how sensitive it is. Since every bike's resistance knob is different, one turn might be plenty on one bike, but another will take three.

✳ Tip

Ease into your first workouts and remember that some drills (especially with balance) are more challenging than they look.

⚠ Warnings

Be sure to set up your bike (seat and handlebar position) correctly to avoid injury.

Don't stop pedalling suddenly. Your feet will keep going and you might too.

921 | Do Pilates

Pilates relies on the concepts of concentration, precision and control. The dance world has been practising pilates for decades.

⊙ Steps

1   Keep your spine in what is known as a neutral position, in between flattened and arched, as you do pilates. When your spine moves out of a neutral position, you are at a greater risk of developing back problems, getting thrown off balance and straining your muscles.

2   Make an effort to keep your head aligned with your spine when you do pilates. It may help you to envision your head as part of your neck and spine. This may prevent you from keeping your head curled under your body, unless the exercise you're doing calls for your spine to be curved.

3   Focus the majority of your exercises on what is known as the "powerhouse". The powerhouse is your group of core abdominal muscles. By targeting the powerhouse, you may be able to increase your energy levels and your overall strength.

4   Target your core abdominal muscles by practising simple pilates floor exercises, such as rolling up. You can do this exercise by slowly peeling your spine off the floor while maintaining balanced breathing and pulling your abdominal muscles tightly inwards.

5   Tone muscles all over your body by getting a piece of pilates equipment called a reformer. The reformer uses heavy resistance to help you tone, strengthen and lengthen your muscles without making you appear bulky.

6   Improve your posture by using a pilates ball or barrel. These deceptively simple pieces of equipment help you target muscles deep within your back to correct poor posture. In addition, they may even help you increase your balance and make you more agile.

7   Give yourself a challenge when you've moved past the basics by lowering your legs during your exercises. Whether you're doing mat exercises or using a machine, the lower your legs are, the harder your powerhouse will have to work to keep them balanced.

✳ Tip

Always use a mat when you do pilates on the floor to properly cushion your spine.

⚠ Warnings

Don't use a yoga mat in place of a true pilates mat. Yoga mats tend to be much thinner and may not provide the support you need.

Although pilates appears to be a less strenuous form of exercise, don't think you can ignore a proper warm-up. This could cause you to pull a muscle and may put you at greater risk of a serious injury.

922 | Assume the Lotus Pose in Yoga

The lotus pose, or *Padmasana* in Sanskrit, is a restful yet energising pose that's ideal for meditation.

⊙ Steps

1   Sit on the floor with crossed legs, bending both legs and crossing the left shin over the right.

2   Place your fingertips on the floor near your hips and use your fingers to help you stretch your trunk upwards.

3   Pick up your left foot and place it on top of your right thigh. Press the outer edge of your left foot against the crease of your right hip.

✳ Tip

Placing your hands on your knees with your palms facing upward is energising, but sitting with your palms facing down helps you ground yourself.

4   Pick up your right foot and place it on top of your left thigh, pressing the outer edge of your right foot against the crease of your left hip.

5   Settle your feet as close as possible to your groin, moving your knees closer together.

6   Stretch your torso upwards, keeping your shoulders down and back.

7   Place your hands on your knees with your palms facing upwards.

8   Practise until you can hold the pose comfortably for several minutes.

⚠ Warning

To avoid injury, you should always listen to your body when doing a yoga pose, and not push yourself beyond your limits. When in doubt, consult a doctor.

Survive an Avalanche   923

Even if you've taken precautions and have been on the lookout for an avalanche, there's still a chance you could be caught in one. Here's what to do if that happens.

◎ Steps

1   Make escape plans as you travel. Keep an eye open for protected areas you can head for if you see or hear an avalanche start.

2   Keep your party spread out as you cross avalanche terrain. If one starts, there's a better chance that not everyone will get caught, leaving some-one to search for you. If you are all under the snow – or injured by the avalanche – your chances of being found and dug up are shot.

3   Shout so that others in your group are aware of the danger. It's not true that loud noises will trigger an avalanche (unless you're causing the ground to tremble).

4   Get rid of your ski poles, snowboard, etc. They'll get in your way as you try to stay above the snow.

5   Start swimming to stay on the surface. Head for one side.

6   Try to make your way to the top just as you feel the snow beginning to slow. Because there is so much air in moving snow, fighting while it's still rushing along uses precious energy and achieves very little. Concentrate on keeping the snow out of your mouth and nose if you end up under the surface. As the snow slows, its density increases and that's the time to struggle.

7   Make a space in front of your face if you end up under the snow. This is much easier to do while the snow is still moving.

8   Conserve your air. While it's tempting to start shouting for help, this may not be the best idea because snow has great sound-insulating qualities.

✳ Tips

Discuss and practise a rescue plan with your whole party. There won't be time to go for help – you will be relying on each other.

Carry a rescue beacon, which can alert others to your location. Without the aid of a beacon (and one for each searcher), you have very little chance of being found in time.

Get an up-to-date weather fore-cast and an Internet avalanche bulletin before you leave.

Call for recent condition reports to get an idea of what to expect once you are out on your trip.

924 | Survive a Bear Attack

Depending on the type of bear – grizzly or black – there are specific actions you can take (or avoid) to help you survive.

⊚ Steps

Grizzly Bears

1   Hike with bear pepper spray at the ready – easily accessible in a holster on your belt or in a front pocket. If a bear does attack, you will only have seconds to respond.

2   Aim the bear spray towards the attacking bear. When he is in close range, about 12 m (40 ft) away, begin to fire a cloud in his direction. Hopefully, the super-strength pepper spray will be enough to ward off the attack.

3   Drop to the ground and lie face down if you have no spray, or the bear continues its charge anyway. Cover the back of your neck with your hands and DO NOT move.

4   Play dead. When the bear starts its attack as you lie on the ground, play dead. If he leaves you alone – even for 20 minutes – play dead. Grizzlies are well-known for attacking until the perceived threat is neutralised; if you're no longer moving, you're no longer a threat.

Black Bears

1   Stand your ground; look big; scream and shout – flail your arms about! Do whatever you can to look aggressive and big. If you have a pack or bike or branch, hold it over your head to look bigger. Black bears will usually bluff one or even several charges.

2   Keep your feet on the ground; do not climb a tree! Black bears are excellent climbers.

3   Fight back once the bear is upon you. Do not go quietly into the night. Think last stand, no holds barred. It is very unlikely things will get to this point, but if they do, use your fists, your feet, sticks and stones; bite his nose off if you have to! He's not going to leave you alone otherwise.

⚠ Warning

Do not run. Running creature equals easy prey in the bear's mind and he'll be on top of you like lightning. There is no chance of outrunning a bear.

925 | Survive a Shark Attack

Being attacked by a shark is one of the most terrifying experiences that anyone can go through. However a surprisingly low amount of these attacks are fatal.

⊚ Steps

1   The first thing that you should always do when faced with an angry shark is to start to make your way into shallower water. Most large sharks need at least a couple of metres of water in order to swim and strike properly. In addition, many sharks like to strike their prey from beneath.

2   Most shark attacks tend to happen because of humans getting too close to sharks rather than the sharks actually wanting to eat the humans. With this in mind it is always a good idea to keep a good distance away from sharks when in the water, in order to minimise risk of attack.

✴ Tip

Large sharks only tend to occupy warmer waters of the world.

3   If you have already been bitten by the shark, and the shark is attacking again, then as well as swimming away, fighting the shark is another option. Generally the best option is said to be to rip at the shark's gills and gouge at their eyes, which are the only two real weak points a shark has.

4   Many experts will tell you that punching a shark on the nose is a good way to deter them, although this is generally best reserved for smaller sharks. Given that great whites, for example, can get to over 3,000 kg (7,000 lb), punching isn't terribly effective.

5   Generally the best advice is always to get out of the water, or at least get into shallower water so that the shark cannot attack you so easily. This is particularly important if you are already injured and might be losing blood.

Survive a Crocodile Attack   926

If you spend any time near crocodile-infested waters, you must be prepared to defend yourself against a crocodile attack.

⊙ Steps

1   Stay as calm as possible and try not to panic. It's important to keep a clear mind when facing a crisis situation.

2   Be prepared to escape. The crocodile may strike once then release, giving you a momentary opportunity for escape. Be ready to take advantage of that opportunity.

3   Respond to the attack with a counterattack of your own. Do not passively struggle to get away from your attacker, but rather use force to beat off the croc.

4   Attack the crocodile's eyes, which are the most sensitive area on the animal. Use any available object to hit or poke at its eyes so that it will release you and skulk off.

5   Aim for the nose or ears if you can't get to the eyes. This may not be as effective as attacking the eyes, but it can still produce the desired result.

6   Blow a whistle if you have one on you. Crocodiles are sensitive to sound and will be repelled by the noise.

7   Roll in the same direction as the crocodile if it initiates its signature "death roll". Whatever part of your body is in the croc's mouth is almost certain to be torn off if you don't turn in the same direction as the croc when it starts rolling and thrashing.

8   Do whatever it takes to keep the crocodile on land and out of the water. Crocs feel much more at home in the water, and they usually drag their prey into the water for the kill.

✱ Tips

Stay away from crocodile-infested waters. Even if you must enter the area, avoid going into or near the water.

Keep a sufficient distance from a crocodile if you happen to see one, and avoid surprising it. Crocs don't like chasing their prey, and they use the element of surprise when attacking.

Run away immediately if you discover that you've come too close to a crocodile. Remember, crocs don't like chasing prey, so they will probably leave you alone.

⚠ Warning

Only play dead if all other methods of resistance have proved futile. A croc will fight with its prey until the prey is dead, but you don't want to find out if this tactic will work.

927 Pack for Warm Weather

Think light cottons and comfortable, flowing clothes when packing for a sunshine holiday. Your body should be protected from the sun, but cool enough to avoid heat exhaustion.

Steps

1 Pack one pair of shorts, several t-shirts or tank tops, and a swimsuit.

2 Pack one lightweight, long skirt when travelling abroad, if you're a woman.

3 Take a hat to protect your head and face from the sun. You may want to wear the hat while travelling to avoid crushing it in your suitcase.

4 Take one long-sleeved shirt or sweater. Keep in mind that hot days can turn into cool evenings.

5 Remember insect repellent, since most warm climates have their fair share of insects.

6 Pack sunscreen, lip balm and sunglasses.

✳ Tip

Remember to care for your feet. A good pair of sandals and antifungal foot powder will keep your feet cool and comfortable in hot weather.

⚠ Warnings

Beware of the sun. If you see small white blisters after a day in the sun, seek medical attention immediately.

Drink lots of water to avoid heat exhaustion.

928 Pack for Cold Weather

Focus on packing warm, thin clothes that can be layered when travelling to a cold climate. The trick is to keep your body warm and avoid over-packing.

Steps

1 Pack a variety of warm accessories: several pairs of socks, a hat, gloves or mittens and a scarf.

2 Take a few thin, long-sleeved shirts, turtlenecks and thermals for layering. Avoid packing bulky jumpers and jackets; opt for light jumpers instead.

4 When purchasing long-sleeved t-shirts, buy tight-weave pieces to ensure adequate insulation.

5 Include one set of thermal underwear.

6 Pack one warm fleece jacket or lined gilet.

7 Take a zip pack, which can house lip balm, hand-warmer pads and an extra pair of socks for day trips.

8 Keep sunglasses and sunblock handy at all times, especially when visiting snowy areas.

9 If you're travelling to a cold, rainy climate, pack plastic bags to carry wet clothing.

✳ Tip

Remember that we lose most of our body heat through the head, hands and feet. Keep these areas covered at all times.

⚠ Warnings

If fingers, toes or nose become white or numb, seek medical attention immediately. This could be a sign of frostbite.

Avoid over-packing – you don't want to be stuck with heavy bags and more stuff than you need.

Pack for a Weekend Trip

929

The trick is to pack a few items of clothing that work well with each other and can be interchanged.

⊙ **Steps**

1 Pack both a black t-shirt and a white t-shirt, plus one sweater or cardigan.

2 Throw in your favourite pair of jeans. An additional pair of casual trousers, such as khakis, will serve you well.

3 Take two pairs of shorts if you expect warm weather or a gilet or jacket if it will be cold or rainy.

4 Remember to take three sets of underwear and two pairs of socks.

5 Pack your nightgown or pyjamas.

6 Wear a pair of comfortable, casual shoes such as loafers, trainers or flat sandals while travelling. Take dress shoes if needed.

7 Include a small toiletries bag with just the essentials – hairbrush, toothbrush, toothpaste, soap, shampoo, deodorant, razor, moisturiser and makeup. Pack travel-size toiletries if possible.

8 Take the requisite wallet, ID, cash, organiser, reading material and so forth.

9 Taking a map, driving directions and details about your destination is essential. Get ideas online and then print the information you need before your trip.

✳ **Tips**

Neutral colours work well on weekend trips. Choose a base colour – black, brown, grey or navy – and team it with white, beige or a bright colour.

For women: pack a neutral dress (black, white, beige, gray or navy) that can be dressed up with sandals or dressed down with trainers and a sweater. Wear one pair of earrings that go with everything.

Purchase a space-saving travel bag with compartments.

⚠ **Warning**

Leave expensive jewellery at home, as it's easy to lose on a trip.

Pack a Child's Suitcase

930

Preschool and school-aged children are fairly easy to pack for, as long as you let them join in the process. Follow these few simple ground rules.

⊙ **Steps**

1 Let your child help choose which clothes to take along – explain what the weather will be like where you are going. Retain veto power over the choices, though.

2 Try to plan coordinated outfits in advance for each day of your trip, so there will be no fuss about what to wear each day. Bring a few extra outfits in case of spills or damage.

3 If possible, store each outfit in a large zip-close plastic bag, or a larger bag for older children. This makes it easy for your child to pick a matching set of clothes each day, and provides you with a handy container for snacks or rubbish while you are sightseeing.

4 Give your child a small rucksack or carry-on bag of their own, and explain that they can take favourite toys or books that will fit in the bag, but that they must carry it themself.

✳ **Tips**

If you take electronic toys, make sure you can turn the sound off, or that your child can use them with earphones.

Try to take toys and games that will hold your child's attention for as long as possible. Avoid heavy toys or toys with small parts that can get lost.

⚠ **Warnings**

Never put a child's name on the outside of their clothing or rucksack, as children tend to trust people who call them by name.

5   Sew or print (with a permanent fabric marker) your child's name and emergency contact information inside all their clothes.

6   Pack a few extra snacks and surprises to keep your child happy during the journey. If you're flying, include some boiled sweets or chewing gum to relieve pressure during take-offs and landings.

It's not healthy for a child to carry a heavy rucksack – make sure you check the weight and contents of any bag your child packs for themself.

931 | Pack for Airport Security

Fear of terrorist attacks has caused most countries now to be extra-vigilant in airport security.

⊙ Steps

1   Carry toiletries and liquids in travel-sized bottles. All your containers must fit into one clear, resealable bag.

2   Check in or carry on such electronic devices as mobile phones, cameras, camcorders, laptops, pagers and PDAs. Make sure you pack undeveloped film and cameras housing undeveloped film in carry-on bags, as hold baggage screening damages film.

3   Pack your semi-sharp personal items in either carry-on or hold baggage. Such items, which were previously banned in carry-on bags but are no longer, include nail clippers and files, tweezers, knitting needles and scissors with blades shorter than 10 cm (4 in).

4   Bring gifts for friends and family unwrapped in both carry-on and hold baggage.

5   Declare any firearms and ammunition to the airline before packing them in hold luggage.

❊ Tips

To keep things easy at security checkpoints, pack all unnecessary liquids in your hold luggage.

Once you clear security, rules allow you to bring on the plane drinks and other liquids purchased in the boarding area.

⚠ Warning

Never pack in carry-on or hold baggage explosive materials, inflammable items, including lighters, and such disabling chemicals as bleach, chlorine, spray paint or tear gas.

932 | Select the Right Guidebook

The guidebook you use can make or break a trip. Prioritising the elements of your trip before you shop will help you choose the perfect book.

⊙ Steps

1   Find a local bookshop with an extensive travel section.

2   Locate guidebooks about your destination. Do you want a book about an entire country? Or perhaps a specific city?

3   Check each guidebook for maps to be sure that each city or town is well detailed.

4   Choose guides that cater to your budget. Some books focus on hostels and budget travel, while others review more upscale accommodation.

5   Cross-reference at least two books to make sure you choose the most comprehensive one.

6   Make sure you are choosing the most current edition of each book.

❊ Tip

Call ahead to any hostels, hotels or travel companies to make sure they are still in business before you visit them.

⚠ Warning

Try not to rely solely on any guidebook. Recommendations from friends and associates can be invaluable.

Upgrade an Airline Ticket

933

Airline upgrades are awarded to passengers based on available space, frequent-flyer status and the fare paid.

⊙ Steps

1 Increase your chance of getting an upgrade by using one airline for all your travels.

2 Be friendly to the ticket agent. They are required to follow certain procedures, but a little friendliness might help and certainly couldn't hurt.

3 Ask the ticket agent casually whether there are any seats available in first class.

4 Trade in frequent-flyer miles for an upgrade, if you have miles.

5 Check to see whether your frequent-flyer programme offers special upgrade deals. If the flight isn't full, the agent might upgrade you when you check in.

✳ Tips

If you are a lower-level frequent-flyer member, you may be able to pay for your upgrade and still spend less than what you would have paid for a first-class ticket.

If you are making a connecting flight and the service wasn't great on the first leg of the flight, politely complain to the ticket agent. A ticket agent might give you an upgrade if you have a legitimate complaint about inadequate service.

Book a Trip on Eurostar

934

Eurostar is a high-speed train that travels beneath the English Channel from London to Paris and from London to Brussels.

⊙ Steps

1 Call Eurostar on 01233 617575 or go to their website.

2 Book tickets as early as you can for the best rates. Fares for standard class non-exchangeable, non-refundable tickets across the Channel start at around £50 and go up as seats sell.

3 Purchase tickets online from Eurostar's website. Be aware that the credit-card holder and the credit card must be presented at the station to pick up the ticket. You cannot buy a ticket for someone else online unless you plan to pick it up.

4 Choose seats when you book your ticket. All seats are reserved. When purchasing online, you can choose between window and aisle only. When purchasing on the phone, you can request specific seat assignments. If you don't like your seat, change it before checking in at a station kiosk.

5 Check in at least 30 minutes prior to your trip if you are travelling in standard or leisure-select class. Tickets are taken by an automated ticket machine or at a kiosk. You must pass through security prior to entering the terminal.

6 Pack appropriately. You can carry your own bags on the train and there is no weight limit for baggage. If you wish to check in your bags, there is an extra fee.

✳ Tips

There are three classes for travel on Eurostar: standard, leisure select and business premier. All classes feature comfortable, clean seats. Leisure select and business premier offer additional amenities such as food service and electrical sockets at your seat.

You may book tickets up to 120 days before your trip.

935 | Plan a Boating Holiday

A boating holiday gives you the opportunity to get away from it all, including the land and all the stresses you find on it.

⊚ Steps

1   Consider the time of year you wish to go. Some boat yards operate all year round whilst others only take bookings over part of the year. The typical season runs from mid-March to around late October and this period is also likely to offer you the best chance of good weather.

2   Choose your route carefully. Consider factors such as what you want to see and do on your trip, the difficulty of the stretch of water you're looking to cross and whether or not you'd prefer to encounter locks en route or not. Planning to get from point A at point B in a certain time can often be scuppered if there are numerous locks to negotiate.

3   Think about whether you wish to go from point A to point B or if it's easier to choose a circular route – often referred to as a ring, so that you end up back at the location you started from.

4   Boating is fun and whilst it is relatively safe, it is important to use your common sense and to remember that you are travelling on water. When you get to your boat, you'll be taught how to operate it and there will also be health and safety guidelines on board. You should pay particular attention if you are boating with younger children.

5   For many people, simply cruising along peacefully, mooring up at the end of a day's sailing and getting a good night's sleep are adequate for their enjoyment. Many routes offer you plenty of opportunities to get off the boat and go for a walk, visit a town or nearby city or to take up some physical exercise such as cycling. So, you need to plan your route on a stretch of water that caters for the activities you may wish to pursue.

6   What about your pet dog? Whilst some boat yards allow you to have a dog on board, there are many that don't. And, even if they do, can they be catered for en route? If you get off to visit a local pub, for example, is your dog allowed on the premises?

7   Just as you'll want to relax and might choose to do absolutely nothing, you'll still have to eat and find other supplies, so unless you're planning to take half the contents of your kitchen cupboard with you, you'll need to pick a route in which you can stop off and buy supplies.

✻ Tip

Hoseasons and Blake's Boating Holidays are two well-established companies for arranging boating holidays. Pick up their brochures for additional information.

⚠ Warning

You might contact boat yards direct, as booking this way could save you money. Ask what is included in any final cost; the company you book with may charge for extras of which you might be unaware.

936 | Raise the Mast on a Sailboat

If you're new to sailing, you'll soon realise that there is a lot to learn about this exciting yet challenging type of boating.

⊚ Steps

1   Free up the forestay, shrouds and anything else needed to let the mast be raised.

2   Keep shrouds attached at both ends. Re-attach them if they're disconnected, but make sure they're free and not entangled with any other part of the boat or boat equipment.

✻ Tip

Raising the mast on a sailboat, especially on the first few attempts, is much easier if there are at least two people who can do the job. Find somebody to help you.

How to Do More of *(Just About)* **Everything**

3   Make sure the mast is untied from all supports.

4   Put the mast in its "pre-raised" position. Lay it on top of the sailboat, placing the base close to the mast step on the cabin top, and the mast's top end in the aft mass carrier.

5   Join the mast to the mast foot.

6   Connect the mainsheet to the bow. Make sure you have enough line to attach the mainsheet to the boom.

7   Connect the forestay to the boom's high end.

8   Attach the mainsheet to the forestay's end.

9   Join the boom to the mast's front.

10   Double check to ensure you've freed the shrouds.

11   Make sure that everything is in place then pull to raise the mast.

⚠ **Warnings**

Don't hit any power lines while raising the mast. This is dangerous and potentially fatal.

Wait to make sure the forestay is attached before releasing forward pressure on the mast.

Travel Light   937

Travelling light has all sorts of advantages, especially for those employing air transportation on a trip. How can you get away from it all if you're bringing it all along with you?

❉ **Tip**

Once you get into the habit of travelling light, you'll never want to lug three huge suitcases along with you again!

◉ **Steps**

1   Pick out one piece of luggage you plan to take along, and make a vow not to take any additional ones. It will be easier to prioritise knowing exactly how much space you have to work with.

2   When packing, live by the credo "If in doubt, leave it out". If it turns out you really needed the item in question, odds are you can purchase a new one at your destination.

3   Be smart when it comes to items like a camera (take a digital), book (bring a mass-market paperback) and toiletries. If you're staying at a hotel, for example, that you know will have shampoo and conditioner in the bathroom, don't take up precious space by bringing your own along.

4   Check the weather report of the destination you'll be visiting. If you're going to be in Tahiti for a week with nothing but sunshine in the forecast, you probably won't even need a long-sleeved shirt or trousers.

5   Limit yourself to one pair of shoes in your luggage (in addition to those you're wearing). Nobody needs three or four or even five pairs of shoes on a trip, it's totally unnecessary.

6   On a long getaway – or a business trip that entails bringing extra items along like brochures for a conference – think about shipping some things ahead of time. What it costs you in cash it will save you in hassle.

7   If you end up picking up souvenirs on your journey, again have them shipped back to you. Or save space and probably money too by sticking with small objects like fridge magnets or t-shirts.

938 | Get Through Airport Check-In Quickly

These days, travellers are experiencing more stress than ever as they try to pass through the maze of people, ID checks, luggage scans and personal searches at check-in. Follow these steps to make the process less painful.

Steps

1 Purchase your tickets as far in advance as possible. First of all it will save you money, but it will also decrease the likelihood of a personal search. Last-minute flight changes or ticket purchases often flag a person for a thorough search.

2 Most airlines will allow you to check in online and print your boarding pass at home. Checking in online can help decrease the stress of having to be at the airport hours in advance, and flags airline personnel to delay closing the boarding period if you have not yet arrived.

3 Before you leave home make sure you have proper identification. Once you arrive at the airport prepare to show your boarding pass and identification prior to entering the security checkpoint.

4 Getting through the security checkpoint can be the most stressful part of your trip. Make sure you keep your boarding pass in your hands at all times, use the bins for items like your bag, wallet, the contents of your pockets, belt, mobile phone and shoes. If you brought a laptop make sure you take it out and put the computer in its own individual bin for scanning. Once all your items are in the bins, make sure you watch them enter the X-ray machine before stepping through the metal detector.

5 Now that you've passed the security checkpoint you may have some time to spare for shopping, eating or just sitting and relaxing near your gate. First check the boards of incoming and outgoing flights to find your gate and your departure time. Make sure you allocate your time appropriately until they call for your flight to board over the loudspeaker.

✱ Tips

Try to leave excess items at home. The more you have the more difficult things will be.

Try to carry on your luggage if possible – losing your luggage can be a huge source of stress.

939 | Cope With Flight Delays and Cancellations

We've all been there – you get to your departure gate and there's a big "cancelled" sign next to your flight...

Steps

1 As soon as you see that your flight is cancelled, or that a delay will ruin your flight plans, get to the nearest airline agent. If your gate is totally overwhelmed, go back to your airline's ticket desk on the other side of the security gate, where they may be better equipped to rebook passengers. There are also phones available that call in directly to your airline.

2 Although your inconvenience may feel greater than anyone else's, there is a planeload of people trying to get to the same place you are, and they might beat you to it. There are a limited number of other seats going to your destination.

✱ Tips

Don't panic. You're going to get there, it's just a matter of when.

Work with fellow passengers on your flight – pool your knowledge to find a solution.

Cheap flights sometimes result in shoddy customer service. Avoid booking with airlines that frequently cancel their flights for unspecified reasons.

3   If your flight was cancelled completely, the chances are it may already have rebooked you to a different flight. However, your new flight will not necessarily be convenient – it might even be a day or two away! But remember, this is the ticket that you have, a guaranteed seat, not a standby slot. Hang on to this as a fall-back plan.

4   Talk to the agent about all possibilities. If the flight planned for you by the airline is not optimal, politely ask the agent to check on a few more possibilities. If your goal is to get there as soon as possible and you're willing, let the agent know you'll fly through any city and make any connection. If the agent can't find you anything, politely ask the agent if there is anything available on another airline. Your airline can put you on another airline's flight. Your least-desirable choice is to go on standby, but you will at least want to be put on the list straight away.

5   Call your airline or travel agent for additional help. If you booked through a travel agent, call them immediately and see if they have better luck rescheduling your flight.

6   Getting angry won't help but being polite just might. Your airline representative has dozens of passengers to reroute as fast as they can. If you're polite, accommodating and grateful, they just might go the extra mile to help you out.

7   Deviating from the original flight plan is the most common reason for misplaced luggage. Keep track of your checked bags. When you get a new flight, make sure you ask about luggage that you have checked in. Ask about its current location and how it will get to your destination. If you change airlines, make sure the new airline has the tag number for your bags.

Handle Missing Baggage   940

Missing baggage can be one of the most stressful aspects of flying. Having important information at your fingertips alleviates a good deal of stress when dealing with this problem.

⊙ **Steps**

1   Determine that your luggage is actually missing. Verify that all bags have arrived for a given flight, or speak to the agent at the airline's baggage office. Use your luggage ticket stubs and unique features on your bag to identify your luggage.

2   Once you have determined that you are missing a bag or bags, take your claim checks to your airline's baggage-service office. It is important that you go to the airline that flew you into your final destination.

3   You will need to provide a detailed description of your luggage, as well as contact and delivery information. The airline will give you a contact number and can typically give you an idea of which flight your bag will arrive on.

4   Give your airline at least an hour or two for your claim to trace in its computer system, and then if you haven't heard anything, call the airline.

5   In most cases, you will receive your missing luggage on the same day, but it will obviously depend on where your missing bag is and the

number of available flights that can return your bag to you. If you flew an international itinerary, for example, it may take longer.

6   Simply await the delivery of your bag. If you are not going to be at home, ask the airline if it is acceptable to leave the baggage somewhere on the premises, or even leave a signed note.

7   After a set time – three days for many airlines – if your luggage has not yet turned up, your missing bag file is usually forwarded to a centralised luggage-tracing centre for more extensive tracing. At this point, you will probably be asked for a detailed contents of the bag. If your bag is not found, then the airlines will compensate you for it, within established guidelines. For more details, see your airline's contract of carriage.

⚠ Warning

Most airlines are not obligated to pay for clothes or other supplies that you are missing because of your delayed luggage until after the first 24 hours. This time-frame may vary, so you should read the airline's contract of carriage to be sure.

941 | Prevent Deep Vein Thrombosis When Flying

Often referred to as "Economy Class Syndrome", deep vein thrombosis (DVT) is the formation of a blood clot in a deep vein that can develop after sitting still on long flights.

⊙ Steps

1   Get fit before you get going. You can help reduce your overall risk of developing DVT by maintaining a healthy weight, giving up smoking, taking steps to lower your blood pressure if it's high and enjoying regular exercise.

2   Ask your doctor if he or she recommends the use of compression stockings that can help increase circulation, particularly if you're at high risk of developing DVT. Make sure you get measured properly so the stockings provide a comfortable fit, and try on the stockings with the shoes you intend to wear during the flight.

3   Get moving. Sitting scrunched up, accordion-style, for long periods of time is not only uncomfortable, but it can be dangerous especially if you're at risk of DVT.

4   Stay well-hydrated by drinking plenty of fluids such as water and juice, as dehydration can result in the thickening of blood and the narrowing of vessels. Avoid alcoholic and caffeinated drinks as they can be dehydrating.

5   Engage in exercise at your seat. Point your toes up and then down to a flat position. You can also try flexing your leg muscles and lifting your knees periodically throughout the flight. Rotating your ankles is another good way to keep the blood flowing. Don't cross your legs as that action restricts blood flow.

6   See your doctor immediately following a trip if you have any signs of DVT. These may include swelling in one or both legs, leg pain or tender-ness, red or discoloured skin or warmth in the leg that's affected. Half of all DVT patients, however, show no symptoms.

⚠ Warning

This is a serious condition, so these steps should be taken by everyone taking a long flight.

942 Take an Eco-Friendly Holiday

Whether you're heading to a nearby lake to pitch your tent for the weekend, going shopping in New York or floating down the Amazon on a raft, there are numerous ways to keep your eco-impact to a minimum while supporting local businesses and cultures.

Green Travelling

- Do your research up front. Read up on environmental, political and social issues in destinations you're considering. Guidebooks that offer this kind of information include Lonely Planet and Rough Guides.

- Book with travel companies specialising in sustainable tourism. Green tours may make a bigger dent in your wallet (they can cost up to 20 per cent more), but you'll be doing your part to preserve the planet's beautiful wild places as well as its cultural hotspots.

- Stay in a green hotel that not only promotes energy- and water-conservation, but also offers guests a variety of eco-friendly amenities, including organic cotton sheets and gourmet meals made with locally grown ingredients.

- Respect the natural environment. Whether you're in a city park or hiking the Himalayas, refrain from touching or harassing animals, leave plants and other natural features as you found them and always dispose of waste responsibly.

- Buy sustainable souvenirs. Avoid crafts, clothing and other items that were derived from protected or endangered animal species. Likewise, buy locally made items that support the people who live nearby, as well as local green organisations. Long-distance shipping of products burns fossil fuels and contributes pollutants to the atmosphere.

- Frequent local businesses. This includes eating in local restaurants, shopping at local markets, attending local events, and using local buses, car rental companies, and tour guides.

Green Certifications

- The Rainforest Alliance, an international conservation organisation, promotes ecologically and socially responsible best practices for Latin American tourism businesses. Search for tour operators that have signed an agreement with the Rainforest Alliance to conserve biodiversity and reduce tourism's negative impacts.

- Sustainable Travel International provides a list of member tour operators and travel companies that are committed to sustainable travel. Some have received certification through the organisation's voluntary Sustainable Tourism Eco-certification Programme (STEP).

- Travel Choice lists eco-tourism operators around the world that have signed the TIES Code of Conduct

- Green Globe. Developed in 1993 by the World Travel & Tourism Council, Green Globe certifies environmentally responsible travel businesses and destination communities worldwide. Search for tourism providers that follow Green Globe's strict standards and bear its logo.

- Blue Flag. Search for over 3,200 beaches and marinas in 37 countries that have earned the Blue Flag eco-label (awarded by the non-profit Foundation for Environmental Education). Certified properties follow stringent criteria for water quality, environmental education and safety.

- Eco Tour is an online Directory of eco-tours and eco-lodges all over the world. Tour companies pay for a listing but must demonstrate their commitment to environmental, social and economic concerns where they operate.

reference

943 | Stay in Touch While Travelling

Jet-setters and business travellers alike face the ongoing dilemma of keeping in contact with friends and loved ones back home. Here are a few tips on staying plugged in.

⊙ Steps

1 Know the time difference. How annoying is it for Dad to get an alarming phone call in the middle of the night, only to realise it's only you from Bali, calling to shoot the breeze? Be considerate of when you decide to check in.

2 Email is the best for travellers. Relating any non-urgent issues, checking in or giving contact information is usually best done via email. While wireless isn't universal, most hotels have at least marginal Internet available, and Internet cafés are a great option for more rustic locales.

3 For homesick folks or new parents, nothing beats video messaging. Newer laptops have built-in cameras and microphones, and many Internet cafés also offer this option. Get your technology in order before your trip to avoid frustration abroad!

4 One word: Skype. Install the software and make free calls to any other Skype user. Skype offers great deals on non-Skype calls and video calls, too.

✱ Tip

Depending on where you're travelling it's not always easy to find ways of staying in touch – but the people back home will appreciate the effort.

944 | Carry Valuables While Travelling

The rule to follow when travelling with valuables is to take what you need and hide it well. Leave the rest – including irreplaceable treasures and excess credit cards – at home.

⊙ Steps

1 Carry traveller's cheques and one or two major credit cards instead of hauling around loads of cash.

2 Create two lists of the serial numbers of your traveller's cheques. Leave one with a friend or relative at home and carry a copy with you. Cross the numbers off as you cash the cheques.

3 Make two copies of your passport identification page, airline tickets, driving licence and credit cards. Leave one photocopy with family or friends at home; carry the other in a place other than where you carry your other valuables.

4 Lock your passport, cash and credit cards in a hotel safe whenever possible. If you have to carry them, keep them in your inside pockets, in a money belt around your waist, or around your neck and tucked under your shirt.

5 Avoid storing valuables in handbags, bumbags and outside pockets; these are easy targets.

6 Take small amounts of money from ATMs. Avoid taking out large amounts for all to see.

✱ Tips

If travelling for an extended period of time, think about renting a safety-deposit box.

Try to travel light. You'll move more quickly and will be more likely to have a free hand.

Avoid standing out as a tourist. Dress like a local, if possible.

⚠ Warning

Pickpockets target wallets kept in the back pocket or in a backpack.

Avoid Bad Water While Travelling

945

When visiting areas with poor sanitation, take extra precautions when handling or drinking water.

⊙ Steps

1   Consider the following safe to drink: commercially bottled water with an unbroken seal, carbonated drinks, beverages made with vigorously boiled water and beer.

2   Order bottled water at restaurants and make sure the seal is opened in front of you.

3   Avoid ice and any drinks made with tap water, such as mixed drinks.

4   Don't use tap water when brushing your teeth. Instead, use bottled water, or add purifying tablets or iodine additives to tap water. You can also boil tap water for 20 minutes to make it safe.

5   Try not to swallow water when showering or bathing.

6   Consider non-disposable glasses and cups unsanitary; drink from original containers and use sanitary straws, or carry your own cups.

✳ Tips

Consider any water in an unfamiliar area unsafe unless you know otherwise.

For boiling water, consider purchasing an immersion coil. If you are travelling to a foreign country, you may need to buy a plug adapter and current converter to make it work.

If you insist on forcing your body to adapt to the water, allow at least four weeks to adjust.

Prevent Malaria While Travelling

946

Each year, 300 million to 500 million people catch malaria, and several million die from it, especially children under five years of age. There are ways to stay safe from this disease, however.

⊙ Steps

1   Take anti-malarial medication one week before you plan to arrive in a subtropical or tropical country. The kind of anti-malarial drug your doctor chooses to prescribe depends partly on what country you will be going to and your prior medical conditions. Always take pills on a full stomach, and never skip a dose.

2   Take anti-malarial medicine once a week while in the tropical or sub-tropical country, and continue once a week for four weeks once you have returned home.

3   Buy your anti-malarial drugs in your home country. Drugs from foreign countries may not be as reliable.

4   Protect yourself against mosquito bites while travelling to malaria-risk areas. Wear long-sleeved shirts and long trousers, especially between early dusk and late dawn. Apply mosquito repellent liberally, and reapply after you swim or shower. Keep screens on open windows and doors, and use mosquito netting around outside living areas.

5   Spray residual insecticides indoors and out to ward off mosquitoes.

✳ Tips

Symptoms of malaria resemble the flu: fever, chills, headache, lethargy and muscle ache. If you feel like you have the flu after your trip, even one full year later, see your doctor.

Because malaria can sit dormant in your system for a long time, you will not be allowed to donate blood for up to three years after returning home from a trip to a malaria-risk country.

⚠ Warnings

Take your anti-malarial drugs exactly as prescribed.

If you think you might have malaria, see a doctor immediately. Delaying treatment can result in serious health consequences.

947 | Respectfully Take Photographs While Travelling

Adopting a respectful attitude about photography when travelling will help you take better and more meaningful photos.

⊙ Steps

1 Cultivate an attitude of respect for locals by imagining what it would be like if a group of strangers showed up in your home or office and began taking photos of you without introducing themselves.

2 Give yourself time to take in your surroundings on your own before snapping a photo. This may mean that you keep your camera tucked away for days or weeks before you start to photograph particular places or people.

3 Carry your camera in an inconspicuous way so that it is not the first thing people see when you approach them.

4 Make contact with the people you wish to photograph before introducing them to your camera. Greet people as you come and go in restaurants or pass them on the streets; sit with them, if possible, before requesting to take a picture.

5 Ask before taking photos of people, even if you suspect they won't see you. If you don't speak the language, you can still point to the camera and point to them and give a questioning look.

6 Consult locals for guidance when you are uncertain whether taking a photo of a particular person, site or object will be disrespectful.

7 Consider letting the potential subject take photos with your camera. Your camera may be an interesting piece of technology to this person, and showing them how to look through the lens or adjust the focus can be fun for all.

8 Think about carrying a Polaroid so you can take photos of people or families and give these to them on the spot. You can then request that you take photos of your own with your preferred camera.

9 Assess the implications of paying someone for their photograph as opposed to establishing a human connection: do you really want them to be a posed model or a souvenir object to be taken home? What would you like the person's memory of you to be?

✱ Tips

Learn a few phrases in the local language and don't be shy about using them. This will go a long way in demonstrating your respect and interest in local culture, and will facilitate genuine contact with the people you wish to photograph.

Be agreeable if someone refuses to let you take their photograph. A person should not have to explain why they don't want to be captured on film.

⚠ Warnings

Avoid taking photos of military complexes, prisons, police stations and bridges. This is illegal in some countries and may result in having your camera and film confiscated.

Avoid taking photos within temples, mosques or churches, or of representations of sacred figures. Ask a monk, nun, priest or devotee before assuming that you can pull out your camera.

Don't offer to send someone a copy of a photo unless you are certain you will follow through on the request.

948 | Communicate in a Foreign Country

It's always a good idea to learn a few words of the local language when you'll be travelling in a foreign country.

⊙ Steps

1 Use body language: pointing, gesturing and pantomiming will all help you get your point across.

2 Carry around a pad of paper on which you can write figures and draw pictures.

✱ Tip

If you carry around a small phrase book or dictionary, you can look up words when you're at a standstill.

3   Hand your pen and paper to the person across the counter when you don't understand how much something costs; most people will get the idea and write down the number.

4   Go to travel shops and look for books or laminated cards with pictures of items related to food, lodging, transportation and entertainment; these are especially useful in restaurants and hotels.

5   Be aware that many English words and name brands are understood almost universally: English, taxi, sexy, Coca-Cola, OK. String these together creatively and you'll be surprised how much you'll be able to get across.

6   Let pictures tell the story. Take photos of your home, your family or whatever else is important to you to share with people you meet on the road.

⚠ Warning

All these instructions require that you have a willing partner who will put in the effort to figure out what you're trying to communicate. If the person you're "talking" to isn't interested, you may have to find someone else.

Hitchhike When Travelling Abroad

949

There are some places in the world where hitchhiking is relatively safe, inexpensive and a good way to meet locals.

◉ Steps

1   Research thoroughly whether hitchhiking is considered safe in the area you will be visiting by checking a variety of sources. Your best sources will be other travellers experienced with budget travel in the area, but also check guidebooks and travel advisories issued by your country's consulate or embassy.

2   Always hitchhike with at least one other travel partner, even if travelling in a country with a reputation for safe hitchhiking.

3   Learn the culturally appropriate hand signals for asking for a ride in the region where you are travelling. An extended thumb will only get you confused looks in some parts of the world.

4   Have a local write down your destination if you don't speak or write in the local dialect. Indicate when asking for a ride that you want to go "towards" or "in the direction of" a particular place so that you have the option of taking a ride part of the way and then hitching other rides.

5   Ask locals where the best roads and times of day are for catching rides. If catching a ride on a truck or tractor that will be picking up other passengers along the way, the earlier you go looking for a ride the better.

6   Find out bus and train fares to your destination, and use these as guidelines for settling a price with your driver, if compensation is expected.

7   Split your group into smaller units if trying to catch a ride for three or more people. It's easier to flag down a vehicle if there are only two of you, and then negotiate taking more people from there.

8   Carry a map that marks roads so that you are familiar with your route. Also bring plenty of water and an extra layer of clothing to maximise health and safety while you wait for a ride.

9   Be prepared to chat with your driver and his companions. If you share a common language, chances are you will be expected to socialise.

✳ Tip

Be a socially responsible traveller by researching the way in which hitchhiking works in the local culture and economy before negotiating payments. In some regions, rides are given to locals for free, and an offer of payment by a "rich foreigner" may make it difficult for locals to find affordable transportation; in other regions, payment makes it possible for private drivers to provide cheap and efficient transportation alternatives.

⚠ Warnings

Hitchhiking in many parts of the world is a dangerous activity. Consider hitchhiking only if you are an experienced traveller and are certain it is legal, common and safe where you are.

Plan in advance how you will deal with sleepy or intoxicated drivers. Options may include asking to be let off earlier than you planned, paying for a meal break or singing very loudly.

Stay awake during the ride to ensure your own safety and to ensure that you arrive at your desired destination.

950 | Tip in a Foreign Country

When you're abroad, tipping can be a perplexing experience: in some countries it's expected, in others it's an insult – and the rules are constantly changing.

⊙ Steps

1 Recognise that tipping is, more or less, mainstream. As corporate mentality replaces traditional ideology (that the honour of providing hospitality is reward itself), tipping etiquette has become more mainstream.

2 In Europe and the South Pacific, tip 10 per cent to 15 per cent, even if a service charge has already been added. Italy tends to be a bit lower.

3 In most Asian countries, don't plan on tipping. Japan sometimes includes a service charge, but don't expect to tip. South Korea doesn't charge for service and doesn't expect a tip, either.

⚠ Warning

Double-check the tipping protocol at South Pacific and Asian hotels. Many prohibit tipping to prevent staff from hassling guests for money.

951 | Bribe a Foreign Official

In many third-world countries an unofficial travel "tax" is *de rigueur*. Although every bribery situation is unique, there are a few universal rules you'll want to follow to successfully negotiate a mutual agreement.

⊙ Steps

1 Verify that bribery is customary in the country you'll be travelling through. The X-rated magazine you proffered up to get you past a Mexican army checkpoint would get you imprisoned in a communist country. Travel guidebooks are typically good sources of information about dealing with foreign officials.

2 Determine who is in charge before offering a bribe. If you deal with anyone other than the superior, you may offend him and create a face-losing confrontation. Be extremely careful not to insult or upset anyone.

3 Identify exactly what the problem is. If you're in violation of some law, ask to pay the fine on the spot. If you're carrying something they want, offer some of it. Your ultimate goal is to agree with the official on both the problem and a mutually beneficial solution.

4 Offer a legitimate explanation for the bribery to put a veneer of legality to the situation. For example, say that you're afraid the fine will get lost in the post and that you'd rather pay the proper authorities right now. The way in which you offer a bribe is sometimes more important than the bribe itself.

✱ Tip

Carry small amounts of sterling currency to offer as bribes. Offer cash first, then other items.

⚠ Warning

Only reveal the amount of money you're willing to part with. If you show the official £500, the fine will most likely be £500. Hide the bulk of your money along with all valuable personal items.

Survive in the Ocean **952**

Finding yourself stranded in the ocean can be a terrifying and life-threatening experience. Here's how to survive.

⊙ Steps

1   Keep your boat afloat. You need to have a boat or life raft otherwise you will be dead in hours, not days.

2   Ration your supplies. Make sure that you do not eat and drink all your resources too quickly. It is much better to be miserable and be rescued with resources left over than to run out in a couple of days and not survive the week you need before you are discovered.

3   Use the ocean water. You can consume up to 1 kg (32 oz) of ocean water a day, but only for five days at a time. You can also reduce thirst by soaking in the water for a short time every day.

4   Eat the plankton. Plankton can be caught using a small net or piece of clothing. Plankton can be eaten without negative consequences and can provide the nourishment you need to survive in the ocean.

5   Stay as still as possible. Moving around can take enough energy that you will need an extra meal or two to survive. By remaining sedentary you can conserve energy and thus require less food.

6   Keep faith alive. Never give up hope that you can be found. Hope has kept people alive for days. Once you lose hope you lose the will to fight.

✳ Tip

Following these steps may help you survive in the ocean for up to a month.

Holiday on a Secluded Island **953**

Secluded destinations are becoming more popular than ever as places to escape the stresses of everyday life.

⊙ Steps

1   Research all options available for spending your holiday on a remote and private island. The costs can vary from surprisingly inexpensive such as Pandan Island in the Philippines to the other extreme such as Musha Cay in the Bahamas, where even a one-day stay will cause you to remortgage your home to pay for it. You can reserve most in a middle price range for an average holiday.

2   Indulge in fantasy land by beginning in the Pacific and Asia. Discover your private tropical island in the sun by heading for the seclusion of Motu. These tiny islands in the South Pacific are a secret getaway with fewer tourists and total privacy than the well-known and built up Tahiti and Bora Bora. The islands off Thailand are another alternative for privacy.

3   Think of Africa as a confidential destination. On its eastern shores, the Seychelles consists of 155 exotic and secluded islands in the Indian Ocean. There are many self-catering properties available, and one island – Denis Island – has 350 acres of untouched foliage, exotic flowers and heavenly white sandy beaches offering swimming all year round.

✳ Tips

You could stay at a resort and charter your own boat in the Caribbean while discovering your own private islands for a sunset dinner, or anchor and snorkel on a tropical reef.

An island can be as eventful or as relaxing as you wish. Choose your location wisely.

⚠ Warning

Make sure you use a reputable travel agent as you will only have access to photos and descriptions prior to your trip.

4   Venture to the best of the best with top-quality amenities for you and your party in the Caribbean. Your options are as unlimited as the waters that surround the islands. Within the Bahamas there are 1,000 islands alone off the beaten track. Dunbar Rock is one of the Caribbean's most unique dive resorts and situated on a rock off Honduras, Central America, with only a six-bedroomed villa on it and is moderately priced. Necker Island in the British West Indies is owned by Sir Richard Branson and is available at a phenomenal price. Salsa into South America for your retreat. Many private island rentals sit along the Atlantic coast near Brazil and Argentina. On the west coast, Chile offers the Juan Fernandez Islands, which were the basis for the tale of Robinson Crusoe.

5   Imagine losing yourself after a tough day touring the chateaux in France and return by speedboat to the tranquillity of your private island. Consider that the best places for seclusion need not be in the tropics or on an idyllic beach front – there are other places, too. Outside Stockholm in Sweden are thousands of private islands with picturesque wood cottages along the waterfront, which can provide you with your own private boat. If you get a hankering for civilisation, take the boat over to Stockholm for some culture and a Swedish smorgasbord.

6   Spend time in North America. Republic Island in Michigan is nestled in the woods on a secluded two-acre island along the river, in a quiet and serene atmosphere of the north woods. Brandy Hill Island is one-acre island paradise located in the north-east corner of Connecticut, which is a delightful holiday to view the autumn foliage. Tuck yourself away in Maine and indulge in catching a lobster for an evening meal. Ontario has remote islands that are accessible by the Algoma Central Railway's wilderness passenger train or by float plane. Honey Bee is a beautiful, historic, private island nestled in the very heart of the Thousand Islands – just one example.

954 | Build a Campfire

Man's oldest foe can be tamed. What once only caused forest fires can now bring light, warmth and hot beans.

⊙ Steps

1   Situate your fire at least 3 m (10 ft) away from tents, trees, roots and other inflammable items if there's no fire ring available. Clear a space 60–80 cm (24–32 in) across.

2   Don't make a ring of rocks if one isn't already there, and don't build against a boulder or other rocks. This will needlessly char the rocks without adding any significant containment to the fire.

3   Gather firewood and kindling if necessary, using only fallen branches. Note that many parks and wilderness areas even forbid gathering fallen material, which plays an important role in the ecosystem.

4   Build a small, loose pile of kindling, making sure you allow space for air to feed the fire. Include paper scraps, dry plant matter and other small, inflammable items.

✳ Tip

Using a gas stove instead of a campfire to cook food in the wilderness is recommended – it's easier to use, cleaner and better for the environment.

⚠ Warnings

Always have someone watching your campfire – never leave it unattended.

Be sure to familiarise yourself with the fire regulations of the area you're camping in before starting a fire.

5   Construct a pyramid of dry twigs and small sticks around and above the kindling pile.

6   Light the kindling with a match.

7   Add increasingly larger sticks and then logs as the fire grows in strength, always leaving enough space between them for the fire to breathe.

Sing Campfire Songs

955

Sing campfire songs to entertain and bond with your party – and keep skittish wild animals away to boot.

⊙ **Steps**

1   Firstly, familiarise yourself with the rules and regulations of the area in which you're camping, particularly with regards to having a fire burning. the last thing you want is your revelry interrupted by angry park rangers or other officials.

1   Compile a list of campfire songs that are easy to sing. Your list should include a wide variety of songs, including slow songs, silly songs, loud songs, rounds, ballads and hymns.

2   Build a large campfire and have your group form a circle around it. Take care that no one sits too close to the fire.

3   Choose a song leader to pick which songs will be sung and when. Ideally, this leader will be the person with the guitar.

4   Begin the session with slow yet light-hearted warm-up songs like "If You're Happy and You Know It".

5   Build energy with songs sung in the round, such as "Row, Row, Row Your Boat" and "Frere Jacques".

6   Move on to more energetic and silly songs like "Do Your Ears Hang Low?" and "John Jacob Jingleheimer Schmidt".

7   Move on to slower and more meaningful songs like "This Land Is Your Land" and "Puff, the Magic Dragon" as the fire begins to fade.

8   Sing slow hymns or reflective songs like "Kum Ba Yah" and "The Ballad of Tom Dooley" as the fire fades to embers.

⚠ **Warning**

Always follow proper safety rules when burning a campfire.

956 Take a Gap Year

Taking a year off between the completion of your degree and diving into the corporate jungle is an international trend, supported globally as a means of self discovery, bridging the gap between education and the "real world".

Getting Started

- Decide exactly what it is you hope to accomplish in the time you're taking for yourself. Is it about enhancing your CV? Accomplishing something you've always dreamed of? Just getting away from the norm, branching out and discovering something about yourself?

- It should now be clear whether you should be packing hiking gear or office attire. Once you know what you're looking for, you can begin to explore potential jobs, mountain trails or whatever it is you've decided to look for.

- If you're going to travel and see as many places as possible, figure out what it will take to get there and how long you want to stay in each place. Do you want to explore your own nation or go abroad, for example?

Getting There

- Finances are going to be your single biggest challenge. There's no rule stating you have to depart for your gap year the day after graduation. Find a way to save until you have the amount you need to get yourself there and stay supported.

- Find as many books, websites, and discussion boards as possible with information pertaining to your plan. This will help you draw up your financial estimates, figure out how to pack and provide invaluable advice.

- Set up the first night's accommodation and travel before you leave.

- Create a timeline for departure and return. You don't have to stick to it exactly, but it's important to have an idea of when you plan to go and when you want to return.

Once You're There

- Make sure you've found housing and transportation that you can rely on. Check this out as soon as you get there.

- Check the medical resources nearby, just in case. Disaster is unlikely to strike, but it's best to know where to go if it does.

- Even the most frugal run out of money sometimes. Make sure there's an emergency fund or a means to make more if you're living on savings.

- You created a plan before you left, and it's always there to refer to when you feel like you've hit a dead end. However, if the plan starts to feel stuffy, change it. This year is about you, not your obligations!

- Get out there and enjoy everything about your new experience!

Returning to Earth

- Though it may be difficult to return to the norm after your adventure, most people find themselves re-energised and ready to enter the workforce.

- Some people find the transition to normal life more difficult. Give yourself time to adjust. Accept that life will have gone on in your absence. Expect changes in the lives of your family and friends and try not to feel like you've missed out. Remember – you've been off having your own adventure.

- If you've been offered a permanent position at your internship in Greece, for example, or just can't stand the idea of leaving Indonesia, then just remember, you don't necessarily have to. It could be the thing you discovered about yourself while abroad is that you want to stay abroad.

Plan a Romantic Getaway

Do some research and plan a few surprises. Whether it's your first trip together or your 50th wedding anniversary, a well-orchestrated romantic trip will not soon be forgotten.

⊚Steps

1 Consider your options for romantic destinations. Do you want to drive or fly? Do you want to create the mood in an urban setting like Paris, or a rugged place like the Grand Canyon?

2 Research bed-and-breakfasts, small inns and private cabins or condos in your destination area, once you have chosen a destination.

3 Ask about special room features: large baths, fireplaces, king-sized beds and patios with sweeping views.

4 Research idyllic beach walks, gentle mountain trails or picnic areas in the area you will be visiting.

5 Investigate cosy restaurants in and around your destination, and make a reservation for two.

6 Allow for plenty of relaxation time on your trip. If you are travelling for a weekend, but have a long drive, skip out early on Friday.

7 Arrange for special treats to greet you when you arrive. Champagne, chocolates and flowers are quintessential romantic treats.

8 Bring scented candles, bubble baths and incense to create an extravagant setting within your hotel room.

✳ Tip

For added mystique, plan a romantic trip as a surprise. Ask your significant other to pack a bag, and then blindfold him or her and lead the way!

Book an Adventure Holiday

If you'd rather be rock climbing than rumba-ing, camping than cabana-ing or sailing than sunning, choose a holiday that pushes you more than coddles you.

⊚Steps

1 Decide on your level of adventure and choose a destination. Trips range from Italian bicycle tours to an Everest expedition. Be realistic about your budget, tolerance for adversity, stamina and abilities. If you get in over your head, the trip may become expensive, scary or dangerous.

2 Research the climate. For example, avoid the monsoon season in tropical regions when travel becomes unpredictable.

3 Choose a primary activity such as kayaking, rafting, bicycling, mountain climbing, skiing, sailing, scuba diving or camping. An activity you're familiar with is good, but it can also be fun to push yourself and try something new.

4 Consult a travel agent or do your own research. Search the Internet using key phrases such as "climb Denali", "ocean kayaking", "adventure travel for women" and so on.

✳ Tips

Don't try to impress your adventure guide with how much you know. Most groups seem to have one customer who wants to act like a guide. Don't be this person.

Look for travel options that fit your lifestyle and interests, such as seniors, students or singles.

⚠ Warning

Don't assume travel companies in other countries are subject to safety regulations. In some countries, there's nothing to stop an unqualified person from acting as a guide. As always, you're responsible for yourself.

5   Keep it fun. If your holiday involves a new or physically challenging activity, don't overestimate your ability. Talk to prospective travelling companions about what you hope to accomplish and what your abilities are.

6   Create a budget, including extra for unexpected events. Base your budget in part on how much gear you must buy or can rent from the guide company. The hassle and expense of transporting gear on an aeroplane can make the rental option attractive. Ask yourself whether you expect to use the equipment for future adventures (and how much enjoyment you get out of owning cool gear).

7   Choose how secluded you want to be. Do you want to be out of touch with the world – no phones, email, radio or TV? Seclusion might mean serenity, but it also means fewer amenities and difficult evacuation in case of trouble.

8   Decide on the level of hardship or deprivation you can sustain. Is there fresh water for washing? What are the bathrooms like? What kind of food will you eat? How are meals prepared and by whom? How brave are the insects and rodents?

959   Take a Hot-Air Balloon Ride

A hot-air balloon ride gives you a stunning, bird's-eye view of a large geographical area, not to mention a chance to do something a bit out of the ordinary.

⊙ Steps

1   Search online or in the Yellow Pages of your destination to find ballooning companies. (They are usually listed under "Ballooning".) Even better, ask friends for references, especially if you'll be in an area where ballooning is extremely popular and a lot of companies are vying for your tourist cash.

2   Call to reserve your flight. Prices generally start at £100 per person for a basic ride of about an hour. You'll probably pay more if you want a charter flight, or if you add goodies such as wine, champagne or even a full-blown picnic. Customising your ride will also cost extra.

3   Ask about packages. Many companies offer half-day trips, all-day trips that include a picnic, or other special packages.

4   Be prepared for an early start time – most ballooning groups will ask you to be at the launch pad before sunrise, when the wind is light to non-existent. Adverse weather conditions are likely to cause a cancellation.

5   Wear clothes that can be layered. The burner for the balloon will often keep the basket warm, even in cool weather, but you should be prepared with at least a light jacket.

6   Bring binoculars, a camcorder and a camera; make sure you have fresh batteries and lots of film if you're not using a digital camera.

7   Use the toilet before your flight.

8   Enjoy the view!

✳ Tips

Don't worry about falling out – the basket won't sway very much.

Book early if you are planning a trip to a popular destination.

Although balloons generally go where the wind takes them, there should be a ground crew (or "chase" crew) following your balloon as it flies. This crew is usually in touch with the balloon pilot by radio.

Even though you may be prone to motion sickness, people seldom get airsick on a hot-air balloon. If you are concerned, take a dose of motion-sickness medication before boarding.

⚠ Warning

If you have a deep-seated fear of heights, you may want to reconsider this activity.

Enjoy a Whale-Watching Trip 960

Nothing could be worse than being caught offshore without things you need to make your whale-watching excursion a pleasant journey. Plan ahead, make a list and enjoy your trip!

Steps

1 Find out what is available on the boat before you pack. If there is a galley or snack bar, you may be able to avoid carrying snacks or drinks, making your pack lighter.

2 Avoid taking anything larger than a day pack. You are not likely to have much storage space and won't want to keep track of a large bag while trying to watch whales.

3 Bring things that will keep you warm and dry (unless you're whale watching in the tropics). Jackets, rain ponchos, warm shoes and socks, and even gloves may be appropriate, depending on where you are.

4 Wear as much as you can to avoid packing it. A jacket (light or heavy depending on where you are), poncho, hat, sunglasses, binoculars and even cameras can be worn or carried when you board the boat.

5 Take food items that will help you avoid seasickness, such as crackers or ginger snaps, even if you've taken a seasickness remedy prior to boarding. Plan to snack every 15 to 30 minutes to keep something in your stomach.

6 Make sure the necessary equipment is readily accessible. If your video camera is stuck at the bottom of a camera bag, you're likely to miss some great shots.

✽ Tips

Although you can take seasickness remedies with you on the boat, "mal de mer" is best dealt with before your trip. Whether you're using a prescription patch, wrist pressure bands or a common remedy such as ginger, avoid waiting until you're aboard ship or feeling nauseated to start anti-seasickness measures.

Remember that there is likely to be sea spray on the boat, so you should have a way to protect your optical equipment when necessary. Plan to put cameras and binoculars under ponchos, inside jackets or into your pack when spray is heavy.

⚠ Warning

Be extremely cautious if you have a condition – such as diabetes – that might make you seriously ill if you get seasick.

Backpack Through Australia 961

Backpacking is a favourite Australian pastime, and it's one of the best ways to experience the country while visiting.

Steps

1 Keep your thumbs to yourself. While hitchhiking is only illegal in a few areas of Australia, it is generally discouraged because of the dangers of taking rides from strangers, especially in the Outback. If you must hitchhike, do not do so alone.

2 Look into the variety of hostels available as you backpack through Australia. Check out YHA Australia's website for listings of registered hostels, rate, conditions and even bunk availability. Most hostels will allow you to stay for very little cash, but may ask for simple household chores in exchange.

3 Dress appropriately. Australia's weather is quite diverse depending on the section of the continent through which you are backpacking. Northern Australia can get hot and dry, so dress in layers and have a jacket available for the cool nights.

4 Wear sunscreen and a hat. Australia is much closer to the hole in the ozone layer than Europe, so the dangers of sunburn are much more

✽ Tip

Hostels will usually ask you for a small rental fee for sheets. You can avoid this fee by making your own "sleep sheet". Just take a full- or queen-sized flat sheet, fold it in half and sew up the edges to make a sleeping bag. It's light and easy to carry, and can be used for all kinds of things in an emergency when you're out on the road.

prevalent here. Be sure to bring plenty of sunscreen to avoid burns and sunstroke as you backpack through Australia.

5 Stay hydrated. Bring plenty of water, especially if you're planning to backpack through the Outback, which is notorious for its vast open spaces and miles to a good watering hole.

6 Gear yourself properly. Hiking rucksacks are light and carry their loads high on your back to evenly distribute the weight. Sleeping bags are a necessity as are torches, matches, maps and a first-aid kit.

7 Map out your route before you leave. Knowing where you're going or at least where you are is always key to a successful backpacking trip. Getting lost means extra energy and use of your supplies, so plan ahead to avoid any problems. Check out Backpack Australia's list of top 10 destinations to help inspire your plans.

8 Consider working for a little extra cash. If you apply for a working holiday visa as opposed to a normal visa you'll be able to take on intermittent work to earn some extra cash as you travel. Explore the Visa and Immigration website for more information.

962 Have Fun in Phuket

An exotic resort spot, Phuket exemplifies what makes Thailand an Asian must-see. Go ready to experience anything, and find out where this intoxicating blend of the Far East and island mystery will take you.

⊙ Steps

1 Play in the ocean to your heart's content. You can rent a wave runner or go parasailing, or choose from many other aquatic activities. Or you can just take it easy, floating on your back in the ocean.

2 Take a day trip. Among the many exotic choices are sea canoeing and white-water rafting. You can also visit Khao Phra Thaeo, the luscious national park, and swim in a waterhole or take a ride on an elephant.

3 Get a massage. Get another massage. Repeat. You can find massage parlours all around the island, and you can even get a massage while relaxing on the beach if you are so inclined.

4 Shop till you drop at the extensive open-air markets. You can haggle with the merchants to come away with some great bargains on clothing, luggage, handbags and jewellery.

5 Dine at one of the beachfront restaurants. You will be mesmerised by the ocean views and sounds as you enjoy authentic Thai cuisine.

6 Participate in the local culture. Try to plan your trip around one of the national festivals, such as the Loy Krathong festival in November. Eat local speciality foods and learn a few words of Thai. Immersing yourself in the culture will add depth to your holiday experience.

7 Commune with the creatures of the sea by scuba diving or snorkelling. The marine life in the waters surrounding Phuket is extensive and beautiful, and you should not miss the opportunity to have such close contact with this underwater world.

✳ Tip

Don't worry about planning excursions prior to arriving in Phuket. Kiosks are stationed on the streets to facilitate day-trip booking. These excursions are surprisingly inexpensive, and you can book one the day before you want to take it, allowing you to keep your trip spontaneous yet fun-filled.

Get Around Paris on the Cheap

Paris is a huge, often confusing city, but once you figure out how to navigate through the *arrondissements* and how to use the métro, you should be able to find your way around fairly easily.

⊚ **Steps**

1 Buy a Paris Visite card before you leave home. Similar to the London Travelcard, this pass gives you unlimited travel on the métro and RER trains and SNCF Ile-de-France buses, as well as the bus parisiens (RATP) networks. Fares vary, depending on the number of zones you need to cover.

2 Purchase métro tickets in a booklet, or *carnet de billets*, of 10. Not only will this save you money, but you won't have to queue for tickets as often.

3 Walk whenever possible. Paris is a very large city, so you probably won't be able to walk everywhere you want to go, but do explore the city on foot as much as you can.

4 Get a detailed street map of Paris that shows the city divided into its neighbourhoods, or *arrondissements*. Also carry a pocket métro map to help you plan longer trips.

5 Carry a French phrase book with you, and learn a few helpful phrases. This will be useful if you need to ask for directions, because it may be difficult to find an English-speaking Parisian who can help you.

6 Take a Paris L'Open bus tour, offered at a discount to Paris Visite card-holders. Although it's not exactly cheap, it's a good way to see the city, because you can get on or off the tour as many times as you like along the way and catch a later bus when you are ready to carry on. Commentary is in English and French, and the full journey lasts two hours and 15 minutes.

7 Ride the Noctambus line if you plan to be out late at night; this bus line covers most of Paris and the surrounding area and operates between 1:00 and 5:30 a.m.

✳ **Tips**

Two people travelling together can share a *carnet de billets*, so it may be worthwhile buying one even if you are making just a few métro trips.

From the top of the Eiffel Tower, you can see the whole of Paris spread out beneath you. The Tower is a classic tourist trap, but it's worth the price of admission to see just how much ground you may get to cover during your stay in the city.

⚠ **Warnings**

Avoid travelling during the morning or evening rush hour; the métro and buses can be uncomfortably crowded.

Like many other underground systems around the world, the métro is a favourite hangout for pickpockets; keep your valuables in a money belt, and be alert to the people and activities that surround you.

Enjoy Venice After Dark

Venice is one of the world's most enchanting cities. Its beauty, architecture and slow pace are incredibly intriguing.

⊚ **Steps**

1 Pick up the free pamphlet "Un Ospite di Venezia" from the Venice tourist office in Marco Polo airport. This guide to what's happening is distributed every 15 days. "Un Ospite di Venezia" lists all music, opera and theatrical productions, along with local exhibits and special events.

2 Soak in the atmosphere at a café in Saint Mark's Square. Many cafés have full orchestras that play in the late evenings while you enjoy a drink or snack. Caffe Florian is Venice's most famous café.

✳ **Tips**

The best way to find good places is to ask the locals. They're happy to help.

Use an Italian phrase book if you need help ordering food or getting directions.

3   See a late-night opera at the famed Teatro de La Fenice.

4   Drink a Bellini at the original Harry's Bar. Harry's Bar has been around since 1931 and is the proud creator of the infamous Bellini. This Venetian hot spot is often frequented by celebrities.

5   Participate in a unique Venetian tradition – the pub crawl. A "giro di ombra" (pub crawl) is an entertaining way to spend an evening in a city with no cars. Start in Saint Mark's Square, where watering holes are plentiful. Walk from wine bar to wine bar sipping on small glasses of wine and devouring light snacks like cheese and crackers.

6   Gamble in a casino. Venice is home to two rival casinos: Casino Municipale and Vendramin-Caleri Palace. Both are open through the wee hours of morning.

⚠ **Warnings**

Most bars are closed on Sundays.

Venetian bar owners have a reputation for overcharging, so check your bill carefully before you pay.

Most restaurants and bars in Italy include gratuity in the bill.

965 | Visit Britain's Stately Homes

In previous centuries, the British aristocracy and upper classes lived amidst sumptuous and sprawling splendour. Many of these stately properties are now open to visitors.

◉ **Steps**

1   Access the websites of the Historic Houses Association (HHA), National Trust, English Heritage, Historic Scotland, Cadw (Welsh Heritage) and the National Trust for Scotland. These organisations protect and promote over 300 member houses and gardens throughout Britain.

2   Become a member or "friend" of these organisations. Many listed properties offer free entry if you are a member.

3   Click on the Places to Visit or Properties tab to find stately homes from regions around Britain listed in the online directories. You can search properties by a vast number of options.

4   Access the websites of the individual properties as well for more detailed information. Read about the historic and architectural significance of each property and about other special features like art collections, gardens, gift shops and restaurants.

5   Decide where you want to go and contact the property directly for clarification or additional info and how to book. If possible, make your booking online to save time and avoid queues.

6   Make reservations for accommodation in advance if you plan on staying in the area for a while. Some stately homes offer accommodation as well, but pre-booking is advised. For phone enquiries, call on weekday mornings when the property is open to visitors.

7   Many of the stately properties are private homes and the owners are descendants of those who built the property centuries ago. Often the owners will themselves host the tour or be involved in the visit.

✳ **Tips**

Opening times and entry prices vary for each stately home. Children under five are usually admitted free.

If you're coming from abroad, get an Overseas Visitor Pass and enjoy free access for seven to 14 consecutive days to the properties listed on the English Heritage website.

⚠ **Warnings**

Some stately homes like Blenheim Palace, Shugborough Estate, Knebworth House and Belvoir Castle have special Christmas events from 12 November to 11 December.

Don't take photographs of the interiors, wear high-heeled or ridged footwear.

Large bags or suitcases must be left at the house entrance.

See the Grand Canyon

The Grand Canyon, located in the Colorado Plateau of Arizona, is one of the most dramatic, beautiful and most-visited sites in the United States.

◉ Steps

1 Plan for your visit to the Grand Canyon by getting information from the National Park Service website and the Grand Canyon Chamber of Commerce website. Order travel brochures and maps to help you see the Grand Canyon.

2 Stop by a visitor's centre once you arrive at the Grand Canyon. For the South Rim, the main visitor's centre is Canyon View Information Plaza, located near Mather Point. For the North Rim, the main visitor's centre is the North Rim Visitor's Centre. Both centres can provide you with maps and literature as well as additional information on visiting the canyon.

3 Drive your car around the Grand Canyon. You can see several parts and scenic spots of the Grand Canyon from the car. Desert View Drive on the South Rim is one location, as is Point Imperial on the North Rim. Find specific details about car routes and scenic viewpoints online.

4 Take a day hike on a trail at the Grand Canyon. There are many trails on both the North and South Rims of the canyon. Some of these are even handicapped accessible. There's a list of trails on the National Park Service website, along with specific information about each trail.

5 Be part of a guided tour of the Grand Canyon. The Grand Canyon Field Institute, a part of the Grand Canyon Association, gives guided tours to visitors and covers topics ranging from canyon history to canyon geology. Find information on choosing a tour or signing up for one on the Grand Canyon Association's website.

6 Experience the Grand Canyon on a mule. Mule rides are available for canyon visitors on both the North and South Rims. These mule trips can be from one hour long to overnight trips, depending on what you're looking for. Schedules and sign-ups are on the National Park Service website.

7 Raft the Colorado River in the Grand Canyon. These river trips range from one to 25 days and fill up quickly. People interested in a river trip have to enter a lottery on the National Park Service website. Details about this lottery and the types of river trips offered can be found online.

8 Go on a helicopter tour of the canyon. The Grand Canyon Chamber of Commerce has information on helicopter and other air tours of the Grand Canyon.

✳ Tips

Directions to the Grand Canyon, information on weather and road conditions near the Grand Canyon are on the website for the National Park Service.

Be sure to plan ahead for your trip to the Grand Canyon. Mule trips, helicopter tours and river trips fill up very quickly.

Visit the online bookshop of the Grand Canyon Association for books and maps of the Grand Canyon before you visit.

Request brochures about the Grand Canyon from the Grand Canyon Chamber of Commerce.

How to Do More of *(Just About)* Everything

967 | Plan a Visit to Angkor Wat

Angkor Wat, itself the single largest religious structure in the history of mankind, is the crowning gem of a much larger body.

⊙ Steps

1   Decide if you are going to Cambodia, or attaching Angkor Wat to a visit to another Southeast Asian country. Angkor Archaeological Park is near the town of Siem Reap, which has an international airport. In the nearby area, you can fly there from Laos, Thailand, Vietnam, Malaysia and Singapore. These are all close enough that a run to Angkor can be added. If you are planning a holiday in Cambodia you are probably making Angkor your main priority and adding the rest of Cambodia on after that.

2   Take those anti-malarials. Angkor sits in a tropical forest, there is malaria around, and while you aren't likely to catch it, it's better safe than sorry.

3   Bring suitable clothing and sunblock. It is hot out there, and touring Angkor will mean being out in the heat all day, and the sun for part of it. Wear suitable clothing, bring your sunblock as well as your insect repellent, and don't forget the water.

4   Engage a *tuk tuk* (motorcycle with passenger trailer) driver or rent a bicycle. The hardy should consider exploring the Angkor ruins by bicycle. It is a pleasant way of getting around if you don't mind pedalling in the heat. Everyone else should find and negotiate for the services of a *tuk tuk* driver. These guys are not guides, but they do drive you from site to site.

5   Get your own guidebook so you won't need a guide to tour each individual ruin.

6   Develop a thick skin. Everywhere you go in the Angkor ruins, you will be confronted by louts and scam artists, and kids trying to guilt you into buying something from them. Don't have a hard heart about this, but at the same time don't let your exposure to Cambodia's poverty take all the joy out of your visit.

7   Don't buy your park pass from anyone except the park authorities. Scammers and counterfeiters are out there.

8   Decide how much time you want to spend in the ruins. Park passes are available for one day, three days and one week. The one-day pass should never be considered: there is simply too much to see, and if you don't have the time to spend at least two days at the park, you should not bother going. A week is for serious archaeological buffs, or people intent on sketching or painting things. The following major sites should be on your itinerary: Angkor Wat, the Bayon, Ta Prohm, Angkor Thom and sunset from Phnom Bakheng. Try to spread them out, mixed in with smaller attractions, to avoid developing "it's just another cathedral" syndrome. Get an early start on each day. Getting to Angkor Wat at 8 a.m. means being ahead of the tour buses by a full hour, and once you are out in front of the crowds you can try to stay there.

△ Warnings

While Cambodia is not dangerous there is a lot of poverty. Keep all valuables on your person at all times.

Never walk off of trails or roads as there are still some land mines left over from the Khmer Rouge occupation.

Climb Mount Kilimanjaro

968

More than 25,000 people per year try to climb Mount Kilimanjaro – Africa's highest peak. Less than half succeed. Here are some tips for standing on the roof of Africa.

⊙ Steps

1 Choose an operator. There are hundreds of companies that service the mountain; selecting an operator can be a daunting task. You want to be sure that your operator staffs experienced, competent guides, who practise high safety standards and treat porters well. Don't select strictly based on price. Avoid the cheapest operators – some are downright dangerous. But do not assume a high-budget operator is superior either.

2 Choose a season. The best times to climb Kilimanjaro tend to be the warmest and driest months – January, February, and September. The primary issue is safety, as the risks associated with climbing increase significantly when the weather is foul. The effects of rain, mud, snow, ice and cold can be very strenuous on the body.

3 Choose a route. The Kilimanjaro routes each have different characteristics that may or may not appeal to you. Consider the difficulty, scenery and traffic when you select your route. Lemosho, Machame and Rongai are recommended. Marangu and Umbwe are not. The longer routes are not only considered the more scenic routes, but give you a better chance of summit due to altitude acclimatisation.

4 Decide how many days your want to spend climbing. Seven or more days is recommended. Do not book the minimum number of days. Chances are, you will not enjoy your climb nor will you reach the summit. Statistics show that each additional day you spend acclimatising increases your probability of success substantially.

5 Choose a private climb. A private, small-party climb is the best way to climb Kilimanjaro. Most climb operators run group departures for up to 12 people. Once they add the support staff, a "small" group of 12 climbers becomes almost 50 people total! That's hardly the way to enjoy the mountain.

6 Get your gear together. This is difficult for many climbers because there are many aspiring to tackle Mount Kilimanjaro who have little or no backpacking experience. Simply follow the gear list provided and resist the temptation to bring more. You won't need it and it is just extra weight that you or your porters must carry.

7 Learn about acute mountain sickness (AMS). Altitude sickness is potentially fatal. However, most climbers will get some form of mild AMS while on the mountain. Your guide will monitor you closely during the duration of you climb. However, you should be aware of the symptoms of mild, moderate and severe AMS.

8 Train for your climb. It is very hard to gauge the mental and physical strength needed to climb Kilimanjaro. Two months of training is usually sufficient. If you can do day hikes for four to six hours, with moderate elevation changes while carrying an ordinary pack, or if you can walk on a stairmaster for two hours, at 30 steps per minute while carrying the pack, then it's likely you'll have no problems with the physical part of the climb (altitude acclimatisation is unknown, however).

✳ Tips

The guides are there to provide expertise and assistance, but they're not babysitters. Be aware of your limitations and your surroundings, and rely on your own judgement.

The drinking tubes on hydration packs often freeze solid. Bring Nalgene bottles to carry water as well or you won't have any to drink.

969 | Travel the Silk Road

The Silk Road, a vast and ancient network of overland trade routes, spreads over Europe and Asia and passes through numerous present-day countries.

Steps

1   Collect Silk Road literature. Numerous academic and popular works cover this subject, including art histories, anthropological studies, economic investigations and historical novels.

2   Study a map of the region, available online from the Silk Road Project (silkroadproject.org), and choose your route.

3   Read up on the countries that you plan to pass through. Knowledge about the currency, culture, ancient history, current situation and geography will all be helpful and interesting. Use a separate guidebook for each country – those from Lonely Planet Publications offer well-rounded information.

4   Pick a method of travel. Determined adventurers might outfit a sturdy vehicle or even a motorcycle. More casual travellers may choose to break the trip into a series of train trips, stopping in the more interesting cities). Luxurious charter trains also offer all-inclusive tours.

5   Focus on a single country if you want a less involved trip. Many countries are proud of their Silk Road history and promote it as a tourist experience. For example, the Tajikistan website provides contact information for the National Tourism Company as well as basic history and information about the country.

6   Prepare for mountain weather. Many areas of Turkmenistan, Afghanistan and Tajikistan are rugged mountains and subject to severe weather. Travel in the summer if your route crosses any high mountain passes.

7   Use your guide books to gauge where you'll find amenities. Large cities are accustomed to travellers and provide a wide range of services. Smaller towns are likely to be less visited by travellers and may offer pleasingly low prices but fewer services.

8   Convert a small amount of currency for each country before you go. You won't need to carry a lot of cash if your ATM card is linked to a global network. Check with your bank.

✳ Tips

If you wanted to pass through the fewest possible countries, your journey would still take you through Syria, Iraq, Turkmenistan, Iran, Afghanistan, Tajikistan and China.

The Chinese city of Xian is the old assembly point for huge caravans preparing to make the westward journey. Today the city is home to silk factories as well as famous archaeological sites.

Plan a Catholic Wedding   `970`

The Catholic Church views marriage as the joining of souls, and as such, it is a very holy and permanent event.

⊚ Steps

1 Begin your wedding preparations a year or more in advance.

2 Obtain copies of both of your baptismal certificates by calling or writing to the church where they are kept.

3 Consult with a priest and explain your intention to be married.

4 Select a site for the reception.

5 Enrol in a Pre-Cana, or marriage-preparation programme, which is designed to help you prepare emotionally, spiritually and socially for marriage.

6 Add the Pre-Cana documents to your other records once you have finished the programme.

7 Discuss with your partner your views about having children, since the Catholic Church only recognises marriages in which procreation is a possibility.

8 Order wedding invitations, mass booklets and thank-you notes four to six months prior to the wedding date.

9 Arrange a premarital investigation with the priest prior to the wedding. Bring along all your records, including information about the parish to which you belong and whether you are both free to marry in the eyes of the Church.

10 Ask the priest any questions you have about the teachings of the Church and its role in your marriage.

11 Select readings for the wedding and ask family members to do the honour of reading them at the ceremony.

12 Plan a receiving line on the steps of the church so you can personally greet all your guests.

✳ Tips

Send invitations out at least six weeks prior to the wedding.

Following the ceremony, the officiating priest will send notice of your marriage to the parish where your records are kept so it can be added to the Baptismal Register.

Plan a Hindu Wedding   `971`

Hindu weddings are steeped in important rituals and customs. Some couples choose to have the typical Hindu ceremony that spans several days, while others have a condensed version that lasts only a few hours.

⊚ Steps

1 Arrange the proposal so that the whole family feels included in the event. In this way, you will receive approval from elders, and the family will also be able to determine whether they think you and your partner are compatible for marriage.

✳ Tips

In the past, most Hindu marriages were arranged by the family. Today, though, it has become more acceptable for couples to meet on their own. Yet even in modern "love marriages", the family remains an important part of the wedding ceremony.

2   Check with an astrologer to match your horoscopes and determine an auspicious date and location for the wedding. Many Hindu ceremonies take place at the bride's house or at a hall.

3   Decide if you will have guests sit on the floor, as is typical at Hindu weddings, or whether you would prefer to go the more modern route and provide chairs.

4   Include the 15 rituals that traditionally make up a Hindu wedding ceremony. Or, if you prefer, select only those that have special meaning for you as a couple.

5   Provide a sari bought by the groom for the bride to change into during the ceremony. (The outfit she arrives in will typically be bought by her parents.) The change of clothes is very meaningful, since it signifies the shift of responsibility from the parents to the husband.

6   Offer food and entertainment to occupy the guests during the wedding ceremony. Eating, drinking and talking during the ceremonial events is accepted practice at Hindu weddings.

7   Order garlands of flowers that the bride and groom will exchange during the ceremony, often along with rings to symbolise acceptance and welcome.

8   Bring a gold necklace if you would like to include the "tying the knot" ritual, in which the groom ties the necklace around the bride's neck.

9   Include a portion of the ceremony (known as the *saptapadi* portion in Hindi) in which the bride and groom take seven steps together towards a long and happy marriage, praying for blessings such as wealth, happiness, strength and devotion with each step.

10 Prepare a mixture of honey and yoghurt, which the bride offers the groom to ensure his good health and a sweet start to their marriage.

11 Offer food to the gods during the ceremony to obtain their blessings. In the Hindu religion, there is one supreme being, with all other gods being aspects of this one.

12 Provide a stone for the bride to stand on to signify her faithfulness and loyalty to the marriage.

13 Ask the groom's brother to sprinkle puffed rice for prosperity and flower petals on the couple after they exchange vows, following an ongoing Indian tradition.

14 Create a marriage mark on the bride's forehead with *sedhu*, or orange powder, to announce to the world that she is now married. After the mark is applied, the couple should touch each parent's feet and receive their parents' blessings.

15 Prepare a large feast to serve the guests following the ceremony. Expect family and friends to help make the food.

Prepare an edible dowry for the bride to give to the groom's family. This can include pastries and other tasty treats.

Remember that a Hindu wedding is more of a community gathering or party than a quiet event.

Plan a Muslim Wedding 972

A Muslim wedding is typically a multi-day event, but traditionally the ritual itself, called a *nikah* in Arabic, is quite simple.

⊙ Steps

1. Anoint the bride with turmeric paste during the *Manjha* ceremony. This happens at the bride's house two days before the wedding. The groom's family provides the paste of turmeric, chameli oil and sandalwood.

2. Apply henna to the bride's hands and feet. Only unmarried women participate in this. A spot is also applied to the groom as a symbolic token. The bride isn't allowed to leave her house until the wedding ceremony.

3. Have family and friends proceed with the groom from his place to the ceremony location. If there isn't a concrete-covered area available, erect a *shamiana*, which is a large decorated tent.

4. Beat drums and play musical instruments while the groom arrives. The groom then exchanges a glass of *sharbet* and money with the bride's brother.

5. Start the ceremony as the priest asks the bride and groom if they're happy with the arrangement and agree with the marriage. The priest then reads a selection from the Qu'ran.

6. Register the marriage. The groom and two witnesses sign it immediately. The bride signs it at a later time. The groom gives gifts and money to the bride's sisters.

7. Seat the bride and groom together following their first meal. Use a long scarf to cover their heads while the priest has them read prayers. The couple is permitted to see each other through the reflection of mirrors.

✳ Tips

The groom's family provides the bride with her wedding-day clothing.

Two men and a lawyer or eminent person must witness the reading of the Qu'ran.

Serve dinner separately to the women and men. The groom's family also eats separately.

Plan a Jewish Wedding 973

Jewish weddings can vary a great deal, depending on whether the bride and groom are Orthodox, Conservative or Reform in their beliefs. But there are some important Jewish traditions that many bridal couples want to uphold.

⊙ Steps

1. Select a location – a synagogue or temple, club, hall, restaurant or hotel.

2. Have a *ketubbah* (wedding contract) prepared. This describes the rights and responsibilities of the bride and groom.

3. Include all members of your immediate families in your wedding party. Typically, the parents of the bride and groom walk them down the aisle.

4. Have a *huppah*, or wedding canopy, in place for the ceremony.

5. Have *yarmulkes* on hand for guests who do not bring their own.

6. Allow time prior to the ceremony for a veiling ritual, in which the groom places the veil over the face of his bride after confirming she is indeed the woman he plans to marry.

✳ Tips

The bride's family and friends sit on the right side and the groom's on the left.

Jewish weddings may not be held during the Sabbath, which runs from Friday at sundown to Saturday at sundown. Most Jewish weddings take place on Saturday night or on a Sunday.

7   Use plain gold wedding bands, without any engraving or stones, for an Orthodox wedding. Place the ring on the index finger of the right hand. Following the ceremony, modern brides move the ring to the left hand.

8   Ask wedding guests to read the seven blessings.

9   Bring a glass for the groom to break at the conclusion of the ceremony. This reminds people of the destruction of the Temple and also calls attention to the fragility of life and the need to care for relationships, which can be broken beyond repair.

10 Following the ceremony, the bride and groom retire to a separate room where they can be alone and eat some food (usually broth) before rejoining their guests at the reception. This period is known as *yihud*, or union.

11 Make sure the reception site has enough room for circle dancing.

974 | Plan a Military Wedding

Military weddings are distinguished from most other types of wedding by the formal uniforms worn by the bride and/ or groom and by the special traditions that are woven into the ceremony.

Steps

1   Decide if you want to get married in a military chapel, at a military academy or in your own civilian place of worship.

2   Meet with the chaplain as soon as possible, if you do decide to get married in a chapel, to discuss the ceremony and arrange premarital counselling sessions.

3   Ask for permission to have wedding flowers, music and photography inside the chapel. Rules vary from place to place.

4   Select a site for the reception. You might consider officers' clubs on base or traditional restaurants or hotels in the area.

5   Order traditional (non-military-style) invitations, but don't forget to include any military titles or ranks held by you, your fiancé or either set of parents.

6   Include "Full dress uniform invited" on your invitations to indicate that guests are welcome to come in uniform.

7   Determine the types of uniforms the groom and members of the wedding party who are in the service will wear. Typically, full ceremonial dress uniform is chosen.

8   Decide on the bridal wear. Many brides who are in the service prefer to wear a traditional bridal gown instead of their uniform. If this is the case, select a formal-style gown with a flowing train and veil to complement the formal men's attire.

9   Have men in uniform wear their military decorations.

10 Ask honour guards to form an archway with swords or sabres outside the ceremony location for the wedding couple to walk through on their way out. This symbolises safe passage into married life.

☀ Tips

Try to secure your site at least a year in advance, since many places book up quickly – particularly military academies.

Consider accenting your cake with military-couple figurines representing different branches of service.

Remember to always verify your plans with the proper military authorities.

11 Seat military guests at the reception according to rank and title.

12 Have a sword or sabre ready at the reception for you and your new spouse to use to cut the wedding cake. This is a dramatic touch that guests particularly enjoy.

Plan an Outdoor Wedding

975

When exchanging vows under the sun or the stars, be sure to expect the unexpected. But with some creativity, planning and foresight, you can have the wedding of your dreams.

⊙ Steps

1 Consider your wedding date. If you have your heart set on a January wedding, you may want to forgo the oceanside ceremony.

2 Scout out several possible locations – even outdoor wonderlands can get booked up far in advance.

3 Examine each location carefully. Is there a major road nearby? Is the place prone to bad weather? Are there lots of mosquitoes? Will there be construction work in the area on your wedding day?

4 Calculate the costs of outfitting an outdoor site before you choose a location. Do you plan on providing a tent? What about lawn furniture?

5 Consider weather and have a back-up site ready. If you have chosen a rain-prone site, make a note on the invitation: "In case of rain, please join us at…".

6 Make your site homelike: rent amenities such as chairs, tables, linen, an electric generator, a dressing trailer, a portable dance floor and portable toilets.

7 Designate a central location where guests can gather for cake-cutting, dancing, bouquet-tossing, etc.

8 String lights between trees, hang Chinese lanterns in the branches, rent some spotlights or scatter scores of votive candles – the possibilities are endless!

✳ Tips

Check for hidden costs, such as charges for permits to hold the ceremony in a public place.

Choose wooden rather than metal seats, which tend to absorb heat and cold.

Check with people in your wedding party about any allergies they may have.

⚠ Warning

Remember that there will be costs associated with outfitting the location and making it accessible to guests.

Elope

976

Eloping can be impetuous and special without the traditional trappings of a wedding. Elope if you are looking to get away from it all, or save yourself from extra expenses and stress.

⊙ Steps

1 Decide if eloping is right for you. The main drawback is that you may hurt the feelings of your close family members if they are not invited. Also, there is something to be said for all the planning and the ceremony of a formal wedding, including getting dressed up and having pictures done – you may appreciate the memories when you are older.

✳ Tips

Many places offer elopement packages. They'll handle everything, including the licence, ceremony, honeymoon and even travel and accommodation.

2   Get a marriage licence at least a week or two in advance of your wedding date.

3   Find a venue. Las Vegas is a popular place to elope and you'll find loads of chapels on the Internet. But if Vegas seems sleazy to you, you might want to look into resorts. Gretna Green just over the border in Scotland is a traditional destination for eloping couples from all over the world, and could be a romantic idea.

4   Plan a honeymoon. Kick off your marriage right! Plan a destination for you and your new spouse after the ceremony.

5   Book your travel. Buy plane tickets and make reservations as soon as possible.

6   Get married. Make sure you take your licence with you and anything else you need.

Go ahead and keep your marriage a secret from your family, but let flight attendants and hotel clerks know! They might boost you up to first class or give you extra perks with your room service.

⚠ Warning

Don't rush into a bad decision. If you are unsure, maybe eloping isn't right for you. Make sure you want to go through with this.

---

977   Decide Who to Invite to Your Wedding

You agreed to have no more than 125 guests at your wedding, but you've realised that between you, you have 300 people on the list. Now what?

◎ Steps

1   Sit down with your intended and list everyone you can think of who you want to invite.

2   Use the one-year rule for friends: if you haven't had a meaningful conversation with this person within the last year, don't invite him or her.

3   Ask your parents on both sides to help you cull people from the list.

4   Avoid the "If I invite this cousin, I must invite all cousins" trap. And don't feel obligated to invite people who invited you to their wedding. Relationships change.

5   Exclude children if possible. Suddenly a family of six is a manageable party of two.

6   Address the invitations only to those you intend to invite. If your single friend rates an invitation and isn't seeing anyone seriously, you don't have to include "and guest".

7   Make sure that the same number of people are invited from each side. This will prevent in-laws from feeling cheated.

8   Keep in mind that on average, about 25 per cent of your guests won't be able to make it.

9   Make a first and second list. Put the absolutely-must-invites on the first list, and as the RSVPs come in, send an invitation from the second list for each regret.

✳ Tips

Remember that these are people you're sharing your special day with. Beyind immediate family members, you aren't obliged to invite anyone.

As a thoughtful gesture, set aside a group of six to 10 invitations for the parents to send to whoever they like that didn't make it on to the guest list.

⚠ Warning

People will bring their kids unless you spell it out for them.

Decide Whose Name to Take When You Get Married   `978`

Tradition dictates that the bride assumes her husband's name at marriage, but today, not only are some women keeping their maiden names, but some men are taking their wives' family names.

⊙ Steps

1   Think about how much your name means to you. If you've built a business or reputation that thrives because of name recognition, you might not want to start all over again with a new name.

2   Listen to how your new name will sound if you change it. Are you willing to be called Mrs Robinson the rest of your life? Will you be taken seriously as Rosa Sosa, or are you tired of being Bruce Wayne?

3   Ask your partner if people frequently mispronounce his or her name. If so, are you willing to tolerate that?

4   Talk the name change over with your partner and both your families. A woman with no brothers may opt to carry on the family name. A son's decision to give up his last name might offend or hurt his parents.

5   Discuss what last name you'd like your children to have. Some couples opt to combine their names, or give daughters their mother's name and sons their father's name.

6   Think about the broader social implications, if that's important to you. Do you believe that it's important for everyone in a new family to have the same name? Or do you feel that relinquishing a name implies inequality or loss of identity?

✳ Tips

Consider hyphenation, but be careful. Very long names won't fit on forms with boxes to fill in, and too many syllables can be a real mouthful.

Some women choose to use their maiden names for business and their married names in their personal lives. This arrangement might be the best of both worlds, but it could also cause confusion when people know you by different names.

⚠ Warning

Don't bow to pressure from your spouse, family or friends. A name is very personal; choose the one that feels right for you.

Choose a Wedding Photographer   `979`

You've already bought the ring and popped the question. Now you want to find someone who can capture the events of your wedding through the art of photography.

⊙ Steps

1   Sit down with your fiancé and determine what you want from the photographer. You will need to know how many pictures you want them to shoot, how you want those pictures printed and how you want them bound, among other things.

2   Analyse the venue you have chosen for your wedding. Note the lighting, the ambiance and the space in which a photographer will be working.

3   Compile a list of local photographers for hire. Search their portfolios – several of these photographers will have photo samples online – to find examples of photos taken in similar environments as your venue.

4   Use that list and make contact with each photographer. Set up a consultation meeting and advise the photographer of the environment in which they will be shooting. Get price quotes on printing, what kind of photo paper will be used, cost per hour or event, and ask how much time it will take to get photos back in their completed form.

✳ Tip

Most photographers will charge a flat fee to attend the wedding and take pictures. You purchase the specific pictures you want at the sizes you want afterwards.

⚠ Warning

Make sure the photographer is on the level – your wedding day will only happen once, so make sure you don't hire someone shady.

5   Compare prices, but keep in mind that photography is expensive. Since wedding photographers usually operate on a fee for the wedding, and a per-photo system after the wedding, make sure you're going to get quality as much as the right price.

6   Hire the photographer, and reiterate the date of the wedding often. Be very specific in your consultations – they will need to know exactly where to be and when, and if there is a surprise or a special event planned.

980 | Choose Readings for Your Wedding Ceremony

Readings lend a traditional as well as a personal touch to the ceremony, letting you use someone else's words or your own to communicate the deep, symbolic sentiments of your union.

⊙ Steps

1   Consider your values. There are certain readings that are conventional according to religions or family tradition. But you may also want to consider your own personal experience and feelings leading up to your wedding ceremony.

2   Browse popular selections on the Internet.

3   Consult with your officiate. Some priests or vicars have a selection of readings that they would prefer you to pick from. Others are more flexible, but run your choices by them anyway.

4   Analyse your text. Make sure you understand the layers of meaning in your reading. Ask a librarian or an academic for help or suggestions.

5   Finalise your choice and choose a reader. Once you are confident about your selection, choose someone to read and have them practise in the upcoming months.

✳ Tips

Coordinate your vows with the readings. If the readings call for one partner to uphold a certain value, the vows should answer to that and affirm it.

Ask your parents what they read at their wedding. It might be nice to follow in their footsteps.

⚠ Warning

If you decide to choose something unique or self-crafted, be sure it is appropriate. Read it to some friends or family beforehand to make sure it's proper.

981 | Hire a Band for a Wedding

The right kind of music will fuel your reception and can make the difference between "just another wedding" and an unforgettable night of fun dancing.

⊙ Steps

1   Get names of recommended bands from friends, newlyweds, site coordinators, clergy and wedding consultants.

2   Check with your wedding venue for any noise or space restrictions.

3   Decide what kind of atmosphere you'd like to create based on the music you choose. Do you want your guests grooving in group dances to country music? Do you prefer a more raucous atmosphere, courtesy of your favourite local band? Or do you want a mellow reception with jazz in the background?

4   Ask to listen to CDs or view video tapes of the bands' performances. Pay attention to how they interact with the audience.

✳ Tips

Look for performers who are fun, excited, sensitive to the crowd and open to your suggestions.

Hire a band that has played wedding receptions before – they will be familiar with the flow of events and can serve as emcees.

Have the band arrive at least an hour prior to the time you want them to begin playing, and check their availability to play overtime.

5   Ask to see the playlist – ideally, you want a wide variety of songs that will appeal to guests of all musical tastes.

6   Discuss room size and equipment needs. Will you have enough outlets? Is the stage big enough to support the entire band?

7   Make a contract that includes dates, times, breaks, musicians, song commitments, emcee duties, clothing, equipment, food, rates and cancellation and refund policy.

Get People Dancing at Your Wedding | 982

With dazzling music and a glowing attitude to match, you can ensure your guests will remember the joy of your wedding day, even if they don't recall the details.

☉ Steps

1   Select an experienced band or DJ – performers who can assess the mood of the crowd and play accordingly.

2   Work closely with the DJ or band to produce a playlist. Whether you're aiming for an overall sound or selecting an assortment of tunes, have a plan.

3   Begin the evening with "after-dinner" music of classy, romantic tunes, followed by upbeat, contemporary songs.

4   Pepper your selection with special dance songs that encourage group participation, including some of those old favourites.

5   Put your bridesmaids and ushers to work getting people on their feet and into action; have them invite other guests on to the dance floor.

✱ Tips

Start the dancing by getting out on the dance floor with your new spouse. Your guests may feel uncomfortable dancing before you do.

Explore the many eras of music history and play a variety of tunes that will appeal to a wide range of ages.

Choose Flowers for Your Wedding Reception | 983

Planning a wedding means many, many days of preparation, brainstorming and stress. One of the details is choosing flowers for your wedding reception.

☉ Steps

1   Figure out a colour scheme for the entire wedding reception. This will help you decide what type of flowers you need to purchase.

2   Develop a budget. Plan on how much you are willing to spend on the reception flowers. Consider how much you are spending on the bridesmaid's bouquets and other floral arrangements for the wedding.

3   Decide the size and the number of bouquets you want to be placed in the reception area. For this step, you must consider how much free space you have, and how the size and shape of the bouquets will follow the theme of the wedding reception.

4   Decide where exactly you want to place the flowers within the reception area. Consider such places as the toilets, tables, chairs, doorways or other places that could use a bit of touching up.

✱ Tip

For a nice touch, consider adding vases around the tables with the same flowers you used in the wedding ceremony. This will add to the overall flow of the wedding reception.

⚠ Warning

Be careful not to overdo the amount of flowers in your reception area. Do not overwhelm your guests with flowers.

984 | Design Your Own Wedding Cake

Creating a customised cake for your wedding is a great way to make your big day stand out from the crowd.

⊙ Steps

1 Start clipping pictures from cake magazines and catalogues to determine the style, colour and overall theme you want to create.

2 Decide on a cake filling. Review your options with the person baking and making your wedding cake, and pick out two or three fillings you are most interested in.

3 Choose a cake icing and colour. Whether you're looking for a classic cake with royal icing or a contemporary cake with chocolate icing, take the time to pick something that reflects your tastes.

4 Estimate how many servings you need. This will be based on the size of your wedding party, and you will need to add or remove tiers from the final design accordingly.

5 Sketch your cake. This is the blueprint for your cake designer and needs to include the number of layers, tiers and any special accessories.

6 Add colour to your drawing with pencils or markers. The more detailed you can make this, the easier it will be to create it in real life.

7 Keep a copy and take the second to your cake designer or specialist.

8 Place your order with all the details and confirm the design.

✴ Tip

Some cake designers are willing to help you design the cake from scratch.

⚠ Warning

Some cake specialists do not make custom cakes without a considerable amount of advanced notice; find out what the requirements are as soon as you have a wedding date in mind.

985 | Stay Calm the Night Before the Wedding

Relax with loved ones, but don't forget to take some time out for yourself – you've planned the perfect wedding and you owe it to yourself to relax before the big day.

⊙ Steps

1 Pamper yourself with a manicure or massage.

2 Take time at your wedding rehearsal to delight in the company of family and friends.

3 Come home, light some candles, put on some relaxing music and draw up a warm, luxurious bath. For an extra indulgence, soothe your senses with aromatherapy.

4 Have a glass of warm milk or hot herbal tea to calm those nerves.

5 Follow your usual night-time routine before going to bed.

6 Get a good night's rest – even if you can't sleep, just resting will help.

✴ Tip

Keep out negative thoughts with positive visualisation – conjure up a picture of serenity in your mind, and remember to take deep breaths.

Choose a Wedding Dress

Buying a wedding dress can be a long process, so start looking at least seven months prior to the wedding if you are having the dress made.

⊙ Steps

1 Cut out pictures from bridal and fashion magazines, shop online and look at old family photos to zero in on your preferred style.

2 Ask friends and family for references on dressmakers and designers if you are having the dress made.

3 Bring a friend whose opinion you trust to shop with you at bridal stores. Include your mother if appropriate.

4 Bring shoes with the same size heel you expect to wear at the wedding.

5 Look through gowns on the rack and visit specialised wedding charity shops. You could save a lot of money.

6 Try on a variety of dresses.

7 Discuss alteration charges with the shop, once you choose your dress.

8 Allow six months for dressmaking if the dress is being made for you.

9 Be ready to pay about 50 per cent of the cost of the dress as a deposit.

10 Take home a fabric swatch to match with your shoes and veil.

✱ Tips

Avoid taking too many friends shopping with you. They may never agree on the same dress, and you might end up confused and frustrated.

If the dress is being made, give the shop a wedding date that is two weeks before the actual wedding. This trick will ensure that the dress will be ready in plenty of time.

⚠ Warnings

When asked to make a deposit on a dress, ask about deposit refunds. Most deposits are not refundable.

Avoid being talked into buying a dress that costs more than you can afford.

Choose a Veil

Whether it wards off bad luck or simply serves as ornamentation for your wedding gown, a veil is a popular accessory for the wedding ensemble.

⊙ Steps

1 Try on lots of veils at your initial dress fitting – you can choose from tulle or organza, decorated with everything from lace or satin to crystals.

2 Choose a veil that complements your dress and doesn't obscure any special detail. Simple gowns look radiant in either a plain or ornate veil, but if you will be wearing a more elaborate dress, consider topping off your ensemble with a plain veil.

3 Use the type of wedding ceremony as another guide. At a very formal wedding, splurge on a full-length veil of any kind; at a formal wedding, don a long veil; exude simplicity at a formal daytime wedding with a fingertip veil or hat.

5 Aim for a narrow cut, which creates an illusion of length and slimness, as well as delicate trim and less puffiness.

6 Have a friend with you to examine the look of your veil from every possible angle. A veil that flatters your face may not flatter the back of your gown, and vice versa.

✱ Tips

At the fitting, wear your hair in a style similar to the way you plan to wear it on your wedding day.

Attach the veil to an additional headpiece so you can remove the veil and still have some decoration at the reception.

988 | Choose Proper Lingerie for Your Wedding

Focus on fit. When you feel good, you look fabulous. Choose wedding lingerie that is beautiful and comfortable.

◉ Steps

1 Begin by choosing a bra that offers enough support and is the right style for your dress, preferably from a brand name with which you are already comfortable.

2 Slip on a strapless bra if your dress has a low or wide-cut neckline, or slender straps. The most versatile strapless is one with removable straps that you can make into a crisscross or halter bra. Buy underwired if you are full-busted or full-figured.

3 Select a backless bra that hooks at the waist if your dress has a low-cut back. Let them see skin, not bra straps.

4 Slim down with a Lycra or spandex slimmer. This modern-day corset will keep you looking trim; just make sure it's comfortable for an extended period of time, and take it along to your fittings – it can change the fit of your dress.

5 Wear underwear that is comfortable, stays in place and doesn't show through the dress in any light.

6 Purchase a slip if you are wearing a long sheath dress.

7 Pick hosiery of any style, as long as its colour flows harmoniously with your dress.

8 Try on a variety of styles under your dress once you've chosen the proper type, and move, move, move. The bra should be comfortable and stay in place at all times.

✱ Tips

Try your bra on with your dress to be certain the fit is perfect.

Spend a little extra if you wear a garter; the less expensive ones tend to slide around and leave you with sagging stockings.

989 | Walk in a Wedding Dress

With a little practice – and the right shoes – you can glide down the aisle with grace and elegance.

◉ Steps

1 Buy a dress that fits you well.

2 Shop for comfortable courts, flats or ballet shoes. Avoid very high heels.

3 Scuff the soles of those slippery new shoes using sandpaper or a kitchen knife.

4 Maintain good posture – head high and shoulders back! This way, the dress hangs on you correctly instead of getting in your way.

5 Grasp the sides of your dress and pull them up when climbing stairs.

6 Bustle the train with hooks, poppers or buttons – if you don't have a detachable train – so that you can move around at the reception.

7 Slip on that dress and shoes, and practise walking and dancing at home. Get a feel for how the dress fits and moves.

✱ Tip

Consider purchasing cushioned insoles for extra walking comfort.

Write a Wedding Announcement 990

Follow these easy steps to writing and sending out a special announcement to family and friends, sharing the good news about your recent marriage.

⊙ Steps

1 Make a list of all of the people who should receive announcements.

2 Order custom-printed announcements. You can get these from small print shops and some card shops.

3 Expect to pay around £200 for 50 cards, depending on the quality of the paper and the design you select.

4 Allow two weeks or more for the cards to be ready.

5 Include important details such as your full name and that of your spouse, your parents' names and the date of your marriage.

6 Decide whether to include more specifics, such as the wedding time and location. If you're sending these to people who weren't invited, take care not to make them feel left out.

✳ Tips

Wedding announcements are typically sent out after a couple elopes, to tell people about their new status. These announcements are also appropriate after a small wedding to which many of your family and friends were not invited.

Check with both sets of parents for names of people they would like to receive an announcement.

Save Money on Wedding Stationery 991

Wedding stationery can very easily take a huge chunk out of your wedding budget. Here are a few ideas to help you save money on stationery for your wedding.

⊙ Steps

1 Start shopping for wedding stationery as early as possible. If you wait until the last minute you may have a harder time finding a good deal. Begin looking for wedding stationery as soon as you know you are getting married.

2 Check bridal shows for good deals on wedding stationery. If there is a bridal expo in your area, this is a great place to start.

3 Check out mail-order catalogues for wedding-stationery discounts. They usually offer great deals when you buy large quantities.

4 Visit online stores for wedding-stationery deals. There are a number of sites that offer discounts for ordering online.

5 Visit your local church and ask about wedding stationery. Churches sometimes offer wedding stationery as part of a fundraiser.

6 Make your own wedding stationery. If you have a computer and a good printer, you can save a lot of money by printing your own. This is also a good way to personalise it all.

✳ Tips

Get an idea of what you want your stationery to look like and try to find something close. You can save money by buying stationery that is not exactly what you were looking for.

Don't get set on one style of wedding stationery. Have an open mind and you will have a better chance to save money on wedding stationery.

992 | Decline a Wedding Invitation

Being invited to a wedding is an honour, but if you can't make it – for any reason – you need to decline as graciously as possible.

⊙ Steps

1 Upon receiving the wedding invitation, determine whether or not you want to attend, need to attend or simply cannot attend.

2 Don't make the mistake of ignoring a wedding invitation that doesn't spark your interest. Sometimes silence from guests is interpreted as an acceptance. Be considerate. You're special enough to be invited. Don't prove to them that they're mistaken in that assumption.

3 Don't delay on your response. The couple needs to know the guest count to give to their caterer. Give them enough time to invite others.

4 When you know way in advance that you cannot attend the wedding, complete the RSVP card as soon as you can. Return the completed RSVP card by post.

5 If the couple did not provide RSVP cards, you are still expected to send a formal reply. Look for and buy formal stationery to use in declining the invitation. Indicate a reason why you cannot attend.

6 When your decision to decline falls within two to three weeks before the wedding day, if the couple offers phone, email and online RSVP options for convenience, choose one of the options and reply accordingly.

⚠ Warning

A wedding invitation is one that requires a response. If you can't make it, don't just ignore it.

993 | Buy the Perfect Wedding Gift

Buying the perfect wedding gift is actually very simple. Follow these few tips, and the happy couple will be thrilled with your generosity.

⊙ Steps

1 If possible, buy a gift from wedding list that the couple has set up. Brides spend a substantial amount of time selecting items they love and that will match their style and décor. Don't think you know better than the bride what she wants.

2 If you can't afford anything left on the list, or for some reason there is no registry or suggested charity or other hints from the couples, then consider Christmas decorations or gift certificates, or even money.

3 If sending a gift, from the list or otherwise via post, order or ship no less than two weeks before the wedding. If it is a destination event or the couple is travelling away from home for the wedding, calculate accordingly so that the gift arrives comfortably before they leave. It is too stressful for them to try and deal with gifts brought to the reception.

❋ Tip

Make sure you sign your gift. If you're given the option of including a note on an order from a wedding list, do so.

⚠ Warning

Art can be a wonderful gift, but don't do it without the couple's direct input – art is very personal.

Buy a Wedding Gift for Someone You Don't Know   994

Your wife's long-lost cousin? Your co-worker's son? With a little effort you can settle on the right way to mark the union of someone you don't know well.

⊙ Steps

1 Find out whether there's a wedding list. If there is and you're comfortable choosing from it, this is the best option. If there's nothing in your price range or the good stuff's already gone, at least you've learned a little about the couple's tastes.

2 Ask people in the know. Get an idea about the couple's interests and shop for a gift certificate to match.

3 Get them a gift certificate from a shop with something for everyone.

4 Take yourself to the mall or shop online, if you really want to pick out a gift yourself. Make sure it's returnable, though. No one needs extra items that don't fit their taste lurking around the house.

5 Avoid regifting that clunky glass vase; save that for the car-boot sale.

6 Give the gift of money if you don't have much time to choose or want to be certain they'll make use of your gift.

⚠ Warning

Don't think you can get away with not buying a gift to avoid the problem. Such omissions are always noticed!

Collect Gifts at a Wedding   995

Wedding days are filled with responsibility, and one thing that is sometimes overlooked is the collection of the gifts.

⊙ Steps

1 A couple of weeks before the wedding, designate a guest as the person responsible for collecting the gifts at your wedding. Choose someone close to you and also someone who is not going to be inundated with other responsibilities on the day (like the best man).

2 At your wedding reception, there should be a special table where the gifts are to be placed. Make sure your designated person knows exactly where it is in the reception area. If you want to give them an extra-special job, allow them to decorate it using the themes and colours of your wedding.

3 Over the course of the night, make sure your designated person keeps a loose eye on the table to be sure that's where gifts are being placed. As people enter the reception area, perhaps even have the designated person refer your guests to the table. If your designated person sees someone who is still holding a gift or envelope, have them gently refer that guest to the gift table.

4 At the end of the evening, have your designated person – with the help of others – carry the gifts to the bridal suite so they will be waiting for the bride and groom upon arrival.

✳ Tip

Have oversized bags on hand to help carry gifts.

996 | Plan a Tropical Honeymoon

Tropical honeymoons are a popular choice for newlyweds seeking rest and relaxation after the stress of wedding planning.

⊙ Steps

1 Narrow your destination to a select tropical area. Consider the Bahamas, Jamaica, Hawaii or the South Pacific.

2 Consider all-inclusive resorts for couples for a romantic, tropical holiday without the coordination stress.

3 Ask about special couples-only features: his and hers spa treatments, isolated bungalows, private dinners.

4 Research water sports and other activities in the area where you're travelling. If you are looking for an active honeymoon, make sure that there is adequate opportunity for sports and activity.

5 Consider hitting two or more islands via charter plane or boat. Some tour operators can arrange a visit to a private island for a night or two.

✱ Tip

Take your marriage licence, or other proof of marriage, when travelling for the first time as husband and wife.

⚠ Warning

Keep valuables at home, or locked safely in your hotel. Many island dwellers prey upon unsuspecting tourists.

997 | Merge Money After the Wedding

Have a candid discussion about money with your partner. Be tolerant and sensitive to each others' views, especially if you have different backgrounds regarding money.

⊙ Steps

1 Conduct a financial review. Together, you should take a close look at your financial picture. Make time to jointly review all individual bank statements, assets, debts, insurance and investments. It's also a good idea to review credit reports, which can impact you as you apply for car loans, mortgages and even property leases. If one or both of you have a lot of debt, commit to an aggressive plan to knock it out.

2 Compare individual spending tendencies. Are you a spender? Is he a saver? You need to discuss spending habits and determine how you will function financially as a couple. Sometimes different spending styles can cause tensions to run high, especially if there is little communication on the subject.

3 Set a budget and address how money will be allocated among bills, investments, savings, fun-money, etc. Make sure you understand your differences and be willing to compromise. It's always a good idea to set aside money for an emergency fund.

4 Decide how to manage your funds. To share or not to share? That is the question. You must decide how the two of you together are going to handle your money.

5 Determine how the bills will be paid. Some couples prefer to sit down together monthly to take care of this task. Other couples designate one person to manage the money. Some take turns.

✱ Tips

Discuss long-term goals and dreams. Be creative and willing to compromise.

Schedule financial talks with each other to check progress.

⚠ Warning

Unexpected expenses will occur, so be be willing to be flexible.

Pay Off Wedding Debt 998

These days, it's easy to spend thousands of pounds on a wedding ceremony and reception, but with a practical plan and a lot of determination, it's possible to pay off your wedding debt.

⊙ Steps

1   Stop using credit. With typical interest rates ranging from eight to 30 per cent, paying off these cards is next to impossible if you continue to increase the balance. Commit to a moratorium on credit cards now and you will reap financial rewards later.

2   Save for an emergency fund. Most people have at least one credit card "in case of emergency". A better alternative is to achieve a healthy savings account for unexpected expenses. Try to save £1,000 to get started and don't touch this money unless you truly need it for an emergency.

3   Pay more than the minimum payments on credit cards. Making only the minimum payment will take years to pay off the balance. Paying more than the minimum will knock the principal balance down faster, and you pay less interest in the long run.

4   Set budget and stick to it. Sit down each month and assess the bills that need to be paid. Pay as much possible towards credit cards and other debt, but still allow enough money for the basics such as food, utilities, household necessities and fuel.

✱ Tip

Work as team to meet your financial goals. Attack your debt together and celebrate your achievements when you have success. Remember, you don't necessarily have to spend a lot of money to celebrate!

Deal with Post-Wedding Blues 999

Getting married is a big adjustment – from a busy engaged couple to a happily married couple – and it's only natural to feel out of sorts during the transition.

⊙ Steps

1   Ease yourself into the transition. For quite a while you've busied yourself with plans for the wedding and it can be a bit of a let-down once the hustle and bustle ends. Take some time to go through your wedding photos. Have fun fitting your new wedding gifts into your home. Talk about the wedding day with your husband and friends and family.

2   If you paid for your own wedding or honeymoon, or contributed to it financially, you may get a shock once the excitement ends and the bills start rolling in. Now would be a good time to sit down with your new spouse and figure out a household budget and a plan for getting the wedding bills paid in a timely fashion.

3   It's normal to feel a sense of loss for a few weeks. Be kind to yourself. Don't worry that this means that you don't love your partner; it's just a natural part of the transition from being single to becoming married.

4   If the two of you didn't live together before marriage, finding your way in your new household can seem challenging. It's going to take some time for each of you to find your place, and there will be times that you don't agree or you knock heads on some issues. It will all work out in time, just remember to keep the lines of communication open.

✱ Tip

Don't worry if you feel down for up to a couple of months after the wedding. If your blues last longer, though, you should seek help from a professional.

1000 Survive the First Year of Marriage

The first year of marriage can seem like an uphill struggle, full of resentment, dissatisfaction and displacement.

⊙ Steps

1 Never stop talking. Recall how much you talked when you were dating. Make it a constant and not just a memory.

2 Listen to each other. You are in a partnership and both partners should be fully aware of the other partner's thoughts and feelings. Now that you are married, you need the input of your partner in order to make decisions that affect you both.

3 Realise you did not get married just to get presents, pay bills, advance your career or make babies. Love had a lot to do with the situation that you are in now, so don't put it on the back burner. Practicality must be tempered with care.

4 Respect each other. Just like parents and siblings, it is easy to take advantage of your spouse and not appreciate their part in your life together. Always give your spouse consideration and defend them when they are not around.

5 Show that you are in it for the long haul. Young marriages can be full of empty threats of divorce and abandonment. This develops from frustration, not a lack of love, so never stop communicating your commitment.

6 Recall that your lives are equally important. Before you married, you had social networks and participated in activities that you enjoyed. Allow each other the time to enjoy friends and pastimes, as they provide a great release to marital tension.

✳ Tips

You won't lose face by apologising. Saying sorry is a quick way to relieve tension.

Think one good thought about your spouse every day. This will provide you with a checklist of reasons not to murder your spouse when that thought first arises.

1001 Celebrate a Wedding Anniversary

Celebrate your love for one another and look forward to more happy years.

⊙ Steps

1 Decide with your spouse whether you want to exchange gifts or buy something together. Consider looking up the traditional gift for your anniversary year and buying something that relates; if you decide to buy something as a couple, exchange small tokens like cards or flowers.

2 Plan a quiet evening or getaway together. Many couples like to observe their anniversary in a private manner, especially early anniversaries.

3 Arrange a small party for your closer family and friends, if desired. If you decide to have a get-together, begin by inviting the bridal party from the wedding.

4 Plan a large party if celebrating a landmark anniversary, such as the 10th, 25th or 50th.

5 Consider reaffirming your wedding vows if you'd like to recreate your wedding, or have the large wedding you never had.

✳ Tips

Couples generally prefer that guests don't bring gifts to anniversary parties. Politely include this request on a small slip of paper in the invitation rather than printing it on the invitation itself.

Set an email reminder or devise some other method to stop you forgetting your anniversary.

⚠ Warning

Don't expect your friends and family to remember your anniversary. In fact, it may be better if they don't.

How to Do More of *(Just About)* Everything

Index

Index

ACKNOWLEDGEMENTS

The packager would like to thank the following people for their help in the creation of this book:

Sarah Bayliss
Mike Cannings
Mia France
Charlotte Goulette
Matt Goulette

Gemma Heynes
Jon Hughes
Dominic Janssen
Katie Janssen
Thomas Jordan

Samantha Lacey
Rob Philpott
Kate Skillman